SECOND EDITION

FAMILIES, PROFESSIONALS, AND EXCEPTIONALITY

A Special Partnership

Ann P. Turnbull

H. Rutherford Turnbull, III

Beach Center on Families and Disability
Bureau of Child Research
Department of Special Education
The University of Kansas

Merrill Publishing Company
Columbus • Toronto • London • Melbourne

Cover: The interweaving arrows of the logo represent the dynamic and constant reciprocity that exists between people with disability, their families, their friends, professionals, and society. The heart-shaped form represents feelings—the warmth, caring, commitment, embracing, recharging energy that comes from the reciprocity and that, in turn, fuels it.

Published by
Merrill Publishing Company
Columbus, Ohio 43216

This book was set in Italia.

Administrative Editor: Ann Castel
Production Editor: Doug Lantry
Art Coordinator: Raydelle Clement
Cover Designer: Russ Maselli

Library of Congress Catalog Card Number: 89–63525
International Standard Book Number: 0–675–21207–3
Printed in the United States of America
1 2 3 4 5 6 7 8 9—94 93 92 91 90

COLLABORATORS

First Edition
Jean Ann Summers
Mary Jane Brotherson
Holly Anne Benson

Second Edition
Jean Ann Summers
Mary Jane Brotherson
Holly Anne Benson
Julie F. Sergeant
Betsy Santelli
Marilyn S. Shank
Lori Unruh
Christine Walther-Thomas
Laurie Ford
Charles D. Rhodes
Gloria Marie Graves

To Jay, Amy, and Kate—
Each exceptional, each our family, and each our teacher, making positive contributions.

To Mary Boone Patterson and Ruth W. Turnbull—
Who gave inherent strength to their families and who, though gone, are everlasting.

To Elizabeth M. Boggs—
Family advocate and our mentor, who taught us about choices by telling us about shoes.

To Richard L. Schiefelbusch—
Whose pithy aphorisms reveal great expectations and teach that every problem is an opportunity.

To Marianna and Ross Beach—
Whose compassion, competence, and commitment have created relationships for people with disabilities not just in Kansas but throughout the hemisphere.

To James MacDonald Fowler, "Jamie"—
Deserving of full citizenship but denied it, not because of his disability, but because of society's—a denial that this book seeks to overcome.

PREFACE

Families, Professionals, and Exceptionality: A Special Partnership concerns families, people who are exceptional, professionals, and ways they can work together more effectively. Although this topic is not original, the focus of this book is unique and the book itself is different from previous works in important ways.

This edition is explicitly value-based. We identify and operationalize six values that guide our research, training, and dissemination efforts at the Beach Center on Families and Disability at The University of Kansas. These values enable us to see families in a different light and then help them better. The values are:

- *Positive contributions*—Persons with disabilities contribute positively to their families. They enrich not only their families, but also their communities and society.

- *Great expectations*—Visions can become realities. Families need new perspectives of what life can be as well as support to fulfill these dreams.

- *Choices*—Families can direct their own lives. Enabling families to act on their preferences allows them to build on their strengths.

- *Relationships*—Connections are crucial to family unity. Family members need to be connected to each other and to friends in the community.

- *Full citizenship*—"Less able" does not mean "less worthy." People with disabilities and their families are entitled to full participation in American life.

- *Inherent strengths*—Families have many natural capacities. Nevertheless, they may need support to affirm positive contributions, achieve great expectations, obtain full citizenship, act on their choices, and enjoy relationships.

Throughout the book, we point out ways to incorporate these values into professional practice.

This second edition also places greater emphasis on *applying* family-systems theory in professional practice. Much has been learned in the last three years about family-systems theory and about how it can be applied. This text teaches you what our research and practice have taught us about applying theoretical concepts in everyday interactions with families. It addresses the needs of a much wider range of families, with particular attention and sensitivity to their cultural, racial, and socio-economic differences. Certainly, respecting family diversity is one of the major responsibilities of educators.

The first and second editions also have many elements in common. We deal with exceptionality in broad terms, addressing all types of disability (mental, cognitive, emotional, physical, language, and sensory) and characteristics of those who are gifted. We regard people with exceptionality as having many similar characteristics with respect to how they affect and are affected by their families and professionals. Accordingly, when we refer to individuals with exceptionalities, we include people who have disabilities as well as people who are gifted. But we recognize that there are distinctions that make a difference. People are different because of the type and extent of their exceptionality. We address their differences as well as their similarities.

We do not confine our discussion to a particular age range. We address the needs of families and people with exceptionalities throughout their life cycles, from infancy through childhood and school years and into adulthood. Although the subject matter requires that some aspects of the book have a deliberate school-years focus, for the most part, we deal with families at different life stages.

We take into account the enormous variety and diversity in families and guide professionals through a systematic and scholarly analysis of families. We apply the family-systems approach in the context of exceptionality across the life cycle. In doing so, we present state-of-art knowledge and reality-tested practice in family-professional relationships. We combine theory and application, not just in the four chapters that specifically address the family-systems concept but throughout the book, showing in many chapters how professionals may work with families within that framework.

We address the family in all its diversity: size, cultural background, geographic location, values, interaction styles, met and unmet needs, and the changing characteristics of a given family over time. By addressing the family as a system, we are not bounded by a focus on one family member, typically the person with an exceptionality. Indeed, we seek to show the complex interrelatedness of all members in a family and the importance of adopting a comprehensive view of professional interventions. We stress that each family must maintain its own critical balance, its unique center of gravity in order to allow any professional intervention to be beneficial to a family member or to the entire family. We encourage professional support of families.

In using a broad approach to exceptionality and families, our aim is to make this book useful to a wide range of professionals—to people working in special education, social welfare, psychology, counseling, health, and in related professions such as ministry and gerontology. Our orientation is interdisciplinary, relying on the most recent research in education, social work, counseling, law, and ethics, and providing relevant illustrations, suggestions, and resources.

We draw heavily on the published and unpublished stories of families. Accordingly, we have seasoned the book with a compelling real-life flavor. We undergird its theories and concepts with the reality of the living laboratory, the reality of family life. Our own experience has added to this combination of theory and reality—our three children are all exceptional, each in a different way. Our son Jay, who has mental retardation, and our daughters, Amy and Kate, have been our catalysts for personal insights into the ways in which disability impacts family relationships.

We have synthesized wide-ranging subjects in the 14 chapters of this book. First, we emphasize the history of parental roles in exceptionalities (Chapter 1), then family-systems concepts (Chapters 2–5). After tying those concepts to family-professional communication skills and strategies (Chapters 6–7), we present the dominant legal framework within which families and professionals must work (Chapters 8–11), concluding with a discussion of family support strategies (Chapters 12–13) and an analysis of moral issues in family and professional relationships (Chapter 14).

To accompany this edition we have compiled an Instructor's Manual that is available from Merrill Publishing Company. This manual provides ideas for how to teach the content of each chapter of the book and is especially helpful by providing family vignettes, small-group problem solving, and role plays that can enliven the didactic content. One of the special features of the Instructor's Manual is that it provides suggestions for how best to use *Parents Speak Out: Then and Now* (Merrill Publishing Company) and pair the two into a comprehensive instructional sequence. (*Parents Speak Out: Then and Now* is a collection of essays written by family members. It provides candid accounts of issues associated with disability. The experiential content of *Parents Speak Out* is highly complementary to the instructional content of this textbook.)

Descriptions and results of research and training projects at the Beach Center on Families and Disability at The University of Kansas, which we co-direct, are incorporated throughout the chapters. The Beach Center is involved in over a dozen research projects related to the six values stated at the beginning of this preface.

Finally, throughout the book we convey optimism, hopefulness, and enthusiasm about families, people with exceptionalities, and family-professional relationships. In this respect, we emphasize the positive contributions that individuals with exceptionalities, their families, and professionals make to each other, rejecting the focus of so much other literature in this field on pathologies and negative stereotypes related to exceptionality.

Our goal has been to organize knowledge so that it is value-based, scholarly, understandable, holistic, relevant, and inspiring. Above all else, our hope is that the information we present makes a positive difference in your life and in the lives of the professionals and families with whom you interact.

We invite you to communicate with us about ways by which we can enhance the relevance of the content of this book in future editions.

Acknowledgments

Because it represents the contributions of colleagues and friends, this book symbolizes the collegial atmosphere at the Beach Center on Families and Disability, the Bureau of Child Research, and the Department of Special Education at The University of Kansas. We want to acknowledge many of those individuals and to state that countless others have also influenced our thinking and provided catalysts for the directions we have taken.

Substantial contributions have been made to the first and second editions by graduate students who are emphasizing family and policy issues in their graduate studies in the Department of Special Education at The University of Kansas. The book has grown out of our interactions with students, and we hope that these interactions will continue for many years. We truly believe that they are part of our collegial family as well as our textbook family.

Since this second edition includes a significant portion of the original work, we would be remiss if we did not acknowledge the helpful assistance we received with the first edition of this book. In the first edition, we were greatly aided by the collaboration and contributions of our colleagues and friends, Jean Ann Summers (Chapters 2, 5, and 13), Mary Jane Brotherson (Chapters 3 and 4), and Holly Benson (Chapters 6 and 7). At that time, they were doctoral students working with us, now they are professional colleagues. We also acknowledge the cheerful and conscientious efforts of a number of people in preparing the first edition manuscript, including Mary Beth Johnston, Dorothy Johanning, Marilyn Fischer, Connie Roeder-Gordon, Harriet Shaffer, Thelma Dillon, Lori Llewellyn, Joni Randel, Barbara Bartz, Lisa Wilshire, Jon Gaines, and Kiesa Harris. Further, we are indebted to the following for their constructive criticism: Cindy Bernheimer, University of California at Los Angeles; Pam Winton, University of North Carolina at Chapel Hill; Joan Safran, Youngstown State University; George Sugai, University of Oregon; and Jane Morse, Lawrence, Kansas.

Invaluable contributions have also been made to the second edition by a number of authors. These include Julie Sergeant (Chapters 1 and 12 and Appendix A), Betsy Santelli (Chapters 6 and 7), Marilyn Shank (Chapters 5 and 10), Chriss Walther-Thomas (Chapters 3 and 4), Lori Unruh (Chapter 9 and Appendix B), Chuck Rhodes (Chapter 13), Laurie Ford (Chapter 2), and Gloria Graves (Chapter 11). We underscore the contributions of Julie Sergeant in helping us coordinate the entire revision process. Her competence and conscientiousness made a critical difference in our ability to make substantial revisions. Manuscript preparation was superbly handled by Mary Beth Johnston and Opal Folks. We acknowledge with gratitude the photographic expertise of Karen Sorenson. In addition, we thank Liliano Mayo, Nancy Richards, and the staff of Families Together, Inc. (Topeka, Kansas) and the Special Education Early Childhood Intervention Program at The University of Kansas for assisting with photographs. Others who helped with the numerous revision tasks include Dorothy Johanning and Susan Shaffer.

We are convinced that we are surrounded by the most supportive and stimulating colleagues anybody could wish for. We salute and thank our colleagues at the Beach Center on Families and Disability, the Bureau of Child Research, and the Department of Special Education. Likewise, the quality of our work is continually enhanced by the problem solving and networking of our superbly qualified Project Officer, Naomi Karp, at the National Institute for Disability and Rehabilitation Research. We also value the opportunity to have worked with our previous administrative editor at Merrill Publishing, Vicki Knight, and our current editor, Ann Castel. We appreciate the competent and cheerful assistance of all the staff at Merrill, in particular editorial assistant Brenda Rock. Finally, we express gratitude to the reviewers who helped shape and improve the second edition: George Sugai, University of Oregon; Sandra W. Gautt, University of Missouri, Columbia; Diane Klein, California State University—Los Angeles; Raymond Dembinski, Northern Illinois University; Annette Tessier, California State University—Los Angeles; and Kent Gerlach, Pacific Lutheran University—Tacoma.

CONTENTS

CHAPTER 3   FAMILY INTERACTION   53

CHAPTER 4   FAMILY FUNCTIONS   79

CHAPTER 5   FAMILY LIFE CYCLE   103

CHAPTER 6   COMMUNICATION SKILLS   143

FAMILIES, PROFESSIONALS, AND EXCEPTIONALITY

A Special Partnership

HISTORICAL AND CURRENT ROLES OF PARENTS

The photograph is of Dr. Elizabeth Boggs and her son, David. This book is dedicated to Dr. Boggs because of her instrumental contribution to shaping the historical and current roles of parents.

Sharing the Journey

Interdependence
not independence
is the reality of this world.
I have a shared destiny
touching the lives
of countless others
as ripples in a pond
fan out in ever-widening circles.
We live in
one another's company.
Together we can diffuse the pain
and multiply the joy
of being.

Brenda Neal

Brenda Neal is a founding member of *Let's Face It,* a support network for people with facial disfigurement. Born with neurofibroma, she understands the reciprocal impact individuals have on each other. We hope that you, as a professional, will consider the importance of the interdependent relationships you will encounter in your work and life, and that you will recognize the inherent strengths that families possess. We hope that you will strive to make these relationships effective ones that will enable families to envision great expectations for their sons and daughters, realize the positive contributions that family members with a disability offer, and expand the choices available to their families as a whole.

There are several reasons why it is important for you to know about the history of parent roles in the care and education of children and youth with exceptionalities. First, history helps us understand issues and approaches; indeed, many current issues relating to family adjustment and family-professional relationships are legacies from the past. Second, many of the challenges that families and professionals face can be aided by the lessons of history. Third, history provides insight into the fickle nature of seemingly entrenched approaches, for the pendulum has swung numerous times on family issues. Today's approaches may seem as improbable to the 21st century as previous approaches seem now.

Upon completion of this chapter, you will be able to answer the following questions:

- What are eight major roles which have been cast upon and assumed by parents of children with exceptionalities?

1

- How might these roles influence the lives of families that are affected by them?
- What implications does knowledge of these historical roles hold for you, as a professional who works with families?

Parents have assumed or have been expected by professionals to assume eight major roles: parents as (a) the source of their child's problems, (b) organization members, (c) service developers, (d) recipients of professionals' decisions, (e) learners and teachers, (f) political advocates, (g) educational decision makers, and (h) family members. These roles did not develop during, and do not represent, discrete time periods, each with a clear demarcation of beginning and end. Rather, there is significant overlapping of roles and eras. There is, however, a general and approximate chronological order of their respective beginnings, peak period of emphasis, and decline. With this general background in mind, we will describe each of these eight roles.

PARENTS AS THE PROBLEM SOURCE

The eugenics movement (1880–1930) contributed greatly to the view that parents are the source of a child's disability. The intent of the eugenics movement was to "improve" the human race through selective breeding. According to Scheerenberger (1983), it was based on (a) genealogical investigations such as Goddard's (1912) study of the Kallikak family, (b) rediscovery of Mendel's heredity laws, and (c) studies indicating that delinquent behaviors were strongly associated with "feeble-mindedness" (MacMurphy, 1916; Terman, 1916). Indeed, the eugenics movement asserted that heredity is the cause of mental retardation. Barr (1913), a leading physician during the eugenics movement, linked heredity with mental retardation:

> A knowledge of causation and the assurance that many pathways lead to one condition of ill, idiocy—a condition which may be doubled and quadrupled through inheritance—should surely have its influence in inducing the adoption of means of prevention, wiser and more humane than those practiced by older nations to preserve the integrity of society. Not by destroying the life of the weakling but by refusing to allow him to perpetuate a maimed existence; next by a simplification of all life, be it the pursuit of wealth or learning, of occupation or amusement—a conservation in lieu of a dissipation of energy; then, after this elimination of harmful influences, such selection in mating, as shall insure only the survival of the fittest. (p. 123)

The eugenics movement resulted in laws restricting the marriage of persons with intellectual disabilities, requiring compulsory sterilization, and causing a sharp increase in institutionalization. Based on U.S. Department of Commerce (1923, 1934) data, Scheerenberger (1983) reported that 9,334 persons with mental retardation were institutionalized in 1900 and 68,035 in 1930.

The policies and practices of state institutions and hospitals, such as limiting and supervising visiting hours, further reinforced the view that families negatively influence their sons and daughters:

> On Thanksgiving Eve I was notified twenty minutes before the holiday pass was to start that all holiday passes had been cancelled by the doctor for sixty days. This covered two major holidays and birthdays for my daughter and myself. I was given five minutes to notify the social worker which one hour I would come and visit in the next four days. Since my holiday had just been thrown into turmoil, I refused to do so and therefore had no contact at all with my daughter over the long Thanksgiving weekend. . . . From the staff's viewpoint they are "protecting me" from my daughter despite the fact she is worse when we have no contact and that has been confirmed repeatedly.

> Once the doctor ordered no contact at all—visit, phone call, or mail. (This was before phones had been installed on the wards.) When I pointed out my daughter's legal right to receive mail, I was "requested" not to send any. I refused.

In other areas of exceptionality, parents were scorned during this period for maladaptive personality traits and child-rearing practices. Often they were viewed as the source of their children's problems, particularly when the children had autism, asthma, or emotional disorders. It was typical in the 1940s and 1950s for professionals to describe parents of children and youth who are autistic or psychotic as rigid, perfectionistic, emotionally impoverished, and depressed (Kanner, 1949; Marcus, 1977). Leading professional Dr. Bruno Bettleheim (1950, 1967) contended that a child who had autism characterized by severe withdrawal possessed these tendencies as a response to the stress created by parental attitudes and feelings. He even advocated "parentectomy," institutionalizing the child to replace parents with institutional staff and professionals considered more competent and caring. By contrast, a recent definition of autism states that "no known factors in the psychological environment of a child have been shown to cause autism" (National Society for Autistic Children, 1977). In light of that definition, Frank Warren (1985), whose son has autism, discusses his reaction to Bettleheim's theory of causation:

> That means we didn't do it, Bruno. . . . We, the parents of autistic children, are just ordinary people. Not any crazier than others. Not "refrigerator parents" any more than others. Not cold intellectuals any more than others. Not neurotic or psychopathic or sociopathic or any of those words that have been made up. It means, Dr. Bettleheim, that you, and all those

others like you who have been laying this incredible guilt trip on us for over 20 years, you are wrong and ought to be ashamed of yourselves. (p. 217)

During this century the impact of causation theories has sent many parents on a tremendous "guilt trip" and, in turn, has produced barriers to constructive parent-professional relationships—resentment, low self-esteem, lack of trust, and defensiveness.

Of course, some disabilities in children may be traced to the parents. For example, some conditions (e.g., cystic fibrosis) are clearly genetic in nature. Excessive maternal use of alcohol or drugs during pregnancy may cause children to have disabling conditions such as fetal alcohol syndrome or cocaine addiction. Malnutrition during pregnancy or in the child's early life may lead to mild mental retardation or motor impairment (Peterson, 1987). However obvious the association between the child's environment and her current situation may seem, the professional must be aware that some children who are exposed to extremely detrimental environments early in life mature relatively unscathed by their experiences, whereas other children who are subjected to less stressful environments may fail to thrive and experience developmental delays (Ensher & Clark, 1986).

Although causation theories have declined over the last 20 years, each of us can help eradicate erroneous accusations wherever they occur—whether in professional literature, teachers' lounges, or parent-professional conferences. Through our own family and professional experiences, we have come to the conclusion that parents do the best they can with the numerous and competing responsibilities they are facing, and that it is impossible to judge another person until we have "walked a mile in her moccasins."

PARENTS AS ORGANIZATION MEMBERS

Largely because of inadequate public and professional responses to their children's educational and other needs, and as a result of their own needs for emotional support, parents began to organize on a local level in the 1930s and on the national level in the late 1940s and 1950s. In 1933, five mothers of children with mental retardation in Cuyahoga County, Ohio, organized a group to protest the public schools' exclusion of their children. Their efforts led to a special class that they themselves sponsored. In 1950, 42 parents and other concerned individuals from 13 states met in Minneapolis to establish the National Association of Parents and Friends of Mentally Retarded Children (now, ARC/USA—The Association for Retarded Citizens).

TABLE 1–1   Milestones of the Association for Retarded Citizens

---

MILESTONES

The Association for Retarded Citizens of the United States has a rich history of improving the lives of people with mental retardation and their families. The ARC also led the way in research and has educated millions regarding prevention of one-half of the known causes of mental retardation. The following are some of ARC's major historical events and accomplishments.

1954   The first National Headquarters opened in New York City. President Eisenhower declared the first National Retarded Children's Week.

1956   "Federal Program of Action for America's Retarded Children and Adults" was presented to Congress. Testimony was provided on bills to expand teaching and research in the education of children with mental retardation.

1959   ARC published a landmark report, *Decade of Decision,* describing the Association's accomplishments and prospects for meeting the service needs of persons with retardation.

1956–1961   Federal support for mental retardation services and research increased from $14 million to $94 million.

1964   Membership totaled 100,000. The first interorganizational conference on mental retardation convened with representatives from 28 national organizations.

1969   ARC opened a governmental affairs office in Washington, D.C., to increase ARC visibility in our nation's capital and to attempt to influence federal policy toward helping persons with mental retardation and their families.

1974   Reflecting its growing service to adults as well as children, ARC's name was changed to the National Association for Retarded Citizens.

In the mid-**1970**s, the Association worked for two major programs that significantly impacted on the lives of people with retardation—Supplemental Security Income and Title Twenty Social Services.

1975   The Association's Research and Demonstration Institute was founded. ARC members' hard work to secure the right to a public education for all children, regardless of their handicap, was rewarded by passage of Public Law 94–142.

1982   The death in Indiana of a baby born with Down syndrome sparked renewed efforts by ARC toward protecting the lives of other so-called "Baby Does" born with mental retardation and other defects.

1985   ARC advocated for persons with mental retardation when the U.S. Supreme Court heard the Cleburne case, in which a group home was denied a permit to operate in Cleburne, Texas. The Court ruled the city of Cleburne's opposition was unconstitutional.

1986   A banner year for key legislation with no less than 11 major laws enacted by Congress and signed by President Reagan. That total included the Education of the Handicapped Act Amendments of 1986 (P.L. 99–457).

Note. From "Milestones," 1987, Arlington, TX: Association for Retarded Citizens. Adapted by permission.

Over the years the ARC has exerted a powerful influence at the national, state, and local level to represent the interests of persons with mental retardation and their families. Table 1–1 highlights ARC's major accomplishments.

United Cerebral Palsy Associations, Inc. (UCP) has a somewhat similar history. It was founded in 1949 largely through the efforts of Leonard H. Goldenson, the father of a child with cerebral palsy. Here is what he related about UPC's beginnings:

> One day, realizing the cost of driving our child into New York City from Westchester, my wife said to me, "Leonard, I know we can afford to do this but what about the poor people? How can they afford to do it?" And she added, "Why don't we look into the possibility of trying to help others in this field?"
>
> It was on that basis that I started to investigate the whole field of cerebral palsy.
>
> Upon investigation, I found there were probably only twenty-some-odd doctors in the entire United States who knew anything about cerebral palsy. I found there were only a few local parents groups in the country that were trying to do something about it. But the parents were so involved with their own children and had to take so much time with them, they could not get out to raise money and inform the public about the subject. (Goldenson, 1965, pp. 1–2)

Other parent groups have been organized—the National Society for Autistic Children in 1961, the National Association for Down Syndrome in 1961, and the Association for Children with Learning Disabilities in 1964.

Parents continue to recognize the benefits of unity. In December 1988, approximately 60 parents and professionals interested in children and youth with emotional, behavioral, or mental disorders met in Arlington, Virginia. After intense discussions, this group decided that there was a major need for a national organization that focused on the needs and issues of these children and youth. A steering committee of parents was formed that later led to the establishment of the Federation of Families for Children's Mental Health. The mission statement of the Federation is included in Table 1–2. After attending the initial meeting, one parent rejoiced:

> We now have a national organization that places our children as its number-one priority. With the determination of parents and professionals working with us as partners, our "invisible children" have a greater chance of being seen and served appropriately in their own community and in their own homes.

Undoubtedly, parent groups have exerted a profound influence by creating opportunities for children and youth and providing hope and support to families. (Two major areas of impact are service delivery and political advocacy, which will be discussed separately in two later sections.)

TABLE 1–2 Mission Statement, Federation of Families for Children's Mental Health

---

- To ensure the rights to full citizenship, support and access to community-based services for all children and youth with emotional, behavioral, or mental disorders and their families.

- To address the unique needs of children and youth with emotional, behavioral, or mental disorders from birth through the transition to adulthood.

- To provide information and engage in advocacy regarding research, prevention, early intervention, family support, education, transition services, and other services needed by these children, youth and their families.

- To provide leadership in the field of children's mental health and develop necessary human and financial resources to meet its goal.

Note. From "Mission Statement" by the Steering Committee for the Federation of Families for Children's Mental Health, March, 1989. Alexandria, VA: Federation of Families for Children's Mental Health. Reprinted by permission.

However, parent organizations do not meet the needs of every parent. For instance, one mother is very satisfied with her role in a parent organization:

> I am proud to be the only person who has been continuously active in some volunteer capacity with the National Association for Retarded Citizens since I participated in its founding in 1950. I believe that NARC has a unique role to play, and that the existence of a strong lay advocacy group which continues to recognize and respond to the great diversity of need among persons called retarded is the single most essential element in securing their future. I have jealously guarded my amateur status within the association even when positions as a consultant and lecture fees have come my way on the outside. In the early days I carried out many unbudgeted assignments which are now executed by paid staff. In recent years I have been able to accentuate multiple linkages with other agencies and movements that no one with ties to a paid position could have made. The cause has taken me to 44 states, plus Puerto Rico and 10 foreign countries. It is hard to put a job title on the role I've played. One could say that I've been a social synergist with a predisposition toward communication and collaboration rather than confrontation. (Boggs, 1985a, pp. 39–40)

By contrast, another mother is not satisfied at all:

> My first phone call to my local unit produced a pleasant enough response from the office secretary and a promise of some information to be mailed. This material consisted of a short summary of the unit's programs and services and a long questionnaire on which I could indicate areas in

which I would be delighted to volunteer. There were numberless areas where I would be useful to the unit; there seemed little they had to offer me. The meetings sounded dull and preoccupied with large and small bureaucratic issues; nothing seemed to have a bearing on Kathryn's development until she could attend a nursery class three years hence. The message was clear: a parent in my circumstances, trying to cope with a trauma of uncertain dimensions, should marshal her forces, muster her energies, and get out and work for the cause. . . .

If I had had an unretarded baby, I'd never in a million years have thought of volunteering for anything during that period. Now that I had Kathryn, why in the world would I be expected to do anything of the kind? Yet in the face of minimal help from the organization, it was telling me I should help it. And numb from shock and diminished self-confidence, I did my best to comply. (Bennett, 1985, p. 163, 164)

Moreover, a government committee's findings indicated that parent organizations tend to consist primarily of white, middle-class parents, and that minority parents and parents who are very rich or very poor typically do not join (President's Committee on Mental Retardation, 1977). Keep in mind that some parents, but not others, are helped by parent organizations. The "parent movement" is helpful to many parents, but it is not for everyone!

PARENTS AS SERVICE DEVELOPERS

Another parental role, developed largely through the concerted effort of parent organizations, involved helping to develop services for persons with exceptionalities. The emphasis in the 1950s and 1960s was on creating education programs for children who had moderate and severe disabilities and who were excluded from public schools. Local parent groups organized classes in community buildings or church basements and solicited financial support from charitable organizations. Over the years, parent organizations initiated services in education, recreation, residential living (group homes), and vocational alternatives. Some parent organizations started the necessary services and family members have devoted a substantial portion of their time to operate them. Other organizations adopted the role of acting as a catalyst for services, working with other community organizations such as public and private schools, recreation agencies, and social service agencies (President's Committee on Mental Retardation, 1977). Still others combined the two roles, serving as advocates and watchdog agencies while providing services to satisfy unmet needs.

It is important to recognize the profound impact of parental organizations on the development of special education services, an impact described by Samuel Kirk (1984), a distinguished special educator for the last five decades:

> I found a satisfaction in associating with many intelligent and knowledgeable parents in these organizations. I found that through association with other parents they learned what the best programs were for their children. If I were to give credit to one group in this country for the advancements that have been made in the education of exceptional children, I would place the parent organizations and parent movement in the forefront as the leading force. (p. 41)

Although the role of service developer and provider interests some families, professionals should not expect families to start services within the professionals' realm of responsibility. For example, parents should not be expected to start a supported employment program for students with disabilities, just as parents of other children would not be expected to start a college preparatory curriculum in their local high schools. Families have full rights to collaborate with professionals in creating educational, vocational, and recreational opportunities, but they should not have to assume full responsibility (as did Elizabeth Boggs and her fellow parents in the early 1950s).

Currently, many families within and outside of parent organizations devote substantial efforts to the development of services other than education; for example, the catalog of adaptive equipment, and appropriate technology and job index services offered by the American Foundation for the Blind; or the Epilepsy Foundation of America's involvement with programs for camping and respite care (American Foundation for the Blind, 1989; Epilepsy Foundation of America, 1989). Almost all parent organizations are involved with public information and support programs. Such involvement requires professionals to be especially aware of the time binds that constrict many parents due to innumerable family and work responsibilities (A. P. Turnbull & Winton, 1984). Many parents simply do not have the time to be service developers.

PARENTS AS RECIPIENTS OF PROFESSIONALS' DECISIONS

During the 1950s through 1970s, a primary role of parents was to enroll their sons and daughters in programs and comply with the professionals' decisions. This role applied particularly to parents whose children had mild disabilities and were served by the public school system. Many professionals expected that parents should defer decision making to them, as expressed in a leading methods textbook of this period:

> Should it be judged that special class placement will probably be of most benefit to the child, then placement should be made without delay. . . .

The entire program should be explained so the parents will understand what lies ahead for the child and so they can support the efforts of the teachers with the child. (Kolstoe, 1970, p. 42)

Another example from the 1960s addresses the alternative roles of educators and parents of students who are gifted in making placement decisions:

Some "guts" to speak straight from the shoulder would be helpful to the educators in this situation. Then the lay groups probably would realize they must delegate some of their authority to the educators to make necessary decisions for improving the education of students. For example, an overwhelming majority of parents do not have the sophistication in educational matters to decide whether or not their youngster would be better off educationally if placed in a differential program for the gifted. . . . Parents could better spend their time: a) supporting parent organizations for raising funds and influencing state and federal legislation, and b) learning techniques to aid their own youngsters toward high achievement. (Lucito, 1963, pp. 227–228)

These passages reflect a tenor of the times—first, professionals were expected to make educational decisions and then interpret these decisions to parents; and, second, parents were expected not to question professionals and to be appreciative recipients of services.

The expectation that families assume a passive role has decreased during the last 10 to 15 years; however, it still exists in practice. Professionals who believe that parents should be seen but not heard convey this message both directly and indirectly. Moreover, they create an important psychological barrier to effective parent-professional relationships (A. P. Turnbull, 1983).

PARENTS AS LEARNERS AND TEACHERS

The role of parents as learners and teachers emerged in the late 1960s, peaked in the 1970s, and appeared to be declining in the 1980s. Several factors have contributed to the development of this role. In education and psychology, the influence of the environment on intelligence was receiving increased recognition (Hunt, 1972). And, in political debates, the New Frontier and the Great Society of the Kennedy and Johnson administrations were introducing compensatory education programs, such as Head Start.

A premise of these programs was that the needs of families from economically deprived backgrounds and the problems associated with low socioeconomic home life resulted in child-rearing environments lacking in opportunities available in middle- to upper-class homes. Thus, programs such as Head Start offered parent training programs, directed at teaching parents how to be better teachers of their children, so that their children would, in turn, make more progress (N. L. Peterson, personal communication, February 10, 1989).

This approach to economically deprived parents was generalized to families of children with exceptionalities. Parents were viewed as agents for increasing children's progress and achievement; the professional view was that parents must first learn before they can teach. Parent training programs, therefore, taught behavioral principles to parents, who then were expected to work with their son or daughter at home. Enthusiasm was sparked by encouraging results that documented the effectiveness of parents as teachers of their children (Bricker & Bricker, 1976; Shearer & Shearer, 1977). Professionals, more emphatically than parents, served as proponents of the parent-as-teacher role.

Because parents *could* be effective teachers, many professionals believed that parents *should* be teachers. They also believed that "good" parents taught their children frequently (Benson & Turnbull, 1986).

The use of the term *parent* is actually a misnomer in this context. It is more correct to say that "good" *mothers* taught their children frequently. The professional emphasis was on the mother being her child's teacher. The literature of this period contains almost no reference to the role of fathers in their children's development.

Early childhood education programs have stressed parent training. Consider the following passage describing the type of parent involvement expected in the Handicapped Children's Early Education Program Network (early childhood projects), funded by the U.S. Department of Education:

> It thus becomes mandatory that projects develop training programs for parents with the objective of teaching parents to be effective in working with and teaching their own child. (Shearer & Shearer, 1977, p. 213)

Given the strong emphasis on the parent-as-teacher role, Karnes and Teska (1980) identified the competencies that parents need to acquire to fulfill this role:

> The parental competencies required for direct teaching of the handicapped child at home involve interacting with the child in ways that promote positive behavior; reinforcing desired behavior; establishing an environment that is conducive to learning; setting up and maintaining a routine for direct teaching; using procedures appropriate for teaching concepts and skills; adapting lesson plans to the child's interests and needs; determining whether the child has mastered knowledge and skills; keeping meaningful records, including notes on child progress; participating in a staffing of the child; communicating effectively with others; and assessing the child's stage of development. (p. 99)

It is important to note that these are less than half of the parental skills the authors identified as essential to the home-teaching role. You may be interested in comparing these competencies to the ones in your professional training programs. We question whether it is realistic to expect parents to develop such elaborate didactic skills.

The impact of the parent-as-teacher role on parent-child relationships has received negligible professional attention. Anecdotal accounts from some parents indicate unintended consequences, such as guilt and anxiety if they are not constantly working with their son or daughter. Other parents have found the role as their child's teacher to be very satisfying. As we repeatedly point out, different roles have different impacts on different parents.

One reason why the role of parents as learners and teachers has declined recently is the relatively low attendance rate at training sessions (Chilman, 1973; Rosenberg, Reppucci, & Linney, 1983). It appears that many parents have increasingly less time to carry out the learning and teaching roles—especially parents working outside the home and single parents. Yet, many families would like to have more information (not necessarily formal classes) on various topics.

The almost exclusive emphasis on behavioral training programs in the 1970s has changed so that today training opportunities are available on topics such as educational advocacy, homework, and future planning. In addition, the orientation includes fathers, brothers and sisters, and extended family members. Chapter 12 addresses the information needs of families and strategies for information exchange.

PARENTS AS POLITICAL ADVOCATES

Parents are tremendously successful as advocates in the political process, but they have had to work for many years and in many different advocacy forums to obtain services. For example, during the decade from 1949–1959 the number of states providing special education for students with mild retardation rose from 24 to 46 and for students with moderate mental retardation from very few to 37 (President's Committee on Mental Retardation, 1977). Still, services for students with severe and profound disabilities lagged behind during this period.

An advocacy landmark occurred in the late 1960s when parents of students with mild to severe mental retardation, in collaboration with the Pennsylvania Association for Retarded Children, sued the state to obtain a free appropriate education for children with mental retardation (*Pennsylvania Association for Retarded Citizens v. Commonwealth of Pennsylvania, 1972*). The parents won their lawsuit, and the court held that all children with mental retardation must be provided with a free public program of education and training.

Thereafter right-to-education suits were brought in almost every state, usually successfully. Thus the time was right to establish by federal legislation what had been decreed in the courts as state law and federal constitutional right (H. R. Turnbull, 1990). Parent organizations representing all areas of exceptionality, particularly the ARC-USA, joined forces with parents who were not organization members as well as with professionals, particularly the Council for Exceptional Children, to seek comprehensive federal legislation mandating that all students with disabilities be provided a free, appropriate public education. These groups were immensely successful, and Congress passed the Education of the Handicapped Act in 1970, an amendment in 1973, the Education for All Handicapped Children Act (P.L. 94–142) in 1975, and three amendments since then (1978, 1983, and 1986). (We discuss this legislation in detail in Chapter 8.) It is a tribute to parent advocacy—greatly aided by and sometimes led by professional organizations—that these laws have been passed and improved, that the parent organizations were able to form coalitions with each other and with professional groups, and that all of this has been accomplished over such an extended period of time in a continuous and consistent manner.

In addition to education, parent advocacy has targeted the standards of treatment in institutions, community services to meet the needs of individuals with a disability and their families, personnel training, research in prevention and amelioration, Social Security entitlements, employment opportunities, and residential options in community neighborhoods.

The role of families as political advocates continued in the 1980s with a strong and powerful constituency. Lowell Weicker (1985), a former United States senator from Connecticut and the father of a son with Down syndrome, described the impact of political advocacy on the attempts by the administration of former President Reagan to deemphasize the federal role in special education:

> The administration did not get its way. Why? Because the disabled people in this country and their advocates repudiated a long-held cliché that they were not a political constituency, or at least not a coherent one. It was assumed that in the rough and tumble world of politics they would not hold their own as a voting block or as advocates for their cause. But that assumption was blown to smithereens in the budget and policy deliberations of 1981, 1982, and again in 1983. In fact, I would be hard-pressed to name another group within the human service spectrum that has not only survived the policies of this administration but has also defeated them as consistently and as convincingly as the disabled community has. Indeed, it has set an example for others, who were believed to be better organized. (p. 284)

PARENTS AS EDUCATIONAL DECISION MAKERS

The role of parents as educational decision makers was established in 1975 when Congress enacted the Education of the Handicapped Act (EHA). This revolutionary law contains numerous requirements granting active decision-making rights to parents of children and youth with disabilities. But the law also is very traditional, because it recognizes the critical role families play in their children's development and the necessity of subjecting schools to parental oversight. Parents have traditionally had oversight opportunities through mechanisms such as local school boards. (Although children who are gifted are not included in the federal laws for children having disabilities, they do receive aid under other federal and state laws.)

An analysis of the testimony recorded in the Congressional Record prior to the passage of the EHA revealed the intentions of Congress in granting these pervasive parent rights (H. R. Turnbull, Turnbull, & Wheat, 1982). Congress's basic premise was that families of children and youth with disabilities could make no assumptions that the public schools would educate their children—that schools would allow parents to enroll their children, much less that schools would educate the children appropriately. Thus, Congress viewed parents as agents for accountability, as persons who should or could ensure that professionals provide an appropriate education. This view, promoted by the political advocacy of some parents, reflected a major switch in expectations about parents' roles. No longer were parents to be passive recipients of professionals' decisions concerning services to their children. Now, they were to be educational decision makers.

Many parents are keenly aware of this change. Prior to the EHA, they were told by school administrators whether and how their children were to be educated. They knew that their sons' and daughters' education depended on the discretion of the administrators. But now with passage of the EHA, given their children's right to an education and their rights as parents, parents' relationships with professionals have become more equal; and parents, by and large, are justified in believing that they can help shape their children's present and future capabilities (see Chapter 8).

Similarly, federal laws dealing with the training, habilitation, and rehabilitation of adults with disabilities also give parents and guardians—and, of course, the people with disabilities themselves—a right to participate in the development and implementation of individualized habilitation programs. Again, these laws stress the role of parents as partners of service professionals.

Just as all parents are not eager to be teachers of their children or serve as political advocates, neither have all parents embraced the role of educational decision maker (A. P. Turnbull & Turnbull, 1982). A study comparing the types of involvement of parents with children in special education classes versus those of parents with children in non-special education classes revealed that parents of children enrolled in special education programs were more likely to be involved in teacher conferences and IEP meetings, advocacy efforts, and helping with the program than the other parents who participated in the study (Salisbury & Evans, 1988). However, research over the last 10 years indicates that the majority of parents participate in educational decision making in a passive rather than an active style (Goldstein, Strickland, Turnbull, & Curry, 1980; Lusthaus, Lusthaus, & Gibbs, 1981; Lynch & Stein, 1982).

Significant barriers hamper active decision making by parents (see Chapter 10). Carol Michaelis, a mother of five children, one of whom has a disability, identified some of the problems associated with this role:

> Since funding for Special Education was tenuous, it also meant that to keep (my son) Jim in the class, I had to be involved. I lobbied at the school board and in the legislature. Keeping Jim in school also meant leaving housework and babies to attend parent conferences across town. No wonder I didn't have time to even try to mainstream myself into the coffee-cup conversation in the neighborhood kitchens. . . . Although so-phisticated services are being implemented in many places, the Individual-ized Education Program conferences, the school visits, and the parent groups take more time for already busy parents. Early intervention means all of this starts sooner and it is possible that the parent and the child are labeled and out of the mainstream even sooner. (Michaelis, 1981b, p. 15)

The roles of parents as educational decision makers as well as learners/teachers and political advocates have focused primarily on the needs of the child or youth with a disability. Thus, parental expectations have been defined in relation to that one individual. The parent perspective revealed by Michaelis indicates that parents have needs in addition to those associated with any of their children.

PARENTS AS FAMILY MEMBERS

Currently, professionals and parents alike are recognizing and emphasiz-ing the role of parents as family members. This role is based on the premise that successful family life requires that the needs of all family members, including parents, be identified and addressed. This premise is consistent with family systems theory, which views the family as a social system with unique characteristics and needs. A basic premise is that the individual members of a family are so interrelated that any ex-perience affecting one member will affect all (Carter & McGoldrick,

1980; Goldenberg & Goldenberg, 1980; Minuchin, 1974). For example, a mother might be so heavily involved in teaching her child and participating in educational decision making that she neglects to spend adequate time with her husband and other children and ignores her own personal needs. Whereas the earlier focus was almost exclusively on the parents (or mother) and their involvement with their child with an exceptionality, now more attention is being given to the diverse needs of each family member and the competing demands in terms of time and responsibility placed on parents. Ann Turnbull (1985b) illustrates the importance of this perspective:

> After Jay returned home (from a private institution for preschoolers, there being none available locally), Rud and I found ourselves overwhelmed with advocacy responsibilities which we felt were our duty as parents of a retarded child. We had meetings on an average of four or five nights a week. We were actively involved with the Association for Retarded Citizens, the group home and sheltered workshop boards of directors, a day-care coalition, a special education task force for the local schools, and a coalition aimed at legislative impact. We were constantly on the go and had little time for family relaxation. It occurred to us that we had brought Jay home from an institution only to leave him with a baby sitter while we went out and advocated for him. I could not help wondering why I saw so few of my professional colleagues at these evening meetings. Rud and I began to question whether the concept of normalization applies to families of handicapped individuals as well as to handicapped persons themselves. There was nothing normal about our schedules. We were not just consumers; rather we were consumed by the need to establish programs and services for Jay. When we reached the point of exhaustion and frustration, we realized that family priorities had to take precedence over advocacy needs. (p. 134)

This example demonstrates the essence of a family systems perspective—it is responsive to family priorities of *every* member of the family, not just the individual with an exceptionality.

Our view of the fallacy of past practices and the wisdom of a family systems perspective is encapsulated as follows:

> The term *parent involvement* sums up the current perspective. It means we want parents involved with *us*. It means the service delivery system we helped create is at the center of the universe, and families are revolving around it. It brings to mind an analogy about the old Ptolemaic view of the universe with the earth at the center. . . .
>
> Copernicous came along and made a startling reversal—he put the sun in the center of the universe rather than the Earth. His declaration caused profound shock. The earth was not the epitome of creation; it was a planet like all other planets. The successful challenge to the entire system of ancient authority required a complete change in philosophical conception of the universe. This is rightly termed the "Copernician Revolution."

Let's pause to consider what would happen if we had a Copernician Revolution in the field of disability. Visualize the concept: The *family* is the center of the universe and the service delivery system is one of the many planets revolving around it. Now visualize the service delivery system at the center and the family in orbit around it. Do you see the difference? Do you recognize the revolutionary change in perspective? We would move from an emphasis on parent involvement (i.e., parents participating in the program) to family support (i.e., programs providing a range of support services to families). This is not a semantic exercise—such a revolution leads us to a new set of assumptions and a new vista of options for service. (A. P. Turnbull & Summers, 1987, pp. 295–296)

We and our colleagues have synthesized the sociology literature on family systems theory with the special education literature on the impact of children and youth with exceptionalities on their families (Benson & Turnbull, 1986; A. P. Turnbull, Summers, & Brotherson, 1984; A. P. Turnbull, Brotherson, & Summers, 1985). As a result, we have proposed a framework, depicted in Figure 1–1, to organize family systems concepts. This framework leads us to a new set of assumptions and a new vista of options for services.

Here are the four major components of this framework:

1. *Family characteristics*—the descriptive elements of the family, including characteristics of the exceptionality (e.g., type, level of severity); characteristics of the family (e.g., sizes and forms, cultural backgrounds, socioeconomic status, geographic locations); personal characteristics (e.g., health, coping styles); and special challenges (e.g., poverty, abuse). From a systems perspective, resources can be thought of as the *input* into family interaction.

2. *Family interaction*—the relationships that occur among subgroups of family members on a daily and weekly basis. These relationships, the *process* of interaction, are responsive to individual and collective family needs.

3. *Family functions*—the different categories of needs the family is responsible for addressing. The purpose, or *output*, of family interaction is to produce responses to fulfill the needs associated with family functions.

4. *Family life cycle*—the sequence of developmental and nondevelopmental *changes* that affect families. These changes alter family characteristics (e.g., a child is born) and family functions (e.g., mother stops working outside the home, which provides more time for child-rearing but less family income). These changes, in turn, influence how the family interacts.

Chapters 2–5 focus on these four components of the family systems framework. These chapters emphasize family system concepts and

FIGURE 1–1   Family Systems Conceptual Framework

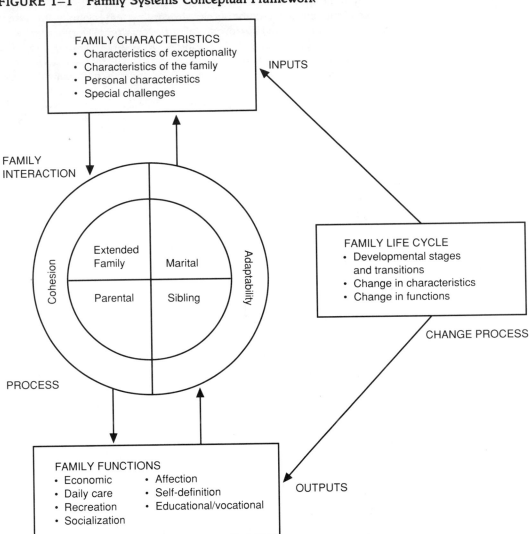

Note. From *Working with Families with Disabled Members: A Family Systems Approach* (p. 60) by A. P. Turnbull, J. A. Summers, and M. J. Brotherson, 1984, Lawrence, KS: The University of Kansas, Kansas University Affiliated Facility. Adapted by permission.

the application of these concepts to professionals working with families. The major contribution of the framework is to help you develop a comprehensive and relevant knowledge of the strengths and needs of families. It is an organizer for understanding the unique characteristics, patterns of interactions, functions, and the change process inherent in every family.

Recognizing that parents are family members with myriad responsibilities and individual needs and preferences has a profound influence on parent-professional relationships in special education settings. The same concept of individualization that the field of special education embraces as pertinent to children and youth also applies to parents and other family members. A family systems philosophy suggests that an understanding of family characteristics, interaction, functions, and life cycle can serve as the basis of meaningfully individualizing parent-professional relationships for the benefit of all concerned—the child, parents, other family members, and professionals. Furthermore, we can begin to consider *family*-professional relationships rather than merely *parent*-professional relationships.

SUMMARY

Many different parent roles have prevailed during this century. These include parents as: the sources of their child's problems, organization members, service organizers, recipients of professionals' decisions, learners and teachers, political advocates, educational decision makers, and family members. No role can characterize all parents. Families vary in the roles they assume, and professionals vary in the roles they consider appropriate and, in turn, recommend to and expect from parents.

The pendulum has swung back and forth along several dimensions:

1. from viewing parents as part of the child's problem to viewing them as a primary solution to the problem
2. from expecting passive roles to expecting active roles
3. from viewing families as a mother-child dyad to recognizing the presence and needs of all members
4. from professionals seeing family needs in a general way to them allowing for individual needs from each family member.

Parents and professionals alike may feel caught up in time-zone changes, much like world travelers. Avis (1985) describes the concept of "deinstitutionalization jet lag," referring to parents who were told years ago the state institution was best for their child, and who now are told the community is preferable. Professionals also experience "parent-role jet lag." Expectations and philosophies have drastically changed since the eugenics movement and the formation of parent organizations. Understanding the distance that has been traveled in this chapter paves the way for the forthcoming journey into the family-systems orientation. This journey starts by considering the vast diversity in resources that characterizes family life.

CHAPTER 2

FAMILY CHARACTERISTICS

Family traditions are influenced by the cultural background of families. These influences can be a source of strength for the family.

S ixteen-year-old Ming-Mei, an honor student, rushes home from her sixth-hour advanced calculus class. She needs to be there when the bus drops off her 6-year-old brother, Wei-Kong, who has cerebral palsy. Wei-Kong's cerebral palsy has left him with severe physical impairments which require the use of a wheelchair and limits many of his self-help skills such as unlocking the door or fixing a snack. Ming-Mei and Wei-Kong's mother works as a manager at a local department store and frequently puts in long hours of overtime to help make ends meet. She has been divorced from their father since Wei-Kong was 10 months old and is the sole financial support for the family.

Traditionally, the word *family* brings to mind the nostalgic picture of a mother, father, and two or three children living together at home. The father works during the week and spends evenings and weekends repairing things, mowing the yard, and playing with the children. The mother keeps house and nourishes body and soul with home-cooked meals and plenty of love. Grandparents are nearby—ready to take the kids fishing, bake cookies, and dole out wise counsel. On Thanksgiving all the aunts, uncles, and cousins gather for a day of family solidarity and joyous feasting.

The truth is that few American families today fit this nostalgic picture. Instead, families such as Ming-Mei and Wei-Kong's are more and more common. People in this country have decried the "decline" of the idealized nuclear family since the American Revolution, yet it is doubtful that a "typical" American family ever existed (Hareven, 1982).

In working with families who have a member with a disability it is critical to individualize your approach to families. An understanding of how families differ and how such differences shape the impact of the family member's exceptionality on the family is important. After exploring the various descriptive elements of the family in this chapter, you should be able to answer the following questions:

- What are four important variables that underlie the way an exceptionality affects a given family?
- In what ways do the characteristics of the exceptionality shape the family's reaction to the exceptionality?
- In what ways do the characteristics of the family shape their reaction to the exceptionality?
- In what ways do the personal strengths and needs of individuals within a family shape their reaction to the exceptionality?
- In what ways may families with special needs differ in their reaction to the exceptionality?

21

The families of today are very diverse. Thus, an attempt to characterize them in any single way would be futile (Benson, 1988). The
American family has changed dramatically in the last half century. For
example, many are delaying marriage or choosing to live alone. In
1986, it was estimated that 67% of all married women between the
ages of 18–34 years were employed outside of the home. Of those
women who are married with children under the age of six years, 60%
are in the labor force. Based on current trends, this number is expected
to increase to 80% by the 1990s (Frost, 1986). In addition, the divorce
rate has increased with almost 55% of marriages ending in divorce
(*Marriage and Divorce Today*, 1987). The result is that one out of every
five families with children under 18 is headed by a single parent (Norton
& Glick, 1986). In 1986 one out of every nine children under 18 lived
with a natural parent and a stepparent (Norton & Glick, 1986). Whether
or not we are witnessing fundamental changes in family structure, we
must recognize that few people live in a "traditional" nuclear family.

Beyond their demographic characteristics, families vary in a multitude of other ways. They differ in religion, ethnic background, education,
and wealth. They differ in their location—rural, urban, suburban. They
differ in values—what they think is important in life—and in their beliefs
about how people should and should not behave. Moreover, they differ
in number of friends and extended family members. They differ in their
personal idiosyncrasies and orientations toward daily living. Given all
the different ways in which families can vary, it is probably safe to say
that every family is idiosyncratic, if not unique.

Yet, although statistics about divorce and working mothers are familiar features in the media, and although most of us were raised since
grade school with stories about the American melting pot and its rich
cultural diversity, the nostalgic image of the "traditional" family continues to cloud professional-family relationships. Family support and
parent-involvement programs for families with children with exceptionalities often are best suited for nuclear two-parent, one-worker, middle-
class families—a minority today. The first step in working with families,
then, is to understand their diversities. The idea of diversity leads to the
conviction that you need to individualize your approach to families.

Four important variables underlie the way an individual with an exceptionality affects a family. These are highlighted in the "Family Characteristics" section of the Family Systems Conceptual Framework in Figure 2–1. First, the characteristics of the exceptionality itself shape the
family's reaction. *Exceptionality,* a broad term, includes persons who are
gifted as well as those with severe and multiple disabilities. Exceptionality includes non-normative conditions of a person's senses (hearing
and sight), health (heart, lungs, or other internal organs), body (limbs),
mind (mental capacity or learning ability), affect (emotional disorder),
and language (speech). In the first section of this chapter we will ex-

FIGURE 2–1 Family Systems Conceptual Framework

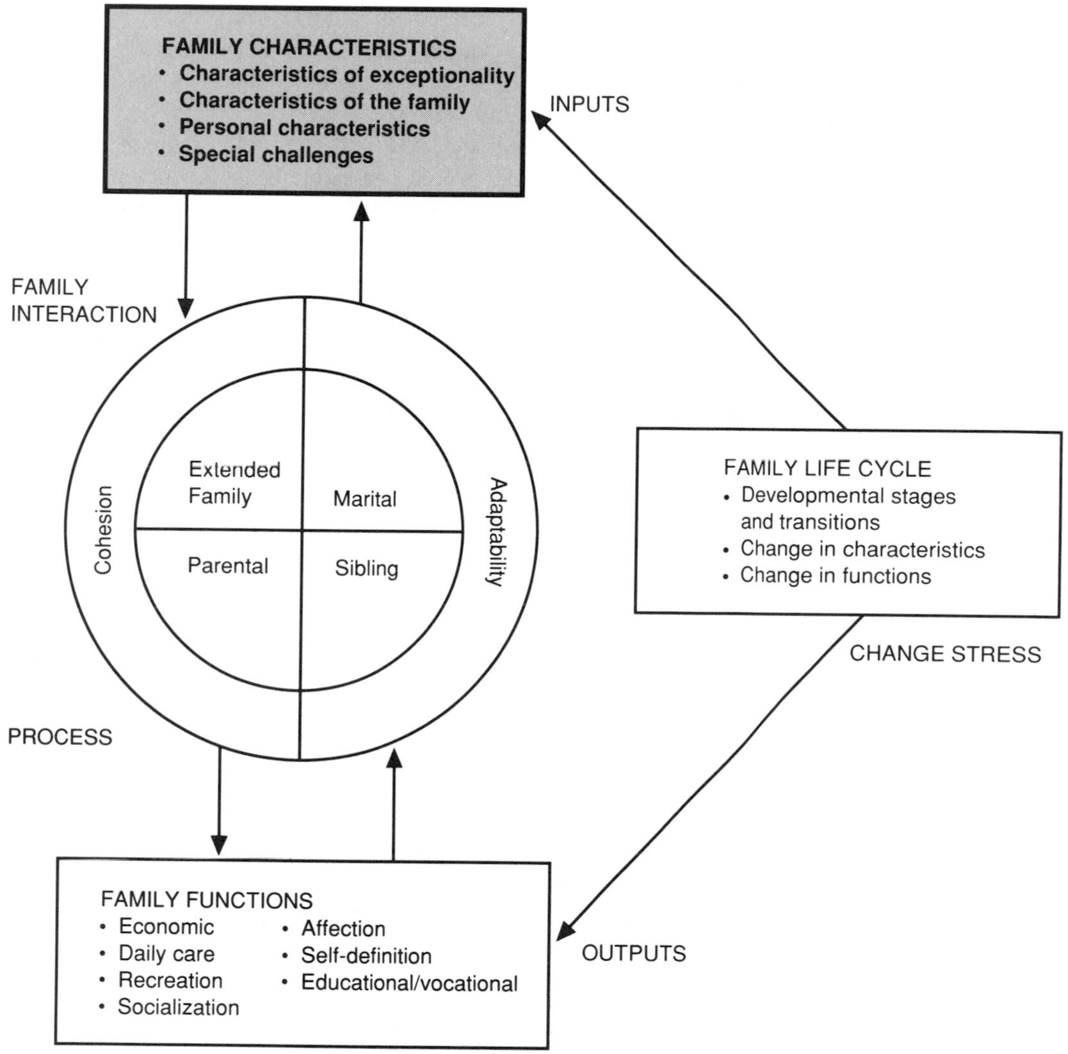

Note. Adapted from *Working with Families with Disabled Members: A Family Systems Approach* (p. 60) by A. P. Turnbull, J. A. Summers, and M. J. Brotherson, 1984, Lawrence, KS: The University of Kansas; Kansas University Affiliated Facility. Adapted by permission.

plore how the nature of the exceptionality may create different effects on families.

Second, the characteristics of families shape their reaction to the exceptionality. The family's cultural background, socioeconomic status, size, and other characteristics can have either negative or positive effects on the way the family copes with their child's exceptionality. Some of these characteristics, such as membership in a minority culture or single-parenthood, also create special issues concerning family-professional partnerships. The possible differences in any family member's reaction to exceptionalities, and special considerations for professional-family relationships as a result of these family characteristics, will be the topic of the second section in this chapter.

Third, every family is composed of individuals, each of whom has unique strengths and needs. These personal characteristics must be explored along with the individual styles of coping with the exceptionality. These issues will be explored in section three.

Finally, many families present special needs which may shape their reaction to the exceptionality. For example, a parent may have a disability, the family may live in poverty or the family may be involved in abuse or neglect which may present special challenges. The final section of this chapter explores these issues.

CHARACTERISTICS OF THE EXCEPTIONALITY

The characteristics of the exceptionality itself will shape a family's reaction to the exceptionality. Characteristics include the nature of the exceptionality (e.g., is the student considered gifted?); the severity of the exceptionality (is the student's condition considered mild or severe?); and the demands of the exceptionality (does the child need someone present at all times?). Each of these areas raises special issues in regard to a family's reaction to the exceptionality. Many times professionals view the disability as having a negative impact on the family, it is important to remember that children and youth with exceptionalities may make positive contributions to the family and enhance family strengths as well.

Nature of the Exceptionality

The nature of the exceptionality influences the family's reaction to it. For example, an uninsured condition requiring frequent medical attention may be a severe drain on the family's resources. A child with a terminal illness poses issues related to grief and loss. A child with a hearing impairment presents a communication problem that pervades everyday existence—how to understand what the child wants and how to make sure the child understands the rest of the family. One father expressed his frustration when his daughter with profound deafness was hospitalized with meningitis:

> Right now, when we needed to communicate with her the most, we could not. Our own daughter—and we hardly knew her! What if she never recovered? She could lip-read several hundred isolated words, but she couldn't speak her own name. She had never said "I'm tired," "I'm hungry" or "My tummy hurts." She had never said, "I love you." She had never asked for a doll or a stuffed teddy bear. She had never told us what she liked or wanted or who she played with.
>
> Communication! That's what we had been denied. An uncontrollable anger welled up within me. We had been cheated—it wasn't fair! Why? Why? Why? (Spradley & Spradley, 1978, p. 189)

A child who is gifted does not preclude stress for a family. Families may be concerned about the extent to which they can or should sacrifice the needs of other family members in order to develop a child's musical or artistic talent. The family may be exhausted by a young child's continual questions and explorations. Or, if the family has traditional values about sex roles, they may be concerned about the career ambitions of a daughter who is gifted and her potential to attract a husband (Perino & Perino, 1981).

When considering the nature of exceptionality, it is important to remember that different exceptionalities bring different kinds of challenges for families. Each exceptionality poses its own special needs and may make its own positive contributions. Take for example the vignette at the beginning of this chapter. This mother may be able to handle Ming-Mei's unique talents better than Wei-Kong's physical impairments, while Ming-Mei may have a better understanding of her brother's special services because she receives special services as well.

Severity of the Exceptionality

In addition to the nature of exceptionality, its severity creates differences in families. One is tempted to assume that a severe exceptionality means a more intense family impact, but such reasoning is not always valid. The issue is not that simple. The severity of a disability may result in qualitative, not quantitative, differences. For example, if a child has a severe disability, it may be apparent at birth and parents must deal immediately with the shock (Fortier & Wanlass, 1984). When the disability appears later, such as a hearing impairment or a learning disability, the parents may feel not so much shock as a sense of relief that their doubts have been resolved (Lonsdale, 1978). On the other hand, when the exceptionality is discovered later, families may have to cope with a complex set of mixed emotions. With a learning disability, for example, the parents may experience confusion and frustration at the discovery that their child, who appears capable in so many ways, indeed has a disability. Other families may be relieved to learn that there are reasons for the problems they have observed, among these some may feel a sense of guilt because the disability was not identified earlier (Walther-Thomas, Hazel, Schumaker, Vernon, & Deshler, in press).

Also, severe exceptionalities are often more visible than milder disabilities. On the one hand, this may excuse a child's inappropriate public behavior. On the other hand, it may cause the family more social stigma and rejection. Further, milder exceptionalities may be invisible, leading siblings to worry whether something is wrong with them, also (Powell & Ogle, 1985). With a severe disability, the family can adjust fairly early to the idea of their child's future dependency (A. P. Turnbull, Summers, & Brotherson, 1984). But with a milder disability, the family may find itself on a roller coaster of expectations, with hopes for the future alternately raised and dashed as the child makes progress or falls back (Wadsworth & Wadsworth, 1971).

Demands of the Exceptionality

The demands of a child's exceptionality also affect its impact on the family. Beckman (1983) found that 66% of the variance in mothers' stress could be accounted for by the unusual caretaking demands of infants with disabilities, including fussiness, irritability, and lack of responsiveness. An older child with a physical disability may require feeding, toileting, catheterization, medication, lifting, bathing, dressing, or other physical care that most children of the same age provide themselves.

For a child who has an emotional disorder, caretaking needs are very different, yet also extremely demanding. A young mother describes this effect graphically:

> I can't remember the last full night's sleep I've had. How can a four year-old be so destructive? He won't sleep or even sit still for very long. I can't have friends over anymore. The last time I did he tore up the living room and wouldn't stop hitting me. I don't even know what starts most of his tantrums. All I know is I can't control them. I guess it's good we don't have any close neighbors, they'd probably think I'm killing him. I thought it would stop as he got older, but it just seems to get worse.

As the child grows older, the issue of behavior control becomes more crucial. Thus, for a youth with autism, episodes of tantrums or aggression may be less frequent, but are often more devastating because of his or her size (Neulicht, 1984). Families may go out in public less often because they fear the occurrence of one of these episodes (Bristol & Schopler, 1983).

In addition to its effects on their own quality of life, many parents are concerned about the impact of behavior problems on their child's opportunities for independence and acceptance in the community. Lyn Isbell (1979c) describes her efforts to control the behavior of her son with Down syndrome:

> Walter's way of admiring a man's tie is to say "TIE!" and give it a strong yank. When he does so, the inevitable sequence of events is this:
>
> 1. The man turns purple.
> 2. The man quickly loosens his necktie knot and turns normal color again.
> 3. Walter's parent-in-charge-right-then says, "Walter, don't do that. That's rude!"
> 4. The man says, "Oh no, that's all right. I don't mind."
> 5. Walter smirks.
> 6. Parents feel helpless. Man feels embarrassed. Walter wins . . . and loses . . . and loses . . .
>
> It hurts people to see you spanking that poor little handicapped child, and people don't like to be hurt. These same people, however, don't live with the vision of the poor little handicapped child growing into a poor large handicapped adult with no idea in the world why he hasn't got much of a fan club. (Isbell, 1979c, pp. 48–49)

You need to be aware of some of the family implications of a student's exceptionality. Instructional objectives that could help the student and family (e.g., improved communication, social skills, or behavior control) perhaps should be given high priority. Some families may be interested in educational programs for behavior management at home (Chapter 12 includes a discussion of the types of programs available for this purpose). Other families might welcome information about services in the community, such as respite care or personal-care attendant services. The nature and extent of each child's exceptionality and unique characteristics carry special implications for the family. Consequently, services and instructional objectives must mitigate negative while enhancing positive effects of the exceptionality on the family.

CHARACTERISTICS OF THE FAMILY

By *family characteristics*, we mean characteristics of the family as a whole: its size and form, cultural background, socioeconomic status, and geographic locations. Each shapes the family's responses to an exceptionality, and each serves as a potential resource to help the family cope. We will consider each of these characteristics in turn.

Family Size and Form

One of the major issues that must be addressed in any discussion on family characteristics is family size and form. As mentioned earlier in this chapter, family structure varies in many ways. The number of children, the number of parents, the presence and number of stepparents, the extensiveness of the extended family, and preferences and extensiveness of live-in family members who are unrelated by blood or marriage all influence the family's reaction to an exceptionality.

Some research on families with members with exceptionalities suggests that larger families tend to be less distressed by the presence of a child with an exceptionality. Why this is so is unclear. It may be that in large families more people are available to help with chores and any special adaptations required by the exceptionality. Or it may be that a large number of children creates a greater atmosphere of normalcy (Trevino, 1979). A larger number of siblings may absorb parents' expectations for achievement that, in two-child families, often fall on the shoulders of the only child without an exceptionality (Powell & Ogle, 1985). Parents may be more philosophically accepting of the exceptionality when the presence of other children without exceptionalities serves as evidence that they are capable of producing "normal" children. Finally, other children may give parents a frame of reference which reminds them that their child with an exceptionality is more like than unlike the brothers and sisters in the family (A. P. Turnbull, Summers, & Brotherson, 1984).

One father of an adolescent daughter with William's Syndrome noted that the problems of his daughter with a disability are often no greater or perhaps even less difficult than the problems his other children experienced during adolescence.

> Adeliza had been, in many respects, the easiest of our six children. As she was the fourth daughter with two younger brothers we as parents were "old pros" at raising teenage daughters by the time Adeliza turned 13. She doesn't date and is not as rebellious as our other three daughters. Instead of being another stressful situation, her teenage years have, in general, been a very positive experience for our entire family.

Finally, when the child with an exceptionality is one of the younger children in the family, the experience of parenting may give parents the skills to cope. One mother, whose premature child was blinded at birth by an overdose of oxygen, noted:

> It was fortunate that she was not our first child. As parents of four, we had had experience; and perhaps I had developed a kind of knack with children. Two premature babies before Elizabeth had taught me that they

may, at first, resist cuddling. They are stiff and unrelaxed because they have had weeks of lying on the hard surface of an isolette where they are handled as little as possible to avoid infections. If a mother doesn't realize this, she may feel disappointed when her baby seems to prefer the crib to her arms. . . . Elizabeth was like that at first. . . . But I was determined not to give up. (Ulrich, 1972, pp. 22–23)

In addition to the number of children, the number of parents (single parent vs. two parents) in the household may cause a difference in a family's reaction to the exceptionality. The presence of a supportive husband—even when he does not participate in child care—seems to be an important predictor of a mother's ability to cope with an exceptionality (Friedrich, 1979; Kazak & Marvin, 1984). Further, positive adaptation to a child's exceptionality appears to be better in two-parent families (Trute & Hauch, 1988). Given the high divorce rate, you are certain to encounter single-parent families in your work with students having an exceptionality. Whether working with single or two-parent families, Meyer (1986) suggests that the impact of the child's disability differs in mothers and fathers. However, the literature is unclear as to the exact nature of such differences. In most programs for children with disabilities "parents" equals "mothers" (Bristol & Gallagher, 1986). Mothers and fathers of children with disabilities agree that fathers should take a more active role in the family, but neither group appears to know what form that involvement should take (Bristol & Gallagher, 1986). An awareness of these issues is important for professionals working with students who have exceptionalities.

A majority of single parents with custody of children are women, although a small but increasing percentage of fathers are maintaining custody (Simpson, 1982). Single-parent families hold a disadvantageous position in society relative to two-parent families because they are frequently characterized by a high rate of poverty, minority representation, mobility, and low education (Hanson & Sporakowski, 1986). Due to their generally low earning power, single mothers face these problems more often than single fathers. Because of the special demands of raising a child with an exceptionality, single mothers of children with a disability may have less choice about working than other single mothers (Vadasy, 1986). Thus, these single mothers must often face the strain of raising a child with a disability alone along with work responsibilities (Vadasy, 1986). Given these pressures, single parents may have neither the time nor the emotional energy to be heavily involved in their child's education. We encourage you to take these factors into consideration; for example, switching from a home-based to a center-based early intervention program may relieve some parental pressure. Respite care and involvement in support groups might also be important sources of help for parents who feel isolated (see Chapter 13). Finally, time-efficient communication, such as notes or phone calls, might take the place of more traditional parent-teacher conferences for parents whose responsibilities mean severely constrained schedules (see Chapters 6 and 7). Table 2–1 offers suggestions on how to work with children from single-parent households.

An opposite situation—more than two parents—exists in families in which one or both parents in the original family have remarried. Since 80% of people who divorce remarry (Visher & Visher, 1982), the likelihood of encountering a remarried or blended family is very high. Of all households with children under age 18, remarried families represent 17.4% (Glick, 1984). In such situations, a bewildering array of family variations and emotional situations are possible. For example, the blended family may include children from two or more marriages. Children may see acceptance of a stepparent as disloyalty to their biological parent (Benson, 1988). They may have to adopt rules and lifestyles in two different households, or give up adult roles they may have assumed while the custodial parent was single (Visher & Visher, 1982). Parents, in turn, may be uncertain about their authority over their spouse's children; or, with a "ready-made" family from the first day of marriage, may not have the privacy or time to establish their new relationship. In addition, issues of financial obligations regarding the previous mate(s) may cause jealousy or resentment (Sager et al., 1983). The resentments among all the adults—both former and current spouses—may surface

---

TABLE 2–1　Do's and Don'ts for Educators of Single-Parent Households

---

DO

- Identify the single-parent children.
- Periodically update school records to reflect family changes.
- Be aware of your attitudes, feelings and language.
- Initiate class discussions and activities regarding different family lifestyles and compositions.
- Focus projects and activities on the family rather than on mothers and fathers.
- Adopt policies regarding noncustodial parents and removal of the child from school.
- Offer before and after school extended care programs.
- Make referrals to mental health counselors when needed.
- Keep communication open with the family; offer a variety of communication options.
- Schedule family-teacher conferences at times when working parents can attend.
- Consider inviting substitute care providers to conferences.
- Have books available in the library.

TABLE 2–1 (Continued)

DO

- Be supportive of parents' situation.
- Teach feeling words in the classroom.
- Consider sex of the teacher when placing children in classrooms.
- Use non-school resources.
- Be aware of the symptoms/reactions to divorce/separation in children.

DON'T

- Blame all problems on living in a single-parent family.
- Make light of the situation.
- Pry or intrude into family privacy.
- Give advice or suggestions.
- Bring up sensitive issues.
- Break the child's confidentiality.
- Get involved in taking sides.

Note. From "20 dos and don'ts that will lessen the burden of grief for single–parent children," by S. Yehl, *Rainbows for All God's Children.* Schaumburg, IL: Rainbows for All God's Children. Adapted by permission.

in conflicts over the children, including visitation schedules, discipline, lifestyle, and so on (Sager et al., 1983).

Be sensitive to possible tensions in a remarried family and make accommodations both for the children's academic and behavioral performance and for the implications for parental involvement (Simpson, 1982). If both parents and a stepparent are involved in educational decision making, for example, an individualized education program (IEP) conference may range from being an amiable discussion about the child's best interests to a family power struggle where professionals are thrust in the middle.

Because of the variations of remarried families in terms of configurations, issues being faced, and ranges of emotional tension or comfort, it is difficult to develop any general rules for how best to work with them. It is important, of course, to avoid taking sides with one parent or another in any conflicts. But, how do you answer such questions as, Should the noncustodial parent be allowed to pick up the child after school or have access to the child's records? Probably such decisions should only be made by the custodial parent (see Chapter 14 for a possible ethical dilemma surrounding this question). In general, encourage involvement by everyone, including stepparents (Simpson, 1982), whenever such an arrangement is possible and agreeable to all parties. The positive side of a remarried family is that a wide circle of interested family members can potentially offer support both to each other and to the person with the exceptionality.

Approximately one out of five children is a stepchild. Thousands of new stepfamilies are formed each week. If these trends continue stepfamilies will represent the most common family structure (Albert, 1988). In your work with families, remember that no family should be considered "broken" whether it is a nuclear, remarried, adoptive, or foster family. The home atmosphere, the quality of the family's interactions, and the family's perception of itself affect the quality of the family life. Albert offers the suggestions listed in Table 2–2 for helping children adjust to a stepparent (Albert, 1988).

Strengthening Stepfamilies (Einstein & Albert, 1986) is a training program which includes readings, recordings, and activities counselors might use to teach stepfamilies the skills and strategies needed to insure a healthy and high-quality family.

TABLE 2–2   Guidelines for Parents Helping Children Adjust to a Stepparent

---

- Recognize the importance of the other biological parent and respect children's right and need to love that parent. Support the time they spend with their other family and invite that parent and other family members to milestone ceremonies—recitals, play-offs, graduations. At such events, focus only on the children and put aside unfinished emotional business between adults present.

- Never speak negatively of the other parent in front of the children; control any resentment you may feel.

- As a stepparent, acknowledge the strong bond between your new spouse and his or her children. So children won't feel left out, avoid monopolizing your mate's time.

- Plan "alone time" with your stepchildren so you can get to know one another better. *Invite* them to do things with you—don't pressure them or make demands.

- Understand that family life cannot always be happy. When conflict arises, it doesn't mean that your family is failing or that your stepchildren hate you.

- Don't expect "instant love"; allow time for relationships to develop. Concentrate on learning to accept, respect, and like your stepchildren.

- Reject fairy-tale myths and unrealistic media portrayals of stepfamilies. Forgive yourself for being imperfect. Realize that you learn when you make mistakes. So does your spouse, and so do the children.

Note. From *Strengthening Stepfamilies* (p. 2) by L. Albert and E. Einstein, 1986, Circle Pines, Minnesota: American Guidance Service. Copyright 1986 by American Guidance Service. Reprinted by permission.

Cultural Background

Individual family members usually have a sense of belonging to a family group; in turn, the family as a whole may have a sense of identity with a larger group within society (McGoldrick, 1982). Ethnic background and religion influence a family's daily life in terms of foods eaten, rituals and traditions celebrated, and so on. Cultural background lays a foundation of values and perspectives of the world that help the family define who they are. Such values and perspectives, in turn, play an important role in shaping a family's reaction to an exceptionality.

As in many other areas, variations exist in the way individuals from different cultural backgrounds view an exceptionality. In addition, within each culture of the larger society, various subcultures exist with their own beliefs, values, attitudes, and norms. Most of the literature on families who have a member with a disability has ignored variations in subcultures (Seligman & Daring, 1989).

The population of the United States is experiencing a shift in demography. In 1987, black students composed 16% of the public school enrollment, Hispanics 10%, and Asians and Pacific Islanders 3% (DBS Corporation, 1987). It is projected that by the turn of the century one out of three Americans will be nonwhite (Rodriquez, 1987). This growth of traditional minority populations is evident in states, cities, and neighborhoods. Thus, the number of minority students in many large city school systems is nearly 80% (Ramirez, 1988). As professionals working with children with exceptionalities, it is important to note the disproportionate representation of culturally diverse children in special education programs (Reschly, 1988).

It is difficult to understand cultural differences without sometimes glossing over differences and promoting stereotypes. Professionals working with the families of children with exceptionalities must be aware of cultural and subcultural differences, yet be careful to avoid stereotyping. Individuals within a given cultural group will not share all the values and beliefs held by the group as a whole (Staples, 1988). It is important that you recognize the potential for differences in values among families that may create a very different set of expectations and goals from those held by school professionals. It is also important to consider how some lifestyles may serve as strengths in the family's attempt to cope with the implications of an exceptionality. We recommend that you search out opportunities to become acquainted with the ethnic cultures represented in your community. Local newspapers and community bulletin boards will advertise cultural events and guest speakers who are interested in promoting public awareness of their community.

Although we are increasingly encouraged to celebrate our ethnic heritage, schools and other human-service agencies tend to mirror the dominant Anglo culture. Agencies' policy-makers are often white, middle-class community leaders, and a large proportion of professionals also come from white, middle-class backgrounds.

Some of the values of the Anglo culture include an achievement orientation, competition, work ethic, verbal competence, a belief in individual autonomy and independence, a focus on the future, and a belief in controlling the environment and one's self through a rational, scientific approach (McGill & Pearce, 1982). These values permeate special education curricula and other interventions from large issues, such as selecting instructional goals to enhance independence, to daily learning activities, such as competitive learning games.

Deviations from these values, or from those held by a given professional, have a number of implications for both educational programming and for relationships with families. For example, many Mexican-American families' traditional attitudes toward childrearing differ from those of the cultural mainstream. Many of these families have a more relaxed attitude toward achievement of developmental milestones and self-reliance in addition to a basic acceptance of a child's individuality (Falicov, 1982). A student from such a family background, therefore, may be frustrated by the competitive learning situations encountered in many American schools.

In many instances, parents from ethnically diverse backgrounds tend to be less knowledgeable about and involved in their child's education program than other parents (Lynch & Stein, 1987). As professionals working with such families, it is important to be aware of the values and attitudes they practice. Find ways to encourage families of diverse cultural backgrounds to participate in programs to a greater extent (Ramirez, 1988), while being sensitive to parental preferences for degree of involvement.

We will illustrate some of these points within the context of Native American traditions. Although Native Americans cannot be viewed as constituting a single subculture, individual tribes are often more similar to each other than they are to the cultural mainstream (Seligman & Darling, 1989). Table 2–3 lists differences in values between Native Americans and the American middle class according to Pepper (1976) and Price (1976) among others.

In particular, professionals working with Native American children should recognize that family involvement may include not only the natural parents but also other extended family members. For example, it is not uncommon for the primary caretaker to be the grandmother (Walker, 1988). Plan well and be persistent when trying to involve the families of Native American children.

Finally, families from Asian cultures may have difficulty assuming control of family-professional decision making, because they often see professionals as authority figures to be respected and obeyed (Deiner, 1983). However, because they typically accord such respect to teachers,

TABLE 2–3 Differences in Values Between Native Americans and American Middle Class

NATIVE AMERICAN	AMERICAN MIDDLE CLASS
Cooperation	Competition
Harmony with nature	Control over nature
Adult centered	Child centered
Present-time orientation	Future-time orientation
Expression through action	Verbal expression
Short childhood	Extended childhood
Education for knowledge	Education for grades

Note. From *Ordinary Families, Special Children* (p. 202) by M. Seligman and R. B. Darling, 1989, New York: Guilford Press. Copyright 1989 by the Guilford Press. Reprinted by permission.

families will often follow much of their advice. Thus, as educators, you can make a tremendous impact on these parents' treatment of their children with disabilities and their understanding of the child's disability (Yee, 1988).

Asian-Americans also value the family very highly. Problems are often regarded as private and to be resolved within the family (Shon & Ja, 1982). Counseling the family of a student with an emotional disorder may be difficult. However, this does not necessarily mean that a family will not accept more "technical" medical or therapeutic services. For example, Seligman and Darling (1989) note that one Vietnamese family in an early intervention program was very receptive to physical therapy and other services offered to their daughter, who had cerebral palsy.

Because Asian families often have difficulty accepting their child's disability, many may initially resist professionals' attempts to meet with them and even deny the existence of the disability (Yee, 1988). While the family must be allowed to cope in their own way, you should be supportive and provide necessary information about the disability when the family is ready (Yee, 1988).

Especially with families from minority cultures, it is important to recognize that families may approach the school or another service agency with caution due to past discrimination. Overrepresentation of minority students in special education programs has been well documented (Mercer, 1973; Reschley, 1988). It is for these reasons that the Education of the Handicapped Act requires nondiscriminatory evaluation and specifies that parents must be notified in their own language of evaluations and educational planning conferences. (See Chapter 8 for a discussion of these legal issues and Chapter 9 for evaluation practices designed to avoid discrimination.)

Overcoming the effects of discrimination requires more than laws, however. It requires that you cultivate rapport and trust with parents whose ethnic background may be different from your own; that you be aware of your own cultural biases; and that you learn many of the verbal or nonverbal styles found in the cultures represented in your school or agency. Respect, for example, may begin by taking care to address parents as "Mr." or "Mrs.," and avoiding patronizing tones and educational jargon (Deiner, 1983).

Family values and lifestyles in some cultural groups may serve as sources of strength in coping with an exceptionality. For example, the stereotype that black families are typically matriarchies (i.e., the major power figure is a strong mother or grandmother) is generally untrue. But this faulty perception may have arisen from the flexible role structures found in many black families and their ability to adopt a wide variety of family arrangements as situations demand (Williams & Stockton, 1973). The implication of these variations for educational involvement is that other family members (e.g., an aunt or a grandmother) might be included in educational decision making, especially if they are the ones who have day-to-day responsibility for the child. Also, black families tend to have strong kin networks into which a child or an adult with an exceptionality can be enfolded and receive financial, child-care, or emotional support (Utley & Marion, 1984). Families with these resources may not have a great need for formal community services such as respite care. Instead, they may be better served by help that strengthens their own system of coping, for example, teaching positioning or motor-therapy exercises to extended family members who are caring for the child. Again, however, they may not prefer community services. Table 2–4 lists some recommendations for how to develop increased sensitivity to the cultural subgroups in your community.

In summary, successful relationships with families require a great deal of self-awareness on the part of professionals. Your own values and communication styles may not be shared by others, and it is important to realize that "different" does not mean "bad." In fact, a close look at the values and customs of other cultures reveals many strengths—such as cooperation or supportive extended family networks—that may make these groups more resilient than the dominant culture in the face of an exceptionality. The realization that you can learn from all persons with whom you interact is the beginning of a sense of respect that should characterize all family-professional relationships. (More information on culturally sensitive communication is included in Chapter 6.)

Socioeconomic Status

A family's socioeconomic status (SES) includes its income, the level of family members' education, and the social status implied by the occupations of its wage earners. Such a definition implies that a higher SES

TABLE 2—4 Suggestions for How to Increase Sensitivity to the Cultural Subgroups in Your Community

---

- Learn about other cultures; share this information within your program.
- Learn how other cultures value children with disabilities, their childrearing practices, the different roles of family members in relation to the child with a handicap, and the value placed on education.
- Through your materials and public awareness, invite members of minority cultures to become involved in your program as staff, board members, volunteers, consultants, participants, etc.
- Learn at least a few words of different languages, especially common greetings, and the phrase "I really want to help."
- Learn about the culture before you design your program; gain the support and participation of the minority community in planning and outreach.
- Become familiar with your community. Find out what cultures are represented, how they are perceived by the professional community, and who the leaders are.
- Examine your hiring practices. Make an effort to hire minority members in a variety of positions.
- Work with members of other cultures to inform professionals of different cultural values and practices.
- Examine ways to remove barriers to accessing services for minority cultures, both through empowering parents and by simplifying the service systems.
- Recognize that we all have our prejudices and believe our values are right. Recognize the tendency to judge other cultural practices as superstitious.
- Learn about the resources within your community and help families access them.
- Remain sensitive to the complexities of being a minority within a majority; raise others' consciousness to the issues of minority cultures.

Note. From "Implications for Parent Training and Information Centers." Compiled by S. Lehr from parents' comments during *We the Parents . . .,* a conference conducted by the Institute on Multicultural Issues (TAPP), 1987, December. *Coalition Quarterly,* 6(2 & 3), 23. Adapted by permission.

family may have more resources available to cope with an exceptionality than a family with a lower SES. Indeed, the ability to pay for services and a higher level of education (leading to knowledge about the exceptionality) are definite resources. But the equation is not that simple; higher SES does not guarantee better coping skills. Lower SES families have resources also; they may have large families and extensive support networks. In addition, values come into play and shape the family's reaction to exceptionality.

Because higher SES families are often more achievement oriented, they may consider an exceptionality that involves a mental or physical disability a severe disappointment of their aspirations for their child's future. This is what Farber and Ryckman (1965) called the "tragic crisis." Lower SES families, on the other hand, tend to regard achievement as being less important than such values as family solidarity or happiness (Lee, 1982; Rubin, 1976). Therefore, to them a disability may represent less of a "tragic crisis" than an additional problem of how to care for the child: a "role organization crisis" (Farber & Ryckman, 1965). Conversely, a child who is gifted may be more stressful to a lower SES family with few resources to help the child develop natural talents.

Another difference between higher and lower SES families may be a sense among many higher SES families of having control of the environment and of the future. Consider the reaction of one father, a professional, to his son's diagnosis of Down syndrome:

> In those first days, my initial reaction was to control. I wanted to understand. I wanted to control the situation by the intellectual process with which I was familiar. But what I learned was not very helpful. . . . While every child's future is uncertain, my son's future seemed hopeless. I could not imagine for him a life so very different from my own. (H. M. Isbell, 1979, p. 22)

Many working-class families may not believe in the possibility of controlling their environment, with the corollary that very few plan for any child's future, let alone for the future of a child with an exceptionality (Rubin, 1976). For example, one factory worker recalled the financial fears he has had since his daughter with a physical disability was born.

> We were not prepared for a child with disabilities. But, we gave her the medical attention she needs. It hasn't been easy and it has caused us to have even more financial problems, but it doesn't stop us from doing all we can and more. Our family works very hard to keep our little girl happy. It has changed our lives. Any little new thing she learns, no matter how small gives us great joy. It is a lot of stress, who knows where the money will come from. People say they understand how rough it is but no one knows the pains and the worries of a parent of a child with disabilities.

On the one hand, therefore, higher SES families may be more stressed by an event, such as an exceptionality, that contradicts their belief that they are in control of their lives. Lower SES families, on the other hand, may have difficulty considering future options for their child and might be caught unprepared when it is time for their child to enter new programs (e.g., finding a long waiting list at an adult service program). Furthermore, a belief that it is useless to try to control a situation or to plan ahead may make lower SES families less active participants in educational decision making.

Geographic Location

As a result of electronic media and increased mobility in most segments of society, regional differences in family values and forms are becoming less and less apparent. Yet traces of regional stereotypes remain: Southern hospitality, Yankee stoicism, Midwestern conformity, and Western independence are values still discussed by family therapists and sociologists (McGill & Pearce, 1982). The same influences can be seen as homogenizing the values of rural and urban families. For example, while farm families once tended to value having many children partially because of their usefulness in working on the farm, modern farm technology has reduced the need for large numbers of children (J. A. Miller, Bigner, Jacobson, & Turner, 1982). Furthermore, the image of rural life as a peaceful existence is fast disappearing. Instead, farming is now considered to be in the top 10% of high-stress occupations, as farmers struggle with complex machinery, computerized operations, huge debts, and new definitions of the role of farm wives in the farm business (Wiegel, 1982).

One of the reasons for diminishing differences (in family characteristics) among geographic locations is the increased mobility of families. Some families move in order to find services. One mother, who had two children with hearing impairments, remarked:

> We lived in a small town in . . . , where they had almost nothing for handicapped children in the schools. We decided that if our children were to get an education, we would have to move; so we started looking at programs all over the country. . . . Finally we settled on Starr King because it had a first-rate oral program. My husband had to quit a good job; we moved to . . . , he had to search for another job and take a cut in pay. But it was worth it! (Spradley & Spradley, 1978, pp. 214–215)

When a family relocates, the stress of finding a new home and settling into a new community may be compounded by the difficulty of finding new services for the child with an exceptionality. Military families, migrant farm workers, and others whose jobs require frequent moves face this problem repeatedly. For example, the Knighton family's military career (Knighton, 1985) required six major moves during Denise's childhood. Each move meant a search for a new program; each move was a gamble that Denise, who had aphasia, could continue the progress she was making. Aside from the possible interruptions in the child's instructional program, moves may mean that parents repeatedly have to provide family and medical histories to new people, and learn the personalities and support potential of new staff. Yockey (1983) described an unfortunate encounter with an uncaring professional in his daughter's new school, and commented:

> As I write this today, certain descriptive adjectives and a few phrases of street vernacular come to mind, but none of them really do justice to the man. Why, you might ask, did we not respond to this unmitigated arrogance by simply telling the "good doctor" to go straight to hell? Because we were in a strange city, in a strange part of the country, in a new school, meeting with a group of people we didn't know, Barb with all the worries of a new house, me with a new job, both of us trying to get off on the right foot. That's not an apology, merely an explanation. (Yockey, 1983, p. 85)

It is helpful to be aware of the anxiety that often accompanies a family's relocation. Communication with and receipt of records from the student's previous school is essential. The interdisciplinary team should avoid routine family and medical history questions except when information is missing or when families appear to appreciate the opportunity to retell their story to new professionals. In addition, every attempt should be made to provide the relocated family with tours of facilities, descriptions of programs, and introductions to staff and other families in the program. The process of "settling in" a new child and his or her family should be as painless and smooth as possible.

This description of family characteristics has emphasized some of the many ways in which families can vary, as well as issues for your consideration. Large or small families, single-parent or blended families, different cultural backgrounds, and the family's geographic location (or relocation) each presents unique sets of challenges. The underlying themes in individualizing your approach are: respect for divergent values, an understanding of some of the many other issues—in addition to their child's exceptionality—the family may be facing, and a creative willingness to capitalize on some of the unique strengths and resources which can usually be found in even the most problem-bound family.

PERSONAL CHARACTERISTICS

The diversity of family units resulting from variations in cultural and other characteristics is multiplied as family members present their idiosyncracies. Thus, each family member has a state of mental and physical health that affects his or her tolerance to stress, an intellectual capacity to understand what is happening, and styles of coping with pressure.

These personal characteristics can be either strengths or drawbacks for the family as a whole, and all of them affect the family's reaction to an exceptionality, as well as appropriate professional approaches to the family.

Family Health

People who do not feel well have more difficulty coping with stressful situations. Conversely, stress produces physiological responses that can make people ill. Parents of children with exceptionalities often report suffering from headaches, lower back pain, depression, and other stress-related problems (Bristol & Schopler, 1983; McAndrew, 1976). Whether a parent's physical problem is caused by worry about the child's exceptionality or whether its source lies elsewhere, the result is the same: reduced ability to cope. To help stop the escalating spiral of stress buildup, you might recommend family support programs such as relaxation training and respite care (see Chapter 13).

Coping Styles

Stress is highly prevalent; thus the presence of an individual with an exceptionality may be only one among many pressures impinging on a family. *Coping* is defined as any strategy a person chooses to reduce feelings of stress (Pearlin & Schooler, 1978). Some family members may take positive action to solve a problem, while others may change the way they think about a situation to make it seem less stressful.

Olson and associates (Olson et al., 1983) developed the following categories of coping styles:

- Passive appraisal (ignoring a problem in the hope it will go away)
- Reframing (changing the way one thinks about a problem in order to solve it and/or to make it seem less stressful)
- Spiritual support (deriving comfort and guidance from one's spiritual beliefs)
- Social support (receiving practical and emotional assistance from friends and family)
- Professional support (receiving assistance from professionals and human service agencies).

These individual coping styles have many implications for developing family support programs. In Chapter 13 we will explore those coping strategies and consider ways they can be strengthened. Here the main point is that not everyone uses the same coping strategies. The following statements made by parents who have a child with a disability illustrate the use of different coping strategies:

> I frequently find myself comparing my son to others with Down syndrome. I find it encouraging to see older Down's kids working in the community . . . I hope Jeff Davis will have a job someday.

*   *   *   *   *

> Our family's strong faith in God has helped us deal with Amy's encephalitis and spinal meningitis. Each person must find their own strength, test it, and if it's not sufficient for the need then they must find it in another source. My source is God's strength and I've found that it never runs out and that it's always sufficient.

It matters little what the preferred strategy is as long as the result is the same: reduced stress.

We encourage you to be sensitive to the variety of ways that help people cope, and to work toward enhancing preferred styles rather than focusing on support that may not be useful to a given family. (In Chapter 13 we will recommend how to do that.)

SPECIAL CHALLENGES

The diversity that exists among families has brought several groups to public attention because they present special characteristics and needs which raise unique issues for professionals working with individuals from these groups. Families who live in poverty, families in rural areas, families where abuse occurs, and families where a parent has a disability will be considered in this section. Adding the demands of a child with an exceptionality to the challenges already facing these families clearly underscores the importance of learning how to support these families.

Families in Poverty

Beyond value differences, the harsh survival problems of families who live in poverty present yet another set of considerations. For these families, a child with an exceptionality may seem to be the least of their worries. Indeed, human-service providers are hard pressed to attract families in poverty into educational programs. For example, Rosenberg et al. (1983) reported the efforts of a program designed to provide parent education to low-income families whose children were at risk for developmental delay, abuse, or emotional disturbance. The program had a capacity to serve 130 families, but even though professionals agreed that there was a great need for the program, only 25 parents attended one or more group meetings in the first year. Rosenberg et al. (1983) speculated that their immediate problems were too overwhelming to allow these parents to attend to more long-term needs.

Families who struggle to meet the most basic needs of their children such as food, shelter, and health care are often unable to do the "extras" which are asked of families who have members with exceptionalities. As a result, although they may want to attend parent groups and teacher conferences, often they simply do not have enough time or energy.

As with families with different cultural backgrounds, it is important that you keep your own values and judgments in proper perspective when working with families in poverty. Parents who do not participate in educational programs do not necessarily care less about their children than those who do. Rather the daily responsibilities of sheer survival often take precedence over educational concerns. Witness the comments of a single mother with 10 children who had recently lost her job at a local supermarket:

> It's not that I don't want to know about my kids' schooling. It's just hard to find the time to go up there for meetings. I can't afford a babysitter and I usually can't find a ride. My oldest has a real nice teacher, I think she understands. She sends home notes and even came to our house one time to tell me about Carlton's classes. It sure makes it easier on me.

Generally headed by women, homeless families, another subgroup of families in poverty, may account for one third of the estimated homeless population of 2.5 million people (Bassuk & Rosenberg, 1988). Homeless people are poor people. Although children make up only one fourth of the U.S. population, four out of 10 poor people are children, and small children have become the fastest growing sector of the homeless (Kozol, 1988).

In the book *Rachel and Her Children: Homeless Families in America,* Kozol (1988) tells stories of homeless people based on his interviews and personal experiences with the homeless. One child tells of the room in which she lives with her mother and three other children.

> Ever since August we been livin' here. The room is either very hot or freezin' cold. When it be hot outside it's hot in here. When it be cold outside we have no heat. We used to live with my aunt but then it got too crowded there so we moved out. We went to welfare and they sent us to the shelter. Then they shipped us to Manhattan. I'm scared of the elevators. 'Fraid they be stuck. I take the stairs. (Kozol, 1988, p. 62)

Given the complexities facing families with limited resources, it seems a discouraging question to ask what, if anything, you can do. On an individual level, you may begin by building rapport and trust. On the school level, support and related-services staff should be available for nonthreatening visits with families, counseling, and nutrition consultation. On the community level, especially families with multiple problems underscore the need for workable interagency collaboration. Finally, social services, health agencies, and schools must cooperate to serve these families more effectively. (See Chapter 9 for a description of types of interagency cooperation.)

Families in Rural Areas

Rural areas typically are populated by disproportionate percentages of students from poor families and many times a large number of Hispanic migrants and other non-English speaking populations or other minorities such as Southern blacks and Native Americans (Helge, 1988). Some very different problems are associated with providing special education in rural areas, often having their roots in scarce services and the distances between families who have children with exceptionalities. Thus, rural families may experience a great sense of isolation if there are no other families in the immediate community whose children have similar problems. One mother of a five-year-old girl with autism who lives in the rural western Oklahoma panhandle expressed her feelings of loneliness and social isolation.

> I just want another person to talk to who really understands what it's like to have an autistic child. I have to drive four hours just to take Celeste to a doctor who really understands what autism is. I'm tired of people feeling sorry for me. I don't want pity, just another person who knows what it's like and can help me know what to do.

Providing services over great distances to a few families requires creative approaches. Latham (1981) pointed out that parents in rural areas may be the only resource available to provide therapy or instruction during the child's early childhood. He described a model in Utah using a combination of in-home video instruction tapes, self-instructional manuals, a WATS line, and a family newsletter. The problem with rural service models of this type is that rural families may be as busy—if not more so—as most other families (see Chapter 4 for a discussion of the many responsibilites families face); hence taking on major responsibility for their child's instruction may be too much unless backed by extensive support.

Families with Abuse

Another issue related to the family's mental health and well-being is family abuse. It is not a small problem. The American Association for Protecting Children (AAPC) (1980) reports the following:

- Approximately 1,727,000 cases of child maltreatment were reported to child protection agencies in the United States and its territories in 1984, representing a 16.93% increase over the preceding year's statistics.

- On a national level, 43% of the children involved in abuse were under 5 years of age; 33% were 6–11 years of age, and 24% were 12–17 years of age.

- Professionals—including medical personnel, social workers, school personnel, law enforcement officers, and child care providers—reported 49% of the suspected cases of child maltreatment. (Krents, Schulman, & Brenner, 1987, p. 79)

The causes of abuse are complex. Often abusing parents were themselves abused as children (Meier & Sloan, 1984). Consider the comments of a mother who had herself been physically and sexually abused by both her parents as a child:

> He was a very fussy child. His screaming drove me crazy. I can remember screaming back at him. I tried so hard, but it was just like being a kid again. Trying so hard to make somebody like me, and he just hated me. . . . His screams reminded me of my own screams as a kid. I wanted so much to do the right thing, but I was failing just like I did when I was a kid. Failing to make my parents love me, be proud of me, or even like me. . . . I remember throwing a Melmac dish against the wall in his general direction and watching it break against the wall. I was holding myself in the corner and thinking, "Oh God! I am just like her." (Harrison & Edwards, 1983, p. 43)

Frequently, abusing parents are young and have few friends. Abuse occurs at all socioeconomic levels and within all cultural groups (Embry, 1980). Various research studies have found that the percentage of abused children who show physical or intellectual problems (some type of exceptionality) ranges from 8 to 55 (Frodi, 1981). Johnson and Morse (1968) suggested that the most likely targets of abuse are children who are hyperactive or difficult to control. Although inconclusive, evidence suggests that children with physical disabilities are at risk for abuse or neglect (White, Benedict, Wulff, & Kelley, 1987). Even children who are gifted may be marked as sufficiently different to be singled out for abuse. Here are the comments of a woman who was abused as a child:

> The summer after my ninth grade year, I went to a community college. I had to do something to keep out of the house, and college classes were

much cheaper than trying to go to summer camp. I loved it there! Mom didn't think I could pass my college classes. I was taking three sections on earth science. I did pass. She nicknamed me "smartass" that year. I decided that I didn't want to go to high school; I wanted to stay in college. I applied for a grant which I received. Mom said that I couldn't go. . . . "Who do you think you are?" she would yell at me when I pleaded with her . . . (Harrison & Edwards, 1983, pp. 32–33)

Researchers suggest that abuse may result when children with exceptionalities are slow to respond to parental instructions (Meier & Sloan, 1984), when the parent-child bonding process has been interrupted due to temporary separation at birth (Blacher & Meyers, 1983), or because some infants—particularly premature babies—do not have a cuddly appearance and often emit a high-pitched and aversive cry (Frodi, 1981). Other researchers, however, point out that abuse and neglect may cause developmental delay due to brain damage, emotional trauma, or lack of early stimulation (Meier & Sloan, 1984). Both sets of dynamics are likely to be involved: Some exceptionalities may arouse aggressive responses in parents who are predisposed to violent reactions, while others may be the result of abuse.

Zirpoli (1986) suggested that because children with a disability present a long-term family crisis, they may be at greater risk for abuse for longer periods of time. However, it is important not to make an erroneous twist of reasoning. Statistically, it is true that a large percentage of children and youth who experience abuse also have exceptionalities. But the reverse conclusion—that a large percentage of children with exceptionalities are abused—does not follow. The vast majority of families whose members have exceptionalities do not abuse them (Embry, 1980). Whether exceptionality is the cause or the result of abuse is of vital interest to researchers who are attempting to find ways to prevent abuse. But, in dealing with the end result—people who are both battered and have exceptionalities—the cause makes little difference. The issue is: what to do?

First, all states have laws requiring school and health professionals to report cases of suspected abuse. But what constitutes "suspicion"? Table 2–5 lists some of the physical and behavioral indicators of different types of abuse.

It is important to remember that many students who are not abused can and do show any one of the signs listed as indicative of abuse. But the presence of many of these indicators, over time, should trigger further inquiry. Most schools maintain written policies and procedures on this issue, and each state has different laws on when, how, to whom, and under what circumstances, to report suspected abuse. You should be familiar with these policies and laws. If students confide in someone at school, they should be taken at their word. A school professional who

---

TABLE 2–5 Characteristics of Abused and Neglected Children

Abused or neglected children are likely to share some of the following characteristics:

- They appear to be different from other children in physical and emotional makeup, or their parents describe them as being different or bad.
- They seem afraid of their parents.
- They may bear bruises, welts, sores, or other skin injuries which seem to be untreated.
- They are given inappropriate food, drink, or medication.
- They are left alone with inadequate supervision.
- They are chronically unclean.
- They exhibit extremes in behavior: cry often or cry very little and show no real expectation of being comforted; they are excessively fearful or seem fearless of adult authority; they are unusually aggressive or extremely passive or withdrawn.
- They are wary of physical contact, especially with an adult. They may be hungry for affection yet have difficulty relating to children and adults.
- Based on their experiences, they feel they cannot risk getting close to others.
- They exhibit a sudden change in behavior, exhibit regressive behavior, such as wetting their pants or bed, thumb-sucking, whining, or becoming uncommonly shy or passive.
- They have learning problems that cannot be diagnosed. Their attention wanders and they easily become self-absorbed.
- They are habitually truant or late to school. Frequent or prolonged absences from school may result from the parent's keeping an injured child at home until the evidence of abuse disappears. Or they may arrive at school early and remain after classes instead of going home.
- They are tired and often sleep in class.
- They are not dressed appropriately for the weather. Children who wear long sleeves on hot days may be dressed to hide bruises or burns or other marks of abuse, or they may be dressed inadequately and suffer frostbite or illness from exposure to the weather.

Note. From *Child Abuse* (p. 65) by R. Harrison and J. Edwards, 1983, Portland, OR: EDNICK Publications. Copyright 1983 by EDNICK Communications. Reprinted by permission.

has been so entrusted should be straightforward with the child about what will happen next and how long the process will last. Referral to a social-service agency does not automatically mean the child is removed from the home, but rather that the agency will look into the allegation. Although school counselors and social workers should be involved in suspected abuse cases, it is important that school policy be flexible enough to allow the continued involvement of the professional the child trusts most (Harrison & Edwards, 1983).

Second, when it does become necessary to report suspected abuse or neglect, the question arises as to how—and whether—to tell the parents a report has been made. Schools have different policies on this issue. Although, in most states, the source of the report is kept confidential, it is often not difficult for parents to guess who made the report. As a result, many advisors recommend telling the parents (Harrison & Edwards, 1983) where the report originated. The professional conducting this conference should explain the school's legal obligation without casting blame, and offer the school's concern and support (Harrison & Edwards, 1983).

Third, curricula are available to teach children about abuse. Specifically, they focus on helping students distinguish between discipline and abuse, assuring them that abuse is not their fault, and emphasizing that the adult who is doing the abusing needs help too, and can get it if the child confides the problem to someone in authority. If you teach such a curriculum, you should invite parents to attend class and/or give them a description of the course.

Abuse and neglect are some of the most difficult of family-professional relationships to deal with. It is important to remain non-judgmental and respectful. Parents who engage in abuse are as much victims of the cycle of violence as their children are. You must make the assumption that they do not want to abuse their children. They need your support as much as their children do.

Parents with Disabilities

The rights of people with a disability are expanding, resulting in an increased likelihood that they will become parents. Consequently, you are likely to have an opportunity to work with parents who have a disability (Thurman, Whaley, & Weinraub, 1985). When a parent has a physical disability, the effects on the professional-family relationship only involve logistics: providing accessible meeting rooms and, perhaps communicating through the most accessible means, such as the telephone. But when parents have sensory or intellectual deficits, there are special issues to consider.

Parents with visual or hearing impairments rely on their children in many situations. For example, parents with visual impairments may ask their children to read prices in grocery stores and otherwise guide them through daily transactions. Further, they may depend on an older child to provide care for younger siblings. Such children may be brought into the parental subsystem (see Chapter 3) and expected to act as "little adults." Whether this is detrimental depends, of course, on the individual family and whether parents can also allow the children on whom they depend time to be "just kids."

The child's role as the parent's assistant does have implications for your consideration. Such children may not have the time to participate in school extracurricular activities, for example. Another illustration involves a teacher who told of a parent-teacher conference with a mother who had a hearing impairment:

> We didn't have anybody who had sign language because our district's deaf education teacher was strictly from the oral school. So I asked Jeannie to interpret at our conference, since I knew she was very good at sign language. Unfortunately, what I needed to tell Jeannie's mother was that I had some concerns about her behavior in class. . . . The mother just nodded and smiled. I didn't understand her reaction. . . . It was only later that I discovered that Jeannie had not, to say the least, translated accurately what I was saying!

Parents who have mental disabilities pose a more difficult set of problems. Partially, the difficulty centers around separating prejudice about parents who have been labeled mentally retarded from the real difficulties they may experience. As discussed in Chapter 1, there are long-standing taboos and discriminations against parenthood for people with mental retardation. Thus, persons with mental retardation have been barred by law in many states from having children, yet the same laws do not pertain to individuals with other problems, such as alcoholism or a tendency to abuse, who may have difficulty caring for their children (Haavik & Menninger, 1981).

Normalization, deinstitutionalization, and integration into the mainstream of the school and community has resulted in a growing number of adults with mental retardation electing to become parents (Lynch & Bakley, 1989). It is very difficult to separate parenting difficulties due solely to mental disability from other factors—such as low income status, a lack of experience with children, or inadequate models of parenting—which people with low IQs tend also to experience (Haavik & Menninger, 1981). Child-protection workers and other professionals seem to operate from a prejudgment that parents with mental retardation will not be "fit" (Budd & Greenspan, 1984). In fact, in some areas, proof that a parent has a mental disability is adequate grounds for removal of a child from the home (Budd & Greenspan, 1984).

However, a low IQ is not necessarily an indicator of poor parenting skills. Rosenberg and McTate (1982) commented that "concern and willingness" to place a child's need ahead of one's immediate wants are often more important predictors of the ability to improve child-care skills than is intelligence. Yet, Budd and Greenspan (1984) noted that the problems experienced by parents with mental retardation are often due to low IQ. For example, poor social skills may make it difficult for a parent to negotiate successfully with a professional. Similarly, poor practical skills resulting from lack of experience or inability to foresee consequences may lead parents with mental retardation to feed or clothe their children improperly or to leave them in hazardous situations. In one example, a mother punished her child by standing him in a corner for many hours, because this was how she had been punished when she was in an institution (Rosenberg & McTate, 1982). In spite of this gloomy picture of individuals with disabilities who become parents, many become effective parents (Lynch & Bakley, 1989).

The number of programs designed to teach parenting skills to adults with mental retardation is increasing. Training for parents with mental retardation should involve very concrete instructions, demonstrations, and feedback. One program designed to address issues related to the environmental circumstances of many individuals with mental retardation and to develop models of service delivery and support for those parents was Project IINTACT (Infant Interagency Network Through Accessing Computer Technology) in San Diego, California. The project provided services to a small group of families in which one or both parents had mental retardation (Lynch & Bakley, 1989).

Project IINTACT was a cooperative project between the staff from the Regional Center for the Developmentally Disabled of San Diego and IINTACT personnel. Each family in the project received home visits from a special educator collecting information about parental and child needs. After an initial data gathering, trained paraprofessionals visited with the special educator and gradually assumed the main home-visit responsibility. Home visits typically focused on parental concerns such as relationships, housing, transportation, employment, and child management. Visits also provided an opportunity to provide instruction and directly teach parents specific skills such as food preparation and how to bathe and diaper an infant (Lynch & Bakley, 1989).

Support for parents with mental retardation should constitute an integral part of general services for adults with developmental disabilities. The social, self-advocacy, and other independent living skills generally taught for adult life will also serve the adult well when he or she becomes a parent. It is important for schools that serve the children of parents with mental retardation to work closely with community programs working with adults.

SUMMARY

Every family-professional relationship requires an individualized approach. Families have diverse characteristics arising from different exceptionalities; family sizes and forms; cultural backgrounds; socioeconomic status; geographic locations; individual characteristics, such as health and coping styles; and such special challenges as poverty and abuse. The multitude of possible combinations and permutations of all these factors creates infinite variations that make each family as unique as a snowflake or a fingerprint.

The concept of individualizing is very familiar to professionals who work with special students. Individualized instruction is not only of value for maximizing each student's potential; it is also a legal requirement. If students benefit from individualized approaches, why not also individualize approaches to their families? Doing so requires an appreciation of the unique characteristics of each family as well as a respect for diverse values, lifestyles, and cultures. Beginning from a base of self-awareness about one's own values and background, it is possible to forge family-school relationships that are rewarding for everyone involved.

While understanding families' unique characteristics is important, it is not sufficient to ensure complete understanding of how a family system operates. Family characteristics shape how a family interacts with its own members and with persons outside the family, such as yourself. We will discuss family interaction in the next chapter.

FAMILY INTERACTION

In Hawaiian culture, the word *ohana* represents the extended family system which sometimes includes close friends who are "adopted" into the family network. The concept implies acceptance, nurturing, and willingness to support those in the ohana. Strong extended family ties can be a source of social support for a family.

The radio alarm goes off right on schedule. Softly, music fills the dark bedroom. "Honey . . . wake up. It's your turn." Laurie nudges her sleeping husband. He mumbles something about work and continues to sleep. "Come on, get up. Take Steven to the bathroom." Several minutes pass and the radio announcer notes, "It's 2:11 and 28 degrees." Laurie is now fully awake. She breathes a frustrated sigh and gets out of bed. She shuffles through the darkness to the kids' bedroom and stands for a moment in their doorway. She surveys the small room where her three children are sleeping. The baby has a cold and is breathing loudly from her crib in the corner. Laurie's eyes have adjusted to the light from the street. She scans the bed before moving to make sure 3-year-old Dinah isn't sleeping too close to the edge of the bunk. Since they started Steven's toilet training program, Dinah has been sleeping in the top bunk. Twice she has fallen out of bed. Next, Laurie moves to the edge of Steven's bed. She takes a long, deep breath. She knows that toilet training is important for her 5-year-old son, who has a severe emotional disorder. Staying dry is important—just like his teachers have said. The whole family will be happier when he is toilet trained, but it feels very hard in the middle of the night! Laurie's goal is to pick up sleeping Steven and get him out of the bedroom before he begins to kick, hit, scream, and wake up his sisters—This works about half the time—maybe it will work tonight. "OK, let's go," she whispers.

The typical focus in special education has been on student outcomes or on student-mother interaction. But, as this example points out, a disability can have effects on other family members as well. Steven's parents have agreed to follow the toileting procedures that Steven's teachers use in the classroom where he is required to sit on the toilet for 10 minutes every two hours. This daytime schedule changes to every four hours during the night. Carrying the program out at home interrupts the sleep of other family members. The lack of sleep is likely to have negative affects on the parents' work efficiency, as well as the patience, energy, and enthusiasm of both parents and children in the family. You need to be aware that student interventions often affect the other family members, therefore, home-intervention programs should be planned with this in mind. Programs need to be beneficial for all family members.

The family is a unit consisting of many interactions—an interactional system. Events affecting any one member can have an impact upon all family members (Carter & McGoldrick, 1980; Minuchin, 1974). Why is knowledge about a family's interactions important to professionals who work with children and youth who have exceptionalities? Because, as professionals, it is important that you focus not exclusively on the student with an exceptionality, but also look at the student within the context of the family.

This chapter will examine family subsystems. After reading this chapter, you should be able to answer the following questions:

- What are family subsystems?
- What are the unique features of each subsystem?
- How do subsystems affect general family interaction?
- Why are cohesion and adaptability important elements of family interaction?
- How can educators help families improve interaction within subsystems?

FAMILY SUBSYSTEMS

From a systems perspective (Figure 3–1), the various relationships that exist for family members are referred to as "subsystems." Within the traditional nuclear family four major subsystems can be identified (A. P. Turnbull et. al., 1984):

1. marital subsystem—husband and wife interactions
2. parental subsystem—parent and child interactions
3. sibling subsystem—child and child interactions
4. extended family subsystem—whole–family or individual–member interactions with extended family, friends, neighbors, and professionals.

These subsystems are the component parts of a family's interaction system. Interaction within families differ based on the subsystems that exist. The configuration of a family's subsystems will depend on each family's idiosyncratic structure. For example, in a family with only one child, there is no sibling subsystem. Although single parents do not have a formal marital subsystem that influences the family, they may share an unofficial marital-type relationship with significant partners.

Husband and Wife Interactions

The marital subsystem consists of interactions between husbands and wives. As marital partners, both husband and wife have needs and roles. The presence of a child or youth with an exceptionality, however,

FIGURE 3–1   Family Systems Conceptual Framework

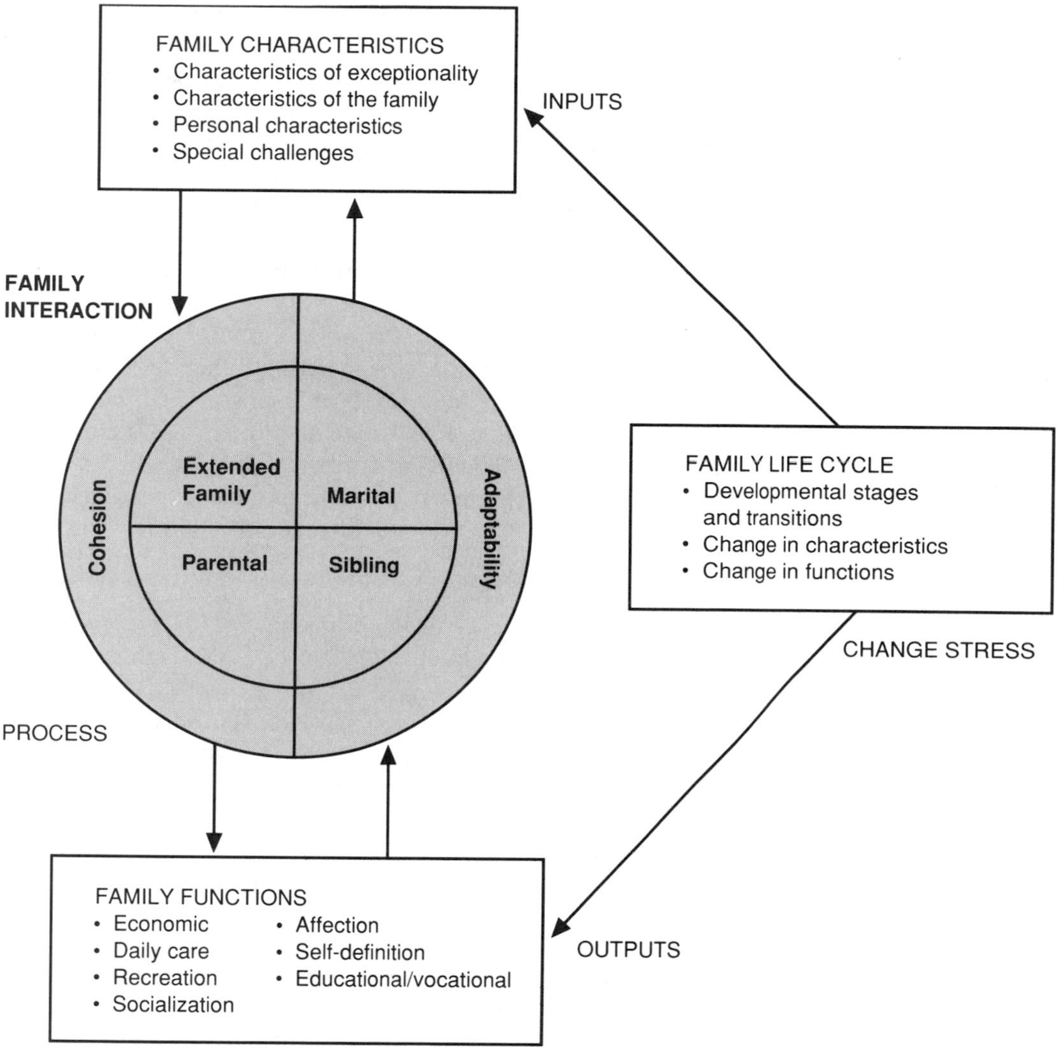

FAMILY CHARACTERISTICS
- Characteristics of exceptionality
- Characteristics of the family
- Personal characteristics
- Special challenges

INPUTS

FAMILY INTERACTION

Cohesion

Extended Family   **Marital**

Parental   **Sibling**

Adaptability

FAMILY LIFE CYCLE
- Developmental stages and transitions
- Change in characteristics
- Change in functions

CHANGE STRESS

PROCESS

FAMILY FUNCTIONS
- Economic
- Daily care
- Recreation
- Socialization
- Affection
- Self-definition
- Educational/vocational

OUTPUTS

Note. Adapted from *Working with Families with Disabled Members: A Family Systems Approach* (p. 60) by A. P. Turnbull, J. A. Summers, and M. J. Brotherson, 1984, Lawrence, KS: The University of Kansas: Kansas University Affiliated Facility. Adapted by permission.

can influence their relationship and interactions. Studies have indicated that having a child or youth with an exceptionality can have a negative impact on the parents' marriage. Featherstone (1980) noted:

> A child's handicap attacks the fabric of a marriage in four ways. It excites powerful emotions in both parents. It acts as a dispiriting symbol of shared failure. It reshapes the organization of the family. It creates fertile ground for conflict. (p. 91)

The role of divorce, marital disharmony, and desertions by husbands has been reported to be disproportionately high in marriages where there is a child or youth with an exceptionality (Gath, 1977; Murphy, 1982; Reed & Reed, 1965). One study assessed marital harmony in 59 couples soon after the birth of a child with spina bifida and again nearly a decade later (Tew, Payne, & Lawrence, 1974). Contact was maintained with these couples as well as with 58 control couples. The couples who had a child with spina bifida demonstrated lower marital harmony and twice the divorce rate as the control group couples. Thus, it appeared that the birth of a child with spina bifida presented a serious challenge to marital stability resulting in many marital needs and activities being subordinated to the child's needs.

Although some studies indicate that having a child with an exceptionality can have a negative impact on marriage, other studies suggest a positive impact on marriage as a result of having a child with an exceptionality. Some husbands and wives feel their marriage is closer and stronger, and Summers (1987b) found that parenting a child with an exceptionality was a source of pride for some couples. Successfully having weathered the experience, one parent reported: "We feel our marriage has been tested. We hung wallpaper together and had [Haley]" (p. 269).

Gath (1977) compared 30 couples of infants with Down syndrome and 30 couples of infants without exceptionality. Although she found marital disharmony in nine of the couples who had infants with Down syndrome and none among the control couples, Gath also noted positive effects in the couples with children and youth with exceptionalities. Almost half of these couples reported that they had been drawn closer together and that their marriage was strengthened rather than weakened by their shared experience.

Kazak and Marvin (1984) compared marital stress in 56 couples with children with spina bifida and in 53 couples with children without exceptionality. The results revealed no significant difference between the groups in total marital satisfaction. Analysis of the subscales, however, indicated that the couples with children having spina bifida actually experienced somewhat higher levels of marital satisfaction. These findings are in direct contrast to the study discussed earlier (Tew et al., 1974). According to Kazak and Marvin (1984), their results lend support to the idea that having a child with an exceptionality may function, in some cases, to strengthen marital relationships.

Comparing a matched sample of 60 families with and without children with disabilities, Abbott and Meredith (1986) found no significant differences between the two groups on measures of marriage strength, family strength, or personality characteristics.

These mixed research results highlight a very important warning to professionals—do not automatically assume that couples experience a negative impact on their marriage as a result of their child. Marriage may be strengthened by a child with special needs. It is also important to recognize that spouses have specific needs and roles to fulfill (e.g., affection, socialization, and self-definition) as marriage partners. Therefore, interventions with families should demonstrate respect for these needs and roles, despite the presence in the family of a child with an exceptionality. Table 3–1 provides some suggestions for how to meet some of those needs.

Parent and Child Interactions

The parental subsystem is composed of interactions between parents and their child or children. In each family, parents assume certain roles as mother or as father or as both. These roles are either explicit or implicit, and can change with time (Minuchin, 1974). The presence of a child with an exceptionality has impact on parent roles, and may affect fathers and mothers in different ways.

The sex of their child can affect parents' interactions with the child differentially. On some fathers, regardless of social class, the initial impact of the disability is greater if their child is a boy; for mothers it is greater if the child is a girl (Farber, Jenne, & Toigo, 1960). Tallman (1965) found fathers to be more adversely affected by the disability of a son than a daughter, and to cope less skillfully than mothers in raising either a son or a daughter.

Fathers, to a greater extent than mothers, have been found to be more concerned about the stigma their family may face as a result of a child with a disability (Gumz & Gubrium, 1972; Tallman, 1965). This stigma may be accentuated by the sex of the child or youth. Cummings (1976) reported that fathers of children with exceptionalities experienced lowered self–esteem. This was particularly true when the child was

---

TABLE 3–1 Suggestions for Recognizing the Needs of the Marital Subsystem

---

- Encourage parents to consider activities they may wish to engage in separate from their child or children.
- Make information available to couples on community respite care or child-care services.
- Consider the time and energy implications of home interventions on the needs of the couple.
- Seek ways to offer flexible scheduling or alternatives if a planned school activity conflicts with a couple's plans.

---

first—born, a namesake, and male. Mothers and fathers may remember their own interests, hobbies, and skills at various ages and make unconscious comparisons between themselves and their same—sex children. One father of a son with a physical disability expressed disappointment that he was not able to share his hobbies with his son:

> I would have liked to have taken him fishing and hunting. I try not to think about it. It is one of the things you put up with. (A. P. Turnbull et al., 1984)

Robin Pulver, mother of a 5-year-old son with mental retardation, noted the disappointment she felt in not being able to experience some aspects of the usual mother-son relationships:

> Most days are too real. The frustrations—days spent trying to teach David a simple skill most of us take for granted. The usual things that people say now strike horror in my heart:
>
> "They grow up so fast!"
> Some do not!
> "I wish I could keep him/her at this age forever."
> No, you don't.
>
> I will not reap the normal rewards of parenting my son. Chances are there will be no reflected glory at graduation or wedding ceremonies. There will be none of the sweet, sad poignancy of seeing him go off to college. (Pulver, 1988, p. 61)

Past research with mothers and fathers suggests that the presence of a child or youth with exceptionalities tends to highlight differences in traditional parent roles (Gallagher, Cross, & Scharfman, 1981; Gumz & Gubrium, 1972). Historically, parent roles have been characterized as expressive or instrumental (Parsons & Bales, 1955). The *expressive* roles, often filled by mothers, included activities related to the internal affairs of the family (e.g., affection, physical care, and self-definition). The *instrumental* roles, in turn, often filled by fathers, included those activities that related to the external affairs of the family (e.g., financial, educational, and vocational).

In one study Gumz and Gubrium (1972) compared the attitude of 50 mothers and 50 fathers of children with mental retardation. They found that mothers were significantly more concerned than fathers with emotional family strain, additional child—care time, and ability to maintain family harmony and integration. Fathers showed a higher degree of concern about their child in activities outside the family than within the family.

Gallagher et al. (1981) compared 50 mothers and 50 fathers of preschool children with exceptionalities and found similar parent role differences. Specifically, fathers predominantly were the providers, protectors, and maintainers of outside–home equipment, whereas mothers tended to keep books, shop for and prepare food, maintain the inside of the home, serve as social hostess and nurse, provide transportation, and select clothing.

The results of both studies parallel the traditional parent–role differences of mother–expressive and father–instrumental. However, these traditional parent and child interaction patterns may be changing. In the Gallagher study (Gallagher et al., 1981), when asked to state their "ideal" parent role allocation, both mothers and fathers agreed that fathers should take a more active expressive role (Table 3–2).

In addition, a study involving 23 fathers and 25 mothers of young adults with exceptionalities found no significant difference between mothers and fathers when addressing the adult needs of their child (Brotherson, 1985). Thus, mothers as well as fathers addressed both instrumental and expressive needs when planning for the future of their son or daughter with an exceptionality.

Fathers of children and youth with exceptionalities, similar to fathers in general, may be assuming a role that increasingly focuses on expressive needs (Eversoll, 1979). Pruett (1987) reports that the bond between father and child can produce positive effects upon the child's self-esteem, sexual identity, cognitive growth, curiosity, and social skills. Men are increasingly enjoying more active expressive involvement with their children (Hornby, 1988; May, 1988). At the same time, mothers of

---

TABLE 3–2 Suggestions for Recognizing the Needs of the Parental Subsystem

---

- Help parents develop alternative activities when traditional roles are inappropriate due to the needs of their child with an exceptionality. For example, a mother may not be able to play ball games with her child with a severe physical disability, but they could attend sports events together.

- Provide and encourage visiting opportunities at school for both mothers and fathers.

- Develop flexible scheduling to accommodate both working fathers and mothers for IEP, evaluation, or parent–teacher conferences.

- Aid both fathers and mothers in locating information about their child's exceptionality. (See Chapter 12 for more discussion on exchanging information with families.)

- Provide parents with opportunities to discuss their concerns, successes, and experiences in raising a child with an exceptionality with other parents. One strategy involves setting up father, mother, or parent support groups. Another strategy is to access Parent–to–Parent programs in which a veteran parent is matched with a new parent to provide emotional and informational support. (A Directory of Parent–to–Parent programs is described in Chapter 12.)

---

children and youth with exceptionalities may be assuming roles that increasingly focus on instrumental needs (Brotherson, 1985). Parents may be beginning to share more of the same care roles.

In general, couples approach parenthood with expectations regarding mother and father roles based on their own experiences as members of their families of origin (Carter & McGoldrick, 1980). However, some of the parenting skills and roles couples learned from their own parents may not be effective or relevant when dealing with a child with an exceptionality, either because of differences in the child or changes in society. As Gallagher et al. (1981) note, "the traditional father roles of physical playmate and model for the male child are largely diminished or not present at all with moderately to severely handicapped children" (p. 13). You should plan services and programs that respond to each parent's strengths and needs. Parents should not be approached as a homogeneous pair. As illustrated, their unique roles and interactions as a mother or as a father can be quite different. A father may share many of the same needs and strengths as a mother, but may also be affected quite differently by certain issues and challenges (Cummings, 1976; Cummings, Bayley, & Rie, 1966; Gumz & Gubrium, 1972).

Brother and Sister Interactions

The sibling subsystem is composed of sibling interactions—the interactions between brothers and/or sisters in the family. Powell and Ogle (1985) describe siblings as "socialization agents," who provide the first and perhaps the most intense peer relationships children experience. By providing a context for social-skills development, these relationships give children the opportunity to experience sharing, companionship, loyalty, rivalry, and the expression of feelings (Powell & Ogle, 1985).

Siblings experience the impact of a brother or sister with an exceptionality in many different ways. Powell and Ogle (1985) have suggested that the affect on siblings may be either positive or negative, depending on "a number of contributing factors, including parental attitudes and expectations, family size, family resources, religion, severity of the child's handicap, and the pattern of interactions between siblings" (p. 41).

The impact that a child with exceptionality can have on brothers and sisters often has not been understood or recognized by professionals who work with families (Vadasy, Fewell, Meyer, & Schell, 1984). For example, parents may be less sensitive to their other children when focusing on the needs of the child with an exceptionality. Often brothers and sisters keep their worries and problems to themselves, making it difficult for parents or others to understand their private concerns

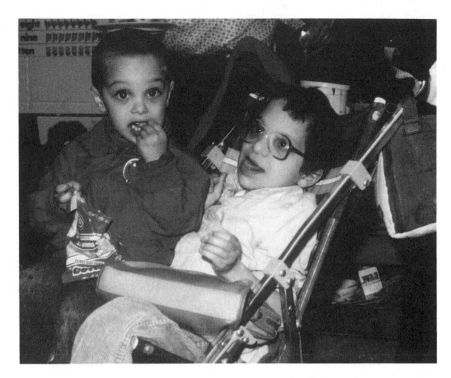

The positive relationship between these brothers will influence their entire family—as will their Islamic background.

(McHale & Gamble, 1987). Similarly, siblings may find it difficult to discuss their confused and often contradictory feelings. Such reactions are illustrated by the comments of a young sister whose brother contracted dystonia, a neurological disorder, at age 14:

> When Tony started going through the beginning stages of his condition, I was unaware how serious the situation would become. My feelings on this are somewhat kept inside. I've never really come to terms in accepting the dystonia. I remember going on vacation and expecting that the dystonia would be gone when I returned. For many years I never believed he would always have it. I thought it would go away. Kind of like hanging a sign, "Wake me up when it's over." I have felt a lot of jealousy for all the attention Tony has gotten, but it's different now. Oh, I still feel frustration, anger, and sadness but my main purpose for Tony is to be his sister. I still worry that someday I'll get it, or if not me, then the kids I hope to have someday. (Engelhart, 1985, p. 3)

Although brothers and sisters may not always reveal their needs, the research on siblings suggests that they may have some special concerns as a result of their brother's or sister's exceptionality. However, in addition to an increased risk for emotional problems and added demands for caretaking among siblings, they can experience some very positive outcomes as a result of their brother's or sister's exceptionality.

Grossman (1972) conducted one of the most well-known sibling studies with 83 college-age siblings of brothers and sisters with exceptionalities. Approximately 45 of the siblings reported that they had benefited from having a brother or sister with an exceptionality. Benefits included increased tolerance and compassion, greater understanding of others, heightened awareness of prejudice and its consequences, and greater appreciation of their own health and intelligence.

A college freshman recently wrote about some of the lessons he had learned from his younger sister with cerebral palsy that had influenced his adjustment away from home:

> Stacy has taught me to never judge people without understanding them first. A hasty judgment of Stacy does not reveal her acute perceptiveness. . . . As a result I hesitate to classify other people too quickly. . . . I always laugh when my Hopkins roommate suddenly turns to me and says, "That guy is gay," or "Jack's a nerd," after seeing them but once. So many people judge books by their covers. Stacy has taught me not to. (Levitt, 1988, p. 55)

Grossman's (1972) study also revealed that 45 of the siblings reported negative experiences as a result of having a brother or sister with an exceptionality. These negative experiences included resentment and guilt, fear that they too might be exceptional, shame, and a sense of being neglected by their parents. Sometimes the time, energy, affection, money, and other family resources that are given to the child with an exceptionality can create resentment in brothers and sisters. In other situations, siblings can develop an understanding and appreciation of life that is far above their years.

One mother described the following conversation when her 8-year-old daughter told her that she felt sad because her younger brother was unable to attend kindergarten at their neighborhood school:

> When I walk by those kindergarten rooms and see all the drawings on the wall my heart hurts too. Sometimes I wish there were a pill we could give him to make his brain all better. "Me to," said my daughter, "but then I'd probably miss my good old brother." (Pulver, 1988, p. 59)

Cleveland and Miller (1977) found that having a brother or sister with an exceptionality affected siblings' life goals. Brothers and sisters who interacted daily with their sibling with an exceptionality ranked learning to accept hardships and devotion to a worthwhile cause as higher life goals than siblings who had less frequent interactions.

Early sibling studies showed that brothers and sisters were expected to take responsibility to help with physical and caretaking needs of their brother or sister. Older sisters of the child with an exceptionality were the most vulnerable to increased responsibility (Cleveland & Miller, 1977; Farber, 1960; Gath, 1974).

School is the social arena children understand best. Some siblings may feel stigma from having a brother or sister with an exceptionality in the same school, or they may feel embarrassed or be reluctant to bring friends home (Lonsdale, 1978). Differences in sibling ages, exceptionality, birth order, and appearance can affect the degree of social stigma. One father noted that the differences in sibling acceptance and loyalty seemed to depend more on the individual personalities of his sons:

> My oldest son has been very sensitive about his brother being different and has been embarrassed at times. My youngest son isn't. He has never given a flip what other people said. (Summers, 1987a, p. 270)

Siblings have expressed concern and worry regarding their future responsibilities for their brother or sister with an exceptionality. Even at the age of 7, one sister shared her worries about whether her brother would hold a job and have nice clothes and a good place to live. She added, "He won't have to worry because I'll give him my money. I don't want him to be a bum" (H. R. Turnbull, 1985b, p. 123). To examine the families' future plans, McCullough (1981) administered questionnaires to parents and siblings in 23 families with a child with an exceptionality. Only 41% of the parents thought their sons or daughters without disabilities would assume at least partial care for the child with an exceptionality, while 68 of the brothers and sisters thought they would assume some responsibility. (Chapter 5 discusses in detail some of the concerns of brothers and sisters for the future of their sibling with a disability.)

For some siblings, it may be important to be included in interventions and/or be asked to attend their brother's or sister's IEP conference. Such involvement may help them understand their sibling's needs better and may provide them with an opportunity to discuss their own needs. Barbara Buswell described her 10-year-old son's concern about his brother who has a disability:

> Following the discussion after his brother's IEP meeting, Wilson's brother, Brooke, told us that he didn't like the school Wilson was attending. "Isn't he good enough to go to our school?" he asked. We thought about this question a lot and it was one of the reasons why we insisted on changing Wilson's placement—his brother wanted him to go there. When we explained why we wanted to have Wilson integrated into our school, the administration personnel noted that there was "nothing in the law about respecting a sibling's wishes." We persisted, and the change was made. It has been a positive move for both of our sons.

Research has indicated that brothers and sisters can be very effective in implementing home training programs (Schreibman, O'Neill, & Koegel, 1983; Swenson–Pierce, Kohl, & Egel, 1987). Thus, several reports suggest that when siblings are involved in training and therapeutic programs, the entire family benefits (Miller & Cantwell, 1976; Weinrott, 1974). With approximate planning, siblings can assume active roles in the education and skill training of the child with an exceptionality.

Addressing siblings' needs is one important way of enabling the entire family to help the child with an exceptionality grow and develop. To plan effective interventions for brothers and sisters, recognize their feelings and needs. (See Appendix A for resource materials for helping children benefit from their sibling experiences.) Table 3–3 provides some suggestions for how to address the wide variety of special needs siblings present.

TABLE 3–3   Parental Strategies for Recognizing the Needs of the Sibling Subsystem

1. *Be open and honest.* Siblings need parents to be available for questions and to provide honest answers to their questions.
2. *Value each child individually.* It is natural to compare children, especially their physical features, strengths, and weaknesses.
3. *Limit care-giving responsibilities.* When one child has a severe disability, siblings may be recruited to perform a number of direct-care activities.
4. *Use respite care and other supportive services.*
5. *Be fair.*
6. *Accept the child's disability.* If parents do not accept their child's disability, it is doubtful if other family members will.
7. *Put together a library of children's books on disabilities.* One of the best ways in which parents can share information with their nondisabled children is to provide literature for them to read.
8. *Schedule special time with the siblings.* Everyone recognizes that children with disabilities require extra parental time.
9. *Let siblings settle their own differences.* Fighting between siblings is natural and, in many cases, healthy.
10. *Welcome other children and friends into the home.* The siblings' relationship with others outside the family is a universal concern.
11. *Praise siblings.* All children need parental praise.
12. *Recognize that you are the most important, most powerful teacher of your children.*
13. *Recognize the uniqueness of your family.*
14. *Listen to siblings.* The way siblings know the child with a disability differs from the way their parents know the child.
15. *Involve the siblings.*

TABLE 3–3 (Continued)

---

16. *Require the child with a disability to do as much for himself or herself as possible.*

17. *Recognize each child's unique qualities and family contributions.*

18. *Encourage development of special siblings programs.*

19. *Help establish a sibling support group.* Through their contact with other parents and professionals, parents are best able to facilitate the establishment of sibling support groups.

20. *Recognize special stress times for siblings and plan to minimize negative effects.* From what is now known, sibling stress seems to be greatest when:
    a. another child is born;
    b. the child with a disability starts to school;
    c. the sibling starts to date;
    d. friends reject the child with a disability;
    e. friends ask questions about the child with a disability;
    f. the child with a disability becomes critically ill;
    g. problems related to the child are handled in secrecy;
    h. parents die;
    i. siblings marry.

21. *Use professionals to help siblings cope when problems arise.*

22. *Teach siblings to interact.* Many siblings need help in learning how to interact socially with their brother or sister who has a disability.

23. *Provide opportunities for a normal family life and normal family activities.* Problems with siblings tend to develop when all of the family's energy and resources are focused on providing care to the child with a disability.

24. *Don't expect siblings to be saints.*

25. *Join sibling-related organizations.*

Note. From *Brothers & Sisters—A Special Part of Exceptional Families* (pp. 177–182) by T. H. Powell and P. A. Ogle, 1985, Baltimore, MD: Paul H. Brookes. Copyright 1985 by Paul H. Brookes Publishing Co., Inc. Adapted by permission.

Extended Family Interactions

The extended family subsystem is composed of family or individual-member interactions with relatives, friends, neighbors, and professionals. Each family will vary in the size of its extended family subsystem and the degree to which it is dependent on it. Extended family relationships can make a major contribution to the quality of life of the child with an exceptionality, as well as provide parents with a network of support. One young father described the support provided by his extended family:

> Our whole family has been involved in her progress, not just our immediate family, but the grandparents, aunts, cousins, all of them. From the

very beginning, there was no question she was accepted, just like any other child born in our family. I remember how the whole family rallied. They sent us cards and flowers and gifts and did all the things you do when a baby is born. And I think that was so important, because, after all, she was a baby first, and then a baby who had problems. (Meyer & Vadasy, 1986, p. 7)

Relatives, friends, and neighbors may experience many of the same reactions to exceptionality as people in general. Often misinformation or lack of information and experience create attitudes of fear, mistrust, dislike, or condescension. In addition, these potential support givers may have to deal with their own feelings of grief, shock, anger, or disappointment (Meyer & Vadasy, 1986).

Think of the roles that relatives, close friends, and neighbors play in your life and the lives of many families. Often, these are the persons who provide care and supervision for the children if emergencies arise or if the parents need to go out for a while. They are the persons who plan picnics, start ball games, or suggest nature walks. They share recipes, hand-me-down clothes, and personal stories. They listen, care, and can be counted on when times are tough.

Involvement of extended family members can be a positive learning and growing experience for all participants. Educating family and friends should be an ongoing process. It may be difficult for family members to realize the long-term impact of the exceptionality. Unless extended family members are educated, the pleasures of infancy and early childhood may give way to feelings of fear, disappointment, or disgust as the child reaches adulthood. One frustrated and hurt parent noted:

We called Jay's parents at Christmas, really excited. Paul is four years old and he'd just learned how to hold himself up in a sitting position. We said, "Paul is sitting up now!" And they said, "Well, when is he going to walk?" They really haven't accepted his disability at all. (Simons, 1987, p. 30)

Grandparents often play important roles in extended families. Because of their experience, they can share valuable and practical advice about child care and child development. Vadasy and Fewell (1986) found that grandmothers were ranked high on the support list by mothers of children with visual and auditory sensory losses. Grandparents of children with exceptionality need information to help them deal with their own feelings in addition to developing supportive roles (George, 1988; Meyer & Vadasy, 1986; Urwin, 1988). Grandparents' or family members' ideas about people with disabilities may have been formed when they were growing up, hence they may be outdated and inaccurate (Meyer & Vadasy, 1986).

Accurate information concerning the problems associated with disabilities and chronic illnesses needs to be shared with extended family members. Increased knowledge concerning the financial, social, emotional, and physical stresses of these families can help all family members deal more effectively with their own needs and facilitate supporting between family members (Seligman & Darling, 1989).

Although families never experience life events in exactly the same manner because of the unique differences of each family unit, a certain level of understanding and empathy can be shared by sensitive people in similar circumstances. Although research in this area is limited, it appears that families of children with similar exceptionalities often are good sources of support (Abbott & Meredith, 1986; Brotherson, 1985). Vadasy, Fewell, Meyer, and Greenberg (1984) reported that both mothers and fathers displayed less stress after the fathers participated in a "fathers only" support group and served as part of each other's extended families. Similarly, a common support model is based on the idea that parents of older children can be good sources of support for parents of younger children. Thus, the Parent–to–Parent or Pilot Parent model (Carter & Reynolds, 1984) matches a trained "veteran" parent with a parent whose child was recently diagnosed with a similar exceptionality. The weekend retreat is another popular family support model whereby families are provided with a combination of respite/recreational, educational, and support activities (e.g. Turnbull & Summers, 1985).

Families of children with similar exceptionalities can share experiences, parenting "tips," and resources. They can laugh at each other's funny stories about the child with an exceptionality without feeling uncomfortable, they can cry with each other and not feel embarrassed, and they can cheerlead for each other's successes with unabashed enthusiasm. Such relationships can help allay fears and remind nervous, new parents that they are not alone. Families who become acquainted in this manner often are included in each other's extended family groups.

One mother reports:

> I think our biggest help was a mother my own age (26 then) who has a son with Down syndrome who came to visit us. He was five and really calmed our fears. We are good friends and see each other quite often. (Nebraska Department of Education, 1987, p. 1)

Levels of extended family support and understanding may vary based on the information extended family members possess. Extended family members need accurate information and emotional support to deal with their own feelings while also being able to provide support to the young children and their immediate families. Services often focus on the children and youth and neglect the stress that can develop for care givers and family members. Urwin (1988) reports that the responses by family members to children and/or parents with AIDS vary, but all members are affected to some degree. Many support services have been geared toward adult males with AIDS, whereas resources for children and youth with AIDS are not readily available. While community resources for children and youth will increase as more children become afflicted with AIDS, support services for extended family members is also needed so that these people can provide support for young children and their immediate families.

Programs are being developed to help extended family members. Research on a support-group program for grandparents (Vadasy, Fewell, & Meyer, 1985) found that about half of the grandparents surveyed had never visited a medical professional (52%) or an educational professional (48%) regarding their grandchild's exceptionality and/or specific needs. Fifty-seven percent reported they had doubts that they were doing the right things for their grandchild. Sixty-seven percent understood some of their grandchild's needs, but they wanted many questions answered. Some of their questions for professionals, as reported by Vadasy et al. (1985), included:

> How can we help him in therapy? What is the earliest program we can find? What kinds of programs are most effective? What is his potential? What can we do to develop her talents? How can we avoid sheltering the child too much? (pp. 14–15)

Many extended family members, close friends, or neighbors can provide support to the child and the family when some of their needs for knowledge, experience, and skills have been met. Addressing these needs represents an important strategy for helping children and for supporting families.

Parents and educators can help extended family members learn to accept the child with the exceptionality more fully. Parents must realize

---

TABLE 3–4   Suggestions for Recognizing the Needs of the Extended Family Subsystem

---

- Provide parents information to help them better understand the needs and reactions of extended family members.
- Provide information for parents to give to interested friends and relatives about exceptionality, the needs of children, and the needs of families.
- Encourage the development of grandparent and/or extended-family-member support groups. Such groups might be facilitated by school social workers, psychologists, PTA volunteers who are grandparents, or extended family members of students with exceptionality.
- Encourage extended-family participation in IEP conferences, classroom visits, and parent training programs.
- Provide library materials for extended family members.

that, in spite of their best intentions, friends and family members do not share their own intimate perspective. By trying to recall their own feelings shortly after their child's exceptionality was diagnosed, parents may learn to understand the feelings of extended family members (Nebraska Department of Education, 1987). Clear and accurate information should be provided in a supportive and nonthreatening manner. Extended family members' questions should be encouraged and answered as completely as possible.

Table 3–4 includes some suggestions on how to provide extended family, friends, and neighbors the necessary information and skills to enable them to support the child and family.

COHESION AND ADAPTABILITY

We have described the subsystems—the people who interact in the family. Now we will discuss *how* they interact. We will start by explaining two elements of interaction—cohesion and adaptability—and discuss implications for professionals. The degrees of cohesion and adaptability in a family describe the ways the subsystems interact (Olson, Russell, & Sprenkle, 1980).

Within families, certain "boundaries" serve as lines of demarcation between elements that belong to a subsystem and those outside it. These boundaries are often defined by the roles played by the members of the subsystem (Minuchin, 1974). For example, the two adult members in a traditional nuclear family may interact with each other in the roles of husband and wife and with their children as father and mother. Boundaries may be open or closed, that is, they may be accessible to interaction with elements outside the subsystem or they may not allow such interaction to take place. Ideally, subsystems should be open enough to allow individual autonomy and closed enough to provide support for members (Summers, 1987a). These boundaries help define the bonding relationships in families. Thus, feelings of closeness to group members is greater than feelings for those outside one's unique system of subsystem relationships (Kantor & Lehr, 1975). This element of family bonding is referred to as *cohesion* (Olsen, Sprenkle, & Russell, 1979).

Cohesion

Family cohesion refers to both the close emotional bonding that members have toward each other and the level of independence individuals feel within the family system (Olson et al., 1980). It can be visualized on a continuum, with high disengagement on one end and high enmesh-ment on the other. One author uses the physical metaphor of "the touching of hands" to describe cohesion in the family (Carnes, 1981):

> The dilemma is how to be close yet separate. When the fingers are inter-twined, it at first feels secure and warm. Yet when one partner (or family member) tries to move, it is difficult at best. The squeezing pressure may even be painful. . . . The paradox of every relationship is how to touch and yet not hold on. (pp. 70–71)

Some families end up not "touching" enough and consequently be-come disengaged. Others become too intertwined and become en-meshed. However, most families operate in the wide swath in the center of the continuum.

ENMESHMENT.   When a family is highly enmeshed, the boundaries or lines of demarcations that exist between subsystems become blurred or weak (Minuchin, 1974). For example, consider a family situation where a mother with many physical-care demands for a child with an exceptionality hands over many of the responsibilities to an older daughter. The daughter may have less parent–child and other–sibling interactions because she has been drawn into the parental subsystem. As a result, her own needs as a child and as a sibling may be over-looked or subordinated.

Interactions in families that are highly enmeshed are often charac-terized by overinvolvement and overprotection. Family members are al-lowed little privacy, and all decisions and activities are family focused. In such situations family members often have difficulty developing a sense of self or individuality. Many professionals encounter families they de-scribe as overprotective. Overprotection occurs when the family protects or isolates the child from demands and situations that require indepen-dence or risk taking by the child (Fotheringham & Creal, 1974). Risk taking can be frightening for individuals as well as for families. When working with families that are overprotective and have difficulty permit-ting risk taking by the child, you may need to consider developing risk-taking skills in small steps. For example, a teacher may want to encour-age a child assigned to a self-contained setting to spend more time in the regular classroom. The family fears academic frustration and rejec-tion by classmates. The teacher may need to problem solve with the family to find solutions with which all participants feel comfortable. For example, peer tutors may be assigned to ease the academic and social adjustment. With risk often comes unpleasant consequences—the child may experience some frustration and rejection. Teachers cannot abdi-cate responsible supervision and goal setting, but everyone learns through failures and successes. It is part of attaining autonomy and independence.

Families who are highly enmeshed also may organize interactions around the exceptionality as though it were the focal point of the family. This may be true in part because the effort to locate, organize, and implement services can be time-consuming for some or all family members. Also, certain types of exceptionality can be stigmatizing for a family, disconnecting it from contact with others.

For example, Philage and Kuna (1985) noted that the pressures on families of children or adolescents with learning disabilities may result in decreased interactions with others outside the immediate family. Thus, some parents choose to maintain relationships primarily with immediate family members and those facing similar problems, often leading to feelings of isolation and "the LD-focused family." The needs of the child coupled with the parents' frustration, disappointment, and isolation can result in the child inadvertently becoming a target of parent and sibling frustrations (Philage & Kuna, 1985).

For families who experience enmeshment, Silver (1974) suggested helping parents identify members in their extended family subsystem who can help meet some family needs. In addition, professionals may help family members identify friends as well as activities they may want to pursue both individually and as a family. While participation in family support groups can be a very positive experience, not all parent or family activities need to be centered around the exceptionality (e.g., advocacy work, parent support group, or friends who are families of children with exceptionalities).

DISENGAGEMENT. A high degree of disengagement also can have a negative impact on family interactions. Families who are highly disengaged maintain very rigid subsystem boundaries (Minuchin, 1974). For example, consider a family where the child with an exceptionality is isolated from the emotional support and friendship of other family members. Limited interaction leaves such a child without the support, closeness, and assistance needed to develop independence. A poem by Fritz Perls (1969), "Gestalt Prayer," characterizes family disengagement:

> I do my thing you do your thing
> I am not in this world to live up to your expectations
> And you are not in this world to live up to mine
> You are you and I am I
> And if by chance we meet, it's beautiful
> If not, it can't be helped. (p. 4)

Interactions in families that are highly disengaged often are characterized by underinvolvement, few shared interests or friends, excessive privacy, and a great deal of time apart. Few decisions require family input and involvement. For all family members, particularly the member with an exceptionality, such a family situation can be both lonely and difficult.

Disengagement can take place within and between subsystems. For example, disengagement within a subsystem exists when a father denies the child's exceptionality and withdraws both from parental and marital interactions. Disengagement between subsystems, in turn, may be found when the members of the extended family subsystem are unable to accept the child with an exceptionality leading to the sharing of increasingly fewer family celebrations. As suggested earlier, information, skills, or greater opportunities to observe and share may help family members and friends increase their interactions with the child with an exceptionality and build positive and healthy relationships with him/her.

IMPLICATIONS OF COHESION.   There are two reasons why it is valuable to understand cohesion in families with children with exceptionalities. First, it is important to recognize the levels of cohesion both between and within subsystems in order to be able to help the family as a whole meet its needs as well as the child's needs. A balance between the extremes of enmeshment and disengagement characterizes well-functioning families (Olson et al., 1980). Boundaries between subsystems in such families are clearly defined, and family members experience both a close bonding and a sense of autonomy.

Jane Schulz describes how she felt giving both autonomy and closeness to her adult son with an exceptionality. It is a balance that is not always easy to achieve:

> Is anything comparable to the anguish parents feel when their children leave home?. . . . Handicapped children and their parents don't know what to expect from separation. . . . My definition of anguish is seeing Billy, suitcase in hand, climb the steps of the group home and then receiving this phone call:
>> "Mom, I had a dream about you last night and cried a lot."
>> "I'm sorry, Billy, what's wrong?"
>> "A little bit homesick. Have to stay here. Fred said."
>> "Oh"
>> "I love you, Mom."
>> "I love you too, Billy."
>
> Although I look upon the two years' separation with all its problems and uncertainties as the most painful experience of my life, I now see it as a vital part of Billy's growth and of mine. (Schulz, 1985a, pp. 16–17)

There are several important points to remember about cohesion. First, most families fall somewhere within a wide normal range on the continuum of cohesion (Olson et al., 1980). In a survey of 1,000 families, Olson et al. (1983) found that those with younger children were more cohesive and flexible while families with adolescents tended to be disengaged and rigid. This finding makes sense conceptually: young families are developing bonds and young children need parents to stay close. During this time parents are often establishing careers and trying to integrate parenting/family styles from two families of origin. This requires flexibility. Families of adolescents, on the other hand, must be more disengaged as youths seek greater autonomy. At the same time, parents must guard against excessive flexibility as teenagers "try their wings." Family values and cultural background also influence cohesion (Rotunno & McGoldrick, 1982). Some Italian-American families may value close family ties and family-centered activities more than families from other ethnic backgrounds (Rotunno & McGoldrick, 1982). In contrast, British-American families value autonomy and self-reliance; family means nurturing individual achievement (McGill & Pearce, 1982).

Second, by considering the degree of cohesion that exists in a family, professionals will be able to examine the appropriateness of possible interventions. Does a particular intervention or program encourage enmeshment or disengagement in a family? For example, mothers involved in early childhood programs are often reinforced for establishing enmeshed relationships with their young children. That is, they are encouraged to spend a lot of time in the classroom, attend mothers' groups, provide home interventions, and transport children to numerous services. When they spend all this time with the child, what happens to their own needs and the needs of other family members? On the other hand, if they do not perform all these tasks, they run the risk of being labeled uninterested in their child's needs. Further, these same mothers may later be criticized for being overprotective or not letting go.

Adaptability

Family adaptability refers to the family's ability to change in response to situational and developmental stress (Olson et al., 1980). It is the family's ability to plan and to work out differences when these occur (Carnes, 1981). Similar to cohesion, adaptability is influenced by family values and cultural background. Like cohesion, adaptability can be viewed on a continuum—at one end are those families who are unable or unwilling to change in response to situational or developmental stress, they may be characterized as rigid, and at the other end are families who are constantly changing, chaotic (Olson et al., 1979). Again, most families fall in the wide swath of balance in the center.

FAMILIES CHARACTERIZED AS RIGID.   Families who are characterized as being rigid demonstrate a high degree of control and structure, and their interactions often are governed by many strictly enforced rules. The power hierarchy in such families is rigidly delineated and negotiations are seldom tolerated. Roles are also rigidly defined and there is little role sharing. Consider the example of a son who becomes physically disabled by a diving accident. This change in the family requires new energies to meet many demanding physical and emotional needs. If, in the past, meeting such needs was primarily the role of the mother, the added demands may be more than she can handle. If the family is highly rigid, members will have difficulty changing or sharing the new roles with the mother, thereby creating stress and difficulty for her and other family members.

For two primary reasons, the rigidity of the family power hierarchy must be considered as educational programs are developed. First, families must learn to adapt their power hierarchies over time. For example, an adolescent needs have a greater voice in family decision making than a young child. As persons with exceptionality enter adolescence or adulthood, you need to consider their abilities to choose and make decisions for themselves. Often family members and professionals tend to keep the child low on the hierarchy of power even into adulthood, treating persons with exceptionality like children long after they have ceased to be children. Second, it is helpful to identify the person or persons (e.g., parent, parents, grandmother, or uncle) who maintain(s) control over family decisions and rules. For example, a teacher might ask a mother to work on procedures to implement a home-based language program. If her husband, who maintains strict leadership in the family, rejects the program, it is unlikely that it will be effective. Indeed, if the mother carries out the intervention against her husband's wishes, he may say or do things to undermine her efforts. As suggested earlier, it is important to examine the impact of a home intervention on every family member and to understand pertinent family values and goals. You and the family must work together to develop interventions that will be consistent with their interaction patterns. In this respect, support from all family members is vital if home interventions are to be successful.

FAMILIES CHARACTERIZED AS CHAOTIC.   In contrast to rigid families, chaotic families demonstrate a low degree of control and structure. Their interactions often are characterized by few rules, which in turn are seldom enforced and often changing. Promises and commitments are often unkept, and family members cannot depend upon one another. Frequently, there is no family leader, negotiations are endless, and roles are unsure and often changing. One of the signs of a family characterized by chaos is that members do not plan together for their future (Carnes, 1981).

All families can experience periods of chaos during stressful life events, for example. But, when chaos is a consistent way of life, the consequences can be negative on the family and the student with an exceptionality. Consider the example of a mother with a son who has a severe learning disability. The child has difficulty academically and socially. The mother has a live-in boyfriend who is the family's primary source of financial support. During the last two years the boyfriend has begun to drink heavily and abuse family members. When the boyfriend begins to fight, existing rules are suddenly harshly interpreted for the child. When the fighting escalates, the rules change—survival being the main concern. Later, the remorseful boyfriend becomes extremely indulgent—creating a third set of rules. The instability and chaos continue. Because of his learning disability, the boy already experiences difficulty reading social cues accurately and his chaotic family life style only exacerbates his problems.

IMPLICATIONS OF ADAPTABILITY. Well-functioning families are characterized by a balance between the two extremes of rigidity and chaos (Olson et al., 1980). However, to help those families whose interactions are extremely rigid or chaotic, three actions are generally helpful. First, refer them for family counseling. This may be difficult to do. Some school districts are reluctant to suggest counseling because of the costs they may have to bear. Other districts provide family counseling and family education services. Be familiar with your local counseling resources. Second, help families plan for change. If possible, discuss schedule changes and transitions well in advance of the time they will occur. Ask yourself, "Is this change too sudden or radical for this family's current level of adaptability?" If so, some students and families may benefit from gradual transitions. When a student will be changing classrooms or school buildings, start with a gradual transition, one day a week, before making the complete transition. If a child needs to begin to learn how to ride the bus, and the family cannot adapt to this change, identify intermediate steps: riding only part of the way or riding with a friend or a family member. Third, encourage families to learn how to examine alternatives. Many families that lack adaptability also may not know how to examine alternatives (Walsh, 1982). These families might benefit from learning a problem-solving process (see Chapter 13). For example, a single mother was experiencing a very frustrating morning routine with her 4-year-old daughter with an emotional disorder. The little girl often refused to dress or be dressed. After generating several alternatives, the mother and teacher agreed to send the child to preschool in the morning in her pajamas. This decision improved interactions between mother and child, and after a period of time, the dressing-routine procedures the child learned at preschool were put into practice at home.

SUMMARY

This chapter has described many of the issues and concepts related to family interaction. We have discussed the family-interaction subsystems and pointed out how cohesion and adaptability are important parts of family interaction. Family interactions vary greatly depending upon a family's resources, the characteristics of the exceptionality, family values, and ethnic background. Family subsystems change as the family moves through the life cycle. For example, the needs, roles, and interactions of families raising young children usually differ from those of families in the process of launching adult children from the home. Balance is essential. Well-functioning families are those that are able to maintain a balance between cohesion and adaptability in their interaction (Olson et al., 1980). Remember that the family consists of interactions—that is, it is an interactional system.

Family members must be considered and involved as student intervention programs are developed. Students cannot be approached in isolation, for they are part of an interacting system that must function as a whole to meet the many needs of each member. Consequently, addressing the needs of parents, siblings, grandparents, close friends, and other extended family members ultimately will nurture and assist the growth and development of students with an exceptionality. We encourage you to broaden your concept of "who is the client" from the individual with an exceptionality to encompass the whole family. Needs of the family will be discussed in more detail in Chapter 4.

FAMILY FUNCTIONS

This group of mothers from the Centro de Educacion Especial "Ann Sullivan" in Peru meet regularly to help make educational materials for the school. Some families' socialization needs may be met through family support groups.

Riding the 7 o'clock bus home on Friday night from the market, Maria closed her eyes and listened to her four children excitedly making plans for the weekend. Kickball was high on the list. So was baseball, TV, and playing "army." Maybe a trip to the zoo would also be good, one of them suggested. Eight-year-old Elisa patted her mother's arm, "Mama, could we? Could we take the bus to the zoo on Sunday?" "I don't think so. I don't know . . . we will have to see," Maria sighed. She was much too tired to think about the zoo. Between cleaning the apartment, doing laundry for five, going downtown to pick up Loretto's new glasses, and getting everyone ready for church on Sunday, a trip to the zoo sounded about as likely as winning the lottery tonight!

Families exist to meet the individual and collective needs of their members (Caplan, 1976; Leslie, 1979). The tasks families perform to meet these needs are referred to as *family functions*. These functions generally fall into seven broad categories: (a) economic, (b) daily care, (c) recreation, (d) socialization, (e) self-definition, (f) affection, and (g) educational/vocational (A. P. Turnbull et al., 1984). Within each of these categories, family activity generally serves two purposes. First, activities are designed to meet current family and individual needs at a reasonable level. Second, they are designed to ensure training and transfer of the responsibility for meeting those needs from the older to the younger generation (Brotherson, Backus, Summers, & Turnbull, 1986).

After reading this chapter, you should be able to answer the following questions:

- What are the major areas of family functioning?

- How can areas of family functioning be positively or negatively impacted by the presences of a family member with an exceptionality?

- What are some of the ways educators can help students and their families meet their family functioning needs?

- What kinds of information can educators provide to help families learn about community services and/or develop new skills?

THE IMPACT OF EXCEPTIONALITY ON FAMILY FUNCTIONS

Each category of family functions is distinct; however, in many ways these functions are interrelated (Figure 4–1). As a result, problems in

FIGURE 4–1   **Family Systems Conceptual Framework**

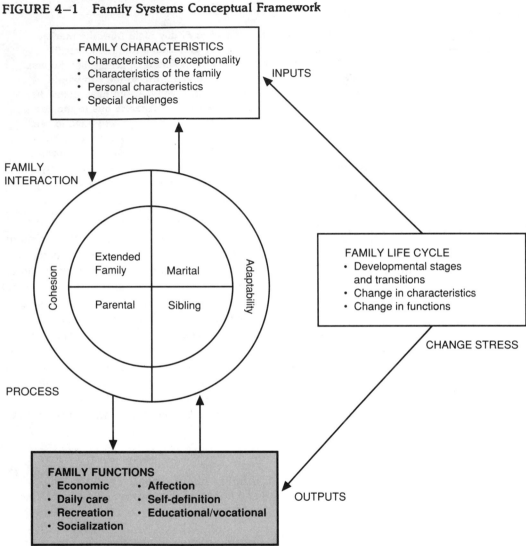

Note. From *Working with Families with Disabled Members: A Family Systems Approach* (p. 60) by A. P. Turnbull, J. A. Summers, and M. J. Brotherson, 1984, Lawrence KS: The University of Kansas, Kansas University Affiliated Facility. Adapted by permission.

one dimension of family functioning can, and often do, impact other dimensions. For example, economic difficulties can negatively impact family members' social or recreational functioning because of limited funds. The category of affection may also be impacted as a result of stress or depression related to the financial worries. Each of the family functions can also be impacted by the presence of a family member with an exceptionality. This impact may be positive, negative, or sometimes neutral (Featherstone, 1980; Grossman, 1972; Kibert, 1986). The impact may be affected by many factors such as those associated with family characteristics (these factors were discussed in Chapter 2) and family interaction (discussed in Chapter 3). Table 4–1 will help you understand the tasks associated with family functions.

It is important for educators to consider family functions as student intervention plans are developed. Often our professional view is so narrowly focused on the student's academic needs that we fail to consider the larger family context in which the student is immersed. Such a limited scope may obscure many critical family needs and responsibilities of students and their families. Dunst, Vance, and Cooper (1986) noted that inadequate resources needed to meet basic family needs can negatively impact on the time, energy, and personal commitment of parents to follow through on home intervention plans. If we do not give adequate consideration to the student's family and existing family-function needs and responsibilities, our best teaching efforts may produce only limited positive results or may even exacerbate students' difficulties. For example, Isa's teacher recommended that his father spend 15 minutes each night working on his expressive language. She sent home a packet of "fun" materials for them to use. Although this may not sound like an unreasonable request, it may be more than this newly divorced parent can handle. By the time he has picked up his three children from the day-care center, cooked their dinner, washed the dishes, and supervised their nightly baths, the father is exhausted and the children are already behind schedule for bed. What can he do? Does he keep Isa up later to do the language activities? Does he skip the bedtime story the children love? Or does he just feel guilty and resentful about being an inadequate parent one more day?

Each time we ask parents to do something at home with their children, they must be willing to give up some other activity that currently occupies that time. Time spent on home interventions may mean less time and energy to address basic family functions such as affection, self-definition, or recreation. This chapter discusses how family members with exceptionality may influence the way families attend to functions. The chapter also suggests how you may help families meet their functional needs more satisfactorily. If functional family needs and relationships (Chapter 3) are considered when school programs are designed for individuals with an exceptionality, such interventions are more likely to meet the needs of students and families in an appropriate and balanced manner.

Economic Needs

Most families need to earn a living and decide how money is spent for family needs. Today in most two-parent homes both parents are em-

TABLE 4–1   Tasks Associated with Family Functions

ECONOMIC	DAILY CARE	RECREATION
• Generating income • Paying bills and banking • Handling investments • Overseeing insurance benefit programs • Earning allowance • Dispensing allowance • Saving for the future	• Purchasing and preparing food • Purchasing and preparing clothing • Maintaining health care • Providing safety and protection • Transporting family members • Maintaining and cleaning home	• Participating in individual and family-oriented recreation • Setting aside demands • Developing and enjoying hobbies • Building skills and talents
SOCIALIZATION	**SELF-IDENTITY**	**AFFECTION**
• Building relationships • Developing social skills • Engaging in social activities	• Establishing self-identity and self-image • Recognizing strengths and weaknesses • Belonging to groups • Developing self-confidence	• Nurturing and loving • Sharing companionship • Enjoying intimacy • Expressing emotions

EDUCATIONAL/VOCATIONAL

- Continuing education for parents
- Completing homework
- Developing cultural appreciation
- Building social responsibility
- Making career choices
- Developing work skills and attitudes
- Supporting career interests and problems
- Developing family values

Note. From *Working with Families with Disabled Members: A Family System Perspective* (p. 36) by A. P. Turnbull, J. A. Summers, and M. J. Brotherson, 1984, Lawrence, KS: The University of Kansas. Adapted by permission.

ployed. Frost (1986) estimated that by 1990 80% of all married mothers of children under 6 will be employed. The economic pressures that two-parent homes face are much greater for single parents. By 1990 it is predicted that approximately one-half of the children in America will live in single-parent homes (Frost, 1986). The vast majority of single parents are mothers, many of whom are financially disadvantaged (Kamerman, 1985; Zigler & Black, 1989). It comes as no surprise, therefore, that single parents have been shown to be at significantly greater risk for financial problems, stress, and depression (Dunst et al., 1986; Quine & Paul, 1985; Schilling, Kirkham, Snow, & Schinke, 1986).

The presence of a family member with an exceptionality can create special economic needs by increasing the family's consumptive demands and decreasing its productive capacity (A. P. Turnbull et al., 1984). In a national evaluation of services for children and adolescents using ventilators, Aday, Aitken, and Weggener (1988) found that 47% of the parents reported that "out-of-pocket" expenses (i.e., those not covered by medical insurance) presented "serious financial problems" for their families during periods when the children were hospitalized. Thirty-eight percent of the parents reported similar financial problems when ventilator care services were provided in the home. Types of expenses included lost income from work, transportation, extra phone costs, lost vacation time, child-care for siblings, meals and motels, accumulating debts, medications, and increased utility bills. Other research investigations have shown that the expenses related to special needs of individuals with exceptionality can create financial hardships for families (McAndrew, 1976).

When one father of a son with a physical disability was asked to name the most stressful factor in planning his son's future, he answered:

> Finding finances. I don't know where the money is going to come from. We've had to have help over the years. I quit counting when Ron's hospital bills topped $600,000. (Brotherson, 1985)

When considering expenses a family may incur because of the special needs of a family member with an exceptionality, we usually think of severe exceptionalities involving physically and/or medically related factors. While the costs in such situations can be astronomical, families of children and adolescents with mild to moderate exceptionalities often experience increased financial responsibilities. For example, students with learning disabilities may need special support services such as tutoring, summer programs, medication, personal and career counseling, calculators, and word processors. Kaslow and Cooper (1978) noted that parents sometimes feel that they have to allocate inordinate amounts of family resources to help their son or daughter with the learning disability. Further, Margalit (1982) suggested that the costs of providing special educational support for these students can contribute to disruption of family equilibrium.

Just as the presence of a family member with an exceptionality can negatively affect the amount of money the family has to spend on other needs, so it can negatively affect the amount of money a family can produce. Some families have reported sacrificing careers to care for the child or to relocate in a geographic area where appropriate services are available (Turnbull et al., 1984). One study found that 27% of the families believed their work performance was affected as a result of their having a child with an exceptionality (Lonsdale, 1978). This study included children with a variety of disabling conditions and levels of severity. Parents mentioned such factors as "lack of concentration, needing to take a lot of time off work, needing to take a less well-paid job" as affecting their work (Lonsdale, 1978, p. 117).

While professionals usually cannot directly reduce the economic impact of exceptionality, they can provide information on financial assistance available to families who request it. Some families may need information about social security disability benefits or other sources of governmental assistance. Others may need advice on wills, trusts, and estate planning. Some may be eligible for school-district or community programs to provide eyeglasses, winter coats, dental care, and other important items and services at no cost or at reduced cost. Others may live in states where family subsidy programs are available for families whose children have severe disabilities and are at risk for institutionalization. Such programs provide a cash payment to families each month to help cover extraordinary caretaking expenses (Slater, Bates, Eicher, & Wikler, 1986). As we discuss in Chapter 12, you need to be familiar with the resources and programs available in your area. Table 4–2 provides suggestions professionals may offer to families regarding financial information/resources.

TABLE 4–2   Suggestions for how to Address Economic Needs

- Identify appropriate community contacts and provide parents with names and telephone numbers of persons to contact regarding estate planning, disability benefits, or family subsidies.
- Provide information on financial planning as part of the family resource library.
- Encourage parents who have been successful in obtaining financial sources or who have completed financial planning to speak with other parents.
- Provide information to help families investigate scholarships and financial aid.

Daily Care Needs

A basic function of families consists of meeting the physical and health needs of their members. This includes the day-to-day tasks of living: cooking, cleaning, laundry, transportation, obtaining medical care when needed, and so forth.

Daily care giving for persons with exceptionalities can be a burden for family members. In some families the daily care needs of individuals with exceptionalities are no different than for other family members. However, for those with severe disabilities, care, assistance, and supervision of daily care is needed over prolonged periods of time (Benson, 1989). The chronicity of this responsibility can take a toll on the well-being of care givers, especially mothers who have maintained much of the responsibility for meeting these needs (Willer, Intagliata, & Wicks, 1981). Although traditionally these chores have primarily fallen on mothers, fathers are taking more active roles in this dimension of family life (Hornby, 1988). Siblings and extended family members may also be involved in the daily care process.

The extent and nature of responsibilities for daily care will vary depending on a variety of factors such as the age of the child or youth and the type, degree, and severity of the exceptionality. The family's expectations and their level of commitment to help members develop skills also influence the division of the daily care tasks. One mother who was working diligently on a campaign for group homes was gently, but firmly reminded by her son that it was time for her own 16-year-old daughter with mental retardation to take responsibility for her share of family dishwashing.

As children with exceptionality grow and develop more self-help skills, family daily care responsibilities often decrease. Helping these children develop daily care skills is an important part of family and teacher responsibilties and should be discussed on an ongoing basis. Willing siblings can often serve as teachers and role models in this area. School-age children have been shown to be effective in helping their brothers or sisters with exceptionality develop basic self-help skills after school while their parents were at work. Such skills included snack preparation, bed making, and tooth brushing (Swenson–Pierce et al., 1987).

Seligman and Meyerson (1982) noted that the responsibilities associated with the care of children with exceptionality may impact parents' psychological, physical, and financial well-being over time. Researchers (Gallagher, Beckman, & Cross, 1983) have found that the stress which parents of children with exceptionalities experience is related to the amount of care-giving demands required and the degree of inappropriateness of the child's behavior. Further, the chronicity of care giving for individuals with severe disabilities and/or chronic medical needs (e.g., dialysis) has been related to increased parental stress (Quine & Paul, 1985; Ventura & Boxx, 1983) and family burnout (LePontois, Moel, & Cohn, 1987). When parents are busy meeting the daily care needs of their children, they sometimes overlook their own needs.

One mother describes the exhaustion she experienced when she finally submitted to her physical need for rest:

> I can remember having to restrain my child at 5:00 in the morning be-
> cause he had paced all night. I was exhausted and there was nothing left
> to do except restrain him. In his bed he finally drifted off to sleep. (Blue-
> Banning, 1985, p. 6)

Respite services provide temporary care for persons with developmental disabilities for the purpose of providing relief from care to the family or primary care givers (Cohen & Warren, 1985). Publicly sponsored respite services are available in 20 states (Slater et al., 1986). Benson (1989) found that families who lack other sources of informal and formal social support and experience stress as a result relied more on respite care services than families for whom social support was not a problem. During interviews with families using respite services, Benson found that the majority felt respite care had positively benefited their families and had helped reduce stress levels.

However, just because children can create greater stress in the family function of daily care needs, this is not always the case. In fact, children can make many positive contributions to this family function. For example, they can help with housekeeping, yard work, laundry, or the needs of younger siblings. As a single mother reported:

> Of my three children, the one with autism is my lifesaver when it comes
> to housework. He believes that everything has a place and belongs in it.
> His room would pass any army inspection. He organizes drawers and
> pulls weeds out of the flower beds. On the other hand, the clutter and
> mess in the bedrooms of my normal kids is shameful. When I ask for
> their help, they consider it an infringement on their social life.

Table 4–3 provides suggestions on how to help families meet daily care needs.

Recreation Needs

The family serves an important function as an outlet for members to relax and be themselves. Sometimes this function is curtailed due to the presence of a family member with an exceptionality. For example, some families have reported that they have difficulty enjoying family outings

---

TABLE 4–3 Suggestions for how to Address Daily Care Needs

- When selecting self-help or personal-care goals at school, discuss priorities with family members. Encourage families to bring their list of priority goals and objectives to the IEP conference.
- Work with family members to identify those skills needed by the student to contribute to the daily-care functions (e.g., taking out the trash, assisting with laundry, cleaning bedroom or feeding a younger sibling).
- Provide practical suggestions and information on how to meet care needs through the family research library.
- Arrange for experienced parents to share their successes at parent groups or through mentorships between sets of parents.
- Send a notebook back and forth from school to homes. Let family members (e.g., parents, siblings, grandparents) share their successes and suggestions with other families in a collective classroom notebook that travels between families.
- Remind parents that *all* family members have physical and health-care needs. Parent needs are legitimate, too. Encourage parents to do positive things for themselves (e.g., exercise, read, visit friends, or take classes).
- Provide information about respite and child-care options in the community through social-service agencies, volunteer groups, or church groups.
- Choose goals that will help students become more independent.

---

such as trips to the beach, picnics, or trips to the swimming pool or cinema (Dunlap & Hollingsworth, 1977; Lonsdale, 1978) as a result. While this function may be curtailed for some families, for others, the exceptionality can enhance their ability to rest and recreate.

Healthy families are able to relax and have fun together. A number of researchers have found relationships between stress and family psychosocial environments (Bristol, 1984; McCubbin et al., 1980). Bristol (1984), for example, compared dimensions of family relationships, personal growth, and family-system maintenance in families of children with autism. Well-adapted families were able to express their emotions, engage in social and recreational activities outside the home, and provide emotional support for each other.

One mother reported her daughter's recreational influence on their family:

> Because of Susan's reading disability, school has always been very hard for her. She reads now—slowly—but for a long time she never thought she would read at all. To make matters worse, Della and Melinda, her younger sisters, have always been star students—both of them are in the gifted program at their school. Because of these things, I really wanted to

---

TABLE 4–4   Suggestions for how to Address Recreational Needs

---

- Gather information from students and families regarding home leisure-time activities, and help students build on those interests. Identify skills in both the school and home environments that the students could use to meet their own recreational needs in the future (e.g., supporting music interests by teaching the student to handle tapes and records, and to store and to use stereo equipment independently).

- Students who are gifted may have a wide range of interests but may have problems concentrating in one area (Stewart, 1986). Encourage these students to follow through on recreation and leisure activities for mastery rather than going through many hobbies or sports activities in a short time.

- Provide information about community offerings for activities such as horseback riding, day camps, canoeing, dancing, camping, and tours. Parents may not be aware of available community recreational opportunities, or that their son or daughter is eligible for enrollment in these programs.

- Provide mainstreamed recreational options such as Scouts, 4-H clubs, arts programs, and dance lessons for children and youth with exceptionalities. These options are sometimes overlooked by families and professionals alike.

---

find the places where Susan could shine too. When she showed an interest in swimming, I encouraged her. She took swimming lessons at the YWCA and we all started swimming a lot as a family. Now she swims on a team for the city during the summer and next year she's decided to try out for the swim team at her high school. She has a lot of confidence in this area. She swims circles around most of her friends and all of her family! But I'm a lot better swimmer today than I would have been without her influence.

Integrated recreational opportunities are important sources for socialization and learning to persons with and without exceptionality. Such activities help meet the psychosocial needs of the child or youth with an exceptionality, and provide valuable experiences for their peers. If classmates of students with disabilities have positive experiences with them in recreational, social, and academic areas, the classmates will be more receptive to integrated work environments (A. P. Turnbull & Turnbull, 1988).

Janet Bennett states:

A long time ago I stopped looking at newspaper listings of special programs for retarded children. Now I just notice what Kathryn might like. All kinds of courses are given by community schools, YMCAs, or churches. Grandparents and teenagers, beginners, or those with some familiarity with the subject—all take the same course. Though there may be beginning, intermediate, or advanced levels, nobody would notice or care if someone took the same course several times. For most of us, and especially retarded children, taking enough time is more important than special techniques. (Bennett, 1985, p. 171)

Educational objectives for leisure and recreation often have been accorded low priority in the educational process, yet this is a very important function of family life (Ball, Chasey, Hawkins, & Verhoven, 1976). Remember to include books on family recreation and leisure in your parent library. Encourage families to pursue hobbies, games, and physical activities together. Ask families what they like to do together as a family and try to build on current interests. Keep them posted on recreational opportunities in the community.

Often educators are so narrowly focused on school-based curriculum that we forget how important family leisure time can be as a way of building new skills, strengthening family relationships, and bolstering self-esteem. Table 4–4 provides suggestions that may help meet recreational needs.

Socialization Needs

Socialization is vital to the overall quality of life for most individuals. Families are the base from which individuals learn to interact with others and keys to the achievement of socialization for all members (Skrtic, Summers, Brotherson, & Turnbull, 1984).

Many families experience stress in attempting to meet the socialization needs of their child or youth with an exceptionality. A review of the literature on social development of children having disabilities concluded that "almost all exceptional children, regardless of their disability, have significant social handicaps" (Strain, 1982, p. 2). Similarly, Brotherson (1985) found that, after residential options, socialization was the greatest need identified by parents for young adults with mental retardation. As one mother said: "People with disabilities are lonesome, lonesome people" (Brotherson, 1985, p. 119).

Persons with exceptionalities of all ages need opportunities to develop and practice social skills—just like everyone else. Well-developed social skills and the friendships that can result when we use these skills effectively are important for full lives and personal happiness. As a result, families and teachers need to help children and adolescents develop good social skills and provide them with opportunities to practice these skills with peers if meaningful friendships are to develop.

Some parents may need encouragement and guidance in this area. Often, even enthusiastic and supportive parents focus on other important areas of their child's development and, unwittingly, ignore the social dimension. They may need to know how their child acts in peer group situations as this behavior may be very different from what they see at home. You can also provide them with information about extracurricular activities at school and in the community where students can socialize. Adrienne Asch (1989), a professional in special education who is blind, wrote about the important role her family played in helping her develop friendships:

> I feel very fortunate to have grown up knowing and becoming friends with children who were disabled and children who were not. Because my family valued having friends and a social life, they took seriously my interests in having a social life, and worked with me and with the school to encourage them. Without active efforts, it is unlikely that simply proximity in class or clubs will be enough to turn acquaintances into friends.
> (p. 195)

Lack of socialization options can be caused by specific skill deficits (e.g., lack of mobility or verbal skills) or be attributed to negative attitudes among community members, neighbors, and relatives toward persons with an exceptionality. In one study of 116 mothers, one third felt their relationships with friends were adversely affected. Friends were reported to be "frightened, embarrassed, and don't know how to approach us" (McAndrew, 1976, p. 229).

Overcoming these barriers can be difficult. In addition to the negative reactions parents may experience when they take their child into the community, they may also find it difficult to meet their own socialization needs. One third of the mothers in McAndrew's study (1976) also reported that their child's disability had placed restrictions on their socialization opportunities, primarily because of the difficulty involved in finding someone to stay with their child.

One mother states: "There are simply times we don't do things because of our son. He requires so much, it's exhausting to just sit down and explain to a babysitter what has to be done. It's just easier not to do it" (Blue-Banning, 1985, p. 1). Even families of children and youth with exceptionalities that are viewed as mild to moderate can experience socialization difficulty. Limited time is an issue for most families, but it may be even more so for families with members who have exceptionalities or are chronically ill (Goldfarb, Brotherson, Summers, & Turnbull, 1986).

Exceptionality can also have positive effects on socialization for family members. Thus, many parents have reported that parent programs were the catalyst for friendships that have lasted long after their children left the programs. Parent organizations also offer parents an avenue to building friendships and reducing isolation. Similarly, Vadasy, Fewell, Meyer, and Greenberg (1984) noted that both fathers and mothers benefited from a series of "fathers only" social support meetings.

All members of the family need an opportunity to socialize. As one mother of a young child with autism reported, "When I'm with my friends that's when I can release my feelings and problems and be my-self" (Goldfarb et al., 1986). Cobb (1976) reviewed the role of socialization and the benefits of social support in illness, hospitalization, pregnancy, childbirth, unemployment, and bereavement. He noted that in all cases, people with more social support made it through crises or life changes with less stress than those who lacked a social support network. Chriss Walther-Thomas related the following story about her daughter and her daughter's friend Bernie:

> Lyndsey and Bernie were 4 years old when they started preschool, and we formed the neighborhood car pool. Within several months, Lyndsey's father had died suddenly and Bernie was diagnosed as having a rare form of leukemia. During the next four years, Bernie's mother, Tamar, and I often remarked how our real lives felt like a bad movie. We leaned on each other a lot for friendship, child care, and moral support. We gave each other a safe and caring place where it was OK to be sad or angry or even to laugh out loud even when there wasn't anything very funny going on.
>
> The children also shared a rare and special friendship. They were able to talk comfortably with each other about things that most children don't understand and grown-ups don't want to hear. Lyndsey went to the hospital with Bernie two or three times a week as a distraction from his chemotherapy treatments. Because of the side effects of chemotherapy, Bernie's appearance changed dramatically. He quickly lost his hair, gained 20 pounds, and had very little energy. Our house was one of the few places where he continued to feel comfortable spending time. Together Bernie and Lyndsey spent hundreds of hours having a great time watching videos, looking at books, making PlayDoh sculptures, and chatting about his rotten disease, her Daddy, and life at school.

Table 4–5 provides suggestions for you to use to help family members with their social needs.

Self-Identity Needs

Persons perceive their competence and worth by the way they define themselves. Family membership plays an important role in helping individuals establish who they are as well as their worth as people. Exceptionality can have an impact on the self-identity of all family members. Parents of children and youth with an exceptionality often experience difficulty with their feelings of worth and self-esteem. For example, parents of infants may have difficulty developing a self-identity as competent parents, possibly because infants with exceptionality are sometimes less responsive to soothing or stimulation, and their cues are often difficult for parents to read.

TABLE 4–5   Suggestions for how to Address Socialization Needs

- Suggest that parents provide information to extended family members to help them become more confident in providing care for their child or youth with exceptionality. Invite interested friends or relatives to the classroom to observe some of the techniques you use.

- Some children or youth may engage in inappropriate behaviors that make it difficult for family members to take them into the community. Offer training to parents (or other family members) on behavior management techniques that would make it easier to take the child to social activities (see Chapter 12).

- Conduct family support-group meetings so that families may exchange ideas about how they handled uncomfortable social situations.

- Provide home learning activities where family members can discuss and/ or role-play social situations and explore ways to handle difficult situations.

If all or most family activities revolve around the exceptionality (e.g., parent groups, friends of children with exceptionality, advocacy efforts, home programs), the exceptionality may become the major identifying characteristic of the family. Further, if its identity remains tied to the person with exceptionality, the family may have difficulty encouraging the young adult to exercise independence (A. P. Turnbull, et al., 1984).

In addition, siblings may be at risk for self-identity problems if family activities revolve exclusively around the sibling's exceptionality. Kronick (1976) noted that siblings of children with learning disabilities may feel less important and less loved because of the parental attention given to the child with the exceptionality. Some siblings even develop somatic complaints in an attempt to gain parental attention (Luterman, 1979; Marion, 1981; Sourkes, 1987).

Some studies have suggested that siblings may worry about "catching" their sister's or brother's exceptionality (Featherstone, 1980; Lechtenberg, 1984; Sourkes, 1987; Western Psychological Institute, 1980). Tew et al., (1974) found that it was more difficult for brothers and sisters of children and adolescents with mild to moderate exceptionalities to differentiate themselves from their siblings than for children whose siblings had more severe exceptionalities. A study by Wallinga, Paquio, and Skeen (1987) showed that parents believed siblings of children with an exceptionality coped better than the siblings actually considered themselves to be. To avoid misconception and fear, children need clear and specific information regarding the nature and consequences of their brother's or sister's exceptionality, opportunities to discuss their feelings, and parental support (Seligman & Darling, 1989). Such an approach will facilitate both the development of positive sibling relationships and healthy self-identities.

Parents of children who are gifted may also experience difficulty with self-identity. Most parents anticipate raising "normal" children; if they are confronted with raising a child who is gifted, therefore, they may feel uncertain and even threatened (Dettmann & Colangelo, 1980). Parents' inability to accept an exceptionality may also greatly affect the ability of the child or youth with an exceptionality to develop a healthy self-identity. If parents have difficulty showing pride and pleasure in their child's uniqueness, their child will grow to view his or her exceptionality or "differentness" as a defect and a societal deviance (Rousso, 1984). A young woman with cerebral palsy makes this point clear:

> My mother was quite concerned about the awkwardness of my walk— which she feared would subject me to endless teasing and rejection. To some extent it did. She made numerous attempts over the years of my childhood to have me go for physical therapy and to practice walking more "normally" at home. I vehemently refused all her efforts. She could not understand why I would not walk straight. Now I realize why. My disability, with my different walk and talk and my involuntary movements, having been with me all of my life, was part of me, part of my identity. With these disability features, I felt complete and whole. My mother's attempt to change my walk, strange as it may seem, felt like an assault on myself, and incomplete acceptance of all of me, an attempt to make me over. I fought it because I wanted to be accepted and appreciated as I was. (Rousso, 1984, p. 9)

Assisting children and youth with exceptionalities, as well as all family members, to develop positive self-identities is critical to enduring quality of life. Table 4–6 provides suggestions for how to help families meet their self-identity needs.

TABLE 4–6 Suggestions for how to Address Self-Identity Needs

- Encourage all family members to develop self-identity in areas other than the exceptionality by pursuing their own interests, hobbies, or personal goals.

- Encourage children and youth with exceptionalities to identify and develop interests that give them pride and self-esteem. One strategy might be to place the student with an exceptionality in the role of helper rather than recipient of help.

- Encourage children and youth with exceptionalities to express their own choices as a strategy to enhance their self-identity. Allowing children and youth to choose what is important to them affords them greater control and independence.

Affection Needs

Families provide a very important environment in which to meet the needs of physical intimacy (e.g., touching, hugging, and kissing) as well as to express feelings of unconditional love and esteem. An individual with an exceptionality can have both a positive and negative impact on a family's ability to be affectionate (A. P. Turnbull, et al., 1984). For example, a family can be drawn together and experience a close sense of bonding as a result of the exceptionality.

As one sibling put it:

> We siblings were a care group for Grace, largely by choice but also out of necessity because both Mom and Dad worked full-time, and we had to help out . . . all eight of us were part of the action. The most important influence Grace has had on me is that she has convinced me that everyone . . . deserves the same as all of us: to be loved, to have fun, to tease and be teased, to have our abilities challenged, to be given a chance to try. This has molded not only my career choices but also in what I simply call "keeping a Grace-ful perspective" on what is important in life. (Osborne, 1988, p. 2)

Members who are exceptional may have a negative impact on families. For example, some families fail to establish affectional bonds with the child who is exceptional either because of fear that the child will die or leave the family, or because the child is physically deformed (Featherstone, 1980). Families play a critical role in expressing affection to young children with an exceptionality. Rousso (1984), a social worker with a physical disability, points out the contribution of the family to meeting affection needs:

> In particular, disabled children need to have their bodies, disability and all, accepted, appreciated and loved, especially by significant parenting figures. (p. 12)

Affection shown by our parents, siblings, and extended family members helps satisfy many important emotional and physical needs. Family expressions of affection also provide important learning models. We learn a lot about affection from watching our parents and from our relationships within the family. As adolescence and young adulthood approach, many parents find it difficult that interest and affection begin to be directed toward friends outside the family. This is often more difficult for parents of youth with exceptionality. As children with exceptionalities grow older, their needs and means of expressing affection are often complicated by emerging sexuality. Sexuality is a difficult topic for many families, but in families with children who are exceptional it can be even more difficult. Ann Turnbull comments about her son, who has moderate mental retardation:

> He is physically mature, even more so than most sixteen-year-olds. Puberty has created tumultuous emotions for him, partially because he does not understand what is happening. His rapid physical changes stand in stark contrast to his slow cognitive growth, and the imbalance has been difficult for me to adjust to. (A. P. Turnbull, 1985a, p. 139)

Other parents may refuse to acknowledge the special needs and changes in affection and sexuality that accompany adolescence. As one mother of an adolescent son with a disability said:

> He has no needs along this line. I don't see any sexual desires expressed. He asked, "Will I ever get married?" and I said, "No." Besides, it is against the church. (Brotherson, 1985)

A lack of adequate information and experience can have detrimental affects on adulthood. An attractive 38-year-old woman with a severe learning disability talked about the frustration and fear she experiences because of limited skill in this area:

> I lived at home with my parents until three years ago when I had a chance to move here and work for my cousin. I think Mom and Dad thought I'd always live with them. Sometimes I miss them alot. I miss their hugs and their encouragement, but I do like being on my own— feeling like a real adult. I have an apartment and a job but what I'd really like is a husband and a family. I'm Catholic, so having children would mean a lot to me. When I'm feeling lonely I really wish that I was in love. I get depressed sometimes because I don't think that will ever happen. I'm getting pretty old and I hardly even know how to meet men or how to act around them. I get really nervous. I've been on about three dates in my entire life. Mom wouldn't let me go out when I was in school. She was afraid that boys would take advantage of me because I seemed young for my age. When I got out of school I just didn't meet guys very often. I know that sometimes when I am around guys I act too interested and sometimes I act too shy. They frighten me a lot. I wish I could take a class somewhere on how to find a boyfriend.

Families need to address issues of affection and sexuality. Because these are sensitive topics, they also tend to be avoided by teachers and schools, and are not addressed often during IEP discussions or parent-teacher conferences. Many, if not most, parents need information. You can help families by providing parents with useful printed material and information on local resources. Offer information during meetings, in newsletters, or make materials available in a resource library. Encourage school personnel and community social services and mental-health agencies to develop groups for parents and/or students to discuss affection, intimacy, and relationships.

Table 4–7 provides suggestions for helping families meet their affectional needs.

Educational/Vocational Needs

The area of educational/vocational needs is often emphasized by professionals more than families (A. P. Turnbull et al., 1984). Such an emphasis is appropriate if it is consistent with the family's values and cultural priorities (see Chapter 2). If not, the difference between the focus of school, other service agencies, and home can cause strain or conflict in the home and school relationship. Indeed, many parents or students respond negatively to a perceived overemphasis on educational/vocational needs. Professionals should remember that the educational/vocational needs are only one function families must address. Maddux and Cummings (1983) warn:

> If academic learning is required in both the home and the school, a child who has difficulty learning gets very little relief. The home ceases to be a haven from scholastic pressures. Imagine how most of us would feel if the most frustrating, least enjoyable, and most difficult thing about our work were waiting for us when we came home each day. (p. 30)

TABLE 4–7   Suggestions for how to Address Affection Needs

- Recognize the needs all family members have for affection; for example, if a parent-child home teaching program each night interferes with a busy family's only opportunities to catch up on the day's events, play games, or snuggle on the couch together reconsider the plan to achieve a balance in meeting all family needs, not just educational needs.

- Provide materials in the resource library and arrange discussion groups involving resource persons that can help parents and students with an exceptionality gain a better understanding of sexuality. Young adults or adolescents with exceptionality, depending on age, type, and severity of exceptionality, benefit from accurate and sensitive information about sexuality and affection.

- Help parents identify their child's positive contributions to affection as well as other family functions. Encourage family members to discuss what positive contributions each makes. For example, suggest that at breakfast family members think of at least two things they like about each of the other members during the day. After dinner, the family shares the ideas they have generated and talk about similarities and differences in each person's list.

A. P. Turnbull and Turnbull (1986) have expressed concern about the "fix-it approach" whereby children with exceptionalities are almost continuously placed in quasi-teaching situations by well-intentioned teachers, family, and friends. Every event is considered a new and meaningful opportunity for learning. These perpetual efforts to make him or her "better" may lead the child to experience feelings of inadequacy as a person. Because the exceptionality cannot be "fixed," ultimately both the parent's and the child's self-image may be negatively impacted.

However, it is important for educators, early in students' educational careers, to help families and students think about the importance of educational/vocational decisions and explore the broadening range of opportunities for all students with exceptionality. According to A. P. Turnbull and Turnbull (1988) family decision making about educational/vocational priorities is strongly influenced by the nature of their expectations. Families of persons with exceptionalities may be confused about what to expect in terms of educational and vocational integration. Often low expectations may have developed as a result of previous thinking by professionals, former policies, and outdated public attitudes. Therefore, to increase substantially the nature and extent of integration professionals must make a concerted effort to help raise family expectations (Forest, 1988; Reynolds, 1988). Turnbull and Turnbull noted:

> High expectations describe a mind set that policy, families, and professionals should adopt—not just to put pressure on the status quo in order to change it, but also to inject a note of optimism into life and to be an antidote to the usual cautions to be "realistic." Because "realistic" implies being satisfied; and people who have been satisfied never created new worlds. (A. P. Turnbull & Turnbull, 1988, p. 4).

Families and professionals need to start teaching students skills in decision making during early childhood and continue systematic instruction in this area throughout the educational program (A. P. Turnbull & Turnbull, 1988). Students of all ability levels and their families need up-to-date information about resources, encouragement from informed professionals, opportunities to see and talk with successful models, and volunteer and paid work experiences. Such skills and experiences will help students make educational and career decisions that will turn great expectations into realities. Chriss Walther-Thomas related the following story about a college student with whom she worked at the University of Utah:

> Early Saturday one morning one of my students brought a box of her graduation announcements to my house to show me how wonderful they looked. As her advisor, I knew that Jill had worked hard to earn a master's degree in special education and how proud she was of this accom-

plishment. She was a top student and I knew she would be an excellent teacher. "I bought a lot of these," she said. "There's a long list of people back home I'm going to send them to!... People, especially teachers and counselors, who told me and my parents that I would never graduate from high school. Boy, I'd love to see their faces when these announcements arrive!" Despite a severe reading disability, Jill had achieved an important career goal. Taped textbooks, accommodations on some exams and assignments, and a campus support agency had all helped make it a little easier but she did it largely because she believed she could and because the people who loved her encouraged her to try.

Table 4–8 provides some suggestions on how to meet educational/vocational needs.

Three points need to be remembered as you implement the suggestions in this chapter:

TABLE 4–8   Suggestions for how to Address Educational/Vocational Needs

---

- Check out the family's willingness to participate before proposing home intervention programs. Ask if they have the time and desire to teach their child at home. Take the same approach with family support-group meetings or meetings held for the purpose of sharing information. If the family is not interested, generate other alternatives to address the child's educational needs. Learn more about the family's high-priority needs.

- For families who choose greater participation in educational/vocational planning, provide a variety of strategies for involvement. Strategies for involving families in IEP conferences are included in Chapter 10; suggestions for how to exchange educational and vocational information with families in Chapter 12.

- Expose students to a variety of possible future jobs through books, field trips, class projects, or classroom visits by different professionals or craftspersons. Students need opportunities to choose areas of vocational interest and to explore them. Start early in a child's educational career to identify skills that will be needed for specific jobs, postsecondary training, or education.

- Discuss regularly long-term goals and aspirations parents have for their children with exceptionalities. Students should be included in these discussions. Talk about the necessary steps to achieve goals. For example, a 6th-grade student with a learning disability wants to follow in his mother's foot steps and pursue a career in science. This goal needs to be considered as summer plans are selected. Learning computer skills, volunteering at a natural history museum, or finding a scientist willing to serve as a mentor may all facilitate the achievement of the student's educational and/or vocational goals.

---

1. the importance of balancing family members' needs;
2. the importance of using a social support network to help whenever possible; and
3. the importance of identifying the positive contributions of children and youth having an exceptionality to each family function.

SUMMARY

Just as families vary in their resources, size, values, and interaction patterns, so they also vary in the way they meet family functions. Families of children and youth with exceptionalities may focus more intensely on certain functions and may have difficulty attending to certain functions. Families vary in the functions they consider important as well as in the intensity with which they experience stress associated with these functions.

Parents may assume that educational professionals do not have available the resources they need to meet many of their family needs (Vincent, Laten, Salisbury, Brown, & Baumgart, 1981). But you, as a professional representing one of the many systems that serve children and families, have a responsibility to be familiar with the referral resources in your own or surrounding communities. You also have a responsibility to acknowledge that families have many needs to fulfill both collectively and individually for all members. Remember that each time you intervene with families and children, you potentially enhance or hinder their ability to meet family functions. Helen Featherstone (1980) describes a situation where she felt the school asked too much:

> I remember the day when the occupational therapist at Jody's school
> called with some suggestions from a visiting nurse. Jody has a seizure
> problem which is controlled with the drug Dilantin. Dilantin can cause the
> gums to grow over the teeth; the nurse had noticed this overgrowth, and
> recommended, innocently enough, that [his] teeth be brushed four times
> a day, for 5 minutes, with an electric toothbrush. The school suggested
> that they could do this once on school days, and that I should try to do it
> the other three times a day; this new demand appalled me; Jody is blind,
> cerebral palsied, and retarded. We do his physical therapy daily and work
> with him on sounds and communication. We feed him each meal on our
> laps, bottle him, bathe him, dry him, put him in a body cast to sleep,
> launder his bed linens daily, and go through a variety of routines designed
> to minimize his miseries and enhance his joys and his development. (All
> this in addition to trying to care for and enjoy our other young children
> and making time for each other and our careers.) Now you tell me that I
> should spend 15 minutes every day on something that Jody will hate, an
> activity that will not help him to walk or even defecate, but one that is

directed at the health of his gums. This activity is not for a finite time, but forever. It is not guaranteed to help, but "it can't hurt." And it won't make the overgrowth go away but may retard it. Well, it's too much. Where is that 15 minutes going to come from? What am I supposed to give up? Taking the kids to the park? Reading a bedtime story to my eldest? Washing the breakfast dishes? Sorting the laundry? Grading students' papers? Sleeping? Because there is not time in my life that hasn't been spoken for, and for every 15-minute activity that is added one has to be taken away. (pp. 77–78)

As Featherstone shows, you need to recognize the impact you can have on a family's abilities to meet all of their functions. You need to ask, therefore, "Am I asking too much or giving too little to aid the family in the many needs they must fulfill? Are my suggestions consistent with their priorities? Are those priorities changing?" In the next chapter, we examine that last question—change over the family's life cycle.

FAMILY LIFE CYCLE

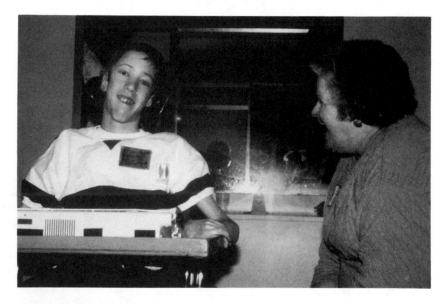

Keith, with the assistance of his communication board, is telling his grandmother about his date for the upcoming high-school prom. Sexuality and dating issues often arise during adolescence.

$\mathbf{T}$ hree-year-old Miguel stares at nothing and at everything. He seems vulnerable and self-sufficient at the same time to Anita. She shudders as she recalls the doctor's words: "Your son has infantile autism." Through her tears she tries to envision the man Miguel will one day be.

The needs of a family with a young child who has an exceptionality are not the same as the needs of a family with a young adult who has an exceptionality. Understanding how a family with an exceptionality changes over time will enable you to provide appropriate support services to each family member. After exploring a family's changing needs in this chapter, you will be able to answer the following questions:

- What developmental stages are represented by family members?
- How may these stages interact to strengthen or cause problems within the family?
- What needs do family members have as a result of the developmental stage of the member with an exceptionality?
- Is the family undergoing a life-cycle transition that needs to be addressed?

A PORTRAIT OF FAMILY CHANGE

The last three chapters presented a portrait of the family system (Fig. 5–1) and how it is affected by exceptionality. The predominant image is one of complexity. First, the many ways in which families can differ—in size, membership, ethnicity, values, personal idiosyncrasies, to name a few—create such a wide range of diversity that we can truly say every family is unique. Second, every family is an interactive system, which means that anything happening to one person reverberates in one way or another throughout the system. Third, every family is busily engaged in a variety of activities designed to fulfill a number of tangible and intangible needs.

Yet another layer of complexity impacts the family system—change. The portrait of diversity, interaction, and wide-ranging functions is only a snapshot of what should more accurately be portrayed as a full-length motion picture. All families experience change as members are born, grow up, leave home, bring in new members through marriage or other

FIGURE 5–1   Family Systems Conceptual Model

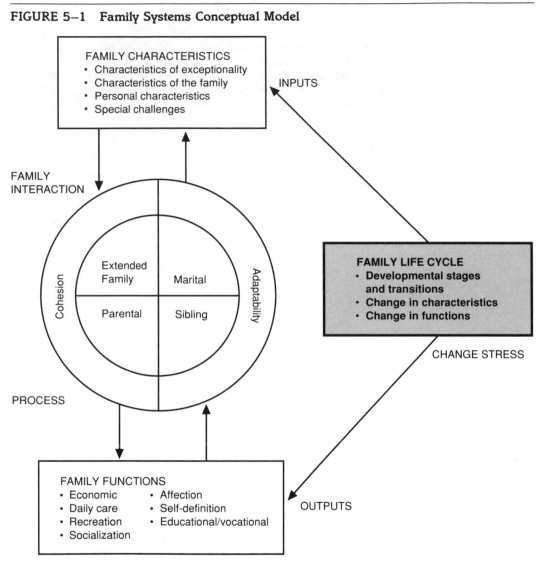

Note. From *Working with Families with Disabled Members: A Family Systems Approach* (p. 60) by A. P. Turnbull, J. A. Summers, and M. J. Brotherson, 1984, Lawrence, KS: The University of Kansas, Kansas University Affiliated Facility. Adapted by permission.

permanent relationships, retire, and die. In addition, families may experience unexpected or sudden changes that drastically alter their lives. Couples may divorce. Families may be separated by war, immigration, or job transfers. Unemployment, natural catastrophes, or a windfall inheritance may suddenly decrease or increase a family's resources. Likewise, religious conversions, political movements, or an unusual education (for a given family) may cause shifts in family values and attitudes.

In this context, exceptionality is in itself an event that may profoundly change the family experiencing it.

Understanding of families and change falls within the domain of family life-cycle theorists. A family's movement through time is its life cycle. Life-cycle theorists usually begin with a consideration of the particular life-cycle stages of each member in a family, typically in three generations (Terkelson, 1980). For example, the oldest members of a family might be entering old age and facing the task of preparing for their own death and that of their peers; their children may be facing mid-career shifts and the prospect of an "empty nest"; and their grandchildren may be leaving home and experiencing the first travails of independent adulthood. But the family life cycle involves more than the sum of each person's life cycle. It encompasses the interactions among all changes in the family (Carter & McGoldrick, 1980). In the example of the three generations, the "middle" generation may face the need to take responsibility for increasingly dependent parents while also beginning to "let go" of their responsibility for their own children. As responsibility shifts, values and approaches to life are transmitted down the generations. Thus, the basic identity of the family is preserved while the main characters change (Terkelson, 1980).

A father who was simultaneously caring for his 81-year-old mother, 21-year-old son with a developmental disability and 13-year-old teenage daughter while also working 50 hours a week commented:

> I felt whipsawed. No matter how much I did for one generation, there was always another whose needs cried out to me with such fervor that I felt I couldn't fulfill all of them. In a sense, my mother had become my son because she had the greater disability and because he was becoming more independent.

A genogram, as depicted in Figure 5–2, is a visual representation of the life cycle of a family. Genograms are often constructed by family therapists as a way to understand family relationships and changes.

Have you ever commented that a family member is "going through a stage?" Actually, the family life cycle may be considered a series of developmental stages. These are periods when the family's life style is relatively stable, and each member is engaged in a series of developmental tasks related to that period of life (Duvall, 1957). For example, in a family whose children are preschoolers, the parents are learning how to care for their offspring and what it means to be a parent. Typically, children are learning how to walk and talk, to dress themselves, and to explore their environment within the safe parameters established by their parents. The family's style of interaction may change with the developmental tasks of a given stage. For example, as one member enters adolescence, the family may need, on one hand, to become more flexible and allow the young person more freedom (adaptability), yet on the other hand, to maintain a family identity for all members (cohesion).

FIGURE 5–2   A Family Genogram

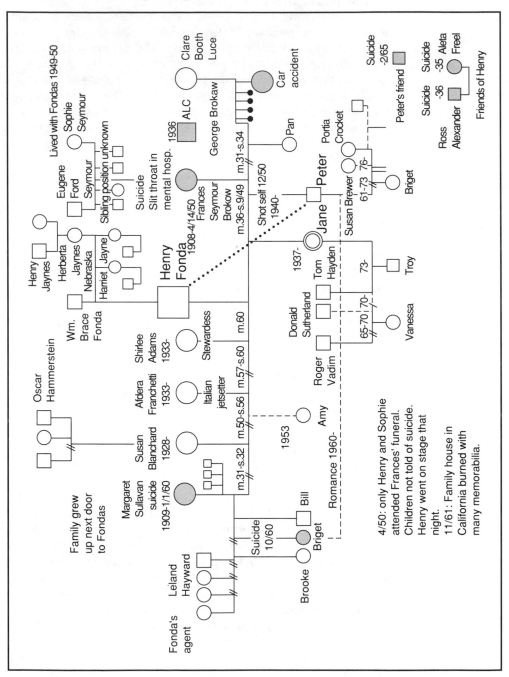

The exact number and the character of individual life-cycle stages are arbitrary. Thus, theorists have identified as many as 24 and as few as six (Carter & McGoldrick, 1980). Life-cycle stages are also culturally and historically specific. A hundred years ago, when people tended to have large families and shorter life spans, a "post-parental" life stage—when there were no dependent children in the household—was rare (Hareven, 1982). Also, in ethnic groups placing a strong emphasis on close extended families and less value on independence, children may not leave home (Falicov, 1982). Further, in blended or remarried families, particularly those with older children from a previous marriage, several life-cycle stages may occur at the same time (Sager et al., 1983).

In short, family theorists have not been able to identify anything uniquely distinct about the particular life-cycle stages. Each one is necessarily a generalization drawn to help us understand the process of change. With this caution in mind, we will present our own generalizations about life-cycle stages and the possible demands of exceptionality on each one. We will concentrate on the four major life-cycle stages during which the family is most likely to experience contact with schools: birth and early childhood, childhood, adolescence, and young adulthood. Following these sections, we will consider the general issues of transition from one stage to another and how exceptionality affects, and is affected by, the family's ability to adjust smoothly to change. As you read, keep in mind the fluidity of the life cycle. A person who is exceptional may progress through these stages earlier or later than normally expected.

BIRTH AND EARLY CHILDHOOD

For most families, the early childhood years are a period of intense absorption with the inner workings of the family (Olson et al., 1983). If the family is not a blended family, the childless couple has explored the parameters of their relationship (we hope), welded the norms of two families of origin into one new unit, and learned how to respond to each other's needs (Duvall, 1957). Now, suddenly, one or more small newcomers arrive on the scene, each dependent on the parents for his or her physical and emotional well-being. While the children are engaged in learning to master their bodies and their immediate environment, the parents are faced with the task of nurturing their children and meeting their needs without forgetting their own.

In addition to these expected developmental tasks, a family who has a member with an exceptionality faces three major issues. First, early childhood is often the time when the exceptionality is discovered and the time when the family needs to come to terms with the diagnosis. Second, the exceptionality may bring the family into contact with the bewildering world of medical, educational, and social services for the first time. Third, the family must develop great expectations for the child with the exceptionality during this period. These issues are interrelated, but each has implications for the family's ability to face the lifelong tasks of living with the impact of an exceptionality.

Discovering the Exceptionality

EARLY DIAGNOSIS: THE GRIEF CYCLE.   For some children, the exceptionality may be apparent at birth or soon after. Parents' reactions to the news of their child's exceptionality has been likened to the experiences of people who lose a loved one through death or some other separation (O'Hara & Levy, 1984). Presumably, in the case of an infant with an exceptionality, the loss refers to the fantasized mental image of the perfect child—the baby who will be cute and adorable, excel in school or sports, and otherwise exceed his or her parents' own achievements (Bristol, 1984). This perfect child has "died," and in its place is a baby with apparent and frightening problems and unknown prospects for the future. The feelings of grief may be complicated by guilt as parents mourn the lost perfect child, while the child with the exceptionality is very much alive and making his or her demands for affection and care (Trout, 1983). Help parents see that their feelings of grief are natural and that expressing those feelings is a healthy step toward resolution. One mother described her feelings:

> Shock, grief, bitter disappointment, fury, horror—my feelings were a mixture of all these after my doctor told me that our new little son, Peter, was born with Down syndrome. I was afraid to have him brought from the nursery. . . . I didn't want to see this monster. But when the nurse brought in this tiny, black-haired baby with up-tilted, almond-shaped eyes, my heart melted. . . . But the grief and fear didn't go away just because we fell in love with our son. They came in great, overwhelming waves. I felt a deep need to cry it out—to cry and cry until I had worked this immense sorrow up from the center of my being and out into the open. . . . I think we should give honest and full expression to our grief. I suspect that when, in our attempts to be brave and face the future we repress our feelings, these feelings of pain and sorrow last longer. All I'm trying to say is that there's a time for weeping and then a time for pushing ahead, and I don't think you can do the second without going through the first.
> (Vyas, 1983a, p. 17)

The various "grief models" applied in cases of loss hypothesize an orderly sequence of stages, leading from initial shock to the final acceptance of reality. Thus, clinicians have identified from three to seven stages through which parents must pass on their way to acceptance of their child with an exceptionality (see Blacher, 1984b, for a review). In general, these stages include: (a) feelings of shock, denial, and disbelief; (b) feelings of anger, guilt, and/or depression; and (c) a reorganization of thoughts from self to others (i.e., the child with the exceptionality) with constructive attempts to seek services and otherwise incorporate the exceptionality into the reality of daily life (Blacher, 1984a). Seligman and Darling (1989) describe the phenomenon of *anomie* or rootlessness which occurs when families learn they have an exceptional member. *Anomie* is characterized by a sense of meaninglessness and powerlessness.

Whether or not the proposed stages are real and experienced in a similar sequence by all parents is open to controversy. Some commentators point out that, as in any effort to classify events, the nature of families resists simple categorization (Trout, 1983). Others note the chronic sorrow that stays with parents throughout life (Olshansky, 1962). Some parents may re-experience the grief cycle as various developmental milestones are not attained.

A parent describes this pain:

> The hardest times for me have been when he's gone for evaluation—watching him not be able to perform or do things. It's not anybody's fault, but it hurts. It's good if a parent knows that's just the way it is. It's not complaining to the Lord; I wouldn't trade places, but the hurt is a part of it.

At the point of diagnosis, however, professional controversy about the particular stage of grief a family is experiencing is irrelevant. What parents need is full and honest communication as well as permission to express their feelings about their child's exceptionality. Attempts to spare their feelings by withholding information are usually misguided. In retrospect, many parents wish they had been told about the exceptionality earlier, more fully, and with greater empathy (Lonsdale, 1978). Indeed, frank and specific communication about the diagnosis appears related to faster and fuller acceptance of the exceptionality (Lipton & Svarstad, 1977).

Professionals must also make sure that their presentation of the information about the exceptionality is balanced. Consider how Ruth Johnson, a mother of a 15-year-old with Down syndrome, learned about her son's exceptionality:

> About 8 p.m. the doctor came in and said abruptly: "Read the numbers on the baby's ID bracelet and the one on your wrist. See, it's the same. This baby is yours. This happens to women your age. You may want genetic counseling, and you'll probably want to put it in a home."

Ruth was alone when the doctor told her.

If you had been this mother, how would you have wanted the doctor to respond? You would have wanted him to tell you the truth about the exceptionality, of course. But would it have helped if he had held your son in his arms while he talked to you? Would you have wanted him to remark about how cute your son was? Perhaps you wish he had pointed out to you what a valuable member of a family a person with Down syndrome can be. By encouraging a family with positive realistic expectations about the child with an exceptionality, you will not only help the family accept the diagnosis, but will also pave the way for a supportive environment for the child. Other suggestions for how to explain the diagnosis are listed in Table 5–1.

LATER DISCOVERY: GRADUAL AWARENESS.   While the discovery of an exceptionality at birth is dramatic and has received much attention in the literature, many families notice their child's exceptionality much more gradually. Accumulated evidence is frequently not confirmed for

---

TABLE 5–1   Suggestions for how to Explain the Disability Diagnosis to Families

---

- Provide full and honest information about the condition of the child.
- Repeat the information in many different ways and at many different times.
- Try to tell both parents at the same time.
- Encourage parents to ask questions.
- Avoid using educational and/or medical jargon as much as possible; explain those terms that must be used.
- Present a balanced perspective—discuss possible positive outcomes as well as limitations.
- Avoid a patronizing or condescending attitude.
- Encourage parents to join a support group or introduce them to a family who is coping successfully with a son or daughter who has a similar exceptionality.
- Realize the parents will need time to consider the diagnosis; set up another conference.
- Allow parents time to express their feelings and be accepting of those feelings.
- Understand that parents may respond with displaced anger; the attack is on the diagnosis, not you.
- If parents respond with anger, avoid being defensive; continue to be supportive and accepting.
- Discuss how to tell brothers and sisters and other family members.
- Suggest reading materials and other resources.
- Assure families that you will be available as a resource to them in the future.

---

several years—perhaps not until the child enters school or even upper-elementary grades. In the case of children who are gifted, for example, a father might be startled by his son's walking at 8 months, or a mother might feel badgered with incisive "why" questions from her 3-year-old daughter, or be irritated by a preschooler's incessant proclivity to collect things (Perino & Perino, 1981). Grandparents, in turn, might be astounded by a 4-year-old's advanced vocabulary and liberal use of adjectives. But the label "gifted" may not enter the minds of family members until it is placed there by school personnel.

Other exceptionalities besides being gifted may not be evident at birth. In the case of autism, for example, a child may appear to be developing normally for the first year or two of life. Likewise, in some instances of learning disabilities the only evidence in the preschool years might be irritability or clumsiness. In others, no evidence is apparent until the child experiences difficulty in school. Perhaps the ambiguity of this exceptionality is one reason why Switzer (1985) found that parents of children with learning disabilities had difficulty understanding the diagnosis. In still other exceptionalities, the problem becomes gradually more noticeable as children increasingly fall behind their age peers in development of motor skills or language (Donnellan & Mirenda, 1984).

When awareness of an exceptionality dawns gradually, parents' grief tends to differ from that experienced at the loss of an imagined child. For some parents the diagnosis, when it finally comes, is less a blow than a relief. The nagging doubts now have a name. The parents find they weren't irrational after all.

This was the experience of Rud Turnbull:

Another early warning sign was [Jay's] plain dullness—not that he wasn't a beautiful child with an abundance of blond curls; it is just that he didn't turn over, move about, push himself up on his elbows, or do the other things that my friend's children of his age had done. His pediatrician . . . seemed to pooh-pooh my concerns. . . . Had it not been for Dr. Neal Aronson, the neurologist who leveled with me, the entire staff of Johns Hopkins Hospital might have kept me in eternal ignorance. . . . He let me know so gently that all I felt was absolution, the soft vanishing of my present and past anxiety—not the pain of the future. (H. R. Turnbull, 1985a, pp. 109–110)

Parent narratives are rife with stories about professionals who discounted the parents' concerns or labeled them "overanxious." Time and again, they are told "he'll grow out of it," or "all babies develop at their own rate."

One mother expressed her feelings about such treatment:

A mother is supposed to be behind her child 100% of the way. I wanted to believe my kid was the brightest, smartest, fastest, the one who could do no wrong in my eyes. Yet, I was the one who was constantly pointing out the negatives to professionals who just couldn't see anything wrong. I resented very much being put in that position.

When a diagnosis does finally arrive, it may be incomplete. The professional may deliberately suppress part of the information on the assumption that he or she knows how much parents can handle, or, conversely, the diagnosis may be elusive because the exceptionality is complex, rare, or slow to unfold (Donnellan & Mirenda, 1984). Parents may react to this ambiguity by taking their child to another specialist and then another, in a search for answers to their questions. Such parents may be labeled "shoppers"—people who have failed to accept their child's exceptionality (Blacher, 1984a) or who are simply seeking more information about the exceptionality (O'Hara & Levy, 1984). In order to facilitate a true partnership with parents, you must accept—and respect—parents who disagree with you. Table 5–2 provides suggestions for how to help parents who seek additional opinions.

Accessing Early Childhood Services

Learning about the exceptionality is only the first of a lifelong series of interactions with professionals. Families with young children whose ex-

---

TABLE 5–2   Suggestions for how to Help Parents Who Seek Additional Opinions

---

- Recognize the reasons for seeking additional opinions:
  - Disagreement with the diagnosis.
  - Desire to have as much information as possible about the exceptionality.
  - Desire to work with professionals who share the same values or communication style.
- Accept and respect families that disagree with you.
- Ask yourself honestly in case of doubt about your conclusions.
- Consider the possibility that you might have used ambiguous terms such as "slow" or educational/medical jargon which might have left the family confused.
- Encourage families to seek a second opinion if they desire it.
- Compare and contrast with the family the results of the various assessments they have obtained.
- Work constructively with the parents.
- Avoid defensiveness; remember, your goal is not to prove yourself, but to obtain appropriate services for the child.

---

ceptionalities have been identified are likely to be plunged almost immediately into the world of infant stimulation, early intervention, preschools, respite services, medical services, and so on. As of March
1988, 56% of women with preschool children and 51% of mothers with
infants under age one were working outside the home (Staff Report of
the Select Committee on Children, Youth, and Families, 1989). The involvement of families in general with preschools and day-care centers,
therefore, is not unusual. But in the case of a young child with an exceptionality, such involvement is much more systematic. Families sometimes learn to think of their child's development less as natural growth
than as a sequence of skills that must be deliberately taught. Therefore,
the early intervention program and/or the preschool must be selected
with an eye toward its ability to meet such developmental needs. Parents must consider such issues as mainstreaming or special programs,
availability of support services, class size, opportunities for individualized instruction, and teacher qualifications and attitudes (Winton, Turnbull, & Blacher, 1984).

Further, because family support is rapidly becoming the *sine qua
non* of early childhood services, families are likely to find themselves
quickly and intensively involved once they have selected a program.
Service providers look to families on theoretical grounds because parents are "the single most important educational influence on the lives of
children" (Latham, 1981, p. 26).

Some parents, especially those with young children, may gladly embrace the opportunity to become intensively involved as a way of doing
something concrete. Such involvement, however, is not an unmixed
blessing.

One mother expressed her ambivalence this way:

> I found the infant stimulation program to be very helpful in providing an
> opportunity to learn parenting skills. (Peter was our first child.) It also
> helped our morale in that it gave us specific things to teach Peter, and so
> we could see steady progress in his development. This created strong
> feelings of guilt in me because I felt that if I wasn't working with him at
> every opportunity, then I wasn't doing enough. If his progress was slow, I
> felt it was my fault. (Vyas, 1983b, p. 51)

From the point of view of some parents—even those who are eager to be involved—parent involvement is neither cheap nor convenient
(A. P. Turnbull et al., 1985). Chapter 4 has amply illustrated the many
responsibilities families pack into their daily lives. Yet, many service providers continue to expect families to sacrifice other needs to become
involved with their children's program.

One single mother explained her reluctance to participate:

> I work full-time. When I get home in the afternoon, I'm tired and I have
> to fix dinner. Sally has been in a situation all day where she's had some-

one telling her she has to work on this and that. I don't feel like she's ready for more education at night. I think it's time for fun and enjoying Mommy for awhile. Plus, I don't think children learn as well from their parents on some tasks that are particularly difficult. Parents tend to want to do the work for their children rather than watch them suffer. (Winton et al., 1984, p. 6)

The importance of early intervention for reducing the impact of exceptionality is not being minimized here. We concur with McDonnell and Hardman (1988), however, who stated that "standardized programs will be successful only to the degree that they are adaptable to varied consumer needs" (p. 334). These researchers suggest the following four guidelines for providing peer-and family-referenced early childhood services: (a) make curriculum relevant to the individual child, family, peers, and community; (b) utilize parents as full partners for educational planning and decision making; (c) systematize communication between family and professionals; and (d) incorporate the child's skill development into the family's typical daily routines.

Moreover, early intervention is a time for preparing families with an exceptionality for the marathon ahead. By helping families focus on their long-range needs, you may enable them to avoid the burnout that can occur from exerting all their efforts into a 100-yard-dash type of early intervention program (Weyhing, 1983). Table 5–3 provides a list of suggestions for how to assist families in developing the slow and steady pace needed to attain their goals (A. P. Turnbull, 1988a).

TABLE 5–3   Stamina-Enhancing Skills for Families

- Meeting the basic needs for food, shelter, health, and security.
- Taking time to reflect on the strengths and limitations of the family.
- Learning to love the child with an exceptionality unconditionally.
- Establishing relationships which will provide the foundation for future support.
- Experiencing and benefiting from the wide range of emotions which accompany having a child with an exceptionality.
- Learning to take charge of the child's education and development.
- Anticipating the future and learning transitional planning.
- Establishing balance and equity in the family by learning to juggle time and attention among the members.

Note. Adapted from "Accepting the challenge of providing comprehensive support to families," by A. P. Turnbull, 1988, *Education and Training in Mental Retardation,* 23 (4), 261–272.

SETTING GREAT EXPECTATIONS

The typical "fix-it approach" of many early intervention programs may cause families to wonder: Is having a disability an acceptable way for a person to be? Thus, families may need reassurance from you that the answer to this question is a resounding *yes*. Early intervention programs should provide opportunities for families to establish and capitalize upon the child's positive contributions. Research with families (H. R. Turnbull, Guess, & Turnbull, 1988) has identified six categories of positive contributions a young person with an exceptionality can make to a family.

- Being a source of joy
- Providing a means of learning life's lessons
- Giving and receiving love
- Supplying a sense of blessing or fulfillment
- Contributing a source of pride
- Strengthening the family

The long-range potential benefits to the family can touch parents, brothers and sisters, and the child with the exceptionality. Ruth Johnson, whose experience with a doctor was described earlier, discusses the contribution her son Joel has made to her family:

> As the doctor explained that we had a boy with Down syndrome, the Lord reminded me of His Word: "Every good gift and every perfect gift is from above, and cometh down from the Father of lights, with whom is no variableness, neither shadow of turning" (James 1:17). We are learning from Joel as he is growing—learning about love, and understanding, and giving, and trusting, and many more "heart lessons" that God has to teach us.

Ann and Rud Turnbull describe the contributions their son Jay has made to his sister Kate:

> Her ability to embrace difference is one of Jay's contributions to her. Other contributions Jay has made to Kate include an enthusiasm about helping others, a sense of pride in individualism and nonconformity, creativity as a problem solver, and a vital sense of humor. (A. P. Turnbull & Turnbull, 1985, p. 24)

Perhaps most important in this respect are the positive contributions for the individual with the exceptionality.

One man wrote:

> [This disability] is the greatest thing that has ever happened to me. For without these limitations, I would not have been able to acquire some of

the important character qualities of life. (A. P. Turnbull & Turnbull, 1985, p. 18)

As you work with a family, share your insights about the positive contributions the child with the exceptionality has made for you. Encourage the members to reflect on the value of the child within their family. As they learn to view their child in a positive way, they will begin to hold great expectations for the child. *Visions can become realities.* Families will benefit from new perspectives of what life can be as well as from support for fulfilling their dreams.

CHILDHOOD

Entry into school, a hallmark of childhood, often marks a widening of horizons for a child. Unless the child has had preschool experience, he or she may be spending a major portion of the day away from home for the first time. Where previously learning had been an incidental part of the child's daily experience, it now becomes a more structured responsibility. The elementary years also mark an escalation of the development of close friendships. From the parents' point of view, these years are the beginning of a long "letting-go" process, in which parents must turn over responsibility for their child to others, and begin giving more and more responsibilities to the child.

For families who have a child with an exceptionality, entry into school may mark their first encounter with many of the issues to which we have devoted whole chapters of this book. For example, the elementary years are a time when some parents learn to participate in their child's individualized education plan (Chapter 10), to understand their legal rights (Chapter 8), and to acquire information (Chapter 12). The experiences of parents in the early elementary years will shape their expectations about their relationship to the school for many years.

School-Related Issues

The specific issues families face when a child with an exceptionality enters school are tied closely to the nature of the exceptionality. If the child has been involved in an early intervention program, the family may have to adjust to a program in which family support is much less intense. Busy elementary teachers may not have the time to exchange daily communication at the classroom door. School-bus transportation also contributes to the scarcity of face-to-face encounters between teachers and parents. In addition, parents may need to shift from a noncategorical early intervention program to the categorical approach which labels their child. Teachers may no longer make systematic home visits. Also, the parent support group which was a part of the preschool program may no longer be available to the family whose child is in elementary school.

When the exceptionality is not identified until the child enters school, parents may experience all the same reactions at this time that other families experienced in the preschool years. As a child slips farther behind his or her classmates, parents and teachers may come into increasing conflict over a solution. If a child has not yet been identified as gifted, the parents may become concerned at their child's apparent boredom and restlessness in school (Perino & Perino, 1981).

A mild exceptionality brings ambiguity. With "hidden" exceptionalities such as learning disabilities, family members may have difficulty accepting the diagnosis (Switzer, 1985). While parents may be relieved to learn a reason for the difficulties their child has experienced, they may also feel guilt that the problem was not discovered sooner (Walther-Thomas et al., in press).

The elementary-school years may also be the first time brothers and sisters encounter social stigma, especially when the child with an exceptionality rides the same school bus or attends the same school as they do. Many siblings may feel a strong need to defend their brother or sister from teasing or ridicule (Skrtic et al., 1984). They may be asked to carry medication, relay messages to parents, and serve as a classroom aide to the sibling with an exceptionality. Such "singling out" can be acutely embarrassing to the sibling (Powell & Ogle, 1985). School professionals should allow siblings to make their own choices about the extent of their involvement with a brother or sister with an exceptionality. Any interactions that are necessary should be handled with discretion.

> I want kids to like me. I even want to be popular. I also have to always look out for Kristen [who is in sixth grade]. When the kids start teasing her on the bus, I want to punch out their headlights and I also want to evaporate. By the time I get home, my stomach always hurts.

School professionals' perceptions about families may be an additional source of strain to parents. For example, professionals may judge parents as "good" or "bad" according to the degree to which they involve themselves with their child's education (A. P. Turnbull & Summers, 1985). If parents' expectations for the child's achievement are higher than the professionals', the parents are perceived to have failed to accept the reality of their child's exceptionality. If, on the other hand, their expectations are lower than the professionals', they are perceived to be overprotective. Some parents may indeed be overprotective, unaccepting, or uncaring, but it is important for you to begin your professional relationship with them by ignoring such possibilities. Placing a higher priority on responsibilities other than education does not make parents "bad." The parents' perceptions about their child's potential is not necessarily inaccurate, nor is it an indication of a parental adjustment problem. Instead, it should be viewed as different—not necessarily wrong— and efforts should be made toward narrowing the gap between reality and perception through increased awareness on both sides of the parent-professional relationship. Also, concentrating on the strengths of the family will improve the members' confidence in dealing with the exceptionality as well as facilitate a family/professional partnership.

Developing Friendships

Making friends is a critical task during childhood. As children with exceptionalities establish friendships, they are forming a support system that will enable them to cope more effectively with life-cycle changes as well as everyday stresses. As Mest (1988) succinctly commented: "The bonds formed by and between persons with retardation [or other exceptionalities] should be regarded as crucial—people need people whether they are disabled or nondisabled" (p. 124).

Mainstreaming has been emphasized as a means to facilitate the "normalization" of children who are exceptional; and yet, placement in a classroom of children without exceptionalities can serve to augment "differentness."

Dave highlights this dilemma:

In junior high I didn't have a whole lot of friends; as a freshman, I was already a misfit. With congenital glaucoma, I didn't lose my sight all at once. When it finally happened, some people didn't believe I had really lost my sight. When I went back to school, some of the kids thought I was carrying the white cane for sympathy. A bunch of rednecks gave me a lot of s—t about it. They were in my social studies class, and one day the teacher talked to everyone about it—including my perceptions of it, while I was there. It was a good thing, even though I may have felt uncomfortable at the time.

Dave's social studies teacher played an important role in his successful adjustment in the classroom. You can facilitate friendships among students with and without exceptionalities in three ways: (a) develop a cooperative learning approach; (b) model respect for the student with an exceptionality; and (c) teach students how to be a friend to someone with an exceptionality.

Using the cooperative learning approach, students learn in pairs or in small groups (Johnson & Johnson, 1986). They are responsible for helping each other master the material and work together to achieve shared goals. A criterion-referenced evaluation system is employed. This instructional approach serves to develop positive interdependence among students in the following ways:

- Positive goal interdependence exists when students perceive that the goal of the group is to ensure the learning of all group members.

- Positive reward interdependence exists when all group members receive a reward based on their overall achievement.

- Positive resource interdependence exists when resources are distributed so that coordination among members is required.

- Positive role interdependence exists when members are given specific complementary roles to play in the group.

- Positive task interdependence exists when a division of labor is structured so that the actions of one member have to be completed if the next group member is to complete his or her responsibilities. (Johnson & Johnson, 1986, p. 555)

Because of the supportive, positive interactions involved in this type of learning, friendships may develop.

Another way you can help students who are exceptional develop friendships is by modeling respect. If you are threatened by the young person in your class who is gifted, your students cannot be expected to have a different attitude. If you are impatient with a student who has a behavior disorder, more than likely your other students will also be irritated with their classmate's behavior. However, if you treat all your students as valued members of the class, your students can learn to do the same.

A third suggestion for helping students develop friendships is to teach them how to be a friend to people with exceptionalities. In many cases, this task also involves some unlearning.

> Jack is 4 years old. He and his harried mother are shopping for new shoes. Suddenly Jack notices something he has never seen before—a chair that has wheels on it like a car! The man who is sitting in it looks nice. Jack decides to ask him, "Mister, can I have a ride in your chair?"
>
> Jack's mother's face turns bright red. She grabs Jack by the arm, whisks him to another department, and hisses through her clenched teeth, "Don't ever do that again! It's not polite!"
>
> Jack learns his lesson well. Stay away from people who sit in car chairs!

In Dave's case, the teacher helped by providing open and frank discussion about his visual impairment. Table 5–4 provides a list of questions

---

TABLE 5–4   Suggestions for how to Evaluate Friendship Attitudes

---

- As you build a friendship with a disabled person, do you see your relationship as casual, close, or intimate? Knowing what level of friendship you have will help you to meet your friend's needs more appropriately.

- Do you think that disabled people deserve pity? What is your view of the "good life"? Physical perfection and flawless accomplishments with unending possibilities of success?

- Do you think that all disabled people have "hearts of gold"? Do you feel that when your friend acts ungraciously, he should be marked off as unappreciative of what everyone is doing for him?

- Do you believe it's best to leave handicapped people alone—that they want to be with their own kind?

- Do you view your disabled friend as a "project" into whom you can invest time and attention, hoping for results of your labor and love? Or is your goal to love with no strings attached?

Note. From *Friendship Unlimited: How You Can Help a Disabled Friend* (pp. 17–18), by J. Eareckson-Tada, 1987, Wheaton, IL: Harold Shaw Publishers. Copyright 1987 by Harold Shaw Publishers. Reprinted by permission.

---

that may be asked to determine personal attitudes about establishing friendships with someone who has an exceptionality. These questions come from the book *Friendships Unlimited* by Joni Eareckson-Tada (1987), a woman with quadriplegia. Her book is replete with recommendations that could be incorporated in class discussions such as the one described by Dave.

Mest (1988) learned that adults with developmental disabilities choose their friends not because they share the same labels, but for the same reasons other people do—"common work, interests, contexts, and experiences" (p. 123). Thus, people with exceptionalities are more like those without exceptionalities than unlike them. In fact, some young people with exceptionalities may be able to teach others without exceptionalities the meaning of friendship.

> Joel, a teenager with Down syndrome, once commented to his mother, "I have *so* many friends."
>
> His mother remarked, "Joel counts his friends by those he loves, not by those who love him."

ADOLESCENCE

Adolescence is the next life-cycle stage in the individual's growth. This period can bring some difficult changes—not only rapid physical changes, but also many psychological changes. Puberty, the beginning of sexual maturity, usually marks the start of adolescence, which is accompanied by a host of developmental tasks including: (a) development of self-identity, (b) development of a positive body image, (c) adjustment to sexual maturation, (d) emotional independence from parents, and (e) development of mature relationships with peers of both sexes.

Adolescence in general can be stressful for both the youth and the family. Parents may find their authority challenged as adolescents experiment with new-found sexuality or begin to assert their independence. In addition, parents may be facing problems of their own as they enter mid-life. Thus, they see their children becoming attractive adults as their own perceived attractiveness and youthfulness begin to decline (Figley & McCubbin, 1983). In a national study conducted with over 1,000 families in the general population (Olson et al., 1983), parents reported that the life-cycle stages of adolescence and young adulthood were the two stages with the highest amount of stresses and strains.

An exceptionality may either compound or mitigate some of the typical storms of adolescence. For example, with certain exceptionalities, parents might not be confronted with rebellion and conflict because the youth may have fewer peers after whom to model such behaviors (A. P. Turnbull et al., 1984). In other cases, adolescence may bring greater isolation, a growing sense of "differentness," as well as confusion and fear about emerging sexuality. Some of the issues families often face in the adolescent years surround (a) sexuality, (b) growing stigma, (c) increased need for physical care, and (d) developing self-advocacy skills.

Sexuality

Emerging sexuality may be a difficult problem in any family. When the adolescent has an exceptionality the problem may be compounded. Some parents may not even recognize that it is possible for their child to have sexual needs (Brotherson, 1985). Even for those families who do recognize their child's growing sexual maturity, both parent and child may have difficulty reconciling an adult body with a less rapidly developing mind. Lyn Isbell (1979a) expresses this conflict:

> His handicap sometimes makes him slightly more patient with mine (which my children would probably label as "motherhood—moderate to severe"). I remembered that the year before he had been very excited about one school dance because he had danced with his teacher whom he greatly admired. So I said, "Well, Walter, are you going to dance with your teacher today?" He stopped admiring his slicked down hair in the toaster and turned to me. He looked at me with the loathing usually reserved for some slimy creature that crawls out from under a large, damp rock. Veteran mommies will be familiar with the look I mean. And he said, "No dancing with teacher, Mom. Dancing with girlfriend."

Retarded people grow up. Adolescence hits them with all the double-barreled confusion we remember from our own early teens. They, like we did, want girlfriends and boyfriends. They want to go to dances at school and eventually out on dates. Most of us parents of retarded people, who were just getting used to the problems of retarded children, go into momentary shock at this realization. "He's going to be a man. She's going to be a woman. And what am I supposed to do about it. . . . What am I going to do about sex? I forgot sex!" (p. 133)

For girls with exceptionalities, families may fear that the vulnerability arising from their need for acceptance may lead to sexual exploitation (Gardner, 1986). For boys, parents may fear their sons will exhibit inappropriate sexual behavior such as masturbating in public or making public affectionate advances on women (Haavik & Menninger, 1981).

All of these issues require programs in sex education, both for the youth and the family. While sex education is important for everyone, for adolescents with exceptionalities it is doubly so, since parents may need help in teaching their sons or daughters about sexuality. A number of good sex education programs are available. However, if the school is contemplating providing a sex education program, the parents should be involved in curriculum planning and implementation at every step (Haavik & Menninger, 1981). Rousso (1982) discusses the problems adolescents with disfiguring exceptionalities may face because they feel different and ill at ease around able-bodied teenagers. Her suggestions for how families can help are listed in Table 5–5.

Some teenagers with an exceptionality learn to be resourceful. Dave tells how he turned his visual impairment to an advantage when he entered college:

TABLE 5–5 Suggestions for how to Help Adolescents with Disfiguring Exceptionalities

---

- Create a comfortable, inviting environment at home so teenagers will want to visit.
- Help the adolescent find friends who consist of both able-bodies and disabled peers.
- The adolescent will mingle, date, and struggle with social problems. Expect and support these experiences.
- Provide candid information about sex, pregnancy, and birth control.
- Help the teenager distinguish between normal bodily changes and the disability.

Note. Based on information from "Taking on the Social Scene" by H. Rousso, 1982, *The Exceptional Parent, 12* (1), pp. 21–25.

I thought it was hard dating. In my situation, I couldn't pick up what others were thinking from visual clues. I guess people with other disabilities-have their own unique problems. Otto was a factor. I guess I encouraged him to be a "social dog," and he did his job well. He was very cute, very lovable and had big brown eyes and floppy ears. Girls missed their dogs—especially freshman girls. Otto would sit in the door of my dorm room, and look out with those soulful eyes. It was a great conversation starter and a way to meet people. You use what tools you have.

Growing Stigma

While the adolescents themselves may be more aware of their growing differences at this time of the life cycle, family members also become more aware of them. For many, the stigma of exceptionality grows as the child grows. Community services may be more difficult to use, both because of inaccessibility and for fear of the attitudes of community members. Some family members have reported that their communities are more understanding when their children are younger (Suelzle & Keenan, 1981).

One mother cites a specific example of this growing stigma:

The community accepts our children much more easily when they are small and cute. People are apt to be fearful around him. . . . It's very hard to give a shot to a six-foot, two-hundred-pound man who doesn't want one. Babyish mannerisms are no longer acceptable. Lind has had real problems with his social relationships. He simply does not know how to initiate a friendship. He has difficulty maintaining a sensible conversation with his peers. He doesn't handle teasing well, so he is teased unmercifully. (Anderson, 1983, p. 90)

One strategy to help reduce stigma for both the individual with an exceptionality and family members is to provide age-appropriate activities and materials. For example, adolescents should wear clothing that is socially acceptable for someone in their age group. Likewise, adolescents should be given opportunities to participate in leisure-time games or activities that are consistent with those of their peers. Age appropriateness, however, may conflict with the choices of some adolescents with exceptionalities. If autonomy is the real goal, then choices of the adolescent and the family should be respected, even when they are not age appropriate.

Adolescents who are gifted experience a different kind of stigma—being singled out as "the brain." This "differentness" can alienate them from their peers and make coping difficult (Perino & Perino, 1981). Some young people even begin to hide their abilities in order to be more like their peers. Underachievement in girls who are gifted frequently begins by fourth or fifth grade and becomes a general trend by junior high (Bell, 1989). Girls also struggle with traditional sex roles. Erin Efaw shares her thoughts:

> To most people I seem to have it all together—I'm smart, pretty, outgoing, and have leadership abilities. What they don't see is the conflict in me between intellect and emotions. Just because I'm smart doesn't mean I don't have the same dreams and ideals of an average 16-year-old girl . . . A lot of times I feel lonely and left out as I listen to my friends talk about the great times they had going out the past weekend. It's hard to realize there's not something wrong with me that makes boys keep their distance as far as dating goes. Intellectually, I know that high-school dating is relatively trivial and that most boys don't want to date a girl that dominates them mentally, but emotionally I long to be just an average girl, going out on weekends, having a boyfriend, and doing what everyone else is doing.

You may need to devote time to helping students who are gifted balance social and academic pursuits during this stressful period.

The stigma surrounding an exceptionality attaches not only to the individual but to the family as well. The effect on a family that has a young member with AIDS can be especially devastating:

> In Ray White's case, for instance, townspeople slashed the tires of his family's car and pelted it with eggs. Schoolmates taunted him; someone even fired a bullet through the living room window. Eventually, the family left town and moved to another state. (Kermani, 1988, p. 153)

Growing Physical-Care Needs

Another concern of adolescence—growing physical-care needs—occurs as children with severe exceptionalities become older, larger, and heavier. More physical energy is needed to provide care and to meet their needs. Family members may experience greater fatigue with such day-to-day tasks as bathing, dressing, and leaving the house. Kathryn Morton describes the toll of physical and psychic demands on parents over the years:

> The sapping of energy occurs gradually. The isolation it imposes does, too. As I work professionally with young mothers, I see them coping energetically with the demands of everyday life. They are good parents, caring ones, doing everything possible to help their retarded child reach full potential, sometimes doing more than they have to; and if they have other children, they are doing the same for them. Most of these young

mothers even get out, see friends, attend meetings, volunteer in the community, and do all the things their friends and families expect them to do. All this is at least possible when one's child is little, though it demands enormous energy. But to look at the mothers of children who have turned into teenagers is to see the beginnings of the ravages. Their life style is changing. They go out less, see fewer people, do less for their children. They are stripping their living to the essentials. And to look at parents of retarded adults still living at home is to see lives that are far removed from those of their peers. The physical and psychic effects of 20 or more years of extraordinary demands on their energies are visible, and they have given up the struggle to be normal. (Morton, 1985, p. 144)

For adolescents who have a severe disability, the physical-care needs will probably increase over time. Part of the stress of increasing care needs is accentuated for some families by the realization, at a time when many parents are launching their children "out of the nest," that their child will continue to be dependent on them. When working with these families, help them build their coping strategies, particularly by using a social support network. (Coping strategies are described in more detail in Chapter 13.)

All adolescents with an exceptionality, however, do not demonstrate greater physical needs as they mature. For many, adolescence is a time of growing independence, as they assume more responsibility for meeting their own needs. It is a time when many begin to strike out on their own, seeking less interference from their parents. As discussed in Chapter 4, greater independence can also mean greater risk for failure. But risk taking is part of independence, and possible failure is something that adolescents experience.

To help family members prepare for the risk taking and independence that adolescents typically experience, opportunities for both should be given prior to adolescence. A 14-year-old girl with a physical disability may want to go to summer camp for two weeks, but her parents find this adventure too frightening. Possibly other experiences could gradually bring up to this young girl's independence. Such experiences might include spending the night with friends, going camping for the weekend with friends or neighbors, or spending several days with an aunt in a nearby city. *Successive approximation*—breaking a desired goal into smaller, attainable steps—is a strategy that builds confidence as well as supports families while learning to cope with change during the life cycle.

Developing Self-Advocacy Skills

Self-advocacy skills include (a) understanding the nature of one's exceptionality along with personal strengths and limitations, (b) setting and striving for realistic goals, and (c) assertively stating personal needs. Although self-advocacy skills can and should be developed in childhood, such skills become more important as the student enters adolescence and frequently encounters situations in which a teacher or parental advocate is not readily available. Also, as the student matures, self-advocacy skills will facilitate participation in IEP decision making (see Chapter 10).

Numerous approaches have been developed to teach and strengthen self-advocacy skills. Techniques for helping students understand their learning disabilities, for example, are provided in Table 5–6 (Tomlan, 1985).

Hoy (1986) emphasizes the need to provide opportunities for students to explain their exceptionality to others such as parents or sensitive regular classroom teachers. Students should be allowed to rehearse what will be said to the selected adult. She contends that adolescents can learn to explain both the nature of their exceptionalities and any program modifications they might need. The Technical Assistance for Self-Advocacy Project at the University of Kansas has produced *The Self-Advocacy Workbook,* a resource to assist parents and professionals in their task of teaching these skills to students (Gardner, 1980).

The matrix in Table 5–7, developed by Corn (1985) to teach self-advocacy skills to students with visual handicaps, can be adapted for other exceptionalities. Her method teaches students to consider (a) their

---

TABLE 5–6   Suggestions for how to Help Students Understand Their Learning Disabilities

---

- Honesty and consistency are crucial.
- Your explanation needs to be as concrete as possible.
- The students need to know, first of all, what a learning disability is **not** (e.g., blindness, retardation, or something to be "grown out of" [p. 203]).
- Discuss student strengths before mentioning weaknesses.
- Work samples can help students understand their problems.
- Do not use work samples when talking to a group.
- Watch student body language for cues as to the right moment to present information.
- Employ eye contact and make sure your presentation is sincere.
- Avoid patronizing. Remember to treat students as the young adults they are.
- Use questioning to determine if students understand the information and are ready to go further.

Note. Based on information from "Self-Awareness, Self-Understanding, and Self-Concept" by P. Tomlan, 1985, *Academic Therapy, 21* (2), pp. 199–204.

TABLE 5-7 The Independence Matrix

	Resources	Problem Solving	Self-Advocacy	Social Skills
Travel				
Reading				
Writing				
Speaking				
Recreation				
Planning				

Note. From "An Independence Matrix for Visually Handicapped Learners" by Anne L. Corn (1985). *Education of the Visually Handicapped, 17* (1), 5, 1985. Reprinted with permission of the Helen Dwight Reid Educational Foundation. Published by Heldref Publications, 4000 Albemarle St., N.W., Washington, D.C. 20016. Copyright © 1985.

resources, (b) alternatives to solve the problem, (c) the demands for self-advocacy created by each alternative, and (d) what social skills they will need. Family members can learn to use this chart too to facilitate the student's self-advocacy skills at home as well as at school. Table 5-8 provides examples of how the matrix in Table 5-7 can be used.

Consumer groups have also been formed to teach self-advocacy skills to individuals with mental retardation. This growing movement strengthens peer support, sense of identity, and understanding of the responsibilities of being a responsible citizen (Browning, Thorin, & Rhoades, 1984).

One unsettling study reported that school personnel rarely respond to student-initiated expressions of choice or preference (Houghton, Bronicki, & Guess, 1987). Self-advocacy involves, therefore, a change in perspective by professionals as well as individuals with exceptionalities

TABLE 5–8 Hypothetical Use of the Independence Matrix

Event: Going to the lunchroom with classmates, unescorted by teacher (4th grade)

SUBJECT	RESOURCES	PROBLEM SOLVING	SELF-ADVOCACY	SOCIAL SKILLS
Travel	• Use a cane • Sighted guide • Walk independently	• Which method is most efficient? • Which method is preferred? • How much time do I have? • Is there someone available as a guide? • Are there any consequences I need to consider, e.g., a child's refusing to walk with me?	• If I choose a sighted guide . . . • Can I locate and request assistance? • If a teacher stops us in the hall, how do I explain the sighted-guide approach?	• Can I join in the conversation on the way to the lunchroom? • If the classmate with whom I am walking is not a friend, do I leave him upon entering the lunchroom or tag along throughout lunch and playtime?

Event: Research paper assignment (5th grade)

SUBJECT	RESOURCES	PROBLEM SOLVING	SELF-ADVOCACY	SOCIAL SKILLS
Reading Assignment	• Check RFB catalogue for a taped copy of the book. • Ask my itinerant teacher if the book is available in braille. • Ask a classmate to be a reader. • Ask if the book could be put onto a cassette for the Versabraille. • Hire a reader.	• Which takes the least time to obtain a book? • Which is the more efficient way to do the assignment? • Is there a difference in my comprehension if I use a reader or read from a brailled copy?	• If I choose to locate a reader . . . • Can I locate a reader and explain my needs, e.g., assignment deadline, location for reading, any necessary or appropriate exchange of favors?	• Am I able to maintain a relationship with a reader? • Do I have appropriate social skills so as not to make the reader uncomfortable, e.g., by using excessive mannerisms? • Can I return the favor in some way?

Note. From "An Independence Matrix for Visually Handicapped Learners" by Anne L. Corn (1985). *Education of the Visually Handicapped, 17* (1), 5, 1985. Reprinted with permission of the Helen Dwight Reid Educational Foundation. Published by Heldref Publications, 4000 Albemarle St., N.W., Washington, D.C. 20016. Copyright © 1985.

and their families. On the one hand, family members and professionals "must give up the authoritarian, omniscient role for one that is supportive, enabling, and consultive in nature" (Siegel & Kantor, 1982, p. 453). On the other hand, the individual with an exceptionality "must be willing to disregard the 'patient,' 'child,' or 'sick' role for a role that is more adult-like, that is, one that assumes responsibility for actions, for making decisions, and for responding to other people's needs and opinions" (p. 453).

Tomlan (1985) describes the benefits of teaching self-advocacy skills:

> I waited to hear Susan explain her language-learning disability with more depth of understanding than "I don't read too good." Armed with the appropriate information, she came to discuss her handicap with insight and confidence not only to her teachers, but to her boyfriend, her parents, and her employer. (p. 202)

ADULTHOOD

Adulthood is the next life-cycle stage in the individual's growth. Culturally, adulthood can be attained in many ways (e.g., getting married, becoming a parent, entering the armed services), but we will define adulthood as starting at the age of 21. This age marks the end of school eligibility in most states for learners with exceptionality.

For most adults in our majority culture, moving into adulthood means finding employment and moving away from home. For the young adult this represents a process of attaining greater independence and responsibility, for the parents a process of "letting go" of their son or daughter. This stage can be difficult in any family, but it is especially challenging for families with young adults who are exceptional. Some of the issues the individual and his or her family might have to resolve include (a) the right to grow up, (b) full citizenship opportunities, and (c) relationship with and implications for brothers and sisters.

The Right to Grow Up

The right to grow up—to attain the status of adulthood—is taken for granted by most adults in our society. With the move into adulthood comes the responsibility for meeting one's own needs to the greatest extent possible. Also, the move into adulthood brings opportunities for greater choice and control. The decisions regarding how to divide independence and responsibility among the young adult with an exceptionality, the family, and other support systems can be difficult. But some families (and professionals) fail to reach this point because they continue to view the young adult as a child. Cultural values strongly influence the concept of growing up and what it means to family relationships as illustrated by these quotes from Latin American families.

- There is a relationship between parents and children that never breaks.
- We never separate from our children. We never cut the cord.
- Young, married couples live at their parents' home; it is Latino tradition. (H. R. Turnbull & Turnbull, 1987, p. 13)

Planning for adulthood to involve possible separation of parents and child must begin early, not when the young adult reaches age 21. In this respect, several parents have reported that it was important, already in the early years of their child's life, to observe other persons with exceptionalities living and working independently in the community.

Full Citizenship Opportunities

No matter how much planning for adulthood takes place, current services for adults with exceptionalities are inadequate. Thus, families report much stress as they search for appropriate services and opportunities to meet their young adult's needs (Brotherson, 1985). The reality of less adequate services being available as the adolescent enters adulthood strikes many families. Not surprisingly, therefore, research has indicated that parents at later stages of the life-cycle experience greater burnout, less support, less community acceptance, fewer services, and more isolation (Bristol & Schopler, 1983; Suelzle & Keenan, 1981).

The individual with an exceptionality and his or her family face many barriers and questions at this stage. One of the authors (Rud Turnbull) shares some of the concerns he feels:

> Jay will pass too soon from public school to adult services. He will move from a school system that must serve everyone to a nonsystem of multiple programs with usually inconsistent goals, functions, eligibility criteria, funding and governing authorities, and accountability—programs that need not serve him but must merely practice nondiscrimination. He will go from a relatively protective system to one that may impose responsibilities on him that he cannot meet. And he will graduate from a system in which I can legally and functionally command services and accountability to a system that is far less amenable to my importunings. Will there be a group home for him, a job, entitlement benefits, recreation, and other opportunities for growth and protection? Frankly, the answer is

unclear, and the pending transition from some certainty to great uncertainty is profoundly disquieting to me. (H. R. Turnbull, 1985b, p. 119)

As parents take on the task of creating adult opportunities, they may be faced with inadequate public funds, sluggish bureaucracies, and social stigma. One woman described her battle at a zoning hearing, attended by people who were opposed to the establishment of a group home in their neighborhood. She describes the bigoted statements and hurtful remarks parents must endure as they advocate for services:

> We have come to this room to beg. All of us are proud men and women, and it is hard for us to beg. We have done it many times before. . . . We have come once more to be told, "I read in the paper that 'these people' can't tell right from wrong." We have come to listen to the old lie, "Everybody knows 'those kids' have superhuman strength and may get violent." . . . I look at the members of the commission. I look at the flag. I cannot look at these angry neighbors. I cannot speak. My mouth is dry. Finally I look across the room at my friend. Her retarded child is only 4; mine is 14. She is weeping. It is her first time. . . . (L. Isbell, 1979b, pp. 237–239)

For some exceptionalities the issue of creating adult opportunities blends with plans for postsecondary education. For students who are gifted, career development and planning should begin early, with explorations of a variety of career options. Perino and Perino (1981) advocate that we help students to think about swiftly developing technology and to prepare for flexible careers that will allow them to adapt to change. Others have noted the need to sensitize students who are gifted to the needs of humanity, moral courage, and responsibility to others (Bruch, 1984).

Beyond making decisions about future careers, planning for a postsecondary education implies selecting a program and finding financial resources. Such planning cannot begin in the last year of high school. Students planning to attend postsecondary programs require guidance in weighing programs at different colleges and universities; such a process might require careful study over a period of several years. Parents and students alike need advice about scholarship opportunities, loans, and work-study programs.

Students with learning disabilities, sensory impairments, or physical disabilities must consider a variety of other special needs when selecting a postsecondary institution. Is the campus accessible for wheelchair users? Does the college provide special assistance such as tutoring programs for students with learning disabilities or interpreters for students with hearing impairments? Does the vocational rehabilitation program provide financial assistance for personal-care attendants while the student is attending college? High-school counselors should have this type of information available about area colleges, universities, and technical schools. More information on future planning is included in Chapter 12.

In order for young adults with exceptionalities to enjoy full citizenship opportunities, society must change its focus from "antidiscrimination" to "equal opportunity" (A. P. Turnbull & Turnbull, 1988). Further, equality in opportunity must be changed to equality in result. Assisting families in establishing great expectations for their exceptional member will cause them to desire vocational opportunities that provide training and experiences commensurate with those provided for individuals without exceptionalities. Parents should expect that their young adult with an exceptionality will have opportunities for (a) personal decision making, (b) future planning, (c) establishing friendships, and (d) technology that permits the young person to work at his or her potential. As these opportunities are provided, the individual with an exceptionality may be able to take a place in the regular work force rather than in adaptive programs.

Issues for Brothers and Sisters

As members of the family age, brothers and sisters experience unique issues and challenges. They often assume responsibility for the needs of their brother or sister, particularly as they see their parents aging. Powell and Ogle (1985) have divided adult-brother or sister concerns into three broad areas:

1. genetics;
2. long-term care of the brother or sister who is exceptional;
3. how to help the brother or sister with the exceptionality to enjoy quality of life.

To some brother or sisters, the implications of their brother or sister's exceptionality may not have been fully explained. Hence, they may become concerned about the genetic implications of having children of their own. Often these issues reach the forefront when a brother or sister considers marriage.

The long-term care of the dependent brother or sister is another major concern. Family members may be unsure of what their guardianship, financial, and advocacy roles should be and what their options are. If there is more than one brother or sister, they may not know how the roles and responsibilities will be divided. One sibling shares the mayhem that resulted in her family when the death of her mother, the primary advocate and case manager, resulted in unclear roles and responsibilities:

At first we responded to calls from the school in a haphazard fashion.
Family visits were sporadic. Six months would pass without anyone's ar-

TABLE 5–9   Possible Issues Encountered at Life-Cycle Stages

LIFE-CYCLE STAGE	PARENTS	SIBLINGS
Early Childhood, ages 0–5	• Obtaining an accurate diagnosis • Informing siblings and relatives • Locating services • Seeking to find meaning in the exceptionality • Clarifying a personal ideology to guide decisions • Addressing issues of stigma • Identifying positive contributions of exceptionality • Setting great expectations	• Less parental time and energy for sibling needs • Feelings of jealousy over less attention • Fears associated with misunderstandings of exceptionality

LIFE-CYCLE STAGE	PARENTS	SIBLINGS
School Age, ages 6–12	• Establishing routines to carry out family functions • Adjusting emotionally to educational implications • Clarifying issues of mainstreaming vs. special class placement • Participating in IEP conferences • Locating community resources • Arranging for extracurricular activities	• Division of responsibility for any physical care needs • Oldest female sibling may be at risk • Limited family resources for recreation and leisure • Informing friends and teachers • Possible concern over younger sibling surpassing older • Issues of "mainstreaming" into same school • Need for basic information on exceptionality

ranging to see Beckie, and then suddenly everyone would show up at the school's Christmas play. Or one of us would mention to a staff member that we thought Beckie should come home for Christmas and then never follow up on the suggestion, leaving the staff to question our commitment. (Ackerman, 1985, p. 153)

Siblings also have concerns regarding the quality of adult life their brother or sister is likely to have. Thus, they may want their brother or

TABLE 5–9　(Continued)

LIFE-CYCLE STAGE	PARENTS	SIBLINGS
Adolescence, ages 12–21	• Adjusting emotionally to possible chronicity of exceptionality • Identifying issues of emerging sexuality • Addressing possible peer isolation and rejection • Planning for career/vocational development • Arranging for leisure-time activities • Dealing with physical and emotional change of puberty • Planning for postsecondary education	• Overidentification with sibling • Greater understanding of differences in people • Influence of exceptionality on career choice • Dealing with possible stigma and embarrassment • Participation in sibling training programs • Opportunity for sibling support groups

LIFE-CYCLE STAGE	PARENTS	SIBLINGS
Adulthood, ages 21–	• Planning for possible need for guardianship • Addressing the need for appropriate adult residence • Adjusting emotionally to any adult implications of dependency • Addressing the need for socialization opportunities outside the family • Initiating career choice or vocational program	• Possible issues of responsibility for financial support • Addressing concerns regarding genetic implications • Introducing new in-laws to exceptionality • Need for information on career/living options • Clarify role of sibling advocacy • Possible issues of guardianship

sister to live nearby, but have no information about possible residential or work options. Or, if no such options are available in their community, they may be unsure of what role they should or can take in regard to developing options.

Across life cycles many challenges face the child with an exceptionality, his or her brothers and sisters, parents, and other family members. Table 5–9 provides a summary of many of these issues.

LIFE-CYCLE TRANSITIONS

Beyond the developmental tasks that the family and individual members must accomplish at each stage, another important life-cycle concept is the transition from one stage to another. Transitions are the periods of time between stages when the family is adjusting its interactional style and roles to meet the needs and challenges of the next developmental stage (Terkelson, 1980). Usually, these periods are briefer than the stages they interface. However, because these shifts may result in confusion and conflict, the transition period is almost always a time of great stress (Neugarten, 1976; Olson et al., 1983).

Two factors tend to reduce the amount of stress most families feel during a transition from one developmental stage to another. First, in every culture, the roles of the new stage are fairly well defined. Thus, the transition may be marked by some kind of ritual, such as a wedding, bar mitzvah, graduation, or funeral. These ceremonies serve as signals to the family that their relationships following the event will be changed (Friedman, 1980). The interactions and roles for the new stage are modeled by other families with the same previous or present experiences. Thus, the future is not entirely unknown. Second, the timing of transitions is also fairly well expected. In our culture, children are often expected to leave home after they graduate from high school. Death may be expected and psychologically prepared for in old age. Life-cycle transitions seem to be much more traumatic and stressful when they occur at other than expected times (Neugarten, 1976).

For families with a member who has an exceptionality, these naturally occurring reductions in the stress often felt during periods of transition may not apply. Thus, the expected roles as well as the future of the person with an exceptionality may not be as clear, and a ritual to mark the change may be absent. Nor may the transition itself, if it does occur, happen at the expected time. We will consider the implications of uncertain futures and time transitions for families.

Uncertainty about the Future

For many individuals with an exceptionality, the future looms like a frightening unknown. Few norms and models of expected behavior may be available for either the child or his or her family. The common admonition to "take things one day at a time" is particularly apt not only because there are more than enough responsibilities for the family in the present, but also because the future is so ambiguous (Featherstone, 1980). One father shares his perceptions about the reasons why parents may fail to address the future:

Most parents anticipate their children's future with enthusiasm, expecting such happy events as scholastic achievement, success in sports, graduation, marriage, birth of grandchildren, and promising careers. In contrast, parents of a retarded child usually view their child's future with apprehension, anticipating scholastic failure, exclusion from services (educational, social, recreational), inability to work or else menial employment, problems in sexual adjustment, inability to live independently, and a life of loneliness and isolation. (Roos, 1985, p. 252)

Further, the rituals that serve as "punctuation marks" for transitions may be blurred or nonexistent. A time when a transition occurs—or should occur—may not be marked with a celebration, but rather with a fresh bout with feelings of chronic sorrow (Wikler, Wasow, & Hatfield, 1983)—Ben will not be promoted to a new classroom each year. Angela may not graduate, get married, and move away from home. Thus, not only is the family uncertain as to exactly how their interactions might change, they may have no cues that the interactions should change.

Professionals can help families mitigate some of these problems by supporting them and teaching them to plan ahead for transitions when, and if, these occur. For example, school personnel can help families think ahead to next year or 5 years from now by discussing instructional objectives in terms of the child's future needs. Visits to new classrooms or community jobs, meetings with future teachers, and talks with parents of older children with similar exceptionalities can all help to reduce the fear of the future by making it less unknown. Table 5–10 provides some suggestions for how to ease the transitions into and out of each of the life-cycle stages discussed in this chapter.

Off-Time Transitions

Families with a member having an exceptionality are especially likely to experience a life-cycle transition that occurs at other than its expected time. Transitions are often delayed or fail to occur. For example, a young adult might remain at home with his or her parents. Jennings (1987) identified six major sources of stress in such a family: (a) parent's recognition of aging, (b) adult child's life-long dependency, (c) social isolation, (d) lack of respite care, (e) financial/economic needs, and (f) inadequate counseling (pp. 431–432). Bob Helsel (1985) describes how continued dependency becomes more of a problem as a child with an exceptionality becomes older:

In the past [Robin] didn't present any special problems with respect to limiting my life. . . . But he was a member of the family. We had other children, so taking care of Robin didn't place any special burden on us.

But it seems to me as I approach retirement age and would like lots of personal freedom, he will present a problem in limiting my ability to go

---

TABLE 5–10   Suggestions for how to Ease Transitions

EARLY CHILDHOOD

- Begin preparing for the separation of preschool children by periodically leaving the child with others.
- Gather information and visit preschools in the community.
- Arrange for mentorships between veteran parents and parents who are just beginning the transition process.
- Familiarize parents with possible career options or adult programs so they have an idea of future opportunities for their child with a disability.

CHILDHOOD

- Provide parents with the opportunity to view a variety of school-placement options (e.g., mainstreaming, resource room, self-contained classroom).
- Help parents prepare for IEP conferences (see Chapter 10 for suggestions).
- Arrange opportunities for family support groups or mentorships to discuss transitions with others.

ADOLESCENCE

- Arrange family support groups to prepare for the physical and emotional changes of puberty.
- Help families and adolescents identify community leisure-time activities.
- Identify skills that will be needed in future career and vocational programs so that these can be incorporated into the IEP.
- Visit or become familiar with a variety of career and living options.

ADULTHOOD

- Ask families if they need information about guardianship, estate planning, wills, and trusts.
- Assist family members in transferring responsibilities to the individual, other family members, or service providers, as appropriate.
- Assist the young adult or family members with career or vocational choices.
- Address the issues and responsibilities of marriage and family for the young adult.

---

where I want when I want. I am aware of the possible limitations or freedom to leave home. . . . [For parents of normal children] if they aren't out of the nest, they are at least old enough so that the parents can say to them, "Take care of yourselves; I'll see you next month!" But with Robin, we can't do that. (p. 91)

In addition to transitions that are delayed or do not occur, with some exceptionalities a transition may occur earlier than the expected time. For instance, researchers have found that placing a child in a living situation outside the home does not generally reduce the overall stress the family feels (Fotheringham, Shelton, & Hoddinott, 1972). When a child leaves home at 19, it may not be easy for the parents, but at least such a change is expected and seen by our society as desirable. However, when a young child leaves home for an alternative living placement, the parents may experience a sense of guilt and inadequacy. In addition, they may feel that professionals view them as failures because they cannot keep the family member with an exceptionality in the home (Kupfer, 1982). Additionally, they often report feelings of abandonment and loss. Rud Turnbull (1985a) described his feelings when he was forced to place his young son in a residential facility:

> It was at Pine Harbor that, in the most wrenching moment of my life, I performed the most difficult act of my life, and handed Jay to Katie, a teen-age volunteer and an utter stranger; crying, burbling, stammering, I managed only to say, "Take him, he's yours now." Jay's screams and his look ["Again? You are leaving me again!"] remain with me today—vivid, poignant, immediate. (p. 112)

Another off-time transition occurs at the illness or death of a young child. Illness and death may be expected (though perhaps not accepted) parts of life for an older person, but when they happen to a child they are seen as strange and cruel twists of fate. Helen Featherstone (1980) described her conversation with a mother whose 3-year-old with an exceptionality had died:

> I asked how things had gone since the spring.
>
> "Last summer was very hard, but when fall came, things started to get good."
>
> "You missed Ellie a lot?" "Well, no. I felt tremendous relief and then tremendous guilt about the relief."
>
> Catherine went on to say that Peter had been miserable, too, because he really did miss Ellie very much. His grief intensified her self-reproach. (p. 132)

Mixed feelings of relief, guilt, and grief are common. Counseling or therapy may be needed for family members to resolve their feelings both about the young person's death and toward each other. Tremendous pressures are felt in a family with a young person who is terminally ill. You can assist in a family's successful adjustment by encouraging an atmosphere that allows open communication of feelings and permission to grieve and express anger. The time you give to such a family in nonjudgmental listening will be a valued gift.

The anguish of parents is portrayed by Frank Deford (1983) who describes his daughter's life and death in *Alex: The Life of a Child,* a book that both celebrates and grieves:

> The life had floated away, free. Alex's body stayed up for an instant or two more, but she was already up there with God. Imagine being eight years old and dead.

And then her little body, the skin and bones, tumbled over on my right leg, and all this vile mucous, all this yukky that had hurt her and killed her, over all the years, all that began to ooze out of her mouth and onto me. Oh, I was so glad. Even if it was too late to matter, I wanted that evil poison out of her. "Oh, Carol, she's died, thank God," I said. (p. 191)

A brother or sister of a young person who dies may be "the 'silent' family member who seems to be coping well but may be in considerable distress" (Seligman, 1985, p. 276). Lois Wright's 2-year-old brother with a rare form of dystrophy died when she was 12. Lois reflects on the experience:

Before Gary died, I tried to figure out how I was supposed to respond when he finally did die. Was I supposed to cry? Would people watch me? I periodically wanted Gary to die so Mom would stay home instead of going to the hospital and sometimes so my family could go on weekend trips and vacations. I felt guilty for thinking about the good things that would happen if Gary died.

After Gary died, I experienced a deep loss and great sorrow. It was much worse than I imagined. I worried about my mom because she was so sad, and I wondered how to act when I went back to school.

My parents did a good job of helping me through this hard time. They seemed to perceive almost all my feelings and tried to counteract them. They encouraged us kids to talk about how we felt and never rebuked us for expressing those feelings. They made special arrangements for me to visit Gary [at the hospital] and, thus, spend time with my mom. I will always treasure those special moments.

A family who has a young member who dies from AIDS suffers additional problems—funeral planning, body preparation, and negotiations with hospital and insurance systems (Lane, 1989). The stigma associated with AIDS can contribute to an increased sense of isolation. Thus, the need to "tell the story," the first step in the grieving process, may not be met (Lane, 1989, p. 6). Guilt and denial can also hamper the grieving process in such families. The support you provide in your professional role may be the only encouragement such a family receives.

SUMMARY

The process of change in a family is a complex phenomenon. As members enter and leave the family system, and as they grow and change, so too must the family's interactional style and approach to life. The needs of a family with a young child with an exceptionality are very different from the needs of a family with an older child or a young adult. At each developmental stage the family must accomplish a number of tasks and face a number of issues associated with the exceptionality. Under the best of circumstances, transitions are difficult to negotiate. And when the family has a member with an exceptionality, transitions may be made more difficult due to the uncertainty of the future and the off-schedule nature of change.

You can help mitigate some of the stresses families experience as they cope with change. You may be able to help families anticipate change by describing what the future holds, inviting parents to visit future classrooms or adult programs, and encouraging planning. (Chapter 12 describes the future planning process in greater detail.)

By recognizing when families are in transition, you may be able to help them cope with new or changing roles. In the face of uncertainty and change, perhaps what families need most from professionals is a little firm reassurance that help will always be available.

The concepts of change and the life cycle complete the portrait of the family system drawn in Chapters 2 through 5. Briefly, the major assumptions of family systems and their implications for professionals are:

1. Every family brings a different set of characteristics, values, and styles to their experience with exceptionality; thus, you will need to individualize your approach to working with families.

2. Families have an interactional style that dictates the way the members fall into subsystems as well as their preferred levels of closeness and flexibility. To be effective, you will find it helpful to encourage balance and to adapt interventions according to family needs and preferences.

3. Families have a variety of coping skills that enable them to meet their tangible and intangible needs. Respect each family's priorities and encourage the family to attend to the different needs of all its members.

4. Families change over time; therefore, families will need you to help them meet the needs of the different developmental stages and also to ease the stress of transition from one stage to another.

Because of the importance of these elements of the family system, you will need to develop trusting relationships with family members so that you can get to know them as individuals. A key aspect of a trusting relationship is positive and open communication. The next two chapters will help you develop skills in that area.

CHAPTER 6

COMMUNICATION SKILLS

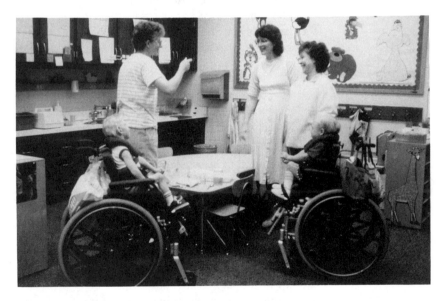

Active listening is an important communication skill that serves as the basis for supportive relationships with families.

What has really helped me the most is having someone to talk to—to share my highs and lows with. Talking to someone who really listens and accepts my feelings just as they are has gotten me through many a tough moment. To me, that's what communication is all about.

This chapter covers communicating—talking and listening—in open, genuine, and meaningful ways with families of children and youth with exceptionalities. The ability to engage in such communication is not easily acquired. On the contrary, many go through life seeking to develop this quality in themselves and to inspire it in others. But, as suggested by the young father introducing this chapter, when the ability to communicate effectively is achieved, it becomes a special gift to the family–professional partnership. Communication is the vital link between your understanding of the unique diversity of families, based on the family-systems framework, and your ability to support families in the manner most relevant for them.

Communication is a process by which people send and receive information. Because of the special needs of family members with exceptionalities, many families and professionals have frequent opportunities to communicate with each other. Unfortunately, communication among families and professionals is often perceived as less than adequate (Sonnenschein, 1984; Vaughn, Bos, Harrell, & Lasky, 1988). Research conducted with special education and regular teachers has indicated that teachers rank communications with parents as a major source of job stress (Bensky et al., 1980). Interestingly, parents report the same feelings of stress when working with teachers and other professionals (A. P. Turnbull, 1983).

An Asian mother shares her frustration:

Communication . . . that's a real simple word. I mean we communicate every day. But why is it when something really important in life comes along, something that needs to be expressed and shared with an open line of communication—everyone clams up? Take my daughter for example. She was born with Down syndrome, and do you know it took almost three days before they told me about it?

If we are to meet the challenge of interacting with families in meaningful ways, then we must find ways to transform inadequate communication among families and professionals into communication that is open, genuine, and meaningful. When families and professionals communicate openly with one another, a true partnership is formed.

143

After reading this chapter you should be able to answer the following questions:

- What are the benefits of positive communication to:
  families?
  the person with a disability?
  professionals?
- What are some important prerequisites to effective communication?
- What are some ways to:
  know yourself?
  know families?
  develop respect for and trust in families?
  use communication skills in difficult situations?
- What are some examples and applications of:
  nonverbal communication skills?
  verbal communication skills?

FORMING A FAMILY-PROFESSIONAL PARTNERSHIP— BENEFITS OF EFFECTIVE COMMUNICATION

When family and professionals respect, trust, and communicate openly with one another, a partnership is formed. Both families and professionals have unique contributions to bring to such a partnership, which, in turn, can be beneficial not only for the person with a disability but for families and professionals as well.

Many researchers have described the multiple benefits of family–professional partnerships for (a) the family, (b) the family member with a disability, and (c) the professional (Bailey & Simeonsson, 1984; Heward, Dardig, & Rossett, 1979; Kroth, 1985).

Benefits for the family include opportunities to:

- receive information about parental rights and responsibilities,
- receive information about the disability,
- learn about program activities for the family member with a disability and about ways other family members can be involved,
- learn how to bring positive program activities into the home,
- learn how to teach new skills to the family member with a disability,
- receive information on other important resources for the family member with a disability.

Benefits for the family member with a disability include opportunities to:

- learn and grow in the consistent environments of home and school,
- participate in other community resources and services.

Benefits for professionals include opportunities to:

- learn more about the strengths and needs of the family as a system,
- learn more about the strengths and needs of the family member with a disability,
- plan programming activities that may also be carried out at home,
- meet the legislative mandate requiring parental involvement in the family-professional partnership in a way that will provide all parties with the opportunity to work with one another.

Family-professional partnerships provide all participants with the opportunity to work cooperatively with one another in a relationship that can benefit each member of this important partnership.

A SYSTEMS PERSPECTIVE ON COMMUNICATION

When families and professionals interact, a host of variables come together. The social, economic, educational, ethnic, racial, and religious backgrounds of families and professionals can affect the establishment and maintenance of effective partnerships. Moreover, the family's past experience in dealing with professionals, the professional's past experience in dealing with families, the level of interpersonal communication skill possessed by families and professionals, their personalities and values, and the expectations and stereotypes that families and professionals hold for one another all play a role in determining the nature of their relationships (Seligman & Darling, 1989).

When family-professional relationships become problematic, there is a tendency to place the blame on either party, to define the problem as existing in either the professional or the family. How a problem is defined will determine, to a large extent, what people do about it (Germain & Gitterman, 1980). If professionals take the position that it is families who are responsible for the problems that arise in interactions, they are likely also to believe that it is families' responsibility to ameliorate the problems. It is probably safe to assume that the same is true when families see professionals as the cause of a conflict. When this happens, conflicts often not only remain, but become larger and ultimately more difficult to solve. The systems perspective on communication provides an alternative method of viewing problems and problem resolution.

From the systems perspective, communication breakdowns represent a faulty system rather than faulty people. Consequently, the locus of communication problems is viewed as residing in the interactions between people, not within people. This is not to say that individuals cannot, and do not need to, improve their interactions with others; on the contrary, much can be done. But from a systems perspective, when problems arise between people, the emphasis is on changing their interactional patterns rather than changing one individual or the other. The systems perspective leaves no room for placing blame when communication is less than optimal. In fact, attempts at placing blame for the problem are seen as counterproductive to its resolution. Instead of focusing on the issue of blame, one is free to explore the variables that may be contributing to the communication breakdown. Such exploration provides professionals and families with the opportunity to see how the problem appears both to themselves and to each other.

Sometimes it is easy to identify the variables that are contributing to a problem, such as when parents cannot participate regularly in school meetings because they have no telephone or transportation. In other cases, the variables may be more difficult to identify and address, such as in situations involving a personality clash between the parent and professional. By recognizing that the communication breakdown is due to problems within the interaction system and not within the people, all parties involved are better able to work together to explore and restore the breakdown. By engaging in mutual problem solving, both parties have the opportunity to express and fulfill their needs. Furthermore, a willingness to share responsibility for breakdowns in communication maximizes the probability that families and professionals can work toward mutual solutions in a nonthreatening and nondefensive manner.

The process of confronting and solving problems is difficult and painful, yet when we solve problems, we learn and grow. When we solve problems together, we learn and grow together. Mutual problem solving between families and professionals is ideal, therefore. Professionals who endeavor to establish good communication with families must be willing to work zealously in situations in which there appears to be difficulty. This requires demonstration of a willingness and openness to accept mutual responsibility for both the problem and its resolution. Evidence of this willingness alone can often do much to influence the behavior of others. In addition, it is helpful for professionals to have some degree of insight into the prerequisites to positive communication.

PREREQUISITES TO POSITIVE COMMUNICATION

Developing positive communication among families and professionals involves a number of prerequisites: (a) knowing yourself, (b) knowing the families, and (c) using your knowledge to develop mutual respect and trust.

Knowing Yourself

The first prerequisite for learning to communicate effectively and work with others is learning to know and work with yourself. The more you know about and appreciate yourself and your behaviors, the better you can understand and appreciate the personalities and behaviors of others (Seligman & Darling, 1989).

Developing self-awareness and self-acceptance can be a difficult and painful process that requires commitment and perseverance. It is a task that most of us will never complete in our lifetimes. Fortunately, according to Rogers (1951), complete self-awareness and acceptance is not a prerequisite for persons who are in positions of helping others. What is important is a willingness to look at and understand your own perceptions, attitudes, and values, and to reflect on how they may be affecting your family-professional interactions.

UNDERSTANDING YOUR PERCEPTIONS. The way in which people view the world varies widely according to a complex interaction of internal and external forces (Webster, 1977). Due to the complexity of this interaction, no two people perceive the world in exactly the same way. First, we perceive our world through our sensory receptors. Although this accounts for much consistency in perception among people, it is possible that differences exist even at this very basic level. Such differences are obvious when we interact with persons who experience deafness or blindness.

Through our sensory receptors, we filter and edit information to make sense of what we hear, feel, see, and smell. This part of perception, which can be referred to as "interpretation," characteristically takes the form of impressions, conclusions, assumptions, expectations, and/or prejudices. It is important to recognize that interpretations are different from observations: two people may observe the same event but interpret it differently. For example, a professional may interpret a child's crying as attention-getting behavior, whereas the parent may see it as an expression of pain and frustration. When we acknowledge our tendency to interpret sensory data, we realize that our interpretations may not always be accurate and may not be the same as the interpretations of the family.

Many of us seldom question our perceptions of the world around us. Thus, we generally accept our perceptions and interpretations as a true representation of reality. This can and does lead to problems when we interact with others who do not share our view of reality. It becomes even more problematic when we insist that others agree with our projected images. An important prerequisite, then, for developing productive communications with others is a willingness to admit that our perceptions and interpretations, by nature, may be inaccurate, or at least incomplete, as well as different from others. Because everybody perceives reality differently, it is likely that families and professionals will continue sometimes to disagree. By understanding your own perceptions and recognizing that differences in perceptions are a natural outgrowth of the human condition, you may be able to alter your approach when differences in perception arise, however. Instead of viewing differences in perception as problems, differences can be viewed as opportunities for both families and professionals to sharpen their perceptual worlds through their interactions with one another.

UNDERSTANDING YOUR ATTITUDES.   Because the attitudes and feelings people have about themselves tend to determine the nature of a relationship, a second prerequisite to positive communication is an awareness of your own attitudes about the families with whom you interact. Sonnenschein (1984) describes seven categories of attitudes and assumptions sometimes held by professionals that may stand in the way of effective family-professional partnerships. We present these not because we want to lay a "guilt trip" on you, but because your consideration of each of these attitudes may help you in your own self-awareness efforts.

The seven categories as conceptualized by Sonnenschein (1984) are: (a) the parent as vulnerable client; (b) the parent and "professional distance"; (c) the parent as patient; (d) the parent as cause; (e) the parent as less observant, less perceptive, and less intelligent; (f) the parent as adversary; and (g) the parent as "pushy," "angry," "denying," "resistant," or "anxious."

The Parent as Vulnerable Client.   In Sonnenschein's (1984) words, "There seems to be a natural imbalance between the helper and the helped, the powerful and the powerless, the expert and the novice that is difficult to overcome" (p. 130). As a result of this unequal power distribution, parents often feel uncomfortably vulnerable. It is important for you to be aware of some parents' tendency to feel vulnerable when asking for help, and to be aware of how your own attitudes and behaviors may contribute to this reaction.

The Parent and "Professional Distance". The belief that professionals must maintain "professional distance" when interacting with families is another attitude that may be more detrimental than beneficial to effective family-partnerships. According to many parents, this distance typically is accompanied by lack of empathy on the part of the professional, and many parents suffer when professionals fail to demonstrate genuine empathy. A mother of three children with muscular dystrophy, two of whom also had mental retardation, writes:

> When we are injured, we need nurturance—whatever age we are. I think one of the dilemmas for the professional dealing with parents of handicapped children is that they have to try to help parents, who may also acutely need nurturance themselves, to give extra care and nurturance to the child. Some of the professionals who worked with us let us know that they understood our pain, and that was often all the care we needed. But sometimes the concern for the child became the total focus, and I felt drained and discouraged. (Weyhing, 1983, p. 127)

To minimize the distance between yourself and families, it will be important for you to allow yourself the normal feelings and warmth that occur between people who care about each other.

The Parent as Patient. A third attitude that may hinder the development of meaningful family-professional partnerships is the expectation that parents who have children with exceptionalities need treatment themselves. Although this may be the case for some parents, it is not the case for the majority. In fact, evidence suggests that some parents may become emotionally stronger as a result of their experiences with family members with a disability (Wikler et al., 1983).

As professionals, positive communication will necessitate that you develop an awareness of any tendencies you may have to view parents as sick or in need of treatment. In Sonnenschein's (1984) words, "If parents sense that they are being perceived as 'troubled' or 'coping badly,' they may do their best to hide any signs of struggle or, perhaps, will feel as helpless and disturbed as they are judged to be" (p. 134). Capitalizing on the family's strengths rather than weaknesses in both subtle and obvious ways can do much to change both the family's and your own perspectives. Inquiring about unique positive contributions the child makes and asking the family to share ways in which they have coped successfully are two means of accomplishing this.

The Parent as Cause. A fourth attitude that, if present, may undermine the success of the family-professional partnership is the notion that the parent is responsible for the condition of the family member with a disability. This view is held not only by some professionals, but by some parents as well. It will be important for you to be sensitive to the tendency among some parents to feel guilty about their child's problems, and to make every effort not to reinforce, nor to invalidate, such feelings. According to Moses (1983), "the temptation on the part of most professionals is to try to take away the guilt. Only the very exceptional person is able to validate the legitimacy of the parent's feelings without seeming to confirm a judgment of fault. To offer such a relationship is to offer a unique opportunity that facilitates growth" (p. 21).

The Parent as Less Observant, Less Perceptive, and Less Intelligent. According to Sonnenschein (1984), some professionals tend to discount whatever parents say about the family member with the disability, a tendency that may cause parents to feel that their opinions and impressions are not useful. Yet, as has been demonstrated in numerous studies, many parents of children and youth with disabilities are extremely observant, perceptive, and intelligent, and have much useful information to share (Bailey & Simeonsson, 1984; Barna, Bidder, Gray, Clements, & Garner, 1982; Connolly, Morgan, Russell, & Richardson, 1980; Vadasy, Fewell, Meyer, Schell, & Greenberg, 1984).

An important prerequisite for positive communication, then, is that you acknowledge and appreciate how much parents know about their child with a disability and how observant, perceptive, and intelligent they are about the child's strengths and needs. An ideal partnership is one in which both parties feel needed, respected, and valued. If you wish to establish such relationships with families, you must let parents know how vitally important and useful their contributions are.

The Parent as Adversary.   Sometimes professionals in fields related to exceptionalities view parents as adversaries competing with them in various ways and for various purposes. Sometimes parents view professionals as adversaries. As Sonnenschein (1984) points out, it is possible to understand how adversarial, or competitive, relationships can arise between parents and professionals since both have vested interests in the child's welfare and progress.

As a prerequisite for positive communication, it is important that you be cognizant of this tendency to compete, as competition can only result in negative effects upon the family-professional partnership as well as upon the family member with a disability. A helpful alternative for both families and professionals might be for all parties to reflect upon their mutually shared interest, commitment, and dedication to helping the family member with a disability.

Parents as "Pushy," "Angry," "Denying," "Resistant," or "Anxious." This tendency to label parents often results in more harm than good, particularly when labels based on inaccurate interpretations of parents' behaviors are applied. In Sonnenschein's (1984) words:

> Parents who disagree with a diagnosis or seek a second opinion are "denying;" those who refuse the kind of treatment that is suggested are "resistant;" and those who are convinced that something is wrong with their child despite inconclusive tests are "anxious." A belief that the parents' perception or suggestion may be the better or more accurate one is rare. (p. 136)

As a prerequisite to positive communication we encourage, whenever possible, to resist the temptation to label parents. Labeling does nothing to enhance or improve relationships, no matter how accurate the label may be. Rather than label, if you wish to develop good relationships with families, try instead to accept the parents' expression of positive as well as negative feelings. Your acceptance will do much to enhance and encourage free and open communication.

Each of the attitudes presented by Sonnenschein (1984) may hinder the development of meaningful family-professional partnerships. As a prerequisite to positive communication, we encourage you to consider your own attitudes about families and to evaluate them in relation to their contribution to the establishment of effective, collaborative family-professional partnerships.

UNDERSTANDING YOUR VALUES.   According to Aponte (1985), values are the standards by which a person directs his actions and defines, interprets, and judges all social phenomena. As such, values serve as important guideposts for everyday behaviors and interactions with others. Because values guide your selection of goals for every aspect of your life, positive communication with families requires you to understand your own values about families and disability and how they may affect your interactions with families.

One way to clarify your own values about families and disability is for you to consider the underlying values of the Beach Center on Families and Disability that are presented in the preface of this text.

- persons with disabilities make positive contributions to their families and to society;
- persons with disabilities and their families need support to develop and maintain expectations and dreams for the future;
- persons with disabilities and their families have the right to full citizenship;
- families and persons with disabilities are capable of making meaningful choices and acting on their preferences;
- connections both within families and between families and their various support networks are crucial;
- families who have a family member with a disability possess inherent strengths.

Your personal attitude toward these values will have an impact on how you interact with families. Moreover, when you have clarified your own values for yourself, it will be easier for you to understand the values that are important to the families with whom you work.

Knowing Families

A second prerequisite to effective family-professional partnerships is learning to know and understand the family. Just as it is important to know and understand yourself as one of the partners, so, too, is it imperative that you understand the family as the other half of the partnership.

To develop a comprehensive picture of the family, you will need to understand: (a) the family as a system, (b) cultural and socioeconomic differences; and (c) the logistical constraints on the family's life.

UNDERSTANDING THE FAMILY SYSTEM. The family systems model, as presented in Chapters 2 through 5, provides a useful organizing scheme for understanding families. According to this framework, you need to be aware of (a) the characteristics of the family as a whole and each of its members; (b) the interaction patterns between and among family members as well as between and among family members and those outside of the family; (c) the capacity of the family to deal with the many functions that relate to daily living; and (d) where the family is in the family life cycle. Information about each of these facets of the family as a system will provide you with a greater understanding of the family as a whole and enable you to respond with greater sensitivity to the needs of all its members.

To gain an understanding of the family as a system in ways that are "family friendly," or not intrusive to the family, you will need to be aware of many different strategies for gathering this information. For example, a discussion guide for gathering information about families, such as the one shown in Appendix B, can be used to remind you of the types of information that may be helpful. As you begin your interactions with the family, more specific kinds of information may also appear to be helpful.

Table 6–1 provides a summary of various kinds of information about families needed for an effective family-professional partnership. In addition, the relevance of this information for the educational program of the family member with a disability is also pointed out.

Information about the family as a system may be gathered in one or more of the following ways, depending on the needs of the family.

- Information about the family may be collected through unstructured, informal conversations with the family over a period of

TABLE 6–1 Gathering Information Using a Family-Systems Approach

Examples of the kind of information that may be gathered from families:	Educational rationale/implications for the development of educational programs:
FAMILY STRUCTURE	
• Who are the members of the family?	• May determine whom to invite to IEP meetings, and whom to involve in home intervention programs.
• What are the ages and sex of the family members?	• May determine the family's ability/willingness to participate in the educational program.
• What is the educational background of family members?	• May determine the family's ability to understand and/or carry out certain educational interventions.
• What are the general attitudes of significant others toward the disability?	• May determine approaches for working with the family. For example, attitudes of denial may be approached differently than attitudes of indifference or anger.
FAMILY FUNCTIONS	
• What is the impact of the disability on regular performance of duties within the home?	• May determine the kinds of skills training the student needs as part of the educational program.
• Does the disability create any restrictions on the family's desire to engage in recreational/leisure activities such as vacations and/or evenings out?	• May determine the kind of recreation/leisure goals to include on the child's IEP and the family's need for respite care.
• Who takes primary responsibility for caring for the member who is disabled?	• May determine whom to invite to IEP meetings and other educationally relevant activities, as well as who in the family may be in greatest need of a break from the usual care-giving demands.
• Does the disability create any financial restrictions for the family?	• May determine the family's need for financial support.
FAMILY INTERACTION	
• Do family members provide emotional support to each other? How is this given?	• May determine how to relate to the student as well as to other family members.
• Do individual schedules permit much time together at home as a family?	• May determine the number and kinds of home intervention programs to recommend.

TABLE 6–1   (Continued)

FAMILY INTERACTION

- Do family members openly discuss the disability?

- What is the nature of the relationship between siblings and the member who has a disability?

- May determine the need for caution and sensitivity when interacting with families in which the disability is not openly discussed or acknowledged.

- May determine how well the child is incorporated into the family and the type of intervention programs that might be most appropriate.

LIFE CYCLE

- Does the family relate to the member with a disability in an age-appropriate fashion?

- What is the family's perception of the future for the member who has a disability?

- May determine the family's understanding and approval of educational objectives that are chronologically appropriate.

- May determine the kinds of skills and goals the family thinks are important to include in the educational program.

Note. From "Assessment Guide for a Family Systems Approach" by H. Benson, 1986, Lawrence, KS: The University of Kansas. Adapted by permission.

weeks or months. Telephone conversations, before and after school contacts, and other informal meeting times all provide opportunities for you to get to know the members of the family as friends and partners. Many families appreciate these informal opportunities to "talk story", and you may find the families' stories to be rich with information about the families' strengths and needs.

- If your program routinely utilizes an intake interview when the child first enrolls in the program, some information about the family as a system can be collected from this procedure.

- If and when a family appears comfortable with home visits, sharing family-systems information during a home visit is sometimes easier than in a meeting at school.

- Some information may be available from existing records or from other professionals who have been, or may currently be, involved with the family. It is important to communicate and collaborate with others who are involved with the family to avoid unnecessarily gathering information that is already available.

You will likely use a combination of these methods since different family situations will require different strategies and combinations. Since some information about the family system may be sensitive for the family, it is important to allow yourself and the family sufficient time for a level of trust to be established before broaching any potentially sensitive areas. A period of several weeks or months and several contacts may be required. Families may never be comfortable sharing sensitive information, and they always should maintain the right to decline to discuss topics which they consider private. The role of educators is not to conduct an intrusive, formal family assessment; on the contrary, educators should seize the opportunity to gather information in a friendly, relational, and supportive way.

UNDERSTANDING CULTURAL AND SOCIOECONOMIC DIFFERENCES.   Because the United States is one of the most culturally diverse nations in the world, and because nonmajority ethnic groups are typically overrepresented in special education classes, it is especially important for you to be responsive to different cultural and ethnic styles.

As a professional, you bring your own set of values to your encounters with families whose cultural background differs from yours; and your own values will influence your responses to families. By taking the time to know yourself and your own ethnicity and its influence upon you, you will be taking the initial step to becoming more culturally aware and more sensitive to cultural differences. The second and equally important step in this connection is to learn about and become more responsive to cultural and ethnic styles.

When you interact with families from cultures that are different from your own, it will be important for you to be aware of a number of characteristics that are specific to different cultures. As you work to build partnerships with culturally diverse families, it may be helpful for you to consider each of these characteristics and to reflect upon how they may be affecting the family's responses to you and the services you provide. Table 6–2 provides a summary of these characteristics.

Many excellent resources are available to help you become more familiar with the traditions, customs, beliefs, and values of different cultures. We encourage you to explore some of the resources presented in Appendix A. Supplement your readings by participating in ethnic festivals, attending community classes on various cultures, visiting museum exhibits, and perhaps most importantly, learning about the characteristics of cultural experiences from the families themselves. Your enhanced cultural enlightenment will enable you to respond with greater sensitivity to all families.

Socioeconomic status has a tremendous impact upon a family, affecting most aspects of the family system—resources, interaction patterns, family functioning, and the family's life cycle. Thus, in the same way that it is important for you to understand characteristics that are specific to different cultures, so too, is it essential that you recognize the far-reaching effects of poverty upon families.

TABLE 6–2   Suggestions for Cultural Considerations

CULTURAL CONSIDERATIONS	EXAMPLES	MAY DETERMINE
Meaning of the disability	Disability within a family may be viewed as shameful and disgraceful, or as a positive contribution to the family	The level of acceptance of the disability and the need for services
Attitudes about professionals	Professionals may be viewed as persons of authority or as equals	The level of family members' participation may be only minimal in the partnership out of respect and fear
Attitudes about children	Children may be highly valued	The willingness of the family to make many sacrifices on behalf of the child
Attitudes about seeking and receiving help	Problems within the family may be viewed as being strictly a family affair or may be easily shared with others	The level of denial may work against acknowledging and talking about the problem
Family roles	Roles may be sex specific and traditional or flexible. Age and sex hierarchies of authority may exist	Family preferences may exist for which family member takes the leadership role in the family-professional partnership
Family interactions	Boundaries between family subsystems may be strong and inflexible or relaxed and fluid	The level of problem sharing/solving in families. Family members may keep to themselves and deal with problems in isolation or problem solve as a unit

Families in poverty are often struggling to meet basic survival needs. Because the presence of a family member with a disability compounds this daily struggle, many families from low SES groups do not have the energy to focus on the specific needs of the family member with a disability. What may appear to be a lack of interest in establishing a family-professional partnership on the part of the family, therefore, in reality may be an effort by the family to tend to other external factors critical to their very survival. A lack of understanding of the influence of poverty upon a family's capacity to participate in the service-provider system may mean that these families are written off as unreachable. In

TABLE 6–2 (Continued)

CULTURAL CONSIDERATIONS	EXAMPLES	MAY DETERMINE
Time orientation	Family may be present or future oriented	Family's willingness to consider future goals and future planning
Role of the extended family	Extended family members may be close or far, physically and emotionally	Who is involved in the family-professional partnership
Support networks	Family may rely solely on nuclear family members, on extended family members, or on nonrelated persons. Importance of godparents	Who can be called upon in time of need
Attitude toward achievement	Family may have a relaxed attitude or high expectations for achievement	The goals and expectations of the family for the family member with the disability
Religion	Religion and the religious community may be a strong or neutral factor in some aspects of family life	Family's values, beliefs, and traditions as sources of comfort
Language	Family may be non-English speaking, bilingual, or English speaking	The need for translators (Smith & Ryan, 1987)
Number of generations removed from country of origin	The family may have just emigrated or be several generations removed from the country of origin	The strength and importance of the cultural ties
Reasons for leaving country of origin	Family may be emigrants from countries at war	Family's readiness for involvement with external world (Valero-Figueira, 1988)

contrast, by being aware of the influence of poverty on a family and being flexible and creative in offering meaningful opportunities for involvement in the family-professional partnership, professionals may be able to reach families who are perhaps most in need of family-centered support.

UNDERSTANDING FAMILY LOGISTICAL CONSTRAINTS. Another important prerequisite to positive communication is an understanding of any logistical constraints on the family's capacity to participate fully in the family-professional partnership. Sometimes families, although ready and motivated to participate fully in the family-professional partnership, are unable to do so because they have no transportation, or their own employment schedule interferes, or they cannot get a babysitter. Such logistical constraints may determine whether or not the family is able to participate in the family-professional partnership. As you become aware of such constraints, you may be able to help the family find practical solutions—solutions that will, in turn, foster positive communication. Specific solutions to logistical constraints are suggested in Chapter 10.

Developing Respect and Trust

Become familiar with, and appreciating who we are as well as the families with whom we work forms the basis not only for effective communication with others, but also for the development of mutual trust and respect (Traux & Mitchell, 1971). Trust and respect are essential to the development of effective and meaningful communication among parents and professionals. In Ann Turnbull's (1985b) words:

> When professionals interact with parents, respect is a necessary ingredient. . . . One of the most meaningful interactions I have had as a parent with a professional since Jay has been home was with a psychologist. As I shared some very personal concerns with her related to planning for Jay's future, tears came down her cheeks. We sat in silence for a long time, both considering the course of action that would be in Jay's best interest. The silence was beautiful. It confirmed that she was hearing what I was saying and was sharing my feelings on the subject. There was no easy answer. An immediate response, telling me not to worry about things, would have insulted my sensibilities. I knew she respected me when she poignantly shared my feelings. The result of that interaction was that my respect for her as a professional grew one hundredfold. (p. 133)

Without mutual trust and respect, the probability for the development of meaningful and productive communication among families and professionals is severely compromised (Simpson, 1982). Moreover, lack of trust and respect affects not only the family and the professional, but the child as well. In Rutherford and Edgar's (1979) words: "when teachers and parents find themselves in adversary roles, distrusting each other, children suffer" (p. 20).

Building a trusting and respectful relationship with families is an interactive process that involves the mutual sharing of ideas, information, and feelings (Margolis & Brannigan, 1986). This process cannot be rushed, and yet, when given time to evolve at its own pace, it will significantly strengthen the family-professional partnership. During this process you will use the knowledge and awareness you have about yourself and the families with whom you work to cultivate a cooperative relationship built upon a foundation of understanding and genuine concern.

Margolis and Brannigan (1986) have identified eight strategies and behaviors that can be used for trust building with families. These strategies are summarized in Table 6–3.

Seligman and Darling (1989) also recommend some specific techniques to facilitate the development of trust and respect, especially in relationships with families from diverse cultural backgrounds. These strategies are presented in Table 6–4.

The idea of using other parents as peers in a parent-to-parent relationship to facilitate the development of the family-professional partnership is especially useful in the early stages of the relationship. Often if the first few contacts are with a parent who speaks positively of the family-professional partnership, then the family members are more able to feel confident about their own family-professional relationship. Sharing common values and traditions with the family and similar experiences living with a family member with a disability gives peers more credibility. The strategy of building relationships based on cultural and familial similarities is becoming widely used in Parent-to-Parent programs throughout the country. By matching "veteran" parents with "new", or "referred" parents based upon similar family and life experiences, Parent-to-Parent programs provide information and emotional support through unique relationships built upon trust and mutual understanding. As one father of a child with Down syndrome shared:

> At that point (the time of diagnosis), what we needed most was to be able to talk and cry with someone who really knew and understood our

---

TABLE 6–3 Suggestions for Developing Trust and Respect

- Accept families as they are.
- Listen carefully and empathetically for the cognitive and emotional content of the family's message.
- Help families feel comfortable by sharing information and resources with them when legally permissible.
- Prepare for all meetings so that your knowledge will be obvious at the right moments.
- Focus on the hopes, aspirations, concerns, and needs of family members. Attending to concerns communicates caring.
- Keep your word. Return calls promptly and share materials as promised.
- Allow the family's expertise to shine.
- Be there when needed.

Note. From "Building Trust with Parents" by H. Margolis and G. Brannigan, 1986, *Academic Therapy, 22*(1), 71–75.

TABLE 6—4 Suggestions for Trust Building with Culturally Diverse Families

---

- Speak and provide written materials in the family's native language.
- Use community representatives and/or peers to develop initial relationships.
- Be especially sensitive to the logistical constraints and be flexible in working with the family to find viable solutions that are comfortable for the family.
- Encourage families to share with you their view of their situation. Such a sharing of the family's story and perspective may reinforce to the family your genuine interest and concern.
- To the greatest extent possible, take the "shoes test" and try to assume the family's point of view.

Note. From *Ordinary Families, Special Children: A Systems Approach to Childhood Disability* by M. Seligman and R. B. Darling, 1989. New York: The Guilford Press. Copyright by The Guilford Press.

own sorrows and our fears for the future. As supportive and helpful as our friends and family were, and the medical people were trying to be, we always felt as though there were gaps. And, for us, the only way to bridge the gaps was to connect with someone on the same side.

INTERPERSONAL COMMUNICATION SKILLS

Having identified some of the prerequisites to effective communication among families and professionals, we turn our discussion to the importance of good interpersonal communication skills. We strongly believe that good communication skills are especially important for persons who work in helping professions. The more accurately you are able to communicate thoughts and feelings, the more able you will be to help others. Some individuals seem to have a natural ability to communicate well, most persons must work consciously to develop this ability, however. Fortunately, it has been demonstrated many times that communication skills can be learned and applied by a variety of professionals and nonprofessionals alike (Edwards, 1986; Lombana, 1983).

For example, Edwards (1986) investigated the effects of training on special educators' interaction skills and found that participation in a training component on interaction skills resulted in positive changes in the professionals' nondirective interviewing skills. Similarly, in a study by Hirsch and Altman (1986), graduate students were trained in communication skills for sharing diagnostic information and recommendations with families. Again, professionals and parents both attested to the effectiveness of the training program for improving the students' interaction skills.

Although it has been scientifically demonstrated that many communication skills can be taught, many theorists contend that effective communication is an art, not a science (Brammer, 1988). Effective use of communication skills as an art relies heavily upon the user's attitudes and personal qualities. Therefore, it is important for you to try to master both the art and the science of communication skills and to incorporate these techniques and qualities into your personal style so that they become natural and spontaneous. To integrate these elements successfully into your personal style requires systematic practice and use of the skills. The advantage of learning communication skills is that they demand no special equipment and can be practiced anywhere—at home, at work, and during leisure time. We strongly urge you to practice and use the communication skills that we will now share with you.

Nonverbal Communication Skills

Nonverbal communication includes all communication other than the spoken or written word. As we communicate verbally, we also communicate nonverbally through the use of gestures, facial expressions, voice volume and intonations, physical proximity to others, and posture. According to Knapp (1972), in a typical conversation between two people, less than 35% of the social meaning is transmitted by words, while 65% is communicated through nonverbal forms of communication. Thus, nonverbal behaviors can strongly influence interactions between people. Many of the nonverbal cues that we transmit to others are largely beyond our conscious awareness (Hepworth & Larsen, 1982). Therefore, if you wish to improve the nature of your interactions with families, you will need deliberately and consciously to use nonverbal communication skills consistent with your feelings and intentions.

Examples of nonverbal communication skills that can help foster the total communication process are: (a) physical attending, (b) listening, and (c) experiencing and expressing empathy.

PHYSICAL ATTENDING.   Physical attending is a basic nonverbal communication skill that consists of several components: contact, posture, and gestures (Ivey, 1986).

The contact component involves both eye contact and the degree of physical contact, or closeness, between people who are communicating with one another. Because your eyes are a primary vehicle for communicating, maintaining eye contact is a way of showing your interest in another person. In a similar way, adjusting the physical space between yourself and family members with whom you are communicating may also convey a particular level of interest. A relaxed posture, one in which you lean forward and face the other person squarely, and well-timed, unexaggerated body movements or gestures may also influence the overall comfort level of families with whom you communicate.

When considering the components of physical attending, it is important to remember that different cultures have different norms for each component. In some cultures, eye contact is considered offensive; in others, a physical distance of less than 6 feet may make participants uncomfortable. These factors make it especially important that you be aware of, and sensitive to, cultural preferences.

LISTENING.   Listening is the "language of acceptance" and, as such, is considered by many to be one of the most essential ingredients for an effective helping relationship (Gordon, 1970). Unfortunately, true listening rarely occurs naturally or spontaneously. To listen to another person with genuine, undivided attention is a difficult task that requires both diligence and practice. According to Benjamin (1969), genuine listening requires three conditions: (a) that we attend to the other person without preoccupation; (b) that we are aware of the way things are said, the tone in which they are said, and the expressions and gestures used; and (c) that we hear what is not said, that which lies beneath the surface. Ultimately, the goal of listening is to understand.

Gordon (1970) and Kroth (1975) have identified two varieties of listeners—active and passive. Although some persons may tend to be one kind of listener or the other, most unconsciously fluctuate between the two varieties. Indeed, truly effective listeners have mastered both listening styles and are able to select the style that is most effective in a given situation.

Passive listeners are the "silent types" who say very little, but remain actively involved in the communication exchange through the use of nonverbal attending skills, silence, and minimal encouragement. According to Gordon (1970), saying nothing can often communicate acceptance which, in turn, can foster constructive growth and change. Simpson (1982) points out that, while this type of listening style may not be appropriate for all situations, it may offer parents of children and youth with exceptionalities what they need most, "the chance to talk about their attitudes and feelings relative to having an exceptional child to an interested, yet quietly accepting professional person" (p. 94).

Active listeners, on the other hand, assume a much more involved and direct role in the process of communication. In contrast to the passive listener, the active listener is animated, makes comments, asks questions, and may even share personal experiences. According to Gordon (1970), active listening encourages people to accept and express their thoughts and feelings, facilitates problem solving, promotes friendliness and warmth, and builds constructive and mutually supportive relationships. It is important to realize that active listening is not merely a set of techniques; rather, it is a method of communicating some very basic attitudes that are essential prerequisites for active listening. Gordon (1970) describes these attitudes as follows:

- You must want to hear what the other person has to say.
- You must sincerely want to help the person with his/her problem.
- You must genuinely be able to accept the other person's feelings, no matter how different they are from your own.
- You must trust the other person's capacity to handle, work through, and find solutions to his/her own problems.
- You must realize and appreciate that feelings are transitory in nature, consequently you need not fear them.
- You must view the other person as separate from yourself with alternative ways of perceiving the world.

EXPERIENCING AND EXPRESSING EMPATHY.   Intimately related to the listening process, and another important aspect of effective family-professional relationships, is the ability to experience and express empathy. Empathy requires that you set aside your own internal frame of reference and try to understand and experience the world from the other person's point of view. Empathetic listening, therefore, is completely nonjudgmental and nonevaluative. When you listen empathetically, you do not agree or disagree, but rather attempt simply to understand what it is like to be in the other person's shoes. When you listen empathetically to a family, you convey genuine interest, understanding, and acceptance of the family's feelings and experiences. This does not mean that you will necessarily approve of, or agree with, the family's point of view, but that you will try to understand the family's situation from the family's point of view—not your own. Listening to understand without judgment or evaluation is difficult, but can be learned, beginning with an awareness of your own inner states and outer behaviors. It is a behavior that is critically important for productive and meaningful relationships with families.

If you wish to improve your communications with families, you must recognize both desirable and undesirable nonverbal behaviors. To assist you in evaluating and improving your nonverbal behaviors, we have included in Table 6–5 an inventory of desirable and undesirable nonverbal communication behaviors developed by Hepworth and Larsen (1982).

Verbal Communication Skills

Although the nonverbal communication skills of attending, listening, and expressing empathy are effective and essential means for communicat-

---

TABLE 6–5   Inventory of Practitioner's Nonverbal Communication

---

DESIRABLE	UNDESIRABLE
Facial expressions	
Direct eye contact (except when culturally proscribed)	Avoidance of eye contact
	Eye level higher or lower than client's
Warmth and concern reflected in facial expression	Staring or fixating on person or object
	Lifting eyebrow critically
Eyes at same level as client's	Nodding head excessively
Appropriately varied and animated facial expressions	Yawning
	Frozen or rigid facial expressions
Mouth relaxed; occasional smiles	Inappropriate slight smile
	Pursing or biting lips
Posture	
Arms and hands moderately expressive; appropriate gestures	Rigid body position; arms tightly folded
	Body turned at an angle to client
Body leaning slightly forward; attentive but relaxed	Fidgeting with hands (including clipping nails or cleaning pipe)
	Squirming or rocking in chair
	Slouching or placing feet on desk
	Hand or fingers over mouth
	Pointing finger for emphasis
Voice	
Clearly audible but not loud	Mumbling or speaking inaudibly
Warmth in tone of voice	Monotonic voice
Voice modulated to reflect nuances of feeling and emotional tone of client messages	Halting speech
	Frequent grammatical errors
Moderate speech tempo	Prolonged silences
	Excessively animated speech
	Slow, rapid, or staccato speech
	Nervous laughter
	Consistent clearing of throat
	Speaking loudly
Physical proximity	
Three to five feet between chairs	Excessive closeness or distance
	Talking across desk or other barrier

Note. From Direct *Social Work Practice Theory and Skills* (p. 77) by D. H. Hepworth and J. A. Larsen, 1982, Homewood, IL: The Dorsey Press. Copyright 1982 by The Dorsey Press. Adapted by permission of Wadsworth, Inc.

ing with families, certain situations demand verbal responses in order to facilitate communication. Examples of verbal responses include furthering responses, paraphrasing, response to affect, questioning, and summarization.

FURTHERING RESPONSES. Furthering responses indicate attentive listening and encourage people to continue to speak and examine their thoughts and feelings. There are two types of furthering responses:

1. *Minimal encouragers,* sometimes referred to as the "grunts and groans" of communication, usually include short but encouraging responses such as "Oh?," "Then?," "Mm-hum," "I see," or "and then?" Minimal encouragers can also be nonverbal and take the form of head nods, facial expressions, and gestures that communicate listening and understanding.

2. *Verbal following* involves restating the main points or emphasizing a word or phrase contained in what the family member has said, using the language system of the family. Verbal following not only encourages the family member to go on speaking, but also provides the professional with a means of checking listening accuracy. An example of minimal encouragers and verbal following is provided:

   FAMILY MEMBER: I've had a really rough day.

   PROFESSIONAL: Oh?

   FAMILY MEMBER: Jason woke up with wet sheets and cried all through breakfast. To top it off the bus came early and I had to send him to school without any lunch.

   PROFESSIONAL: You've had a really rough day.

PARAPHRASING. Paraphrasing involves using your own words to restate the family's message in a clear manner. In paraphrasing, the emphasis is on the cognitive aspects of the message (e.g., ideas, objects) as opposed to the affective state of the speaker (Cormier & Cormier, 1979). The goal in using paraphrasing is to feed back the essence of the family member's statements. Paraphrasing responds to the implicit meaning of what is said as well as the explicit message. Some examples of paraphrasing follow:

   FAMILY MEMBER: I don't know what to do with Elena. One minute she's extremely hyper and the next minute lethargic.

   PROFESSIONAL: Elena's behaviors are pretty inconsistent.

   FAMILY MEMBER: Everything seems to be a burden these days, doing the housework, taking care of the kids, paying the bills. I just don't know how much longer I can take it.

   PROFESSIONAL: You're almost at the end of your rope.

Paraphrasing is an extremely useful technique in clarifying content, tying a number of comments together, highlighting issues by stating them more concisely, and checking one's perceptions. Most importantly, paraphrasing communicates interest in, and understanding of, what the family member is saying.

RESPONSE TO AFFECT.   Response to affect involves (a) the ability to perceive accurately and sensitively the other person's apparent and underlying feelings; and (b) the ability to communicate understanding of those feelings in language that is attuned to the family member's experience at that moment. Attention is paid not only to what the family member has said, but also to how it is said. When you use this technique, try to verbalize the family member's feelings and attitudes, and use responses that are accurate and match the intensity of the family member's affect. Developing a vocabulary of affective words and phrases can be helpful. Some examples of response to affect follow:

> FAMILY MEMBER: I've been so wound up since Becky went into the hospital. I have all this nervous energy, but there's not one thing I can do to help.
>
> PROFESSIONAL: You're feeling really anxious and helpless right now.
>
> *   *   *   *   *   *   *
>
> FAMILY MEMBER: Ever since Elliot was born, my family and friends have become extremely distant. I have no one to turn to and don't know what to do.
>
> PROFESSIONAL: You're feeling very alone with no one, or no place, to turn to.

The purpose of responding to affect is to provide a mirror in which family members can see their feelings and attitudes. This reflection, in turn, helps them move toward greater self-understanding (Benjamin, 1969). In addition, this technique can work to assure family members not only that their feelings have been recognized and understood, but also that their feelings are legitimate and acceptable to the professional. Lastly, response to affect can serve as a tool for professionals to check their own perceptions of the family member's feelings.

QUESTIONING.   Questions generally fall into two categories: closed-ended questions and open-ended questions. *Closed-ended questions* are mostly used to ask for specific factual information. Skillful communicators keep their use of closed-ended questions to a minimum, because this type of question limits responses to a few words or a simple "yes" or "no." Moreover, overuse of closed-ended questions also can make an interaction seem like an interrogation. While closed-ended questions can restrict conversation and often yield limited information, they are appropriate when used sparingly and propitiously. Some examples of appropriately used closed-ended questions are as follows:

"When did Carlos first start having seizures?"
"How old is Betty Sue?"
"Would a ten o'clock meeting be okay for you?"

Unlike closed-ended questions, *open-ended questions* invite family members to share and to talk more. Some open-ended questions are unstructured and open the door for family members to talk about whatever is on their mind (e.g., "What would you like to talk about?," or "How can I be of assistance?"). Other open-ended questions are more structured in that the professional imposes boundaries on possible responses by focusing the topic (e.g., "What are some of the specific methods you've tried to control Matthew's behaviors?"). According to Hepworth and Larsen (1982), open-ended questions can be formulated in three general ways: (a) by asking a question ("How is Miko getting along with her new wheelchair?"); (b) by giving a polite command ("Would you please elaborate on your feelings about the new bus route?"); or (c) by using an embedded question ("I'm interested in finding out more about Ansel's toileting program at home.").

Open-ended questions generally involve use of the words "what" and/or "how." Benjamin (1969) recommends that practitioners stay away from "why" questions as much as possible, as it is common in our society for the word "why" to connote disapproval, displeasure, blame, or condemnation (e.g., "Why don't you listen to me?" "Why are you late?"). Therefore, the word "why" may evoke a negative or defensive response from the person with whom you are speaking. Below are two examples of open-ended questions in response to comments initiated by a family member:

FAMILY MEMBER: I just don't know if I'll be able to carry out Megan's feeding program at home.

PROFESSIONAL: What are you concerned about?

* * * * * * * *

FAMILY MEMBER: I'm really excited about our new house, we're moving in on Saturday.

PROFESSIONAL: I'm so pleased for you. Tell me more about your new house.

SUMMARIZATION. Summarization is a recapitulation of what the family member has said, with an emphasis upon the most salient thoughts and feelings. While similar to paraphrasing, summarization is different in one important respect—summaries are substantially longer.

Summarization serves a number of different purposes. For example, summaries can be used as a stimulus to explore a particular topic; they can communicate to family members that you are interested in, and listening to, what they are saying; they can serve as a perception check for you; and they can synthesize and integrate information that has been shared (Simpson, 1982). Summarization is particularly useful: (a) to recall the highlights of a previous meeting; (b) to tie together confusing, lengthy and/or rambling topics; and (c) to acknowledge the point at which a topic has become exhausted.

Using Communication Skills in Difficult Situations

Your knowledge and application of the nonverbal and verbal communication skills presented in this chapter will provide you with a whole range of options for interacting meaningfully with families. Each interaction will be unique and will require its own blend of skills. As a skilled communicator, you will need to choose the communication skills that seem most appropriate with each family and life situation.

While sensitive use of communication skills is vitally important to the success of any family-professional interaction, they are particularly important during times of crisis. For when families are in crisis they may respond to you with anger, hostility, fear, and/or resistance, making meaningful communication between you and the family more difficult to initiate and/or maintain.

Hepworth and Larsen (1982) suggest during difficult interactions with families that it may be helpful to use the whole spectrum of communication skills. Defining this collection of communication skills as "empathic communication", Hepworth and Larsen note its importance in staying in touch with families and in knowing how to respond to the sometimes volatile emotions being expressed. Moreover, as you interact with families who may be combative or withdrawn, it is important to gauge the effectiveness of your use of empathic communication by observing the family's response immediately following your interaction.

Some family responses that suggest that your use of empathic communication is beneficial to the family include:

- willingness to explore a problem or stay on the topic;
- expression of pent-up emotions;
- willingness to look within themselves;
- spontaneous sharing of more personally relevant material;
- verbal or nonverbal affirmation of the validity of your response.

On the other hand, if your use of empathic communication is not particularly helpful to the family, you may see the family engaging in some or all of the following responses:

- rejecting, either verbally or nonverbally, your response;
- changing the subject;
- ignoring the message;
- becoming more emotionally detached;
- continuing to express anger rather than looking at the relevance of the feelings involved.

Your sensitive observations of the family's responses will help you determine the effectiveness of your interactions with the family.

When you are dealing with families in crisis, you may find that other communication skills are helpful, including assertiveness, conflict resolution, negotiation, and ways to diffuse anger and aggression. Table 6–6

TABLE 6–6 Suggestions for Dealing with Aggression

DO

- Listen.
- Write down what they say.
- When they slow down, ask them what else is bothering them.
- Exhaust their list of complaints.
- Ask them to clarify any specific complaints that are too generally stated.
- Show them the list and ask if it is complete.
- Ask them for suggestions for how to solve any of the problems they have listed.
- Write down the suggestions.
- As much as possible, mirror their body posture.
- As they speak louder, you speak softer.

DON'T

- Argue.
- Defend or become defensive.
- Promise things you can't produce.
- Own problems that belong to others.
- Raise your voice.
- Belittle or minimize the problem.

Note. From University of New Mexico Institute for Parent Involvement, Albuquerque, NM, 1979. Adapted by permission.

contains some valuable tips for how to deal with aggression. Table 6–7 describes some recommendations for how to interact with families in crisis situations. We cannot guarantee that these tips will completely resolve conflict or diffuse a crisis, but when used effectively they can do much to return the interaction to the point of workability.

There is not sufficient space here to discuss more fully the issues of assertiveness, conflict resolution, negotiation, and dealing with anger, but much has been written about these topics (e.g., Gordon, 1970; Kroth, 1985; Lombana, 1983; Simpson, 1982; Warschaw, 1980). We encourage you to use this information and to consult Appendix A for additional related materials.

Improving Communication Skills

We have summarized specific communication tools that have proven useful and effective in a variety of circumstances. It should be clear that no one skill or approach is appropriate in every situation or with every individual. Nor is every approach comfortable or well suited for every professional. As emphasized earlier in this chapter, it is up to you to incorporate these skills into your unique personal style by combining them with your own experience and knowledge.

TABLE 6–7   Suggestions for Crisis Intervention

- Establish rapport.
- Assess the problem.
  (a) Who is affected?
  (b) What are the unmet needs of the affected member?
  (c) What kind of crisis is it?
    - unexpected loss
    - prolonged stress
    - life-cycle transition
  (d) severity of the crisis:
    - critical
    - serious
    - mild
- Identify resources and strengths.
- Develop a plan of action based upon the intensity of the crisis.
  critical—direct intervention
  serious—persuasion to influence the course of action
  mild—offer assistance
- Evaluate the plan of action.

One method that has proven helpful to persons seeking to develop their communication skills is the use of audio and/or videotapes. While audiotapes are ideal for practicing and evaluating verbal communication skills, videotapes offer the additional advantage of feedback on both verbal and nonverbal behaviors. Ask a friend or colleague to spend 10–20 minutes talking over an issue or problem with you. Tape your conversation. As you talk, practice using one or two of the skills we have described. Following your conversation, review the tape critically taking note of the positive contributions you made as well as those that seemed less positive. Set personal goals for improvement. In addition, ask your friend to provide you with feedback on your performance. As you begin to feel confident about the skills you have practiced, try adding more skills to your repertoire. Over time, and with enough practice, these skills can become a natural and spontaneous part of your communication style.

SUMMARY

Probably one of the most important attributes you can possess as a professional is the skill of effective interpersonal communication. Development of effective interpersonal communication skills is a complex and ongoing process that requires knowledge, experience, practice, and commitment. Effective communication skills are a necessary prerequisite to positive family-professional partnerships. In this chapter we have discussed the multiple benefits of family-professional partnerships, some of the prerequisites to the development and maintenance of positive partnerships, and specific skills that can help you communicate more effectively with the families of the students whom you serve. In the next chapter we focus on some strategies that have proven effective for establishing and maintaining communication among families and professionals.

STRATEGIES FOR COMMUNICATION

Parent-professional conferences, which can enhance relationships between families and professionals, may take place at school or in the home. They should be conducted in the parents' primary language to the greatest extent possible.

"Look, Daddy! That's my picture!"

I smiled at Anna who was stroking the paper on the refrigerator as though it were a prized kitten. I'd heard that comment at least 30 times but I didn't mind. Last week's edition of the classroom newsletter that Mrs. Cornell sent to parents featured Anna's drawing on the front page. I wondered if Mrs. Cornell had any idea how much that crudely sketched cow meant to Anna—and to me.

Professionals use a variety of strategies to establish and maintain communication with parents and other family members. Examples include school conferences, home visits, weekly telephone calls, daily log books, and occasional newsletters such as the one for Anna and her family. Some communication strategies can be rather formal in nature and require advanced preparation. Others involve comparatively little preparation and are relatively informal. Because families differ in their needs and preferences in communications with the programs that serve their children (Benson & Turnbull, 1986; MacMillan & Turnbull, 1983), no single approach is appropriate for all families. Nor is a single approach appropriate for all professionals, for they too differ in terms of preferences, needs, and styles of communication. For these reasons, it is important to have a wide selection of communication alternatives. This chapter presents a variety of useful communication strategies and provides guidelines for how to work cooperatively with families to determine the most effective strategies. After reading this chapter, you should be able to answer the following questions:

- What does the current research indicate about parent preferences for involvement?
- How can family preferences for communication be identified?
- What are the three major phases of a planned conference; what are the components of each?
- What are some strategies for being prepared for unplanned conferences?
- What are some nonconference strategies for communication?
- What are some strategies for effective use of the telephone when communicating with families?

CURRENT RESEARCH ON PARENT PREFERENCES FOR INVOLVEMENT

A. P. Turnbull, Winton, Blacher, and Salkind (1983) surveyed 100 parents of kindergarten children regarding their preferences for personal involvement in their child's educational program. Parents ranked as most important (a) informal and frequent communication with teachers, and (b) the opportunity to relax each day with the knowledge that the child's educational needs were being met by the kindergarten program.

In a study conducted in 1986, McCarney investigated the communication preferences of parents of students with emotional disorders from four states. Respondents were asked to rate each of 20 types of parent/ teacher communication strategies on a survey form. According to the results, parents preferred the traditional direct communication of parent-teacher conferences and the convenience of telephone contacts with professionals. They also preferred open houses at school, work or notes sent home by the teacher, classroom observations, and informal teacher contacts. In contrast, parents gave low rankings to the traditional, but less direct, communication strategies of parent group meetings and parent-teacher meetings other than those held at school or home.

Seeking to determine parent/staff ratings of current and preferred parent involvement strategies, N. Horner (1987) collected data from 124 parents of children in special education placements in a large metropolitan school district. Parents preferred a significantly greater level of involvement in decision making, program activities, and more frequent communication than they were experiencing.

In 1988, Vaughn et al. sought to determine whether the actual nature of parent involvement practices had changed in the 10 years since such involvement was mandated by federal law (see Chapter 8). The investigators consequently examined parental participation in the initial placement and individual educational program (IEP) conferences by observing 26 conferences for children referred for possible learning disabilities. According to the results, parent participation at these conferences over the 10-year period remained at the same low level, with parents continuing to take a passive stance, asking few questions, and responding minimally. Similarly, examining the extent of family participation in their children's special education programs, Lynch and Stein (1987) found that 50% of the parents were not participating in the development of the IEP and only 34% actually offered suggestions during the IEP meeting.

Chapey, Trimarco, Crisei, and Capobianco (1987) surveyed parents of students who are gifted about their involvement in family-professional partnerships in the educational programs. These parents reported that, despite expanded opportunities for direct involvement with the professionals, they chose such indirect activities as checking and signing homework and responding to invitations to parent-teacher conferences and open houses.

In summary, based on these findings, most parents prefer informal and frequent communication with their child's educational programs. Activities such as giving and receiving information tend to be preferred over activities that require active decision making. Despite current policy requiring formal and active participation by parents, a more passive role appears to be the one most preferred by the majority of family members (A. P. Turnbull & Winton, 1984). Perhaps there is a need to reevaluate parent-involvement policy and practices to ensure proper individualization of involvement options. In Lynch and Stein's (1982) words:

> Perhaps the next step for educators is to review the definition of active participation as it relates to parent involvement. Can "active" be operationalized to fit all parents, or is active involvement an individually defined phenomenon that varies from parent to parent and family to family? Could the same model of individualization that is used to develop the child's special education program be expanded to provide for some individualization for the family? Instead of measuring and judging parental involvement by the numbers and kinds of comments made at the planning meeting, it may be time to assess the families' present level of involvement, ask them to describe their preferred level of involvement, and mutually develop goals and objectives that will allow them to participate as actively as they choose. This would allow for differences in family preferences and needs while still supporting and encouraging the concept of joint decision making. Despite the mandates and assumptions about the rights and roles of parents in the development and monitoring of their child's educational program, it may be time to recognize that parents, too, have the right to individualization. (p. 62)

Reassessing current parent-involvement policy and practice and recognizing the importance of individualizing for families is an important first step in learning to work successfully with families. However, knowing that families differ in their preferences for participation is not enough. It is important to determine the particular ways in which families differ, as well as the specifics relative to a family's needs and preferences. In the next section we discuss methods for gathering this type of information.

IDENTIFYING FAMILY PREFERENCES

A variety of methods may be used to identify family preferences for communication with the service-delivery program. We encourage you to consider the ideas presented in Table 7–1 to learn about family preferences. Whatever method is used, you should recognize that family preferences may vary over time and, therefore, will need to be monitored and reidentified on a somewhat regular basis. Moreover, if you elect to use formal inventories, avoid including options that you are unable to deliver. For example, do not give families the option to choose a daily communication strategy if you are unwilling, or unable, to communicate that frequently. When deciding which communication options to offer

---

TABLE 7–1   Suggestions for how to Assess Family Preferences for Communication

---

- Use the Discussion Guide in Appendix B to talk with and listen to families.
- Talk with family members, individually or in groups, about their needs and preferences.
- Seek the advice of professionals who have worked successfully with families in the past.

---

families, it is important to take into consideration your own, as well as the family's, preferences and needs.

SPECIFIC COMMUNICATION STRATEGIES

Individualizing approaches to communication with families who have diverse preferences and needs requires that professionals be skilled in a number of communication techniques or strategies. In the next section we present a variety of commonly used formal and informal strategies for establishing and maintaining effective communication with families. We have divided the discussion into two main sections: (a) strategies for communicating with families via family-professional conferences, and (b) nonconference strategies for communication.

The strategies presented here are meant to be practical techniques to assist you in your endeavor to work effectively with families. You are the best judge of whether or not these techniques can work for you, and we urge you to evaluate continually the effectiveness of each strategy for your purposes. Whenever possible, modify the strategies to suit your personal style and the unique characteristics of your program. Although the development and personalization of strategies requires an initial investment of time and energy, we believe that use of many of these techniques will help you to conserve time and energy in the long run. Thus, effective communication strategies can be viewed as means of prevention. By providing avenues for sharing concerns between the family and professionals in an ongoing fashion, issues can be aired and dealt with while fresh and before they become more complex.

Family-Professional Conferences

Conferences are one of the most effective and commonly used methods to facilitate productive partnerships between families and professionals.

Family-professional conferences can provide a variety of important opportunities to:

1. share and receive information about the environments and activities pertinent to the student's development;
2. work together to enhance the student's learning;
3. develop rapport and partnership;
4. cooperate to prevent and solve problems.

Research has shown that conferences not only enhance family-professional relationships, but also have an impact on student performance. A study conducted by Iverson, Brownlee, and Walberg (1981) investigated the effects of teacher-parent conferences on reading achievement of several hundred low-achieving elementary-school students. Results indicated that more frequent contacts between the parents and professionals resulted in significant gains in reading performance. The existence of a positive relationship between school achievement and parent-teacher conferences was also validated in a similar study by Anchor and Anchor (1974). However, although the results of these studies appear positive, more research is needed before definitive conclusions can be drawn.

Because of the many potential benefits of family-professional conferences, conferences should not be limited to the beginning and end of the school year. Regularly scheduled conferences can do much to maintain and enhance family-partnerships (Heward & Orlansky, 1984). We encourage you to participate in planned as well as unplanned family-professional conferences throughout the year.

Planned Conferences

Conscientious planning is the key to effective family-professional conferences. In planning a conference, you will need to consider the three major phases of a conference: (a) preconference, (b) conference, and (c) postconference. Each conference phase consists of a number of steps that require skill and planning on your part. A description of these phases and steps follows:

PRECONFERENCE.   Preconference preparation is an essential ingredient of conference success. Kroth (1985) suggests that professionals perform four basic preconference steps to ensure a smooth and productive conference. These steps are: (a) *notify*, (b) *prepare*, (c) *plan agenda*, and (d) *arrange environments*.

Many elements go into *notifying* parents that a conference will be called. Probably the most important task is to inform the parents of the

---

TABLE 7–2   Suggestions for how to Notify Families about Conferences

---

- Hold an informational parent group meeting.
- Send a written notice about the date, time, place, and length of the meeting.
- Be specific in the notice about the purpose of the meeting.
- Include in the notice the names and responsibilities of other professionals who may attend the meeting.
- Ask the family's advice about the other family members who should attend the conference.
- Decide with the family if the student should attend the conference.
- Pick a time for the meeting when all parties can attend.
- Provide a list of suggested activities that parents can complete to prepare for the meeting.
- Follow up the written notification with a telephone call.

---

purpose of the meeting. Many school systems schedule conference days for parents of all students to discuss progress. Typically, notice of these meetings is provided in the school calendar at the beginning of the year. When this is not the case, every attempt must be made to tell the parents in a clear, understandable, and nonthreatening manner about the purpose of the meeting. This step is particularly important because, based on their own past experiences with schools and teachers, many parents are reluctant to attend such conferences (Mattson, 1977). As one parent of a child with a learning disability noted:

> I didn't like going to school when I was a kid. And I don't like it any better as an adult. There's just too many unhappy memories.

In a workshop designed to help parents and teachers develop communication skills, Flake-Hobson and Swick (1984) asked parents to describe what they thought and felt when their child's teacher called them for a conference. Some of the parents' comments were: "I feel worried." "I feel guilty that I haven't done enough to help my child in school." "I feel nervous, I think that Roddy has done something wrong." "I think that Dorene is not doing her work" (p. 142). Of the group of 50 parents, not one parent described experiencing positive thoughts or feelings when asked to attend a school conference.

Several strategies may be implemented to reduce unnecessary stress for families. These are summarized in Table 7–2.

McNamara (1987) suggested that prior to the notification of the conference, family members be invited to attend an informational group meeting at which the professionals explain the purpose of the individualized education program (IEP) and inform parents of their legal rights. This meeting could also be used to tell parents about the steps used by the school district in planning and implementing the IEP, as well as about various community resources.

The written notification of the conference should include specific information about the date, time, place, purpose, and persons attending the meeting. Moreover, McNamara (1986) suggests including in this notice a request for parental input about topics to be discussed, family members and professionals who should attend, and any other thoughts or concerns the family may have.

By following up your written notification of the conference with a telephone call, you provide family members with an opportunity to ask questions and to more fully understand the intent of the meeting. It will be important, too, to decide with the family which family members and professionals should attend the conference, including whether or not the student with a disability should be in attendance. This, too, may be done over the phone.

Involving the student with an exceptionality, when appropriate, in conference discussion and problem solving (including IEP conferences) can help ensure that the decisions made are consistent with his or her own preferences and interests. Moreover, inviting students to attend and participate in conferences presents them with excellent opportunities to learn and practice the decision-making skills that are so important to independent living (A. P. Turnbull & Turnbull, 1988).

Providing families with a list of suggested activities that they can complete to prepare for the conference may also reduce parental anxiety. In a 1986 study, Kinloch observed that parents who received a preconference awareness packet (containing information about what would happen at the conference and suggestions about how to prepare for the conference) prior to the conference had significantly higher rates of attendance than parents who did not receive such preconference suggestions. Nye, Westling, and Laten (1986) recommended that parents be provided with a list of (a) "cue questions" to ask before and during their annual review conference, and (b) "clarification questions" to use while the conference was underway to clear up any misunderstandings. Table 7–3 presents a listing of activities that families can do before the conference to prepare themselves (Kroth, 1985).

The second step in preparing for the family-professional conference involves *professional preparation.* Insufficient preparation generally is obvious to everyone and can have unfavorable results. Hence it is essential that you spend a sufficient amount of time preparing for conferences with families. Table 7–4 summarizes a number of logistical and psychological tasks that can be completed as a part of professional preparation.

TABLE 7–3   Suggestions for Parental Preparation for Conferences

- Review records on past conferences.
- Talk with family members about what questions to ask and what information to share.
- Make a list of questions to ask.
- Make a list of information to share.
- Ask another person to go to the meeting with you.
- Take all relevant records with you to the conference.
- Bring pencil and paper.
- Check the time and place of the conference.

Note. From *Communicating with Parents of Exceptional Children* (2nd ed.) (p. 187) by R. L. Kroth, 1985, Denver: Love Publishing Co. Copyright 1985 by Love Publishing Co. Adapted by permission.

Planning and developing an agenda is the third major step of pre-conference preparation. An agenda is important for two reasons: (a) it notifies participants about what topics are to be covered at the conference, and (b) it serves as a guide for structure and sequence during the conference. The agenda should be flexible enough to accommodate last-minute additions or changes and should include topics that families have mentioned as important.

The final preconference preparation step consists of *arrangement of the physical environment.* The purpose behind this step is to establish

TABLE 7–4   Suggestions for Professional Preparation for Conferences

- Review the student's cumulative record.
- Assess student's progress.
- Gather examples of student's work.
- Prepare conference materials (reports, data sheets, etc.).
- Outline items to be discussed.
- Talk with other involved professionals to coordinate conference proceedings.
- Plan how to talk about delicate issues (e.g., suspected child abuse, proposed change in educational placement).
- Mentally rehearse the conference and review materials and items to be discussed.
- Wear comfortable clothes.
- Relax.

TABLE 7–5 Suggestions for how to Conduct Home Visits

- Talk with family members about the home visit before scheduling the appointment.
- Make home visits only if they are scheduled with the family ahead of time.
- Arrive and leave on time.
- Cancel home visits only when absolutely necessary.
- Dress appropriately and comfortably.
- Respond with sensitivity to offers of food and beverage.
- Expect distractions.

---

an atmosphere that will enhance communication among families and professionals. A number of factors may be considered when completing this task. The first is to decide where to conduct the meeting. Family-professional conferences can be conducted at the family's home, at the school, or in a neutral location in the community such as the library or community building.

Conferences held at the family's home may be necessary or preferred by families who lack transportation or who are reluctant to come to the school/program. Although home visits may mean more distractions (e.g., the TV, the telephone, neighbors dropping by), they also provide you with the opportunity to gather a more complete picture of the student's environment and family life. Table 7–5 provides some guidelines for home visits.

In some cases, you may want to consider bringing another person (e.g., a social worker or school nurse) along with you on the home visit. Bringing a second person may be particularly important when the topics to be discussed are apt to cause conflict or when there is a history of misunderstandings between the family and the professional. This person may serve as a witness to events, a support person, or a mediator in case of serious disagreements.

When making home visits, it is particularly important to recognize that some parents are uncomfortable opening their homes to you and may find home visits intrusive. Responses to home visits are often determined by how you present them to the families. A mother of an adolescent with an emotional disorder shared this reaction:

> When Kristi was first evaluated for a special education program, the school social worker called to say that she was coming to our home for a visit. She did not say why she was coming and I did not ask. I only knew that social workers normally visit a home to see if it "passes inspection." I cleaned for days, baked cookies and had coffee, tea, and home-made

---

TABLE 7–6   Suggestions for how to Prepare the Setting

- Make arrangements for a quiet and private room: one in which the doors can be closed and the windows are not facing out to frequently used areas.
- Gather all necessary materials prior to the meeting and make arrangements not to be interrupted.
- Be sure that both the temperature and the lighting are comfortable.
- Choose adult-sized chairs and tables.
- Arrange the furniture in a manner that reflects equality. Avoid placing the "professional's chair" behind a desk or at the head of a table.
- Have tissues, beverages, papers, and pens available for all participants.

> lemonade ready for her visit. The joke was on me. She had only come for a social history. She did not inspect my home or even eat a cookie. How much easier my life would have been if she would have explained to me why she was making her visit.

When family-professional conferences are held at the school or agency, the professional is responsible for preparing the setting. Probably the two most important considerations are privacy and comfort. Unless an atmosphere that is confidential, comfortable, and free of interruptions can be arranged, it may be difficult to establish rapport and trust with parents. Consider the steps presented in Table 7–6 when preparing the environment for a family-professional conference.

CONFERENCE.   Stephens and Wolf (1980) describe four major components of parent-professional conferences: (a) *rapport building,* (b) *obtaining information,* (c) *providing information,* and (d) *summarizing and follow-up activities.*

The *rapport building* phase sets the tone for the remainder of the meeting and is, therefore, very important. Shertzer and Stone (1981) described rapport as essential in the development of comfortable, unconditional relationships between families and professionals. Rapport, defined as "a condition of mutual understanding, respect, and sustained interest between individuals" (Shertzer & Stone, 1981, p. 187), is established and maintained through the professional's genuine interest in, and acceptance of, the family. As such, rapport must be natural, not artificial or forced.

Rapport with families is not achieved in the first meeting. Moreover, rapport building is a process that is dependent on many intangible variables both within yourself and within the families you serve. By knowing, understanding, and accepting yourself and the families with whom you are interacting, and by using the communication skills presented in Chapter 6, you will have the necessary tools for establishing rapport with families.

Roberds-Baxter (1984) suggests that educators can build rapport and invite a "parent connection" with parents by:

1. designing the structure of the conference by considering the needs of both the family and yourself when deciding on locations, time constraints, get-acquainted topics, and topics for the agenda. A well-designed structure will allow you to concentrate more fully on the interpersonal dynamics of the meeting.

2. enhancing your own well-being by engaging in personal growth activities such as relaxation and visualization techniques and setting personal goals for honing your interpersonal skills. These activities will help you enter a conference feeling calm, confident, and attentive.

3. ensuring parental comfort by taking time to build the rapport that encourages psychological comfort in parents. Family members who feel respected, understood, and important may find it easier to participate more fully in the conference.

Some specific strategies for building rapport appear in Table 7–7.

A second component of the conference entails *obtaining information* from the families. Such information provides you with the opportunity to practice many of the communication skills described in Chapter 6. Encourage families to share information by asking open-ended questions. Demonstrate your interest in their replies both verbally and nonverbally (i.e., maintain eye contact and an open posture, use minimal encouragers such as head nods and "um-hums," ask relevant questions). When unclear regarding a family member's point of view, ask for clarification or for specific examples. Do not make assumptions based on limited or unclear information. Respond empathetically if and when families have difficulty expressing a thought or a feeling. Provide feedback to the families regarding their ideas and, most importantly, reward their contributions. Use summarization as a means of checking out the accuracy of your perceptions and to let the parents know that you are listening attentively and are interested in what they have to say.

Sharing information with families, a third component of the conference process, should be accomplished through the use of jargon-free language. Lavine (1986) noted that people's ability to attend to, organize, and understand information presented verbally can be negatively affected by the use of jargon. It is important, therefore, to take time to translate the information into language that everyone present understands. When sharing information, begin on a positive note, such as pointing out the child's strong points, before mentioning areas of deficit

---

TABLE 7-7 Suggestions for how to Build Rapport

- Know, understand, and accept yourself and the families you serve.
- Make contact with families early by sending positive messages, via the telephone or written notes about their students.
- Design the structure of the conference (location, time, participants, agenda items, etc.) with the needs of all persons in attendance in mind.
- Practice relaxation and visualization.
- Offer to take coats; have coffee or tea available.
- Allow time for getting acquainted by talking informally about topics that establish parents as individuals and stress the positive attributes of the family member with a disability.
- Introduce all conference participants and explain their roles.
- Thank parents for their interest and attendance. Let them know how much you value their contributions.
- Review the purpose of the meeting.
- Encourage parents to participate by asking questions and providing opportunities for them to express their opinions.
- Let parents know if you wish to take notes during the meeting. If you do so, take notes openly. Use carbon paper or offer to copy them for the family.

---

or concern. Provide specific examples either by telling anecdotes or by showing the family members examples of the child's work. Be aware of and responsive to the impact of what you are saying on the family. If they are frowning or appear puzzled, stop for a moment to provide an opportunity for questions or comments. As much as possible, encourage a give-and-take atmosphere in which all participants in the conference can interact and share information.

The last component of the conference involves *summarizing and follow-up activities.* In summarizing, you should review the high points of the meeting with special emphasis upon next-step activities. It is important at this point to restate who is responsible for carrying out next-step tasks and the date by which they are to be completed. Options for follow-up strategies should also be discussed and agreed upon. If another meeting is to be scheduled, use this time to decide on the time and place. End the meeting on a positive note. Be sure to thank the family for their interest and contributions and offer to be available should any relevant questions or issues arise.

POSTCONFERENCE. Several tasks need attention following the conference: (a) *reviewing the meeting with the student,* (b) *sharing the out-*

come of the meeting with other professionals, (c) *recording the conference proceedings*, and (d) *evaluating the conference.*

If the student did not attend the family-professional conference, it may be appropriate to *spend some time talking about the meeting with the student.* Explain the decisions that were made, and talk about how they will impact on the student's activities. Be sure to allow time for any questions the student may have, and be ready to respond to any concerns.

In addition to meeting with the student, it may also be appropriate to *share the outcome of the conference with other professionals* who are involved in the student's program. Reviewing the decisions made at the meeting, as well as any resulting changes in the student's program will help to ensure continuity and consistency. Such contacts can be made in person, over the telephone, or through a written report.

Recording conference proceedings is another important postconference task for family-professional accountability, particularly in the event of a due process hearing at some later date. Proceedings should be recorded as soon as possible following the meeting when the information is still fresh in your mind. The written proceedings should include the time of the meeting, the location, agenda topics, nature of interactions, and decisions made. Further, it is a good practice (a) to keep a permanent file of each of your meetings so that you can access them at some later date, (b) to mark your calendar for agreed upon follow-up dates, and (c) to list the tasks you agreed to complete as a result of the meeting.

A fourth important postconference activity is that of *evaluating the conference.* Ideally, both families and professionals should be given the opportunity to consider what went well during the conference and to make suggestions for improvements. Figure 7–1 provides a sample form that professionals may use in evaluating family-professional conferences. This form could easily be modified for families to use. Many other similar forms are available for other types of conferences, or you may wish to develop your own. Regardless of which procedure you select, we are confident that you will find conference evaluation a valuable process to help you identify ways to modify and improve future conferences.

Unplanned Conferences

Unplanned conferences with parents or other family members inevitably occur, and you need to be prepared for them. Preparation is particularly important because unplanned conferences can often serve as a forum for families to manifest their most intense thoughts and feelings (Simpson, 1982). Unplanned conferences can occur at any time and in any

---

FIGURE 7–1   Conference Evaluation Form

Date of Conference: Length of Conference:
Purpose of Conference:
Persons Attending Conference:

Please rate your satisfaction with your performance on each conference activity using the following scale:

1. Unsatisfied
2. Somewhat unsatisfied
3. Somewhat satisfied
4. Satisfied

PRECONFERENCE PREPARATION

1. Notifying Families

Conference informational meeting for families	1 2 3 4
Conference notice	1 2 3 4
Follow-up telephone call to confirm the conference time/date	1 2 3 4
Information packet sent to parents prior to conference	1 2 3 4

2. Preparing for the Conference

Review of cumulative records	1 2 3 4
Assessment of student progress and areas of concern	1 2 3 4
Examples of student work	1 2 3 4
Written conference materials (reports, data sheets)	1 2 3 4
Agenda outline	1 2 3 4
Consultations with other professionals	1 2 3 4
Plans for dealing with sensitive issues	1 2 3 4
Conference rehearsals	1 2 3 4
Relaxation strategies	1 2 3 4

3. Planning the Agenda

Planning and development	1 2 3 4
Length	1 2 3 4
Content	1 2 3 4
Flexibility	1 2 3 4

4. Arranging the Physical Environment

Location	1 2 3 4
Privacy	1 2 3 4

---

place. Parents may unexpectedly drop in at school before, during, and after school hours; you may receive telephone calls at home in the evenings and on weekends; and you may be approached by families with child-related concerns at such unlikely places as the beach, the theater, and the grocery store.

FIGURE 7–1   (Continued)

Comfort	1	2	3	4
Room arrangements	1	2	3	4
Availability of supplies (tissues, beverages, papers, pens)	1	2	3	4

CONFERENCE ACTIVITIES

1. Developing Rapport

Know, understand, and accept yourself	1	2	3	4
Know, understand, and accept the family	1	2	3	4
Make positive contacts with family prior to the meeting	1	2	3	4
Design conference structure to meet the needs of all involved	1	2	3	4
Include informal get-acquainted time	1	2	3	4
Introduce conference participants	1	2	3	4
Express appreciation of the family's role in the meeting	1	2	3	4

2. Obtaining Information from Families

Use of open-ended questions	1	2	3	4
Demonstrate interest in nonverbal ways	1	2	3	4
Demonstrate interest in verbal ways	1	2	3	4

3. Providing Information to Families

Use of positive statements	1	2	3	4
Use of jargon-free language	1	2	3	4
Use of specific examples to clarify meaning	1	2	3	4
Encouragement of a give-and-take atmosphere	1	2	3	4

4. Summarizing and Follow-Up

Review of high points to determine next steps	1	2	3	4
Restate responsibilities for next steps	1	2	3	4
End meeting on positive note	1	2	3	4

POSTCONFERENCE FOLLOW-UP

Review meeting with the student	1	2	3	4
Share conference outcome with other professionals	1	2	3	4
Record conference proceedings	1	2	3	4
Evaluate conference procedures	1	2	3	4

Although it is probably impossible to avoid being caught somewhat off-guard at such times, there are a number of things you can do to prepare for these encounters. The first step is deciding what is acceptable to you as a professional, given the other demands on your time and energy. It is often helpful to talk with other professionals regarding their strategies for handling such issues. You may decide, for example, that telephone calls at home on weeknights are acceptable, but that conferences at the beach are out of the question. Make a list of options that you consider to be: (a) open to consideration or (b) not open to consideration. Once this is done, set your priorities and seek support from the administration of the program. This support is important both for your own sense of security and in the event that future problems arise concerning these issues. In addition, some administrators wish to have this information on file to ensure consistency across programs.

Once priorities have been established and endorsed by the administration, it is important that you inform the parents of your preferences. Ideally, you should do this at the beginning of the year before any unplanned conferences have had a chance to occur. Preferences should be communicated both verbally and in written form to avoid misunderstanding and to allow the parents to ask questions. When communicating preferences, be sure to cover the following topics: First, explain your philosophy regarding unplanned meetings in noneducational settings accompanied by a rationale. A rationale for your unwillingness to engage in these conferences can be stated simply: "I want to be able to meet your needs and answer your questions as well and as completely as possible; however, I am not able to do so without sufficient preparation and access to your child's records." Second, specify the times and conditions under which you will and will not receive drop-in visits at school and telephone calls at school and/or home. Third, clarify any rules, guidelines and/or protocol regarding meetings during class time and/or classroom observation.

Drop-in meetings by parents during class time can be especially disruptive to professionals as well as to students in the program. To avoid potential disruptions, Simpson (1982) suggests adopting a policy that requires all visitors to the school or agency to check in at the central office. This requirement makes the administration responsible for deciding whether or not a conference is needed. Moreover, the administration can provide you with advance notice that the parent has arrived. When communicating preferences about unplanned meetings and contacts, be specific and use many examples to ensure that parents know what you mean. The better a parent understands your preferences, the greater the chance is that your preferences will be respected.

Having well-organized files, data sheets, permanent products of the student's work, schedules, graphs, and charts can make a difference between disastrous and successful unplanned conferences. In addition, often it is helpful to have community resource guides and names, addresses, and phone numbers of other agencies, families, and professionals who may be of assistance to families. Sometimes an on-the-spot referral to a school or community-based professional may be more appropriate and wise than attempting to assist a family with a problem that may be more adequately addressed by other professionals.

**TABLE 7–8   Suggestions for how to Prepare
for Unplanned Conferences**

- Decide what options are acceptable to you.
- Seek support from your program administrator.
- Inform families verbally and in writing of your preferences.
- Share with families the reasons for your preferences.
- Specify time and conditions for:
  telephone calls
  informal meetings
  formal meetings
  observations
- Keep well-organized files of student work, charts, data sheets, etc.
- Maintain a directory of available community resources.
- Practice and use positive communication skills.

Last, but not least, is the importance of good communication skills for unplanned conferences. Without good communication skills even the best prepared professionals can fail in their attempts to meet the needs of families. Table 7–8 summarizes some strategies for managing unplanned conferences.

NONCONFERENCE STRATEGIES FOR COMMUNICATION

Most parents appreciate receiving information regularly about their child's activities and progress at school. Likewise, most professionals appreciate information and feedback from the home. Since weekly conferences are time-consuming and impractical, it is necessary to develop alternative strategies for keeping open the lines of communication between families and professionals. Many different nonconference strategies for communication may be used, but generally they can be divided into two categories: written messages and telephone contacts. Since some parents may not read and other families may not have a telephone, it is necessary to adapt communication strategies to fit the specific needs and desires of the families in your program.

Written Strategies for Communication

Of the many different written strategies for communication, we will present six: (a) handbooks, (b) handouts for specific situations,

(c) newsletters, (d) letters, notes, and log books, (e) progress reports, and (f) occasional messages.

HANDBOOKS.   Most programs have developed handbooks for families that outline general administrative policy and procedures. However, such handbooks typically do not include information about the various educational options available within the program. For this reason, it is often helpful to develop a handbook containing information specific to your program activities that accompanies, and does not duplicate, the general program handbook. Kroth (1985) emphasizes that such a handbook should be concise, attractive, and written in simple and understandable language. If your program serves children and youth who speak English as a second language, consider having the handbook printed in other languages. Translation services are becoming increasingly available, and sometimes bilingual parents may assist in producing the handbook in different languages.

Many different kinds of information can go into a handbook. For example: personnel, classroom procedures, classroom supplies needed by students, transportation, lunch or snack information, methods of reporting progress and sharing information, and any additional topics that are unique to your program.

HANDOUTS.   A second written strategy for communication is the use of handouts for specific situations (Kroth, 1985). Handouts can pertain to a variety of subjects, including resources in the community; safety and travel tips; tips for preparing a child for trips to the dentist and eye doctor; a list of restaurants, shops, movie theaters, and museums that are accessible to wheelchairs; places to go on field trips; and summer enrichment programs and activities for rainy days. Be creative when selecting or compiling handouts for families. Individualize them by placing stars next to items that are particularly pertinent to specific families or family members. While the collection and compilation of handouts may require some time and effort on your part, such time and effort will undoubtedly be noticed and appreciated by many of the families with whom you work. Often the small, thoughtful gestures indicate to parents that you care and have their best interests in mind.

NEWSLETTERS.   Probably one of the most enjoyable and useful ways to encourage family-professional communication and to provide information and support to families is to create and disseminate a newsletter. The results of a survey of single-parent families conducted by Nelson (1986) indicated that the newsletter *Solo Parenting* was an effective way to meet their needs for information and emotional support. Newsletters can be developed by an individual teacher and class, an entire grade, or an entire school. A variety of information and formats can be included in newsletters, such as drawings, quotes, and essays written by the students; comic strips; announcements of upcoming special events; children's birth dates; a parent column; horoscopes; updates on ongoing school projects; and an advice column. If family members are interested, recruit them to help with the editing, translating if necessary, and development of the newsletter. This often is a good way to give parents the message that their input is valued and needed. Figure 7–2 includes a sample newsletter developed by Lois Orth-Lopes for the Assessment-Learning Classroom at the Edna A. Hill Child Development Laboratory Preschool at The University of Kansas.

Newsletters can also be created by family members, containing such information as tips for other families, stress-reduction techniques, descriptions of adaptive devices, advertisements for toy swaps, methods of managing child behaviors, announcements of workshops and seminars, and an opportunity to brag.

LETTERS, NOTES, AND LOG BOOKS.   Letters, notes, and log books are other options for ongoing communication with families. These methods are particularly good vehicles for exchanging information and strengthening relationships. Some professionals and families prefer log books over notes and letters since the latter are sometimes difficult to locate and hence may be more easily lost or misplaced. In addition, log books offer a record of communication over time that some families like to keep at the end of the year. It is a good idea to involve families in deciding how frequently to write, who will write, and what kinds of information to be exchanged. Encourage all family members to write notes if they are so inclined.

Examples of topics appropriate for sharing through notes and log books include information regarding details of routine care (e.g., eating and toileting habits), special accomplishments, and special activities. As much as possible, strive to communicate positive information about the student while attempting to keep negative comments to a minimum. When necessary, negative comments are best relayed in person, where there is an opportunity for the parents to ask questions and seek clarification. Likewise, sensitive, confidential, or controversial information is best reserved for private, face-to-face conferences. A sample of log book entries appears in Figure 7–3.

A mother's reaction to a log book she used indicates the potential value of this approach.

> When I reached in Tony's backpack to get the log book, I looked forward to what I would find. His teacher told us the highlights of the day, and there was always something there that let us know—"She really is proud of Tony." It may sound strange, but I always thought of the log book as my friend. The log book provided confidence for the present and hope for the future.

FIGURE 7–2   Sample Newsletter.

Young Jayhawks

Volume 5, Number 6   Lois Orth-Lopes, Editor

ACTIVITIES FOR THE WEEK

We have planned large group activities that will help the children to get to know each other, including the songs, Who I Am and Friends. We will also learn a new song, Sky Bears, and play the bells as we sing.

SHARING TIME ON TUESDAY

Last week, Ryan, Tanya, and Leilani put their sharing things in paper bags and gave clues to the other children. Everybody had a great time guessing. Ryan brought in a photograph of his twin aunts. Tanya shared an animal that she calls Foozy. Leilani showed the children a book that plays music.

This week, Michael, Muhammad, Chad, Annie, and Elizabeth will have a chance to share. Remember to send the sharing item in a paper bag so that the other children can guess what is in the bag.

ARTIST CORNER

The drawing for this week is by Mark. He used felt-tipped markers to make this bear. The original work is on the wall outside our classroom.

THE ZIPPER BEARS

The children have been learning how to zip their coats without any help from their teachers or friends. When they are successful for four days, a zipper bear is hung beside their name on the art wall. Many of the children have been working very hard and will have a zipper bear by their name soon.

In Manuel's daily battle with his zipper on his coat, October 16, 1988, Manuel won! His zipper bear proudly hangs on the wall.

PARENTS NIGHT A SUCCESS

We were very pleased to have so many parents, brothers, sisters, and grandparents come to Parents Night last Tuesday. It was a nice opportunity for us to get to know you better even though the time was short.

If you were not able to come, or even if you were there and have questions or concerns, please feel free to call. Our number at the office is 864-3831. If it is more convient, you can call Lois at home (842-7137).

SNACK MENU

Our cook, Yvonne, prepares a nice variety of snacks for the children each week. The menu for this week is:
Monday: chex mix, orange juice
Tuesday: fresh fruit, graham crackers, water
Wednesday: muffins, apple juice
Thursday: mixed vegetables, crackers, water
Friday: crackers with peanut butter, lemonade

Note. From *Young Jayhawks* by L. Orth-Lopes (Ed.), 1988, Assessment Learning Classroom, Edna A. Hill Child Development Laboratory Preschool, Dept. of Human Development, The University of Kansas. Reprinted by permission.

FIGURE 7–3 Sample Log Book

Date	Name	Event
3/26	Marsha (teacher)	Mia was so happy with herself today at snack time. As the snack helper, she poured juice for all the children and didn't spill a drop! She kept saying to all who would listen, "Did it, did it." See if she will show you tonight.
3/27	Angela (mother)	Yes, Mia did show us her new trick, and you are right. She was so proud. Thanks for suggesting that a small pitcher with just a little water might make pouring easier for her. Now she wants to move on to watering the plants with the big pitcher.
3/28	Marsha (teacher)	How about letting her practice with a big pitcher in your sandbox?

PROGRESS REPORTS.   Progress reports are a more traditional means of providing families with feedback about how their child is doing at school. These reports can be complex or simple, and can be sent home once a day, once a week, or once every few weeks. Information may be communicated about a single subject or area of development, or about many. A sample of a progress report is included in Figure 7–4.

OCCASIONAL MESSAGES.   Finally, professionals may wish to use occasional messages to inform parents specifically about positive aspects of their child's performance. These messages can take many forms including mini-diplomas, certificates of recognition, sticker cards, and mock telegrams. Hochman (1979) recommends sending "happy grams" home to parents and many school supply companies sell "happy grams" for this purpose. An example of an occasional message format is provided in Figure 7–5.

FIGURE 7–4 Sample Daily Progress Report

ABOUT MY DAY

Name: _____   Date: _____

I did really well today on:

I still am working hard on:

Parent Signature _____   Teacher Signature _____

FIGURE 7–5   Sample Occasional Message

JUST FOR PARENTS

Date _____
Time _____

PURPOSE _____
_____
_____
_____
_____

Occasional notes may be used to identify special events that parents need to know about, to notify parents of special meetings that will be occurring, or to thank parents for support or feedback.

The Telephone

The telephone can be a convenient and effective tool for communicating with families and thereby provide information and emotional support. Occasional telephone calls to families may even result in improved student performance. Heward and Chapman (1981) noted that the use of recorded telephone messages increased parent-teacher communication and improved students' spelling performances. Likewise, Fuller, Vandiviere, and Kronberg (1987) found that a call-in telephone service ("talkline") that provided developmental guidance and referral and general information to parents was valued by the users and used with increasing frequency during the 8-month study period.

As a general rule, telephone conversations with parents should be brief and to the point. Longer, more involved conversations are more effectively conducted in person. It is a good idea to make prior arrangements for the times at which you will call in order to avoid disrupting the parents' schedule. Be sure to inquire whether a parent wishes to receive telephone calls at work. Conversing over the telephone poses some disadvantages, such as not being able to see the parents' nonverbal reactions and messages. For this reason, it is particularly necessary to listen carefully and to check out perceptions by asking questions and summarizing. Table 7–9 contains suggestions for use of the telephone as recommended by the Parent Center of the Albuquerque, NM, Public Schools (1985).

Heward and Orlansky (1984) suggest using the telephone to organize a telephone tree. A telephone tree is an efficient way to get infor-

---

TABLE 7–9 Suggestions for Use of the Telephone

- Treat every message (incoming or outgoing) as an important call.
- Always identify yourself as you place a call or answer one.
- Personalize your conversation at every opportunity by using the caller's name.
- Don't use the telephone for criticism. Criticism is tricky enough even in an eye-to-eye encounter. When the parent must depend completely on your voice, criticism is doubly difficult.
- Be sure to ask the parent if you have called at a convenient time. If not, ask him to name a time when he'll be free to talk.
- Jot down in advance what you want to find out from the parent and what you want to tell the parent.
- When taking down information, briefly double-check your notes.
- If it is necessary to leave the line during a call, explain the reason and excuse yourself. When you return, thank the caller for waiting. (On long-distance calls, make every effort to avoid putting a parent on "hold.")
- Always offer the caller or person being called your help or assistance.
- Allow time for the parent to ask you their questions.
- Return all calls promptly; the exception, of course, is if you are involved in the classroom with students.
- Give definite information and offer positive information.
- Avoid the use of vague statements that may force the caller to dig for information. Vague statements are irritating and waste time.
- As the conversation ends, thank the caller before you say good-bye.

Note. From The Parent Center of the Albuquerque, NM, Public Schools, 1985. Adapted by permission.

mation to several people with little effort. Using the telephone tree, the professional phones 1–2 parents with a message; those two parents, in turn, each call two or more parents and so on until all parents have been contacted. This system has the additional advantage of providing parents with opportunities to get involved and interact with one another.

A third way to use the telephone as a communication tool is to record daily messages on an automatic answering machine that parents can access. In the Heward and Chapman (1981) study, the teacher of a primary class for students with learning disabilities recorded messages such as the following on an answering machine:

> Good evening. The children worked very hard today. We are discussing transportation. They enjoyed talking about the airport and all the different kinds of airplanes. The spelling words for tomorrow are: train, t–r–a–i–n;

plane, p–l–a–n–e; truck, t–r–u–c–k; automobile, a–u–t–o–m–o–
b–i–l–e; and ship, s–h–i–p. Thank you for calling. (Heward & Chapman,
1981, p.13)

During the 6-week program, the teacher received an average of 18.7
calls per week, compared with an average of 0.16 calls per week prior
to intervention. In addition, scores on daily spelling tests improved for
all students. Prior to the study spelling lists were sent home each day
with a request for parents to assist their children in studying without
similar results.

SUMMARY

The importance of effective communication between families and professionals cannot be emphasized strongly enough. Good intentions and
fond feelings are necessary elements for good communication, but they
are not enough. To establish and maintain productive and meaningful
partnerships with families, you must acquire and use communication
skills as well as a variety of strategies for communicating. In Chapters 6
and 7 we have provided information about communication skills and
strategies that have proven both valuable and effective. We encourage
you to strive to master these skills for the benefit of the students and
families with whom you work as well as for yourself. In the next chapter, we discuss special education law and its implications for family-
professional interactions.

THE LAW OF SPECIAL EDUCATION: THE EDUCATION OF THE HANDICAPPED ACT

Ryan enjoys working as a library assistant in his high-school library. Integration is one outcome of special education legislation.

It is the year 1973, and a mother and father come to the office of a school superintendent in Anytown, USA. With them is their son Kevin. He has multiple disabilities, including profound mental retardation, head-banging, need for gastronasal tube feeding, and need for kidney dialysis on a daily basis. They ask, "May Kevin attend school? He's now 7 years old, and our other children began their education at that age." The answer, "No, we don't have programs for children like your son."

It is now 1989, and a different set of family members come to the office of the same school superintendent. With them is their daughter, Becky. She has multiple disabilities, too, including severe mental retardation, poor language, and poor motor skills. They ask, "May Becky attend school? She's now 3 years old, and we understand you have a preschool program for students with disabilities." The answer, "Yes, we have a good and long-standing program for Becky and children like her."

What's the difference? It is not the superintendent; she's the same in 1989 as in 1973. It is not the children; both have serious disabilities and clearly need intensive special education and related services. It therefore must be the passage of time and what has happened during the 16-year interval. What did happen? What happened was simple: Congress passed laws that made it possible for Becky to do what Kevin could not do—attend public schools.

In this chapter, we will explain those laws. After reading it, you should be able to answer the following questions:

- What is the Education of the Handicapped Act?
- Which students does it benefit?
- What are the six major principles of the Education of the Handicapped Act?
- In what ways do the education rights of students who are between 3 and 21 years old differ from those of infants and toddlers (from birth through 2 years old)?
- What are the rights of parents and other family members in regard to the education of their sons and daughters with disabilities?
- What are the rights and duties of schools and professionals under the Education of the Handicapped Act?
- How should you conduct yourself with parents and other family members in order to carry out your rights and duties under the Education of the Handicapped Act?

We have emphasized the history of family-professional relationships, described the family as a system, and discussed important skills and strategies for communicating with families. We are now going to introduce another system that affects family-professional relationships, a legal system established by federal laws regulating the education of students with disabilities. Those laws so dominate professional practice in all states that they deserve full attention. This chapter will discuss the reasons for the laws, early responses to educational discrimination, and the six principles of the federal laws.

The major federal special education law is the Education of the Handicapped Act (EHA). That law has been amended many times, the most important amendments being passed in 1975 and 1986. The 1975 amendments, called The Education of All Handicapped Children Act, P.L. 94–142, created the basic structure of today's law and the six principles that we will discuss later in this chapter. The 1986 amendments added new provisions for infants and toddlers, for children from 3 through 5 years of age, for youth in transition from school to adult life, and for enforcement of the EHA. We will point out the special impact of the 1986 amendments when we discuss the EHA as amended in 1975.

Other laws affect the education of students with disabilities. The most important of these is the federal antidiscrimination statute, Sec. 504, which is part of the Rehabilitation Act. Generally, Sec. 504 prohibits any state or local agency that receives federal financial assistance from discriminating against any "otherwise qualified" person with a disability, solely on the basis of the person's disability. Since the EHA covers almost all issues involving families, professionals, and students with disabilities, and Sec. 504 basically follows the EHA, we will not discuss Sec. 504 in this chapter. Under the EHA, Part B (ages 3 through 21), parents are authorized to be involved in their children's education. Although parents may share with other family members their responsibilities for their children's education, they may not delegate their rights to others. Schools will recognize only parental rights, the duly authorized agents of parents (e.g., their privately hired psychologists or lawyers), or individuals who are the legal equivalents of parents (e.g., adopting parents or permanent foster parents). Thus, we refer in this chapter to *parents,* but recommend that you consider, in your work, not only the legal parents but also those individuals who act as parents and who support parents.

The 1986 amendments (Part H, Infants and Toddlers) extended rights to family members, not just to parents. If you are working with infants and toddlers (birth through 2), you will be dealing with, and recognizing the rights of family members. We will point out these distinctions throughout this chapter.

These federal special education and nondiscrimination laws do not affect the education of children who are gifted and talented, unless those students also have a disability. Some states, however, include children who are gifted and talented under their special education laws. In many instances the way states define "gifted and talented" and the rights to which these students are entitled (e.g., an individualized education plan or due process) varies from year to year. Also, state and local laws often supplement federal laws and regulate the education of all children. You will need to know whether your state law covers gifted and talented students. As you read this chapter, remember that federal laws apply only to students with disabilities.

REASONS FOR THE FEDERAL LAWS

There are four major reasons why Congress decided it is appropriate for the federal government to play a role in the education of children and youth with disabilities.

First, for many years and in many ways schools had excluded students with disabilities from any form of education. These were practices of "pure exclusion," such as excluding from school any child who could not walk, was not toilet trained, had behavior problems, or was deemed unable to profit from the educational program offered. Indeed, when Congress enacted the Education for All Handicapped Children Act (P.L. 94–142) in 1975, it found that one million children and youth with disabilities were receiving no education at all.

Second, Congress found that nearly half of the nation's children and youth with disabilities were not receiving an appropriate education. The denial of an appropriate education is "functional exclusion"—that is, the child is included in a school program in name only and is not truly benefiting from it and is, therefore, excluded from the "function" of the program (H. R. Turnbull, 1990).

Third, schools were using psychological or intelligence tests incorrectly and with inappropriate results. For example, a child who speaks only Spanish might be given a test in English; a child with a learning disability might be required to take a test in the same way and within the same time limits as children who have no disabilities; poor black children might be asked questions that are appropriate only for white middle-class children; or a teenager with cerebral palsy might be asked to write answers to a test although she has so little manual dexterity that she cannot hold a pencil. In these and similar circumstances, the test could not measure the student's abilities or disabilities. The results, therefore, were not educationally reliable.

Fourth, the education of children and youth with disabilities and the provision of services to their families makes good sense in terms of other federal policies and for the nation as a whole. Ever since Congress enacted the Rehabilitation Act after World War I to help veterans with a disability get back into the job market, the federal policy regarding people with disabilities has been, in large part, to enact laws and help states conduct programs that help people with disabilities be more independent, productive, and integrated into society. With the exception of some laws that are counterproductive to this general policy (such as laws that support mental retardation residential centers instead of putting money into community programs), special education law, in general, seeks to provide an appropriate education so that children will grow into adults who can be more independent, productive, and integrated.

It may be difficult to understand the reasons for educational discrimination against children with disabilities, hence a brief explanation. Historically, schools discriminated against children with disabilities for many reasons (Children's Defense Fund, 1974; Milofsky, 1974; H. R. Turnbull, 1990). For example, the cost of educating children with disabilities was (and still is) higher than the cost of educating other children, and the governments that funded schools were unwilling to spend the extra money. Also, children with disabilities had relatively little political power in legislatures or in school systems. A third reason is that many educators did not believe that children with disabilities could learn well or fast enough to be educated. Finally, children and youth with disabilities were not regarded as important enough to educate as a matter of public policy. As Blatt, Biklen, and Bogdan (1977), Gliedman and Roth (1980), Sarason and Doris (1979), and H. R. Turnbull and Wheat (1983) all argue, the very fact that a child was mentally disabled was sufficient reason to practice all sorts of discrimination. Indeed, Elizabeth Boggs (1985a), Janet Bennett (1985), and Frank Warren (1985) illustrate how pervasive a form discrimination may take. Elizabeth Boggs (1985b) describes the situation of "pure" exclusion in New Jersey in 1950 as she speaks about the special education provided by a local Association for Retarded Citizens:

> The charter members of the Essex (County, N.J.) Unit were a remarkably foresighted lot. By the time (my husband) Fitzhugh and I came on board late in 1949, they had organized an interdisciplinary diagnostic clinic, to which a hardy band of professionals were contributing their time. The initial applicants were accepted by age groups so that the needs of a group could be identified for service planning. Soon there were enough six- to nine-year-olds identified as trainable to justify organizing some classes.
>
> These children had been denied admission to local schools. However, we had a social mission in mind, so we, too, had some eligibility criteria. The children had to be toilet-trained and able to understand simple commands. Our mission was to persuade the county superintendent of schools, and through him the local superintendents, that such children could respond to skillful teaching in a classroom setting and should be accommodated in public schools. (pp. 45–46)

EARLY RESPONSES TO EDUCATIONAL DISCRIMINATION

Early in the 1970s children with disabilities were faced with such widespread discrimination in education that their advocates decided on a new approach. Led by the Pennsylvania Association for Retarded Children (here, parents were in the role of advocates—see Chapter 1), they sued school officials, claiming that children with disabilities have a legal right to an appropriate education under the federal constitution.

One basis of their claim was very simple. Because the states have chosen to educate children who do not have a disability and even to educate some (but not all) children who have a disability, schools violate the equal-protection clause of the Fourteenth Amendment to the United States Constitution when they fail to educate all children with disabilities. The equal-protection clause says that no state shall deny the equal protection of its laws to any citizen. The courts generally agreed with these advocates. They held that there is a violation of equal protection when children who are not disabled are given an education, or when some children who are disabled are given an education, but other disabled children are not; that is, some children (the excluded children) are treated less equally than the included children (*Pennsylvania Association for Retarded Children v. Commonwealth*, 1972; *Mills v. D.C. Board of Education, 1972*).

A second basis for their claim was also quite simple. The Fourteenth Amendment prohibits states from depriving a person of due process (courts had come to interpret due process as an opportunity for a fair hearing before a right or privilege is taken away). Because the denial of an education adversely affects the child, the schools violate the due process clause of the Fourteenth Amendment when they deny the child an education without giving a reason for that action or granting the child's advocates an opportunity to protest the denial (*Lebanks v. Spears*, 1973; *Maryland Association for Retarded Children v. Maryland*, 1974).

The courts quickly ordered important remedies. They generally required school systems to (a) identify all school-aged children and youth with disabilities; (b) give them nondiscriminatory tests; (c) provide them with an appropriate education; (d) educate them with students not having disabilities to the greatest extent beneficial for the children with disabilities; (e) notify parents of proposed changes in educational classification, programming, or placement; and (f) give parents opportunities to consent to or protest against schools' decisions (H. R. Turnbull, 1990; Weintraub, Abeson, Ballard, & LaVor, 1976).

As H. R. Turnbull (1990) and Weintraub et al. (1976) have demonstrated, even before these legal victories Congress had been sensitive to the problems of special education. In 1966 it enacted P.L. 89–750, Education of the Handicapped Act. This law provided federal grants to help states initiate, expand, and improve special education. A later law, P.L. 91–230, Elementary, Secondary, and Other Educational Amendments of 1969, had a similar purpose—namely, to stimulate the states to develop special education programs.

In 1973, Congress enacted Section 504 of the Vocational Rehabilitation Act. Section 504 is a civil rights act for people with disabilities which prohibits any recipient of federal funds, including schools, from discriminating against people solely on the basis of their disability. For example, discrimination solely on the basis of disability occurs when a school bans a student with a learning disability from competing for a place on an athletic team; the disability does not make the student unathletic, and the ban cannot be justified on the basis of protecting the student from injury.

By 1974, however, Congress had become so dissatisfied with the states' efforts, and so aware of the major victories that advocates for children and youth with disabilities had won in the courts, that it realized the need for more significant laws. In that year, therefore, it substantially increased federal aid to the states, requiring them to adopt a goal of providing full educational opportunities to all children with disabilities as a condition of receiving the federal funds (P.L. 93–380, Education Amendments of 1974).

In 1975, Congress acted with such finality that the education of children with disabilities and the schools of the nation were forever changed. It enacted P.L. 94–142, Education of All Handicapped Children Act. Not all of the legal requirements of federal special education law are contained in these laws, since Congress could not write laws with such specificity; however, the Department of Education has implemented it with specificity by promulgating regulations that are published in the *Code of Federal Regulations* (1984). P.L. 94–142 was an amendment to Education of the Handicapped Act (the original 1966 law). Many refer to P.L. 94–142 as though it were the only federal law. It is not, and, to be accurate, we refer in this book to the federal law as the "EHA"—the Education of the Handicapped Act, as amended (20 U.S.C. Secs. 1401–1461), and as implemented by U.S. Department of Education regulations (34 CFR Part 300, Subpart A).

THE EHA: PART B AND PART H COMPARED

The EHA generally provides benefits for students who have a disability and need special education and related services. It does so by creating two sets of rights, according to the age of the students. One set is under Part B. The other is under Part H.

Part B of EHA provides for the education of children and youth from age 3 through age 21 or until the student leaves school or graduates before age 21. (Students who are 3 through 5 years old are, in 1989, provided education in a state's discretion. By 1991, however, they must be educated; states no longer will have discretion to exclude them. Thus, we include them in the *age* group of students, 6–21, whom the states must educate.)

By contrast, Part H (enacted in 1986) provides for the education of infants and toddlers, from birth through 2 years of age. Moreover, Part B and Part H create separate and different sets of rights.

Part B

Under Part B, children and youth with disabilities are those who, because of a disability, require special education and related services. The disabilities that may cause such a need are mental retardation, hearing impairment, speech impairment, visual disability, serious emotional disturbance, orthopedic impairment, other health problems, and specific learning disabilities.

Part B defines *special education* as specially designed instruction that meets the student's unique needs, including classroom instruction, physical education, home instruction, and instruction in hospitals and institutions. The law defines *related services* as those designed services that may be required (they must be stipulated in the student's individualized education program) to assist the student to benefit from special education. Designated services are transportation, early identification and assessment of disabling conditions, and when required, speech pathology, audiology, psychological services, physical and occupational therapy, recreation, parent counseling and parent training, and medical services (medical services may be only for the purpose of diagnosis and evaluation).

Part H

Special provisions apply to children from birth to 3 years. Under Part H (created by P.L. 99–457 and implemented by regulations adopted on June 22, 1989, published as Vol. 34, Part 303, *Code of Federal Regulations*), infants and toddlers have special rights.

Those infants and toddlers who qualify for the services must need early intervention because they either (a) experience developmental delays or (b) have diagnosed physical or mental conditions that have a high probability of causing developmental delays. In addition, each state has the option of serving infants and toddlers who are "at risk" for developmental delays. Developmental delays must fall in the following areas of development: cognitive, physical, language and speech, psychosocial, or self-help. Although the states may otherwise define "developmental delay," they must include delays in those areas of development.

Under Part H, *early intervention services* are those that (a) are designed to meet the infant's needs in one or more of certain areas of development (physical, cognitive, language and speech, psychosocial, and self-help); (b) comply with state standards; (c) include at least 10 different types of intervention; and (d) are provided by qualified personnel. Also, early intervention services are those designed to meet the family's needs related to enhancing the child's development in the stated areas, are selected in collaboration with the parents, are provided under public supervision by qualified personnel, are provided in conformity with an individual family service plan (IFSP), and are free unless the state establishes a sliding fee scale of payment.

The 10 different types of intervention include family training, counseling, and home visits; special instruction; speech pathology and audiology; occupational therapy; physical therapy; psychological services; case management services; medical services only for diagnosis and evaluation; early identification, screening, and assessment services; and health services necessary to help the infant or toddler benefit from the other intervention services.

The regulations make it clear that professionals have new or expanded roles and responsibilities with respect to families. Specifically, they are expected to consult and train parents, participate in assessment of a family and development of the IFSP, provide case-management services, make available psychological and social work services, and offer special instruction to the child and information to the parents about special instruction. The regulations also point out that the list of services is not exhaustive; other services, such as respite and other family support services, may be provided. In addition, parent-to-parent support personnel may provide those services, not just professionals or paraprofessionals. Finally, services to families also may include family training, counseling, and home visits. In short, the regulations not only expand what professionals must offer, but also who may offer it.

The personnel authorized to provide these services include those who have qualified as special educators, speech-language pathologists, audiologists, occupational therapists, physicians, physical therapists, psychologists, social workers, nurses, and nutritionists.

States that have not yet mandated early intervention or preschool special education as a matter of their own laws have the option of participating in Part H (infants and toddlers, ages birth through 2) and in the early childhood programs for children from ages 3 through 5. As of March, 1989, each state had elected the option of participating in Part H.

It is important to contrast the broad eligibility provisions of Part H with Part B (ages 3–21). Under Part H, those infants or toddlers who have or may experience developmental delays or are at risk for such delays are entitled to receive services. Each state may determine which children are "at risk." The federal law does not define those children.

But, under Part B, only those children and youth who have disabilities that cause a need for special education are entitled to the law's benefits. This means, for example, that a student who has AIDS but who experiences no adverse effect in education because of the disability is not entitled to the EHA. Very few students fall into this category.

PART B'S SIX PRINCIPLES AND THEIR RELEVANCE TO PART H

The EHA established new ground rules for schools, parents, and students with disabilities. H. R. Turnbull (1990) refers to these rules as the six principles of special education law:

1. *Zero-reject:* Schools must educate all students with disabilities and may not exclude any school-aged student with a disability solely because the student has a disability.

2. *Nondiscriminatory evaluation:* Schools must test and classify students fairly, essentially by administering nonbiased tests in ways that do not put students at a disadvantage, but allow them to display their educational abilities and disabilities.

3. *Appropriate, individualized education:* Schools must provide each student with an individually tailored education.

4. *Least restrictive educational placement:* Schools must educate students who have disabilities with their peers who do not have disabilities to the greatest extent consistent with their educational and social needs.

5. *Procedural due process:* Schools must provide opportunities for students' parents to consent or object to their children's educational identification, classification, program, or placement.

6. *Parent participation:* Parents of children with disabilities may participate in various ways in their child's education.

Because Part H does not provide infants and toddlers and their families with the same rights provided by Part B to children and youth and their parents, the six principles of Part B do not apply fully to Part H. We will point out the differences and similarities in the remainder of this chapter. We will describe these six principles and their implications for professional-family relationships later in this chapter and in Chapters 9, 10, and 11. For now, note that the six principles essentially require professionals to act professionally and schools to follow a course of conduct that is both logical and helpful. They must enroll the student, evaluate fairly, provide a beneficial education, integrate to the maximum extent appropriate, follow fair procedures, and allow parent participation.

Zero-Reject

The zero-reject principle of Part B requires schools to provide a free education to *all* school-aged children and youth with disabilities. It prohibits schools from excluding any such child solely because the child has a disability. Thus, Kevin (the young boy in the introduction to this chapter) has the same rights as Becky (whom we also met in the introduction). He may not be excluded.

The zero-reject principle rests on the proposition, first announced in *Pennsylvania Association for Retarded Children v. Commonwealth* (1972), that all children with disabilities can learn, and that state and local educational agencies, therefore, have no right to exclude any of them from school. Consequently, Kevin will not be turned away today, as he once was.

The zero-reject rule means that no child may be denied education if the child meets the age and need standards as explained above. State and local school systems ultimately must bear the entire cost of the education, even if the child is enrolled in programs operated by other state or local agencies or is placed in a private school at the request of the schools. As a general rule, courts have been willing to rule that every child with a disability is entitled to the benefits of the EHA. But there are some present and possible exceptions to the rule of zero-reject.

The first exception concerns the "educability" issue. Despite previous court decisions, some school authorities have argued that some children are not educable (i.e., they cannot and never have benefited from any educational intervention, no matter how good the intervention). In one case, *Timothy W. v. Rochester School District* (1988), the schools were temporarily successful and persuaded a trial court to rule that they did not have an obligation under the EHA to provide any program for the student. The decision was reversed on appeal, the appeal court holding that neither the law nor the facts about the child justified exclusion and a violation of the zero-reject role. The case may foreshadow other similar attempts to exclude some children.

School authorities also have challenged the zero-reject rule in another way. They have argued that some children and youth with disabilities are disruptive and should be excluded from school, and that the zero-reject rule does not prohibit the schools from suspending or expelling them. The courts (*Honig v. Doe*, 1988) have ruled that school authorities may suspend or expel a student who has a disability only when the student's behavior is not caused by a disability. Thus, if the child's disability caused the behavior that leads to threatened suspension or expulsion, the student is protected by Part B and may not be expelled. But his educational placement may be changed.

Similarly, school authorities have persuaded courts that even though a student may have a disability (such as AIDS), the schools do not have to provide special education under the EHA if the student's disability does not cause a need for special education. Thus, to be eligible, the student not only must have a disability, but also need special education on account of the disability (*Board v. Cooperman,* 1987; *District 27 v. Board,* 1986; and *Parents of Child v. Coker,* 1987).

Finally, courts also have allowed state and local schools to administer minimum-competency tests (i.e., examinations that measure acquired learning) to children and youth as long as the school allows accommodations in the way the tests are administered and provides adequate notice of the tests so the students can prepare for them. If students fail the tests, the schools may withhold graduation diplomas (*Brookhart v. Illinois St. Bd. of Education,* 1982; *Board of Education v. Ambach,* 1982).

These provisions offer professionals many ways to work with parents. For example, they may help parents enroll children for school, obtain services for preschool children, plan for the transition of their children from school to adult services, work with their children on school discipline, plan for appropriate extracurricular or athletic activities, and work with students who are given competency tests. The key is this: Parents now may assume their child will be educated at public expense and appropriately, and professionals now must respond to the child's legal rights to be educated appropriately.

COVERAGE.   *All* children and youth are entitled to a free appropriate public education, no matter where they are educated. Thus, a child who is in a hospital because of a long illness, or confined to home because of a chronic illness, is entitled to an education. Likewise, children in state institutions for people with emotional disorders, mental retardation, blindness, or deafness are entitled to an education. Similarly, children placed in private schools by public schools are entitled to an education. In addition, students for whom no special education program exists locally have the right to attend an appropriate program elsewhere, such as at a private school, a state school or institution, or a regional cooperative school. In short, the place where the student happens to be—whether hospital, home, institution, or private school—does not affect the student's rights to education under the EHA.

CHILD CENSUS.   School systems, working in cooperation with health, social service, and other child-service agencies, must identify all school-aged children and youth in their jurisdictions. In addition, they must plan for the education of those students and allow them to enroll when they are age eligible.

SERVICE PRIORITIES.   State and local school systems are required to spend their federal funds on two types of children and youth (the so-called "service-priority" children). First, they must provide funding for any age-eligible student who is not receiving a free, appropriate education. Second, they must provide funds for these children who have the most severe disabilities within each category of disability.

Professionals may work with parents of unenrolled children to ensure these children are included, and with parents of all children, particularly those with severe disabilities, to obtain appropriate services. Professionals must bear in mind that (as a legal matter) they do not thereby impair the claims of other students, because the state and local agencies must provide for those students even if it means using nonfederal funds (as it usually does).

SINGLE-AGENCY RESPONSIBILITY.   The state educational agency (SEA) is ultimately responsible for the education of all children and youth with disabilities. It usually does not operate programs itself, although in some states the SEA is the "local school board" for state schools for students who are deaf or blind. LEAs (local educational agency) directly operate special education programs and are responsible in the first instance for providing for each eligible student.

Sometimes, parents have been unable to enforce their child's right at a local level, usually because of local school resistance or inability. In such situations, the SEA is responsible for educating all eligible children and youth. It does this by "direct services" to the students (*Honig v. Doe*, 1988).

Parents and professionals may work together with the knowledge that, ultimately, the SEA is responsible for making the student's education appropriate. Thus, they may look to the SEA to give advice, help monitor LEAs, provide assistance and information to professionals and parents, render other technical assistance, coordinate the providers of related services, enforce compliance with federal and state law, and generally be both helper and watchdog for LEAs and professionals.

PERSONNEL DEVELOPMENT.   The SEA and the LEAs are required to develop and implement personnel development programs, particularly inservice training of professionals and parents (the program referred to as the Comprehensive System for Personnel Development).

PART H.   The zero-reject rule has a somewhat different meaning for infants and toddlers. It is not until the fifth year of a state's participation in Part H that it must have in place a program to serve all age-eligible, disability-eligible infants and toddlers. Since all states have chosen to participate in Part H (as of March, 1989), 1991 is the target year for full compliance. This means that during the first four years of a state's participation, some eligible infants and toddlers may not receive any direct services. (Each state may drop out of Part H after a planning, start-up period. This means that some states may later decide not to serve infants/toddlers.)

Moreover, although Part B provides for services free of charge to parents, Part H allows the state and local agencies to establish a system of payments for early intervention services, including a schedule of sliding fees. Some services must be free, such as child-find, evaluation and assessment, and case management, as well as certain administrative and coordinative functions. If state law, however, provides for free early intervention services, the state law prevails and a state may not use the federal law as permission to charge fees.

EFFECTS OF ZERO-REJECT PRINCIPLE.   Parents now may make the following assumptions: their child will be given free access to the schools; education will be free; they will work with professionals to provide a free appropriate public education to children; some preschool education may be provided by the schools.

The father of one young man (now 21 years old) reflected on the fact that the schools excluded his son in 1974 but had to accept him in 1975:

> I remember very well that the superintendent turned us away in one year and was about to do so the next. But before he could tell us "no" again, I pulled a copy of P.L. 94–142 out of my briefcase and told him that things had changed, my son had rights, and I would gladly sue him and his school board and would win if he didn't have the school bus at our house on the first day of school. You know, the bus arrived on time, and it did so for 14 years thereafter, day after day. Now, that's zero-reject in practice.

The following comments relate the experiences of a mother in a large city in the northwest. Her 18-year-old daughter has had four brain surgeries, been classified first as having a rare condition (Sturge-Weber Syndrome) and, after the last surgery, as having been cured of that but acquired cerebral palsy:

> I learned early on that I had to know Belena's rights. We were very lucky that P.L. 94–142 came along when it did. Otherwise, she never would have gone to school.

The issue for parents no longer is whether the schools will educate their children. That problem has been laid to rest by the law. The issues now center on *quality* and *duration:* what type of education will be provided, where, and by whom; and how soon will education be furnished and for how long.

A careful review of data on the topic of zero-reject shows the massive effect of the principle. One result of the zero-reject rule is that the number of students with disabilities who are educated by the nation's schools or other educational programs (such as institutions or hospitals) has risen each year since the 1975 amendments. Moreover, the numbers have increased dramatically; for example, in 1976–77, the number served under the EHA was 3,485,088; in 1986–87, a decade later, the number was 4,166,692 (Office of Special Education, 1988).

The largest number of students served under the EHA have learning disabilities; the next largest, speech or language impairment; and the third largest, mental retardation. In descending order, the other major conditions are emotional disturbance, multiple disabilities, hearing impairment, orthopedic impairment, other health impairment, visual disability, and deaf-blind combined disability (Office of Special Education, 1988). During the decade from 1976–77 to 1986–87, the number of students in several categories of disability decreased (mental retardation, orthopedic disability, and other health impairment). During the same period, the greatest increase in the number served by category was in learning disability and emotional disturbance (Office of Special Education, 1988).

The number of students served is lowest at age 21, with substantial decreases in numbers beginning at about age 16; and the largest number served falls in the age group of 6 through 17. However, numbers have increased in all age groups (Office of Special Education, 1988).

The zero-reject principle has had other parent-professional effects. It imposes a duty on professionals and creates a legal right for parents and children. It abolishes the *privilege* of an education, replacing it with a *right* to an education. Many a parent now says, "I've got rights," and many a professional now replies, "Yes, and I've got duties." Not long ago, parents and professionals would have talked about "privileges" and "charity," not rights and duty.

Zero-reject changes professional practices as they affect children and parents. It gives rise to the potential for the student to be integrated with others who are not disabled and to receive education for an extended period of time. It is a means to the mainstream of adult life and the first step in a lifetime of services to people with disabilities. It therefore allows and encourages growth, not only in the student but also in the parents and professionals. And, for that reason, it changes the norms of schools and society by saying that it is normal to include persons with disabilities. It also changes the form of society by integrating students with and without disabilities in the nation's schools. The difference is profound: children and parents today are served, not excluded.

**TABLE 8–1   Suggestions for how to Implement
the Zero-Reject Principle**

- Offer to help families during child-find and school enrollment, and by providing information and making referrals to appropriate private and public providers.
- Demonstrate the educability of your students, particularly to families, showing their positive contribution and abilities.
- Work on student discipline, with family participation, if there is behavior that threatens the student's suspension or expulsion from school.
- Plan an appropriate curriculum, one that ensures an educational benefit in the least restrictive alternative setting and in the family home.

Table 8–1 includes suggestions of how you can implement the zero-reject principle.

Nondiscriminatory Evaluation

The principle of nondiscriminatory evaluation exists to help professionals accurately assess the student's strengths and weaknesses. That goal has several rationales. That type of assessment—and nothing less—is necessary to assure that students are not wrongly identified as disabled (when they are not) or as having a certain type or extent of disability (when they do not). In turn, fair evaluation is necessary to assure proper placement, which, of course, helps provide an appropriate education. The principle of nondiscriminatory evaluation is a means to an end, and the key is for professionals to translate evaluation results into appropriate instruction.

In addition, you may use the nondiscriminatory evaluation to defend any categorical label assigned to the student. There is much disagreement about whether labeling is acceptable professional practice, and many states have resorted to noncategorical (i.e., label-free) identification of students as having "special needs" or "exceptionalities." But other states still adhere to categorical labeling (e.g., the categories of the EHA—learning disabled, hearing impaired, health impaired). In those states, professionals may classify students on the basis of the evaluation results.

The EHA requires professionals to adhere to multiple strategies to assure nondiscriminatory evaluation. These are included in Table 8–2.

PART H.   The requirements for nondiscriminatory evaluation of infants and toddlers are set out in its regulations, not in the statute. These regu-

---

TABLE 8–2   EHA Requirements for Assurance of Nondiscriminatory Evaluation

---

1. Testing and examination materials and procedures must be selected and administered so as not to be racially or culturally discriminatory.

2. Materials and tests must be given in the student's native language or mode of communication (e.g., signing) unless it is not feasible to do so.

3. No single evaluation procedure may be used as the only criterion for determining an appropriate educational program.

4. Only those materials and tests may be used that have been validated for the specific purpose for which used.

5. Tests must be administered and interpreted by trained personnel in conformance with the instructions from their producers.

6. Tests must be administered in a way that accommodates the student's manual, speaking, or sensory disabilities.

7. All evaluations must be made by a multidisciplinary team or group of persons, including at least one teacher or other specialists with knowledge in the area of the student's suspected disability.

8. The student must be assessed in all areas related to the suspected disability, including, where appropriate, health, vision, hearing, social and emotional status, general intelligence, academic performance, communicative status, and motor abilities.

9. No student may be placed in a special education program until a complete and individual evaluation, which meets the above standards, has been completed.

10. Professionals must draw upon information from a variety of sources about the student, including aptitude and achievement tests, teacher recommendations, physical conditions, social and cultural background, and adaptive behavior.

---

lations require tests (a) that be administered in the parents' native language or other mode of communication, (b) that tests not be racially or culturally discriminatory, (c) that no single evaluation procedure be used, and (d) that qualified personnel administer the tests. Evaluation is for the purpose of determining a child's eligibility for Part H; assessment is for the purpose of identifying the child's needs, the family's strengths and needs, and the services needed to meet the child's and family's needs.

Special rules apply to evaluation and assessment of the child and of the family. Generally, with respect to the child's evaluation and assessment, appropriate personnel must administer nondiscriminatory procedures and use *informed clinical opinion*. With respect to the family's assessment, the purpose is to determine the family's strengths and needs related to enhancing the child's development. The family assessment must be voluntary on the family's part, and it must be based on information provided by the family through a personal interview and incor-

---

TABLE 8–2 (Continued)

---

11. Professionals must ensure that information obtained from all those sources is documented and carefully considered.

12. Professionals must ensure that the placement decision is made by a group of people, including those knowledgeable about the student, the meaning of the evaluation data, and the placement options.

13. Professionals must obtain the consent of the student's parents for the initial evaluation for special education programs.

14. Professionals must reevaluate the student, in conformity with these requirements, every 3 years or more often if "conditions warrant" or the student's parents or teachers request reevaluation.

15. In the case of students with suspected or documented learning disabilities, professionals must adhere to special requirements for nondiscriminatory evaluation. You should comply with your state and local rules as well as the special federal rules for assessing learning disabilities. Schools must include the student's regular education teacher on the evaluation team, or if the student does not have such a teacher, a regular education teacher. Also, schools must include at least one person qualified to conduct individualized diagnosis of students (e.g., school psychologist). There also are additional requirements (a) defining specific learning disabilities; (b) requiring a member of the team, other than the student's regular education teacher, to engage in direct observation of the student in the regular education program; and (c) requiring the evaluation team to prepare a written report of the results of the evaluation.

16. Parents have the right to have their child evaluated by an independent professional free of cost to them. Those circumstances are when the school's evaluation has been challenged and found inappropriate in an administration hearing or in court. Of course, parents always have a right to an independent evaluation at their own expense.

---

porate the family's description of its strengths and needs with respect to enhancing the child's development.

As a general rule, child and family evaluation and assessment must be completed within 45 days after the state lead agency has been notified of the family's application for services.

EFFECTS OF NONDISCRIMINATORY EVALUATION PRINCIPLE.   The principle of nondiscriminatory evaluation has had many salutary effects (H. R. Turnbull, 1990). For example, it has required professionals to be more careful in classifying and providing curriculum and related services for children and youth. It has led to fewer students being classified as mentally retarded or speech impaired who otherwise might have been so classified. At the same time, it has led to many children being classified as learning disabled.

The same principle has validated the use of standardized tests (*PASE v. Hannon,* 1980). However, in some states legal objections have been raised to using those tests without special safeguards to assure that they do not discriminate against ethnic minority children on the basis of their ethnicity (*Larry P. v. Riles,* 1984). It has not, however, prohibited school authorities from using standardized tests for the purpose of classifying students in school, even though the results of the tests have been that more students of racial minority groups have been classified as disabled (*Georgia State Conference of Branches of the National Association for the Advancement of Colored People v. Georgia,* 1985). But it also has recognized that intelligence testing has a potentially hypnotic effect on its users (i.e., professionals will pay too much attention to a student's IQ), and it has tried to mitigate that effect by requiring that other procedures be brought to bear in classification.

As a result of the nondiscriminatory evaluation principle, professionals are required to spend more time in evaluation and classification. But that extra effort should have the effect of giving you a more comprehensive picture of the student and, therefore, a greater ability to identify the student's strengths (and build on them) and weaknesses (and remediate them). Thus, it also has required you and parents to work together and in particular to evaluate more carefully a student's strengths and weaknesses. In turn, it has required professionals to make more relevant, data-based, and objective educational decisions.

It has given parents and other family members an opportunity to participate in the evaluation process and its outcomes; it has been a bridge to greater family-professional partnership.

Not all of the hopes for parent-professional interaction during assessment have been fulfilled. A mother who lives in a major metropolis in the south recently made the following comments regarding assessment of her 15-year-old son who has learning disabilities and some attributes of severe emotional disturbance.

> I kind of had to push my way through the door into assessment. I had some bad experiences. I was told I had to have a degree in psychology if I were to understand my son's assessment. But I know my son, and I don't believe that I need a college degree. I've got my 'degree in motherhood' and that's enough to qualify me to be involved with the school people.

A similar observation was made by a black mother of a 7-year-old who has attention deficit disorder and a mild learning disability and attends school in a large metropolis:

> Aaron clearly had the same problems he would have had without regard to his race. But when his evaluation was done, it was interpreted without consideration of our family life. The psychological evaluations were not culturally sensitive. I had to question whether the psychologist understood Aaron's environment and family and whether she could do a complete and accurate assessment without understanding them.

TABLE 8–3   Suggestions for how to Implement the
Nondiscriminatory Evaluation Requirements

- If you have any doubts about the evaluation of the student, ask family members about the student's strengths, needs, and positive contributions, and about the family's and student's expectations for the future.
- If you have any doubts about the family's native language, ask the family what its preferences are for language or other modes of communication.
- Document all observations that you use in evaluation, so that "soft data" such as your observations will be supported by current and relevant facts in the record.
- Be sensitive to family racial, socioeconomic, or ethnic differences with respect to yourself, other school staff, and the student body; and about how those differences affect your assessment and evaluation of the student and the student's educational placement and program.

One purpose of the nondiscriminatory evaluation requirements was to ensure that minority students are not overclassified into special education; that is, that there are not a disproportionate number of them in special education as a percentage of all of them in the total school population (Gottlieb, 1981). Yet, data show that minority students continue to be overclassified, particularly in programs for students with mental retardation or emotional disability (MacMillan, Henrick & Watkins, 1988).

Suggestions for how you can implement the nondiscriminatory evaluation principle are included in Table 8–3.

Appropriate Education

Enrolling and evaluating a student is of little value, unless an appropriate, individualized education is also provided. Under Part B, the cornerstone of the principle of appropriate education is the individualized education program (IEP). We describe parent participation in the IEP and explain the process of developing IEPs in Chapter 10. Here, we will describe only the legal requirements for an IEP in addition to other ways in which the law defines "appropriate education."

IEP.   The IEP is a written document developed in a team meeting. A representative of the school who is qualified to provide (or supervise the provision of) special education and the student's teacher (or teachers) must attend. Parents must be invited and may attend. The student may also attend, at the discretion of the parents. In addition, the school and parents may invite others (including other family members) to attend. When the student is evaluated for the first time, the IEP committee also must contain a member of the team that performed the nondiscriminatory evaluation. The purpose of the special requirements for the first IEP is to ensure that the evaluation results are translated into the student's program.

The IEP must contain the following statements regarding (1) the child's present levels of educational performance; (2) the annual goals and short-term instructional objectives in each area requiring specially designed instruction; (3) the specific educational services to be provided and the extent to which the child will be able to participate in regular education programs; (4) the projected date for the beginning, and the anticipated duration of, such services; (5) appropriate objective criteria and evaluation procedures; and (6) schedules for determining, at least on an annual basis, whether the instructional objectives are being met.

The IEP may be revised annually or more often if warranted in the judgment of the professionals or parents.

If the public schools enroll the student in a private school, special provisions require the public and private agencies to work together to develop and ensure that the IEP is carried out. Of course, the public school pays the private tuition.

Because the law places a high premium on parent participation, special requirements assure that a student's parents have a chance to attend the IEP conference. These include advance notice of the meeting, mutually convenient scheduling, and arranging for interpreters for deaf or non-English-speaking parents. If parents are unable to attend, they may still participate through individual or conference telephone calls.

IEP meetings may be held without the presence of the parents only when it can document that it unsuccessfully attempted to have the parents participate. Such documentation should include detailed records of telephone calls, copies of letters to or from the parents, and the results of visits to the parents' home or place(s) of work. The school must give a copy of the IEP to the parents, upon request.

The student's right to attend the IEP conference arguably assumes that the student has the ability to contribute to the meeting in a meaningful way. Often, however, students do not participate. Since the EHA assumes that student rights are protected by parents and school personnel this is legal, but usually student participation would be helpful. It could, for example, ensure (a) that the student's perspective is taken into account; (b) that the other participants focus on the student's rights and needs and not on what they themselves want or find convenient; and (c) that the student obtain practice in decision making. Flemming and Flemming (1987) make some useful suggestions for student participation.

The IEP is the most important vehicle for an appropriate education as made clear by the law itself. The EHA defines *appropriate education* as an education that (a) is provided at public expense, under public direction and supervision; (b) meets the standards of the state educational agency; (c) includes preschool, elementary, and secondary school; and (d) is conducted in conformity with the requirements for the IEP. This statutory definition, however, does not flesh out the meaning of appropriate; it is just a skeleton.

DETERMINING WHAT IS APPROPRIATE.   Another definition of "appropriate" education is the "process definition" (H. R. Turnbull, 1990) whereby the student's education is deemed appropriate if the specified procedures of the EHA are followed. (a) Specifically, if professionals make a nondiscriminatory evaluation; (b) develop the IEP with the proper people, at the proper times, and in a proper way, using the evaluation results; (c) place the student in the least restrictive environment; and (d) grant parents' rights to due process and to participate in the development of the student's IEP. This approach to an appropriate education was sanctioned by the United States Supreme Court in the very first special education case it decided, *Board v. Rowley* (1982).

In the *Rowley* case, the Court was faced with a claim that Amy Rowley, a teenaged girl with significant hearing loss, required an interpreter as a "related service" in order for her to have an appropriate education. Without an interpreter, Amy heard only 59% of what transpired in her class; however, she had passed from grade to grade without ever being held back and without using an interpreter. The Court ruled that Amy did not require an interpreter. In doing so, it affirmed that "process definition," stressing that all the professionals involved in developing Amy's IEP were of the opinion (a) that she could be educated appropriately without an interpreter; (b) that the law allowed her parents to be involved in her education in multiple ways; and (c) that in fact they had been so involved.

The Court also ruled that Congress intended only that the EHA open the doors of public education to children and youth with disabilities, giving them a *reasonable opportunity* to learn. Congress did not intend for the schools to develop students' capacities to their *maximum*. Accordingly, Congress' intent is satisfied when professionals provide students with a reasonable opportunity to learn. Since this had been accomplished in Amy's case (as proven by her passing from grade to grade), the school had satisfied the EHA's requirements of an appropriate education, hence an interpreter was not required.

"Reasonable opportunity" is proven when the student receives some "educational benefit" from the program offered by the school. As *Rowley* makes clear, "educational benefit" was proven in Amy's case as she had progressed from grade to grade without the benefit of an interpreter. But this kind of progress is not required of every student. Instead, there must be proof that there is more than "trivial progress" (*Polk v. Central Susquehanna Intermediate Unit 16,* 1988). Other cases emphasize that there also must be some real benefit as measured by taking into account the student's present placement, diagnosis, disability, and capability (*Thornock v. Boise USD,* 1988; *Board v. Diamond,* 1986).

This "reasonable-opportunity" rule has taken on a new meaning in the few states that have been ordered by courts to provide summer schooling to students with severe disabilities. Here courts have ruled that the law's requirements of individualized education mean that schools must provide summer schooling to pupils whose disabilities are so severe that they will experience significant regression in their learning unless their education continues during the summer (*Armstrong v. Klein,* 1980, 1981; *Georgia ARC v. McDaniel,* 1983). In these instances, "reasonable opportunity" and "individualized education" are the bases for summer training.

In *Tatro v. State of Texas* (1984), the Court ruled that an appropriate education depends on the availability of related services. In that case, the issue was whether clean intermittent catheterization for a child who has spina bifida and cannot toilet herself constitutes a related service or a medical service (the latter is not considered a related service unless it is performed for diagnostic and evaluation purposes). The Court ruled that catheterization is a related service, since it is required to assist Ambur Tatro to benefit from special education.

However, not all health-related services are provided to the student at the school's expense. For example, although a school may be required to clean and suction a student's tracheostomy tube (*Department of Education of Hawaii v. Katherine D.,* 1984), a school need not provide services so that a student may use a ventilator or a respirator in school (*Detsel v. Board,* 1987; *Bevin H. v. Wright,* 1987). Nor have schools always been required to provide psychotherapy services; indeed, in most cases, they are not.

The critical distinctions between *related services* and *nonrelated services* include (a) the complexity of the service, (b) the cost of providing it, (c) the expertise required to provide it, (d) the risk of liability for the provider (school) and of damage to the student if the service is not correctly provided, and (e) the constancy or frequency with which the service must be provided.

Recognizing that schools resist paying for related services that affect a student's health because of the cost of the service, Congress amended the Social Security Act in 1988 by enacting the Medicare Catastrophic Coverage Act of 1988, P.L. 100–360. This law allows schools to charge the state's Medicare fund for the cost of certain services for certain students: the services must be reimbursable under the state's Medicare plan and the students must have IEPs that call for the services.

Thus, there are four ways to define "appropriate education": (a) by the language of the law itself, which requires individualization and relies greatly on the IEP; (b) by the process definition; (c) by the "reasonable-opportunity" rule; and (d) by the availability of related services (H. R. Turnbull, 1990).

PART H. Part H (infants and toddlers) requires a basically similar approach to individualization and appropriateness. We will describe the regulations in this chapter and discuss the major differences that affect professional practice in Chapter 10. The major difference is that Part H requires an IFSP, not an IEP.

The regulations implementing Part H are very specific about the IFSP and, because they are so new, deserve extended discussion.

The IFSP must:

- be developed by the family and appropriate qualified providers of early intervention services;
- be based on the multidisciplinary evaluation and assessment of the child and the assessment of the family; and
- include the services that are necessary to enhance the child's development and the family's capacity to meet the child's special needs.

In addition, the IFSP must contain specific content as follows:

- a statement of the child's present levels of physical, cognitive, language-speech, psychosocial, and self-help development, based on professionally acceptable objective criteria;
- a statement of major outcomes for the child and family and the criteria, procedures, and timelines used to determine the degree of progress and whether modifications or revisions of outcomes or services are necessary
- a statement of specific early intervention services necessary to meet the child's and the family's unique needs, including the frequency, intensity, location, and method of service delivery;
- payment arrangements, if any;
- to the extent appropriate, a statement of medical and other services that the child needs, but that are not required to be provided under Part H. If necessary, a statement of the steps to be taken to secure those services through public or private resources;
- a statement of the projected dates for beginning the services and their duration;
- the name of the case manager assigned to the family;
- a statement of steps to be taken to support the child's transition from early intervention services to preschool or other services, including discussions with and training of the child's parents re-

garding future placements and other matters relating to the child's transition.

An important note is added to the regulations on the IFSP, reminding you that family members play a variety of roles in enhancing their child's development. It also points out that it is important that the degree to which the family's needs are addressed in the IFSP be determined in a collaborative manner with the full agreement and participation of the child's parents.

The participants in the initial and in each annual IFSP meeting must include the following:

- the child's parent or parents;
- other family members as requested by the parent(s), if it is feasible to include them;
- the case manager;
- a person(s) directly involved in conducting the child and family evaluations and assessments; and
- as appropriate, persons who will provide services to the child or family.

If a required person is not available to attend the meeting, other means for participation must be used, such as telephone conference calls, attendance by a knowledgeable representative, or pertinent records made available at the meeting.

The initial meeting to develop the IFSP must take place within 45 days after the child or family is referred to the state's lead agency. Thereafter, periodic review is available in two ways: (a) every 6 months the IFSP must be reviewed for progress and appropriate revision, by a meeting or other means agreeable to the parties; and (b) annually a meeting must be held to evaluate the IFSP and review it as appropriate.

All meetings must be scheduled at times and places convenient to the family. The family's native language or other mode of communication must be used. And the meetings must be arranged so as to allow the families enough time to plan to attend.

Special rules specify how to provide services before the evaluation and assessment of the child and family are complete. Specifically, services may begin before evaluation and assessment if the parents agree, an interim IFSP is developed (naming the case manager and demonstrating that the services are needed immediately by the child and family), and the evaluation and assessment are in fact completed within the 45-day period.

Every agency or person having a direct role in providing early intervention services is responsible for making a good-faith effort to assist each eligible child in achieving the IFSP outcomes. But no agency or person may be held accountable if the child does not achieve the growth projected by the IFSP.

Part B (IEP) and Part H (IFSP) differ in two important ways with respect to rights. First, Part H services must be those that are "necessary" to most of the child's and family's needs. This is different from Part B, which requires "appropriate" education (a higher standard than "necessary" services). Second, the requirements for case management and transition planning do not appear in Part B.

Yet it is clear that the IFSP and Part H have potential for strengthening families by helping them (a) develop great expectations for their infant-toddler and themselves; (b) see the positive contributions that the infant-toddler can make to the family, its friends, and society; (c) choose how they want to be involved in their infant-toddler's life; (d) establish relationships with professionals and with others who are not in the disability service-providing business; (e) learn what their strengths and needs are; (f) learn what new strengths can be developed; (g) determine how they cope with difficulties and learn new coping skills; (h) improve or develop new communication techniques within the family and with professionals; (i) see the possibilities for the integration and independence of the infant-toddler, and, indeed, of the whole family; (j) secure and coordinate services from a variety of disciplines, service providers, and funding streams; (k) learn how to take charge of their situation and become their own case manager if they so wish; and (l) be launched successfully as families affected by a disability.

Moreover, the IFSP also recognizes that families play a crucial role in their child's development and will continue to do so. The IFSP extends the notion of "parent participation" to that of "family participation," subject to the final decision by parents. It recognizes, as this whole book does, that families are systems and that no one member of the family (the infant-toddler) truly can be helped unless all members of the family are strengthened.

EFFECTS OF PRINCIPLE OF APPROPRIATE EDUCATION. The effects of appropriate, individualized education have been far-reaching. H. R. Turnbull (1990) discusses them in detail. Among others, it generally has turned schools into child-centered agencies. The student is no longer required to fit the school, but the school is required to fit the student. Second, by becoming providers of a wide range of services, (e.g., related services) schools have become more than vehicles for traditional academic training, they have become multiservice agencies, providing education, health, mental health, social service, and other programs to children and families. As a result, professionals now work in multidisciplinary teams and with many types of professionals. Third, the requirements of an appropriate individualized education has made it possible for you and families to establish new relationships, ones that recognize the necessary and legitimate roles of shared decision making.

Fourth, it has recognized that students themselves have legitimate roles to play in shaping their own special education and their own lives. Finally, it has overcome the practice of "functional exclusion" by assuring the provision of services that are truly beneficial to students.

Research results indicate that the principle of appropriate education has brought other results. The number of students receiving related services is large. For the school year 1985–86, for example, approximately 4.6 million students were receiving related services. Students with learning disabilities received the highest number of related services, followed by those with mental retardation (and, in declining order, emotional disturbance; speech or language impairment; multiple disabilities; hearing impairments; orthopedic disabilities; visual impairments; health impairments; and deaf-blind) (Office of Special Education, 1988).

Among related services, diagnostic services were the most common; other services, in descending order, were counseling, transportation, psychological, school social work, speech-language pathology, school health services, recreational, audiological, occupational therapy, and physical therapy (Office of Special Education, 1988).

Still, some family members may feel dissatisfied with the right to an appropriate education and the results of the IEP. One mother, whose daughter has many health problems and is classified as "other health impaired" and "medically fragile," commented:

> I have spent a great deal of time at my daughter's school. I saw them using aversives like pinching and spraying vinegar into the students' faces. I don't condone those practices. And they aren't written into the IEPs either. Still, it is very important to have a written IEP because it is your legal protection. But the heart and soul of the teacher must be in your child's education or else all you have is a legal document.

And another parent commented about the IEP:

> Until my son was 15 years old, all the IEP did was look at his weaknesses. That's hard on a youngster, especially when he needs to have such good self-esteem.

Suggestions for how you can implement the appropriate education principle are included in Table 8–4.

Least Restrictive Environment

The principle of the least restrictive environment (LRE) is a technique for preventing the unwarranted segregation of students with disabilities from their peers who do not have disabilities. There are three important

---

TABLE 8–4 Suggestions for how to Implement the IEP Requirements

---

- Be sure to comply exactly and in spirit with the rules concerning the development of the IEP and IFSP
- Ask families who they want to attend IEP and IFSP meetings and schedule those meetings to be convenient to the family and those people it wants to attend them
- Be sure that families are notified of and know their and the student's rights to an appropriate education
- Be sure that the IEP offers at least a reasonable opportunity for the student to benefit (this is the minimum requirement by law, so you may want the IEP to offer the opportunity for the student to develop to the maximum)
- When working with students with technology-support systems or challenging behaviors, be sure to learn how to work with the students by taking full advantage of family information and advice and opportunities for personnel development

---

reasons for preventing segregation by disability. First, segregation can have an adverse effect on the ability of students with disabilities to learn. Second, segregation can have an adverse effect on their ability to associate with classmates who do not have a disability. As H. R. Turnbull (1990) pointed out, the LRE principle seeks to maximize the child's educational and social-associational opportunities. Third, it helps hold down the cost of paying for two school systems (special and regular). One of Ryan's parents commented on his experience in an integrated school setting (see the photograph at the beginning of this chapter):

> It's not so much the program that helps Ryan as it is the other students. They respond to him, and he to them, in ways that make his physical disability—his not walking—so minimal.

Moreover, the least restrictive environment rule rests on a basic principle of constitutional law. According to that principle, when any state has a legitimate goal to pursue and that goal requires the state to restrict the liberty or opportunity of any of its citizens, that goal must be pursued in the way that is least restrictive of citizens' rights and opportunities. In Chambers' memorable metaphor, if it is permissible for a state to kill mosquitoes, it must use a fly swatter, not a bazooka, if the fly is on a citizen's back (Chambers, 1972).

In its attempt to carry out the educational and associational goals of the LRE principle and in so doing comply with the Constitution, the EHA and its regulations require schools to assure that (a) to the maximum extent appropriate, all children and youth with disabilities (including those in private schools and public institutions) are educated with those who are not disabled; and (b) special classes, separate schooling, or other removal of a student with disabilities from regular education occurs only when the nature or severity of disability is such that education in regular classes cannot be achieved satisfactorily with the use of supplementary aids and services.

To carry out these two basic requirements, schools must provide (a) a continuum of alternative placements, including regular classes, resource rooms, special classes, special schools, homebound instruction, and instruction in hospitals and institutions; (b) supplementary services, such as speech therapy and adaptive physical education, for a student who is educated in regular classes; (c) education as close to a student's home as possible; and (d) opportunities for a student to participate in extracurricular and nonacademic activities to the maximum extent appropriate. Courts interpret these provisions as allowing the removal of a student to special placements, particularly those in institutions, only when the extent of the student's disability is great and local programs are inadequate.

The most useful case involving the principle of the least restrictive alternative is *Roncker v. Walters* (1983). In that case, the question was whether a student with a severe disability should be educated in a community-based school or in an institution; in other words, whether the child's education could be accommodated in the community or not.

The case was resolved in favor of "mainstream" placement, and the court ordered the student placed in a community-based school program rather than at the state institution for individuals with mental retardation. That is, the court ruled that the EHA's requirement that the student be educated with students who do not have a disability "to the maximum extent appropriate" depends on the "feasibility" of providing the services that initially make a residential or institutional placement appropriate in a nonsegregated setting. If it is feasible to duplicate those services in a community setting, then the institutional placement is not appropriate. *Feasibility* is determined by the student's needs and the school's ability to modify its program to meet those needs. This is a strict test: the school must be able to show that it cannot meet the student's needs after modifying its program. There are three ways in which the school can show this: (a) the student would receive no benefit even if the program were modified; (b) even after a modification, an institutional setting would offer greater benefits; or (c) the student demonstrates disruptive behaviors in the integrated setting.

The LRE principle has been criticized for legitimatizing special schools, institutions, and other nonregular education settings and programs (Taylor, 1981). At the same time, however, the LRE principle is a constitutional principle that can be the last line of defense against those who seek separate placement (H. R. Turnbull, 1990).

Throughout this book and particularly when we discussed family system concepts in Chapters 2–5, we emphasized the variety and complexity of families and the implications of such diversity for your work. In the context of this chapter, it is sufficient to point out only a few points that relate to families and the principle of the least restrictive education of their children.

Some parents will want their children in the "most normal" program possible (i.e., as close to regular education and the "mainstream" as possible), but others will prefer separate education, even institutional placement (Abramson, Willson, Yoshida, & Hagerty, 1983; Boggs, 1985a, 1985b; A. P. Turnbull & Winton, 1983; Ziskin, 1985). Professionals should acknowledge that through these choices parents are expressing a preference for certain values—either educational or associational—related to their child or their other family members.

A mother in a large urban school district had pushed hard for integrated education for her son with learning disabilities and, after she won her point, she commented that, in a separate school, "My son would never have been a success with his peers in the neighborhood. He always would have been regarded as different."

And a parent whose daughter had been placed in a separate program because of her physical disabilities reflected:

> I don't like to say it, but in the separate school she was becoming weird. She was picking up autistic-like behaviors, developing poor social skills, and acquiring a poor opinion of herself and other students. We changed all that, but only after a fight. LRE is the most important thing that can happen to my child. If I were starting her off in school now, for the first day of her life, I would never allow her to go to a special education class. It did more harm than good.

Some families have great expectations for their children and believe that their hopes can come true only if their children are educated in integrated ("less restrictive") settings. They may hope, for example, that their children will hold real jobs, with real wages, working beside nondisabled people. They will see integrated education as a means for achieving that dream: no other form of education will prepare their children adequately for working in an integrated setting, doing competitive work with or without support.

Other families may want their children to be "full citizens." They may understand that certain people with disabilities, including perhaps their own children, still experience "second–class" citizenship, in that they are segregated in work, residential living, and personal relationships. To help overcome segregation, these families may insist on integrated education. Some also may have had negative experiences in segregated programs. They may have seen their children become isolated from their neighborhood peers and family friends because they were separated from other (nondisabled) children in school; or they may have seen their children lose skills or display inappropriate behavior in segregated settings but not in integrated settings. For these parents, their children's skills and personal relationships require integration.

But parents also may say that their child's educational placement reflects their needs and those of their other family members. As several parents have noted in *Parents Speak Out: Then and Now* (H. R. Turnbull & Turnbull, 1985), a delicate balancing of values and individual interests occurs when special education placement is determined. But parent preferences also may take into account that some necessary educational or other services are not available. Leah Ziskin (1985) is a physician whose daughter, Jennie, has severe mental retardation. After having Jennie at home for 10 years, here is what she said about balancing family interests:

> When Jennie was almost ten years old, the family had an opportunity to accompany my husband to Australia on his sabbatical leave. We obtained guest-placement status for Jennie at a state institution during the four months that we were away. From all reports Jennie's adjustment was uneventful; she did well. However, we missed her. Someone didn't always have to be watching her or feeding her; in other words, we felt suddenly unburdened. When we returned to New Jersey, we brought Jennie home. But our attitudes had changed—probably mine most of all. I realized that our family had interacted better when Jennie was not always there. In retrospect, it appears that we did not realize how we were functioning as a family when we were dealing with Jennie on a full-time basis. (p. 76)

Professionals should be particularly sensitive and tactful when they discuss special educational placement with parents, remembering that values, competing interests, and service availability are three important components of parental decisions. Where the parents' preferences are based on values, professionals should acknowledge the legitimacy of those values, even when they differ from their own. Where parents' preferences are based on problems of service availability, professionals should try to make services available so parents' values can be realized.

You may want to explore with parents their preferences for special or regular placement, what can be done to respond to those preferences so that the law can be carried out, and the student's experiences and preferences so that they can be responsive to the student as well as the parents. Professionals also may want to suggest to their supervisors, principals, superintendents, school board members, or state department of education personnel how changes can be made to accommodate individual needs in LRE placements. Further, they may want to urge parents to become involved in state or local advisory boards that specify needs and how they can be met.

PART H. The regulations under Part H create a strong preference for community-based services, to the extent appropriate for the child. Thus, to the extent appropriate, services must be provided in the types of settings in which infants and toddlers without handicaps would participate. Thus, early intervention centers, hospitals, clinics, and other settings appropriate to the child's age and needs are permissible settings. "And the Department of Education recommends that services be community-based and not isolate a child or family from settings or activities in which children without handicaps would participate."

EFFECTS OF THE LRE PRINCIPLE. The LRE principle has had some important effects. For example, it has enabled parents, regular educators, and special educators to plan for and deliver programs in a collaborative way, and it has made it possible for regular systems to become more integrated. It has enabled many students who otherwise would have received special education to receive an education in regular programs (Office of Special Education, 1983, 1984, 1985, 1986). Further, it has prevented some children to avoid institutional placement (Office of Special Education, 1983, 1984, 1985, 1986). Finally, it has helped students with disabilities receive a more effective education and associate with and enhance the sensitivity of peers who are not disabled (H. R. Turnbull et al., 1983).

Most students with disabilities in the 1985–86 school year received some education in the same building as students without disabilities or in other settings with nondisabled students. Over 26% received special education in regular classrooms; additional 41% were provided special education and related services primarily in resource rooms, while another 24% received special education and related services in separate classes within a regular education building (Office of Special Education, 1988). The extent to which students with disabilities are placed in the various settings depends on the disabling condition. Students with a learning disability or speech impairment, for example, are more apt to be in regular classes or resource rooms than students with mental retardation (Office of Special Education, 1988). Likewise, some states are more inclined to mainstream than others (Office of Special Education, 1988).

Suggestions for how to implement the LRE principle are included in Table 8–5.

Procedural Safeguard and Due Process

Part B of the EHA requires two basic components: (a) general safeguards, and (b) the hearing.

TABLE 8–5   Suggestions for how to Implement the LRE Principle

---

- Be especially sensitive to and nonjudgmental about the family's choice of a particular educational setting for the student.
- If the family wants a segregated or other more restrictive setting, explain the benefits and risks of less restrictive settings to ensure that the family is fully informed, including your professional opinion concerning the most appropriate least restrictive setting.
- Try to provide services in the most integrated setting and demonstrate the benefit to the family and student.

GENERAL SAFEGUARDS.   The procedural safeguards for parents and students include the right to access to the students' educational records. They also include the right to limit access to those records except by people who need to know what they contain in order to be able to provide or monitor services. In addition, parents may obtain an independent evaluation of their child.

Children who have no parents, whose parents cannot be found, or who are wards of the state have the right to "surrogate parents"— people appointed to represent them in special education matters. Professionals should ask these surrogates how they want to be involved in the student's education, remembering that the EHA requires schools to treat surrogates as though they were the child's parents.

Parents (including surrogates) have a right to a written notice whenever schools propose to change or refuse to change the child's identification, evaluation, educational placement, or the provision of a free, appropriate education. Parents' consent must be obtained before any initial evaluation or initial placement of a child in special education. Strategies for how to provide notice and obtain consent are included in Chapter 9.

DUE PROCESS HEARING.   When parents or professionals disagree on a child's identification, evaluation, placement, program, or other elements of a free, appropriate education, they may obtain a hearing (the so-called *due process* or *fair hearing*) to resolve their differences. Schools, not just parents, may call for a hearing. Professionals should become familiar with the procedures for requesting a hearing in their school district or service agency.

At the hearing, both parties (i.e., parents and schools) have the right (a) to be advised by a lawyer and other experts; (b) to call witnesses to testify; (c) to introduce evidence, including documents; (d) to examine and crossexamine witnesses; (e) to receive a record of the hearing; (f) to be provided with written findings of fact by the hearing officer; and (g) to appeal the decision. The decision of the first hearing officer usually is appealed to the state educational agency; from that agency, it may be appealed to a state or federal court.

The parents and service providers must exhaust their administrative remedies before filing a lawsuit in a state or federal court (*Sessions v. Livingston Parish*, 1980). That is, they must go through a due process hearing with a local hearing officer and then complete the appeal to the state agency before they may file their lawsuit. However, they need not exhaust their remedies if the requirement to exhaust their remedies would be futile in that it would have no power to correct the situation (*Miener v. State of Missouri*, 1982).

In spite of such options for reconciliation of differences, the school and parents must adhere to the "stay-put" rule (*Honig v. Doe*, 1988). Neither the school nor the parents may unilaterally remove the student from publicly funded education and make a placement in a program that charges tuition expecting to recover the tuition without first exhausting their administrative remedies (*Foster v. D.C. Board of Ed.*, 1981). Parents must notify the schools before they make a private-school placement (*Evans v. D.C. Board of Education*, 1987). Also, they must accept an appropriate program if offered by the LEA; that is, they must allow an LEA to "cure" its inappropriate placement. The parents' duty to accept the LEA cure exists even if this means withdrawing the student from private school before the end of the school year (*Hudson v. Wilson*, 1987). Further, the parents may not place the student in a school that has not been approved by the state for tuition reimbursement (*Schimmel v. Spillane*, 1987). Finally, the parents always run the risk that the public school program will be considered appropriate, in which case they may not recover tuition at all (*Rouse v. Wilson*, 1987).

The "stay-put" rule allows two exceptions. First, schools or parents may make the unilateral removal and obtain tuition reimbursement if the child's physical or mental health is in serious and imminent danger in the present program (*Anderson v. Thompson*, 1981). Second, parents may do likewise when the school has acted in "bad faith" such as by unreasonably delaying the child's evaluation) (*Doe v. Anrig*, 1983; *William S. v. Gill*, 1982).

PARENTS.   As we point out in Chapter 11, you have many opportunities to work with parents within the due process principle. Be particularly careful about keeping records, and comply with every requirement concerning the child's identification, evaluation, program, and placement to avoid triggering a due process hearing (H. R. Turnbull, Turnbull & Strickland, 1979). This means that you should advise parents about all their rights in a way that is comprehensive and informative—that is, paying attention to what you say and how you say it (H. R. Turnbull, 1978).

HANDICAPPED CHILDREN'S PROTECTION ACT.   The EHA was amended in 1986 to allow courts to order schools to pay the fees of the lawyers whom parents hired to assert their children's rights. The

---

**TABLE 8–6   Suggestions for how to Implement
Due Process Requirements**

- Be sure the family fully understands all its own rights as well as those of the student, providing a combination of face-to-face meetings and information on paper.
- Document all your judgments by current, relevant, and observable facts entered into the student's files and shared with the family.
- Testify only about facts or documented observations and be willing to say to the family everything you would say in a due process hearing.

---

amendments, called the Handicapped Children's Protection Act, acknowledge that the EHA's rights are not worth much if the parents cannot afford a lawyer to help advocate for them. Thus, the general rule is that the school must pay the attorney fees if the parents "prevail" in their dispute with the school. Fees may be awarded for work done in the due process hearing, on appeal from it to the state educational agency, and in trials and appeals in court. Exceptions to this rule require that parents be reasonable about their negotiations with the school.

PART H.   Under the infants and toddlers legislation, the procedural due process rights are very elaborate and will be described in Chapter 11.

EFFECTS OF DUE PROCESS PRINCIPLE.   As evidenced by research, the effects of due process are powerful. In summary (see Chapter 11 for more detail), it has made professionals and parents more accountable to each other. It has required professionals to change the "power relationships" that they had with parents and to be more sensitive and accommodating to parent values, concerns and information. But it has exacted high costs in terms of money, emotions, and time when there have been due process hearings. And it has increased the use of mediation as a way to prevent, contain, and resolve parent-professional disputes.

Suggestions for how you can implement the due process principle are included in Table 8–6.

Parent Participation

Because this book concerns parent-professional relationships and parent participation in the education of students, we will summarize only the most relevant components of the EHA. The book sets out many reasons for parent participation. As H. R. Turnbull et al. (1982) show (see Chapter 1), the EHA assumed that parent participation helps students, parents, and professionals and that it is a way to make schools accountable to parents and students.

Several questions have arisen about who are "parents" and when a biological parent loses, or does not lose, rights under the EHA. If a student has permanent (not temporary) foster parents, they, not the state welfare agency, have the EHA parent rights (*Criswell v. State Department of Education,* 1986). Even if a surrogate parent has been appointed, the student's biological parents are still entitled to exercise their own rights under the EHA, but not the student's rights (*John H. v. MacDonald,* 1986). The parent who has custody of the child usually is entitled to exercise the parental rights of the EHA. However, when a noncustodial parent is responsible for the child's education expenses, that parent sometimes also has parent-participation rights.

The EHA requires that each state establish procedures for consulting with people involved in or concerned with the education of students with disabilities, including parents and guardians. It also requires the state agency to establish procedures for making the state special education plan available to the public and parents, holding public hearings, giving adequate notice of those hearings, and allowing public comment on proposed policies, programs, and procedures before they are adopted.

Further, the EHA also requires that the state agency create an advisory panel related to Part B. This panel must be composed of individuals involved in or concerned with special education, including at least one representative of individuals with disabilities, teachers of students with disabilities, parents of such children and youth, state and local education officials, and administrators of special education programs. The panel is to (a) advise the state agency on unmet needs; (b) comment on the state's education plan, policies, and regulations; and (c) assist in developing and reporting data and evaluations of special education.

PART H.   Part H defines "parent(s)" to be a parent, guardian, person acting as a parent, or surrogate parent. A person acting as a parent may be a grandparent or stepparent with whom the child lives or a person legally responsible for the child's welfare.

There are other Part H rules for parent participation. The law establishes a State Interagency Coordinating Council and requires that family members be on the Council. In addition, all of the parent rights available under Part B relating to access to and confidentiality of information apply to Part H programs.

Parents and other members of the public may have access to information about state and local school special education programs. Not all information about every student is accessible, but generally parents and other members of the public may obtain all information concerning the *programs* the state or local agency runs. (This is different from parents' right to have access to their child's education records. That type of access does not belong to the public.)

Parents have the right to consent or object to the release of personally identifying information about their children. This protects family privacy. In addition to the right to assure confidentiality, parents also have the right of access to their own children's educational records. This assures the basis for a long-term and constructive relationship.

The state also must publish its proposed plan, give notice of when hearings will be held, allow for public opportunity to comment on the plan, hold public hearings, and review and comment on the public comments. It also must establish a public awareness program, comprehensive child-find system, and a central directory of information.

SUMMARY

We have described the six principles of the EHA (Part B) and shown how they relate to the early intervention program established for infants and toddlers under Part H. Further, we have illustrated how the law has been interpreted, summarized the impact of the law on students and families, and suggested how you can work with families in implementing the law. We will now examine in greater detail some of the law's requirements and ways to implement them.

CHAPTER 9

FAMILY INVOLVEMENT IN THE REFERRAL AND EVALUATION PROCESS

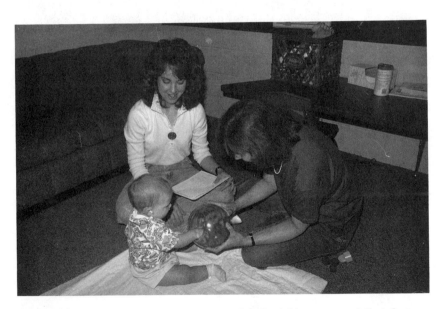

Involvement of parents in the evaluation of their children—especially infants—can help ensure accurate results. Some families, however, may choose not to participate.

Finally, after years of vague doubts and haunting fears, there was a reason why Melissa was experiencing problems. As the psychologist explained the test results to us, our daughter was no longer "lazy" or "crazy." She had a learning disability and there was something we could all do to help. I'll never forget that first conference and I'll be eternally grateful. They gave us more than information—they gave us moral support.

Students and their families enter special education through the process of referral and evaluation. By handling this process in competent and sensitive ways, you can help ensure that families' initial experiences with special education are positive, as in the example above. Thus, the outcomes of referral and evaluation experiences have both short and long-term implications for family-professional partnerships.

This chapter will describe how the referral and evaluation process relates to implementation of the legal requirements discussed in Chapter 8 and how it provides meaningful opportunities to involve families in information dissemination and decision making. The focus will be on the school-age population. The infant and preschool referral and evaluation process, as mandated in P.L. 99–457, is in some ways similar, yet a number of differences warrant separate discussion at the end of this chapter. After reading this chapter you should be able to answer the following questions about the referral and evaluation of students for special education services:

- How is the referral and evaluation process coordinated?
- Why should prereferral interventions be initiated prior to referring a student for an evaluation?
- How should parents be notified of a referral and their consent obtained for an evaluation?
- What kind of evaluation information can be obtained from families?
- How should parents be informed of evaluation results?
- How is the referral and evaluation process conducted for infants and preschoolers?

OVERVIEW OF THE REFERRAL AND EVALUATION PROCESS

The Education for the Handicapped Act (EHA) does not address the referral process, yet it contains many regulations pertaining to nondiscriminatory evaluations. (We encourage you to refer back to Chapter 8, if necessary, to insure that you have a complete understanding of legal requirements.) State and local school districts have established their own policies covering both processes of referral and evaluation. This general process is outlined in Figure 9–1.

This chapter discusses this referral and evaluation process based on the family-systems perspective presented earlier in this book. At each step of this process, it is essential to keep in mind that the individual you are working with is part of an interrelated family system. To better understand and plan for the student who is being evaluated, you must also understand that student's family and consider their needs. For example, if you would have been on the team evaluating Melissa, as described at the beginning of this chapter, it would have been important for you to know about her father's fears and doubts, and how these feelings have affected the functioning of Melissa's family.

Schools are not the only agencies that provide services to students who have a disability and their families. The many other agencies that also deliver services need to be considered in the referral and evaluation process. Students referred for a special education evaluation may already be receiving health, mental health, or social services as well as their regular education services. This is especially true of children being referred to the public school from early childhood professionals. In other cases, you may need to solicit the involvement of other agencies in the process of evaluating the student. For example, Melissa's father's doubts about his daughter prior to the referral and evaluation process might have prompted him to take her for individual counseling with a mental health professional. If so, it would be important to involve this professional in the evaluation of Melissa. Sometimes such services are paid for, in part or in full, by the school in which the student is enrolled. For that reason, and to coordinate the child's various services for maximum effectiveness, school professionals also must deal with representatives from the other service agencies as well as with the student's parents. This cooperation begins during the referral and evaluation stages and continues through the student's involvement with special education.

COORDINATING THE REFERRAL AND EVALUATION PROCESS

The school-based committee with overall coordination responsibility for identification and placement is the special services committee. It typically is comprised of special services personnel (i.e., teachers, psycholo-

FIGURE 9–1 Sequence and Functions of Referral & Evaluation

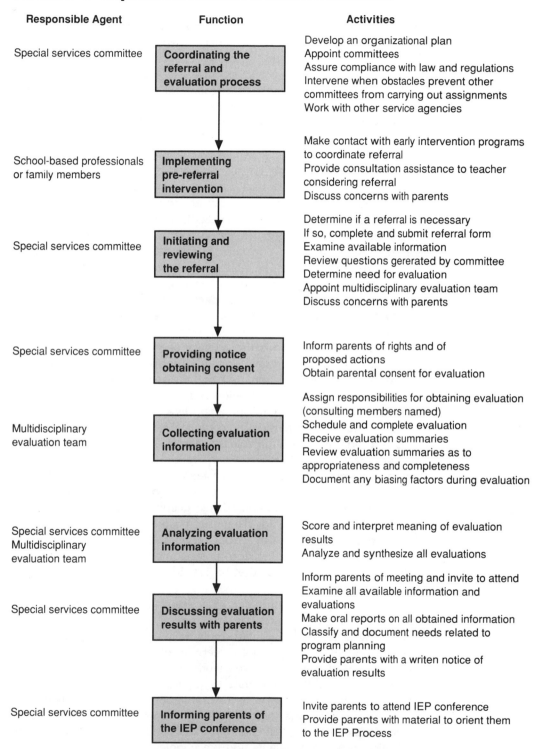

Responsible Agent	Function	Activities
Special services committee	**Coordinating the referral and evaluation process**	Develop an organizational plan Appoint committees Assure compliance with law and regulations Intervene when obstacles prevent other committees from carrying out assignments Work with other service agencies
School-based professionals or family members	**Implementing pre-referral intervention**	Make contact with early intervention programs to coordinate referral Provide consultation assistance to teacher considering referral Discuss concerns with parents
Special services committee	**Initiating and reviewing the referral**	Determine if a referral is necessary If so, complete and submit referral form Examine available information Review questions gererated by committee Determine need for evaluation Appoint multidisciplinary evaluation team Discuss concerns with parents
Special services committee	**Providing notice obtaining consent**	Inform parents of rights and of proposed actions Obtain parental consent for evaluation
Multidisciplinary evaluation team	**Collecting evaluation information**	Assign responsibilities for obtaining evaluation (consulting members named) Schedule and complete evaluation Receive evaluation summaries Review evaluation summaries as to appropriateness and completeness Document any biasing factors during evaluation
Special services committee Multidisciplinary evaluation team	**Analyzing evaluation information**	Score and interpret meaning of evaluation results Analyze and synthesize all evaluations
Special services committee	**Discussing evaluation results with parents**	Inform parents of meeting and invite to attend Examine all available information and evaluations Make oral reports on all obtained information Classify and document needs related to program planning Provide parents with a writen notice of evaluation results
Special services committee	**Informing parents of the IEP conference**	Invite parents to attend IEP conference Provide parents with material to orient them to the IEP Process

Note. From *Developing and Implementing Individualized Education Programs* (3rd ed.) (p. 50) by B. Strickland and A. P. Turnbull, 1990, Columbus, OH: Charles Merrill. Copyright 1990 by Charles Merrill. Adapted by permission.

gists, social workers, counselors, therapists) and administrators, but its membership changes and the number of people involved increases and decreases depending on the function it is serving at a particular time.

As mentioned, other service agencies may also be involved with the student who is being referred or evaluated. If so, it is important that the professionals from these agencies interact positively. The effective professional is interdependent. No professional acts alone; each acts as part of separate, but interlocking systems. For example, consider the case of Deidre, a 16-year-old student with mild mental retardation. She is in her first year at the local high school. She has been involved in prevocational training at the junior-high school and is now receiving vocational rehabilitation during half of each day at school. She also receives services in regular education and is a client, from time to time, in mental health services from a private psychologist. Deidre's special education teacher, regular education teacher, vocational rehabilitation instructor, and psychologist must all be able to work together to adequately provide the educational experiences Deidre needs.

Once a student is referred to special education, the special education system permeates the services the student and his or her family receive and, therefore, serves as the connector of services. In some instances, special education is the primary service system. For example, Deidre's services were primarily provided for through special education with occasional services from the mental health system. In other instances, however special education may be a secondary service system—one that is collateral to but supportive of the primary system. For example, students with medical complications may receive their services primarily from health professionals with only secondary services through special education. Either way, special education tends to be the constant system, always present so long as the student is enrolled in school. And special education is legally responsible, not only for specially designed and individualized instruction but also for the related services, such as health (for diagnostic purposes only), and for linking the student to mental health, social services, and vocational rehabilitation. Therefore, special education professionals play a key role in coordinating services, a process that begins during the referral and evaluation process.

The school-based committee responsible for coordinating the referral and evaluation process is named differently in different schools (e.g., child study team, eligibility team, multidisciplinary team, special education committee). If you are not a member of the special services committee in the program where you work, we encourage you to talk with the chairperson of the committee to inquire about the particular procedures, schedules, and forms used throughout the process illustrated in Figure 9–1. Each of the steps identified in Figure 9–1 will be discussed in this chapter, and we will end with a discussion about the referral and evaluation process for infants and preschoolers.

IMPLEMENTING PREREFERRAL INTERVENTION

A referral is a formal request for multidisciplinary assistance in identifying the special needs of students. Referrals for special services can be initiated by parents, other family members, community professionals, or school professionals. Typically, children with severe congenital disabilities are identified during infancy and increasingly are enrolled in early intervention and preschool programs. Thus, their referral to the public school program frequently comes from early childhood professionals.

A different situation applies to children who manifest characteristics that create concern about their academic or behavioral performance after they enter school. Children identified as having a disability during school years typically have milder disabilities than those identified shortly after birth. Also, later-identified children may live in geographical areas that do not have a comprehensive identification program during the preschool period. School-based professionals need to know the indicators of special needs related to every category of exceptionality (Pasanella & Volkmor, 1981; Schulz & Turnbull, 1984). A major indicator is school achievement significantly below expectation levels. It is necessary to document concerns by reviewing the student's classwork, homework, tests, and behavioral observations in order to pinpoint general levels of performance and any performance patterns that tend to be associated with success or failure (e.g., individual vs. group activities, oral vs. written work). Many schools have checklists to help you identify or document your concerns.

Children who are gifted are usually identified after they enter school. The parents of these children often have some indication that their son or daughter is different prior to entering school, and may be the ones to begin the prereferral process. While this also happens occasionally with children who have mild disabilities, their parents may tend to be more uncertain about the nature of the problem. You must be willing to listen to the concerns of parents and other family members even if these are not concerns that you have identified in the classroom.

Before initiating a referral for a student (made by school personnel or parents), we suggest that schools provide consultation assistance to the teacher for the purpose of developing prereferral interventions. This process involves conducting an assessment of the discrepancy between the student's performance and the teacher's and parents' desired expectations and then implementing an instructional program to narrow this discrepancy (Graden, Casey, & Christenson, 1985). According to Ysseldyke et al. (1983), the recommendation to use a prereferral intervention process is based on the finding that too often the decision to refer a student for a special education evaluation is tantamount to the decision to assign that student to a special education program. Thus, prereferral might lead to the prevention of special education placement.

Effectiveness of Prereferral Interventions

Many states and local school systems have developed prereferral intervention programs. Several research studies have been conducted in an attempt to measure the effectiveness of such prereferral interventions (Graden, Casey, & Bronstrom, 1985; Harrington & Gibson, 1986). Strickland and Turnbull (1990) reported that the following benefits associated with prereferral intervention have been identified:

- Meets legal requirements of P.L. 94–142.

- Helps in refining vague and subjective referral and identification procedures by providing a clear definition.

- Results in programs which are both more appropriate and cost effective than separate special programs.

- Provides less fragmentation in the regular program and in the services provided to students with disabilities.

- Restructures the regular program to broaden the range of accommodation for all students.

An extensive study was conducted in an attempt to evaluate the prereferral process as mandated by the state of Kansas (Cooley, McVey, & Barrett-Jones, 1987). The results indicated wide variability in the way preassessment was being implemented. Successful preassessment practices were differentiated from unsuccessful along three critical factors: (a) accurate description of the student's problem, (b) appropriate interventions, and (c) follow-up of intervention outcomes. These factors are reflected in the general guidelines for establishing prereferral interventions recommended by Strickland and Turnbull (1990):

- Insure that concerns are clearly defined.

- Insure that intervention strategies are appropriate to the concern.

- Insure that the strategies are implemented, monitored, and evaluated in a consistent manner.

- Insure that strategies are as unobtrusive as possible.

The authors also recommended that a prereferral checklist be used to ensure successful completion of all steps leading up to the referral. Figure 9–2 provides an example of a prereferral checklist.

In a review of the prereferral intervention literature, Lloyd, Crowley, Kohler, and Strain (1988) emphasized the need for more research regarding the implementation and effects of prereferral intervention programs. This article raised several questions felt to be in need of future research focus. Two of these questions involved the way parents respond to prereferral systems and whether parents of children with disabilities respond differently to these systems than parents of children without disabilities.

Role of Families in the Prereferral Process

In general, the role of families in the prereferral process has not been dealt with in the literature. Ammer (1984) found that substantive in-

---

FIGURE 9–2.   Prereferral Checklist

PREREFERRAL CHECKLIST

Appropriate activities on this checklist must be completed before referring a student for assessment for special education services. Place the date that activities were completed in the space next to the activity. This form must accompany the referral form.

1. _____ Reviewed student educational records to determine longevity of concern and previous interventions.
2. _____ Established that student has passed vision and hearing screening or referred student for vision and hearing screening.
3. _____ Met with student to discuss concerns and possible solutions.
4. _____ Met with parents to discuss concerns and possible solutions.
5. _____ Collected and analyzed recent examples of student's classwork.
6. _____ Collected specific information from records and performance about student's academic skills.
7. _____ Collected specific information from the record and class about student's behavior.
8. _____ Brainstormed with co-teachers to obtain strategies that have worked in similar cases.
9. _____ Identified in writing the student's specific educational problem.
10. _____ Consulted with counselor regarding student's behavior.
11. _____ Consulted with resource teachers in school to discuss concerns and obtain strategies.
12. _____ Obtained observation by another teacher or school resource to obtain information regarding concern.
13. _____ Developed and implemented instructional strategies with assistance of other educators.
14. _____ Developed and implemented with other educators, a behavior management plan.
15. _____ Obtained or developed instructional learning aids to address this student's problem.
16. _____ List any other modifications, interventions, or strategies you have attempted in order

to maintain this student in the classroom. _____

_____

Note. From *Developing and Implementing Individualized Education Programs, 3rd edition,* by B. B. Strickland and A. P. Turnbull, 1990, Columbus, OH; Charles B. Merrill Publishing Co. Copyright 1990 by Charles B. Merrill Publishing Co. Adapted by permission.

volvement of parents in strategy planning and implementation is not common. We feel that it is important for you to discuss your concerns and possible interventions with the student's parents (and other family members, if appropriate) either at a regular parent-teacher conference or at a specially called conference. The parents may already suspect that their son or daughter is in some way different from other children and can contribute much to the planning of prereferral interventions.

The communication skills and strategies discussed in Chapters 6 and 7 will serve you well in sharing concerns with parents. Parents' understanding can be enhanced by using specific descriptors of performance levels:

> Stuart completed 13 of 100 addition facts on his timed test; every other student in the class was able to complete 85 or more. Stuart hid his paper and appeared to be embarrassed by his score.

You can also show parents samples of their son's or daughter's work. If prior communication on report cards or in conferences about the child's performance has been accurate and explicit, parents will already have initial warnings that their child's performance is not totally satisfactory or that, in the case of children who are gifted, their child's performance is accelerated. One major reason for honest and full disclosure is that it affords parents a more gradual recognition that special help may be needed.

A conference to share concerns with parents also enables them to verify observations at home or information received previously from professionals outside the school with the concerns you have noted at school.

What if the parents do not agree with your concerns and express strong objection to your view of their son or daughter? First, it is important to consider their perspectives carefully. We must always allow for the possibility that their perspective is accurate. As one mother commented to the author:

> Roberta's teacher told me that she wanted Roberta to get special testing because of her poor reading skills. I told her that I didn't think Roberta read so badly. She reads comics, cookbooks, road signs, and written messages on TV. That's what my older kids did when they were in second grade. The teacher didn't believe me—she thought I was just sticking up for Roberta. She said Roberta couldn't do that. I told her that I see it with my own eyes at home. Why would I lie? What she does at school is not everything she does.

This mother has a good point—performance at school is not everything! Often students perform differently in different environments. When parents' observations differ from yours, ask them to give examples of their child's performance and reasons they think may account for the discrepancy. Strive to observe the child at both school and home in order to gather more information to verify or disconfirm concerns.

INITIATING AND REVIEWING THE REFERRAL

The prereferral intervention may be successful and preclude the need for formal referral and evaluation. Preliminary data indicate that the use of prereferral interventions in some schools has substantially reduced the numbers of students who proceeded through the total process of referral, evaluation, and placement (Graden et al., 1985). However, if the prereferral intervention is unsuccessful in improving the student's performance and appropriate modifications cannot be made, a referral for evaluation should be sent to the special services committee. Referral forms vary from school to school; you will need to use the one approved in your school.

To the greatest extent possible, try to obtain parent cooperation before initiating a formal referral. The EHA does not require parent consent for referral; however, some states and local school districts do. Even if consent is not required in your school district, we will shortly discuss the requirement that parents give their consent for their son or daughter to receive an initial evaluation. We encourage you to involve parents in the decision to initiate the referral as much as possible. Since the decision to refer their child for evaluation will create anxious and sad feelings for many parents, your communication with the parents needs to be sensitive to such feelings.

REVIEWING THE REFERRAL

The special services committee is responsible for reviewing the information on the referral form to decide the most appropriate way to address concerns. For example, they may suggest gathering more information on the prereferral intervention, waiting several months on the suspicion that the problem is temporary, providing remedial education rather than evaluating the student for special education, or deciding to pursue a multidisciplinary evaluation of the student. Parents need to be informed if an evaluation is not pursued, the reasons for that decision, and the plans developed to respond to the concerns that initially triggered the referral. If parents disagree with this decision, they can request an evaluation and expect it to be honored since, typically, the special services committee decides in favor of pursuing an evaluation. Thus, one study indicated that 92% of students referred were subsequently evaluated (Algozzine, Christenson & Ysseldyke, 1982).

PROVIDING NOTICE AND OBTAINING CONSENT

As noted in Chapter 8, the EHA allows parents an opportunity to participate in educational decisions for their child. As a result, schools must inform parents of their son's or daughter's performance (notice) and involve parents in decision making (consent). Typically, one member of the special services committee is responsible for communicating with the family. Committee members use various criteria to select the most appropriate person for these responsibilities (e.g., the professional who has already established a positive relationship with the parents; the one who has had the most frequent contact with the parents, or is likely to have such contact; the one whose values or communication style is most complimentary to the parents; or the one who has some time available).

We will now review how the requirements pertaining to notice and consent apply to the evaluation process.

Providing Notice

The EHA requires that schools provide a written notice to parents in their dominant language within a reasonable time period before the student's evaluation status is changed. Parents must be notified when the school:

- Proposes to initiate or change the identification, evaluation, or educational placement of the child or the provision of a free, appropriate public education to the child; or

- Refuses to initiate or change the identification, evaluation, or educational placement of the child or the provision of a free appropriate public education to the child. (*Federal Register,* 1977, p. 42495)

The primary purpose of notifying parents is to provide them with information about the reasons for the special service committee's decision. The EHA statute specifies the content requirements of the notice:

- A full explanation of all the procedural safeguards available to the parents;

- A description of the action proposed or refused by the agency, an explanation of why the agency proposes or refuses to take the action, and a description of any options the agency considered and the reasons why those options were rejected,

- A description of each evaluation procedure, test, record, or report the agency used as a basis for the proposal or refusal, and

- A description of any other factors which are relevant to the agency's proposal or refusal. (*Federal Register,* 1977, p. 42495)

First, "procedural safeguards" refers to the legal rights of parents as discussed in Chapter 8. According to Kabler (1985), these rights include those activities which the school district carries out while providing appropriate notices to parents regarding proposed actions, obtaining informed consent of parents, involving parents in decision making, and providing an impartial review mechanism in the event an unresolvable disagreement develops between the school district and the childs' parents. "The best procedural safeguards are those which strengthen the parent-school partnership leading to collaborative efforts to benefit the child" (Kabler, 1985, p. 242). It is your responsibility to inform parents of their rights. Typically, school districts have a written list of rights they send to all parents. We suggest that you review this list, if available, to assess whether or not you believe it is comprehensible to the parents with whom you work. You might even suggest changes to eliminate jargon and to enhance clarity and relevance.

The second required component of the notice is a description of the school's proposed course of action, rationale, and alternatives. At this point, the proposed action is to evaluate the student from a multidisciplinary perspective to determine whether a disability exists and the most helpful type of individual programming. Even if the reasons for this recommendation have previously been explained to parents during conferences, it is important to iterate them in writing and to identify why other possible options are less appropriate than evaluation. For example, it will essentially help to summarize the information on the referral form and the major points of discussion from the special services committee meeting in your explanation to parents.

Third, the notice must contain descriptions of assessment procedures, data, and other information used to make the decision to pursue a multidisciplinary evaluation. You can summarize information from the prereferral intervention or from the special service committee's discussion. It also helps to include the names and purposes of the tests the evaluation team plans to administer to the student. The purposes of each test will probably be more meaningful to most parents than the actual names.

Finally, any relevant information the special services committee considered in its decision to pursue an evaluation should be shared with families. Aside from academic information, this could include information associated with health status, peer relationships, or other relevant issues.

Obtaining Consent

Requiring parental consent for the initial special education evaluation means that parents must participate in the decision of whether or not to conduct a multidisciplinary evaluation. The EHA definition of consent is:

1. The parent has been fully informed of all information relevant to the activity for which consent is sought, in his or her native language or other mode of communication;
2. The parent understands and agrees in writing to the carrying out of the activity for which his or her consent is sought, and the consent describes that activity and lists the records (if any) which will be released and to whom; and
3. The parent understands that the granting of consent is voluntary on the part of the parent and may be revoked at any time. (*Federal Register,* 1977, p. 42494)

Parental consent must be obtained in the following two instances:

1. Conducting a preplacement evaluation; and
2. Initial placement of a handicapped child in a program providing special education and related services. (*Federal Register,* 1977, p. 42495)

A preplacement evaluation is the initial evaluation following the child's referral. As we discussed in Chapter 8, students must be reevaluated by a multidisciplinary team every 3 years. The reevaluation, unlike the preplacement evaluation, requires parental notice but not parental consent. The initial placement refers to the first time a student is placed in special education. Parental consent is required for the initial placement but not for subsequent changes in placement.

The concept of consent implies both the right to give and withhold it. Consider a conflict that could arise:

> You have been very concerned about Eddie's sullenness and withdrawal. Some days you believe he is pulled so far into himself that you absolutely cannot reach him. He stares blankly, cries frequently, and has practically no interaction with you or his classmates. Meanwhile, his school performance is plunging downward. You have met with his parents individually

on several occasions, as has the school counselor. They refuse to acknowledge his problems and assert emphatically that no child of theirs will ever be identified as having an emotional disorder. You believe it is your professional duty to Eddie to try to locate special help for him and you realize you simply do not have the expertise to deal with his needs. You completed a referral form with thorough documentation and reviewed it with the special services committee. They concurred with your recommendation of a psychiatric and psychoeducational evaluation. When the school counselor met with Eddie's parents to review the notice with them and request their consent, they refused to even consider the possibility of an evaluation. Frustrated, you are caught between Eddie's needs, his parents' needs, and your professional judgment.

What legal options do you have when parents refuse to give their consent? The EHA provides the following options:

1. Where state law requires parental consent before a child is evaluated or initially provided special education and related services, state procedures govern the public agency in overriding a parent's refusal to consent.

2. Where there is no state law requiring consent before a child is evaluated or initially provided special education and related services, the public agency may use the hearing procedures (outlined in the law) to determine if the child may be evaluated or initially provided special education and related services without parental consent. (*Federal Register*, 1977, p. 42495)

We advocate the use of mediation to resolve conflict whenever possible (see Chapter 11). When mediation is unsuccessful, however, it is important to recognize that parental refusal to give consent does not end the process of providing an appropriate education to students with exceptionalities. On the contrary, school professionals may challenge the decisions made by parents. A family-systems perspective can help provide insight into the intended and unintended consequences of such action for the parent-child relationship. (The ethical implications of parent-professional-child conflicts are discussed in Chapter 14.)

Supplementing Written Communication

Even though the notice to parents must be provided in writing and their consent must also be obtained in writing, face-to-face contact can be very advantageous at this point in the evaluation process. All communication does not have to be restricted to a written format. You can consider several options: (a) send parents the written notice and consent form to review and schedule a follow-up meeting to discuss the need for an evaluation and answer any questions; (b) hold a meeting in which you give the notice and consent form to parents and review the written information with them; and (c) schedule a meeting to share information with parents orally and then follow up the meeting with a written notice and consent form. Ask parents which option they would prefer. The face-to-face meeting can be helpful in developing a trusting relationship, providing support for parents' anxieties and concerns, and orienting parents to what they can expect throughout the evaluation and IEP process.

COLLECTING EVALUATION INFORMATION

We discussed the legal requirements for nondiscriminatory evaluation in Chapter 8 and made some suggestions about the meaning of those requirements for professionals. Here, we want to discuss the meaning in greater detail.

The special services committee is responsible for appointing a multidisciplinary team to collect evaluation information for the purpose of determining if the student has an exceptionality and to identify the nature and extent of special education and related services that the student needs. The only EHA requirement for multidisciplinary team composition is that the team include at least one teacher or other specialist with knowledge in the area of the suspected disability. There is no explicit requirement that family members be involved in the collection of evaluation information. However, the team must:

> Draw upon information from a variety of sources, including aptitude and achievement tests, teacher recommendations, physical condition, special or cultural background, and adaptive behavior. (*Federal Register,* 1977, p. 42497)

Family members can provide valuable information from a unique perspective, but often family input is not sought. In a 2-year study examining the EHA impact on nine children and their families representing diverse exceptionalities and backgrounds, Halpern (1982) found that parents' perspectives during the evaluation process were not actively sought. He concluded that parents have to take the initiative to share their perspectives.

Harriet Rose, a mother of a young adult with cerebral palsy, described her desperate attempt to get professionals to accept her opinions regarding her daughter:

> How could I convince them my daughter was bright and capable of learning? What could I say to keep them from brushing my opinions aside be-

cause I was "just a mother?" I decided I was going to have to take an aggressive approach in order to keep from being ignored.

I whisked Nancy inside the center in her wheelchair, gave my interviewer a smashing smile and proceeded to tell her more than she really needed to know about Nancy using all the technical and medical jargon I had learned over the previous 10 years. I also mentioned, very casually, that I had earned my master's degree in special education and had taught school before Nancy was born. All of which was a bare-faced lie.

At first I felt a little guilty about what I had done. It really wasn't fair for me to take out my previous frustrations on those perfectly innocent professionals. But on the other hand, it was sad to think that my opinion as a pseudoprofessional was valued so much more than my opinions as a mother had ever been.

Family Participation in the Evaluation Process

Many options exist for families to participate in the evaluation process. For example, they may share information about the strengths and needs of their family. (Family discussions can follow the protocol included in Appendix B. We recommend that this protocol be adapted to special considerations of a particular family and multidisciplinary team.) Social workers and counselors have special training in working with families and can assume this responsibility within the context of the multidisciplinary team. This interview can provide valuable insight into the families' perceptions and expectations about the evaluation and their son's or daughter's participation in a special education program.

An alternative to an interview is to more informally visit with the family to listen to how they share their "family story." Often the most relevant information evolves from informal conversations about the daily responsibilities facing families and the ways they are meeting those responsibilities.

We advocate including family perspectives as an integral part of the evaluation process to ensure that the child's evaluation is viewed within the ecological context of family life. According to Sattler (1988), the goals of an initial interview with parents can be summarized as follows:

1. to gather information about parental concerns and goals;
2. to assess parental perceptions of the child's problems and strengths;
3. to obtain a case history;
4. to identify problem areas and related antecedent and consequent events;
5. to identify reinforcing events for both child and parents;

6. to assess parents' motivation and resources for change;

7. to obtain informed consent; and

8. to discuss assessment procedures and follow-up contacts. (p. 442)

A third way to include families in the process of collecting evaluation information is to ask them to provide information about their son's or daughter's developmental skills in home and community environments. As we pointed out earlier in this chapter, students perform differently in different settings. Thus, a comprehensive view of a student necessitates collecting performance data from settings outside of the school. Vincent and her colleagues suggest that at least one report from parents or family members be included in every multidisciplinary evaluation (Vincent, Laten, Salisbury, Brown, & Baumgart, 1981).

Most family inventories have been developed for the early childhood level. However, a few are designed for use at the elementary and secondary levels. One resource that lists family inventories is *Family Assessment* by Harold Grotevant and Cindy Carlson (1989). In addition, this book provides information on observational coding schemes, global rating scales, projective techniques, and self-report measures. These inventories were primarily developed to be administered by family clinicians. Since teachers are *not* family clinicians, interviews and informal conversations offer the best ways for teachers to gather information. If you believe more indepth information on a family needs to be gathered, we encourage you to seek assistance from the school counselor or psychologist.

Finally, it is useful to determine the student's preferences and choices. While the best way to accomplish this is to gather it directly from students, parents may be the most helpful informants for young children and for students with severe communication disabilities. Special educators are increasingly recognizing the importance of tailoring instructional programs to student preferences and teaching choice-making skills (Guess, Benson, & Siegel-Causey, 1985; A. P. Turnbull & Turnbull, 1985).

Minority Families and the Evaluation Process

Professionals are increasingly concerned about ensuring that the needs of families from diverse ethnic backgrounds are addressed during the evaluation phase. A significantly higher percentage of minority, as compared to majority, students are referred for psychological testing; however, psychologists contact parents of minority students less often than parents of majority students (Tomlinson, Acker, Canter, & Lindborg, 1977).

When you contact parents of minority students, the contact takes place within a sociocultural context. As we discussed in Chapter 6, communication difficulties due to ethnic, cultural, or socioeconomic differences between you and the parents may arise. Therefore, when evaluating minority students, consider the influences of the family's cultural background, use of language at home, and attitudes towards school and academic achievement (Esquivel, 1985). Sattler (1988) provides the following suggestions for how to work with members of different ethnic, cultural, and social groups:

1. Study the culture, language, and traditions of other groups;

2. Learn about your own stereotypes and prejudices;

3. See the strengths in the coping mechanisms of other groups;

4. Appreciate the minority families' viewpoints and show a willingness to accept a perspective other than your own;

5. Recognize when group membership differences may be intruding on the communication process; and

6. Find ways to circumvent potential difficulties. (p. 462)

Right of Parents to Obtain Independent Evaluations

According to the EHA, parents have the right to obtain independent evaluations of any child who may have a disabling condition. The only way a school system can deny this right is by establishing the appropriateness of their own evaluation through a due process hearing. According to Hepner and Silverstein (1988a), this is one of the most important and underutilized aspects of the EHA. The regulations state that the results of any independent evaluation obtained by the parents must be considered by the school district in any decision made with respect to their child. This right to an independent evaluation applies even if the assessment of the child has already been completed by school personnel. As school personnel, you are required to provide parents with information about where they can obtain an independent evaluation.

Hepner and Silverstein (1988a) cited two major circumstances that might lead parents to seek an independent evaluation. One is concern about the evaluation process, the other is concern about the results and implications of the evaluation. In either case, it is important that, when a parent has engaged more than one professional to work with their child, these professionals be willing to communicate with each other about their evaluation findings and their work with the child (Hepner & Silverstein, 1988b). The importance of cooperation between various professionals is discussed earlier in this chapter.

ANALYZING EVALUATION INFORMATION

The multidisciplinary team assumes responsibility for analyzing evaluation information. This is done at two levels: (a) scoring and interpreting the meaning of each evaluation instrument; and (b) analyzing and synthesizing all evaluations to obtain an overall composite of the student's performance. The first task typically is done individually by multidisciplinary team members whereas the latter takes place at a team meeting. The goal of the meeting should be to determine whether the student has an exceptionality and the particular type of such exceptionality and to develop a profile of the student's strengths and weaknesses for the purpose of individual program planning. This analysis provides the basis of the decision on the appropriateness of the student's placement into special education. It also enables the team to present a composite view to the family rather than a fragmentation of discrete scores from several instruments.

Family members usually do not participate at this point in the assessment process. The scoring, analysis, and synthesis of evaluation instruments requires technical expertise that most families do not have. Some families, however, are knowledgeable in this area and may value the opportunity to participate in this preliminary review of information. Additionally, some families appreciate being present at any discussion related to their child's possible identification for special education, perhaps because they perceive that the best way to ensure that their perspective is considered is to be part of the decision-making process from its earliest point. Parental involvement in analysis of evaluation information can vary depending upon its appropriateness for a given family.

DISCUSSING EVALUATION RESULTS WITH PARENTS

How Parents Are Notified

As we noted in Chapter 8 and in this chapter, parents must receive written notification any time school personnel propose or refuse to change a student's identification, evaluation, educational placement, or the provision of a free, appropriate education. Consequently, written notification (or a written summary) of evaluation results must follow the initial evaluation. (The required content of the notice was described in this chapter.) Reevaluations every 3 years do not require a written notice. However, we encourage professionals to frequently touch base with families. In addition, it is a good rule of thumb always to give families a copy of the reevaluation summary. Full disclosure of information on a continuing basis frequently enhances parental trust and the probability of their making informed decisions.

After initial evaluations are completed, parents must be informed in a written fashion. It is also very important to be able to interpret findings orally to them. As we pointed out, evaluation information can be highly technical, and written explanations may not be fully informative. Another benefit of discussions is that family perspectives concerning the evaluation data can be extremely helpful in validating or disconfirming such data. Specifically, parents can share information on the son's or daughter's special needs, confirm whether or not the performance described by professionals is typical, and make connections between the current and previous evaluations completed by persons outside of the school such as pediatricians and preschool teachers.

What options are available for interpreting evaluation findings to families in a written and oral fashion? The two major options consist of holding an evaluation interpretative conference with the parents or to incorporate the review of evaluation information into the IEP conference. The advantages of a separate conference, particularly for the initial evaluation, is that it allows more time to discuss findings in depth and enables the family to assimilate evaluation information prior to making immediate programming decisions. On the other hand, the advantage of incorporating the interpretative conference into the IEP conference is that it eliminates an additional meeting.

We suggest that you consider a separate interpretative conference in the case of initial evaluations and the multidisciplinary reevaluations if families are interested in this option. Our experience suggests that it is practically impossible to do justice to reviewing and discussing a formal evaluation and planning the IEP in one meeting. Further, most parents (including the Turnbulls) are unable to assimilate the implications of evaluation information quickly enough to translate them immediately into IEP decisions concerning goals, objectives, placement, and related services. When formal evaluations have not been administered, however, a performance update on the student can be shared at the IEP conference.

Now, let us consider strategies for coordinating oral and written notification of evaluation results. Parents may receive written notification prior to the conference, during the conference, or as a follow-up to the conference. Table 9–1 includes a summary of the advantages and disadvantages of each of these strategies. Since it is impossible accurately to second-guess parent preferences, we suggest again that you ask them which approach to sharing information they would find most helpful.

One study found that parents who were able to hear an audio- and videotape replay of the evaluation conference significantly increased their understanding of their child's speech and hearing problems (Marshall & Goldstein, 1969). Thus, mechanical feedback can be used for a

TABLE 9–1 Timing of Written Notification to Families

TIMING OF WRITTEN NOTIFICATION	ADVANTAGES	DISADVANTAGES
A. Send written notification of evaluation results to families prior to the conference.	• Families can review and reflect on results that enable them to pinpoint areas of agreement and disagreement. • They can observe their child as a basis for confirming or disconfirming results. • They can review the report with the child. • They can make a list of questions to ask at the conference. • They can identify important areas not covered by the evaluation. • Essentially, they can be ready to *discuss* the report at the meeting.	• When the initial evaluation is done and parents are receiving "formal" information for the first time, a written notice can seem impersonal and brusk. • Many families may have difficulty reading or comprehending the report. • Families may misinterpret information, creating erroneous impressions about the child's performance.
B. Share written notification of evaluation results with families during the conference.	• Professionals can explain the evaluation results beyond the scope of that in the written notice. • A face-to-face explanation can be helpful and supportive to families who are learning for the first time that their child has an exceptionality. • Providing a copy of the written notice during the evaluation prevents families from having to take notes and provides written clarification for them to refer to immediately after the conference.	• The families' advanced planning is eliminated if they have no evaluation information to consider prior to the conference. • Hearing evaluation results for the first time at the conference may prevent families from being able to pinpoint their areas of agreement and disagreement. This could necessitate an additional meeting.

C. Share written notification of evaluation results with families after the conference.

- Professionals can explain the evaluation results beyond the scope of that in the written notice.

- A face-to-face explanation can be helpful and supportive to families who are learning for the first time that their child has an exceptionality.

- Writing the notice after the conference enables professionals to incorporate family perspectives shared at the conference into the report.

- The families' advanced planning is eliminated if they have no evaluation information to consider prior to the conference.

- Hearing evaluation results for the first time at the conference may prevent families from being able to pinpoint their areas of agreement and disagreement while they are in attendance. This could necessitate an additional meeting.

Note. From *Developing and Implementing Individualized Education Programs* by A. P. Turnbull, B. Strickland, and J. C. Brantley, 1982. Columbus, OH: Merrill Publishing Co. Copyright 1982 by Merrill Publishing Co.

replay of important information. Most people's comprehension is increased from hearing emotionally laden and complex information more than one time.

Parents' Role in Discussing Evaluation Results

Many professionals perceive their role to be one of interpreting evaluation results to parents, but such a perception implies one-way communication—that the conference is designed for professionals to tell parents how their child is performing. On the contrary, the purpose of the conference is for professionals and parents (and others whom they invite) to discuss the evaluation findings and reach the most complete understanding possible of the student's instructional needs. Some parents prefer to be passive recipients of information and their preferences need to be respected. Others, however, want to be actively involved in making evaluation decisions.

Regardless of the level of participation, parents often find the conference to be an intimidating situation. Blair (1989) noted six reasons that may contribute to a parent feeling uncomfortable in conferences:

1. At a meeting, particularly an initial meeting, there are many professionals, most of whom are strangers to the parent.
2. In many instances parents feel their level of knowledge is less than that of the professional.
3. Many parents lack training and/or experience in communicating with professionals.
4. At times parents distrust the intentions of the professionals so they distrust their recommendations.
5. Frequently parents don't believe that what they have to offer will carry any weight; therefore, they may not really understand that their role is to be a part of the team.
6. Sometimes parents come to a meeting with feelings of anger at the professionals who have only seen their child briefly, yet think they know what is best. (p. 6)

When you put yourself in the parents' place, you clearly understand how hearing evaluation results can be a painful and emotional experience. However sensitively the information is conveyed, many parents, particularly those who strongly value academic achievement and success, will be sorely disappointed by the confirmation of a problem. Many parents are starved to hear good news about their child:

> Ramon has been tested so many times. I guess he started a program when he was 7½ months old. I was constantly being updated on where

he was in relation to where he should be. Maybe they were saying strengths, but it seemed to me they were just saying how he compared to others. His weaknesses were in all areas—motor, speech, just everything was delayed. Wasn't there anything positive to say?

Some parents may experience feelings of guilt that they created the problem or could have attended to it earlier. They may worry about their child's future and fear an escalation of problems. A defense mechanism may be to doubt the credibility or expertise of the multidisciplinary team. Some parents will need more time than others to come to grips with the reality of the evaluation results.

Fourteen years ago, when my son was in Junior High, I remember walking into the room with five teachers, a guidance counselor, a vice principal, a psychologist, a social worker and a learning consultant. I was told that my child was a behavior problem, dyslexic, hyperactive and a general "pain in the neck." He was always clowning and disrupting classes. This child was the light of my life, yet no one had anything positive to say about him. No one suggested that his clowning was a need to cover for his feelings of inadequacy. No one realized that it is easier to let others think he was funny than reveal that he couldn't do the work. I looked up and saw the eyes of all ten people upon me. I felt that each of them had not only judged my son but was judging me as a parent. I was a working mother, which elicits some guilt under any circumstances, but in this situation, I believed they were questioning why I was working when my son had problems. I felt guilty, inadequate, angry, frustrated, and most of all helpless. (Halperin, 1989, p. 6)

You can help by responding to the questions that parents have, providing them with clear descriptions and concrete examples of their child's performance, and offering to arrange for additional evaluations by persons not involved in the initial evaluation. Sometimes professionals are frustrated by parents who do not immediately accept the evaluation results. We hope you will strive to put yourself in the parents' shoes and realize how much they love their child and how strong their parental need is to "stack the deck" in favor of their child. Your support and patience will pay off in the end.

Student's Role in Discussing Evaluation Results

Sharing evaluation results with children and youth is also important. According to Sattler (1988), students need evaluation feedback to make decisions about themselves and to make accurate estimates about their abilities. Such information is needed for self-corrective or esteem-building purposes.

A student can get involved in interpretive conferences at many different levels (Teglasi, 1985). First, the parents may be given the test results and instructed on how best to share the evaluation results and recommendations with their son or daughter. Second, the student may be brought in at the end of a conference held initially only with the parent. Finally, separate conferences can be held with the parents and the student. The advantage of the latter approach is that it prevents children and youth from becoming overpowered by the presence of many adults. If separate conferences are arranged, they can be followed by a joint conference where the results are reviewed on the student's level. It does not matter which approach is used as long as you are sensitive to the needs and preferences of children and youth to receive information regarding their evaluations.

Agenda for Discussing Results

It is extremely important that the conference in which evaluation results are discussed with parents (and other family members according to the parents' preferences) is well prepared and well conducted. According to Teglasi (1985), three goals should guide the interpretation of evaluation information to parents: (1) a clear understanding of the student's problems should be promoted; (2) parents should be assisted in the emotional adjustment to the assessment information; (3) the information should be interpreted and communicated so as to facilitate decision making.

THE PRESENTATION OF EVALUATION RESULTS.   The first goal can be obtained by being well prepared and structured in your presentation of the evaluation results. One broad way of structuring the agenda is to include the following components:

- initial proceedings,
- presentation of findings,
- recommendations, and
- summary (Rockowitz & Davidson, 1979).

Whatever structure you use, it is important to include the parent at each level of discussion to get both their reactions to your input and their own input. For example, during the initial proceedings, it is important to ask parents their perceptions of their son's or daughter's functioning. Their answer will provide you with clues to their current level of understanding and can help you take the "shoes test" with them—put yourself in their place. Perhaps you can incorporate some key words they use (e.g., "lagging behind") in subsequent explanations.

Consideration of the parents is also important when reviewing the evaluation results. Hirsch (1981) designed a training program to teach parent-conference skills by combining programmed learning materials and role-play practice sessions. A major component of this training consisted of communicating evaluation results. Hirsch developed a series of steps for professionals to follow which is summarized below:

1. Introduce the skill being discussed including examples.
2. State the student's current level of functioning on the skill and how that compares to chronological age peers.
3. Give examples of skills the child can and cannot perform.
4. Address the importance if any discrepancy is noted between age and achievement and how this will affect the student's development at present and future. (Hirsch, 1981)

The communication skills that we discussed in Chapter 6 are very useful to incorporate into your discussion of evaluation results. Many parents have had many clues that problems exist and usually appreciate direct, yet sensitive communication. Helpful tips include using jargon-free language, offering suggestions for follow-up reading material, and conveying the clear message that you have the child's and family's interests in mind.

PARENTAL ACCEPTANCE OF EVALUATION RESULTS. Most parents experience initial emotional reactions to the assessment information you present. Their ability to adjust to those reactions and accept the results can be enhanced by actions you may take. Teglasi (1985) describes the following general pitfalls to be avoided during parent conferences:

1. Avoid blaming parents (e.g., "You should have read to your daughter more when she was young.").
2. Avoid passive avoidance (e.g., "Your son's disability shouldn't cause any problems for you.").
3. Avoid a tendency toward comforting (e.g., "Everything will work out.").
4. Avoid authoritarian dogmatism (e.g., "Your daughter's test results indicate a severe emotional disturbance.").

From a multidisciplinary perspective, an important consideration in sharing evaluation results is to formulate a composite of the student's strengths and weaknesses rather than a string of isolated discipline-specific reports. The family is dealing with the whole child—not a child segmented into mind, muscles, larynx, eyes, ears, and personality. A parent shared her frustration concerning isolated evaluation reports:

> Specialists see her from their own point of view. I guess the hardest thing is that I want answers. I wanted them to say she is going to make it or she isn't going to make it. I guess the hardest thing is not getting answers and everyone looking at their particular area and no one giving me the whole picture. Everyone is just looking at one area and forgetting she is a whole child.

A major outcome of the evaluation discussion should be to reframe the conception of the student's problem. Fulmer, Cohen, and Monaco (1985) described this reframing as follows:

> Feedback of test results inevitably affects the way in which a family conceives their child's problem. It may serve to answer questions the family has already framed, such as "is he able to perform his schoolwork?" It may also serve to introduce whole new viewpoints from which to see a certain behavior. That is, a child whom the parents see as "bad" or "disobedient" may be reframed by the consultant as "disabled." One who is seen as "lazy" may be reframed as "depressed."
>
> The main purpose of "reframing" a child's problem is to "construct a workable reality" [Liebman, 1975] for the family. That is, to state the problem in a way that permits a solution. (pp. 145–146)

The process of reframing proceeds on different schedules for different families. Again, the majority of parents will need a period of time to integrate the evaluation information fully and develop new perceptions about their child. Switzer (1985) describes a cognitive problem-solving seminar she offered for parents of children who recently received the diagnosis of learning disabilities. The purpose was to provide factual knowledge, decrease feelings of anxiety, and increase receptivity to interventions. She reported a positive evaluation by families. Interestingly, parents recommended that such a seminar be delayed for 2 months after diagnosis to provide needed "distance" before readiness to learn disability-related information.

FOLLOWING THROUGH ON RECOMMENDATONS.   After evaluation results have been discussed, decisions must be made. The more parents feel that they have been actively involved in the evaluation process, the more likely they will be to follow through on recommendations. Teglasi (1985) identified the following factors as being associated with a greater likelihood that parents will carry out recommendations:

- Parents who perceive their child's problem in a manner that is similar to the professional's are far more apt to accept the recommendation than if they disagree with the problem statement.

- The likelihood of following through on the recommendations is enhanced when both parents attend the conference, particularly if there are two or more conferences.

- Precise communication or clarity of interpretive material is important, and

- Families are more likely to act on a recommendation from professionals whom they perceive as caring. (Teglasi, 1985, pp. 419–420)

It may be useful to engage in continuous evaluation of the progress of the evaluation conference as the conference proceeds. The following questions could serve as a guide in such an evaluation:

1. Do the parents understand the results?
2. Do they generally accept the results?
3. Do they understand the recommendations?
4. Do they generally accept the recommendations?
5. What specific areas do they question?
6. What kinds of interventions do they desire?
7. Do they understand their rights under Public Law 94–142?
8. Do they want another evaluation from an independent source?
9. What would they consider successful treatment or remediation?
10. How willing are they to change their own expectations and behavior?
11. Are they willing to be involved in parent training programs or in other skill programs? (Sattler, 1988, p. 453)

Two major outcomes can result from discussing evaluation results: (a) it can be determined that the student does not qualify for special education, the referral concerns can be addressed in an alternative way, and parents can be notified accordingly; or (b) the student can be identified as an appropriate recipient of special education services. In the latter case, the next step in the process is to arrange for an IEP conference. (The role of the family in the conference will be discussed in Chapter 10.)

INFORMING PARENTS OF THE IEP CONFERENCE

The next chapter will discuss the IEP conference in detail. At this point, we want to call your attention to the EHA requirement that parents be notified (in writing or orally) of the IEP conference. Such notice must be provided early enough to allow parents to make arrangements to attend, and it must indicate the purpose, the time, and the location, as well as the persons who will attend. Furthermore, the IEP conference must be scheduled at a mutually agreed-upon time and place. In cases in which a separate evaluation conference is held, the need to inform parents of the IEP conference can be included as one of the recommendations. Since many parents do not know what an IEP conference is, it may be helpful to provide a thorough explanation of what will happen at the conference and to give parents written material so they can prepare for their role in the conference (a discussion of the use of printed material to provide information is included in Chapter 12).

REFERRAL AND EVALUATION OF INFANTS AND TODDLERS

As discussed in Chapter 8, the definitions of evaluation (determination of program eligibility) and assessment (identification of strengths, needs, and services for ongoing program planning) and procedures for nondisciplinary compliance are similar in Part B and Part H of the EHA. There are, however, some major differences between referral and evaluation procedures of infants and toddlers and school-age students that are worthy of note.

First, the *process and timing of referral* is addressed in the Part H regulations but not in the Part B regulations. In terms of *process*, Part H regulations give primary emphasis to a comprehensive child-find system to identify and locate infants and toddlers in each state who are eligible for services. This system is responsible for developing procedures which primary referral sources (hospitals, physicians, parents, day-care programs, local educational agencies, public health facilities, other social service agencies, and other health care providers) can use in making referrals for evaluation and assessment and for services, if appropriate. Two regulatory *timelines* apply to referrals: (a) they must be made 2 working days after a child has been identified; and (b) once the referral is made, the evaluation and assessment activities and the IFSP meeting must be completed within 45 days. We encourage you to contact the lead agency in your state to obtain a description of its child-find program and the procedures developed for the primary referral sources.

The second major difference between the Part B and the Part H regulations is that the latter calls for a *family assessment*, in addition to child assessment. The family assessment must identify the family's strengths and needs related to enhancing the development of the child. According to regulations, such assessment must be voluntary, carried out by appropriately trained personnel, based on information provided by the family through a personal interview, and incorporate the family's description of its strengths and needs as these relate to enhancing the child's development. A related issue is the third major difference which is greater emphasis on *clinical methods* for obtaining information (e.g., the evaluation and assessment of the child must be based on informed clinical opinion) and, as stated above, the family assessment must include a personal interview.

The Part H requirements for a family assessment and the use of clinical methods will require the development of many new practices in the field which will occur after the publication of this book. At the Beach Center on Families and Disability at The University of Kansas, we and our colleagues are working to develop a process for identifying family strengths and needs that is as "family-friendly" as possible. In this effort, our approach has been to talk with families and practitioners around the country and to get a grassroots perspective on preferences (Summers et al., in press).

Families and practitioners are recommending an informal approach with an emphasis on open-ended conversations rather than the completion of paper-and-pencil inventories or even structured interviews. They emphasize the importance of investing time in building rapport and friendship between practitioners and family members. Here are some viewpoints of families:

> At first, I was tense with the professional coming to my home. But it was a nice little conversation. The professional's mannerisms and the way she asked questions was like we were sitting down for a cup of coffee. She got a lot of information without asking.

> She [previous practitioner] came out to the house when [child] was 8 months [old], and she said, he has problems, and I said, no, he don't, he's just a baby. . . . She asks me all kinds of stuff like if I have a crib, how many people live here, and she writes it down. She was a nosy lady—nosy, nosy! I kept hiding from her, and finally I moved so they wouldn't bug me. . . . When she [current practitioner] came out, I thought, oh, gee, here we go again. So I asked her, "What's wrong?" and she just says "nothing, I just want to know if you need anything."

Based on our research, the advice from families and practitioners is consistent with the Part H regulations which emphasize clinical methods—eliciting from families a description of strengths and needs as they see them and using personal interviews. The challenge is to develop family-friendly approaches in which families and professionals can create comfortable opportunities for families to express, through dialogue, their own strengths and needs in light of their daily life. Coles (1989), a prominent psychiatrist and humanitarian, describes the perspective of his mentor: "Why don't you chuck the word 'interview.' Call yourself a friend, call your exchanges 'conversations'!" (p. 32).

Consistent with our emphasis on family-friendly language and concepts, we prefer to avoid the term, *family assessment,* even though it is used in the Part H regulations. To some people the term connotes a formal, standardized, even judgmental process. Since this clearly is *not* the intention of the regulations, we prefer to characterize the process as *identifying family strengths and needs.* The role of early intervention is not to assess families in a traditional sense, but to identify through mutual exchanges the strengths and needs of families that are relevant to consider in planning and providing early intervention services.

At the Beach Center we will be working over the next several years to develop model procedures for family-friendly means of identifying family strengths and needs. That information will be incorporated into the third edition of this text. (We will be happy to send you a bibliography if you contact us.)

We would like to return to the emphasis in the Part H regulations on the use of clinical methods. The child evaluations must be conducted by personnel trained to utilize appropriate methods and procedures and be based on informed clinical opinion. A state-of-art aspect of infant/toddler assessment that has implications for both personnel training and the use of clinical opinion is the *simultaneous* collection of information and sharing of results.

An example of a program that uses this approach is helpful in understanding how it works:

> Project Trans/Team, at Child Development Resources in Lightfoot, Virginia, uses an assessment process that prevents staff from interpreting assessment data and making decisions without the family present. The family and the assessment facilitator work with the child, while the other team members observe. Following this transdisciplinary assessment, the entire team meets immediately to discuss their observations and possible interpretations. The family is asked to share their thoughts and observations first. If staff are uncertain about any aspect of what they saw they share their uncertainty with the family and with each other. (Johnson, McGonigel, & Kaufman, 1989, p. 30)

The "agony" of waiting for results and worrying about what they might be can be alleviated for families when they participate in collecting assessment information and when that information is immediately exchanged.

SUMMARY

This chapter has described the steps involved in the referral and evaluation process. These steps and the activities associated with them for school-age children are summarized in Figure 9–1, and the end of the chapter describes how this process differs for the infant/toddler population. The referral and evaluation process is long, with many component parts, but it is a critically important process. When referral and evaluation are soundly and humanely accomplished, a relationship of trust and collaboration among families and professionals will start on a firm basis. It is upon this strong foundation that the IEP and IFSP conference is built. Chapter 10 will describe this next phase of implementing the legal rights and responsibilities of students and their families.

FAMILY PARTICIPATION IN DEVELOPING THE IEP

IEP conferences are stressful for some families. Parent-to-parent contacts may help relieve some of these feelings.

Elizabeth had always liked her looks. Her thick, raven hair and copper skin had turned more than a few heads. She didn't have much money, but she had been told she made her clothes look good instead of the other way around. Today, however, the mirror reflected somebody different. She combed and combed her hair but she couldn't get it right. The more she tried, the more frustrated she became. She looked at her hands; they were trembling. Elizabeth had been dreading this day for several weeks—in fact, ever since she got the letter saying she had to go to a meeting to help plan her son Tyrone's education. Those important people at that school would never listen to what she had to say; she just knew it. How could she ever make them understand? Tyrone does lots of smart things, and he should be with smart kids—not in a "special" class. But why would they ever listen to her when she dropped out of tenth grade to have him?

Extensive family participation in the IEP process is a hallmark of the Education for the Handicapped Act (EHA). However, passing a law that provides the opportunity for families to participate equally and actively in educational decision making does not ensure that they will (A. P. Turnbull & Turnbull, 1982). After reading this chapter you will be able to answer the following questions about IEP conferences with family members:

- How much do family members typically participate?
- What barriers restrict family participation?
- How can I involve family members more in this important process?

REVIEW OF RESEARCH ON PARENT PARTICIPATION IN IEP CONFERENCES

A policy interpretation of IEP requirements, prepared by the Office of Special Education in the U.S. Department of Education, clarifies the expectations for family involvement:

The IEP meeting serves as a communication vehicle between parents and school personnel, and enables them as equal participants to jointly decide what the childs needs are, what services will be provided to meet those needs, and what the anticipated outcomes will be (*Federal Register, 1981, p. 5462*).

In spite of the emphasis on parental participation mandated by this policy, research demonstrates that many families do not actively participate in the IEP process. Following are three studies that have examined parental participation in IEPs. None involves special interventions to increase parent participation; rather, they portray the nature of parent participation without special attempts to influence it.

The first study surveyed 400 parents of students representing a broad spectrum of types and levels of disabilities, ages (i.e., 4–20), and ethnicity (Lynch & Stein, 1982). Families were interviewed in their homes using a 64-item questionnaire administered in their native language. Highlights of the results are as follows:

- Of the 71 parents who reported participating in IEP development, 14.6% stated they had expressed opinions and made suggestions, 11.2% said they helped and trusted the professionals, 7.5% responded that they listened to and agreed with the teacher's recommendations, and 6.3% maintained that they understood everything that went on;

- Seventy-six expressed that they were satisfied or very satisfied with their child's special education program;

- Parents of students with physical disabilities and parents of 13- and 14-year-old students reported significantly less participation than parents of students in other programs and age categories;

- Caucasian parents were significantly more aware of the related services identified on the IEP than black or Hispanic parents; and

- Hispanic parents tended to offer fewer suggestions in the IEP conference than black or Caucasian parents (the population was too small to allow for statistical comparison).

In another study, Vacc et al. (1985) evaluated 47 conferences conducted for students with learning disabilities. Their results included variables related to (a) length and composition of the conference, (b) participation styles of those in attendance, and (c) discussion content. The length of the conferences was 12 to 49 minutes, with 25 minutes being the average. The typical number of participants in the conference was three; with a special educator and a parent or guardian attending each. Mothers attended significantly more often than fathers. Only six of the 47 conferences, however, met federal guidelines for appropriate participant composition.

Parents and special education teachers were found in this study to contribute more than any other participants at the conferences, but their participation styles differed. Almost 33% of the parental participation was passive in content compared to 3% of the special educators' citations. Parents appeared more likely to respond to comments directed toward them rather than to ask questions or initiate comments.

The discussion content of these conferences reveals important information for professionals. Thus, academic and social functioning was the primary focus, whereas relatively little attention was given to personal information about the student, placement, implementation plans, and plans for integrating students into regular classes. Due process was the least frequently cited topic for discussion. (Such oversights could be avoided by soliciting information about certain topics by open-ended questioning of the parents [See Chapter 6].)

In the third study, 26 conferences of students with learning disabilities were evaluated (Vaughn, Bos, Harrell, & Lasky, 1988). This investigation not only determined length, composition, and parental participation, but also analyzed parental attitudes in greater depth than the 1985 Vacc et al. study. The 1988 conferences lasted from 20 to 110 minutes with the average length of 41 minutes. An average of 6.4 participants were involved. Hence, conferences seem to have increased in length and in number of participants over the 3 years between the two studies.

The passive nature of parental participation was also noted in this study. Parent interactions accounted for merely 14.8% of the conference time or 6.5 minutes. Most of the time was spent initiating comments or making responses. An average of only 4.5 questions was asked by parents. The number of participants did not appear to affect parent participation.

Communication problems may contribute to the passive quality of parent participation. When asked about the school's goals for the parents, 39% replied that they believed school personnel wanted them to help their child with homework. One fifth (19%) said they did not know what the school's goals for them were. Regarding their personal goals for the school, 66% said they wanted the schools to help their child do better; 12% suggested specific areas for improvement; and 35% responded that they wanted their child to be brought up to grade level. The discrepancy between perceived goals of the school and parental goals points to a communication problem that should be addressed during the conference.

Another area of communication difficulty appears to be parental misunderstanding of the terminology commonly used by professionals. Of the parents interviewed, over one fourth thought the term *learning disabled* (LD) meant their child was slow. Only 4% knew the term meant their child had average or above average intelligence. To 12%, the term implied that their child had a physical problem. Some merely responded: "(Learning disabled) is what my child is" (Vaughn et al., 1988, p. 86); 23% had no or an unrelated explanation. These results suggest that clarifying terms for parents is an important aspect of the IEP conference and should not be neglected.

This parental lack of understanding may extend to the child. Parents were asked about their child's knowledge of the IEP process. Almost one fifth (19%) said their children, whose ages ranged from 5 to 16

TABLE 10–1 Possible Reasons for Passive Parental Participation

---

- Satisfaction with conferences and their level of participation causes them to feel no need to contribute more.
- Knowledge about their child's handicaps and of the decisions made during the conference is not enough to allow them to participate.
- School personnel expect parents to play a passive role in the process.
- The classroom teacher, who is frequently not in attendance or is given little status at the conference, appears to be the provider of most information to parents prior to the IEP meeting. Thus, a mismatch of information provision occurs.

Note. From "Parent Participation in the Initial Placement/IEP Conference 10 Years after Mandated Involvement" by S. Vaughn, C. S. Bos, J. E. Harrell, and B. A. Lasky, 1988, *Journal of Learning Disabilities, 21*(2), pp. 82–89.

---

years, did not know they were coming to the conference, and 38% reported that their child did not think a problem existed. Only 15% stated that their child knew about his or her learning disabilities. Thus, students in this study did not appear to be developing self-advocacy skills.

Parental attitudes about the meeting itself varied. More than half (69%) of the parents interviewed were positive and appreciative of the meeting. However, some mentioned being nervous and cautious, while others said they felt confused and overwhelmed. In spite of the discomfort experienced by some parents, 65% felt all their questions had been answered, and the vast majority (92%) believed the school wanted to help their child.

These studies show key trends and parallels. On the whole, parents can be characterized as passive participants in IEP conferences. Table 10–1 delineates possible reasons for such passive participation. Generally, parents report satisfaction with both their child's special education program and their relatively low degree of involvement in IEP development. Trends of negative, disgruntled parental perceptions are noticeably absent from these data. (However, research trends do not represent all parents. Some parents do actively participate in IEP conferences, but the majority of parents do not.) Also, all these studies focused on the IEP conferences of students with disabilities. Research is needed on IEP conferences involving parents of students who are gifted. A major contribution of the Lynch and Stein (1982) investigation is the identification of participation variations according to disability type, family life-cycle stage, and cultural background.

The finding that the majority of parents participate passively in conferences cannot be interpreted as a reflection of the parents' preference. For this reason, we need to explore barriers that prevent more active involvement.

BARRIERS TO PARENT PARTICIPATION

Passive parent participation can be interpreted in many different ways. One way is to recognize the numerous barriers that preclude parents from achieving more active participation. Indeed, Lynch and Stein (1982) found discrepancies between the barriers identified by low-income parents and special education teachers (U.S. Department of Education, 1984). These barriers are identified in Table 10–2.

As illustrated, parents and teachers have different opinions about the sources of barriers. Given the vast variations among parents, professionals, and IEP conference content, we believe that no set pattern of barriers can be identified. Thus, you must recognize all potential barriers and learn strategies for minimizing each one. To help you accomplish this goal, we will address individually each of the barriers identified in Table 10–2.

Parent-Identified Barriers

LOGISTICAL PROBLEMS. Many parents face logistical barriers, such as lack of transportation and child care, that hinder them from attending IEP conferences. Providing these services can increase parent participation in the meetings (Pfeiffer, 1980) and in IEP-related training sessions (Thompson, 1982), especially for parents of low socio-economic status. Suggestions are provided in Table 10–3 for overcoming these obstacles.

Another important logistical issue involves fathers. IEP meetings are almost always attended by one parent—the mother (Vacc et al., 1985).

TABLE 10–2 Barriers to Parental Participation

ACCORDING TO . . . LOW-INCOME PARENTS	SPECIAL EDUCATION TEACHERS
• Logistical problems	• Parent apathy
• Communication problems	• Parent lack of . . .
• Lack of understanding of school system	– time
	– energy
• Feelings of inferiority	– understanding
• Uncertainty about the child's disability	• Devaluation of parent input by school officials
• Concern about how they and the school can help	

Note. From "Perspectives on Parent Participation in Special Education" by E. W. Lynch and R. Stein, 1982, *Exceptional Education Quarterly, 3*(2), pp. 56–63.

TABLE 10–3   Suggestions for how to Overcome Logistical Barriers

TRANSPORTATION

- Meet in the student's home or neighborhood community facility.
- Find a community volunteer group to provide transportation.
- Utilize school funds to defray expenses incurred by the family for public transportation.
- Plan the conference for the time when parents usually visit if the student is in a residential facility (i.e., beginning or end of school year and holidays).

CHILD CARE

- Conduct the meeting in the student's home or in a place where a playground or playroom is accessible.
- Help parents brainstorm alternatives for locating child care.
- Arrange for volunteer helpers through school or community clubs.
- Utilize school funds to pay for child care services.

TIME

- Arrange meetings for the convenience of the parents—including the father and other family members.
- Ensure that meetings are conducted in a time-efficient manner.
- Help families determine priorities for decision-making opportunities.

Yet, the importance of the father's role is recognized in both research and model programs (LaBarbera & Lewis, 1980; Pfeiffer & Tittler, 1983). Parent contributions tend to increase when both parents attend the conference (Pistono, 1977). One father commented:

> I am at the IEP meeting to remind my wife that we are there for our son's best interest. She gets overemotional at the meetings. I help balance her out.

School personnel should schedule IEP conferences when fathers can attend. In the past, professionals have assumed that mothers, because they are homemakers, could attend conferences during the school day and that fathers could not attend because of employment. Given that the majority of mothers of school-age children are employed (Select Committee on Children, Youth, and Families, 1988), both mothers and fathers frequently need flexible scheduling options to attend early in the morning, late in the afternoon, during evening hours, or over the lunch hour.

Time is another logistical barrier for many families. In fact, this is one of the barriers identified by both parents and teachers. Strategies for dealing with this barrier are also included in Table 10–3.

The many functions for which families are responsible, discussed in Chapter 4, make it clear that families have many other demands on their time, attention, and energy than their son or daughter's education. As we also pointed out earlier, education is the only one of seven functions in which guaranteed rights to services exist. This may explain why many parents, facing inordinate time demands, relegate educational decision-making authority to teachers while giving their attention to other family needs. Based on a family-systems perspective, this response may have the consequence of improving the parent-child relationship or decreasing family stress. Such outcomes may be more important or more necessary for some families during periods of major stress than active involvement in IEP conferences. As one parent stated:

> Sometimes I get to the end of my rope and can't handle one more thing. The kids are crying, my husband is down and out with no job, the car is parked because we can't afford to run it, and the doctor tells me I'm pushing my luck to postpone surgery. About that time the teacher calls for me to come talk about Danny. I just can't hack it. She's a good lady and she's helped Danny. But I've got all I can handle at home. (A. P. Turnbull & Summers, 1985, p. 292)

COMMUNICATION PROBLEMS.   We addressed the importance of language and cultural sensitivity in communicating with parents in Chapter 6. Obviously, clear language and cultural sensitivity are critical in the IEP conference. A sometimes overlooked area of cultural difference is religious beliefs. One teacher expresses her experience with cultural insensitivity:

> Sam's expression was wide-eyed when the psychologist who was to test him walked through the door. Sam was not going to perform well for this man, I could tell. I was teaching in a private Christian school, and Sam's parents were fundamentalist Christians. The psychologist was dressed, to put it kindly, casually and very differently from the dress code we had at our school.
>
> I attended the IEP conference with Sam's parents. The results the psychologist reported for the *Wechsler* were inaccurate. I had taught and cared about Sam for almost a year; the psychologist saw him for 2 hours. I knew the score was too low, and I didn't want it haunting Sam throughout his school career. Finally, I was able to convince the other team members that the score was discrepant compared to the other test results. Only then did they stop looking at me condescendingly and listen to my objections. I believe, though, that the score would have been placed in his records without qualification had I not been knowledgeable about assessment.
>
> I have found that some of the people who take pride in their tolerance can be the most closed-minded and provincial. A simple phone call to Sam's administrator, myself, or his parents to ask what might prove offensive to the family's religious beliefs would have established a better rap-

---

TABLE 10–4 Suggestions for how to Minimize Language and Cultural Barriers

---

- Work with churches and outreach organizations within minority communities.
- Make a home visit to encourage parental participation.
- Have a translator present if needed.
- Give parents a concise written summary of the conference in their native language.
- Recognize that each family represents a unique culture; be careful not to assume that a family's culture is similar to your own.
- Avoid stereotypical assumptions; ask to determine preferences and needs.

---

port with all concerned and provided Sam with an opportunity to perform to his capacity during assessment.

Suggestions for minimizing language and cultural barriers in the IEP process are provided in Table 10–4.

Communication problems also occur when families and professionals disagree. Differences of opinion naturally occur during the IEP process. Your ability to handle these differences diplomatically may influence the family's willingness to accept and participate in the IEP process. Bailey (1987) specifies two types of disagreements that can occur during the IEP process—goal-related and method-related. Sources of disagreements include priorities for treatment and values related to treatment. For instance, you suggest to a parent that he review the alphabet, one of the IEP goals, with his daughter at home. He tells you that he believes his daughter should not have homework since she has an exceptionality. A conflict of values ensues. Value conflicts such as this are the most difficult to resolve, but differences in priorities also need to be addressed.

Bailey suggests the following four reasons for differences in parental and professional priorities: (a) parents may lack motivation because they do not see the relevance of the recommended activities; (b) parents may lack time, resources, and/or skills for follow-through; (c) professionals may not understand the needs and priorities of the family; and (d) professionals may not be skilled at challenging and motivating parents. Suggestions for how to resolve differences are provided in Table 10–5.

Bailey also emphasizes that problem solving should be done *with* parents rather than *for* them, especially in the beginning stages of goal setting. *Collaborative goal setting,* "a process by which parents and interventionists jointly determine family goals and the means by which

---

TABLE 10–5 Suggestions for how to Resolve Differences

- Use good communication skills to establish a positive rapport with the family.
- Recognize that differences in values are common.
- Understand that negotiation involves presentation and consideration of multiple alternatives.
- Attempt to come to agreement with the family on functional roles; then, consider family structures which could be employed to reach those goals.
- In cases where a family's values are detrimental to the child, address the problem directly and specifically. (You will be more likely to find the family receptive to your suggestions if a positive relationship has already been established.)

Note. From "Collaborative Goal-Setting with Families: Resolving Differences in Values and Priorities for Services" by D. B. Bailey, 1987, *Topics in Early Childhood Education, 7*(2), pp. 59–71.

they are attained," (p. 63) will help prevent conflicts from developing. When parents feel professionals value their input, they will be more likely to participate in the IEP process. Moreover, this approach helps parents learn to set personal goals and priorities. Table 10–6 lists other ideas for collaborative goal setting.

LACK OF UNDERSTANDING OF THE SCHOOL SYSTEM.   Many parents, particularly those from minority backgrounds, lack information on legal rights pertaining to special education (Budoff, 1979; Mitchell, 1976; Strickland, 1983; A. P. Turnbull et al., 1983). We discuss how to exchange such information with families in Chapter 12. At this point, however, we want to report two research studies that sought to increase parents' understanding of the IEP process.

The first provided training on legal rights and IEP participation skills to mothers of Head Start children who had disabilities (Thompson,

---

TABLE 10–6 Suggestions for Collaborative Goal Setting

- View the family from a systems perspective.
- Consider relevant family needs.
- Employ effective listening and interview skills.
- Reach a joint solution by negotiating values and priorities.
- Serve as a service coordinator to help families find appropriate community resources.

1982). The training involved a one-day workshop for mothers to address competencies related to IEP conference participation. A combination of lecture, discussion, audiovisual, and simulated activities was used. After training the researchers observed IEP conferences involving the mothers who received training and a group of mothers who had not participated in training. The results showed that the mothers who received training made twice as many contributions in the conference compared to mothers who did not receive training. These same mothers also expressed slightly more satisfaction with the conference.

The second study involved the development and field-test of a set of parent education materials designed to encourage parent participation in the IEP meeting (Malmberg, 1984). The materials included two booklets—one for parents and one for a family support person (friend of the family who attends the conference to provide support). The parent booklet covered (a) the procedures to be followed; (b) terminology; and (c) strategies for gathering, organizing, and presenting information about the child. The booklet for the parent support person included information on how a friend or advocate can assist the parent before, during, or after the conference. The field-test involved interviewing a small group of parents and observing their conferences after they had had a chance to read the materials.

The researchers reported that the materials influenced meeting preparations and more active conference participation for some parents. Premeeting planning questions were identified by parents as one of the most helpful portions of the booklets. None of the parents in the field-test sample elected to invite a support person to attend the conference with them; however, they did report reviewing the support materials with a spouse or a friend before or after the conference. A special educator involved in the field-test sample made the following comment on the impact of the materials on conference participation:

> Compared with other parents from this school, the parents know what to do. Usually, where you get to the point when you ask for questions (after the reports), parents tend to be sitting back as if to say, "Oh, whatever you want to do." The booklets appear to have made them focus more on the purpose of the meeting—what's appropriate for the child. (Malmberg, 1984, p. 108)

We encourage you to develop, implement, and evaluate programs designed to maximize parents' understanding. Legal rights are hollow unless families have the knowledge and skill to put rights into action.

FEELINGS OF INFERIORITY.   A number of factors may cause family members to feel inferior to school personnel, including (a) a diminished sense of status or power in decision making, (b) feelings of intimidation associated with being outnumbered by professionals, and (c) guilt feelings related to the cause of the child's exceptionality.

Parents' diminished sense of status and power in decision making has been documented. Gilliam and Coleman (1981) asked IEP conference participants to rank the relative status or importance of the participants. Although parents were rated high in importance before the meeting, they were ranked low in terms of their actual contribution after the meeting. The researchers concluded that parents either do not possess expertise, or are not perceived as possessing expertise, commensurate with other conference members. They also suggest that the most influential roles (e.g., special education teachers, special education consultants, and psychologists) are assigned to those members who are familiar with test scores, diagnostic reports, and cumulative records. They recommended that a case manager coordinate the conference process and provide parents increased access in the assessment and data-gathering phases (Gilliam & Coleman, 1981).

Gerber, Banbury, Miller, and Griffin (1986) corroborated these results. In a study of 145 special education teachers in six states, these researchers found that parent participation was valued only by slightly more than half the teachers surveyed. Seventy-one percent of the teachers agreed to an option to waive parental rights to attendance, and, thus, place decision making totally in the hands of professionals. Moreover, the IEP conference was perceived as little more than a formality by 44% of the teachers surveyed. These two studies indicate that professionals often do not value parental input. A parent commented about the differential power structure as follows: "One group has power and the other doesn't. I think the ultimate lack of power is to have a child who needs" (D. L. Ferguson, 1984, p. 44).

A second reason for some parents' sense of inferiority is that they sometimes feel outnumbered by professionals at IEP meetings. Marion (1979) warns: "The single greatest deterrent to minority parent participation is that they might feel overwhelmed when they walk into a meeting and feel all the school people are lined up against them" (p. 9). He suggests having in attendance only those people who are most familiar with the child with other professionals "on call" to join the meeting upon request.

By contrast, a survey of 243 parents (whose ethnicity was not identified) in Colorado showed that the presence of large numbers of professionals at conferences did not make it difficult for parents to ask questions and did not prevent good discussions. Indeed, some parents viewed the large number as a show of concern and interest (Witt, Miller, McIntyre, & Smith, 1984). Thus, the number of people at conferences affects different families in different ways. The more people present, the greater the breadth of expertise and the greater the chance of including all persons who have implementation responsibility. The benefit of smaller conferences is they can be less intimidating and more focused. Parents' individual preferences must be respected in planning which professionals should attend. (See Table 10–7 for an inventory of family preferences.)

Parents are, indeed, outnumbered even in conferences when only three professionals attend (given that both parents attend) or when two professionals attend (in typical cases when only one parent attends). However, intimidation probably has more to do with the professionals' communication style than with the number of persons attending.

Communication that is sensitive to the inclusion of parents in decision making is an effective conference strategy. A study was conducted to assess the impact of the following two interventions on increasing parent contributions during conferences: First, sending parents questions prior to the IEP conference and making a follow-up telephone call; and second, having the school counselors act as a "parent advocate" (Goldstein & A. P. Turnbull, 1982). The counselors were given a sheet of instructions asking them to engage in five behaviors: (a) introduce parents, (b) clarify jargon, (c) ask questions, (d) reinforce parental contributions, and (e) summarize decisions at the end of the conference.

Forty-five parents of students with learning disabilities were chosen from five elementary schools in one local education agency to be observed at IEP conferences. The parents selected from each school were divided randomly into three groups—(a) questions and a phone call in advance, (b) parent advocate present, and (c) control group. All conferences were observed, and speakers and topics were coded.

Results indicated that significantly more parent contributions occurred in conferences in which a parent advocate was present compared to the control group. No differences in participation were found between the control group and the parents who had received both questions and a phone call prior to the conferences. Thus, adherence to basic principles of good communication during the conference was effective in increasing parent contributions. One interpretation of this result is that parents' feelings of intimidation were reduced.

A third and final factor related to parents' feelings of inferiority is some parents' belief that school personnel blame them for their child's disability. In a study of variables associated with parental satisfaction with conferences, Witt et al. (1984) found that a major variable influencing satisfaction was professionals who attribute blame to sources other than the parents. As we stated in Chapter 1, you need to be particularly sensitive to direct comments or innuendoes that families might perceive as blaming them for the child's problem. In addition, we encourage you to adopt the practice in every IEP conference of making several statements to parents highlighting the positive contributions they make to their child. Table 10–8 delineates other suggestions for helping parents overcome feelings of inferiority.

TABLE 10–7   Inventory of Family Preferences, pp. 281–282

This form is designed to be administered orally—either in person or over the phone—to a parent or guardian of the student with an exceptionality.

1. **Who would you like to have attend the meeting?** (Suggest as possibilities both parents, stepparents, grandparents, the student with the exceptionality, brothers and sisters, other family members, friends, and/or other parental and student advocates. Remind parents to choose people who are close to the student and who can help develop the IEP.)

   NAME   **POSITION**

   _____   _____

   _____   _____

   _____   _____

   _____   _____

2. **What school personnel do you want to attend?** (Ask if they would feel more comfortable if a small number of professionals would attend or whether they want to have feedback from several different professionals. Tell them that by law one teacher and a person responsible for providing special education services must attend. Suggest as possibilities current teachers, paraprofessionals, next year's teachers, psychologist, school social worker, counselor, occupational therapist, speech therapist, physical therapist, adaptive physical education teacher, principal, director of special education, or staff from adult programs.)

   NAME   **POSITION**

   _____   _____

   _____   _____

   _____   _____

   _____   _____

3. **What day of the week would be most convenient for you (and your spouse)?**

   _____

4. **What time of day should we meet?**

   _____

5. **Where would be the best place for us to have the conference?** (Suggest as possibilities the school, their home, or a community building.)

   _____

6. **How can we help with transportation and child care or is our assistance needed?**

   _____

   _____

TABLE 10–7   (Continued)

7. **Some people like to have information about their child's educational program before the conference. Others prefer to wait until the conference to receive information. What is your preference?**

   _____

   _____

   (If parents say they want information before the conference, ask the following; if not, go on to Number 8.)

   Which of the following types of information would you like to have? (Read list.)

   ____ **Evaluation reports of performance on formal tests**

   ____ **Checklist that you can fill out to describe for the other participants your son or daughter's strengths and needs**

   ____ **List of subjects the school personnel plan to cover on the IEP**

   ____ **Summary of your child's strengths and weaknesses in each subject area**

   ____ **List of the goals and objectives school personnel plan to suggest at the meeting**

   ____ **Information on your legal rights**

   ____ **Information on placement options**

   ____ **Information on available related services**

   ____ **Other:**_____

   _____

   _____

   How would you like to receive this information?
   (Suggest letters, phone calls, conferences, brochures.)

   _____

   _____

8. **Do you have some information that might be helpful to share with school personnel?** ____ (If they say yes, ask the following; if not, go to Number 9.)
   What information do you have and how would you like to share it?

   _____

   _____

9. (Close by expressing your appreciation to the family, assuring them of your support and interest, and telling them that you look forward to their participation in the conference.)

TABLE 10–8 Suggestions for how to Help Families Overcome Feelings of Inferiority

PRIOR TO THE CONFERENCE:

- Establish rapport.
- Explain the IEP process.
- Answer questions.
- Complete the *Parent Preferences Inventory* (Table 10–7)
- Emphasize that families can make contributions to the conference that are unique and valued.
- Ask families who would constitute a suitable advocate for them.

DURING THE CONFERENCE:

- Avoid overwhelming the families with a large number of professionals.
- Include a family advocate in the discussion.
- Emphasize perceived family and student strengths.
- Stress that the family knows the student better than anyone else.
- View family members as partners.
- Mention the positive contributions the family has made.
- Avoid blaming the family for the child's difficulties.
- Ask family members for suggestions (i.e., what has worked for them).
- Avoid using jargon as much as possible and explain necessary terms in a matter-of-fact, non-condescending manner.
- Summarize findings and decisions at the end of the conference.

UNCERTAINTY ABOUT THE CHILD'S EXCEPTIONALITY. Many parents—especially those with children who have mild to moderate developmental delay, disabilities of unknown etiology, and no physical problems—experience uncertainty about their child's exceptionality. When you work with families of children who have no clear-cut diagnosis, you will need to be especially supportive. Claire Yaffa (1989) describes the essential role of supportive professionals for her family:

> When Robert was in second grade, a child who was so joyous, happy, and sang all the time, changed. He could not read as well as the other children in the class. He had difficulty following a long list of instructions. We were assured it was just a "developmental phase" or "immaturity" and he would outgrow his problem. He did not sing anymore. His frustrations increased and crying and tantrums took the place of his singing. We sought and received excellent professional help. We were told our son had a learning disability.
>
> Throughout the years of his undergraduate education, because of knowledgeable, caring teachers and professionals, a positive image of himself was learned and reinforced. Though frustrated and discouraged many

times, he never gave up. He learned to believe in himself, and became less dependent on others as he relied on and trusted himself. (pp. 57–58)

A common theme in interviews with mothers of preschool children who have disabilities is the need for competent teachers whose expertise can instill the confidence the mothers lack in themselves (Winton & Turnbull, 1981). One mother explains this need:

You've got to have a staff that is smarter than you. . . . I'm no genius, I mean, my background is giving enemas . . . but you've got to know that the people that are teaching your child know their stuff. Now I leave him off in the morning and I feel like . . . people more competent than me are taking him and that's a great feeling. (p. 15)

You can help parents who experience uncertainty recognize the important contributions they can make. For example, a parent may make the following comment to you:

When Mark gets stubborn, I give him a 2-minute warning. Then he has to do what I say. It usually works.

You then respond:

Thank you for sharing that with us. It's very helpful to know your good ideas. We haven't tried a warning period, but it sounds like a good suggestion. It's also important for both home and school to give Mark consistent messages.

When you respond in such a manner, parents immediately know that their contributions are valued. They also will sense your desire to establish a partnership with them.

Teacher-Identified Barriers

Teachers in the Lynch and Stein study (1982) identified the three major barriers to parent participation as being: apathy; parents' lack of time, energy, and understanding; and devaluation of parent input by the school. The latter two were also identified by parents and discussed in the previous section. Here we will discuss parent apathy and two additional barriers that educators have reported in the literature—constraints on professional time and expertise.

PARENTAL APATHY.   Some parents are apathetic or indifferent about their involvement in IEP conferences. Apathy can occur for a variety of reasons, including those discussed in the previous section. You will most likely encounter parents who are apathetic and unwilling to be involved in decision making you consider important. At times, you may put extensive effort into developing the IEP only to find that the parents do not show any interest in even learning about it. Sometimes you will try every positive step you can think of and still not get a positive response. You are not a failure in such situations. Your job is not to make families do something they choose not to do. We encourage you to use the communication skills discussed in Chapter 6 to try to stand in the parents' shoes and see the issues from their perspectives. Further, the family-systems framework (Chapters 2–5) can assist you in gaining insight into their own unique pattern of family interaction. Perhaps you can come to understand and even accept parental apathy by finding out the family's priorities and responding accordingly. For instance, families from some cultural backgrounds may believe that you are the expert, and that you should make the decisions for that reason. Also, the suggestions provided earlier in Table 10–8 for reducing family inferiority might reduce parents' apathy as they gain confidence in their ability to participate in decision making. We also encourage you to continue to work intensively with the student and maintain contact with the family even when no response is forthcoming.

PROFESSIONAL TIME CONSTRAINTS.   The IEP process can be extremely time-consuming. Thus, the length of time required to develop a new IEP has been estimated as about 6 hours according to data collected in the first several years of EHA implementation (Price & Goodman, 1980; Safer, Morrissey, Kaufman, & Lewis, 1978). One third of the time for IEP development was reported to evolve from the teacher's personal time (Price & Goodman, 1980). Many professionals feel harried by what can seem as overwhelming time requirements to complete IEP-related paperwork. One teacher stated:

> I cannot ask my wife and children to put up with me, depressed and tense for months each spring because I must finish my testing, must begin testing with the new kids we've identified, must get the reports in on time, must complete reams of papers (the law says so, and tells me how much time I have to do it), and can't teach. When I am in class, I am tense and harried because the testing isn't getting done on time. I don't have any time to plan, to diagnose, to remediate, and I can't get on top. (Katzen, 1980, p. 582)

You will need to find a way to resolve the time constraints that work against you. However, Witt et al. (1984) underscored that, compared to five other variables, allowing enough time for the conference was the most important variable associated with parent satisfaction. Therefore, the place to cut corners is not during the conference itself. Suggestions for helping you cope with time limitations are provided in Table 10–9 (A. P. Turnbull, 1983).

TABLE 10-9   Suggestions for how to Maximize Time Efficiency During IEP Construction

- Use computer software that allows for efficient construction of IEPs without sacrificing individualization.
- Dictate reports and have them transcribed by a secretary.
- Use volunteer assistance to schedule and arrange meeting rooms.
- Attend preservice and inservice training on time management.

PROFESSIONAL EXPERTISE CONSTRAINTS.   Interdisciplinary teams are characterized by complex group dynamics for all parties involved (Bailey, 1984; Chase, Wright, & Ragade, 1981). Providing opportunities for individualized parent participation is only one of many challenges. Professionals have been expected to function well in IEP conferences in the absence of adequate preparation. The emphasis in professional preservice and inservice training programs related to parent participation in IEP conferences has been on legal rights as distinguished from educational decision making and communication. A parent shared her perspective on the way professionals conduct conferences:

> Accordingly, these professionals do not tell anything to parents that they do not feel is necessary. They cover the bases legally, though; they rush through a meeting, get the parent's signature, and breathe a sigh of relief as they go on to the next "case." While they might not intentionally mislead a parent, they will withhold important information because it is safer and easier. (D. L. Ferguson, 1984, p. 43)

As an alternative to a hurried conference, we will now discuss six components of IEP conferences and strategies for involving parents in each.

SIX COMPONENTS OF THE IEP CONFERENCE

The IEP conference typically consists of the following six components: (1) preconference preparation, (2) initial conference proceedings, (3) review of formal evaluation and current levels of performance, (4) development of goals and objectives, (5) specification of placement and related services, and (6) conclusion. Structuring the IEP conference into separate components for the purpose of planning and conducting conferences can enhance systematic decision making (Ysseldyke, Algozzine, & Mitchell, 1982). We will provide a brief overview of each component with specific suggestions for how to involve families. These suggestions are summarized in Table 10–10. Readers interested in more detailed information about the IEP process are referred to Strickland and Turnbull (1990). Again, we believe that families should have an opportunity to participate to the extent they want to. More involvement is not necessarily better involvement.

Preconference Preparation

The tasks completed during the preconference period can greatly influence conference success. We suggest you start by appointing a "service coordinator" to assume responsibility for conference planning, implementation, and follow-up (Gilliam & Coleman, 1981; Marion, 1979). (We prefer the term *service coordinator* to *case manager* since no one appreciates being referred to as a "case," nor do they want to be "managed.") Centralizing responsibility with one person helps ensure continuity and coordination. The service coordinator should be a person who: (a) has established a good relationship with the family or is even selected by them, (b) is responsible for a portion of the child's educational program, and (c) has special expertise related to the child's exceptionality. Frequently, the person who assumes this role is a special education teacher, counselor, social worker, or principal. An important aspect of the coordinator's task will be to serve as a liaison between school personnel and the family.

One of your first responsibilities if you serve as the service coordinator should be to solicit information from families concerning their preferences. Consider these ideas for obtaining information: (a) ask families to complete a questionnaire such as the one in Table 10–7; (b) discuss preferences with families open-endedly, such as in a conference or over the telephone; or (c) ask for advice from professionals who have worked successfully with a family in the past (e.g., teachers) or who have a positive current relationship (e.g., social worker, public health nurse). No matter which method you choose, you will need to gather information early enough to carry through the family's preferences in planning (see Table 10–7, *Inventory of Family Preferences*). Especially encourage parents to consider which family members or friends might serve as effective advocates in the conference. Frequently overlooked family members, such as siblings or grandparents, often have valuable perspectives to share and can benefit from having access to educational information about the student with the exceptionality.

Your second task is to consider whether or not including the student is appropriate. Research indicates that the majority of secondary students with mild disabilities prefer to be involved (Gillespie & Turnbull,

TABLE 10–10   How to Involve Parents in the IEP Conference, pp. 288–290

PRECONFERENCE PREPARATION

- Appoint a service coordinator to organize all aspects of the IEP conference.
- Solicit information from the family about their preferences and needs regarding the conference. (See the *Inventory of Family Preferences,* Table 10–7.)
- Discuss the meeting with the student and consider his or her preferences concerning the conference.
- Decide who should attend the conference and include the student, if appropriate.
- Arrange a convenient time and location for the meeting.
- Assist families with logistical needs such as transportation and child care.
- Without educational jargon, inform the family verbally and/or in writing of the following:
  - Purpose of the meeting
  - Time and location of conference
  - Names of participants
- Based on the *Inventory of Family Preferences,* share information the family wants before the conference.
- Encourage the student, family members, and their advocates to visit the proposed placements for the student prior to the conference.
- Facilitate communication between the student and family members about the conference.
- Encourage families to share information and discuss concerns with participants prior to the conference.
- Gather needed information from school personnel.
- Prepare an agenda to cover the remaining components of the IEP conference.

INITIAL CONFERENCE PROCEEDINGS

- Greet the students, family, and their advocates.
- Provide a list of all participants or use name tags.
- Introduce each participant with a brief description of his or her role in the conference.
- State the purpose of the meeting. Review the agenda; and ask for additional issues to be covered.
- Determine the amount of time participants have available for the conference and offer the option of rescheduling, if needed, to complete the agenda.
- Ask if family members desire clarification of their legal rights.

REVIEW OF FORMAL EVALUATION AND CURRENT LEVELS OF PERFORMANCE

- Provide family members with a written copy of evaluation results if desired.
- Avoid educational jargon as much as possible and clarify diagnostic terminology throughout the conference.
- If a separate evaluation conference has not been scheduled, ask diagnostic personnel to report the following:
  - The tests administered
  - The results of each

TABLE 10–10 (Continued)

- Options based on the evaluation
- Summarize the findings including strengths, gifts, abilities, and needs.
- Identify implications of test results for planning purposes.
- Ask families for areas of agreement and disagreement with corresponding reasons.
- Review the student's developmental progress and current levels of performance in each class.
- Ask families if they agree or disagree with the stated progress and performance levels.
- Strive to resolve any disagreement with student work samples and solicit information from families about collecting further samples.
- Proceed with the IEP only when you and the family members agree about the student's exceptionality and current levels of performance.

DEVELOPMENT OF GOALS AND OBJECTIVES

- Encourage the student, family members, and advocates to share their expectations for the student's participation in the home, school, and community.
- Collaboratively generate appropriate goals and objectives for all subject areas requiring special instruction consistent with expectations.
- Discuss goals and objectives for future educational and vocational options based on great expectations for the student.
- Identify objectives to expand the positive contributions the student can make to family, friends, and community.
- Prioritize all goals and objectives in light of student preferences and needs.
- Clarify the manner in which the responsibility for teaching the objectives will be shared among the student's teachers.
- Ask family members and advocates if they would like to share in the responsibility for teaching some of the objectives at home or in the community.
- Determine evaluation procedures and schedules for identified goals and objectives.
- Explain to family members and advocates that the IEP is not a guarantee that the student will attain the goals; rather, it represents a good-faith effort on the part of school personnel that they will teach these goals and objectives.

DETERMINATION OF PLACEMENT AND RELATED SERVICES

- Include the student, family members, and advocates in a discussion of the benefits and drawbacks of viable placement options.
- Select a placement option that allows the student to be involved with peers without exceptionalities as much as possible.
- Agree on a tentative placement until the family members can visit and confirm its appropriateness.
- Discuss the benefits and drawbacks of modes of delivery for related services the student needs.
- Specify the dates for initiating related services and anticipated duration.
- Share the names and qualifications of all personnel who will provide services with family members and advocates.

TABLE 10–10   (Continued)

CONCLUDING THE CONFERENCE

- Assign follow-up responsibility for any task requiring attention.
- Review with the student, family members, and advocates any responsibilities they have agreed to assume.
- Summarize orally and on paper the major decisions and follow-up responsibilities of all participants.
- Set a tentative date for reviewing the IEP document.
- Identify strategies for ongoing communication with the student, family members, and advocates.
- Express appreciation to the student, family members, and advocates for their help in the decision-making process.

1983) and that attitudes of mothers and resource teachers toward IEP conferences were more positive when elementary students were involved (Fifield, 1978). We advocate the inclusion of students whenever possible in light of student, parent, and teacher preferences both as a strategy for teaching self-advocacy skills (Strickland & Turnbull, 1990) and as a means of addressing the student's concerns (Daniels, 1982). Parents who want or need to talk privately with professionals can stay after the student leaves or arrange another conference. A mother of a 12-year-old student with a physical disability stated:

> He knows how to tell what he likes and doesn't like and what he wants to do. It does no good to decide something for someone else. If he decided, maybe he would be more eager to do it. (Gillespie & Turnbull, 1983, p. 27)

One young man with cerebral palsy expressed his frustration to his mother at not being involved in decision making:

> I have never been able to talk to you alone for the most part, anyway. There have always been the middlemen . . . [doctors, social workers] and the others. And, for the most part, your friends and these quacks. How much of the truth comes out when others are listening or asking questions? How much more do you think would come out if you had talked with me privately and asked questions? I can answer questions, too. You [were] always apt to consider the situation much much worse than it really was. Don't you know where this leads when you are unwilling to talk, or listen . . . I just might have something worth listening to!

Van Reusen (1984) has developed and validated an instructional strategy to teach secondary students with learning disabilities how to participate effectively in their own conferences. This instructional strategy teaches students to:

- inventory their learning needs and interests,
- provide their inventoried information during a conference,
- ask appropriate questions during a conference,
- respond appropriately to questions during a conference,
- verbally summarize their understanding of their IEP goals before the conclusion of the conference. (Van Reusen, 1984, p. 11)

The IEP documents of students who demonstrated these skills included more student-initiated goal statements when compared to the IEPs of students who had not received training. Additionally, the other conference participants reported higher levels of satisfaction with conferences in which students had been prepared for involvement. Three considerations must be kept in mind in this regard, however (Strickland & Turnbull, 1990). Does the student possess the requisite communication skills? Will the student be comfortable attending the meeting? Is the student interested in attending the meeting? Suggestions to parents and teachers for including students in IEP conferences are presented in Table 10–11 (Strickland & Turnbull, 1990).

A third task will involve taking into account the items on the questionnaire that address (a) scheduling, (b) size of committee and location of conference, and (c) advance preparation. As the coordinator, remember that professional team members are entitled to their preferences; communicate to families what they are. For example, if it is impossible for the regular education teacher to hold a conference before school in the morning, alert parents to this problem.

It is important to consider the option of exchanging advance information such as draft ideas for goals and objectives. (Advance information about possible ideas for consideration should not be misconstrued to mean completed IEPs.) Although providing advance information might be viewed as extra work, it can be a useful strategy and can save time later. Families frequently find it helpful to have an opportunity to reflect on information—such as current levels of performance, goals, objectives, placement, and related services—so they can feel confident about agreeing or disagreeing with professionals' opinions and recommendations. By exchanging information in advance, families and professionals alike can use the IEP conference time for clarification and decision making. When information is not exchanged in advance, participants are likely to spend the majority of the time reviewing information and generating ideas. Then, they tend to hurry decision making into the last few minutes. When families prefer not to exchange written information in advance, two meetings (barring time constraints)—one to review information and one to make instrumental decisions—would

TABLE 10–11 Suggestions for how to Include Students in IEP Meetings

- The way in which the student is to be involved should be determined on a case-by-case basis. Older students with mild disabilities may be able to participate more fully than younger students and students with limited ability. The parents, IEP committee members, and the student should determine in advance the role the student will be expected to play.

- Parents or teachers can review the agenda and draft goals and objectives with the student prior to the meeting to familiarize the student with what will be discussed and how the student might be involved.

- If the student does not feel comfortable attending the meeting, information related to the educational program can be discussed prior to the meeting and incorporated into the IEP at the meeting. A conference might be conducted with the student prior to the IEP meeting to determine to what extent he or she feels comfortable participating in IEP development.

- The physical setting should be arranged so that the student sits with the rest of the committee as a fully participating member. A warm business-like atmosphere should be established, and IEP committee members should view the student as a full and responsible member of the committee.

- Ask questions of the student which cannot be answered with a yes or no response. Instead of asking, "Do you like math?", ask "What is it that you dislike about math?" Instead of asking, "Do you think this will help you?", ask "How do you think we can help you?"

- Plan time for the student to speak, and do not interrupt while the student is talking. This communicates the message that what the student is saying is important.

- Use brief remarks. Do not confuse the student by using long complicated questions or comments. Clarify, interpret, and summarize what the student says after the student has presented his or her ideas.

- The meeting should be nonthreatening and should stress the student's positive growth and the willingness and commitment of the IEP committee to assist the student in achieving the goals and objectives established.

be useful. Issues of both personal preference and time efficiency need to be considered. Table 10–10 includes suggestions on how families can prepare for the IEP conference in advance.

Initial Conference Proceedings

An atmosphere of open communication must be established during the initial part of the conference. We have discussed the intimidation many families feel during the conference. The service coordinator, therefore, should start the conference in a positive and constructive way to enhance the mutual efforts of all participants in working toward common goals. A clear statement of purpose early in the conference can help direct everyone's attention to the important decisions that need to be made. Surprisingly, observations of conferences indicate that (a) a statement of purpose is usually not made, (b) the roles of team members are not defined, and (c) individuals present are not encouraged to participate (Ysseldyke et al., 1982). A teacher commented on how the roles of team members can create barriers in conferences:

> I was recently at a conference in which a psychologist was also present. It was not until after the conference that we discovered the father thought the psychologist was a truant officer.

Suggestions, as outlined in Table 10–10, include (a) greeting parents and their guests, (b) making introductions, (c) reviewing an agenda, (d) addressing timelines (time schedules) for participants, and (e) providing information on legal rights.

The *McGill Action Planning System* (*MAPS*) (Vandercook, York, & Forest, 1989) provides ideas for developing the IEP. During the conference, the participants are asked the following seven questions:

- What is the individual's history?
- What is your dream for the individual?
- What is your nightmare?
- Who is the individual?
- What are the individual's strengths, gifts, and abilities?
- What are the individual's needs?
- What would the individual's ideal day at school look like and what must be done to make it happen? (pp. 3–4)

This approach encourages a well-rounded perspective of the student as well as active participation by conference members—including family members and their advocates. For example, Vandercook, Fleetham, Sinclair, and Tetlie (1988) discuss the involvement of three friends in 9-year-old Catherine's IEP conference in which MAPS was utilized. Jessica, Julie, and Amy addressed Catherine's mother's worst nightmare that Catherine would be alone some day by reassuring her that they would be willing to live with her when they grew up. The girls also provided practical ideas for how to include Catherine in classroom activities. Thus, the girls gained confidence in their ability to make a difference in Catherine's life, and Catherine's mother was encouraged by their loving support. And the benefits for Catherine? According to Vandercook et al. (p. 19), the first observation from everyone involved with her is: "Cath is *so* happy!"

REVIEW OF FORMAL EVALUATION AND CURRENT LEVELS OF PERFORMANCE

The IEP must include the student's current levels of performance. This information is the direct result of the evaluation process and provides the foundation for developing an appropriate instructional program. The conference chair can consider two options (both discussed in Chapter 9). First, the IEP conference can be used to review formal evaluation results and to develop the IEP. Second, a separate meeting (before the IEP conference) can be held *only* to review evaluation results. The decision of when to report evaluation results should be based on a consensus of family and professional preferences. (Many of the suggestions for this portion of the IEP conference which are included in Table 10–10 are repeated from the discussion of the last chapter.)

Development of Goals and Objectives

Goals and objectives are the heart of the IEP, as they represent the content or substance of a student's educational program. All participants must address the central issue: What are the most important goals and objectives for this student to learn based on the student's as well as the family's current and future preferences and needs? It is important for the service coordinator to direct the group's attention to this issue throughout the conference and to insure that all participants have great expectations for the student's full citizenship throughout school and adult years.

Different conference participants may answer this question in different ways. Phil Roos (1985), the father of a child with a severe disability, shared his perspective on the issue of goals:

> Parents and professionals may have different ideas regarding specific program objectives and their relative importance. For example, professionals may focus on academic and abstract achievements whereas parents may be interested in practical objectives that make the retarded child easier to live with. Professionals may emphasize development of new skills, such as number concepts or color recognition, while parents may wish to eliminate socially inappropriate behavior, such as tantrums or screaming. As a result of these different priorities, professionals may feel a child is making good progress while his parents may feel that nothing is happening. I recall, for instance, that some years ago my wife and I were told with pride that Val was beginning to recognize colors. Rather than reacting with obvious enthusiasm, we expressed dismay that she had managed to yank all her hair from her head. We suggested that eliminating this self-destructive behavior should take precedence over color recognition. (pp. 253–254)

The coordinator can ask families to share their preferences at the conference. Parent and professional preferences need to be merged and translated into IEP goals and objectives (Vincent et al., 1981).

The service coordinator also can consider using a questionnaire, such as the one in Figure 10–1, to aid in selecting the most important goals and objectives for a particular student. Additional criteria can be added or criteria now included can be deleted based on professional and family recommendations. In their present form, the criteria are more geared to older students. The chair may ask all conference participants to complete a questionnaire individually before, during, or after the conference and then collectively discuss the results. Goals and objectives can be selected on the basis of computed scores or through consensus following discussion. The major advantage of this questionnaire is that it makes explicit the criteria for selecting goals and objectives (see Figure 10–1).

Nonacademic and enrichment opportunities need to be considered in formulating goals and objectives in addition to academic areas (Crawford, 1978). Consider Tony's situation:

> Tony is a 17-year-old student with moderate mental retardation. His major needs relate to independent living and vocational skills. Considering his many deficits, it would be easy to identify more than enough goals and objectives for the year in these two areas alone. But Tony also has a special interest and talent in music. He believes that "music is magic." Music was identified as an important subject to include on Tony's IEP. One of the objectives was to teach Tony to play a guitar. As the year progressed, the music program and the guitar—as contrasted to the independent living and vocational programs—provided the spark for Tony to turn off the alarm clock and get out of bed every morning.

Determination of Placement and Related Services

It is critical that decisions concerning placement and related services be made at the IEP conference for two reasons. First, few aspects of educational programming are more important to the student than placement and related services. Second, placement and related services specified on the IEP make the school legally responsible for providing them.

Families who are unfamiliar with placement options need a specific description of the various options available. Based on observations of 34 conferences, a team of researchers (Ysseldyke et al., 1982) concluded that the concept of least restrictive placement was neither explicitly stated nor used as a basis for making placement decisions in any of the conferences. The authors observed: "In general, teams presented data, and then someone on the team recommended a placement. The

FIGURE 10–1   IEP Adult Life Skills Criteria Checklist

Instructions: These IEP goals/objectives should be rated according to their relevance to adult life skills.

Student's name _____

Completed by _____

Date _____

Key   1-Definitely no
      2-Probably no
      3-Maybe/
      sometimes

4-Probably yes
5-Definitely yes
NA-Not applicable
cannot assess

IEP goals/objectives

1. Will acquisition of this skill allow student to function more independently in the residential environment?

2. Will acquisition of this skill allow student to function more independently in the school/educational environment?

3. Will acquisition of this skill allow student to function more independently in the community environment (e.g., social activities, shopping transportation)?

4. Will acquisition of this skill enable student to function in vocational environments?

5. Will acquisition of this skill promote integration with non-disabled peers?

6. Will acquisition of this skill promote integration with disabled peers?

7. Will this skill improve student's quality of life?

efficacy of the placement was seldom discussed" (p. 311). It cannot be assumed that parents know the meaning or implication of terms such as *resource room, mainstreaming, itinerant teacher,* and *job station.* In a survey of 50 parents of kindergarten children with mild disabilities (all of whom were mainstreamed), 90% of the parents indicated they would like to have more information on mainstreaming (A. P. Turnbull et al., 1983).

Furthermore, families may need a new perspective on mainstreaming; recently, *progressive inclusion* and *integration* have become the ter-

FIGURE 10–1   (Continued)

8. Is acquisition of this skill a stated or implied preference by the student?																			
9. Will acquisition of this skill enhance student's ability to make choices?																			
10. Is this skill commonly reinforced in natural environments?																			
11. Is this a skill that will be taught in the natural environment?																			
12. Is this a skill that the student will have an opportunity to practice on a regular basis?																			
13. Is the skill age appropriate?																			
14. Are the settings, materials, cues and strategies that will be used to teach this skill age appropriate?																			
TOTALS																			

Note. Adapted from "A Systematic Procedure for Prioritizing IEP Goals," by J. C. Dardig and W. L. Heward, 1981, *The Directive Teacher,* Summer/Fall, p. 582. Copyright 1981 by Thomas M. Stephens, Publisher. Reprinted by permission.

minology of choice. Reynolds (1988) defines *progressive inclusion* as a "gradual movement toward more inclusive or integrated arrangements" (p. 2). *Progressive* can imply "improvement, success, betterment" or "change through a sequence of stages or gradual movement along a dimension of development" (p. 2). Both of these definitions imply positive growth in the individual—a goal of both regular and special education. The word *inclusion* suggests acceptance rather than rejection by the schools. The value of progressive inclusion in the life of Michael is described by his mother (Skarnulis, 1988):

> From the beginning, I was dissatisfied with Michael's situation, and the nagging doubts grew louder and louder. If he was ever going to live at home and be part of his community, then he needed to learn how to do what is acceptable. But what I saw happening in the special school was that he was learning to be more unacceptable, more different...
>
> Michael came home to live on July 4, 1980, Independence Day. He is now 19 years old and goes to school at Forest Lake High School. He attends regular classes, including art, floral design, and swimming; plays bass drum and timpani in the orchestra; works at a local mail order company; attends football games and concerts; and goes on hayrides, canoe trips and snowmobile rides with friends and family. I'm pleased to say that most people that know Michael share my vision because he has shown them anything is possible. When Michael and I attend planning meetings, the other team members are now invested in actualizing the vision. (p. 4)

Thus, a philosophical change has occurred. According to Forest (1988), *integration* is often thought to imply merely the placement of a child with an exceptionality in a school or classroom with children who do not have exceptionalities. This term now has a deeper meaning— inclusion and belonging. The former concept was simply a placement issue. The latter is a philosophical debate. Forest suggests that instead of asking "How can we do it," we ask the following:

- What kind of school communities do we want?
- Who do we want our children to grow up with?
- What values will we model for our children?
- What do we want the future to look like? (p. 3)

She contends that the *how* will naturally follow an understanding of the *why* of integration.

> The inclusion of those we have labeled and excluded will liberate our hearts and souls. We will all not only read and write better, but we will be a part of creating a more loving and caring world. (p. 4)

TABLE 10–12 Parental Concerns about Integration

- Safety
- Attitudes of regular education students and staff
- Program quality
- Transportation
- District commitment to the integrated model
- Potential for failure

Note. From "Parent Perception of the Integration Transition Process: Overcoming Artificial Barriers" by M. F. Hanline and A. Halvorsen, 1989, *Exceptional Children, 55*(6), pp. 487–92.

Many families will need for you to ease their concerns about integrating the student with an exceptionality. Table 10–12 lists some of the issues that families may want to have addressed. Some of the positive effects of integration are described in Table 10–13. This list might provide encouragement for families as well as the student who will be integrated.

Concluding the Conference

The concluding portion of the conference should be used to synthesize recommendations and develop a plan for follow-up responsibility. Because many important decisions are made at IEP conferences, the ser-

---

TABLE 10–13 Positive Effects of Integration

- Enhancement in learning
- Social skill development
- Increased challenge of school work
- Positive impact on self-esteem
- "Real-life" environment
- Friendships with children and youth who do not have a disability
- Having classmates who do not have a disability as role models
- Increase in parental expectations
- Brothers and sisters who do not have a disability become less concerned about long-term care
- Change of family focus away from the disability

---

vice coordinator should summarize them to ensure that consensus has been achieved. The coordinator also should identify any tasks requiring follow-up attention, (e.g., locating instructional materials, arranging transportation, scheduling) and assign related-service individuals to assume responsibility for each. Finally, the coordinator should make plans to review or revise the IEP and identify strategies for ongoing communication among school personnel and the family about the student's progress. The suggestions in Table 10–10 are designed to help ensure that closure is reached and future steps are identified.

POSITIVE OUTCOMES OF THE IEP CONFERENCE

Surprisingly little research has examined the results of IEP conferences. More research is needed on the outcomes of family participation. Several outcomes, such as professional accountability, parental well-being, and student gain have been suggested in the literature, but they have not been researched thoroughly.

Regarding professional accountability, one study investigated the effect of parental participation in team meetings in a residential institution for persons with mental retardation (Singer, Bossard, & Watkins, 1977). Results indicated that more staff members attended conferences and more recommendations were made when parents were in attendance. A teacher described a similar reaction:

> Whether we acknowledge it or not, our staff puts a lot more effort into evaluations and IEPs when we know that the parents are going to participate actively. It's motivation for us—it helps us do our best.

Parental well-being is suggested in the following viewpoint of a father describing his reaction to the IEP conference:

> Attending the IEP meeting gave me a psychological boost. I looked around the table and felt very fortunate that every person there really cared that Cindy gets a quality education. It made me realize that my wife and I are not alone in our concerns and in our hopes.

Moreover, the high level of satisfaction reported in the studies in the first section of this chapter indicates that parents have a positive perception of their role in the IEP conference. However, one study found a less positive attitude toward the IEP process by parents of students classified as gifted as contrasted to parents of students classified as having a disability (Lewis, Busch, Proger, & Juska, 1981). Susan Efaw describes her disillusionment with her daughter's initial IEP conference.

That was about as much of nothing as one could imagine. They, at that time and I'm afraid still now, had the same goal plan for every student; they really did not know how to ¹un a program although there were some very talented teachers working with gifted. The meeting merely consisted of reporting the score (99+ on the *Wechsler*) and passing around a form which everyone at the table signed.

The results of the IEP meeting can be positive for parents of students who are gifted, however. Betsy Santelli explains why the conference she attended for her daughters was favorable:

As parents of two daughters who had participated for several years in gifted education programs, Jim and I had not had the opportunity to participate in an IEP conference when we moved to Kansas. Although anxious at first about what our roles might be, we were delighted to find a real willingness and genuine interest on the part of the staffing team to learn from us about Maren and Tami's unique and special qualities as well as those of our family. Before any assessment results were shared or questions were asked, time was allowed for informal sharing among all of us as people—not professionals, not parents—just people. Those few minutes helped set the stage for the comfortable sharing of information that followed and continues to this day.

Finally, the ultimate outcome is the determination of whether family participation increases the appropriateness of the student's educational program. Research studies on this important topic have not been reported. It represents a priority area of inquiry for the next decade. Also, research is needed to determine if the philosophical shift from a focus on least restrictive environment to integration will have a positive impact on family attitudes toward the IEP process.

DIFFERENCES BETWEEN THE IEP AND THE IFSP

The regulations for the IEP and IFSP were discussed in Chapter 8. In analyzing those regulations, you will note two major differences between the IFSP and the IEP. First, there are differences in the *target individual(s)* who should be the beneficiary of individualized planning. Whereas the IEP is conceptualized as a document focusing on the needs of the individual student, the IFSP is a document focusing on the strengths and needs of the individual with a disability and the family. Part H requires that each IFSP include: A statement of the family's strengths and needs related to enhancing the development of the child (the regulations specify that this information be included with the consent of the family), major outcomes to be achieved by the child and family, and services to meet the unique needs of the child and family. Additionally, one of the particular services specified in Part H includes family training, counseling, and home visits. Thus, the IFSP places the family in the center of the planning process and moves early intervention from being child-focused to being family-focused. This is an exciting opportunity for the field of early intervention to make a positive difference in the lives of families and to develop family-centered approaches that can be incorporated into service delivery at other life span stages, as well.

Second, there are *substantive* differences between the IFSP and the IEP. The IFSP goes beyond the IEP in the nature of the components that must be included in addition to family strengths and needs, such as a plan for transitioning from early intervention to preschool, specification of a case manager responsible for implementing the plan and coordinating with other agencies and persons, and arrangements for paying for services. Although the importance of transitional planning (see Chapters 5 and 12) case management (see Chapter 13), and clarification of responsibility for paying for related services (Strickland & Turnbull, 1990) are recognized in special education programs for students of all ages, the IEP does not require that these aspects be specified.

The IEP and IFSP will likely differ in the *process* of their development. This process difference emerges from best practices in working with infants and toddlers rather than from the regulations. As discussed in Chapter 9, the IEP process is typically conceptualized as linear (see Figure 9–1), consisting of a series of rather discrete and sequential steps. On the contrary, efforts are under way to conceptualize the IFSP as a more fluid and dynamic process which allows families and professionals to move back and forth between evaluation of the child, sharing information with the family, identifying family strengths and needs, identifying outcomes, and providing services to the family and child (Johnson et al., 1989).

A mother commented:

> Why can't the IFSP be in a 3-ring notebook? It's an evolving document. We should constantly be able to add and delete information.

Dynamic and fluid models will be developed for the IFSP over the next several years.

BEST PRACTICES FOR THE IFSP

At the time this book went to press, best practices for the IFSP were still at a very preliminary phase. We hesitate to make specific suggestions concerning the IFSP document and process because so much work remains to be done. Instead, we can refer you to the available literature at this time that has many helpful ideas, including Bailey and Simeonsson (1988); Bailey, Winton, Rouse, and Turnbull (in press); Dunst, Trivette, and Deal (1988); Johnson et al. (1989); and Winton and Bailey (1988). As noted in Chapter 9, we and our colleagues will be working over the next several years to learn more about how the IFSP can best be developed and implemented. The major challenge at this time is to develop procedures for the IFSP document and conference that meet both the letter and the spirit of the law while simultaneously respecting the continually evolving strengths and needs of families and infant/toddlers. Our hope is that the process for IFSP development and implementation will be more informal than the process described in this chapter for the IEP. We invite you to write us for supplemental information on the IFSP as we attempt to meet this challenge. The address of the Beach Center can be found in Appendix A.

SUMMARY

Research on parent participation in IEP conferences indicates a general trend of passive involvement in decision making. We have discussed barriers to active family-professional partnerships from the perspectives of families and teachers and suggested strategies for your consideration that have been verified by research. Furthermore, we have shared a model that we have found helpful in planning IEP conferences—a model that divides the conference into six components. Suggestions for how to involve families in each of the six components are summarized in Table 10–10. We believe that adherence to these suggestions will increase the relevance and success of conferences. Finally, we have described the major differences between the IFSP and IEP and highlighted current challenges that face the field in developing model procedures for the IFSP document and meeting.

Despite your best efforts, satisfactory agreement will not always be reached in IEP and IFSP conferences. When such an impasse occurs, it becomes necessary to pursue other forums of decision making. Chapter 11 provides you with information on the due process hearing, which is the legally sanctioned mechanism for resolving disputes that can arise in IEP and IFSP conferences or otherwise.

DUE PROCESS: USING THE LAW WHEN THERE IS CONFLICT

Families or school systems may request a due process hearing to receive an impartial resolution to a dispute. In Adam's case, the hearing was requested by his mother.

At the age of six, my son Adam was placed into a self-contained classroom for children with severe emotional problems. I found out that our educational experience was that of an emotional roller coaster. When I was in agreement with the educational team, I experienced many more highs than lows. But, as a black single parent, the lows were devastating because I felt so alone. When I disagreed with the team, I felt overwhelmed and powerless. By the time Adam was in the sixth grade, it was very clear that the educational team was tired of working with him. They refused to implement a program suggested by his therapist. This was a program that had been successful at home. During a school conference, eight professionals told me that my son needed to be placed in a more restricted environment (hospitalization) because of his behavioral problems in school. I asked them to supply me with objective data to support their recommendations. They presented me with a great deal of subjective information. Deep in my gut, I knew Adam didn't belong in an institution and that I had every right to question their decision. I was also painfully aware that the odds were eight to one and the only way my objections and input could carry equal weight would be through a due process hearing.

Gloria Graves, Adam's mother, is quoted throughout this chapter concerning due process, except where otherwise noted.

As we pointed out in Chapter 8, one of the six principles of the federal special education law is due process. There, we gave a short-hand definition of due process as the legal requirement that schools must provide opportunities for parents to consent or object to their children's educational identification, classification, program, or placement. The underlying principle of due process is fairness, as manifest in the opportunity to consent or object. Taking this theme of fairness as the fundamental characteristic of due process, it is helpful to remember the reasons for due process as we outlined them in Chapter 8:

1. Due process is a requirement of the federal constitution.
2. Due process is a way to help parents and schools hold each other accountable to each other. The first four principles of law—zero-reject, nondiscriminatory evaluation, appropriate education, and least restrictive placement—are the "inputs" from the school to the student. Due process is a way for parents to determine whether the school has done its job under those principles. It also is a way for schools to remain accountable, since schools may bring a due process hearing against parents who object to the schools' proposed course of action.

3. Due process is a way of changing the balance of power between professionals, who have traditionally wielded power, and parents, who have felt they could not affect their children's education.

4. Due process is a new way to focus on the rights and needs of students, parents, and professionals, particularly students.

Later in this chapter we will show how these purposes have been accomplished. But we also will point out some of the new problems that due process has created in parent-professional relationships. Throughout this chapter we will suggest how you can minimize the conflict the due process provisions otherwise seek to resolve.

A few important reminders about the Education of the Handicapped Act are in order. First, Part B of the Act deals with the education of students who are between the ages of 3 and 21. Part H deals with the early intervention services available to infants and toddlers who are between the ages of birth through 2; it also authorizes services to their families. If you have any questions about these two Parts, we suggest you review Chapter 8.

Second, Part B gives legal rights to parents or surrogate parents. As we noted in Chapter 8, the word *parents* has been interpreted to include people other than a student's biological parents. Part H, by contrast, gives legal rights to students' parents, guardians, or surrogate parents. We will use the term *parents* to refer to all those people (other than local education agencies—LEAs) who have rights of due process under Part B and Part H. We will discuss the due process provisions of Part B first and then the provisions of Part H.

Finally, Part B and Part H alike apply to LEAs and other agencies that furnish special education or early intervention services. For the sake of brevity, we will use the terms *LEA* or *school* to refer to each such agency.

After reading this chapter, you should be able to:

*   identify the general safeguards for students, parents, and LEAs;
*   apply the rules concerning access to records, confidentiality of records, evaluation, notice, consent, surrogate parents, consultation, and state advisory panels;
*   identify the rules for due process hearings;
*   apply professional practices with respect to hearings and appeals;
*   assess the positive and negative effects of the due process safeguards;
*   define mediation and distinguish it from the EHA's due process safeguards (particularly those relating to the due process hearing);
*   understand basic principles of negotiation.

In Chapter 8, we organized the elements of due process into two categories: general safeguards and hearing rights. We will continue that same scheme here.

GENERAL SAFEGUARDS

The general safeguards relate to access to and confidentiality of student records, evaluation of the student, notice, consent to services, surrogate parents, public consultation concerning state plans, and advisory panels. We will discuss each in detail.

Access to Records

If I had not reviewed Adam's school records, I would not have known that there was so much damaging misinformation in them. That misinformation could have greatly hurt our position in the due process hearing if presented as fact. I demanded it be taken out of his files, and I now review those files regularly. It is good to know what the school has on file about Adam, and why.

Families have the right to obtain access to their child's educational records. Under Part B, parents have the right to examine all relevant records relating to the student's identification, evaluation, placement, and education. Similarly, under Part H, parents may inspect the infant-toddler's records relating to evaluation and assessment, eligibility determinations, IFSP development and implementation, individual complaints dealing with the child, and any other area under Part H that involves records about the infant-toddler and the family. In addition, under the EHA generally, certain information about school programs for all students with disabilities (e.g., the number, ages, and races of all such students) is public information, available to all people, not just parents.

Under Part B, LEAs must notify parents (in their native language) that personal identifiable information is on file. This information includes the student's and parents' names and their address; any personal identifier, like a social security number or student number; and any list of personal characteristics or other information that would make it possible to identify the student. These are essentially the same rules under Part H.

The Department of Education has stated that the regulations implementing the Family Educational Rights and Privacy Act apply to Part H. Thus, each of the following rights is available under Part H.

Schools must explain the type of information they plan to collect and how they plan to use it. A school may collect information on the number of students with a particular disabling condition and may seek data for a description of their educational achievement. Typically, school administrators, not teachers (or other direct-service staff), are responsible for these duties and records.

Schools must give parents a summary of policies and procedures to be used by *participating agencies* (any agency or institution that collects, maintains, and uses or provides information) for storing information, releasing it to third parties, or destroying it, and their plans for protecting personally identifiable information. Schools also must publicly announce, through the newspapers or other appropriate media, any activities they plan for the purpose of identifying and evaluating students who may be disabled. Thus, they are responsible for developing policies for access to system records and protection of student records to be followed by all other agencies involved in children's education. Again, school administrators hold primary responsibility for these duties.

Parents and their representatives (e.g., independent experts or lawyers) have the right to inspect personally identifiable information in the student's records within 45 days maximum after requesting to inspect the records. For example, a parent may want to see the student's records of intelligence testing or other assessment of disabling conditions. If the record includes information on more than one student, the parent is entitled to see or be informed about only the portion relating to their child.

Obviously, you need to be careful to record only information that is accurate, current, and relevant; and impressions or conclusions that can be supported by facts. A good rule of thumb is this: put into the record only what you would be willing to defend in court. Another good rule is to consider whether you would want the information you are about to enter to be filed about you. That is, take the "shoes" test—regard your action as you would if it were taken with respect to you. Both of these criteria—the "defense-in-court" and "shoes" tests—should help you understand the fairness doctrine that underlies the due process principle.

If parents request access to records, inform them that access is available and that the school may have policies that must be followed (and they, of course, should follow those policies), and refer the request to the appropriate administrator. Under no circumstance should you or any professional refuse access. It is proper, however, to follow school policies and inform appropriate administrators of the request.

A school may presume that the parent has access rights unless it has been advised otherwise (e.g., in cases of termination of parental rights, guardianship, separation, or divorce). If you doubt anyone's authority to inspect a child's records, refer the request to the appropriate school administrators.

Parents may request an explanation or interpretation of the information and must be given copies. You and all other school staff should be willing to make explanations, when qualified to do so. A fee for copies may be charged, unless the fee would prevent a parent from having access to the record. Typically, school administrators should handle the billing.

Upon request, parents must also be provided with a list of the types and sources of information collected and used by the LEA. The school must keep a record of who has had access. Again, school administrators usually keep those lists and are responsible for maintaining the access log.

After reading the records and having them appropriately interpreted, parents may ask the school to amend the information in them. The school—acting through its administrators and direct-service staff—must consider the request and give an affirmative or negative response within a reasonable time. If the school disagrees with the request, it must inform the parents of their right to a hearing to protest this school's decision. Thus, parents have rights to challenge the contents of the student records. This again underscores the necessity of your recognizing the importance of your responsibilities for maintaining accurate, current, and relevant student records.

In commenting on the "fairness" element of due process, with specific reference to the provisions for access to records, H. R. Turnbull (1985a) concluded that "access is not only invaluable to parents and professionals, it is imperative as a course of decent conduct between people and as a weapon against charlatanry" (p. 111). When parents and professionals alike have access to records, they can be more equitable in their dealings with each other; this alone can evoke more positive, more respectful, and more decent parent-professional relationships. This is the fairness doctrine at work. In addition, access can be a powerful accountability tool—a way for parents and professionals to assure themselves, by knowing the facts and impressions recorded in the child's record, that they are not being taken advantage of.

A student's records often reveal whether schools have complied with the EHA. Records transmit information from one professional to another; therefore, their accuracy, completeness, and relevance determine the effectiveness of professional intervention. Parental access helps keep the records useful, and that in turn helps professionals. Records also may contain information about the family, not just the student. For the sake of the family, then, access is important. Finally, records reveal much about people.

Confidentiality of Records—Privacy

Federal law also provides for the confidentiality of student records. The EHA and the Family Educational Rights and Privacy Act (FERPA) assure the confidentiality of any personally identifiable data, information, and records collected or maintained by the state education agency, all schools, and all other education agencies. LEAs must give parents, guardians, and, in some cases, pupils access to their own public school records, an opportunity for a hearing to challenge the content of the records, and the right to prevent the release of certain parts of the records without consent. These rights apply under Part B and Part H. (For the sake of simplicity, the term *school* includes providers of early intervention services under Part H.)

One person at each school must assume overall responsibility for ensuring that personally identifiable information remains confidential. This individual might be the director of special education, the director of special services, or some other administrator with similar responsibility. All persons who participate in the collection or use of confidential information must receive training in state and local policies and procedures related to the confidentiality of personally identifiable information. Each school also must maintain an updated roster of persons (and their positions) employed by the agency who have access to personally identifiable information. For example, the list may authorize the teachers or related-service providers who work directly with a student, but not every teacher in the school and certainly not parents of other students. This list must be available for public inspection. You should know who that person is. Teachers, related-service providers, and other professionals who work directly with a student should exercise the right to see the student's records, particularly evaluation data, IEPs, and year-end summaries.

Schools must obtain parental consent before releasing personally identifiable information to anyone other than the officials authorized to collect and use the information. For example, schools should get parental consent to release information about an individual student to researchers, special groups such as Special Olympics, and parent-advocacy groups such as United Cerebral Palsy Association Chapters. Generally, the administrators should prepare the consent forms and, together with the direct-service professionals, give them to parents with the request for parental consent.

LEAs must notify parents when personally identifiable information is no longer needed for educational services; on the parents' request, the LEA must destroy the information. Permanent information that may be kept indefinitely includes a student's name, address, phone number, grades, attendance record, classes attended, grade level completed, and year completed. School officials should advise parents that the student's records may be needed for such purposes as securing Social Security benefits or qualifying for certain income tax deductions. In addition, they should fully explain the safeguards for maintaining confidentiality of records before asking parents to make a decision about whether or not to destroy the records. Typically, school administrators carry out those duties.

The EHA specifies that parents' rights pertaining to educational records automatically are transferred to the student (or his or her legally appointed guardian, if the student has been adjudicated incompetent) at age 18. This requirement has major implications for schools serving students in the 18- to 21-age range. With respect to such students, you should know whether the student has been adjudicated incompetent (i.e., a court has ruled that the student, although having attained the age of majority, is not mentally competent and, therefore, should be placed under the legal authority of a guardian). You also should know who the judicially appointed guardian is. You also should consider whether the student and his or her parents want the parents to continue to have access to records and otherwise exercise the rights of parent participation. It is a good idea for administrators and direct-service staff to confer on these matters and settle upon a uniform course of action.

Evaluation

Under Part B (students aged 3 through 21), parents are entitled to an independent educational evaluation of the student. Evaluation under the EHA refers to procedures used to determine (a) whether the student has a disability and (b) the nature and extent of the special education and related services the student needs. Such procedures are those used selectively with the individual student; they do not include basic tests administered to or procedures used with all children in a school, grade, or class. A person who may make an independent evaluation is any qualified examiner who has no responsibility for educating the student and is not employed by the school. A qualified person is one who has met appropriate state certification, licensing, registration, or similar requirements. Upon request, schools must give parents information about where they may have independent educational evaluations performed. You may give that information to parents and, upon request, you should.

Under some circumstances, the independent evaluation must be carried out at public expense; the public agency either pays for the full cost of the evaluation or ensures that the evaluation is otherwise provided free to the parents. Parents have the right to an independent evaluation at public expense if the due process hearing officer requests one for use in a hearing or if the parents disagree with the school's evaluation. If the school initiates a hearing and if the school can prove that its evaluation was appropriate, the parents may be required to pay for any new evaluation. When parents obtain an independent evaluation at their own expense, the agency must consider this evaluation as a basis for providing the student with an appropriate education, as evidence in a due process hearing, or both.

Adam had had significant behavioral problems in kindergarten. At the age of 5 he was evaluated by the school district and recommended for placement in a personal social adjustment (PSA) classroom. These classrooms are now known as behavior disorder (BD) classrooms. On several occasions, I asked if Adam was also learning disabled and whether learning problems could be causing some of his tantruming at school. I was told by his teacher that it was the opinion of the educational team that Adam's problem was not caused by a learning disability. I continued to request complete evaluations. Finally, I was told the test had been completed and that there was no significant evidence that Adam had a learning disability. After learning about my right to have an independent evaluation, I notified the special education director that I was pursuing an independent evaluation based on the fact that they had made a recommendation to change his educational placement to hospitalization. In addition, I requested a due process hearing in objection to their evaluation process. The hearing officer agreed that the evaluation was needed and the school was required to pay the expense.

The provisions for obtaining and using independent evaluations reflect some of the major purposes of the due process doctrine. They let parents use other experts to challenge the schools and their experts. That is accountability at work. They also allow parents to deal on a more equal basis with professionals. When fortified with their own experts, parents have the ability to change the balance of power between themselves and professionals. In addition, the provisions tend to keep the professionals and parents focused on the student, who is, after all, the person evaluated.

Part H makes no explicit provision for independent evaluations. Parents may obtain their own evaluations, but Part H does not give the same rights as Part B regarding free evaluations or even the rights to be informed where evaluations can be obtained and to have them considered by a service provider.

Notice

Schools must give prior written notice to parents whenever they propose to initiate or change, or refuse to initiate or change the student's identification, evaluation, or placement under Part B, or under Part H the provision of early intervention services to the infant or toddler and family.

The requirements for notice can serve several purposes. First, they make it possible for parents and professionals to speak *with* each other, to have at least the same basic information. Thus, the requirement that the notice must contain certain information (the "what" or the content and substance of the notice are set out in Part B and Part H regulations) and that this information must be provided in understandable ways (the "how" or the method of communication such as in the family's native language are set out in Part B and Part H regulations) is the beginning of a certain sharing; it allows an opportunity for dialogue. Second, the "power relationship" between the professional and the parent can be made more equal. With roughly equal knowledge, parents and professionals can deal in roughly equal ways with each other. Third, knowledge can relieve some of the anxiety that parents naturally feel about the school's authority and the student's education. When working with families, you should not only try to tell them what the school proposes, but you should do so in a way they understand.

Sometimes notice does not enable professionals and parents to communicate with each other because it does not adequately inform. That is usually so because the notice often is written for the purpose of satisfying legal requirements and, therefore, tends to be stated in terms that lawyers or school administrators use with each other. In those instances, you may prefer face-to-face explanations, simplified written notice, or both. You also may have an ethical duty to give more adequate notice (see Chapter 14). Or, notice may not be timely.

> Sometimes the notices came on time. Sometimes they were just a few days ahead of the meetings, and they told me about meetings scheduled at the convenience of the staff.

Of course, some parents will not respond to notices. There may be many reasons for their failure to respond and you should seek to determine why parents do not respond. For example, you may follow a "touch-base" policy of telephoning, making a home visit, asking the student, or consulting other professionals involved with the parents. If you do not learn why parents do not respond, your LEA is legally entitled to seek a due process hearing if parental consent (following notice) is required. Or, you may proceed with your plans if parental consent (following notice) is not required.

Consent

As we discussed in Chapter 9, under Part B (age 3–21) the school must obtain the parents' consent for the initial evaluation and for the student's initial placement in a special education program. Consent may not be required for any other benefit to the student.

Part H (infants and toddlers) has its own rules about consent. Early intervention service providers must obtain parental consent before (a) conducting the initial evaluation and assessment of the child and (b) initiating the provision of early intervention services for the first time. If the parents do not give consent, the providers must make reasonable efforts to ensure that the parent (a) is fully aware of the nature of the evaluation and assessment or the services that would be available and (b) understands that the child will not be able to receive the evaluation and assessment or services unless consent is given. Also, if the parents do not give consent, the provider may initiate a due process hearing or other procedures to override the parents' refusal to consent to the initial evaluation of the child.

Consent as defined in Part B and Part H means that: The parents have been fully informed in their native language, or in another suitable manner of communication, of all information relevant to the activity (e.g., evaluation) for which consent was sought; the parents understand and agree in writing that the activity may be carried out; the consent describes the activity and lists the records (if any) that will be released and to whom; and the parents understand that they give consent voluntarily and may revoke it at any time. Use the consent forms your agencies have prepared, and offer to explain those forms to parents and make careful notes of your conversations when seeking consent. Typically, administrators have those forms and usually prepare them (often with the advice of legal counsel). But the duty to explain does not rest solely with them. All professionals should be available to explain requests for consent.

> With respect to Adam's placement in a school or psychiatric hospital, nobody told me I could make a choice between placements or treatments. When I learned that I had the right to take or refuse what the school offered, I was able to reject their plans and force them to create something else. So the right to consent meant a lot to Adam and me. It gave us a wedge to break up their game plan.

If parents refuse to consent when consent is required, they and the LEA must first attempt to resolve the conflict by complying with any applicable state law. (It is a matter of good professional practice for you to communicate clearly, even repeatedly, to explain the reasons why consent is sought.) If there is no consent, the school may initiate a due process hearing. Should the hearing officer rule in the school's favor, the parents' refusal will be overruled and the school may evaluate or place the student and notify the parents of its actions so that they may appeal. Again, school administrators are responsible for deciding whether to seek a hearing. In reaching these decisions, it is proper, however, for direct-service staff to consult with them, and be consulted by them.

The requirements for consent address some of the purposes behind due process. They help assure accountability by requiring schools to explain what they want to do and why. Thus, they can change the balance of power between parents and professionals by giving parents an opportunity to veto, subject to a due process hearing, what the school wants to do. Finally, the consent provisions mean that schools must focus on the infant-toddler and family under Part H and on the student under Part B, adapting their services to them; they do this by requiring schools to justify themselves.

Surrogate Parents

The appropriate state agency (under Part H, the lead agency; under Part B, the state education agency) must ensure that the rights of an infant-toddler under Part H or a student under Part B are protected if his or her parents are unknown or unavailable or if he is a ward of the state (e.g., when parental rights have been terminated or parents have abandoned their child. The provision does not apply when the parents are simply uncooperative or unresponsive.) The state education agency under Part B may comply with this requirement by assigning a surrogate parent. Under Part H the state lead agency must appoint surrogates. It must devise methods for determining whether a student needs a surrogate and then for assigning one. Two criteria apply to the selection of a surrogate: there should be no conflict of interest, and the individual should have the skill to represent the student.

The surrogate may represent the student in matters affecting identification, evaluation, placement, and right to a free appropriate public education (Part B) and early intervention services (Part H). You should know whether a child has a surrogate parent and, generally, should deal with that person just as you would with the child's own family members (see Chapter 8).

Fundamental fairness calls for protection of the vulnerable student. Consequently, the surrogate also has the same opportunities as natural parents or other guardians to hold the schools accountable, redress any imbalance of power, and require schools to focus on the student.

Consultation Concerning State Plans

Under Part B, the state education agency must establish procedures for conducting consultation with persons involved in or concerned with the education of students with disabilities, including those individuals and their parents or guardians. Each state agency also must make available to the public and to parents its annual plan for complying with the law; for conducting hearings at which the public may comment on the education of such students and the state's annual plan; for giving adequate notice of those hearings; and for allowing the general public to comment on proposed policies, programs, and procedures before these are adopted.

Also under Part B, the state education agency must (a) give public notice of hearings at which it seeks public comment on its special education policies; (b) provide an opportunity for public participation and public comment; (c) review the public comments before adopting the annual plan; and (d) publish and make the plan generally available. In addition, the agency must give assurances that, in giving full educational opportunities to students with disabilities, they will provide for the participation and consultation of the parents or guardians of the students. State-agency professionals generally have input into the state plan, and sometimes so do LEA professionals. All may attend the public hearings and you may want to encourage parents and other interested people to attend.

Part H contains similar rules regarding public participation in the development of the state plan, notice of public hearings, opportunity for public comment, public hearings, and review and reporting on public comments.

Advisory Panels

Each state education agency must create a Part B advisory panel whose members are to be appointed by the governor or other official authorized to make such appointments. The panel must be composed of individuals involved in or concerned with the education of students with disabilities. In addition, the panel should include at least one representative of individuals who have a disability, teachers of students with a disability, parents of such students, state and local educational officials, and administrators of programs for such students. The panel is to advise on the unmet needs of students, make public comment on the annual plan and on pertinent state rules or regulations, and assist the state in developing and reporting relevant data and evaluations. Professionals may attend the meetings of the state advisory panel and may want to encourage parents and other interested people to also attend.

Likewise, under Part H the state must establish an Interagency Coordinating Council. The Council must include at least three parents of infants or toddlers or other children with disabilities aged 3 to 6. You should tell parents about the existence of the state and local advisory committees, their roles, and how to obtain access to them (e.g., the name of the chairperson).

Up to this point, the general provisions of the due process principle have tried to emphasize the fairness component and, in doing so, prevent any conflict between professionals and parents. Advice for observing general safeguards is presented in Table 11–1. But conflict is inevi-

---

TABLE 11–1 Suggestions for Observing General Safeguards

- Do not deny parents access to the student's records but refer them to school administrators when they request copies.
- Record in student records only that information that is accurate, current, and relevant, and only those impressions or conclusions that can be supported by facts.
- Inquire whether a parent has the legal right of custody in cases where you are unsure about the effects of divorce or separation or in other situations involving custody, and refer the matter to the school administrators if in doubt.
- Be willing to explain a student's records upon parental request.
- If you are involved as a professional with a student, exercise your rights to see the student's school records.
- Make sure that you have obtained parent consent to release personally identifiable information about the student to anyone other than school authorities (such as parent advocacy groups).
- Advise parents where they may obtain independent evaluations of the student when they request such information; tell the school administrators that they have made the request and how you responded.
- When you give parents a notice, make sure not only that it tells what the school intends to do or refuses to do, but that it is written in the parents' native language and in such a way as to actually inform the parents.
- If you have doubts about the parents' understanding of the notice, offer to explain it verbally.
- If a parent does not respond to a notice, and a response is required, get advice from the school administrators on how to proceed and offer to make special efforts to obtain consent (telephone, home visit, etc.).
- Use the consent forms that your school has prepared; if you explain them to a parent, keep notes about the conversation.
- Always consult with your school administrators if you believe that a due process hearing should be brought by the school or that one may be brought by a parent.
- If a student has a surrogate parent, deal with that person in the same way you would if the person were the student's biological or adopting parent.
- Encourage parents to learn about the state and local special education advisory committees and offer to give or obtain information about those committees.

---

table in some cases. That is why another component, the "hearing" provisions, provide a means for resolving conflict. We now turn to these "hearing" provisions.

DUE PROCESS HEARING

The EHA's provisions for a hearing address each of the major purposes of the due process principle. First, they advance the fairness doctrine by allowing parents or schools to protest what each other does. Second, they enforce accountability by making it possible for each party to require the other to justify and defend a course of conduct. Third, they seek to redress the power relationship by allowing parents to seek a resolution of a dispute from an impartial person, thus preventing unilateral decision making. Finally, they make parents and professionals alike focus on the student's identification, evaluation, classification, placement, and program.

> I was just scared of due process. I knew I had to win to keep Adam out of an institution. But I didn't know if I could. If I had not protested, he would have been put into an institution. And then I basically would have lost him because he couldn't have survived there. I was desperate, very much so. And I was angry because I felt the staff had been shown that there was another way to work with Adam successfully. But they were basically finished with him and thought they had done me a favor by keeping him in a program. It wasn't a matter of them doing me a favor but of doing their job! I had no choice but to go to due process. It was the only way. Negotiation had failed. Due process was the only recourse.

Hearing Rights

Under Part B, each school must give the parents, guardian, or surrogate an opportunity to present complaints relating to any matter concerning the student's identification, evaluation, placement, or right to a free, appropriate public education. If the parents, guardian, or surrogate file a complaint with the school, they are entitled to an impartial hearing. The school must inform the parents about any available low-cost or free legal aid in the geographical area (e.g., legal aid clinics).

The right to a due process hearing is not limited to parents, guardians, or surrogates. A school also may initiate a due process hearing on its own proposal or refusal to initiate or change a student's identification, evaluation, placement, or free, appropriate public education. Normally, the school's decision to seek a due process hearing is made by its administrative officers. You may be asked to help school administrators decide whether or not to file a due process hearing. In addition, you may request the appropriate administrators to initiate one. For example, schools may want to initiate due process when parents refuse consent for the initial evaluation of a student who has an obvious disability.

Unless the parents and the school agree to an extension, the hearing must be held and a final decision reached within 45 days after the hearing has been requested; and a copy of the decision must be mailed to the parties. (The hearing officer may extend these deadlines.) The time and place of the hearing and each review of that decision (i.e., when parents or schools file an appeal) involving oral argument must be reasonably convenient to the parents and student (e.g., in the local school district, not at a distant state capitol).

You may be involved in due process hearings in a variety of ways. For example, you may be asked to be a witness. You may even volunteer to be a witness, although some ethical issues become involved when you do so (see Chapter 14). Your records may be put into evidence at the hearings. In some instances, you may be asked to give your expert opinions on what should be done for the student. When you serve as expert witnesses, and indeed in all cases where you testify or your records are admitted as evidence, you should be careful to testify from facts and data before reaching a conclusion. While you may feel conflict about your loyalties (see Chapter 14), your professional conduct should be above reproach. If it is, you will have discharged your duties to the student, parents, and schools. It is only natural for you to feel bias toward one party or to experience conflicting loyalties, but your feelings and conduct should be separate.

Typically, professionals like yourself—teachers, other direct-service staff, and school administrators—will be involved in a due process hearing. You will be asked, in most cases, to bring school records to the hearing, testify, and, when appropriate, give opinions. Before the hearing, you will be working with the school's lawyer and perhaps with the parent's lawyer in preparing the school's case. You may feel ambivalent about testifying. Adam's therapist describes her feelings after testifying at a due process hearing:

> I found testifying in a due process hearing to be unpleasant and somewhat stressful. It was frustrating to see how, in some cases, egos, personal convictions, and unsupported theoretical persuasions got in the way of promoting a child's best interests. On the other hand, it was tremendously gratifying to be able to contribute to a due process hearing that eventually resulted in moving a child from an uncompromising and unproductive school environment to one in which gains could be made. In this case, the child changed from being a highly aggressive, unhappy child who kept an entire school staff in an uproar, to a boy, who over a period of 2 to 3 years, was able to function appropriately in self-contained and mainstreamed classes. He was able to take responsibility for his own actions, and learn how to get along with peers as well as to take direction from authority figures. To prevent institutionalization in a case such as this was certainly a worthwhile endeavor.

Hearing Officers

Each school must keep a list of the hearing officers and their qualifications. The hearing may not be conducted by an employee of the school involved in the education of the student. Also, a due process hearing may not be conducted by any person having a personal or professional interest that might conflict with his or her objectivity in the hearing. A person who otherwise qualifies to conduct a hearing is not considered an employee solely because he is paid by the school to serve as a hearing officer. Sometimes hearing officers are employees of other schools or are retired educators, university professors of education, lawyers, or interested citizens with no particularly relevant experience or training.

Hearings and Appeals

At the initial hearing and on appeal, each party has the right (a) to be accompanied and advised by an attorney and by other persons with special knowledge or training with respect to children and youth with disabilities; (b) to present evidence and confront, examine, cross-examine, and compel the attendance of witnesses; (c) to make written and oral argument; (d) to receive a written or electronic verbatim record of the hearing; and (e) to receive a written account of findings of fact. No evidence may be introduced by any party unless disclosed at least 5 days before the hearing. The parents have the right for their child to be present and to have the hearing open to the public. Some parents will want to close hearings because of privacy. Others may select open hearings in order to let the public know about a problem.

> Our due process hearing lasted 2½ days. It was in the school administration building. And it was intimidating. I didn't testify. I was too emotionally spent to get on the witness stand. And I had enough other evidence. At the hearing, everyone wanted to justify their positions, to defend them. It was arm's length. Everyone tried to be cordial, but it was just on the surface.

Unless a party appeals from the initial hearing or begins a court action after the appeal, the decision of the initial hearing is final. After an initial hearing, an aggrieved party may appeal to the state education agency, which is required to conduct an impartial review of the hearing, reach a decision, and send a copy of the decision to the parties within 30 days. The hearing officer on appeal must make an independent decision after reviewing the matter.

The parties thereafter may file a lawsuit in either a state court or a federal district court. The court must receive the records of the administrative proceedings, hear additional evidence if offered, and, on the basis of the preponderance of the evidence, grant appropriate relief. The LEA's decision whether or not to initiate an appeal typically is made by school administrators upon advice by school lawyers. In addition to a careful assessment of the chances of winning, the decision whether or not to go to court is influenced by such factors as cost, time, and effects of prolonged school-parent conflict on the child.

> There was a decision in Adam's favor but there was an appeal. That was frightening, too. I just didn't have it in me to face an appeal. I was so relieved when they withdrew it.

Stay-Put Rule

During the initial hearing or appeal, the student remains in his or her current educational placement unless the school and the parents, guardian, or parent surrogate agree otherwise. When applying for initial admission to school, the student will be placed in the public school program, with the parents' consent, until all the hearings (including appeals) have been completed. The school may use its normal procedures for dealing with children and youth who are endangering themselves or others (e.g., suspension or expulsion; see Chapter 8 on the law regarding suspension and expulsion). In addition, a school may seek appropriate relief in court from the effects of this stay-put rule, such as when the student is dangerous to staff or other students. In that case, the school would ask for a change in the student's placement, despite the rule.

Part H

Under Part H (infants and toddlers), the state must provide for the timely administrative resolution of complaints by parents. States have two options: (a) to adopt the Part B due process procedures; or (b) to develop new impartial procedures for resolving individual child complaints. Under both options, the procedures require that an impartial decision maker resolve the dispute. The service provider is bound by that decision and must implement it unless it is reversed on appeal. In addition, a state that does not use the Part B procedures must nonetheless ensure that its procedures result in speedy resolution of individual child complaints.

A state may offer mediation as an intervening step before implementing due process procedures, but it may not require parents to use mediation (see discussion on mediation later in this chapter). All disputes must be resolved within 30 days after the lead agency receives a complaint. All hearings must be held in places and at times convenient to the parents.

Parents have the rights to: (a) be accompanied and advised by counsel or other people with special knowledge or training in early intervention, (b) present evidence and examine and cross examine witnesses, (c) prohibit the use of evidence not disclosed to them at least 5 days before the hearing, (d) obtain a transcript, and (e) obtain written findings of fact and decisions.

A provider or parent who is aggrieved by a decision may appeal it to a state or federal court.

As in the case of Part B, the infant-toddler also is protected by a specific stay-put rule under Part H. The rule is this: If a complaint is pending at any administrative level or on appeal to a federal or state court, then, unless the state agency and parents or guardians agree otherwise, the infant-toddler is entitled to continue to receive the appropriate early intervention services being provided; or, if applying for initial services, is entitled to receive those services that are not in dispute.

These rules under Part H deal only with complaints about individual children. In addition, Part H's regulations also require the state lead agency to establish procedures to resolve complaints about how the state itself—so-called *systemic complaints*—implements Part H and its site plan.

EFFECTS OF DUE PROCESS PRINCIPLE

There is no doubt about the many powerful effects of the due process principle. At the beginning of this chapter, we stated that due process seeks to achieve the four results of fair treatment, accountability, a new balance of power, and a focus on rights and needs. Has it succeeded? Generally, it has.

Positive Effects

The requirements for notice have been the core of the fair treatment that due process seeks. Without notice, parents would have no way of knowing what schools are doing or proposing to do. With notice, in contrast, parents can acquire such knowledge and, with it, sometimes assure themselves that the schools either are or are not providing a free, appropriate public education to their child.

Due process has sought accountability and achieved it. The fact that parents may take legal action against schools, and schools may likewise against parents, has made it possible for each party to hold the other accountable for its actions.

Due process sought to redress the balance of power between schools and parents. There is some substantial but not conclusive evidence that this goal has been achieved. Budoff and Orenstein (1982) maintained that due process, particularly the system of hearings and appeals, has legitimized the rights of parents and students, lent credence to parents' right to question educators and other professionals concerning the services offered to students, served to bring pressure on political and administrative organizations to become more responsive to students' needs, and caused some school systems to reconsider their modes of operation and to make appropriate changes in their relationships with parents and students.

Due process sought to create a new forum for focusing on the students' rights and needs. It seems to have succeeded on this issue, for the very basis for a due process case is whether the school and parents have responded satisfactorily to students' legal rights. In case after case (H. R. Turnbull, 1990), the courts have required schools to reshape their policies and practices to discharge their duties to students.

If the focus is on the results with respect to students' identification, classification, program, and placement, it is clear that there have been and will continue to be highly positive results. As we point out in Chapter 8, when hearing cases that started out in due process hearings, the courts have prevented exclusion, made evaluations fairer, revised appropriate programming, and slowed the unwarranted segregation of students who have a disability.

> I think there were positive aspects about due process. I had the opportunity to protest and present my case. I had the right to bring my own experts and to take on a whole team of school-district people. Without due process, Adam would have ended up in an institution or out of school and facing truancy hearings. As things ended up, he was placed in a regular school's program for children with severe emotional disturbance, so he is partially mainstreamed. So it did some good.

Negative Effects

In many respects, then, due process has accomplished its goals. But, in so doing, it has caused new problems. In brief, these results have been costly. We will discuss three elements of "costs" in this section. One involves the financial costs the parties must bear when they use the due process hearing and appeals as a method of resolving disputes.

COSTS—FINANCIAL.   Parents and schools alike must pay for attorneys, expert witnesses, independent evaluations, consultations, and communications (telephone and duplicating records) when they enter into a due process hearing. Total costs are affected by the number of participants, length of hearing process, and parent wealth and education. As these increase in quantity so do the costs of hearings (Boscardin, 1987). Early research showed that costs can be as low as $200 or as high as $4,000 per case (Budoff & Orenstein, 1982; NASDSE, 1978; Strickland, 1982; Yoshida, 1979). In addition, some parents must devote so much time to a case that they cannot attend to their job responsibilities and even lose their jobs (Budoff & Orenstein, 1982). In light of the high costs, it is not surprising that the parents who exercise their due process hearing rights generally are from middle to upper-middle socio-economic classes (Budoff & Orenstein, 1982; Lay, 1977; NASDSE, 1978). Parent costs increase with parent wealth and educational level (Boscardin, 1987).

> Given my limited income, participating in a due process hearing was contingent on my ability to juggle bills, borrow money and sell what I had of value. And, two years after the decision, I still struggle to pay off at least $6,000 in bills related to the hearing. However, I *would* do it again for the sake of Adam's future.

Schools also must absorb high financial costs (Budoff, 1979; Budoff & Orenstein, 1982; NASDSE, 1978; Yoshida, 1979). Again, early research revealed costs of up to $8,000 per hearing, with an average of between $800 and $1,000 (NASDSE, 1978). In 1987, some cases cost in excess of $10,000 (Boscardin, 1987). There also are costs associated with staff time, typically 73 hours per hearing (Kammerlohr, Henderson, & Rock, 1983).

COSTS—EMOTIONAL.   Emotional costs also are high. Budoff and Orenstein (1982) report parents and educators experienced emotional trauma and anxiety. LEA staff morale and confidence can diminish, particularly when parents attack professionals who see themselves as advocates for students or when they cast doubt on their professional judgment and competence (Budoff & Orenstein, 1982). But Strickland (1982) has documented that there are also emotionally satisfying aspects to the hearing, for parents and educators alike. And Budoff and Orenstein (1982) note both negative and positive psychic outcomes.

> I did not anticipate the impact that past legal proceedings would have on Adam's program, however. Understandably, the administration wanted to be sure that Adam was adjusting to his new program, but daily questioning about his progress focused so much attention on Adam that it began to interfere with my efforts to make him feel like an ordinary student. He, in turn, picked up very quickly on the fact that he could easily generate anxiety on the part of several adults and thereby gain attention. Time has gradually lessened this problem; Adam now draws no more attention than a regular student. I also have to say that the hearing affected my health. I lost 30 pounds over a few months. I lost sleep. I became emotionally fragile, so bad that I couldn't testify. I lost energy. I spent time on the hearing and on practically nothing else except Adam and my job. For both of us, the hearing was very hard.

OTHER COSTS—REDUCED CONFIDENCE, MORE CONFLICT. There is evidence that the due process hearing reduces not only parents' and professionals' confidence in the approach itself, but also parents' confidence in the schools themselves and their support for public education (Budoff & Orenstein, 1982). Indeed, the due process hearing in some instances has escalated rather than reduced the conflict between parents and professionals (Essex, 1979; Winer, 1982), left professionals feeling cynical and suspicious about parents (Daynard, 1980), widened the gulf between parents and professionals (Budoff & Orenstein, 1982), foreclosed constructive future communication (Budoff & Orenstein, 1982), and created a win-at-all-costs, rather than a problem-solving situation (Budoff & Orenstein, 1982).

> After the hearing, the staff told me they were upset that they could not get me to trust them. By that time, I couldn't trust any of them. That's what I mean when I say, everyone lost.

These results are not universal. For example, Strickland (1982) did not find that the due process hearing caused a significant change in parent-professional relationships—there was neither improvement nor deterioration in the relationships. Indeed, she reported that parents noted a significant improvement in the way they were treated by professionals after the hearing—they were respected as knowledgeable, courageous, and committed, and they were dealt with in a more conciliatory way by professionals because they were regarded as willing "to go to bat" to obtain rights promised by the EHA.

As Budoff and Orenstein (1982) and Strickland (1982) have suggested, one reason why parents and LEAs are dissatisfied with due process hearings is that they essentially have little control over the outcomes. The decision, after all, is rendered by a third party, someone who is not affected by the judgment. And often the attorneys for the parents and LEAs control the proceedings. This lack of self-determination in the hearings can contribute to continuing conflict between the parents and LEA, even after the hearing. In brief, the adversarial process tends to deny the parents and LEA the opportunity to take control of their own situation and increases their dependence on outside authority, namely, the hearing officer.

In addition, persuasive evidence shows that the parents and LEAs who go to hearings enter them with a history of mistrust and failed communication (Fiedler, 1985). Given the win-lose nature of due process hearings, it is inevitable that one of the parties will feel far more dissatisfied with a hearing's outcome than the other, and that those feelings of dissatisfaction will continue after the hearing.

What about the child? Both Budoff and Orenstein (1982) and Strickland (1982) reported that some students experience little to no effects, while others experience negative consequences from due process hearings. Students' attitudes toward school sometimes become more negative during the due process hearings (Budoff & Orenstein, 1982), and they sometimes experience informal sanctions from professionals (Strickland, 1982), such as negative teacher attitudes that are manifest by unwarranted "correction" procedures or unfairly depressed grades.

> After the hearing officer reached a decision which supported our position completely, Adam's teacher and his school psychologist, who were part of the educational team working with children with behavior problems, filed assault and battery charges against him. As a result, my 12-year-old son was thrust into the juvenile court system.

How may you act to reduce these costs? Obviously, any conduct that prevents the need for a due process hearing is a sure way of containing costs. You therefore should act legally and professionally, in the ways we suggest in this book. Such behavior will do much to prevent the causes of conflict. More, you should try to depersonalize any conflict that does arise. Of course, it is difficult not to take personally or not to act defensively at any suggestion of error, misjudgment, wrongdoing, or other negative behavior. But if you try to acknowledge that some conflict is inevitable and regard the due process hearing as a means for working out conflict, you may be less apt to be emotionally injured or to attack and try to emotionally wound a parent or another professional. You may want to try, with renewed vigor, to follow the communication skills and techniques that we discussed in Chapters 6 and 7, particularly after a hearing or mediation.

> If I had it to do all over again, I would go to due process once more. But a part of me would not want to. I would have a sinking feeling because I know what it's like. But I would have no choice. It's my only resource, my only defense.

The feelings expressed by this observation may apply to nearly everyone. Few want to go to due process. Most want to avoid it. Table 11–2 suggests what you can do to avoid some of the negative effects of due process.

MEDIATION

From the start, many people thought due process could harmonize the separate but similar interests of parents, professionals, and students— the interests of each in the student's free, appropriate public education (H. R. Turnbull, 1990). Yet, as we have shown, adversarial confrontation does not necessarily bring these common interests together. Accord-

---

TABLE 11–2 Suggestions for Reducing the Negative Effects of Due Process Hearings

---

- Consult with school administrators when you believe it is appropriate for the school to initiate a due process hearing.

- If you are a witness at a hearing, be sure to testify from facts and data entered into the student's records before stating a conclusion.

- Be sure to meet with the school's lawyers before testifying so you will know what they expect you to say and so you can tell them the basis (data, facts in the record) for your testimony. If the parent's lawyers want to meet with you for the same purpose, behave in the same way with them as with the school lawyers.

- Try to depersonalize the issues in a hearing.

- Renew your communication efforts and employ your best communication skills when working with parents involved in the due process hearing.

---

ingly, some people (Budoff & Orenstein, 1982; H. R. Turnbull & Barber, 1984; Fiedler, 1985) have concluded that mediation, or some other way of informally resolving conflict, is preferable.

The desire for an alternative to the due process hearing has several sources. Some professionals have criticized the over-legalization of special education, claiming that contemporary moral and ethical issues are best decided outside a courtroom or a due process hearing, including education issues (Kauffman, 1984). Others have argued that the due process approach is too rigid and forces an either-or choice, so that one party necessarily wins and another invariably loses (Agard, 1980; Fiedler, 1985; Folberg & Taylor, 1984). Some say that schools practice "defensive education" and concentrate on technical compliance with the law at the expense of "quality" education (Hassell, 1982). Moreover, some have observed that the parties generally do not seek compromise or problem-solving solutions (Losen & Diament, 1978), and some think this is so because they become too intent on "winning" the case (Budoff & Orenstein, 1982). Those who have criticized the due process approach as being too adversarial have suggested that mediation is a preferable approach (Fiedler, 1985), and A. P. Turnbull and Strickland (1981) have even described how to conduct mediation as a type of parent-professional negotiation.

Mediation is a method of settling disputes by negotiation rather than by decision of a neutral judge. It seeks compromise, not victory. Indeed, it requires compromise by the parties. These are among the reasons that many states have begun to use mediation in advance of due process hearings (McGinley, 1987). In addition, there is evidence (McGinley, 1987) that mediation can accomplish what due process hearings cannot: the resolution of conflict over the particular issue and the harmonizing of personal feelings. This is so because, in part, the parties have greater control over the outcomes in mediation than in a due process hearing.

Mediation consists of meetings between those who are in disagreement, with an impartial person, selected by the parties and therefore trusted by them, presiding over the meetings. The mediator tries to find ways of helping to resolve differences by compromise, and the parties are asked by him or her to identify points of agreement, points for compromise, and points that cannot be compromised. Mediation has the advantage of drawing attention to the points of agreement and using them as the springboards for reconciling the points of conflict (A. P. Turnbull & Strickland, 1981). In mediation, some agreement can be obtained, and some differences may remain. When differences still exist, the parties may choose to go to a due process hearing.

For example, the parties may have many differences at the outset. Such differences may concern a student's evaluation (does she have a learning disability or emotional disorder?), program (should he be in a regular classroom or resource room program?), and related services (should the family and child have psychological counseling?). After mediation, differences may only remain about the student's program, in which case the parties may go to due process. As noted earlier, states may offer mediation but not require it under Part H. And mediation may not delay the resolution of an individual child complaint beyond the 30-day period.

Mediation will never fully take the place of the due process hearing, because the hearing is indispensable under the EHA and, ultimately, under the federal Constitution. However, mediation can be a useful prelude to the hearing, because it may make the hearing unnecessary by resolving the parties' differences or it can narrow down the issues. (Of course, it also can prolong conflict!)

If you find yourself in disputes with parents, you would do well to suggest mediation, avoid the threat of a due process hearing, try to identify the common ground, seek (and be prepared to make) compromises on disputed issues, and use the knowledge and techniques for enhancing interpersonal relationships that we have described in this book.

NEGOTIATION

One way to prevent either due process hearings or mediation is to negotiate successfully in situations such as IEP conferences. Many lawyers and others who have become concerned that adversarial confrontations such as due process hearings or even mediation proceedings do not successfully resolve disputes have begun to study the art of negotiation.

One of the most useful results of their studies is the book, *Getting to Yes: Negotiating Agreement Without Giving In* (1981), written by Professor Roger Fisher of the Harvard Law School and William Ury of the Harvard Negotiation Project.

Fisher and Ury describe the usual negotiation postures as either "soft" or "hard." The "soft" negotiator wants to avoid personal conflict, leading to concessions that are too readily made. The "hard" negotiator, on the other hand, wants to win and sees negotiation as a contest of wills; this leads to equally hard responses and injured relationships.

In place of these traditional approaches, Fisher and Ury suggest another: the method of "principled negotiation." This strategy looks for mutual gain whenever possible; and, when there cannot be mutual gain, it insists on results that are based on fair standards that are independent of the will of either party. That is, it asks the participants to see themselves as working side by side, attacking the problem—not each other. It helps them focus on their common interests, not their negotiating positions. It encourages them to find options that will result in mutual gain. And, finally, it insists that any result should be based on some fair standard applied even-handedly to the problem.

If you want to learn how to enter into a successful negotiation and perhaps prevent mediation or due process hearings, we urge you to study Fisher and Ury's paperback masterpiece, *Getting to Yes: Negotiating Agreement Without Giving in.*

SUMMARY

The first challenge for professionals is to prevent conflict by carrying out the skills this book seeks to teach: complying regularly and rigorously with all laws and policies; and seeking parental and professional collaboration. The second challenge is more specific. It implies following the suggestions we have made about how to comply with the law and work with parents and other family members within the law's structure. The third is to make the promise of due process—its purpose—into the reality for each student and family. This means having a strong desire and the skill to deal fairly, to hold oneself and one's employer accountable, to recognize that professionals do not (and should not) have a monopoly of power over the student and family, and to keep one's focus clearly on the student and parents. In keeping that focus sharp, you will want to know how to provide information, a topic we address in the next chapter.

C H A P T E R 12

EXCHANGING INFORMATION WITH FAMILIES

Professionals who work with Hispanic families who request information in Spanish should search out appropriate materials in that language. Alternatives to print media should be made available to any family member who cannot read.

What it all comes down to is this: at no time did *ANY* of the groups who were supposed to provide information actually do their job. Our systems are so fragmented that they could not, or would not, and the situation is not getting any better. If a given agency does not have the *exact* information that you need, or if they don't want to be bothered (and yes, that is the case a shocking number of times), you will not get nothing from them, even though they may know where that information can be obtained. It is a national disgrace, and will continue to be so until enough parents raise enough hell to change it. Sadly, our experiences, and other similar to ours have shown that that is what it is going to take.

The above quote from Bob, a frustrated father who describes his family's search for information about his son's disability, illustrates the need for effective means of exchanging accurate information with parents. You can satisfy an important component of educational programs for children and youth with exceptionalities by providing information to family members in many different ways ranging from informal (e.g., suggestions on how to explain visual impairment to neighborhood children) to highly formal (e.g., workshop on building friendships). It is important to remember, however, that the provision of information is not a one-way undertaking. Educators and other professionals will receive valuable information from families on topics such as student strengths, daily living skills, or the continuity from skills learned in the classroom into the home. This new perspective on *exchanging information* preempts the tradition of providing information to families, which reinforces the role of the parent as a recipient of professionals' decisions. It also preempts the earlier view (discussed in Chapter 1) of "training" parents which often places the parent in the role of a student.

Jane Schulz (1985b), the mother of a son with Down syndrome and a leading teacher educator in special education, shared her view on this issue:

> The current concept of parent training is extremely insulting. Some colleagues told me of an encounter with a young mother and her two boys, aged 7 and 12, both mentally retarded and blind. My associate suggested that parent training was indicated. I wondered at the time who we knew that could tell this mother anything. In fact, I immediately wanted to meet and learn from a woman who had raised children with such complicated problems. Since that time I have had the distinct pleasure of working with her and her children. We pooled our resources; we learned from each other. Parent training? This mother and father were good parents long before I came along. (p. 6)

Models for parent involvement have broadened from clinic-based and formal workshops to include more diverse options for exchanging information. This diversity is consistent with families' preferences based on their schedules, available time, and competing responsibilities. For example, many families want to exchange information through informal conversations rather than participation in didactic sessions.

There has also been a shift from a singular focus on mothers to exchanging information with different family members (e.g., fathers, mothers, brothers and sisters, and extended family). This new emphasis enables family members to address their own priorities, not just the child's progress. A family-systems approach acknowledges the right of all family members to have their needs met and to identify their priorities.

Family members vary in their interest in exchanging information, the priority of their topics of interest, the format of the information to be shared, and the choice of a person with whom to work. We will provide an overview of options to consider when individualizing your approach to exchanging information with families. Upon completion of this chapter, you will be able to answer the following questions:

- What might you recommend to a family who requests information about managing behavior? Establishing a homework routine? Advocating for their child's participation in an integrated setting? Planning for the future?

- What are possible methods of incorporating ongoing opportunities for information exchange with families into your program? How will you take into consideration the diversity of the families involved?

- What would you do if a family member of one of your students asked you for information or support which you did not have or felt you were unqualified to provide?

OVERVIEW OF TOPICS

Many different topics are relevant to the concerns and needs of families. Based on our review of the literature and our own experiences in working with families, we have chose four topics to highlight in this section—behavior management, homework, educational advocacy, and future planning. The families with whom you work may be interested in information on these topics, or they may prefer pursuing others.

Behavior Management

Behavior management interventions seek to change parent-child relationships by modifying parent and child behaviors alike. Parents learn principles that enable them to increase the child's positive behaviors while decreasing or eliminating the negative behaviors. These principles typically include defining the behavior, measuring its rate and occurrence, intervening by arranging consistent consequences, and evaluating the effectiveness of the intervention. This section will describe examples of programs which teach behavior management techniques to parents.

STEPS TO INDEPENDENCE. A comprehensive program focusing on behavior management topics, *Steps to Independence: A Skills Training Guide for Parents and Teachers of Children with Special Needs* (Baker & Brightman, 1989), is based on years of research and feedback from parents of children with disabilities. It is written for both parents and professionals and will be helpful for both those who like to conduct daily, structured learning sessions at home and those who prefer to benefit from opportune learning moments as they present themselves. The book is divided into three sections, each filled with drawings, charts, and examples:

1. Basics of Teaching—includes targeting skills, establishing steps, picking rewards, setting the stage, teaching, observing progress, and troubleshooting.
2. Skill Teaching—includes self-help skills, toilet training, play skills, and independent living skills such as self-care, home-care, and information.
3. Behavior Problem Management—includes identifying, specifying, and measuring behaviors as well as initiating a program.

PARENT AND TODDLER TRAINING (PATT) PROJECT. One project which serves children who have multiple disabilities and visual impairments is the Parent and Toddler Training (PATT) Project (Klein, Van Hasselt, Trefelner, Sandstrom, & Brandt-Snyder, 1988). This early intervention program contains a curriculum for parents or other primary care givers covering issues in early child development, social development, family members' reactions, enhancement of infants' development, and family communication and problem solving as well as behavior management. An effort is made to involve and recognize the needs of the entire family during 2-hour weekly sessions for 6 months. Scheduled social activities often include grandparents as well as siblings.

The goal of the PATT curriculum section on behavior management is to provide a basic understanding of behavioral techniques in order to enable the parent to utilize effectively these strategies at home. The curriculum leaders work with the parents in the design and execution of behavior interventions appropriate for the needs of the family. Booster sessions which occur monthly after the initial 6-month training period allow the parents to express any concerns or questions they might have regarding the curriculum. These sessions are reduced to bimonthly meetings over the following 6 months (Klein et al., 1988).

OTHER PROGRAMS.   Many programs suggest the use of modified behavior management principles in interactions between parents and children at home. Techniques such as being consistent, reinforcing positive behaviors, ignoring problem behaviors, and manipulating the environment can be effective in a nonstructured setting. *Children and Adolescents with Mental Illness: A Parent's Guide* (McElroy, 1987) and *Teaching the Young Child with Motor Delays: A Guide for Parents and Professionals* (Hanson & Harris, 1986) are examples of broad-based materials for parents which recommend the use of behavior-management principles for behavior problems at home. Behavior-management techniques have also been used with success in feeding and nutritional programs for individuals with disabilities. For example, *Nutrition and Feeding of the Handicapped Child* (Crump, 1987) describes a group weight-control program which requires parental involvement in their child's weight-loss program. Contracts are signed by the parents and the child, and weekly graphs visually help monitor weight fluctuations. A resource which suggests simple record keeping as an aid to improvements in mealtime behavior is *Mealtimes for Persons with Severe Handicaps* (Perske, Perske, Clifton, McLean, & Stein, 1986).

Brothers and sisters also have been given opportunities for training on behavior management (Powell & Ogle, 1985; Schreibman et al., 1983). Schreibman and her colleagues (1983) taught behavior-management principles to brothers and sisters of children with autism. The siblings were able to use the behavior management skills effectively, and their brother or sister with autism made consistent progress. Powell and Ogle (1985) provide an excellent review of research on providing information to brothers and sisters and guidelines for setting up programs.

Homework

Damion, a junior-high student who has a learning disability, describes his frustrations with his homework assignments.

Sometimes I take longer with my homework than the other kids. It's not fair. I never talked to the teacher about having too much homework. I just suffer through it. My parents know that I have problems with my home-work because sometimes I get mad and won't do it. They help me with it a lot.

Many parents are interested in learning how to help their son or daughter at home with the skills they are being taught at school. In an observational study of IEP conferences, it was reported that the majority of parents asked how they could help their child at home, but none of them received a definitive response from the professionals at the meet-ing (Goldstein et al., 1980). Parents of students who are gifted are en-couraged to create a home environment that facilitates creativity and is challenging (Takacs, 1986), yet many of these parents experience con-cern and anxiety about how to best support their child's achievement (Dettmann & Colangelo, 1980; Takacs, 1986).

Exchanging information with parents about their son or daughter's homework assignments has the potential advantages of enhancing the child or youth's academic or developmental progress and strengthening the partnership between families and teacher. However, some families' teaching may increase stress and tension. Reflect on your own experi-ence. Was tension ever created in your family when your parents at-tempted to help you with a school assignment? Depending upon family dynamics, involving parents as helpers with homework can be an asset or a liability.

Maddux and Cummings (1983) provide excellent suggestions, con-sistent with a family-systems perspective, of when home tutoring should not be done:

- if there is parental disagreement over whether or not the child should be tutored;
- if no quiet, nondistracting place is available in the home;
- if tutoring might result in neglect of the needs of other family members (in cases where there are many children or where someone suffers from a chronic illness);
- if time spent in tutoring deprives the child of opportunities to make friends with other children or develop necessary social skills. (p. 31)

Another warning is to avoid the "perpetual-patient" syndrome for the students (Gliedman & Roth, 1980), described by Sondra Diamond, a psychologist with a physical disability:

Something happens in a parent when relating to his disabled child; he forgets that they're a kid first. I used to think about that a lot when I was a kid. I would be off in a euphoric state, drawing or coloring or cutting out paper dolls, and as often as not the activity would be turned into an occupational therapy session. "You're not holding the scissors right." "Sit up straight so your curvature doesn't get worse." That era was ended when I finally let loose a long and exhaustive tirade. "I'm just a kid! You can't therapize me all the time! I get enough therapy in school every day! I don't think about my handicap all the time like you do!" (Diamond, 1981, p. 30)

We encourage you to take into consideration individual family situations before implementing mandatory, extensive homework policies. You must realize that families' time constraints and tutoring abilities may create tense learning situations which may lead to guilt feelings on the part of family members, a no-win learning experience on the part of the student and lack of needed recreational time for both parents and students (C. M. Horner, 1987).

Some students, however, benefit from regular homework assignments, and some families enjoy working on assignments together. To insure that these experiences are positive ones, communication between home and school is vital. Several authors have proposed suggestions for successful homework experiences (See Table 12–1).

C. M. Horner (1987) recommends a four-stage model which focuses on increasing students' independent study skills. The four stages are as follows:

Stage I—Establishing Routine

The student records assignments completed in class as well as homework assignments into a notebook which serves as communication between home and school. A weekly contract is devised whereby the student promises to record assignments in the notebook and the parents list a reward to be given at the end of each week. The contract system is eventually faded and replaced with verbal encouragement.

Stage II—Managing Time

A board which can easily be erased for each new day's schedule is fabricated listing household chores, homework, and other daily activities; predicted time required for their completion; actual time the tasks were started and completed; and the total time required. This process continues until students develop an ability to predict the time needed for a specific task.

Stage III—Teaching Problem Solving

Parents can encourage independent study techniques by helping the student devise a study plan. The parents model self-instruction techniques by asking "What is it I have to do?" and "How can I do it?", brainstorming with their child about possible answers to the questions, leaving their son or daughter to practice independently, and then guiding them through self-evaluation of their work.

TABLE 12–1   Suggestions for Supporting Families to Assist with Homework

---

- Meet with families at the beginning of the school year to establish homework policies and to discuss the encouragement of effective study habits in a positive manner at home (Salend & Schliff, 1988).
- Provide feedback to students and parents using a daily report card system (Strukoff, McLaughlin & Bialozor, 1987).
- Tape messages on a telephone answering machine as an aid in the communication of homework assignments to parents (Minner & Prater, 1987)
- Explain assignments thoroughly, so that students clearly understand the reason for the task, and when it is to be turned in, as well as the actual directions for completing the assignment (Salend & Schliff, 1988).
- Discuss the mechanics of the assignment with your students, including the format to be used (e.g., word processor, ink, cursive) and the materials needed (e.g., calculator, colored pencils) (Salend & Schliff, 1988).
- Allow students to begin their assignments in class, answering questions as they arise (Salend & Schliff, 1988).
- Utilize two sets of textbooks—one at home and one at school for students who are frequently absent (Fithian, 1984).
- Obtain periodic feedback from parents regarding their perceptions of their son's and daughter's homework skills (Salend & Schliff, 1988).
- Videotape classroom sessions for students who are homebound (Fithian, 1984).
- Abstain from assigning homework on weekends, giving students and families a needed break (Salend & Schliff, 1988).
- Work in conjunction with parents to assign skill practice which is relevant in home settings (e.g., sorting silverware, measuring ingredients for a recipe) (Salend & Schliff, 1988).
- Review helpful study habits with your class (Salend & Schliff, 1988).

Stage IV—Achieving Independent Study

At this stage, parents and teachers fade their involvement to that of encouragement and occasional monitoring. The student should understand that the parents or teacher will be happy to provide assistance if requested.

This program not only encourages homework completion, but also teaches skills such as problem solving and time management, which are important throughout the life cycle.

A student with learning disabilities may feel discouraged if faced with the burden of a normal load of homework. Damion's stepmother, Valerie, expressed her frustration at this system:

There is no justice. Teachers at the junior high level understand even less about learning disabilities than at the elementary-school level. My son is in books that he can't read, doing assignment sheets that he can barely read, searching for answers in the text he can't read. Don't get me wrong. There have been gains, but I feel like I am the one who has made them happen. Now he's able to give taped book reports so that the teacher can listen instead of deciphering his writing. This requires a lot of work from all three of us. (dad, mom, son). We listen to the taped book or read a book to him, then have him write about what he's heard, then we practice reading it and finally we tape him reading it. All this work for only 10 points a page, that most kids whip out independently in an hour or so.

Students who have learning disabilities may benefit from (a) assignments which have been shortened; (b) a set time period (e.g., 20 minutes) during which to do as much studying as possible each day; or (c) the option to call the teacher at home when frustrated (Stevens, 1984). Damion, a junior-high school student, noted that he would prefer shortened versions of usual assignments, clearly indicating that the option of contact with the teacher outside of school hours was not for him. For other students, this latter option may be preferable.

Students who frequently are absent from school may also benefit from expanded homework programs. Children and youth may miss school due to the nature of their disability; chronic illness, for example, may require a student to spend days or even weeks at home or in the hospital. It is important to maintain an atmosphere of normalcy in these cases, expecting students to keep up with their work (within reason), and grading assignments as if the student were in class (Fithian, 1984).

Teacher characteristics and practices are influential variables in successful homework programs. A willingness to work with families will help ensure positive homework experiences for your students. Sometimes students do get enough instruction or therapy in school and teaching preacademic or academic skills at home might be overkill. All students—those who are disabled and/or gifted—have the potential for "burning out" on learning. As we discussed in Chapters 3–5, balance is the key.

Educational Advocacy

Since the passage of the Education for the Handicapped Act (see Chapter 8), educational advocacy has been a major training emphasis. Specific topics include legal rights, integration, and assertive communication. Ferguson (1984), the mother of a child with a severe disability involved in a parent-run advocacy program, pointed out one reason why advocacy training is important:

Although parents do have a lot of information, it is not the "right" kind. When we go to speak to administrators at school we hear about IEP's,

> MA's, criteria, auditory processing, regulations, and, sometimes, due pro-
> cess. At first, there seems to be no correspondence between what we
> know and what the people in schools are talking about. Difficult initial
> experiences can cause some parents to stay silent. Others begin to search
> out information and eventually learn to speak the language of the
> schools. . . . One of our members suggested, "If you say 'perseveration'
> instead of 'he does it again and again and again and again,' it makes it
> sound as though you know what you are talking about." (p. 41)

Families with advocacy skills are able to represent their child's interests in trying to secure appropriate educational services. Integration is
currently an active area for educational advocates. Barbara, the mother
of a third grader with multiple disabilities who has been successfully
integrated into his neighborhood school in a regular classroom all day
for a year now, explains:

> I don't know of any family whose child is integrated who hasn't had to
> advocate. It's constant. You have to advocate on all levels—kids, families
> in the neighborhood, your extended family, administrators, and teachers.

Although legislation mandates the least restrictive environment for all
students with disabilities, funding is often distributed such that school
districts are penalized for placing students in regular classrooms. One
example is Florida, where in 1985–86 only 28 out of 67 counties mainstreamed students with mental retardation into neighborhood schools.
At the same time, the state supported 77 special centers whose sole
purpose was to educate exceptional students (Burton & Rachlin, 1988).
Circumstances such as this create an educational apartheid where "separate but equal" is being challenged by families and professionals alike.

A comparison between the perceptions of parents of children with
special needs being educated in mainstreamed settings and the perceptions of parents of children in nonintegrated settings produced interesting
results (McDonnell, 1987). Among the parents of children in special
schools, 65% felt that, upon entrance to an integrated setting, their children would be verbally abused by peers without a disability at least
once a month and only 34% expected that their child would make
friends with classmates without a disability in such a setting. By contrast, only 4% of the parents whose children were currently being educated in integrated classrooms reported verbal abuse by classmates on a
monthly basis, and 64% of these parents reported no known incidents
of verbal abuse. Regarding friendships, 74% of this group of parents
explained that their children had friends without a disability at school.
These outcomes were not significantly different when the answers of
parents of children classified as "severely multiply handicapped" were
compared to those whose children were noted as "severely intellectually handicapped" for the purposes of the study (McDonnell, 1987). In

Minnesota, over 90% of classmates of children with severe disabilities felt that integration was a good idea and many expressed that they had benefited from the experience (York, Vandercook, Heise–Neff, & Caughey, 1988).

Family-professional partnerships have proven effective in working towards the instatement of integrated school programs (Hamre–Nietupski et al., 1988). Each member of the parent-professional team contributes important strengths to the teamwork. Hamre–Nietupski et al. note the following:

Contribution of Parents

- commitment to their children and expectations for full citizenship in the community;
- knowledge of their children's needs and how to explain these needs to the community;
- experience and contacts to network with other parents and influence community leaders.

Contributions of Professionals

- knowledge of "the system";
- acquaintance with professional literature and research;
- knowledge of classroom techniques for successful integration experiences

These researchers continue by delineating 11 strategies which, in their experience, have proven a successful means for advocating for integration in a school district where administrative leadership is skeptical. These strategies are outlined in Table 12–2. The success of these strategies was due, in part, to the group's organization, commitment, and efforts to educate others in the community.

Once a school district is integrated, educational advocacy continues to contribute in important ways to the success of the programs, team roles, or other aspects of integration. (Contact the Institute on Community Integration at the University of Minnesota [see Appendix A] for further information.)

An excellent advocacy resource for special education professionals is the federally funded parent center. Usually staffed by parents of persons with exceptionalities, these centers' primary mission is advocacy training. An example of a parent center is the PACER program in Minneapolis, Minnesota. PACER was funded in 1976 based on the philosophy of "parents helping parents." Its main function is to inform parents of their rights and responsibilities related to special education. The primary means of sharing information includes workshops, newsletters, phone calls, and letters. Over 8,000 persons received information from PACER in 1987–88; recipients have evaluated the services very favorably (PACER Center, Inc., 1987).

TABLE 12–2 Strategies for Securing Integrated Options

---

1. Organize an advocacy group
2. Become better informed on integration issues
3. Inform others of integration benefits and strategies
4. Work to influence policies on integration
5. Work with the media
6. Meet frequently with influential school administrators
7. Influence others in the school system
8. Work within other advocacy organizations
9. Consult with a legal advisor
10. Bring advocates to IEP conferences and placement staffings
11. Contact other parents and advocates

Note. From "Parent/Professional Partnerships in Advocacy: Developing Integrated Options within Resistive Systems" by Hamre–Netupski et al., 1988, JASH, *13* (4), p. 253. Copyright 1988 by The Association for Persons with Severe Handicaps. Reprinted by permission.

Parent's comments included:

> I think we got what we needed because PACER was involved. When we knew where we stood regarding laws and rights the district started listening to us. (PACER Center, Inc., 1984, pp. 17, 27)

Educational advocacy is not for all families, however. Given their responsibilities in the fulfillment of other family functions, some families find that advocacy is not a priority. A mother commented on her need to balance priorities:

> I used to run from this meeting to that one. I wanted the people in my community to crown me "World's Greatest Mom of a Blind Kid." I wanted to know deep down in my heart that I was creating a better world for Angela. Then after Angela started acting out really badly, it dawned on me that she needed a mother—not a community organizer. I spend more time at home making sure she gets what she needs. We are both happier.

Engaging in advocacy is extremely demanding of time and energy. One way to assist families who are not able to advocate is to suggest community resource persons who may help them in this area.

Future Planning

The importance of helping families plan for the future is well documented in the life cycle literature. As discussed in Chapter 5, a pervasive concern of many families is the future. This issue needs to be addressed as soon as possible, beginning in early intervention programs. At this stage, parents can benefit from information about possibilities for their child's future. Dreams of a happy, fulfilled life including full citizenship, employment, and independent living opportunities are important for all families. You are in a position to support the family of a student with a disability to envision their child's future and to develop great expectations.

From life-cycle literature we know that transitions or life changes are periods of greatest stress for families. These transitions frequently involve entry into or exit from school programs—preschool, elementary school, secondary school, and postsecondary education or adult services. The value of family involvement in educational transitions has been well documented, although the extent of family participation may vary (Fowler, Chandler, Johnson, & Stella, 1988). Information has been provided to families in a number of ways. Most of the materials developed to date focus exclusively on helping families deal with an educational transition at one particular point in time.

A school-based model to prepare families for making transitions from preschools to kindergarten programs has been the Planning School Transitions project developed by Susan Fowler and her colleagues at The University of Kansas. The project resulted in a series of research and discussion articles which contain procedures for identifying and assessing children's readiness for transition (e.g., teacher expectations regarding child skills necessary for end-of-year points; parent interviews which assist parents or family members to identify and prioritize family needs). These articles are excellent resources for educators: *A Collaborative Model for Providing Support to Parents during Their Child's Transition from Infant Intervention to Preschool Special Education Public School Programs* (Hanline & Knowlton, 1988); *Making the Transition to Preschool: Identification of Parent Needs* (Hanline, 1988); and *Planning School Transitions: Family and Professional Collaboration* (Hains, Fowler, & Chandler, 1988).

The transition from adolescence to adulthood can pose significant challenges. Currently, adult services are not mandated by federal legislation. Thus, where available, services are often uncoordinated and lacking, causing great frustration to families. A study which examined two generations of parents of adults with severe disabilities found that 20 years ago parents did not experience a change of services or relationships with professionals as their children attained adulthood. The reason for the absence of change was that services for children with disabilities were as fragmented as services for adults. The newer generation of parents, however, faced sudden ending of the services to which they had become accustomed. Thus, the transition experience of the older generation was not as traumatic, due to an "ironic consistency" of a lack of services (Ferguson, Ferguson, & Jones, 1988).

A parent of a 21-year-old woman who recently graduated from high school commented:

> At Denise's graduation, I had a flood of confused emotions. I felt elation to know that Denise was a first-generation beneficiary of P.L. 94–142, but I also felt impending doom and dread in recognizing that she was graduating to a waiting list—#168 on the waiting list for supported employment. Would her life ever be full again? Could I keep my job? What would she do to fill so much idle time?

A major part of secondary education should consist of planning for the employment, recreation, interpersonal relationships, and residential options that students with severe disabilities will access after high school graduation. A resource written for families is *Disability and the Family: A Guide to Decisions for Adulthood* (H. R. Turnbull, Turnbull et al., 1989) which includes information on the requirements of decision making in adulthood and ways to support adults who do not have full mental competence; financial planning and government benefits; planning for life in the community including recreation, interpersonal relationships, residential options, and employment; and advocacy. A major theme of the proposed future-planning process is that the student's preferences should be at the heart of all planning. The book contains a comprehensive Preference Checklist that can be used by students and families in prioritizing a range of considerations about future options. Other resources include the book *The Young Person with Down Syndrome: Transition from Adolescence to Adulthood* (Pueshel, 1988) and a journal article in *Teaching Exceptional Children* entitled "Learning Disabled Students Make the Transition" (Neubert & Foster, 1988).

One model which is adaptable to transition situations across the life cycle is the *Rainbow Connection Instructional Guide,* developed by the United Cerebral Palsy of Greater Birmingham to aid professionals in developing transitional services for students with disabilities (Hughes & Beaty, 1986). The Rainbow Connection has received positive reviews (Brown, 1987). The manual contains the following sections plus an extensive appendix:

1. Need for transitional services.
2. Development of constructive relationships between programs.
3. Roles of staff and programs.
4. Selection of students to receive services.
5. Responsibilities of interdisciplinary team members.
6. Encouragement of parental skills and involvement.
7. Timing and delivery of the transitional services.
8. Follow-up and evaluation of services provided and received.

9. Consideration of services for students with severe disabilities.
10. Examples of the Rainbow Connection model from transitional settings across the life cycle. (Brown, 1987; Hughes & Beaty, 1986)

Future planning is of particular importance for parents of students who are gifted. Parents can create early opportunities for these students to explore and identify interests. Indeed, research indicates that individuals who are highly successful in artistic, psychomotor, and cognitive fields have received strong family support and encouragement at an early age (Bloom & Sosniak, 1981). Takacs (1986) cautions against misinterpretation of these findings. She maintains that optimally parents should be willing to investigate new interest areas with their children, warning against overencouragement which may narrow children's fields of exploration.

Parents of students who are gifted can benefit from information on how to encourage career development through such strategies as having biographies available on persons with distinguished careers, helping students become personally acquainted with adults in leadership positions in a variety of fields, arranging an adult mentor relationship with a person whose profession is particularly interesting to the students, and helping with college planning (Karnes & Karnes, 1982). Career choices may be difficult for students who are "multipotentialed." Pask-McCartney and Salomone (1988) discuss the difficulties a student has in making a choice when presented with a wide range of possibilities. These authors cited the following quote from Sylvia Plath's *The Bell Jar,* to illustrate their point:

> I saw my life branching out before me like the green fig tree in the story . . . I saw myself sitting in the crotch of this fig tree, starving to death, just because I couldn't make up my mind which of the figs I would choose. I wanted each and every one of them, but choosing meant losing all the rest, and . . . I sat there, unable to decide. (pp. 84–85)

A curriculum which enables students who are gifted to envision possibilities and organize these options using effective problem-solving strategies is *Futuristics: A Handbook for Teachers of the Gifted and Talented* (Epley, 1985).

College planning is also an issue for many students with learning disabilities and several resources have addressed this subject. *The McGuire-Shaw Postsecondary Selection Guide for Learning Disabled Students* (MSG) stresses the importance of a match between the characteristics of the student, the characteristics of the institution, and the characteristics of support programs available for students with learning disabilities. This guide can be an asset to counselors who work with high-school or community-college students who are exploring the possibilities of university study, or to the staff of colleges who are involved in admitting new students (McGuire & Shaw, 1987). Michael (1987) produced a comprehensive list of questions to aid students and their parents in evaluating postsecondary program choices for students with learning disabilities. In 1988 he expanded on his work, focusing on the importance of adequate library services for college students with learning disabilities (Michael, 1988). Another resource is *Peterson's Guide to Colleges with Programs for Learning Disabled Students* (Mangrum & Strichart, 1988). Assisting with future planning can alleviate some of the family members' concern and worry. Once future options are explored, the future is likely to be less threatening. In addition, identifying future goals can guide students, families, and professionals in designing relevant educational programs to best prepare the student to meet such goals.

But future planning can also present drawbacks for some families. One such drawback, discussed in Chapter 5, is that many families are more present- than future-oriented. According to their ideological style, they "take a day at a time," believing that all things eventually work out. This attitude was expressed by Elsie Helsel, the mother of an adult son with cerebral palsy and mental retardation:

> We have lived long enough and through enough that we are not fretting about what will happen to Robin when we die. There is a limit to what can be accomplished by planning ahead. Who knows precisely what will happen ten years from now, or five years from now, or even tomorrow? We believe that all of us are in God's care and under His protection. Robin's deep, abiding faith in God has helped him cope with a very frustrating existence on this earth. He truly believes that God is his refuge and strength, and that belief will sustain him as long as he lives. (DeWert & Helsel, 1985, pp. 104–105)

Thus, even though some professionals may believe it is important for a family to engage in detailed future planning, the family may not be so inclined. For such families, future planning may be stress-producing rather than stress-reducing.

This section has provided an overview of four topics—behavior management, homework, educational advocacy, and future planning—about which families may wish to receive information. Some families may not want to pursue these topics, but be curious about others, such as learning more about their child's particular exceptionality. Information preferences will vary widely as will families' preferences for how information is shared. The next two sections will present alternatives to consider when individualizing information exchange with families.

METHODS OF EXCHANGING INFORMATION

Professionals who will be designing and implementing opportunities for information exchange with families need to be aware of available settings for providing information as well as the various formats of information presentation within each situation. We suggest a planning process which includes the following five steps:

1. Identify family needs and preferences through conversations with the families, using the *Guide for Gathering Family Information through Dialogue* (presented in Appendix B), if desired.
2. Analyze needs and determine individual and group preferences.
3. Plan informational opportunities consistent with preferences.
4. Provide informational opportunities.
5. Receive feedback from families on the appropriateness of the opportunities provided.

Group, Individual, or Independent Situations

In planning how to share information it is important to consider the benefits and drawbacks of group vs. individual sessions. Studies of behavior-management sessions have examined the relative effectiveness of these two approaches (group or individual sessions). One study randomly assigned parents of children with mental retardation to an individual training group, a 10-session group training, or a control group (Brightman, Baker, Clark, & Ambrose, 1982). The parents receiving individual and group training achieved almost identical results, and both performed higher on outcome measures than the control group. Besides, group training was conducted at half the cost per family and was far more time-efficient for the professionals providing the training.

GROUP SESSIONS.   Group training can provide a supportive environment in which families can learn from and be reassured by other families. As one mother stated in the evaluation of a group training session:

> It helps to know that there are other parents who have the same concerns and problems as I do. It makes me feel normal.

Another advantage of group training is decreased cost and time compared to individual sessions. For some families, however, group training poses problems related to schedule inconvenience, transporta-

Families Together is a federally funded parent training and information center which offers weekends of education, information and relaxation for the entire family. See Appendix A for a state listing of federally funded parent centers.

tion, child care, perceived breach of privacy, and lack of responsiveness to idiosyncratic family concerns.

Group sessions tend to be stereotyped as being offered in the evening for 1 or 2 hours with mostly mothers and some fathers in attendance. However, group sessions may be structured in many different ways. One variable is scheduling. An example of an innovative approach is the Families Together program in Kansas. The goals of Families Together are to strengthen families, provide an opportunity to learn and recreate together, bring professionals and parents together as equals, share information and learn from each other, and reinforce the concept that each family member is an important and vital part of the family unit. To achieve these goals, Families Together provides weekend workshops (Saturday morning through Sunday noon) for the entire family at a motel. Approximately 18 families come together for family recreation, parent discussion groups, sibling discussion groups, and child activities. Parents have identified the major highlights of the weekends to be visiting and talking with other parents, information from resource persons, and a chance to go out and not worry about the children on Saturday night because child respite care is provided. The key to this creative alternative is the balanced emphasis on enjoyment and learning. Another creative alternative to traditional support group sessions is telephone conferencing. This approach is described by Evans, Smith, Werkhoven, Fox, and Pritzl (1986).

A second variable to be given serious consideration in structuring group sessions is the persons for whom the group sessions are designed. In addition to serving as information opportunities for mothers only or for mothers and fathers, workshops have been designed for siblings (Meyer, Vadasy, & Fewell, 1985a, 1985b), grandparents (Meyer & Vadasy, 1986), and fathers (Meyer, Vadasy, Fewell, & Schell, 1985).

INDIVIDUAL SESSIONS.   In contrast to group approaches, individual sessions can enable a family and a professional to develop a closer working relationship (Bernal, 1984) and to focus more specifically on the unique aspects of the family's situation. When working with just one family, professionals can tailor information to the preferences of that one family.

Individual sessions frequently are conducted in the family's home. Home sessions have the advantages of enabling professionals (a) to "get to know the family on their own turf," (b) to assess family and child needs related to educational goals and objectives, (c) to observe family interaction and child-related problems and expectations in the home setting, and (d) to minimize family problems related to child care and transportation.

Portage project.   An example of a home teaching program is the Portage Project, which serves families with children who have disabilities from birth to 3 in five county programs in north central Wisconsin (Shearer & Loftin, 1984). Recently, the Portage Project, which has been replicated in programs across the country and abroad, has modified its procedures as a result of a 3-year demonstration project funded by the Handicapped Children's Early Education Program, Linking Infants and Families Together (LIFT). Portage-LIFT home-based services are carried out by a team composed of an infant developmental specialist, an infant language and feeding specialist, and an infant motor specialist. This team works in a modified transdisciplinary approach with local and centralized tertiary diagnostic facilities to develop the necessary supports and address the assessed needs of the family.

Staff work with the parents in a consultative role to identify needs and services, provide information and resources, and develop a goal-oriented program for both child and family. Each family is assigned a co-case manager who works with the parent or parents to develop an Individual Family Service Plan (see Chapter 10) specific to their needs and desires (Jesien, 1988).

The staff become a consistent and stable source of support, encouragement, information, and resource referral to the family. Every family is assessed on an individual basis, and the program is adjusted to become family-specific and take into consideration belief systems and cultural differences. The staff visits the home as frequently as needed according to a schedule developed jointly with parents. The content of the visits is also largely determined by family needs, typically entailing family support and activities that enhance the child's functional abilities in a responsive play atmosphere (Jesien, 1988).

Family friends program.   A program which utilizes volunteers over the age of 55 as support personnel has met with much success in Washington, DC. The volunteers visit children with chronic illnesses or disabilities in their homes at least once a week, providing support not only for the children but for other family members as well. The older volunteers are trained to assist the families in the areas of social and emotional support, tutoring, recreational activities, advocacy, and self-help skills (Miller & Diao, 1987). Researchers have found that this program is both cost effective and productive. When surveyed, parents generally felt that their children's condition had improved and some reported that their son and daughters were more sociable. Parents also indicated increased family participation in events outside the home and positive attitudinal changes as a result of the program (Miller & Diao, 1987).

We need to remember, however, that all families are not comfortable with home visits. Some families consider their homes to be their own private domain, which they do not want professionals to enter. Professionals have criticized parents for not eagerly anticipating home visits and have interpreted parental aloofness in this regard as "not caring about their child." This kind of generalization is unwarranted. Rather, we encourage you to respect the preferences of families for participating in home visits and remember that they, too, sometimes retreat into the privacy of their homes.

INDEPENDENT OPPORTUNITIES.   Busy schedules and conflicting interests may be a deterrent to group meetings, while invasion of privacy issues may hinder home visits. Families often prefer to acquire knowledge informally, on their own time. An excellent way to transmit information to these families is to provide opportunities for independent study. This may be accomplished in a number of ways. A resource library or room where families can meet may fulfill some families' informational needs. Such a library should contain material on a variety of subjects, in a variety of languages depending upon the cultural backgrounds of the families you serve. It is not necessary to limit the material to printed matter.

As professionals, you need to be creative in devising methods of interaction with the families of the children and youth in your programs. Table 12–3 lists some specific suggestions for how to exchange information with families. The following section presents both creative options and traditional techniques for information sharing.

TABLE 12–3 Suggestions for Exchanging Information with Families

- Maintain a current resource file which lists resource persons and organizations and agencies at the national, state and local levels.
- Network with professionals and families at conferences and other meetings who are able to provide needed information to you or to families. Include their names and addresses in your resource file.
- Subscribe to a computer bulletin board at school and allow your students or their families access.
- Compile a family resource library containing videotapes and machines, books, and brochures which would be of interest to families.
- Provide a few minutes of flexible time before or after class to allow family members to stop and chat with you or each other. An activity, such as music, before dismissal or upon arrival could incorporate family participation for those who are interested.

Formats for Providing Information

PRINT. A variety of printed resources are available. Many of the training projects described in the previous section have developed manuals to serve as a supplement to group training (e.g., Baker & Brightman, 1989; PACER Center, Inc., 1987). The advantage of manuals is they organize material into a succinct format with a substantive core of information. If parents read the material before attending a group session, there may be more time for discussion and such active learning strategies as role-playing, modeling, and group problem solving. Manuals can also be a resource to review and update after a workshop is completed.

A second option involves use of manuals alone, unaccompanied by group or individual sessions. In a study of 106 families of children with mental retardation, families were randomly assigned to one of five training conditions related to teaching behavior principles: control, training by manuals only, manuals and phone consultation, manuals and eight group meetings, and manuals, eight group meetings, and six home visits (Baker & Heifetz, 1976; Baker, Heifetz, & Murphy, 1980; Heifetz, 1977). Families in all training conditions scored higher than the controls on their knowledge of behavioral principles and child self-help skills. Little difference was found in the effectiveness of approaches, however. The families who only received the manuals reported less confidence about their teaching and reported doing less teaching one year later than the parents in the other three groups. The manuals-only group was by far the most cost-effective group.

Professionals from a variety of backgrounds as well as family members have written books and manuals that are available for purchase or through most community libraries. A distinct advantage of parent-written books is that parents reading them may be able to identify with the author as a "person who has been there" and, therefore, having an authenticity derived from firsthand experience (Mullins, 1983). Families vary in their perspectives, however, and many readers may disagree with the views of parent authors. One useful approach is to offer families the option of reading materials written by professionals and/or family members.

Fact sheets and information packets about specific disabilities are available through national clearinghouses and state and local agencies and advocacy organizations. Generally these materials can be photocopied and given to families who request information on any disability from cleft palate to muscular dystrophy to learning disabilities. It is important to be sensitive to family members who do not read or who read at low reading levels or in languages other than English. NICHCY, the National Information Center for Handicapped Children and Youth, distributes materials written at low reading levels or in Spanish on issues of concern to families, such as mainstreaming, P.L. 94–142, or the IEP process. (See Appendix A for information on how to contact NICHCY).

MEDIA.   Media are increasingly being used as a format for sharing information with families. For example, the Navajo community of Rough Rock, Arizona, shared information with families on the availability of special education services through videotaped vignettes (Dunlap, Ondelacy, & Sells, 1979). Families viewed the videotapes on battery-operated equipment in hogans, summer shelters, tents, and outdoors in a field of grazing sheep. The authors described the value of the videotapes as follows:

> The video tape format permitted stopping of the action, rewinding for subsequent viewings, and the selection of vignettes most likely to be of interest to the people being addressed. Moreover, it added a valuable dimension to the message of what special education was at the school. For "special education" is a difficult concept to convey in the Navajo language. Even in English, the term is vague and demands a certain conceptual foundation before it can begin to be well understood. . . . The staff visiting a home or addressing a group used the tapes as a shared experience, which was always followed by a flurry of questions. A home visit alone, without the video component, would probably have been more of a one-way communication than the shared experience sought in the project. (Dunlap et al., 1979, pp. 3–4)

For a description of a video-based parent education program which has been used with families of children with disabilities in developing countries, see McConkey (1988).

In addition to use with individual families, videotapes can be used for mass dissemination. A project of national significance is currently under way at the Young Adult Institute, a social service agency in New York City that provides residential and rehabilitative services to persons with developmental disabilities. Based on a comprehensive national search of videotapes, films, and slide-tape presentations that provide instruction and support to families the Young Adult Institute has compiled a resource directory. (See Appendix A for information on how to order these materials.) The Young Adult Institute has also produced two series of parent-support television programs broadcast in the Northeast geographical area. Videotapes of the two series, on early childhood and transition/employment, and corresponding training manuals are available for national distribution. The use of television has tremendous potential for reaching families in their own homes. Furthermore, since many families own videocassette recorders, it would be helpful for public libraries, tape rental stores, and school programs to make instructional tapes available for rent or loan. Your program may want to budget money to pay the rental fee for families who do not have the resources to purchase or rent videocassette recorders.

COMPUTER TECHNOLOGY. Computer technology offers opportunities for families to receive information as well as to work with children and youth on home-based learning activities. One demonstration project involved home-based teaching of children from birth to 6 in rural areas (Tawney, Aeschleman, Deaton, & Donaldson, 1979). Computer equipment was installed in the homes of 19 families, most of whom were of a lower socioeconomic status, and lived as far as 275 miles from the project headquarters. Instruction of children focused on motor or visual-discrimination skills. The program was designed for parents and children to work on lessons for 15 to 30 minutes each day for 5 days a week. Parents also could discuss concerns through postsession voice communication with program specialists. The authors documented increases in child performance, noting the positive project outcome that families accepted the technology into their homes and worked cooperatively with project staff. A similar program is being implemented in rural Montana to network families of children with disabilities (Green, 1988).

A microcomputer/videodisc-based instructional system has been used with students having learning disabilities in classrooms to teach time-telling skills (Friedman & Hofmeister, 1984). Unlike the computer program described above, the videodisc systems are interactive and can provide spoken instruction dependent upon choices made by the user. We expect this type of instructional system will be available to families through local libraries or through the school systems in the relatively near future.

Families often need assistance in becoming familiar with computer technology. Such training would be an excellent topic for informational sessions. If families are able to meet the financial expense involved in owning a home computer, they can learn to make judicious software selections (Huntington, 1984a) and provide opportunities for their children to increase their academic achievement at home (Huntington, 1984b). Computer resource centers provide a unique method of information dissemination to families and professionals of children and youth with disabilities. The Technology Issue of *Exceptional Parent* (Oct., 1988) describes two such bulletin boards, The National Special Education Alliance, which is sponsored by Apple Computers, Inc. and the Disabled Children's Computer Group; and IBM/Special Needs Exchange, operated by LINC Resources Inc. These resources encourage the use of adaptive technology and networking among families and professionals, answering questions and providing support (Green, 1988; Moore, 1988). You can encourage your school district to subscribe to SpecialNet, a computer-based network which not only provides valuable support to educators, but offers services to parents, such a PIP (Programs Involving Parents), a computerized bulletin board. This SpecialNet bulletin board prints weekly articles and stories of interest to families of children and youth with disabilities, news about parent meetings and resources, and allows parent-to-parent communication (PACER Center, Inc., 1987).

Resources and Referrals

As a professional with training in a specified area such as education, counseling, nursing, or even more specifically, early childhood or physical disabilities, you may be asked by a parent for information outside your area of expertise. In such situations it is essential that you recognize the limitations of your knowledge and be willing to respond "I don't know." Instead, you should have access to and rely upon resources to provide you with information to respond to families' concerns, or to refer families when appropriate. It is a good policy to follow-up on your referrals, asking the family if the information source has been helpful to them and providing further referrals if necessary. Some families may become frustrated with constant referrals and with professionals who do not possess clear answers to questions, as this mother describes:

> Since Bob is in the Coast Guard, our first stop was the local military doctor, who informed us that he had seen many such cases, and that the problem was that we were not being firm enough in our discipline . . .
> Our next stop was the psychology department, and the problem was that we were being much too strict, and needed to "loosen up a bit". . . .
>
> Over the next few years, we looked for information from the entire spectrum of medical arts, both military and civilian, and were always told that the information given us by the *last* person was totally wrong, and that the *current* person had the word from on high, which also didn't work. . . .

Next, we tried various federal, state, and local "social service agencies" (a misnomer if ever there was one), and were always told that our problem was too severe, not severe enough, too common, too complex, not served by that agency, and sometimes just "tough s—t!"... The school system, when we got into that environment, was even worse.

There may be occasions when a family member of one of your students requires information or support of a nature you are not qualified to or would prefer not to provide. In contrast, other families may not be interested in pursuing the types of family-professional interactions you feel would be beneficial to their son or daughter. Keep in mind that, as a professional, your role is to support the children and youth in your program without imposing your personal values into the family system. This section will describe resource persons and helpful organizations at the national, state, and local levels, and offer suggestions for how to cope with challenging situations.

RESOURCE PERSONS.   A variety of resource persons can be contacted to provide information to families in formal or informal ways, such as:

1. professionals—teachers, psychologists, social workers, counselors, physicians, and therapists
2. family members—mothers, fathers, siblings
3. extended family members—grandparents, other relatives
4. individuals with exceptionalities
5. paraprofessionals
6. friends, and
7. clergy.

Be sure the selected resource person fits the topic of interest. For instance, assisting parents in following up on school activities might best be done by a professional; helping parents learn to be assertive with professionals might best be taught by other parents. Certainly, one should not overgeneralize this point—many parents can effectively teach school follow-up skills, just as many professionals can teach assertiveness. Families may not feel comfortable with all professionals or parent leaders. It is important to help families recognize the forms of support available to them, enabling them to choose which resources fit their needs.

NATIONAL RESOURCES.   National organizations provide a wealth of information to families and professionals. Specifically, the National Information Center for Handicapped Children and Youth (NICHCY) disseminates fact sheets about specific disabilities, general information, and referrals to public agencies and organizations at the state level. Some of the information distributed by NICHCY is available in Spanish or in low-level reading materials (National Information Center for Handicapped Children and Youth, 1989). Other organizations which provide information at the national level include the National Information Center for Orphan Drug and Rare Diseases and the National Organization for Rare Disorders (NORD). (See Appendix A for information on how to contact these organizations.)

As discussed in Chapter 1, most specific types of disability are associated with an organization of advocates. These organizations perform various activities, including dissemination of information, research, and referral of parents to local affiliates. Some produce materials, such as the American Foundation for the Blind, which offers a variety of products and publications. For example, *Parenting Preschoolers: Suggestions for Raising Young Blind and Visually Impaired Children* (Ferrell, 1984) is a free booklet offered by this organization which provides information of the sort typically disseminated by advocacy groups. The booklet answers questions commonly posed by parents of a young child who is visually impaired, suggests organizations families can contact for services or referrals, and briefly describes programs and professionals parents are likely to encounter (e.g., home-based services, resource rooms, occupational therapists, ophthalmologists, social workers). Resources for contact with other parents are also listed (American Foundation for the Blind, 1989).

STATE AND LOCAL RESOURCES. The Departments of Education and of Mental Health at the local, county, or state levels should be able to provide you with referrals to agencies within your area. In addition, the phone numbers of these agencies are listed in the yellow pages under "Government" or "School—Public", or in a community or consumer resource section of your phone book. Family members or professionals may contact state agencies for information. A research study which was conducted to analyze the format and content of the material sent out by these agencies found that most material was produced for readers at the 15th-grade or college reading level (McLoughlin, Edge, Petrosko, & Strenecky, 1981). The extraordinarily high reading level of this material represents a comprehension barrier for many families. It is notable that some states may provide material printed in languages other than English.

It is best to try to contact services at the local level before contacting state organizations. Local affiliates of national organizations can be a helpful source of information and support for families of children and youth with disabilities. You may contact them through the national office of the organization or find them in your local phone book. However, when the full name of an organization is unknown or if a parent lives in a rural area where services are scarce, state or national organizations may be the best way to locate information and referrals. Most states have a Parent Training and Information Center, such as PACER, which can access or recommend resource libraries and contact with parents, and provide educational activities and basic support. (We have listed available Parent Training and Information Centers in Appendix A.) We urge you to write centers in your geographical area to inquire about the services they provide and the ways that the families with whom you work, along with yourself and your professional colleagues, can benefit from their services. State Developmental Disabilities Agencies, State Vocational Agencies and Crippled Children's Services also provide information to parents and professionals. NICHCY can provide you with a current listing of these agencies for your state. Families and professionals who work with children with special health-care needs can contact the state department of health for referral to the Title V program in their respective state. Title V programs provide access to the diverse public and private services and funding options designed for children with special health-care needs.

Parent-to-Parent projects, which match a "veteran" parent with a "referred" parent offer emotional and informational support to families which professionals are often unable to provide. The Parent-to Parent National Survey Project, coordinated by Betsy Santelli at The Beach Center on Families and Disability at The University of Kansas, is currently compiling a survey of Parent-to-Parent programs across the country. The results from the survey will be published in a national directory which will be available to families and professionals through the Beach Center.

State universities often administer a variety of programs for children and youth with disabilities. You can contact the University Affiliated Program (UAP) office at your state university to inquire about available programs. Although such programs have the benefit of the most recent research in the field, not all parents have been satisfied with the services received. Barbara Huff wrote about her family's experiences at a university-related medical center.

> We became guinea pigs for students to learn from.
>
> We had four psychiatrists that led teams who watched behind a glass window in every therapy session. . . . The dynamics of the family was what they were studying. We got nowhere. They were only interested in the dynamics and the cause. . . . We felt we were just a test case for the whole educational system. (Donner, 1988, Supplement 3)

CHALLENGING CIRCUMSTANCES.   State and local agencies may also provide support to parents who are substance abusers or who are in need of financial assistance. We encourage you to work through the school counselor who, in turn, can refer parents to these sources based on the parent's preferences. The final decision to seek help, however, is up to the individual involved. In some situations a father or mother, whom you consider to be alcoholic, may not be viewed as having a problem within their particular family system. In child abuse cases, your involvement may be mandated. Educators or other professionals are legally required to report cases of suspected abuse. The decision whether or not to notify the parent in these instances is a personal one which must be made by the professional in each situation, according to individual circumstances.

As a professional, you may encounter parents who do not wish to receive the information you would like to provide. There are many explanations for this seeming reluctance to become involved. It does not mean that the parents are not concerned with their child's welfare. Parents may have more urgent problems (e.g., financial, work-related), they may completely trust professionals to attend adequately to the needs of their son or daughter without their involvement, they may feel powerless and unable to contribute to their child's program, or they may feel uncomfortable within the school setting. Some families may not value the input of "strangers"; and cultural inclinations may lead families to respected and familiar resources rather than to educators. Demonstrating to the parents how you value their involvement and how it can affect their child's progress, and relating positive comments about their son or daughter can help make parents feel more comfortable with the family-professional relationship. Somers (1987) suggests referring families who feel ill at ease in school settings to outside agencies such as the Cystic Fibrosis Foundation, the National Association of the Deaf, or other support groups related to a specific disability; or a state agency such as the State Department of Mental Health. The types of support offered by these organizations may be more acceptable to some parents than the support services available through the school district.

Professionals may become involved with families who are debating a decision about which you have strong feelings, such as trying new medication, corrective surgery, or residential placement outside of the home. Your role should not be that of decision maker; rather, you should act as a resource, providing enough information to enable the family to choose the alternative which is the most appropriate for them. Once the family has made its decision, it is your job to support them in that choice. One mother speaks up for her right to make a decision which may not be popular in the eyes of others:

> Zachariah has not lived at home since he was about 3 years old, when—
> after countless trips to doctors and talks with therapists, social workers,
> special educators—I realized that his needs were so great that taking care
> of him would preclude any semblance of normal life for the rest of us. . . .

I know that I love Zachariah. But I also know that he cannot live at home. This does not make me a bad person. And it does not make me a failure as a mother. (Kupfer, 1988, p. 226)

SUMMARY

This chapter has highlighted the professional's role in the process of information exchange with families.

Because families' preferences vary widely, we have emphasized the need to provide a range of informational topics and formats for addressing those topics. We also suggest a planning process to assist you in organizing your efforts to provide meaningful learning opportunities. A key aspect of planning is to develop a network of professionals and families that work together. We also discussed appropriate resources for information and referrals to assist you when you are questioned about information that falls outside of your area of expertise.

Many families are interested in receiving information, but it is important to realize that increased knowledge is not the only helpful coping strategy. The next chapter will discuss the range of alternative coping strategies available to families.

C H A P T E R   13

FAMILY SUPPORT:
HELPING FAMILIES COPE

Friendships between people with and without a disability can provide social support for the person with a disability, as well as for his family.

Dominique's annual IEP conference had just ended. Dominique and her family had just left and the team of professionals were all sitting quietly around the table in a state of shock. Finally, one professional broke the silence and stated, "I just don't understand it. Dominique's family just doesn't seem to care. It's almost like they are ignoring all of Dominique's problems."

In times of stress families with students who have exceptionalities employ several different types of coping strategies. Understanding these strategies and how they work can greatly enhance your professional relationship with these families. After exploring these strategies you will be able to answer the following questions:

- What are the major internal coping strategies often employed by families with a child or youth who has an exceptionality?
- What are the major external coping strategies often employed by families with a child or youth who has an exceptionality?
- How can you support families to help them develop and use internal and external coping strategies?

In the previous chapter we reviewed a number of programs and strategies designed to help families make meaningful contributions to the education of their children and youth. It should be clear by now, however, that although education is the central mission of a school, it is not a family's only goal, perhaps not even its main goal. Families must meet a variety of demands, ranging from economic survival to the nurturance of self-esteem. Also, other people in families besides persons with exceptionalities have needs which are equally important. The key, as we have emphasized, is *balance*. Family lives that are totally centered around exceptionalities are unfair, not only to all the other family members but also to the persons with exceptionalities. In the long run, how far up the developmental ladder can students with exceptionalities climb, if the people holding up the ladder—their families—fall apart?

Early intervention programs, preschools, and schools have a role in helping families cope with stresses that lie beyond the realm of education. In some cases, professionals at these agencies may take leadership in providing such services. In others, their role may be more peripheral: appropriate referrals and interagency coordination. In still others, their role may be no more (or less) than well-placed empathic comments and moral support. Nevertheless, major or peripheral, these programs can play important roles in family support.

In Chapter 4 we outlined the functions families fulfill, the needs families must meet, and the ways in which exceptionality may shape those needs and the family's response to them. Unmet needs, tangible or intangible, are sources of stress. Most family theorists define *coping* as any activity that reduces stress (Pearlin & Schooler, 1978); we extend that definition to include any activity that results in meeting one's needs.

Families' reactions to situations—how much stress or unmet need they feel, or even any feeling of stress at all—vary widely depending on their perceptions of the event as well as the resources they have available to meet the challenge (Hill, 1949). Further, one of families' key resources for dealing with stress is their arsenals of coping strategies. Using categories of coping styles identified by Olson and his associates, we defined these strategies in Chapter 2 (Olson et al., 1983). Briefly, coping may involve (a) one or more internal strategies designed to make an event less stressful by changing one's perceptions about it or to make it solvable, or (b) one or more external strategies designed to marshal one's resources to address needs directly and thus reduce stress (Olson et al., 1983). In this chapter we will look at internal and external coping strategies in depth and consider family support programs designed to strengthen each one.

INTERNAL COPING STRATEGIES

Internal coping involves thinking about a stressful situation either to change one's perceptions (making the situation feel less stressful) or to make it solvable. Perceptions involve interpretations of the personal meaning of events in our environment. For example, the same event may be interpreted positively, neutrally, or negatively by three different people. If we interpret an event negatively, we think of it as threatening our well-being or creating needs—in other words, it is stressful to us. If, on the other hand, we interpret an event positively, we think of it as enhancing our well-being or satisfying our needs—in other words, we cope. For example, depending on her values and beliefs, a mother with a particular religious background might view her daughter's marriage to someone of another religion as a positive event ("He's such a nice young man!") or as a negative one ("She's marrying outside the faith!"). When we use an internal coping strategy, we revise our interpretations about an event that was originally perceived negatively, so that all or part of it can be perceived positively or at least neutrally. The three major types of internal coping strategies are *passive appraisal, reframing, and spiritual support.*

Passive Appraisal

USES OF PASSIVE APPRAISAL   Passive appraisal involves ignoring a problem or setting it aside, either temporarily or permanently. Looked at pessimistically, passive appraisal might be viewed as a kind of "helpless resignation" (Pearlin & Schooler, 1978), or more positively as a decision to "ride out" a crisis (Olson et al., 1983) in the hope that it will go away (e.g., "maybe he'll grow out of it."). Passive appraisal also could include "checking out," or relaxing, when a situation seems overwhelming by putting one's problems aside for an hour, a day, or a weekend.

One form of passive appraisal is denial. We often see denial at work within the first few days or months after the family learns of their child's exceptionality. Early interventionists or professionals working with individuals who are learning disabled or gifted may see the family denying an exceptionality as they struggle against the idea that their child may be different from anyone else. For example, one father, when told by the school psychologist that his son was eligible for the gifted program, responded:

> Oh, no. You're not going to put any wild ideas in his head that he can go to college or something, because I can't afford to send him. We're just regular people, and we *work* for a living. We don't go around setting ourselves up over other people. Besides, that boy has a smart enough mouth on him already.

As discussed in Chapter 5, denial may be one of the stages in the cycle of adjustment to a distressing event, such as the death of a loved one or the birth of a child with a disability. We can see an example of denial in the reaction of one mother at the birth of her child:

> Finally my pediatrician brought the baby to me and unwrapped him for me to see. I was stunned. This was not my perfect baby! I was still tired from my delivery, and I felt like a spectator in a dream. I just knew I would wake up and everything would be all right. I could not take this baby when I was uncertain that it was mine. (Bristol, 1984, p. 29)

A second form of passive appraisal consists of refusal to think about the future. This behavior may be caused by the difficulty of handling immediate concerns of physical care, finding services, helping the student succeed in school, and so forth, all at one time. The future, therefore, seems to be an expendable item that can be cut from the list of stresses (Featherstone, 1980). Another reason why families may refuse to consider the future is that it represents too great a fear (Brotherson, 1985). For a student with an exceptionality, future adulthood is a great unknown and is, therefore, fraught with uncertainties. Faced with their own mortality, parents may have few clues as to who will continue to provide support and guidance for their child. Adult services are a fragmented maze, besides, they are not mandated as they are for school-aged students. Bob Helsel refers to this fear:

> You mentioned worrying about the future. I suppose this is the biggest worry that a parent of a severely handicapped child has—what happens when I die? And there is no answer to that. As far as I know, there is no way to provide properly for him in that eventuality—at least, I don't know of any way. (Helsel, 1985, p. 90)

Thus, it is little wonder that families often avoid considering the future. "Take things one day at a time" is advice "passed like an amulet" from parent to parent in support group meetings (Featherstone, 1980, p. 29). One mother explained why she hadn't joined a support group:

> I don't go to any parent associations. I couldn't face people saying this is what I went through with my child and then I'd know I'd got it to go through. I'll worry in six years time, but just now I'll take each day as it comes. (Lonsdale, 1978, p. 115)

The third type of passive appraisal, relaxation, is one in which families with children and youth having exceptionalities may indulge less often. Relaxation means taking time out for oneself, stopping to catch one's breath when little irritations or large problems become too weighty. Any activity that removes the mind and body from problems at hand could be considered coping through relaxation. Everyone seems to have a favorite style of "getting away," ranging from watching TV to hobbies like carpentry or gardening. Exercise, sports, eating out, reading, drinking, or smoking are all examples of relaxation. One mother explained her way of coping:

> It makes me more patient and I try to grin and bear it. When things really get bad I go and soak in the bath for an hour. My husband was told I was on the verge of a nervous breakdown but I've never had it yet! (Lonsdale, 1978, p. 108)

It is difficult for many families to find the time to get away. A single mother of two children with behavior disorders speaks of the tremendous demands placed on her family:

> Living in a trailer house with my two boys is quite an experience. At times I get really frustrated because I never seem to get a break. I used to have my mom and my grandma help me out by babysitting for me, but now they won't do it 'cause they say the boys won't mind. I also used to hire babysitters but they all quit on me. I can't find no one,

'cause in this small town word travels fast and my boys already have a reputation. I'm even afraid to talk on the phone the way these two behave, always fightin' and runnin' away. I used to wake up in the mornin' to the sounds of things a breakin' or these two fightin'. Now I just don't sleep. Will I ever get a break?

WORKING THROUGH DENIAL. Professionals are often frustrated when families seem to deny their child's exceptionality or refuse to plan for the future. From the professionals' point of view, the families may be wasting precious time that could be spent more usefully to help the child make developmental or academic progress. It is important to keep in mind, however, that denial may be serving an adaptive function for the people who are engaging in it. Denial provides time for absorbing facts in small, digestible bits and avoiding a more devastating reality (Fortier & Wanlass, 1984). It may also serve as a cushion giving the family a span of time to regroup and gather the necessary energy to go on (Bristol, 1984). Except in rare circumstances, families will turn to more active coping strategies in their own time. In the meantime, it is important to maintain an open line of communication, establish trust, and consistently point out educational strategies that offer realistic opportunities for improvement without promising miracles.

For those few families who do seem "stuck" in a denial stage, we do not recommend that professionals confront them directly with the "reality" of their children and youth's exceptionalities and/or with bleak prospects for the future. Confrontation is a specialized therapeutic technique employed by highly skilled counselors. Its successful use requires hours of trust-building before the confrontation and many more hours of empathic support afterward to follow through with the desired changes (Northern, 1982). Even social workers, counselors, and psychologists on the school's interdisciplinary team should be reluctant to attempt confrontation if there is not adequate time to work with a particular family. If handled without empathy and trust, confrontation may result in alienation, anger, and withdrawal. Instead, the best strategies include building trust; remaining open, supportive, and available when parents make tentative inquiries; and encouraging involvement in support groups. It also may help to show examples of the student's school work, to invite families to observe the class, and to provide parents with information on normative expectation for a particular grade. All of this, of course, should be done with careful attention to the principles of empathic and nonthreatening communication discussed in Chapter 6.

ENCOURAGING RELAXATION. With all the demands on their time—including those made by professionals—families may feel guilty about taking time to get away occasionally. They may need to know that they have "permission" to relax, and that you think it important for families to take some time just for themselves. You might try asking parents what they do to get away from stressful days, and tell about some of the ways you yourself choose. Try to help families understand that pacing their efforts is important and that recreation in whatever form they may choose is an important part of their sense of well-being. For those who protest that they do not have the time, you may suggest some of the ideas discussed in Chapter 4, such as time management strategies, ideas for renegotiating chores, or the use of social support.

Some families might be interested in an organized relaxation training workshop. A number of these are available, either through consultants who specialize in relaxation training or through instructor's manuals with accompanying audiotapes (Osterkamp & Press, 1980). Those who are not interested in such a group activity may select some of the relaxation tapes that are on the market, either with guided-imagery exercises in relaxation or with instructions accompanied by soft music to encourage relaxation. You may wish to consider adding a few of these tapes to your school's resource library. By so doing, you and other school staff would also have access to the tapes.

A final way to encourage relaxation is to refer families to respite-care services in your community. Respite-care services provide temporary care of a person with a disability for an hour, a day, or for longer periods of time, so that the family can get away. Respite care may be provided in the family home, in the provider's home, in an activity program (in which the person with a disability attends a recreation program for a day or an evening, usually on a regular basis), or in a group home (where a "guest bed" may be kept available for respite) (MacDonald & Mare, 1988). Although most families prefer in-home service (Upshur, 1982), all of these types of respite care have value. Respite-care providers are usually trained in such skills as first aid, adaptive equipment, handling, positioning, communication, behavior management, and so forth (Edger, Reid, & Pious, 1988).

Families report a variety of benefits from using respite care, including reduced stress, improved family functioning, and having more time to themselves (MacDonald & Mare, 1988). Unfortunately, most areas of our country still lack organized respite services and sufficient opportunities for parents to locate and use reliable providers (Edger et al., 1988). Further, some parents may be unable to use services because of prohibitive costs. Others may be reluctant to use them because of family values that prevent them from seeking help or because they do not know or trust the providers.

Some schools offer respite services as a component of their overall program. Here the services of volunteers, specially recruited providers, and employed high-school students combine their efforts and provide a respite care service (Edgar et al., 1988). If no school services are available, someone in your school might participate in community planning to start a program. Alternatively, the school's parent group might consider organizing a respite cooperative and drawing upon the experiences of other communities (Ferguson, 1978). Although planning and development is time-consuming, in the long run, it is worthwhile. Encouraging families to relax can help develop a valuable coping skill.

Reframing

Olson et al. (1983) define reframing as "the family's ability to redefine a demanding situation in a more rational and acceptable way in order to make the situation more manageable" (p. 143). Essentially, reframing involves two steps. The first step requires distinguishing situations (or parts of situations) that can be changed from those that are beyond one's control. The second step requires taking action on alterable situations and/or redefining what cannot be changed to make it more acceptable (McCubbin et al., 1980). Families can be assisted in both action taking and redefinition.

TAKING ACTION: BUILDING PROBLEM-SOLVING SKILLS. Systematic problem solving is a technique used in a variety of settings, including individual or group therapy, educational classrooms, and corporate planning (Goldfarb et al., 1986). Many families use problem solving, either formally or informally, in their daily lives. It is also a skill that can be taught, as, for example, when Walther-Thomas, et al. (in press) successfully taught problem solving to families whose children and youth have learning disabilities.

Problem solving essentially employs four steps.

1. *Defining the problem* involves describing the issue completely and—as suggested by Olson et al. (1983)—breaking it into resolvable and unresolvable parts.

2. *Brainstorming alternatives* involves a free-spirited and nonjudgmental listing of all possible options for solutions.

3. *Evaluating alternatives* includes using criteria on which all family members agree in considering the relative merits of each alternative.

4. *Selecting an alternative and taking action* involves assigning responsibility for tasks and following through on them (Goldfarb et al., 1986).

This bare-bones description of the problem-solving process obviously masks a number of nuances and potential complications. Families must use appropriate communication skills to work through the process together. They must be able to negotiate, compromise, and assume responsibility without attributing blame. These skills can be cultivated with practice. Your school may be interested in conducting problem-solving workshops for families (for school personnel, too!) (Problem-solving training manuals are available [e.g., Walther-Thomas et al., in press].) Problem solving can also be an effective tool for resolving such educational issues as (a) selecting and prioritizing IEP goals and objectives, (b) deciding on placement for a student, (c) agreeing on appropriate related services, and (d) reaching consensus on whether to initiate a due process hearing. When it is not possible to conduct a training program or if some families are not interested in attending workshops, commercially available self-help books that focus on problem solving related to disability issues may be an option (Goldfarb et al., 1986).

ENCOURAGING REDEFINITION.   Although the solution to many of the day-to-day problems associated with an exceptionality is within families' control, the presence of the exceptionality itself is not. It, therefore, is a vital part of families' reframing skills to be able to redefine the situation to make it less stressful. Brotherson (1985) examined some aspects of parental planning for adult needs and the relationship of that planning to adult family functioning of 48 parents of young adults with mental and physical disabilities. The results showed a positive relationship between planning for adult needs and family functioning, and a positive relationship between using social supports in planning and family functioning. Positive redefinition was the coping strategy most often used by the families surveyed. There are two ways (positive comparisons and selective attention/selective ignoring) families can redefine their perceptions of the exceptionality and its impact on them, and a number of ways that professionals can help.

Positive comparisons, one type of redefinition, involve considering others' problems and stresses and concluding that our own are not so bad after all (Pearlin & Schooler, 1978). The effect fits the old parable: If we could put our troubles in a bag and bring them to a meeting to exchange with someone else, we would all go home again with our own. One mother philosophically summarized this effect:

> Everybody has got a cross to bear. Some people's are a bit heavier than others. You can always look around and see people worse off. (Lonsdale, 1978, p. 106)

No matter how difficult the exceptionality may seem to an outside observer, many families are amazingly adept at using positive comparisons:

> We're lucky because Carol isn't aware she's different. I know lots of others who are very hurt because they know they're retarded. But Carol is too handicapped to be hurt by her limitations. (A. P. Turnbull et al., 1984, p. 31)

It would be inappropriate to violate confidentiality and point out to families the specific ways in which their student is less disabled, less disruptive, or less troublesome than another student. Professionals can indirectly assist families in making positive comparisons, however. For example, you can avoid implying that a particular student is the "worst one" in regard to a behavioral or academic problem, while highlighting the student's strengths. If possible, help families understand that their student's problems are not uncommon but are shared by many students. Except in very rare cases, this is, after all, true. Such assurances place the problem in a more realistic and less alarming perspective; it helps to know one is not alone.

Comparisons with other students may be equally important for families of children and youth who are gifted. Those families who see their children as "little adults" may find graphic examples helpful in seeing that their children have similar needs to other children for security, assurance, guidance, peer interactions, and time for just plain fun.

A second type of redefinition is *selective attention* and *selective ignoring* (Pearlin & Schooler, 1978). This approach involves more attention to the positive aspects of a situation and less to the negative aspects. Contrary to the expectations of some professionals, there are positive factors associated with exceptionality, and many families recognize this fact (H. R. Turnbull, Guess, & Turnbull, 1988). A single father remarked how his son's learning disability has strengthened their relationship.

> Before Javon's diagnosis, I really did not know my son. I mean, we really were not very close. After I learned of his disability our relationship changed dramatically. I started spending time with him . . . quality time with him. I suddenly realized that relationships are a two-way street . . . that I needed him as much as he needs me. Through the disability, I gained a son that I never knew. Together we have learned that we are both in this together . . . and that love can conquer even the greatest disability.

It is important to encourage families to think of the positive contributions of exceptionality. You will note from the examples that most of these contributions are intangible contributions to understanding, to capacity to love, to meaningfulness, and to career direction. Generally these types of attributes are not mentioned at IEP meetings as part of the student's charateristics. It might be rewarding to list these and also to develop IEP objectives that foster positive contributions.

Families also need to be recognized for their own contributions and successes. It may be more difficult for families to see their own positive attributes than those of their children and youth. Parenthood is so deeply rooted in one's self-concept that the advent of a student with an exceptionality can have a profound effect on one's self-esteem. Even families of children who are gifted may feel inadequate about their perceived responsibility to nurture their children's talents. The threat to families' self-esteem that accompanies an exceptionality makes it vital for professionals to point out the successes families have achieved and to praise their efforts, no matter how great or small. It is also important not to expect too much from families in the way of participation in their student's education because, for families, falling short of professional expectations could be one more blow to an already feeble self-image.

Finally, redefinition may take the form of finding side benefits. Often families that face traumatic or overwhelmingly negative experiences find that many positive side effects result from these experiences. Thompson (1985) noted that negative events can often bring families close together and elicit support and caring from friends and neighbors. They can also teach a valuable lesson and make the family aware of the preciousness of life in a way that routine events cannot. For example, one young man describes the impact that cancer has had on his life.

> At first I thought it was just a dream but then the reality set in . . . it wasn't a dream, but my worst nightmare. How could this happen to me? I was 20 years old, an All-American football player, and I had cancer. I was devastated. Everything that I had identified with was gone. I couldn't play football ever again because of the surgery, hell I didn't even know if I would ever walk again. I spent the next 10 weeks undergoing radiation and chemotherapy. I lost all of my hair, all of my so-called friends, and most of my ambition to live. Then it happened. A very special person came into my life and touched me in a way that words can't describe. This person was Jay, a 5-year-old boy with terminal cancer.
>
> Within the few short weeks before his death, Jay taught me more about life than all the exhorting world ever could. Jay gave me hope and inspiration. Jay made me laugh and cry. But most of all, Jay was my friend . . . a friend like no other. The two of us were inseparable. We shared a camaraderie that few people ever get the chance to experience. We were both battling something that was bigger than both of us. We were in this together until the end. I was there when Jay died. I can remember sitting there, tears pouring down my face, realizing just how important friendships were and how precious the gift of life really was. It's been four years since that time and not a day goes by that I don't think of Jay. Sure, Jay is gone now, but through me his spirit lives.

Spiritual Support

McCubbin et al. (1983) classify spiritual support as an external coping strategy. However, we choose to consider it an internal strategy. The type of support one might receive from *organized* religious participation—from clergy or from fellow religious group members—is really a type of social support and, therefore, a different kind of strategy. In fact, many families have reported that they do not receive much support from organized religious groups and that they may receive rejection or intolerance instead (Bristol & Schopler, 1983; Brotherson, 1985). The type of spiritual support most often employed by families of children and youth with exceptionalities is personal, spiritual, or philosophical interpretation gleaned from reading religious books or drawn from their upbringing (A. P. Turnbull, et al., 1984). In this context, the essence of spiritual support as a coping strategy means an internal interpretation of the meaning of the exceptionality.

People have a strong need to understand the meaning of events in their lives. The advent of an exceptionality is a random event that must be explained somehow. Gardner (1971) suggested that, to some people, feelings of guilt may be preferable to the feeling that the world is out of control. One parent expressed a commonly heard question when he learned of his daughter's leukemia: "Oh, my God, why Ellen? Why us? What have I done to deserve this wrath?" (Zimmerman, 1982, p. 28). Some families lose their religious beliefs after the advent of an exceptionality. One parent commented:

> It shouldn't have happened to me. Why did it happen to me? Crikey, if there was a God there wouldn't be any disabled children. All children are supposed to be perfect. (Lonsdale, 1978, p. 107)

Other families, however, use their beliefs to gain a sense of meaning. For example, one parent said he believed "God has a plan for that boy," and another parent commented, "God must think I'm a pretty strong person, to trust me with all these problems" (A. P. Turnbull et al., 1984, p. 32).

Still other families reframe their beliefs to fit the exceptionality into a new framework. Perhaps one of the most extensive examples of this approach is Rabbi Kushner's (1981) efforts to explain his son's severe degenerative disease in his book, *When Bad Things Happen to Good People*. Kushner notes that when something goes wrong, one need not decide either that God is evil or that the victim is evil and is being punished. Rather, he postulates that even God must follow his own laws of nature and that his omnipotence lies in compassion and support of those who fall victim to random natural events.

More so than other professionals, school professionals have an especially delicate role to play in encouraging the use of spiritual support. Aside from the difficulty of knowing when one is stepping over the boundaries between church and state, spiritual beliefs are personal and are not often discussed in public situations. In addition, such beliefs are highly individual. It is difficult to know the right thing to say, because what might be comforting to one person might seem foolish to another.

Thus, a better strategy is simply to listen nonjudgmentally to families' religious interpretations of the exceptionality and to refer them to religious resources in the community who can provide support and assistance.

Nearly every national religious organization has some curricula available for children and youth with exceptionalities. Special educators and other school personnel might wish to lend their expertise in integrating children and youth in classes in their own religious organizations, making the church or synagogue more accessible, or fostering greater general awareness and acceptance of exceptionalities. This is a type of informal interagency cooperation that should not be overlooked.

EXTERNAL COPING STRATEGIES

The amount of stress a family feels is related to the nature of the event, the family's resources and its perceptions or interpretations of the event (Hill, 1949). In the previous section, we discussed coping strategies relating to perceptions (i.e., the internal strategies of passive appraisal, reframing, and spiritual support). External coping strategies (i.e., coping through the use of social support or formal support) relate to the family's resources. Professionals can help families effectively use both strategies.

Social Support

Social support is a multidimensional construct that refers to the assistance individuals or families can receive in times of stress or need. Informal neighborhood groups, extended family networks, friends, coworkers, and church groups are all examples of typical social-support networks where assistance might be found. Psychologists and other helping professionals have begun to realize that social support offers numerous benefits. Thus, many studies have shown that social support is linked to reducing stress, decreasing physical health problems, and improving emotional well-being (Goldfarb et al., 1986).

In families where there is an exceptionality, social support can be especially important as an exceptionality can add a variety of major or minor stresses to the family. In fact, one longitudinal study (Beckman & Pokorni, 1988) showed that, in some instances, families with a child with an exceptionality who employed social support as a coping strategy during early stages of the life cycle showed decreased family stress during later stages.

The social-support network can provide three types of assistance to families: (a) material support, (b) emotional support, and (c) referral and information. Material support consists of goods and services, that is, the family's social-support network might donate tangible items such as money, food, or physical objects (Schradle & Dougher, 1985). Emotional support, in turn, provides the family with psychological resources (Schradle & Dougher, 1985). For example, friends or extended family may listen to our problems with a sympathetic ear, give us a pat on the back, or otherwise let us know they care. The social-support network can also provide valuable referral and information. For example, families who have experienced similar situations are excellent resources of information about which schools, health agency, or recreation programs provide the best services.

Of all the possible social-support networks available to families with an exceptionality, research has shown that family members provide each other the greatest amount of support. Specifically, Friedrich (1979) found that a good marital relationship was the single best predictor of good adjustment in mothers who had children with disabilities. Similarly, Kazak and Marvin (1984) noted that it was less important to mothers that fathers help with child care than that they provide their wives with emotional support.

The effects of an exceptionality on the family has been well documented in the literature, with the focus of attention generally on the person with the exceptionality and the mother. However, as discussed in Chapter 3, professionals are now realizing the importance of fathers, grandparents, and brothers and sisters on the overall adjustment process of the family with an exceptionality.

Generally speaking, research suggests that the birth of a child with an exceptionality into a family can have a variety of adverse reactions on the father. For example, fathers who are coping poorly may withdraw from their families and fail to provide much needed support. This forces other family members (especially the mothers) to provide additional support resulting in family tension. Furthermore, there is some evidence that fathers may cope better with a daughter who is disabled than a son. Through the use of social-support networks, researchers (Vadasy, Fewell, Greenberg, Desmond, & Meyer, 1986) have shown that fathers can learn to cope better, be more supportive of their family, and attach a more positive outlook to their son or daughter who has a disability.

In addition to the father's role in a family with an exceptionality, professionals are also recognizing the grandparents' role as an extended-family, social-support network. Thus, research indicates that the birth of a grandchild with a disability evokes different emotions than those produced by the birth of a healthy grandchild (Meyer & Vadasy, 1986). This is an important finding because a major concern of parents is how their own parents will accept the child with a disability (Seligman & Darling, 1989). Grandparents may display a variety of responses to both the grandchild and the family itself when faced with the crisis of a disability. According to Meyer and Vadasy (1986), grandparents often deny a grandchild's problem, trivialize it, or fantasize about unrealistic cures. Grandparents may also feel anger, depression, or even resentment toward the parents. Reactions such as these can prove to be difficult burdens to both the parents and the family itself—all of whom are already attempting to cope with the crisis. The family now must attend to their own pain and also deal with the grandparents' reactions (Seligman & Darling, 1989).

The contributions that grandparents can make to the family with an exceptionality are many and varied. For example, grandparents can assist with many daily routines such as shopping, running errands, or child care. They can also provide access to community resources, share coping strategies that helped them in the past, and provide invaluable respite care. Perhaps the most important help grandparents can provide is emotional support. Thus, the support of grandparents adds immeasurably to the parent's ability to cope (Seligman & Darling, 1989).

It is imperative that professionals recognize the natural support system that grandparents can provide to the family with an exceptionality. To this end, workshops could be organized to provide grandparents information about therapies, service opportunities, and general knowledge about their grandchild and his or her disability. Through the use of such workshops, grandparents can learn to cope and, in turn, provide the all-important social support that families with exceptionalities need.

Not only does an exceptionality in the family cause stress to both the fathers and the grandparents, it also has a significant effect on brothers and sisters. In fact, some researchers (e.g., DeLuca & Solerno, 1984) suggest that brothers and sisters of the child with an exceptionality may be at risk psychologically. For example, children who share in the anticipation of a new family member may share the grief and pain that accompanies the birth of an infant who is disabled. They may experience anger or resentment. They may feel guilt that they somehow caused the disability. The may worry about catching the disability and avoid the family member with the exceptionality. Moreover, they may develop anxieties about the future of their brother or sister with a disability. Whatever the case, brothers and sisters of a family member with a disability feel stress and this stress needs to be dealt with.

Sibling relationships are usually the longest and most enduring of all family relationships. The permanence of this relationship makes it possible to exert considerable influence over the family member with a disability through longitudinal interactions (Seligman & Darling, 1989). It stands to reason, then, that it is essential to involve brothers and sisters in the social-support network. One of the easiest ways to counteract childhood stress is to provide an open line of communication among all family members. Far too often, families try to shelter their children from crises. As a result siblings often have a limited understanding of their brother or sister's condition. In contrast, through communication siblings can learn that they are not the cause of their brother's or sister's disability or that they are in no danger of catching the disability. Siblings can also be taught how to relate effectively to their brother or sister and to the surrounding environment as well. They can also be taught how to communicate to family and friends about the disability. In addition, they can be taught how to deal with such discomforting feelings as anger, resentment, and jealousy (Seligman & Darling, 1989; Wasserman, 1983).

Another way of dealing with sibling and disability issues is to form a sibling support network. In such a network, brothers and sisters of families with exceptionalities get together and share experiences and basic information about disabling conditions. Through this network siblings can also educate their peers about disability. For example, Kate and Amy Turnbull (A. Turnbull & Bronicki, 1986; A. Turnbull & Bronicki 1987; K. Turnbull & Bronicki, 1989), the sisters of an older brother with mental retardation, taught elementary-age persons about disability through class science projects. The results of their studies showed that children can teach other children about disability and that teaching helps children have more positive attitudes and feel more comfortable with someone who has a disability. Further, they suggest that "Kid Power," which means kids taking the lead in creating a positive social-support network among other kids, can be organized by siblings and their friends.

Sibling support networks and "Kid Power" groups can be formed at your school if they do not already exist. You can plan meetings during school hours or after school. Social-support networks are very important to the psychological well-being of children and youth with a disability as well as to their brothers and sisters. People with a disability and their families and friends in the community benefit from social-support interactions. Social opportunities with community groups such as softball teams, bowling leagues and church groups can produce positive experiences for everyone involved. Take, for example, the personal experiences of Chuck Rhodes and the fraternity members of Sigma Alpha Epsilon at the University of Kansas.

During the academic year of 1989 at The University of Kansas, the members of Sigma Alpha Epsilon undertook an exciting new initiative in the area of fraternity community service. They decided to "adopt" a young man with moderate mental retardation into their fraternity as a little brother and spend significant time with him. This young man was Jay Turnbull.

At the outset of the project, the members of SAE were often apprehensive in their interactions with Jay. They seemed overprotective and viewed him more as an object of wonder than as a person. As the weeks passed though, these apprehensions disappeared as the brothers of SAE slowly began to realize that Jay was a person just like you and me—only he has special needs. They began to see that Jay was not a project to be worked with, but a person who could be a friend—a truly "special" friend.

As the year passed, Jay became an active part in all fraternal endeavors. He attended football and basketball games with the brothers; he attended intramural and extracurricular activities with the brothers; two times a week he walked to the SAE house from work with a friend to eat lunch and spend the afternoon and evening "hanging out" with the brothers; he and his dad, Rud, attended a formal dinner and were featured as guest speakers; he was even fixed up on a blind date for the brothers' annual spring formal.

Surely, more happened: The list of activities is only the epidermis of something potentially revolutionary in human relationships. Jay and the SAE brothers became involved in each other's lives and by being together, Jay and the brothers grew in ways that college courses, mere physical proximity, and all of the exhorting in the world could not achieve:

- Together they learned how to be friends with people who are different from each other.

- They touched each other's inner selves in ways that inculcate different kinds of compassion, insight, joy, laughter, and understanding.

- They prepared each other for the future. Some of the brothers will have children or other relatives who have disabilities. Some will be asked to ensure that people with disabilities have opportunities for education or work. Some will argue their cases in court. Some will treat them in hospitals. Some will pray for their souls and enrich their spirits. But most all of them will have some contact, however tangential, with people with disabilities.

All have learned again: "We are all in this together." Jay and the SAE brothers learned how to *BE* with each other in newer and better ways—how to be a friend, co-worker, and recreator with people who are different because of the presence or absence of disabilities.

Jay and the SAE brothers engaged in a new form of life and a new form of education. It was one that satisfied the needs of individuals who do not have disabilities, responding to their natural instincts for altruism and compassion, for something beyond their studies and parties. And it was one that satisfied Jay and his family, and other "Jays" and their families, responding to their needs to have their sons and daughters be not just *in* a community but also *of* a community.

In addition to benefits for Jay and the SAE brothers, the experience also had positive effects on Jay's family.

Jay's mom commented:

> The guys give us hope and excitement for Jay's future. They want to share an apartment with him. It's a dream come true for him to have friends to live with.

And his sisters have benefited, too:

> It's majorly cool for Jay to be with the guys. We're proud that Jay has such great friends. They are like our brothers, too. Now it's like we are a normal family and just fit in like everyone else.

We hope that the importance of social support and the role that it plays in the lives of all family members is clear to you. All family members are affected by an exceptionality and positive relationships of any one family member are extremely important to the coping ability of the family as a whole. A knowledge of families' social activities will help you initiate social-support opportunities appropriate for each individual. One person may prefer to be involved in 4-H, while another may prefer to help with Sunday school classes at the family church.

The self-help support group is one of the most popular forms of building social support for families with children who have exceptionalities. These are groups organized with the main objective of providing emotional support for their members as distinct from educational programs. Groups that are established and conducted by a professional social worker or psychologist may have a therapeutic goal (e.g., Intagliata & Doyle, 1984). Other groups may be organized through the leadership of family members (with perhaps a little logistical assistance from a professional) with the major purpose of sharing concerns and advice, planning recreational activities, and assuring one another that "we are not alone." As we point out in Chapter 1, many parent-founded groups perform the self-help function by design.

The majority of these support groups are attended by mothers—even when originally organized as couples' groups. A growing number of schools and other service agencies are organizing siblings' groups, which seem to meet an important need for information and support among brothers and sisters of children with exceptionalities (Powell & Ogle, 1985). A few fathers' groups have been organized, and—even more rarely—grandparents' groups. Support groups are fairly common in early intervention and preschool programs, less common in school-aged programs, and extremely rare among families with adults. These neglected family members and life-cycle stages deserve some attention if your school is considering developing a support program or cooperating with another agency in organizing one.

Another strategy for building social support is a mentorship program, such as the Parent-to-Parent groups. Such programs match a "veteran" parent to a parent with a child whose exceptionality has been newly identified. The parent mentor provides emotional support, information about services and—by his or her mere presence—testimony that one *can* survive and even prevail over parenthood demands. These programs have proven extremely successful. One veteran parent said this about them:

> Parent-to-Parent programs facilitate the establishment of a more intimate social support network for families who have a family member with a disability. Because they share such similar joys and sorrows, parents who participate in a parent-to-parent link receive a quality of support that is unlike that available from either professionals or other family members and friends. Parent-to-Parent programs truly provide empathetic, credible listeners who share their own personal experiences and know-how, at a time when families often need these resources the most.

In addition to helping with family support groups, professionals can help families build their own networks of social support. Encourage families to attend IEP meetings together and to bring a friend or extended family member as well. Consider that interdisciplinary team members often compare notes before or after an IEP meeting and imagine how valuable it would be for parents also to have that opportunity.

One veteran family of many IEP conferences comments on this strategy:

> Having Betsy attend our daughter's IEP conference with our family was the best advice we ever took. Not only did she provide support with just her presence, but having an outside opinion has proven to be invaluable. We have made up our minds that we will never have another conference without one of our friends there.

In addition, the school's resource library can provide information about exceptionalities that families can share with friends to alleviate ambiguity and fear. It is surprising sometimes how much simple information can do to increase the social support available to families. Consider the comments of this stepgrandparent, whose son had recently married a woman with a 9-year-old daughter with cerebral palsy:

> She's such a lovely child. She really wants to spend time with me too, but I'm afraid to. How do I help her take off her coat? How do I help her sit in a chair? I just know I'd break her arm or something (Goldfarb et al., 1986, p. 58).

In a case like this, a brief lesson from an occupational or physical therapist on some basic positioning techniques could produce many hours of respite for the parents, not to mention a rewarding relationship for the child and grandmother.

Finally, it is important to remember that as a professional you provide social as well as professional support. Your encouragement and empathy play a vital role, as discussed in Chapter 6.

Professional Support

USING PROFESSIONAL SUPPORT. When families turn to agencies or private practitioners for help in solving problems, they are using professional support as a coping strategy. Doctors, lawyers, social workers, vocational rehabilitation counselors, and teachers are all examples of professional support. Families may receive tangible assistance with their problems—for example, a training program for their child or youth or Medicaid reimbursement for adaptive equipment. They may also receive emotional support, either formally through counseling designed for that purpose or informally through encouragement from a caring professional. The main distinction between social and professional support is that professionals are paid to help. It is their job to provide support, which is essentially the main focus of the one-way relationship between the professional and the person or family to be helped. Social support comes from family and friends with whom we interact for a variety of reasons, and to whom we also provide support when they face problems. This mutuality and exchange in a relationship is the coin with which we pay for social support. On the other hand, we pay for professional support with appreciation for their help and with money—either tax dollars or our own.

Families of children and youth with exceptionalities are often more familiar than others with the professional support system. From the time of diagnosis through adulthood, a constantly changing plethora of professionals enter and exit their lives. As children with exceptionalities grow older, the most constant—and most trusted—fixtures in this professional scene are educators (Suelzle & Keenan, 1981). Unfortunately, contact with professionals may produce stress. Consider the comments from a foster family of a student who was diagnosed as having an emotional disorder.

> We knew Dee had a problem and all we wanted was a simple confirmation. What we got instead was an endless shuffle from doctor to doctor and not one straight answer. When we finally did get the diagnosis, it was almost like we had to pry it out of the psychologist. And then he actually had the nerve to say that poor parenting skills were at the root of Dee's problem. We have never been so insulted in all our lives!

It is difficult to know how much of this indictment is true. Some of it may be a "kill the messenger" syndrome, in which families have difficulty separating the pain of bad news from the bearer of it. Harris (1985) described this difficulty:

> Like any parent of a handicapped child, I've encountered incompetence and insensitivity as well as genius and saint-like understanding in helping professionals. . . . But I have realized only recently what burning rage I have felt because my daughter is handicapped and how bitterly I have viewed the efforts of any professional who is less than perfect. It's not easy to accept that the world is unjust, that some children are blessed and others burdened. . . . Helping professionals were among the first to get in the way and catch the brunt of my unrestrained anger. (pp. 262–263)

A good strategy to find out what is effective and what is not effective to ask each family as you begin to work with them about their most positive and most negative experiences with professionals. Their answers will probably give you insights into how to establish positive relationships with them through an individualized approach.

CASE MANAGEMENT.   There is one specific facet of professional support that should be discussed here, and that is the need to coordinate services. Effective coordination has been hampered by, among other details, the lingering assumption that families are responsible for finding and coordinating the variety of health, educational, and social services their student may need (Schalock, 1985). Some parents accept and even welcome this responsiblity. For example, one mother comments:

> I have really become quite an efficient case manager. When I first learned of Hector's problem I thought I would let the professionals decide what services Hector would need and when he would need them. What an idea! Someone to coordinate services for my son. After about a month I finally realized no one was going to do this so I took things into my own hands. I decided what doctors, schools, and recreation services would best suit Hector's needs. I made a lot of mistakes and had to change services many time. I guess I've made a lot of people mad at me. But hey, no one else was willing to do it.

However, there is a difference between acknowledging families as the primary managers and decision makers for their children and youth and leaving it up to them to search for, and coordinate services. Some children and youth need a wide variety of services, both within and outside the school. Also, some communities have a large number of professional services that overlap in function. The task of finding services, deciding which is best for a particular person, and then coordinating the various agencies involved can be time-consuming and exhausting.

One promising solution to this problem has been the development of case management services for the purpose of coordinating the interrelationships among all involved service workers, staff, organization administrators, educational institutions, service providers, and clients to integrate and expedite the delivery of needed services (Freedman, Pierce, & Reiss, 1987). The principal agent in such a system is the case manager who serves as an informed mediator for the family and their children and youth and as an informed planner/organizer of the service delivery and financing systems.

Case management services have proven to be a highly effective method of organizing and facilitating appropriate access to and utilization of services. In addition, case management can be a vital component of family support as one family points out:

> The addition of a case manager to our lives has made it possible for us to care for Juanita at home. The burden of coordinating services or even understanding whether we qualify for certain services has been lifted off our backs. We no longer have to worry about finding services. Our case manager does it for us. We can now focus all of our attention on Juanita and our family needs.

Some families choose to be their own case manager, others prefer that a professional serve as the case manager, and in still other situations a family and professional serve as co-case managers. The key is that a range of options be available so that family preferences can be respected.

SUMMARY

This chapter has described a variety of support services within the framework of natural coping strategies by families that may be used to reduce stress. The range of coping strategies, from passive appraisal to professional support, provides families with a wide array of help in meeting individual and family needs. Many families use some or all of these strategies instinctively. You can help build these natural strengths in a number of ways. Some help comes in the form of structured programs, like case management services, respite care, or problem-solving workshops. Other help is more incidental to your day-to-day interaction with families, such as encouraging families to think of the positive contributions of their child with an exceptionality, pointing out successes, and encouraging parents to relax.

Not every family can use every coping strategy, and, even if they do, they might not want it in the format presented to them. For example, some families do not want to be involved with organized support groups and prefer to stay away from the "handicapped establishment" (Bennett, 1985). Others might have no place in their belief structure for spiritual support. Still others may have no need for respite care but feel comfortable getting their rest and relaxation by their own firesides (Lonsdale, 1978). Preferred coping strategies may change over the life cycle, however (McCubbin et al., 1983). Finally, some coping strategies are more useful for some family functions than for others (see Chapter 4). As we have emphasized, you should work with, not against, individual family preferences. The Discussion Guide included in Appendix B includes sections on coping strategies. You can modify it to suit your program offerings and use it to identify family preferences. Furthermore, some coping strategies are more appropriate for some situations than for others. Thus, as much as possible, families should be encouraged to have a variety of coping strategies at their disposal. In a way, reframing is the first step to any action—internal or external—one might take to reduce feelings of stress. The first question is: Is this something we can change or is it something we must learn to live with? Once that question is answered, the next step consists of choosing the coping strategy that will best fit the situation as well as the individual family's style. As a professional, your role is to suggest, not dictate; to provide options, not select. It is through seeing yourself and your school as a resource for coping, rather than as a manager, that you can best provide support.

Throughout this book, we have discussed the strengths and weaknesses of families, the family-systems approach, and family-professional relationships. This chapter on coping is the last chapter on those subjects which offer direct solutions to family-professional problems. In the next chapter, we continue to focus of those relationships, but from a radically different perspective, one that does not identify direct or simple solutions—the moral perspective.

PROFESSIONAL ETHICS AND MORALS

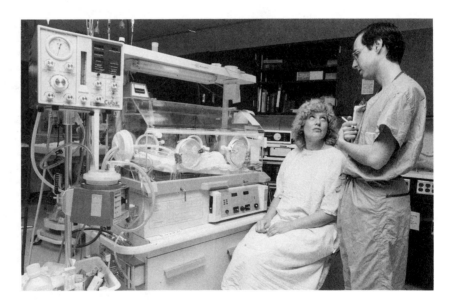

Even with sensitivity to a family's characteristics, interactions, functions, and life cycle; proficiency with communication skills; and knowledge about the law, you may find yourself in situations where there are no right-wrong answers. That is when you will use your ethics to make a moral decision.

Angela, a teenaged girl who has moderate mental retardation, has begun to bite her nails so often and so severely that she has torn her skin and requires bandages that impair her work at school and at her job. A school psychologist suggests to her teacher and parents that the most effective way to stop the nail biting is to shout "no" loudly, shake a finger at the girl, point to her hand, and slap her. The teacher agrees that this strategy would be effective. Her parents have doubts, her mother being inclined not to use the slap; besides her social worker is well known for reporting cases of abuse to the child protection agency and is opposed to the intervention. By contrast, the school principal still practices corporal punishment (which is legal in many states).

In studying this book, you have been introduced to the family-systems perspective, which states that professionals should take into account the interests of all members of a family when addressing the needs of one of them. You also have considered strategies for how to communicate with and provide information to families, so that you can carry out the family-systems perspective. And you have learned about the legal rights of students, family members, and professionals in special education, so that you may act lawfully. Even with all of this information, you may still be asking questions about what is right to do in particular situations. In order to respond to questions like this, you have to look at the morals of special education and other interventions. There are situations that do not have a clear-cut, right-wrong answer, requiring you to exercise professional, legal, and moral judgments. In this chapter, we will discuss some of these problem situations and show you how you can begin the difficult process of making reasoned, articulated, moral judgments about them. After reading this chapter, you should be able to answer the following questions:

- How can moral issues be viewed from a family-systems perspective?
- How can you view problem situations from a moral perspective?
- How do ethics and morals relate to defining a moral perspective?
- What are the sources of ethics and morals?
- How can you reach a moral judgment in problem situations?

A MORAL PROBLEM FOR
FAMILIES AND PROFESSIONALS

Let's begin by considering the problem raised by Angela's behavior. What is the right thing to do? Consider it from the perspectives of the following: the family as a whole, the student's, the teacher's, the mother's, the father's, the social worker's, and the principal's. Will all these people agree with each other? What is best for the family as a system? How do you determine, and who decides, what is right in this situation? What does it matter what is right?

The question "What is the right thing to do?", asks about the ultimate resolution of the problem. "Will they agree with each other?" deals with the issue of a universal right answer as distinguished from a relative right answer. "How do you determine?" Aims at the process for resolving the issue. "Who decides?" includes both the process for decision making and the power to make decisions. Finally, "Why does it matter?" gets at the relevance and, indeed, necessity of making moral judgments when formulating a course of action.

Let us consider those issues. It is unlikely that the people named in this scenario will all agree on whether the intervention is right. After all, each has a different view about whether or not to use the proposed shout-point-slap method. Perhaps they can tell us why they think they are right. For example, the psychologist and the teacher may say it is right to use the intervention because it will be effective (thus, *right* equals *effective*; as we point out elsewhere, efficacy is a fact to be considered, but it may or may not be determinative of a result), but the social worker may say it is wrong because it is not the least restrictive/ drastic intervention (thus, right equals least intrusive, a concept discussed in Chapter 8). It is not clear how they will resolve their differences or who will make the decision.

There are several reasons why it matters what is right. One, the student has a behavior that interferes with her learning, may be socially isolating, and perhaps physically harmful and nonhygienic. Two, no law or codes of professional ethics adequately governs the situation (as long as the slap does not constitute child abuse). Three, a family-systems perspective teaches us that a variety of considerations come into play. These include the wishes of the student, the wishes of the parents, the effect of the procedure on the siblings when the procedure is followed at home, and the effect of the procedure on other functions of the family, such as affection and socialization functions. Thus, we have no choice except to think about right and wrong actions.

From this example, we learn why we should be concerned with the moral right and wrong of professional interventions. Tymchuk (1976) suggested that the reason is to ensure consistent treatment by professionals. Allen and Allen (1979) contended that the extreme vulnerability of students with mental retardation requires that professionals consider the ethics of intervention. Further, Mesibov and LaGreca (1981) made the case that professionals must consider ethical issues in order to be more effective in their work. H. R. Turnbull (1982) argued that the law requires professionals to consider their ethical duties because they set the standards of professional conduct over and above those standards required by the U.S. Constitution as a matter of the child's lawful rights. Heshusius (1982) and Rosenberg, Tesolowski, and Stein (1983) said ethics are important to consider because professionals have a moral duty to be advocates for their clients. According to Bateman (1982) and Guess et al. (1984), ethics are important because the law often does not provide guidance for professionals. Finally, H. R. Turnbull and Guess (1986) have shown how ethical analyses can help resolve difficult problems. And as Table 14–1 shows, there are other good reasons to think about ethics than those sampled in the preceding overview.

DEFINING ETHICS AND MORALS

What do ethics and morals mean? The word *ethics* refers to the science of thinking about and studying morals, whereas the word *morals* involves right and wrong behavior. Thus, ethics is systematic reasoning about right and wrong behavior (Frankena, 1973; Mann & Kreyche,

---

TABLE 14–1   Other Reasons to Consider Ethics

- Other sources of answers to difficult questions may not be available (in this case, the law was not helpful and professional codes of ethics were not sufficiently helpful).

- Thinking about issues of right and wrong usually will provide thoughtful and reasoned answers which generally are better—because they can be defended and justified—than a knee-jerk or gut-feeling response.

- It usually is better to think through problems for oneself and reach a conclusion that is personally satisfactory than to be guided solely by what another person thinks (e.g., in this case, the teacher could have acquiesced with the psychologist and principal, even though neither of them was required to do the shout-point-slap). We become more independent and autonomous when we think for ourselves, especially concerning the difficult questions of right and wrong in education. As Socrates pointed out, the unexamined life is not worth living.

- We ought to do right and not wrong; therefore, we must think about right and wrong carefully because we act as trustees and stewards for children and as caretakers of their bodies and minds.

- The professional who carefully considers moral issues is truly acting in a professional manner by applying broad concepts to a problem in an attempt to answer it.

1966). In this chapter, we refer to decisions about the right or wrong action as moral decisions, and we try to help you reach decisions by using ethics.

Let us apply that definition to Angela. The individuals involved in her life were not likely to reach consensus on whether the shout-point-slap procedure was right or wrong. Even the reasons they gave (e.g., effective is right; least intrusive is right) would not resolve the disagreement. Yet, it is clear that right and wrong matter in this case and that it is important to consider the moral issues involved.

When reasonable people disagree about the right or wrong thing to do in a particular situation, like the one we have described, it will help to think carefully about what you would do and why. To do so, it is helpful to know about the sources of ethics and morals in special education.

SOURCES OF ETHICS AND MORALS: PROFESSIONAL CODES

Some useful sources of ethics and morals are available for special education professionals. For example, the Council for Exceptional Children (CEC), the nation's special education professional organization, has published a Code of Ethics and accompanying Standards for Professional Practice (1983). The Code is based on the obligation of special educators to the student, the employer, and the special education profession (but *not* to the family). These obligations are described in eight principles that are to form the basis for all professional conduct. CEC then lists minimum standards of conduct, the Standards for Professional Practice. Together, the Code and the Standards, according to CEC, "provide guidelines for professional etiquette, for effective interpersonal behavior, for resolution of ethical issues, and for making professional judgments concerning what constitutes competent practice" (p. 205).

CEC is not the only organization that has developed a professional code of ethics. Such codes include those of the American Psychological Association (1981), National Association of Social Workers, American Psychiatric Association, National Association of School Psychologists, Principles for Professional Ethics, and American Speech-Language-Hearing Association.

From some perspectives, right behavior is that which professional organizations recommend—the proposed and alternative interventions are moral only if they are recommended or at least not prohibited by the codes of ethics and professional standards of relevant professional organizations. (This does not mean that professional associations' approval of a professional behavior necessarily makes it right. Moral debate rages around interventions that have received approval by some professional associations, e.g., abortion, aversive behavior modification, nontreatment of some newborns, and denial of treatment in community settings.)

Rather than adopt codes or standards, some organizations have developed statements of policy. For example, the American Association on Mental Retardation (AAMR) has formulated policies concerning the basic rights of persons with mental retardation including the right to habilitation and the use of physical, psychological, and psychopharmacological procedures to affect behavior. Similarly, the Association for Persons with Severe Handicaps has adopted position papers and resolutions concerning treatment, education, habilitation and other issues.

Thus, if you have questions about the ethics of a behavior, you may consult the views of professional organizations. You are not legally bound to follow the organization's codes, standards, or policy positions, which are guidelines and recommendations, not obligations that can be enforced by law. They can, however, be useful to you in defense of what you did if you acted consistently with them. In some cases, noncompliance can result in expulsion from the professional organization.

The codes, standards, and policy positions are valuable in other respects. First, they represent the careful thought of a large number of professionals; obviously, they also represent the accumulated experience and wisdom that goes into the professionals' consideration of the moral problems. Thus, the codes, standards, and policy positions usually have been adopted only after debate and consideration by various delegate bodies or by delegates to professional meetings. This assures that the codes are widely accepted.

Second, the codes deal in general terms with a large number of problems. Although someone might wish that they were specific and answered all the questions an individual may have, that clearly is neither practical nor desirable. It is not practical because such documents cannot address all the problems that may arise. Besides, it is not desirable because individual professionals are responsible for their own behavior and should be encouraged to consider and apply moral solutions to particular problems.

Finally, the codes, standards, and policies have the effect of supplementing the laws of special or regular education by providing moral guidance. Those laws—whether in the form of the Education of the Handicapped Act (EHA) and its regulations, state or local laws and regulations, or court interpretations of those statutes and regulations—do not always apply to a problematic situation. Thus, you may need extra guides to moral conduct; indeed, there are likely to be situations in which the laws do not apply or seem to be inadequate for determining what is right or wrong. After all, in cases where the law does apply but seems inadequate, the laws merely state what is lawful, not necessarily what is right or wrong from a moral perspective. In those instances, a professional may choose between the law or morals. This is a choice of civil obedience or civil disobedience, a topic well beyond this chapter's boundaries.

SOURCES OF GENERAL MORAL PRINCIPLES

Let us assume that you have a moral problem concerning the education of a student and the relationship between the student and the family. After consulting the appropriate codes or standards, you determine that they do not address your problem in a way that seems sufficiently or satisfactory to you. What can you do?

One way to proceed is to begin to think systematically about moral behavior. How do you do this? After all, you are not trained to think about moral behavior. You may have some conceptions about the right thing to do; indeed, you probably do. But you have not been trained to apply your conception of morality to the situation at hand, and you may realize that your conceptions are different from those of other professionals.

It may help, therefore, to have some guidance based on the works of great philosophers. You may want to know, for example, how the classical Greek philosophers would have answered the moral questions. You may want to know whether their answers are consistent with the Judeo-Christian ethical tradition. You may want to apply a utilitarian philosophy. In any case, you want to know the major philosophical principles so you can apply them. In the following sections, we will give you a brief description of each of the major philosophical principles and some guidance about how to apply them to particular cases.

The Greeks, St. Thomas Aquinas, and the Golden Mean

Ancient Greece is a fertile source for philosophy still applied in the western world. Socrates, Plato, and Aristotle were the leading thinkers of Ancient Greece and thus most deserving of attention today. Centuries later, St. Thomas Aquinas reiterated their views. All of them argued, first, that the essence of a human is the ability to reason, the characteristic that sets a human apart from other species. The human faculty of greatest value, therefore, is intellect—the power that enables reasoning, conceptualization, and rational judgment. For this reason, the power of the intellect provides human satisfaction, fulfillment, or happiness; it is also the faculty that has the primary claim for development. This is why Socrates said that the unexamined life is not worth living. To fulfill this unique trait, we must use our reason and intelligence. In addition, the Greeks maintained that, to have a "happy" life, we must act reasonably, with intelligence and thoughtfulness, and we must avoid excesses of action. Thus, we must live according to a Golden Mean—a course of conduct that avoids extremes.

Judeo-Christian Doctrine

The Judeo-Christian ideal is for people to be more like God and it is most often perceived in terms of love between persons. Precepts such as "Do unto others as you would have them do unto you" and "Love thy neighbor as thyself", therefore are the cornerstones of the Judeo-Christian doctrine of reciprocity. Further the Old Testament stresses the concept of the each person's responsibility to each other, whereas the New Testament emphasizes the commandment to treat others as you would want to be treated.

Empathetic Reciprocity

The Judeo-Christian doctrine of love is much like a secular doctrine of empathetic reciprocity according to which we should recognize in other people the same needs to be loved, fulfilled, and respected as we see in ourselves (Allen & Allen, 1979). The doctrine of empathetic reciprocity is secular because it does not explicitly rest on religious authority. But it is like the Judeo-Christian doctrine of reciprocity in that it urges us to put ourselves in the position of others as fully as possible. We should do this by adopting their needs and wants and by laying our own aside. Because this doctrine emphasizes the humanness of each individual as reflected in each person's need for love, fulfillment, and respect, according to this doctrine, therefore, each action we take concerning another is right or wrong to the extent that it contributes to others' capacities to acquire love, fulfillment, and respect.

Kant's Categorical Imperative

The German philosopher Immanuel Kant stated a rule by which to judge maxims of conduct. He argued that an act is moral only if it can be applied to all rational beings without contradiction or exception. Thus, non-dichotomous (i.e., equal or unexceptional) treatment of all people in similar circumstances is the right action. An action is right if a rational person would decide upon and approve that action for all persons in the same circumstance. Any action that one takes toward anyone in a given situation must therefore be appropriate for all others in the same situation.

Utilitarianism

In contrast to the exceptionless nature of the Categorical Imperative are the doctrines of the utilitarians. Jeremy Bentham and John Stuart Mill, English philosophers, were leading utilitarians who argued that the "right" action is the one that promotes the greatest good for the greatest number of people. Thus, we must judge the effect of our actions from the viewpoint of not only their effect on ourselves (the actors) but also their effect on people directly and indirectly affected. In addition, we must also determine what constitutes a good effect or a less good, or bad, effect.

Causalism

A different way to define moral action is to ask about an act, "What harm does the act do?" This approach, called *causalism,* requires that we determine if an action will have a negative effect on society, on the general welfare. If it does, the action is wrong. In this view, the individual is the means to a general welfare. For example, causalism may disallow the nontreatment of a mildly injured newborn who is reasonably likely to become a gifted child, but it may allow nontreatment of children who will always be wholly dependent on others because of their severe disabilities. The only proper perspective according to causalism is societal harm: What harm will an action cause to society?

It is not the role of this chapter to reach final answers; that is something you must do for yourself. Nor is it the role of this chapter to describe fully all the major philosophical doctrines; that is best left to texts on philosophy (Frankena, 1973; Mann & Kreyche, 1966; Taylor, 1967) and to the words of the philosophers themselves. Instead, this chapter seeks only to describe briefly some of the major philosophies of the Western world and show how they might be applied to some of the problems. Thus, it contains these inherent attributes: The description of the philosophies will only briefly show how they might apply; it will not answer for you what is "moral" because that is within the scope of your own professional responsibility. For that reason, we will pose unanswered questions in the hope you will try to answer them for yourself.

Moreover, we do not say what we would do in a particular situation because a more important objective of this text is for you to make your own judgments.

Some readers may criticize us for not disclosing our judgments, the reasons we reached them, and the reasons we rejected other judgments. That indeed may be a shortcoming. (Of course, in some cases our judgments can be inferred.) Nonetheless, we adhere to our plan of setting forth the principles, applying them, and showing how you may reach certain judgments.

We do so because we believe that the family-systems approach makes it undesirable for us to reveal our answers. An advantage of the family-systems approach is that it clarifies professional-family relationships by analyzing families more carefully than most approaches to these relationships. Yet, the approach entails the disadvantage that it complicates the effort to find solutions to complex problems, especially moral problems. We believe we will undermine the essential didactic message of this book—that professionals must take family systems into account in their work with people with exceptionalities—if we state what moral judgments should be reached in each problem we give, when taking a family-systems approach. What is right for one family is not necessarily right for another.

A second reason for declining to give our judgments is that a judgment stated in one case can become a precedent in another. Given our brief statement of principles, cases, and application, we are wary of the precedential problems that judgment-giving can create.

Third, in each of the problems, matters of fact are entwined with questions involving moral judgments. In real life, these are intermingled, as in this chapter. Thus, for example, whether a shout-point-slap intervention works is a matter of fact; whether such a procedure should be used is both a matter of fact (will it work?) and a moral judgment (if it won't, how can it be justified; and if it will, should it nonetheless be used as a moral action?). Because mixed questions of fact and morals are present, we think it best for you to sort out the questions of fact from the moral issues and, having done so, make moral judgments.

Finally, matters of moral judgment are different from matters of taste. We emphatically deny that any one moral judgment is as worthwhile as any other. It may be a matter of political doctrine to establish an all-Aryan race, but that did not make the Holocaust moral. It may be a matter of social preference to want to improve the condition of mankind, but that does not make moral compulsory sterilization of all people who have mental illness or metal retardation. It may be a matter of taste to apply shock therapy for inappropriate behaviors, or even a matter of programmatic desirability, but that does not make the use of shock morally right in every case (H. R. Turnbull & Guess, 1986). Thus, not all matters of taste or desirability can be justified on moral grounds, and, too, matters of taste or desirability must be distinguished from matters of moral judgment. The recent effort at values clarification has tended to accord all values, and hence all moral judgments, equal status, as if they were merely matters of taste. That may be insufficient for some readers, as it is for us, but it has the advantage of forcing readers to clarify for themselves what are matters of taste, what are matters of moral judgment, and when, why, and under what circumstances one or more moral judgments prevail over other plausible ones.

CASES WHERE ETHICS AND MORALS MAY BE INVOLVED

In this section, we will present some of the most common situations where right and wrong may be involved. We will describe a factual situation, ask questions from the family-systems perspective about the right or wrong thing to do, and briefly show how one or more of the major philosophical doctrines can be applied to resolve each situation. As you read the problems and the questions, remember that we are approaching situations from the family-system perspective. That perspective asks you to consider the interests of all affected people; our questions help you do that. Also, remember that reasonable people can disagree about the right action. As you think about the right action, remember that you are increasing both your ability to think as well as your tolerance of other people's different points of view. Those abilities may help you in interdisciplinary team decision making.

When we apply one or more of the principles, we try to accomplish two tasks. First, we show you more adequately the meaning of the principles, as our initial definitions were brief. Second, we show you how a principle might be applied to a particular case. Remember, however, that it is your decision, not ours, whether the case should be approached that way.

You will probably lean toward several responses as you read these situations and our discussion of them. First, you may be overwhelmed by the number of questions we raise concerning the moral thing to do in each situation. Please recall, however, that the family-systems approach requires that you take into account the interests of all family members. You also will notice that, in some cases, we ask you to consider the interests of people outside the child's family, including the interests of various professionals and other children. Considering their interests means that the family-system perspective is not the only legitimate perspective. There are other competing interests.

Second, you may observe that the moral action in each situation depends on which principle you apply and that different results are approved or disapproved by different doctrines. Such a conflict is unavoidable. However, do not give up seeking an answer simply because there are conflicting results. You may prefer to apply one philosophical principle—such as the reciprocity principle or the utilitarian principle—and apply it to all situations. If you do this, you will have chosen to act on the basis of a consistent philosophy. Or, you may prefer to reach a result that consistently is student-centered; you may always rule in the student's favor. If you do this, you usually will not apply consistently any given philosophy but instead, will be acting as an advocate of the student.

Third, you may find that professional codes and standards are sufficient to provide you the needed guidance. That is an understandable result because the code and standards reflect a national consensus that resolves these matters for you from the perspective of a national special education organization. But even then, you are exercising your own independent judgment to adhere to them. Let us now turn to the problems.

Screening, Evaluation, and Referral

An early childhood screening program has been established in your state (where early education begins at age 3 for children with disabilities). The screening consists of cursory examination of each child to determine if there are visual, hearing, motor, intellectual, or emotional problems. Two-year-old Sally is screened, with her mother's consent, and found to have a moderate hearing loss. Unfortunately, Sally lives in a rural community. There are no appropriate diagnostic or treatment clinics within 100 miles of her home or school. In addition, Sally's mother does not have transportation and is a single parent.

Should the professionals tell Sally's mother about the hearing problem? Unquestionably, they should tell Sally's mother the truth about her daughter. For one reason, telling the truth is a matter of moral duty under reciprocity and Categorical Imperative doctrines. For another, not telling the truth, or withholding a substantial portion of it, is indefensible professional conduct as a matter of tradition. There are times, some people think, when falsification or withholding information is defensible (Bok, 1978; Katz, 1984.) By contrast, there are questions about the consequences of telling the truth. Should the professionals make a referral to an agency that is, for all practical purposes, unavailable because it is so far away, or try to intervene in some other way (such as by learning what intervention to use and using it themselves, even though they may not be fully trained and may be doing some harm as well as some good)? What would be the effects for Sally and her mother of doing nothing? Of making an impractical referral? Of putting together a makeshift intervention?

What is the right action? It may be that a Golden Mean approach would require a makeshift intervention because doing nothing or referring Sally to the distant clinic are extremes that do not yield acceptable results. Doing nothing is unacceptable from the standpoint of developing Sally's capacities to hear and, thereby, to use reason and intelligence. Referring Sally to the distant clinic on the other hand, is unacceptable because it is unlikely that any intervention will occur—the distances are too great. But a different result can be defended. Thus, it may be that the "Golden Rule" or reciprocity doctrines would put us in Sally's or her mother's shoes and have us at least make the referral to the distant clinic. Less desirable but more practicable, we might choose the makeshift intervention. Sally's mother may be able to arrange transportation to the distant clinic, and she and the clinicians together might devise a way to carry out the intervention in her rural community. Or, we might conclude as a matter of fact (i.e., after evaluating the efficacy potentials) that a makeshift intervention would do some good until Sally enters the kindergarten program 3 years from now. Note, however, that this is a judgment of fact, not a moral judgment.

Establishing Educational Opportunities

A family recently has arrived in America from Vietnam after surviving the Vietnam war and subsequent internal strife. There is only one child in this family, Kim, a 15-year-old boy whose older brothers and sisters were killed in Vietnam. After two years in public school programs for non-English speaking students, Kim has mastered English and demonstrated a brilliant grasp of mathematics, physics, and chemistry. Kim's teachers urge his father and mother to send Kim to a school for students who are gifted, nearly 2,500 miles from Kim's family's home. There, Kim would receive a full-tuition scholarship, free room and board, and intensive training that almost certainly would qualify him for a full scholarship at any of the nation's best universities.

Kim is ambivalent. His mother and father are strongly opposed to the idea and say that they would lose their only son. It is clear that they have strong values of family togetherness. But the professionals at the school, which has no program for gifted secondary students, are eager to see one of their "own" excel and have these chances.

In this case, there are conflicting values and beliefs about what is important. Kim's parents think that their family's unity is more important than Kim's education; the professionals believe otherwise. Kim is caught in the middle, perhaps feeling (as the only son of immigrants who have lost their other children in war) an obligation to his parents, to himself, and to his deceased brothers and sisters to "make it" in America.

What is the right thing to do (and whose perspective prevails?) when professional, family, and student values conflict? The Greek approach may favor the out-of-home education because that intervention maximizes Kim's intelligence and ability to reason, which the Greeks valued so much. The reciprocity doctrines, however, also can be applied. If Kim's parents adopt a reciprocity approach, they perhaps would favor Kim's intellectual development and allow him to go away to school. But Kim himself may prefer to stay home, also because of reciprocity (putting himself in his parents' place). And Kim's parents might argue that he should stay home because that is what they would do if they were in his position. Thus, the reciprocity doctrine will yield different results, depending on one's perspective. Finally, everybody may be persuaded by the utilitarian argument that everyone will benefit in some way by Kim's leaving home and acquiring benefits for himself, his parents, and his present school.

Establishing Intervention Goals

A very young boy has been diagnosed as brain damaged. There is an early intervention project in his hometown where he would receive fairly typical special education training. His parents, however, have read about the Doman-Delacado method of intervention. Called "patterning," this procedure involves intensive physical intervention for nearly half a day every day. In this case, the intervention requires the assistance of a staff of volunteers. Staff at the local early childhood program recommend that the parents enroll the boy in its program, arguing that they have been effective with children like this and the Doman-Delacado method has not been proven effective. The mother wants the patterning because she believes it could cure her son as well as provide her with a support system of volunteers. The father wants to enroll the boy in the local program, avoid a "parade of do-gooders" coming to his home, and spend the cost of the Doman-Delacado tuition and equipment on their older son's college tuition.

What is the right thing to do when family members and professionals encounter a disagreement over values, and when there are conflicting professional opinions, some of which are supported by research results? Here the utilitarian perspective may favor the father and the local educators, who also argue for spreading the benefits among all family members. This is so because, from the father's perspective, the center-based early education program will help his boy with the disability as well as leave funds for developing his other son's talents. From the educators' perspective, the local program will help the boy (its efficacy is well documented), his mother (who will not have to be so terribly involved in his therapy that she may end up overlooking some of the other members of the family as well as her own needs), and the brother (because family financial resources can be preserved). The reciprocity doctrines may also tip the balance toward the local program because the boy and his mother may benefit from the intervention and from the presence of other people in their lives. From the boy's perspective, it may be good to be the center of so much attention, and it may be beneficial to have the therapy. From the mother's perspective, she also benefits as the key person in her son's therapy and as the recipient of a support system. Obviously, this is a case where the right action will depend on three factors—the perspective taken (the father's, mother's, boy's, brother's, or educators'), the philosophical approach adopted (the utilitarian and reciprocity approaches yield different results), and the efficacy of the therapy. Again, remember that the question of fact (efficacy) must be answered separately from the question of right behavior.

Granting or Denying Access to Information; Dealing with Child Neglect and Custody Disputes

Sean is a 10-year-old with a learning disability. His parents were divorced last year and he lives with his mother, who has legal custody, and her parents. Sean's father, whose interest in Sean's welfare is well known, lives in the same town. He fought hard but unsuccessfully to obtain joint custody and alleged that Sean's mother sometimes neglected to feed Sean during the time Sean was living with her before the divorce hearing. Sean's father comes to your classroom and asks to see Sean's school records. You decline the request and refer the matter to the school principal, who also declines. Sean's father argues that, although the mother has legal custody, he is, after all, Sean's father. Besides, he implies, Sean may be neglected still. In fact, you recently have observed Sean's lethargy and noted in the school records that Sean is extraordinarily hungry at lunch times and perks up after eating. Sean's father also says to the principal, "I know you have talked about Sean and me to a whole bunch of people in this little town because the word's come back to me. If you can blab about us to a bunch of people who have no business knowing about us, why can't I see his school records?"

In this case, it helps to think about (a) the records, (b) child neglect and Sean's welfare, and (c) your role in adversary proceedings. Remember, too, that the family-systems perspective is not the only one; here also is a school-system perspective to consider.

Should Sean's father be shown the records? Here the EHA (as interpreted in some states) denies access to the father, but the father's moral claim may seem more compelling than the mother's legal rights under the EHA. Should the principal discuss Sean and his parents with people who are not involved in Sean's education? It seems clear he should not; the EHA prohibits disclosure, and no moral principle justifies it. Does it make any difference, as the teacher points out, that Sean's maternal grandparents have seen the records without explicit permission by his mother? What is the right thing to do?

Consider the issues of child neglect and child welfare. Should the school professionals file a report of suspected child neglect, as the law requires them to do? Assuming that they comply with the law and file a report, would their action help Sean, who is having adjustment problems because of his learning disability as well as because of his parents' divorce? Suppose you have reason to believe, based on Sean's school and family history, that Sean's health has deteriorated during the time he has stayed with his mother. Since the bottom line is a custody battle, would Sean be better off with his mother or his father?

Would you be willing to go to court to testify that you suspect Sean's mother is neglecting him? Or would you testify only reluctantly, if required to appear in court? Should you volunteer to tell the father about the problem of neglect as you noted it in the records? What if the principal has said to you, "Listen, this case is closed. Let's keep out of the courts and get along with educating Sean." Do you agree that Sean's educational welfare is the school's only business? Would you volunteer to reveal the facts that you have noted in Sean's record if you were called to testify in a new child-custody proceeding? In short, are you willing to defend your actions when faced with issues of private and confidentiality of records, potential or actual neglect or abuse, and custody disputes?

Let us consider Sean's case from the reciprocity perspective. First, Sean is the most vulnerable person in this situation, so we may want to take his point of view as being the most important one. What would he want? What would you want if you were Sean? Clearly, he wants and needs both good health and an education. Without the former, the latter becomes more difficult to obtain. Thus, disclosing the records of the father (probably illegally) and reporting the suspected child neglect (which is legally required) are right from a reciprocity perspective. But consider the parents. We know what the father wants, and we can assume the other objects to disclosure and reporting. If, however, she could be made to understand that those actions would help Sean and perhaps herself, would she object so much?

From the perspective of the Greeks and Aquinas, it is right to report the suspected neglect because Sean could be helped physically, and his physical improvement most likely will help him intellectually. Now consider the case from a utilitarian perspective. Releasing the records might promote a great deal of good, even though it may be illegal. The good might involve Sean's health and education, his father's peace of mind, his mother's getting help, and perhaps even a change in the custody arrangement.

In Sean's case, we suggested that we consider the morality of action from his point of view because he is the most vulnerable of the people involved. That perspective—namely, that professionals have a moral duty to give priority to the most vulnerable of the people in a situation (usually, the child who is exceptional or any child, for that matter)—has been advanced by special educators (Weintraub & McCaffrey, 1976). It is an appealing idea, and one that you might well adopt. It considers the power relationships among people and attempts to rebalance them. It gives professionals a single point of focus, thereby simplifying matters of moral judgment. Finally, it is consistent with the reasons why many professionals entered the business of helping people who are exceptional. On the other hand, this perspective does not necessarily take into account the family-systems theory, which requires careful consideration of the interests of all family members. It make moral judgments on the basis of the needs of one person, not on the basis of principles as applied to problems. And arguably, therefore, it will be too pragmatic and eclectic for many people (although pragmatism and eclecticism are philosophical principles that one may adopt). Despite the shortcomings of the "vulnerability perspective," it has much to recommend it, not the least of which is that CEC seems to have used it as the central point of view for its Code and Standards (Weintraub & McCaffrey, 1976).

Giving Sufficient Information to Get Consent

Under the EHA, professionals must obtain consent from a student's parents to administer an initial special education evaluation and to make an initial special education placement. Knowing this, you (the assistant director of special education in the school district) meet with Hillary's parents to seek consent from them for an initial special education placement out of the "mainstream." Instead of attending regular classes with children who, unlike Hillary, do not have an orthopedic disability, she will be placed in a new "special" school, where all the students have a physical or mental disability. Since this is her first special education placement or identification, parental consent is required.

Hillary's parents (Mr. and Mrs. Beaudelaire) speak only a little English. Before you meet with them, Hillary's teacher recommends continuing her present placement, which is intellectually and socially beneficial to her. The special education director has issued a policy that all school personnel strongly push for the transfer of students like Hillary to the new school. He is under orders to do so from the school board that proposed the new facility and staked its reputation on the bond vote for funds to build it. He also may lose a special education program (in the new facility) that is badly needed by some children if there is not a large enough number of students to justify its cost.

In your meeting with Hillary's parents, they ask you about the benefits and drawbacks of the transfer and about their rights if they do not like the placement. They want to know how Hillary's program will be implemented; they ask about the school district's ability to provide social integration of students who have physical disabilities with students who are not disabled. They ask why you are pressing so hard for consent to the transfer and what alternative placements there are. Finally, they ask the meaning of certain jargon such as "mainstream," "separate self-contained program," "paras," "quads," and "TMR."

Knowing that the "information" element of consent is satisfied by providing a sufficient amount of information in a way the parents can understand (H. R. Turnbull, 1978), you face at least these questions: How much do you say, if anything? How do you say it so it will be understood? How do you avoid a confrontation between the parents, the principal, and school board? How clearly do you define the terms you and others so frequently use (e.g., "para" or "TMR") for the parents?

According to the Greeks and Aquinas, any action that maximizes Hillary's or her parents' intellect is right. Thus, full information is demanded. Obviously, the reciprocity doctrine also favors Hillary and Mr. and Mrs. Beaudelaire. Their futures are at stake, and few people would want to have so much resting on inadequate information. From a utilitarian perspective, full and frank disclosure to occur may also be preferable, as that may help in the education of other children. Conversely, it could cause considerable administrative problems for the school and its teachers, and thereby hurt other pupils. From the causalist perspective, it can be argued that disclosure would cause no harm for Hillary and her parents and only limited harm for the school, but long-term benefit for its students. This, of course, is a matter of fact, not moral judgment (as is the efficacy of aversive therapy in our first illustration). But facts shape moral judgments and, therefore, must be known before judgments are reached. From a causalist perspective, there also is the added argument that Hillary would be at a disadvantage if she were placed in an environment that is intellectually impoverished and not challenging; thus, disclosure is right. Again, matters of fact affect moral judgments.

Dealing with the Cause of a Disability

Two students in your special education program (you are the school special education director) pose interesting problems in working with their parents. Jennie had been classified as having autism. Larry has moderate mental retardation.

In Jennie's case, the cause of her autism is not clear. One psychiatrist, who examined her at the school's request, suggested that her mother is so disturbed herself that she may be a cause of Jennie's disability. Another psychiatrist, however, strongly rejects this theory, saying it is not consistent with current research.

In Larry's case, there is no doubt that his retardation was caused by his mother's excessive alcohol consumption during pregnancy; Larry has fetal alcohol syndrome. In both cases, Jennie's and Larry's parents are committed to their children. In Larry's case, his mother is wholly remorseful and feels exceptionally guilty about the etiology of his retardation. It also is clear that both students and their parents would profit from counseling because both families have multiple psychological problems to resolve. The mothers, however, resist entering school-based counseling (or any other counseling), because they do not see how it would help their children, and they accuse the school of meddlesome interference. You recognize the desirability of having counselors work with the mothers. One of the professional staff suggests that you should "try a little guilt . . . it works wonders" (the so-called "guilt-trip technique"). She argues that, since the mothers were the cause of the disabilities, they should be willing to be the cause of a "cure." You have doubts about the causation, but believe a great deal of good could result from counseling.

Do you blame the parents, using the guilt-trip technique? Do you blame each of them equally, even though the causation in Jennie's case is not clear? Do you use it in the case of Larry, where the etiology is clear? Do you ask, "So what if the parents do not go to counseling—what difference would it make to the students?" After asking that question, do you conclude that it might make a positive difference? Again, we see mixed questions of fact and moral judgment. The lesson is the same: Be sure of your facts before making any judgments. What do you do then?

Here, the classical, utilitarian, and causalist approaches may favor the guilt-trip technique as a means of obtaining a result (therapy) that may be helpful. Specifically, from a classical perspective, counseling may help the parents understand their children and their development. From a utilitarian perspective, the greatest good is the mothers' mental health and their children's development; the greatest number of people helped is four [two sets of mother-child(ren)]. Finally, from a causalist perspective, there will be little, if any, harm to the children or their parents, who as a group already are in need of mental health intervention. But these approaches are disrespectful of the parents and may make their relations with the school and their children even worse; thus, the Categorical Imperative argues against using that technique, since it treats the children as means and not ends—as ways to get to their parents. The Categorical Imperative also disapproves of the guilt-trip technique because it is an exception to the rule that equal treatment of people in similar circumstances fosters respect and improves familial relations.

Also, the same result may be obtained by other means. Finally, the reciprocity doctrine seems ambiguous. Neither parent wants counseling, but both probably would benefit by it, although not if they are brought to that result by these methods.

Treating the "Real" Client

Charles is a 10-year-old child who is both gifted and has a severe hearing impairment. For a variety of reasons, transferring him from the local school, where you are the school psychologist, to the state school for students who are deaf is not possible. You have seen Charles on several occasions—principally to determine the causes of his increased withdrawal from social contact with other students (as a younger boy, he was quite gregarious). You have decided there is little you or anyone else can do for him except to wait out his adolescence. You are pessimistic about his future, knowing that research indicates that, as they grow older, children with severe hearing impairments become more and more isolated from people who hear normally. You have interviewed Charles' parents, Eleanor (who also has a hearing impairment) and Robert (who does not), and you realize that you can do a great deal for them if they will enter into therapy with you (you have an after-school private practice).

Who is the "real" client? Charles, or Eleanor and Robert? Suppose you also have been working with Charles' younger brother, Eric, who also has a hearing impairment but is much more determined and optimistic than Charles about being accepted at school. Do you make comparisons between Charles and Eric when working with their parents? Do you even make comparisons about Eleanor's approach (she is very nurturing with Charles, very sympathetic) and Robert's (he is much more demanding)? Do you side with one parent or the other?

The family-systems perspective suggests that there is no conflict here, no need to decide who the real client is because it considers the family as a whole and says that professionals should try to help the family meet everyone's needs. But Charles is the student and you are employed by the school system to work with students. That seems to mean, from your perspective as a school employee, that he is the real client. From your perspective as a psychologist with a private practice, however, it may appear that Charles' parents are the true clients. And from your perspective, again as a school employee, the true client might be Eric, for whom prevention of social isolation seems desirable and possible.

The problems here are similar to those in the immediately preceding case. But there is the extra dimension of the younger brother, Eric. Does your decision depend on its effect on Eric? If so, how? If Eric can be helped by helping Charles, Eleanor, and Robert, it seems that any decision about them is made more right if it also can help him. This is a utilitarian approach, because it maximizes good among a larger number of people.

The Advocacy Issue

Miguel is the son of Rosita and Hernandez, both of whom recently immigrated to the United States illegally, but have been given amnesty to stay. Miguel was born in the United States, so he is a U.S. citizen. He is educationally puzzling. School evaluations show him to either have mild mental retardation or a significant learning problem. The school district in a southwestern state is under pressure from the state education department to reduce the special education enrollment. Indeed, it has been threatened with a lawsuit if it places too many Hispanic Americans in its programs for students with mild mental retardation or learning disabilities.

You are the director of special education in the district and a firm believer in special education for Miguel and students like him. Research data and your own experience of 15 years in the district convince you that special education placement is preferable to regular education placement because of the individualized instruction provided and the success of eventual phase-out from special education. You know you soon will be asked to make a recommendation concerning Miguel's placement.

Do you have an ethical duty to be an advocate for Miguel, as Rosenberg et al. (1983), Heshusius (1982), and Hyman and Schreiber (1975) argue? Or is the duty to the child based on research data or local experience? Do you have a duty as an administrator to serve as advocate for the school district, which is under extreme pressure from the state education department and may face a lawsuit? Does it make any difference that all local, state, and federal special education funds already have been budgeted, and that special education placement of Miguel may result in withdrawal of funds from regular to special education?

This case poses a difficult question about loyalty. The Greeks' Golden Mean may tell you that some (but not excessive) advocacy is required for Miguel. The reciprocity approach will move you to become an advocate for Miguel only if you put yourself in his shoes alone. But if you consider the district's limited resources, you may reach a different result based on the reciprocity perspective—one that favors the mainstream for Miguel and takes account of the needs of other special education students. Finally, you also may adopt a utilitarian perspective and conclude that the interests of the group of all special education students outweigh the interests of Miguel, individually.

The Dual-Loyalty Issue

You are a classroom teacher in a school district that serves the residents of a black ghetto in one of America's largest cities. Trained in social welfare and special education, you have become increasingly convinced that the district is taking advantage of the parents. For example, its consent forms are full of educational jargon and legalese. Although they may be legal, they are not helpful. In addition, the way in which parents' consent for evaluation, programming, and placement is obtained seems coercive to you. Finally, you have strong reason to believe that the school district routinely violates special education students' rights.

Thus, your concerns are twofold: First, you are concerned about the parents, who have no real control over their children's programs; and second, you are concerned about the inadequacy of the school's programs for the children. In this frame of mind, you attend a meeting of a local teacher-parent group and listen with increasing discomfort to the school principal gloss over problems or misstate facts.

To whom does your loyalty run? To the school, which employs you and provides some programs? To the parents, who may be able to recapture some stake in their children's lives and by collective action improve the school for them and other children? To the children, who may leave the school before any improvements occur and who also may be subject to informal discipline or casual sanctions if their parents become too involved in their education? Would you be willing to attend the next meeting of the parent group and set the record straight? Does it matter what the last teacher who set the record straight, several years ago, still has not been given lucrative summer-school teaching opportunities and has been assigned regularly to the least desirable administrative tasks in school? Does it matter, too, that there is a rumor that the school board will try to fire the next teacher who "gets out of line?"

The dual-loyalty issue is a hard one. Here, we clearly see that the right or wrong action depends on the perspective you take—whether the students' and their parents', or the school's. The doctrines do not give you clear-cut answers.

In addition to the dual-loyalty issue comes the problem of "whistle-blowing" (Bok, 1980; Nader, Petkas, & Blackwell, 1972). The issue is this: Should the employee "squeal" or "blow the whistle" on the employer and should that be done publicly; or are there less noticeable ways to be an advocate (Crary, 1980)?

From the utilitarian perspective, your duty is to the greatest number of people. Therefore, you need to decide if your action in setting the record straight will benefit anyone, and, if so, how many and for how long. From the perspective of the Golden Mean, you need not make a public protest because it suggests that there may be other ways to be effective and that they should be used before resorting to public protest.

The reciprocity doctrines are ambiguous in application. On the one hand, they say that you should be loyal to the students and parents, as you would want them to be loyal to you. On the other hand, you may ask whether the parents and students would put their jobs at risk for you. That is not a proper question under the reciprocity doctrines, because those doctrines do not involve making deals. Yet, many people would ask that very question (make a deal), and that fact alone makes the reciprocity doctrines ambiguous in application though they should not be.

Under the Categorical Imperative, it would be wrong for your co-employees to take formal or informal sanctions against you or the students, since that would use people as a means of retribution and not as ends in themselves or as valued people. But you cannot be sure that the school board will behave as Kant would under the Imperative. Indeed, you think it will not; rather, the school board and some school officials might violate that principle in the way they deal with the students and parents. Finally, causalism may tell you that the harmful effects of your protest would be felt by you yourself as well as by the children and parents. So causalism may dictate that you find other means for correcting the problem.

Consent and Choice by Teachers, Parents, and Students

Renee is a teenager who, for several years has expressed to her parents, Murray and Kirsten, a dissatisfaction with her learning disabilities (LD) program at the high school. In talking with some university faculty who are conducting research in learning disabilities at the school, Renee learns that she has the right under the EHA to attend her own IEP conference if it is "appropriate" for her to do so. She also learns that "appropriateness" has not been defined by law, but that data show that student participation in IEPs is academically and emotionally helpful to the student.

Renee asks you, the LD program director, for permission to attend her next IEP conference. You recognize the critical role that consent and choice play (Guess et al., 1985; Guess & Siegel-Causey, 1985; Shevin & Klein, 1984; A. P. Turnbull & Turnbull, 1984, 1988; H. R. Turnbull, 1981) in the academic, social, and emotional maturation of children and youth. You know that in a year or two Renee will enter a transition phase from school to postsecondary education and that her curriculum next year will be geared to independent living. Besides, you see in Renee a squelched spirit because of constant frustration in her education.

With this in mind, you discuss Renee's wishes and her rights with her parents and the special education director. Her father thinks Renee's participation is "silly—she's still just a girl." But Kirsten, her mother, is keen on it—"she needs to be on her own one day, and we'd all better get ready for it." The special education director is adamantly opposed and cites his experience ("special education kids jut can't have a meaningful role") in the precedent issue ("we'll have every kid in school telling us what to teach and how, and we're the professionals, not the kids").

Putting aside for this case the potential problems related to advocacy and dual loyalty (which we discussed before), what is the "right" thing to do? When and how much consent and choice should the professional give a student? Remember that when the professional does not help the student develop independence by providing training in consent, choice, and decision making, the professional may make the student more dependent on family and professionals, thereby, in turn, also making the family more dependent on the student.

The classical approach will be to include Renee in her IEP conference, if that will increase her capacities. The reciprocity doctrine is ambiguous, and the result will depend on whose perspective you adopt. The Categorical Imperative tends to favor Renee's participation, as she will be treated as a more valued person when she participates. The utilitarian approach also may favor her participation because, in the long run, she will become more independent of school and parents. Finally, the causalist approach may suggest that little if any harm will come because Renee's participation can be controlled or limited by adults and it will not become a precedent for all students.

CONSIDERING ALTERNATIVES

You may have noticed that we have described problems in which you must deal with a given intervention or action by a professional. Perhaps you even remarked to yourself that there may be alternatives to a certain intervention or action. If so, you are correct.

We stated problems that have specific interventions or actions to make you think about the moral thing to do. Now you may want to develop alternative interventions and actions to each situation. For example, in the case of "screening, evaluation, and referral" involving the preschool girl who had a hearing disability and who lived in a rural community, it may have been possible for the mother and local professionals to obtain training about interventions, to make trips to the distant clinic less often but for longer periods of time, or to obtain the services of an itinerant professional. Likewise for the "cause of disability," it may have been possible to persuade the mothers to enter counseling by some means other than the "guilt-trip technique." Similarly, in the case of the "dual loyalty," the professional may secretly approach an "outside" advocate (such as a spokesperson for the parent group), protest to the principal, persuade the principal to correct the impressions he created, remain quiet until he or she has power to correct the situation without being fired, or leave the job. So, in each problem as well as in your professional life, you may seek alternatives. After identifying them, you still may be in doubt whether they are right or wrong. If so, you may use the same procedure for those questions as we have described here.

The questions in the "screening, evaluation, and referral" case involve efficacy, that is, will the proposed action be effective and have the intended results and are there equally effective or nearly effective alternatives? Matters of fact here must be rigorously separated from matters of moral judgment. You must determine the facts (is the intervention efficacious?) before making a moral judgment (is it right to use the intervention?). A central question is this case or in a similar case of an arguable intervention, therefore, is this: Is it your duty to use only the curriculum, procedures, methods, settings, and technology that actually benefit a student, or at least does not harm the student, according to research data and professional experience? The self-evident answer is "yes." But turn the question around: May the professional use an intervention that has no benefit and actually may harm a student without offsetting benefit? The self-evident answer is "no." Yet, nonefficacious treatments (Clark, 1987; Lennox, Miltenberger, Spentler, & Erfanian, 1988) have been used and they have been the focus of moral argument against their use (H. R. Turnbull & Guess, 1986).

In addition, consider the possibility that a curriculum, procedure, method, setting, or technology may also have a negative effect on the teacher or other professional involved. This may be the case when an intervention such as the shout-point-slap procedure so depersonalizes the student-professional relationship that the student becomes an "object" in the professional's mind. (According to a different perspective, depersonalization is a professional coping strategy that allows more consistent application of an intervention and reduces the personal anxiety about the intervention's use.)

Consider, too, the possibility that the intervention may have harmful effects on other students. This would be the case where, for example, the intervention, when carried out in the presence of other students, results in making them so afraid of the professional that any intervention by the professional will be resisted, feared, or avoided and, thus, be less effective.

Finally, consider the family-systems perspective. What effect will the intervention have on the child and other family members individually? What effect will it have on the family as a whole?

In the case of the shout-point-slap intervention for nail biting, the efficacy questions are these: First, does the intervention work—does it stop the behavior? Second, what other effects does it have on the student and are those effects negative (e.g., does the child avoid contact with the professional, thus rendering any interventions ineffective?) Third, what effects does it have on other students and are those effects positive (e.g., does it keep them from similar behavior?) or negative (does it make them want to avoid the professional, thus rendering any other interventions ineffective?)? Fourth, what effects does it have on the professional? Fifth, what effects does it have on family members and the family as a whole? Once these questions have been answered, it is possible to determine if the procedure is right or wrong by following the guide set out in this chapter. Indeed, as we have tried to show, it is possible to apply that procedure, once the facts are known about a situation, to all situations.

Let us now review the process we have described. An example of the shout-point-slap procedure is in Table 14–2.

For each problem, you may want to construct a chart analysis such as the one illustrated in Table 14–3.

Using this technique, you are determining the right or wrong behavior by treating each of the principles equally. That is, there is no greater reason to apply one than another. The right or wrong action will then depend on the totality of the applied principles. You decide which action is right by determining which is more often right than not under each of the principles. This is a very mechanical approach, even somewhat simplistic and, for that reason, it may not be appealing. But it gives general guidance. Of course, you may reject this approach and treat any of the principles as having an exclusive (or a greater) claim to your morals than any other.

TABLE 14–2   Suggestions for Applying an Analytical Approach to Decision Making

---

- State the problem: A student is injuring herself, both physically and socially by severe nail biting.

- State the facts and distinguish them from moral judgments.

- State the ethical issue: Based on our knowledge about an intervention, is it moral to use a point-shout-slap method to correct the problem?

- Consider the alternatives to that intervention: Can other interventions prevent the behavior without having effects on the student, family, other students, and the professional that are more negative than the proposed intervention?

- Repeat the issue: When is a proposed or an alternative intervention moral? Answer the question by applying professional and philosophical principles.

TABLE 14–3 Chart Analysis

Principles	PROPOSED ACTION	ALTERNATIVE A	ALTERNATIVE B
		Does the principle apply?	
1. Classicists	Yes	Maybe	Yes
2. Golden Rule	No	No	Yes
3. Categorical Imperative	Yes	No	Yes
4. Utilitarianism	Maybe	No	Yes
5. Causalism	Maybe	No	Yes

SUMMARY

As you make your decision about the right or wrong of an action, keep the family-systems perspective in the front of your mind. Do this by asking questions about the interests of all the members of the student's family. Remember, too, that there are other legitimate perspectives to be considered, namely, those of the school system and its professionals and those of other students.

We hope we have been successful in accomplishing the purposes of this chapter, which are to:

1. Make you more aware of moral problems in your profession,
2. Help you understand why it is important to consider the ethics of a situation,
3. Help you apply the major ethical perspectives that you might take into account in determining the right thing to do,
4. Show you how those perspectives can be applied, and
5. Help you think in moral terms, so that you yourself will be more able to act thoughtfully when you confront tough issues.

It is now time for an epilogue, a final word about this book and its messages.

EPILOGUE

In the first edition of this book, we suggested that a revolution was happening in the field of exceptionality. That revolution, we said, was the adoption of a family-systems approach to working with people with exceptionalities. It was one that expected professionals to be competent to work not just with the student, but with the student's family as well.

In this edition we also have made another assumption. It, too, contains an element of revolution. We have assumed that families, professionals, and students with an exceptionality should form a partnership on the basis of articulated principles, sometimes called "philosophy" or "values." In the preface, we describe the principles that guide our work and that permeate this book.

We hope that you, the reader, will embrace two fundamental points: First, that the family-system framework is useful and indeed indispensable in your work; and second, that the principles of positive contributions, great expectations, full citizenship, relationships, choices, and strengths are relevant to your work and should be incorporated into it, just as we have incorporated them into this book.

If you are committed to improving the lives of people with an exceptionality and their families, you should emphasize their positive contributions, raise their expectations and your own, strive to have them attain full citizenship, enhance and enlarge their friendships and choices, and help them build on their inherent strengths. By doing all of this, you will change not just theory but yourself and the world as well.

A P P E N D I C E S

A. RESOURCES FOR FAMILIES AND PROFESSIONALS:
    PUBLICATIONS, AUDIOVISUALS, AND
    INFORMATION/REFERRAL CENTERS ON FAMILIES
    AND DISABILITY

B. GUIDE FOR GATHERING FAMILY INFORMATION
    THROUGH DISCUSSION

RESOURCES FOR FAMILIES AND PROFESSIONALS

The following resources (publications, audiovisuals, and information/referral centers on families and disability) will give you access to information not included in the text because of limitations for length and content. This resource list is not exhaustive; it is meant as a starting point for your further studies as a student and for your resource file as a professional.

The printed publications are divided into the following topic areas: coping, family members, families with special challenges, future planning, health-related issues, integration, legal issues, multicultural issues, parent-professional communication, and parent-written books. Publisher's addresses and phone numbers follow the section on audiovisuals, and the information and referral sources include a state listing of parent training and information (PTI) projects.

PRINTED INFORMATION

Coping

Galbraith, J. (1983). *The gifted kids' survival guide.* Minneapolis: Free Spirit Publishing, Inc.

This book, written for children who are gifted, discusses issues surrounding friendship, stress, and school. The appendix includes resources for both children and their families.

Goldfarb, L. A., Brotherson, M. J., Summers, J. A., & Turnbull, A. P. (1986). *Meeting the challenge of disability or chronic illness: A family guide.* Baltimore: Paul H. Brookes Publishing Co.

This self-help book describes a process families can use to identify and address their needs and strengths. Steps in problem solving are explained and supplemented by family examples and self-help exercises.

Greenspan, S., & Greenspan, N. T. (1989). *The essential partnership: How parents and children can meet the emotional challenges of infancy and childhood.* New York: Viking Penguin, Inc.

This work is a sequel to *First Feelings,* a book which describes the six stages of emotional growth of early childhood. *The Essential Partnership* applies these stages to everyday situations that families of young children face.

Kelker, K. A. (1988). *Taking charge: A handbook for parents whose children have emotional handicaps.* Portland State University: Research and Training Center to Improve Services for Seriously Emotionally Handicapped Children and their Families.

This handbook for families of children with emotional disabilities discusses the impact of emotional disability upon the family, legal issues, and types of services available. A bibliography is included for each chapter. Professionals as well as family members will find this guide informative.

Madara, E. J., & Meese, A. (1988). *The self-help sourcebook: Finding and forming mutual aid self-help groups.* Denville, NJ: Self-Help Clearinghouse, St. Clares-Riverside Medical Center.

This guide is a compilation of national clearinghouses and support groups for disability, parenting, women, veterans, genetic disorders, and other subjects. Suggestions for how to develop self-help groups are given.

Perske, R., & Perske, M. (1988). *Circles of friends: People with disabilities and their friends enrich the lives of one another.* Nashville: Abingdon Press.

This book emphasizes the value of friendships between people with disabilities and people without disabilities. Many firsthand examples enhance the relevance and humanness of the information.

Salisbury, C., & Intagliata, J. (1986). *Respite care: Support for persons with developmental disabilities and their families.* Baltimore, MD: Paul H. Brookes Publishing Co.

This book examines respite-care programs from both theoretical and applied viewpoints. The need for services, models for service delivery, and evaluation of programs are discussed.

Silver, L. B. (1984). *The misunderstood child.* New Jersey: McGraw-Hill Book Company.

This book written for families with members who have a learning disability, will also give professionals insight to the many issues facing these families. Topics include: basic questions; psychosocial, emotional, and social development; diagnosis; treatment; and legal issues.

Webb, J., Meckstroth, E., & Tolan, S. (1982). *Guiding the gifted child: A practical source for parents and teachers.* Columbus, OH: Ohio Psychology Publishing Company.

This succinct book is a helpful resource for both families and professionals. It is a winner of the American Psychological Association Book of the Year Award.

Family Members

Einstein, E., & Albert, L. (1986). *Strengthening stepfamilies.* Circle Pines, MN: American Guidance Service.

This comprehensive workshop kit focuses on stepfamily issues. Portions could easily be incorporated into workshops/support group sessions for families with a member who has a disability.

Meyer, D. J., & Vadasy, P. F. (1986). *Grandparents' Workshop: How to organize workshops for grandparents of children with disabilities.* Seattle: University of Washington Press.

This guide provides information to professionals on how to organize support groups for grandparents of children with a disability. Activities and discussions address the concerns of these family members.

Meyer, D. J., Vadasy, P. F., & Fewell, R. R. (1985). *Living with a brother or sister with special needs: A book for sibs.* Seattle: University of Washington Press.

Stressing the positive aspects of living with a sister or brother with a disability, this book provides specific strategies for helping siblings deal with their feelings, better understanding disabilities, and succeeding in living with a sister or brother with an exceptionality.

Meyer, D. J., Vadasy, P. F., & Fewell, R. R. (1985). *Sibshops: How to organize workshops for brothers and sisters of children with special needs.* Seattle: University of Washington Press.

This workshop handbook provides professionals with an understanding of brothers and sisters of individuals with a disability. The guide suggests goals and activities to meet the needs of these often-overlooked family members.

Meyer, D. J., Vadasy, P. F., Fewell, R. R., & Schell, G. C. (1985). *A handbook for the father's program: How to organize a program for fathers and their children with disabilities.* Seattle: University of Washington Press.

This handbook provides professionals, agencies, and fathers with information on how to organize a community father's support program. The guide also helps professionals stimulate new ideas about how best to support all members of the child's family.

Powell, T. H., & Ogle, P. A. (1985). *Brothers and sisters: A special part of exceptional families.* Baltimore: Paul H. Brookes Publishing Co.
This resource will benefit both families and professionals by suggesting techniques and services that will help brothers and sisters of children with a disability better understand the feelings and circumstances which surround the experience of growing up with a brother or sister with an exceptionality.

Families with Special Challenges

Hope, M., & Young, J. (1986). *The faces of homelessness.* Lexington, MA: D.C. Heath & Co.
This book discusses the growing problem of the homeless in the U.S.—the population affected, the causes of the problem, current service systems, and proposals for the future.

Mustin, J. W. (Ed.). (1988). Families of prisoners [Special issue]. *Nurturing Today, X*(1).
This issue is devoted to concerns of families who have a member in prison. Impact on the family, the prisoner, and innovative programs for family support are among the issues discussed.

Sidel, R. (1986). *Women and children last: The plight of poor women in affluent America.* New York: Viking Penguin.
This book describes the lives of women and children who are living in poverty in the United States. Sidel analyzes how and why they came to live in poverty and presents a family policy that will provide aid for this growing segment of our population.

Thuman, S. K. (Ed.). (1985). *Children of handicapped parents: Research and clinical perspectives.* Orlando, FL: Academic Press.
This volume examines research and clinical problems relating to family members whose parents have a disability. Research models and strategies for professionals who are interested in parent-child relationships or family interactions are presented.

Future Planning

Edgar, E., & Heinowski, J. (1985). *Parents as case managers: Training workshop materials.* Seattle: University of Washington Press.
These training materials for parents and/or professionals focus on case management for children exiting special education programs in the public schools. The workshop may be adapted to encompass transition in other situations as well.

Mount, B., & Zwernik, K. (1988). *It's never too early, it's never too late.* Publication No. 421-88-109. St. Paul, MN: Metropolitan Council.

This booklet discusses personal-futures planning for persons with developmental disabilities, their families and friends, case managers, service providers, and advocates. The strategies focus on the gifts and abilities of people with developmental disabilities.

Orlansky, M. C., & Heward, W. L. (1981). *Voices: Interviews with handicapped people.* Columbus, OH: Charles E. Merrill Publishing Co.

Interviews with 53 people with disabilities about their lives, their disabilities, and their hopes and dreams.

Pueschel, S. M. (1988). *The young person with Down syndrome: Transition from adolescence to adulthood.* Baltimore: Paul H. Brookes Publishing Co.

This resource will benefit families and professionals who want to help adolescents with disabilities prepare for independent living, sexuality, employment, recreation, social integration, and self-awareness and esteem in adulthood.

Turnbull, H. R., Turnbull, A. P., Bronicki, G. J., Summers, J. A., & Roeder-Gordon, C. (1989). *Disability and the family: A guide to decisions for adulthood.* Baltimore: Paul H. Brookes Publishing Co.

This guide is an aid to families who are concerned with the interpersonal, recreational, employment, and residential preferences and needs of their family member with a disability. Information is also included on financial planning and decision making when mental competence is limited (guardianship and alternatives).

Health-Related Issues

Beckett, J. (1989). *Health care financing: A guide for families.* Iowa City, IA: National Maternal and Child Health Resource Center.

This resource describes public and private services available to families of children with special needs. Coping with diverse service systems, advocacy, funding options, and resource organizations and agencies at state and local levels are discussed.

Jones, M. L. (1985). *Home care for the chronically ill or disabled child: A manual and source book for parents and professionals.* Washington, DC: Association for the Care of Children's Health.

This book provides a parent's perspective on issues of concern to family members who care for someone with a disability or a chronic illness at home. Suggestions for organization of the home, financial planning, and coping with specific disabilities are given.

Shelton, T. L., Jeppson, E. S., & Johnson, B. H. (1987). *Family-centered care for children with special health care needs.* Washington, DC: Association for the Care of Children's Health.

This book examines family-centered care, with examples of programs and policies. Resources for technical assistance, programs and audiovisual materials are suggested.

Integration

Biklen, D. (1985). *Achieving the complete school: Strategies for effective mainstreaming.* New York: Teachers College Press.
This guide describes proven strategies for effective school integration. The roles of administrators, principals, teachers, and parents are discussed.

Knoll, J. (1987). *Annotated bibliography on community integration for people with severe disabilities.* Syracuse University: Research and Training Center on Community Integration.
This comprehensive bibliography provides detailed annotations of books, manuals, and research articles of interest to professionals and families. Community living, respite care, and case management are among the many interest areas covered.

Perske, R. (1980). *New life in the neighborhood: How persons with retardation or other disabilities can help make a good community better.* Nashville, TN: Abingdon Press.
This book, beautifully illustrated by Martha Perske, examines issues surrounding community integration. Quality of life, property values, sexuality, and neighborhood relationships are all discussed in an easy-to-understand format.

Schaeffer, B., Buswell, B., Summerfield, A., & Kovar, G. (1988). *Discover the possibilities: A curriculum for teaching parents about integration.* Colorado Springs, CO: PEAK Parent Center.
This model of a workshop for educating teachers, administrators, parents, and others about integration is written by parents of children with a disability. The philosophy of integration is described; samples of overheads and a timeline for a workshop are included.

Vandercook, T., York, J., & Mutuszuk, P. (1988). *Integrated education for learners with severe disabilities: Print and media resources.* University of Minnesota: Institute on Community Integration.
This annotated bibliography constitutes a comprehensive resource for parents and professionals who are interested in journal articles, books, manuals, newsletters and audiovisual materials on integrated education. Annual revisions of this bibliography are planned.

Legal Issues

Russell, L. M. (1983). *Alternatives: A family guide to legal and financial planning for the disabled.* Evanston, IL: First Publications, Inc.

This resource addresses the legal and financial issues of wills, guardianships, trusts, taxes, insurance, and future planning facing families with a member who has a disability.

Turnbull, H. R. (1990) *Free appropriate public education: Law and the education of children with disabilities.* Denver: Love Publishing Co.

This book provides a case-law and legislative analysis of the six major principles of P.L. 94–142—zero reject, nondiscriminatory evaluation, appropriate education, least restrictive placement, due process, and parent participation.

Turnbull, H. R. (1989). Technology and children with disabilities: A guide for family members. *Take advantage of the law.* Lawrence: The University of Kansas, Beach Center on Families and Disability.

The first in a series of brief guides explaining disability law to family members, this booklet focuses on P.L. 100–407 and P.L. 100–360. These two laws can help families obtain technology services or devices for members with disabilities.

Multicultural Issues

Ho, M. K. (1987). *Family therapy with ethnic minorities.* Beverly Hills, CA: Sage Publications.

This author examines current theories, models, and techniques relevant to ethnic-minority family functioning and therapy. Cultural values are explored and specific suggestions on culturally significant family therapy skills for each ethnic group are provided.

Mindel, C. H., & Habenstein, R. W. (Eds.). (1988). *Ethnic families in America: Patterns and variation* (3rd ed.). New York: Elsevier Publications.

This anthology on "minority" families examines ethnic family strengths and needs as well as historical background and demographic characteristics.

Toward multiculturalism [Special issue]. (1989). *Coalition Quarterly, 6*(2&3). Boston: Technical Assistance for Parent Programs.

This issue of *Coalition Quarterly* is an excellent source for background information about multicultural issues, overviews of cultural perspectives on the family and disability, and strategies for integration of multicultural sensitivity into a program. Numerous resources for professionals are included.

Turnbull, H. R., & Turnbull, A. P. (1987, May). *The Latin American family and public policy in the United States: Informal support and transition into adulthood.* Unpublished manuscript, University of Kansas, Beach Center on Families and Disability.

A World Rehabilitation Fund (WRF) Grant funded this study and report on the adaptations, coping strategies and use of informal support in Latin American families with a member who has a disability. The Latin American family and its traditions, attitudes, and behaviors with respect to the transition of the member with a disability from adolescence to adulthood are discussed.

Parent-Professional Communication

Berg, K., Gilman, A., & Stevenson, E. (1989). *Get to the point: How to say what you mean and get what you want.* New York: Bantam Books.
This book explains how to influence and encourage the listener to hear what you are saying, instead of reacting to your position.

Des Jardins, C. (1980). *How to organize an effective parent/advocacy group and move bureaucracies.* Minneapolis: PACER Center, Inc.
This manual discusses the nature of advocacy as well as such issues as how to advocate effectively, choose effective leaders, and educate families about their rights.

Fisher, R., & Ury, W. (1981). *Getting to yes: Negotiating agreement without giving in.* New York: Viking Penguin, Inc.
This book discusses effective negotiation without a win-lose attitude and successful negotiation with those you may perceive to be more powerful than you.

Kohn, A. (1986). *No contest: The case against competition—why we lose in our race to win.* Boston: Houghton Mifflin Co.
This book explains how we are socialized to pit ourselves against each other in a competitive situation. The author argues against this unproductive approach and suggests how we can be successful without it.

Strayhorn, J. M. (1984). *Talking it out: A guide to effective communication and problem-solving.* Champaign, IL: Research Press.
This book describes several types of communication skills that facilitate or obstruct problem solving in family, social, and work settings. Examples and role-plays are included to facilitate comprehension.

Parent-Written Books

Bratt, B. (1989). *No time for jello: One family's experiences with the Doman-Delcato "patterning" program.* Cambridge, MA: Brookline Books.

Berneen Bratt, the mother of a son with cerebral palsy, tells the story of her family's search for a cure for her son's condition through the Doman-Delcato "patterning" program. The book helps families weigh the considerations involved in choosing treatment programs for their family members. The importance of programs which are responsive to both the child's and the family's needs is stressed.

Deford, F. (1983). *Alex: The life of a child.* New York: Viking Penguin.

Frank Deford tells the story of his daughter's life and death, and about the ways in which her courage impacted her parents, brother, friends, and the adults around her.

Featherstone, H. (1980). *A difference in the family: Living with a disabled child.* New York: Viking Penguin.

Helen Featherstone, educator and mother of a child with severe disabilities, discusses ways in which families cope positively with their feelings. This book offers reassurance and invaluable guidance to families and helps professionals be more supportive and understanding.

Rose, H. W. (1987). *Something's wrong with my child.* Springfield, IL: Charles C Thomas.

Harriet Rose describes her family's experiences with Nancy, her daughter with a disability. Personal accounts are interspersed among chapters which focus on such issues as grief and marriage in more universal terms. The author encourages parents to see their child first as a child, and to feel adequate as parents even though they are not disability specialists.

Turnbull, H. R., & Turnbull, A. P. (1985). *Parents speak out: Then and now.* Columbus, OH: Charles E. Merrill Publishing Co.

Fifteen essays by parents and siblings, most of whom also have some professional connection to the field of disability provide first-hand anecdotal insights into family impact and adaptation. Two essays are included from most of the contributors—one from 1978 (1st edition) and a second from 1985 (2nd edition). This "longitudinal" approach provides a rare glimpse of family changes over time.

AUDIOVISUALS

Atkins, P. (Producer). (1986). *Seasons of caring* [Film or Videotape, and study guide]. Washington, DC: Association for the Care of Children's Health.

This 40-minute audiovisual focuses on how to raise a child with a chronic illness or a disability. Family adjustment is discussed with an emphasis on the importance of mutual respect between families and professionals. The father's role is stressed.

Forest, M., & Flynn, G. (Producers). (1989). *With a little help from my friends*. Niwot, CO: Expectations Unlimited.

This hour-long video focuses on school integration experiences. Students and teachers discuss their friendships and successes, and an example of a planning curriculum, MAPS, is included.

Godwin, T., & Wurzburg, G. (Producers). (1988). *Regular lives* [Videotape]. Seattle, WA: TASH.

Award-winning documentary on people with developmental disabilities who are integrated into typical school, work, and living environments.

Levy, J. M. (Director). (1987). *Children with special needs* [Videotape series]. New York: Young Adult Institute.

These videotapes provide information and support to families and professionals in a series of 36 half-hour tapes which can be used sequentially or alone. Topics include parent, professional, family, developmental, transitional, and therapeutic issues.

Levy, J. M. (Director). (1987). *On our own* [Videotape series]. New York: Young Adult Institute.

This series of videotapes focuses on adolescent and adult issues such as sexuality and wills and trusts; employment issues such as social and interpersonal skills and the roles of employers and co-workers; and transition issues such as family-support systems and parent/professional collaboration. Training manuals are also available.

PACER Center. (1987). *Parents' voices: A few speak for many* [Videotape]. Minneapolis: PACER Center.

This videotape is designed to promote collaboration between professionals and families of children with severe emotional disorders. First-person accounts of parents' perspectives on the barriers to effective working relationships between parents and professionals are presented.

Samuelson, D. (Director). (1989). *Special kids, special dads—fathers of children with disabilities* [Videotape and discussion guide]. Bellevue, WA: SEFAM Family Support Program.

This videotape, focusing on fathers of children with special needs, discusses issues involving fathers' roles in their families. The importance of increased involvement of fathers in the lives of their children is stressed.

PUBLISHER INFORMATION

Abingdon Press   (800) 672-1789
201 8th Avenue South
P.O. Box 801
Nashville, TN 37202

Academic Press   (800) 321-5068
465 South Lincoln Dr.
Troy, MO 63379

American Guidance Service   (800) 328-2560
Publishers' Building
P.O. Box 99
Circle Pines, MN 55014

Association for the Care of Children's Health (ACCH)   (202) 244-1801
3615 Wisconsin Avenue, N.W.
Washington, DC 20016

Bantam Books   (212) 765-6500
666 Fifth Ave.
New York, NY 10103

Beach Center on Families and Disability   (913) 864-7600
Bureau of Child Research
4138 Haworth Hall
University of Kansas
Lawrence, KS 66045

Brookes Publishing Co.   (800) 638-3775
P.O. Box 10624
Baltimore, MD 21285-0624

Brookline Books   (617) 868-0360
P.O. Box 1046
Cambridge, MA 02238

D.C. Heath & Co.   (617) 862-6650
125 Spring St.
Lexington, MA 02173

Elsevier Publications   (212) 989-5800
655 Avenue of the Americas
New York, NY 10010

Eugene Edgar   (206) 543-4011
EEU, WJ-10
University of Washington
Seattle, WA 98195

Expectations Unlimited, Inc.   (303) 652-2727
6897 Paiute Avenue
Longmont, CO 80501

First Publications, Inc.   (312) 869-7210
P.O. Box 5072
Evanston, IL 60204

Free Spirit Publishing, Inc.   (612) 338-2068
123 N. 3rd St., Suite 716
Minneapolis, MN 55401

Houghton Mifflin Co.   (617) 725-5000
Wayside Rd.
Burlington, MA 01803

Institute on Community Integration   (612) 624-4848
6 Pattee Hall
University of Minnesota
150 Pillsbury Dr., S.E.
Minneapolis, MN 55455

Love Publishing Co.   (303) 757-2579
1777 South Bellaire St.
Denver, CO 80222

McGraw-Hill Book Company   (212) 512-2000
Princeton-Hightstown Rd.
Hightstown, NJ 08520

Merrill Publishing Co.   (800) 848-1567
P.O. Box 508
Columbus, OH 43216-0508

Metropolitan Council   (612) 291-8140
Mears Park Centre
230 East Fifth Street
St. Paul, MN 55101

National Maternal and Child Health Resource Center
College of Law Building   (319) 335-9067
The University of Iowa
Melrose & Byington
Iowa City, IA 52242

Nurturing Today   (415) 861-0847
187 Caselli Avenue
San Francisco, CA 94114

Ohio Psychology Publishing Co.   (614) 224-3288
400 E. Town St., Suite 020
Columbus, OH 43215

PACER Center   (612) 827-2966
4826 Chicago Ave. South
Minneapolis, MN 55417-1055

PEAK Parent Center, Inc.   (719) 531-9400
6055 Lehman Drive, Suite 101
Colorado Springs, CO 80918

Research and Training Center on Community Integration
The Center on Human Policy   (315) 443-3851
Syracuse University
200 Huntington Hall
Syracuse, NY 13244-2340

Research and Training Center to Improve Services
    for Seriously Emotionally Handicapped Children
    and their Families
Regional Research Institute for Human Services
P.O. Box 751   (503) 464-4040
Portland State University
Portland, OR 97207-0751

Research Press   (217) 352-3273
P.O. Box 3177
Champaign, IL 61826

Sage Publications   (805) 499-0721
2111 West Hillcrest Dr.
Newbury Park, CA 91320

SEFAM Family Support Program   (206) 747-4004
c/o James May, Merrywood School
16120 N.E. Eighth St.
Bellevue, WA 98008

Self-Help Clearinghouse   (201) 625-9565
1 Indian Rd.
Denville, NJ 07834

TASH
7010 Roosevelt Way, N.E.   (206) 523-8446
Seattle, WA 98115

Teachers College Press   (800) 356-0409
P.O. Box 939
Wolfeboro, NH 03894-0939

Technical Assistance for Parent Programs (TAPP) Project
Federation for Children with Special Needs
95 Berkeley St.   (617) 482-2915
Boston, MA 02116

Thomas, Charles C.   (217) 789-8980
2600 South First Street
Springfield, IL 62794-9265

University of Washington Press   (206) 543-4050
P.O. Box 50096
Seattle, WA 98145-5096

Viking Penguin, Inc.   (212) 337-5200
40 W. 23rd
New York, NY 10010

Young Adult Institute   (212) 563-7474
460 W. 34th St.
New York, NY 10001

INFORMATION/REFERRAL SOURCES

American Council on Rural Special Education (ACRES)
    Rural Development Institute   (206) 676-3576
Western Washington University
359 Miller Hall
Bellingham, WA 98225

> This institute provides resources and information on rural issues. Publications include a cross-cultural bibliography for rural special educators.

Association for the Care of Children's Health (ACCH)
3615 Wisconsin Avenue, N.W.   (202) 244-1801
Washington, DC 20016

> ACCH promotes quality health care for all children and their families, emphasizing support for the psychosocial needs of families. The organization sponsors an active network of families and professionals and their catalog contains resources of value to professionals and family members.

Beach Center on Families and Disability   (913) 864-7600
Bureau of Child Research
4138 Haworth Hall
The University of Kansas
Lawrence, KS 60045

> The Beach Center is a research and training center based on six fundamental beliefs about families; positive contributions, great expectations, full citizenship, choices, strengths, and relationships. These beliefs are translated into a wide range of research and dissemination and training projects that address family well-being across the lifespan. Newsletters and a publication catalog are available upon request. The Beach Center does not provide case-management or direct services.

Family and Corrections Network   (804) 977-1028
P.O. Box 2103   (703) 943-3141
Waynesboro, VA 22980

> This network provides information about programs serving families with a member in prison or involved in correctional systems. To receive information, write or leave a message on the Network's answering machine with your name, address, and type of information desired.

Migrant Headstart Resource Center   (703) 893-6778
Interstate Research Associates
7926 Jones Branch Drive, Suite 1100
McLean, VA 22102

> This resource center provides training and technical assistance to Migrant Headstart grantees. Through its quarterly newsletter and pe-

riodic mailings, the center disseminates training materials and resource information.

National Center for Clinical Infant Programs
733 15th St., N.W., Suite 912   (202) 347-0308
Washington, DC 20005
> This national center promotes preventive programs for young children. The institute offers training opportunities, publishes a newsletter, and provides other resources for professionals and families.

National Early Childhood Technical Assistance System
The University of North Carolina at Chapel Hill
CB# 8040, 500 NCNB Plaza   (919) 962-2001
Chapel Hill, NC 27514
> NEC*TAS is funded to assist states and HCEEP projects in the implementation of services available to children aged 0–8. The project publishes a directory of selected federal programs in early childhood special education, and monographs and bibliographies on selected topics.

National Maternal and Child Health Resource Center
College of Law Building   (319) 335-9067
The University of Iowa
Melrose & Byington
Iowa City, IA 52242
> This clearinghouse makes referrals, conducts research, and provides a variety of information to families and professionals. Publications are available.

National Information Center for Children and Youth with
   Handicaps (NICHCY)
P.O. Box 1492   (800) 999-5599
Washington, DC 20013
> NICHCY, a valuable resource for families and professionals, offers referrals, state resource sheets, newsletters, and fact sheets about various disabilities at no cost.

National Information Center for Orphan Drug and Rare Diseases
   (NICODARD)
P.O. Box 1133   (800) 456-3505
Washington, DC 20013-1133
> This organization provides information about rare diseases and the drugs used to treat them. Referrals are made, and fact sheets are available.

National Organization for Rare Disorders (NORD)
P.O. Box 8923   (800) 447-6673
New Fairfield, CT 06812
> NORD publishes information sheets for families and professionals on various disorders, makes referrals, and links families for parent-to-parent type support.

Research & Training Center to Improve Services for
   Seriously Emotionally Handicapped Children and Their Families
Regional Research Institute for Human Services
P.O. Box 751   (503) 464-4040
Portland State University
Portland, OR 97207-0751

> This center works to improve services to children with emotional disabilities and their families. Resources for families and professionals include annotated bibliographies, a newsletter, videotapes, and training materials.

Sibling Information Network   (203) 282-7050
Connecticut's University Affiliated Program on Developmental
   Disabilities
991 Main Street
East Hartford, CT 06108

> This clearinghouse publishes a newsletter and provides information, bibliographies of children's literature, journal articles, audiovisual materials, and descriptions of support services to brothers and sisters and other family members of individuals with special needs.

The Exceptional Parent   (617) 536-8961
1170 Commonwealth Avenue, 3rd floor
Boston, MA 01234

> This journal contains articles which describe programs and technology that expand opportunities for children with a disability. Accounts of family experiences focus on family strengths. Letters promote networking among families to share successful experiences.

NEWLY FUNDED AND CONTINUATION PARENT TRAINING AND INFORMATION (PTI) PROJECTS LISTING—ALPHABETICAL BY STATE

Alabama

Carol Blades
Special Education Action Committee, Inc.
P.O. Box 161274
Mobile, AL 36616-2274
(205) 478-1208

Alaska

None

Arizona

Mary Slaughter
Pilot Parent Partnerships
2150 East Highland Avenue
Phoenix, AZ 85016
(602) 468-3001

Arkansas

Bonnie Johnson
Arkansas Disability Coalition
1002 W. Markham
Little Rock, AR 72202
(501) 376-3420

Barbara Semrau
FOCUS
2917 King Street, Suite C
Jonesboro, AR 72401
(501) 935-2750

California

Joan Tellefson
TASK
18685 Santa Inez
Fountain Valley, CA 92708
(714) 962-6332

Northern California Parent Training and
     Information Coalition (NCC)
Florene Poyadue
Parents Helping Parents
535 Race Street, Suite 220
San Jose, CA 95126
(408) 288-5010

Pam Steneberg
DREDF
2212 6th Street
Berkeley, CA 94710
(415) 644-2555

Joan Kilburn
Disability Services Matrix
P.O. Box 6541
San Rafael, CA 94903
(415) 499-3877

Colorado

Judy Martz
Barbara Buswell
PEAK
6055 Lehman Drive, Suite 101
Colorado Springs, CO 80918
(719) 531-9400

Connecticut

Nancy Prescott
CT Parent Advocacy Center
P.O. Box 579
East Lyme, CT 06333
(203) 739-3089

Delaware

Marie-Ann Aghazadian
PIC of Delaware, Inc.
700 Barksdale Road, Suite 6
Newark, DE 19711
(302) 366-0152

District of Columbia

None

Florida

Donna Waghorn
Parent Education Network/Florida, Inc.

1211 Tech Blvd., Suite 105
Tampa, FL 33619
(813) 623-4088

Georgia

Cheryl Knight
Parents Educating Parents (PEP)
Georgia ARC
1851 Ram Runway, Suite 104
College Park, GA 30337
(404) 761-2745

Hawaii

None

Idaho

Martha E. Gilgen
Idaho Parents Unltd., Inc.
1365 N. Orchard, #107
Boise, ID 83706
(208) 377-8019

Illinois

Charlotte Des Jardins
Coordinating Council for Handicapped Children
20 East Jackson Boulevard
Room 900
Chicago, IL 60604
(312) 939-3513

Donald Moore
Designs for Change
220 South State Street
Room 1900
Chicago, IL 60604
(312) 922-0317

Indiana

Richard Burden
Task Force on Education for the Handicapped,
     Inc.
833 Northside Boulevard
Building #1, Rear
South Bend, IN 46617–2993
(219) 234-7101

Iowa

Carla Lawson
Iowa Exceptional Parents Center
33 North 12th Street
P.O. Box 1151
Fort Dodge, IA 50501
(515) 576-5870

Kansas

Patricia Gerdel
Families Together, Inc.
P.O. Box 86153
Topeka, KS 66686
(913) 273-6343

Kentucky

Paulette Logsdon
Kentucky Special Parent Involvement Network
318 West Kentucky Street
Louisville, KY 40203
(502) 584-1104

Louisiana

Sharon Duda
Project PROMPT
1500 Edwards Avenue, Suite O
Harahan, LA 70123
(504) 734-7736

Maine

Deborah Guimont
Special Needs Parent Information Network
    (SPIN)
P.O. Box 2067
Augusta, ME 04338–2067
(207) 582-2504

Maryland

None

Massachusetts

Artie Higgins
Federation for Children with Special Needs
95 Berkeley St.
Boston, MA 02116
(617) 482-2915

Michigan

Patricia Mullen-Lynn
United Cerebral Palsy Association of
    Metropolitan Detroit, Inc.
17000 West 8 Mile Road
Suite 380
Southfield, MI 48075
(313) 557-5070

Cheryl Chilcote
Citizens Alliance to Uphold Special Education
    (CAUSE)
313 South Washington Square, lower level,
    Suite 040

Lansing, MI 48933
(517) 485-4084

Minnesota

Marge Goldberg
Paula F. Goldberg
PACER Center, Inc.
4826 Chicago Avenue South
Minneapolis, MN 55417
(612) 827-2966

Mississippi

Anne Presley
Association of Developmental Organizations of
    Mississippi
332 New Market Drive
Jackson, MS 39209
(601) 922-3210

Missouri

Marianne Toombs
Missouri Parents Act-MPACT
1722 W. South Glenstone, Suite 125
Springfield, MO 65804
(417) 882-7434

Pat Jones
Missouri Parents Act-MPACT
625 N. Euclid, Suite 225
St. Louis, MO 63108
(314) 361-1660

Montana

Katherine Kelker
Parents, Let's Unite for Kids
EMC/IHS
1500 North 30th Street
Billings, MT 59101-0298
(406) 657-2055

Nebraska

Dan Costello
Nebraska Parent Information Training Center
3610 Dodge Street
Omaha, NE 68131
(402) 346-0525

Nevada

None

New Hampshire

Judith Raskin
Parent Information Center

P.O. Box 1422
Concord, NH 03302–1422
(603) 224-6299

New Jersey

Diana Cuthbertson
Executive Director
Statewide Parent Advocacy Network, Inc.
    (SPAN)
516 North Ave, East
Westfield, NJ 07090
(201) 654-7726

New Mexico

Norman Segel
EPICS Project
P.O. Box 788
Bernalillo, NM 87004
(505) 867-3396
Fed Exp: 2000 Camino del Pueblo

Sallie Van Curan
Parents Reaching Out To Help
1127 University NE
Albuquerque, NM 87102
(505) 842-9045

New York

Joan M. Watkins
Parent Network Center (PNC)
1443 Main Street
Buffalo, NY 14209
(716) 885-1004

Norma Rollins
Advocates for Children of New York, Inc.
24-16 Bridge Plaza South
Long Island City, NY 11101
(718) 729-8866

North Carolina

Connie Hawkins
Exceptional Children's Assistance Center
P.O. Box 16
Davidson, NC 28036
(704) 892-1321

North Dakota

Katherine Erickson
Pathfinder Services of North Dakota
16th St. & 2nd Ave., S.W.
Arrowhead Shopping Center
Minot, ND 58701
(701) 852-9426

Ohio

Cathy Heizman
SOC Information Center
106 Wellington Place, lower level
Cincinnati, OH 45219
(513) 381-2400

Margaret Burley
Ohio Coalition for the Education of
    Handicapped Children
933 High Street, Suite 106
Worthington, OH 43085
(614) 431-1307

Oklahoma

Connie Motsinger
Parents Reaching Out in Oklahoma Project
1917 South Harvard Avenue
Oklahoma City, OK 73128
(405) 681-9710
(1-800) PL94-142

Oregon

Cheron Mayall
Oregon COPE Project
999 Locust Street, NE Box B
Salem, OR 97303
(503) 373-7477 (Voice/TDD)

Pennsylvania

Christine Davis
Parents Union for Public Schools
311 S. Juniper St.
Philadelphia, PA 19107
(215) 574-0337

Mentor Parent Program
Salina Rd.
P.O. Box 718
Seneca, PA 16346
(814) 676-8615

Puerto Rico

Carmen Selles Vila
Asociacion De Padres
Pro Biene Star/Ninos Impedidos de PR, Inc.
Box 21301
Rio Piedras, PR 00928
(809) 763-4665

Rhode Island

None

South Carolina

None

South Dakota

None

Tennessee

Roger Blue
Assoc/Retarded Citizens Tennessee
1805 Hayes Street, Suite 100
Nashville, TN 37203
(615) 327-0294

Texas

Janice Foreman
PATH
6465 Calder Avenue, Suite 202
Beaumont, TX 77707
(409) 866-4726

Utah

Stevia Bowman
Utah Parent Center
2290 East 4500 South
Suite 110
Salt Lake City, UT 84117
(801) 272-1051

Vermont

Joan Sylvester
Connie Curtin
VT Information and Training Network,
    Vermont/ARC
37 Champlain Mill
Winooski, VT 05404
(802) 655-4016

Virgin Islands

None

Virginia

Winifred Anderson
Parent Education Advocacy Training Center
228 South Pitt Street
Room 300
Alexandria, VA 22314
(703) 836-2953

Washington

Martha Gentili
Washington PAVE
6316 South 12th Street
Tacoma, WA 98465
(206) 565-2266 (Voice/TDD)

Heather Hebdon
PAVE/STOMP
Specialized Training of Military Parents
12208 Pacific Highway, SW
Tacoma, WA 98499
(206) 588-1741

West Virginia

None

Wisconsin

Liz Irwin
Parent Education Project
United Cerebral Palsy of SE Wisconsin
230 West Wells Street
Suite 502
Milwaukee, WI 53203
(414) 272-4500

Wyoming

None

Note. From *Resources for families and professionals: Publications, audiovisuals, and information/referral centers on families and disability* by J. Sergeant (Ed.), 1989, Lawrence: The University of Kansas, Beach Center on Families and Disability.

GUIDE FOR GATHERING FAMILY INFORMATION THROUGH DISCUSSION

Many of the family-systems characteristics described in this book (Chapters 2–5) may be identified by means of standardized assessment tools and procedures commonly used by mental health professionals such as psychologists, psychiatrists, and social workers. However, most families do not require such a high level of assessment nor do most school programs typically need access to the kind of information these instruments provide in order to work together effectively with families in assuring that children's educational needs are met. We recommend that, unless there is sound rationale for conducting indepth assessments, school programs seek to gather only the information that is necessary in order to: (a) determine the best means of interacting with the family, (b) guide the interdisciplinary team in selecting instructional objectives for the student that also serve the needs of the family, and (c) identify areas of family need that the school or a referral agency can serve. For these purposes, we suggest using a strategy that consists of informal discussions with families to pursue topics similar to those presented on the following pages. In these discussions, your main role is to *listen* to how families tell their own story. Before progressing to those topics, we wish to make some points about their use.

Establishing Rapport

By their nature, the topics are personal, making it easy for families to perceive them as intrusive. Therefore, it is essential that discussions occur in private places, preferably in a comfortable surrounding. Perhaps, if the family prefers, you may meet with the family in their home. It may be desirable to meet with the family several times to gather and exchange information. Emphasize the strict confidentiality in which information will be held. It is also important to explain the use to which the information will be put, its relevance to the student's program, and its value in helping the school serve the family. No topics should be pursued that are not clearly relevant to the purposes you explain to the family. Families should understand that sharing information with you is voluntary and that they are free to refuse to address any topic. In no case should families be pressed to respond to questions when they appear uncomfortable.

Reducing the "Social Desirability Factor"

People tend to provide information in a way they believe will make themselves and their families more acceptable to others. To reduce this tendency (it may not be possible to eliminate it), it is important to take a neutral and nonjudgmental attitude toward all information. You should stress that there are no "right" or "wrong" responses and that the purpose of sharing information is to adapt the school's program and resources to the family's particular needs. Once again, the parents' levels of comfort with and trust in you are vital to the accuracy of the information you will receive.

Choosing the Topics to Discuss

The topics presented here are too numerous to be covered in one session. Select a few topics that seem most important in establishing a good initial relationship with the family. Some topics are not relevant for every family (e.g., issues about relationships in a blended family or issues about siblings for a family with only one child) and should, of course, be deleted. A good strategy may be to select a few of the most relevant topics from each of the five sections of the questionnaire (Family Resources, Interaction, Functions, Life Cycle, and Home-School Communication). You may wish to hold several discussions with the family and perhaps scatter them throughout the school year.

Being Flexible

In an open-ended discussion you should be willing to follow tangents in whatever direction the family's interest seem to dictate. For example, a parent may address other topics in the process of addressing one; in such a case, you should avoid repetition by "formally" bringing up the same topic at a later time. If families refer to some issue or seem especially interested in a particular topic, you should follow up by encouraging them to clarify or provide more information. You can get a better idea of many family-system components from some anecdote or an example a family member may tell you (e.g., the family's communication style) than from directly asking the question itself. It is also a good idea to put the proposed topics into your own words and into words the family will find the easiest to understand. As much as possible, avoid a formal "interview" approach, seeking instead to create a discussion or conversation between a group of people with shared interests and goals.

Reporting Information

Follow school policy on the type of information and formats to be used when you report information for inclusion in the student's permanent record. Avoid interpretive comments in the report and present only facts or actual statements by the families. Guidelines for how to maintain records are included in Chapter 11.

Your ability to use the Family Discussion Guide successfully depends on how well you can organize yourself prior to meeting with the family. The following steps are provided to help you in that organization process.

STEPS FOR USING THE FAMILY DISCUSSION GUIDE

1. Determine the purpose for gathering family information.
2. Determine which family members should be included in the discussion(s) by asking the parents whom they would like to include.
3. Select those topics from each area that are relevant to the purpose for gathering family information and that can be addressed by the persons participating in the discussion.
4. Determine how much time the discussion(s) will take and the number of sessions that will be needed.
5. Determine the best setting for the discussion(s).
6. Determine the best format (i.e., amount of structure) for the discussion(s).
7. Gain the cooperation of the persons participating.

8. Complete the discussion(s).

9. Determine how much of the information obtained needs to be included in the student's permanent records and how to report such information.

10. Determine if follow-up contacts are needed.

DISCUSSION GUIDE

Family Characteristics

1. Names and ages of the immediate family and ages of siblings.

2. Other persons (not necessarily relatives) whom the family consider to be part of their "family."

3. Role of extended family members in connection with the child with an exceptionality.

4. Any issue needing to be addressed about the nature of the child's exceptionality.

5. If there is joint custody, any scheduling arrangements of which the school should be aware.

6. Role of stepparents in the care and education of the child.

7. Any issues associated with the child's reaction to a divorce of which the school needs to be aware.

8. Any other recent changes (such as parental job changes, death of a relative) in the family that may affect the child.

9. Any other members of the family who have exceptional needs.

10. Jobs of family members.

11. The way in which work outside the home influences involvement with the child's educational program.

12. Any special ethnic traditions or customs which should be included in the child's program.

13. Family members or friends who are available to help the child with homework.

14. Description (without using names) of how professionals in the past have been most and least helpful to the child and family.

15. Beliefs about the most important things parents should teach their children.

16. Beliefs about the most important things schools should teach children.

17. Interest in having information about teaching the child at home (e.g., behavior management, self-help skills, social skills, home-work, special needs, providing stimulating experiences, self-concept, self-expectations, sexuality, dating).

18. Interest in receiving information about advocacy and working with professionals (e.g., involvement in evaluation, placement, and IFSP/IEP decisions; legal rights; negotiation; parent or consumer advocacy groups).

19. Interest in information about how to find and use more family support systems (e.g., helping others understand the child's excep-tionality, child care or respite care, support groups, religious orga-nizations, coordination of services, financial support).

Family Interactions

1. Most and least enjoyable aspects of interacting with the child for different family members—parents, brothers and sisters, extended family.

2. Interests and activities of family members.

3. Ways in which family members support each other in reaching goals.

4. Ways in which decisions are made in the family.

5. Kinds of decisions the child with an exceptionality makes and ways in which his or her decision making might be expanded.

6. The family's general daily or weekly schedule.

Family Functions

1. Ways chores are divided and the child's responsibilities for chores.

2. The nature of the family's past involvement in the child's educa-tional program.

3. The way homework or special programs are carried out at home.

4. What the family does for fun.

5. The community activities in which the family, or a member of the family, are involved.

6. The family's strengths in carrying out responsibilities.

7. The characteristics of each member that give the family the most pride.

Family Life Cycle

1. The way the family found out about the child's exceptionality.
2. The most difficult and the most enjoyable times the family has had with the child.
3. The family's short- and long-term goals for the child and for other members.
4. Hopes for the child's life 5 years from now and 10 years from now.
5. Biggest worries and greatest dreams about the future.
6. Interests in information about planning for the future (e.g., educational options; residential and/or vocational programs; colleges, universities, or vocational schools; scholarships or other financial aid, planning for the financial future, guardianship options).

Home-School Communication

1. Preferences for the type of information to be shared between home and school (e.g., special accomplishments, special activities, progress toward educational goals/grades, toileting habits, eating habits, sleeping/napping habits, specific behaviors).
2. Preferences for how frequently to share information (e.g., daily, weekly).
3. Preferences for how to share home-school communication (e.g., home visits, informal school visits, individual conferences, group conferences, telephone calls, logbooks, notes, newsletters, audio tapes, report cards).

C A S E S

Anderson v. Thompson, 658 F.2d 205 (7th Cir. 1981).

Armstrong v. Klein, 476 F. Supp. 583, *aff'd. in part and remanded sub nom.,* Battle v. Commonwealth, 629 F. 2d 269 (3rd Cir. 1980), *cert. den.,* Scanlon v. Battle, 452 N.S. 968 (1981).

Bevin H. v. Wright, 666 F. Supp. 71. EHLR 559:122 (W.D. Pa. 1987).

Board v. Cooperman, 105 N.J. 587, 523 A 2d 655 (S. Ct. N.J. 1987).

Board v. Diamond, 808 F.2d 987, EHLR 557:217 (3d Cir. 1986).

Board of Education v. Ambach, 458 N.Y.S. 2d 680 (N.Y. Sup. Ct., App. Div. 1982).

Board v. Rowley, 458 U.S. 176 (1982).

Brookhart v. Illinois State Board of Education, 534 F. Supp. 725 (C.D. Ill. 1982).

Criswell v. State Department of Education, EHLR 558:156 (M.D. Tenn. 1986).

Department of Education of Hawaii v. Katherine D., 531 F. Supp. 517, *aff'd,* 727 F.2d 809 (9th Cir. 1984).

Detsel v. Board of Education of the Auburn Enlarged City School District, 637 F. Supp. 1022 (N.D. N.Y. 1986), *aff'd,* 820 F.2d 587 (2d Cir. 1987), *cert. den.,* ___ U.S. ___, 108 S. Ct. 495, 98 L. Ed. 2d 494 (1987).

District 27 v. Board, EHLR 557:241 (S. Ct., N.Y. 1986).

Evans v. Board of Education, Civ. Act. No. 76-0293 (D. D.C. June 14, 1978).

Doe v. Anrig, 692 F.2d 800 (1st Cir. 1981), *on remand,* 561 F. Supp. 121 (D. Mass. 1983).

Foster v. D.C. Board of Education, 523 F. Supp. 1142 (D. D.C. 1981).

Georgia ARC v. McDaniel, 511 F. Supp. 1263, *aff'd.,* 716 F. 2d 1565 (11th Cir. 1983).

Georgia State Conference of Branches of the National Association for the Advancement of Colored People v. Georgia, 775 F.2d 1403 (11th Cir. 1985).

Honig v. Doe, 484 U.S. ___, 108 S. Ct. 592, 98 L. Ed. 2d 686 (1988).

Hudson v. Wilson, 828 F.2d 1059 (CA-4 1987).

John H. v. MacDonald, EHLR 558:336 (D. N.H. 1986).

Larry P. v. Riles, 343 F. Supp. 1036, *aff'd.,* 502 F.2d 963, further proceedings, 495 F. Supp. 926, *aff'd.,* 502 F.2d 693 (9th Cir. 1984).

LeBanks v. Spears, 60 F.R.D. 135 (E.D. La 1973).

Maryland Association for Retarded Children v. Maryland, Equity No. 100/182/77676 (Cir. Ct. Baltimore Cty., May 4, 1974).

Miener v. State of Missouri, 673 F.2d 969 (8th Cir. 1982).

Mills v. D.C. Board of Education, 348 F. Supp. 866 (D. D.C. 1972).

Parents of Child v. Coker, 676 F. Supp. 1072 (E.D. Okla. 1987).

PASE v. Hannon, 506 F. Supp. 831 (N.D. Ill. 1980).

Pennsylvania Association for Retarded Children v. Commonwealth of Pennsylvania, 334 F. Supp. 1257 (E.D. Pa. 1972).

Polk v. Central Susquehanna Intermediate Unit 16, 853 F.2d 171 (3d Circ. 1988).

Roncker v. Walters, 700 F.2d 1058 (6th Cir. 1982), *cert. den.,* 464 U.S. 864, 104 S. Ct. 196, 78 L. Ed. 2d 171 (1983).

Rouse v. Wilson, 675 F. Supp. 1012 (WD VA 1987).

Schimmel v. Spillane, 819 F.2d 477 (CA-4 1987).

Sessions v. Livingston Parish, 501 F. Supp. 251 (M.D. La. 1980).

Tatro v. State of Texas, 104 S. Ct. 3371, 82 L. Ed. 2d 664 (1984).

Thornock v. Boise USD, EHLR 556:477 (4th Jud. Dist. Idaho), *aff'd.,* EHLT 559:486 (Idaho S. Ct. 1988).

Timothy W. v. Rochester School District, EHLE 559:480, *rev'd.,* ___ F.2d.

William S. v. Gill, No. 81-C-3045 (D. Mass. 1982).

REFERENCES

Abbott, D. A., & Meredith, W. H. (1986). Strengths of parents with retarded children. *Family Relations, 35,* 371–375.

Abramson, M., Willson, V., Yoshida, R. K., & Hagerty, G. (1983). Parents' perceptions of their learning disabled child's educational performance. *Learning Disability Quarterly, 6*(2), 184–194.

Ackerman, J. (1985). Preparing for separation. In H. R. Turnbull & A. P. Turnbull (Eds.), *Parents speak out: Then and now* (pp. 149–158). Columbus, OH: Merrill Publishing Co.

Aday, L. A., Aitken, M. J., & Weggener, D. H. (1988). *Pediatric homecare: Results of a national evaluation of programs for ventilator assisted children.* Chicago: Pluribus Press, Inc., and the Center for Health Administration Studies, University of Chicago.

Agard, J. A. (1980). Dispute settlement. In S. I. Mopsik & J. A. Agard (Eds.), *An education handbook for parents of handicapped children* (pp. 233–252). Cambridge, MA: ABT Books.

Albert, L. (1988). Strengthening stepfamilies. *Family Resource Coalition Report, 7*(1), 1–3.

Algozzine, B., Christenson, S., & Ysseldyke, J. E. (1982). Probabilities associated with the referral to placement process. *Teacher Education and Special Education, 5*(3), 19–23.

Allen, D. F., & Allen, V. S. (1979). *Ethical issues in mental retardation: Tragic choices/living hope.* Nashville, TN: Abingdon Press.

American Association for Protecting Children (AAPC). (1986). *Highlights of official child neglect and abuse reporting, 1984.* Denver, CO: The American Humane Association.

American Foundation for the Blind. (1989). Facts about the American Foundation for the Blind. New York: Author.

American Psychological Association. (1981). Ethical principles of psychologists. *American Psychologist, 36*(6), 633–638.

Ammer, J. J. (1984). Mechanics of mainstreaming: Considering the regular educator's perspective. *Remedial and Special Education, 5,* 15–20.

Anchor, K. N., & Anchor, F. N. (1974). School failure and parental school involvement in an ethnically mixed school: A survey. *Journal of Community Psychology, 2,* 265–267.

Anderson, D. (1983). He's not "cute" anymore. In T. Dougan, L. Isbell, & P. Vyas (Eds.), *We have been there* (pp. 90–91). Nashville, TN: Abingdon Press.

Aponte, H. J. (1985). The negotiation of values in therapy. *Family Process, 24,* 323–338.

Asch, A. (1989). Has the law made a difference?: What some disabled students have to say. In D. K. Lipsky & A. Gartner (Eds.), *Beyond separate education: Quality education for all* (pp. 181–205). Baltimore, Paul H. Brookes.

Association for Retarded Citizens. (1987). Milestones.

Avis, D. W. (1985). Deinstitutionalization jetlag. In H. R. Turnbull & A. P. Turnbull (Eds.), *Parents speak out: Then and now* (pp. 181–191). Columbus, OH: Merrill Publishing Co.

Bailey, D. B. (1984). A triaxial model of the interdisciplinary team and group process. *Exceptional Children, 51*(1), 17–25.

Bailey, D. B. (1987). Collaborative goal-setting with families: Resolving differences in values and priorities for services. *Topics in Early Childhood Education, 7*(2), 59–71.

Bailey, D. B., & Simeonsson, R. J. (1984). Critical issues underlying research and intervention with families of your handicapped children. *Journal of the Division for Early Childhood, 9,* 39–48.

Bailey, D. B., & Simeonsson, R. J. (1988). *Family assessment in early intervention.* Columbus, OH: Merrill.

Bailey, D. B., Winton, P. J., Rouse, L., & Turnbull, A. P. (in press). Family goals in infant intervention: Analysis and issues. *Journal of Early Intervention.*

Baker, B. L., & Brightman, A. J. (1989). *Steps to independence: A skills training guide for parents and teachers of children with special needs* (2nd ed.). Baltimore: Paul H. Brookes Publishing Co.

Baker, B. L., & Heifetz, L. J. (1976). The read project: Teaching manuals for parents of retarded children. In T. D. Tjossem (Ed.), *Intervention strategies for high risk infants and young children* (pp. 351–369). Baltimore: University Park Press.

Baker, B. L., Heifetz, L. J., & Murphy, D. (1980). Behavioral training for parents of retarded children: One year follow-up. *American Journal of Mental Deficiency, 85,* 31–38.

Ball, E. L., Chasey, W. C., Hawkins, D. E., & Verhoven, P. J. (1976). The need for leisure education for handicapped children and youth. *Journal of Physical Education and Recreation, 47*(3), 53–55.

Barna, R., Bidder, R. T., Gray, O. P., Clements, J., & Garner, S. (1982). The progress of developmentally delayed preschool children in a home-training scheme. *Childcare, Health, and Development, 6,* 157–164.

Barr, M. W. (1913). *Mental defectives: Their history, treatment, and training.* Philadelphia: P. Blakiston's Son & Co.

Bassuk, E. L., & Rosenberg, L. (1988). Why does family homelessness occur? A case–control study. *American Journal of Public Health, 78*(7), 783–788.

Bateman, B. (1982). Legal and ethical dilemmas of special educators. *Exceptional Education Quarterly, 2*(4), 57–67.

Beckman, P. J. (1983). Influence of selected child characteristics on stress in families of handicapped infants. *American Journal of Mental Deficiency, 88,* 150–156.

Beckman, P. J., & Pokorni, J. L. (1988). A longitudinal study of families of preterm infants: Changes in stress and support over the first two years. *The Journal of Special Education, 22*(1), 55–65.

Beckman-Bell, P. J. (1981). Child-related stress in families of handicapped children. *Topics in Early Childhood Special Education, 1,* 45–53.

Bell, L. E. (1989). Something's wrong here and it's not me: Challenging the dilemmas that block girls' success. *Journal for the Education of the Gifted, 12*(2), 118–130.

Benjamin, A. (1969). *The helping interview.* Boston: Houghton-Mifflin Company.

Bennett, J. M. (1985). Company, halt! In H. R. Turnbull & A. P. Turnbull (Eds.), *Parents speak out: Then and now* (pp. 159–173). Columbus, OH: Merrill Publishing Co.

Bensky, J. M., Shaw, S. F., Gouse, A. S., Bates, H., Dixon, B., & Beane, W. E. (1980). Public law 94-142 and stress: A problem for educators. *Exceptional Children, 47*(1), 24–29.

Benson, H. A. (1986a). *Presentation on ethnicity and launching.* Unpublished handout, The University of Kansas.

Benson, H. A. (1986b). Assessment guide for a family systems approach. Unpublished manuscript, The University of Kansas.

Benson, H. A. (1988). The changing American family and students at risk. *Behavior In Our Schools, 3*(1), 7–12.

Benson, H. A. (1989). *An investigation of respite care as a mediator of stress in families with members with developmental disabilities.* Unpublished doctoral dissertation, The University of Kansas.

Benson, H. A., & Turnbull, A. P. (1986). Approachng families from an individualized perspective. In R. H. Horner, L. H. Meyer, & H. D. Fredericks (Eds.), *Education of learners with severe handicaps: Exemplary service strategies* (pp. 127–157). Baltimore: Paul H. Brookes Publishing Co.

Bernal, M. E. (1984). Consumer issues in parent training. In R. F. Dangel & R. A. Polster (Eds.), *Parent training: Foundation of research and practice* (pp. 477–503). New York: The Guilford Press.

Bettleheim, B. (1950). *Love is not enough.* Glencoe, NY: Free Press.

Bettleheim, B. (1967). *The empty fortress: Infantile autism and the birth of the self.* London: Collier-MacMillan.

Blacher, J. (1984a). Sequential stages of adjustment to the birth of a child with handicaps: Fact or artifact? *Mental Retardation, 22,* 55–68.

Blacher, J. (Ed.). (1984b). *Severely handicapped young children and their families: Research in review.* New York: Academic Press.

Blacher, J., & Meyers, C. E. (1983). A review of attachment formation and disorder of handicapped children. *American Journal of Mental Deficiency, 87,* 359–371.

Blair, L. (1989). From a parent's perspective. *Parents Involved Network Newsletter, 5,* 5–6.

Blatt, B., Biklen, D., & Bogdan, R. (1977). *An alternative textbook in special education.* Denver, CO: Love Publishing Company.

Bloom, B. S., & Sosniak, L. A. (1981). Talent development. *Educational leadership, 39*(2), 86–94.

Blue-Banning, M. (1985). [An interview with a family with a child having a disability]. Unpublished raw data.

Boggs, E. M. (1985a). Who is putting whose head in the sand? (Or in the clouds, as the case may be.) In H. R. Turnbull & A. P. Turnbull (Eds.), *Parents speak out: Then and now* (pp. 39–55). Columbus, OH: Merrill Publishing Co.

Boggs, E. M. (1985b). Whose head is in the clouds? In H. R. Turnbull & A. P. Turnbull (Eds.), *Parents speak out: Then and now* (pp. 55–64). Columbus, OH: Merrill Publishing Co.

Bok, S. (1978). *Living: Moral choice in public and private life.* New York: Pantheon Books.

Bok, S. (1980). Whistleblowing and professional responsibilities. In D. Callahan & S. Bok (Eds.), *Teaching ethics in higher education* (pp. 277–295). New York: Plenum Press.

Boscardin, M. L. (1987). Local-level special education due process hearings: Cost issues surrounding individual student differences. *Journal of Education Finance, 12,* 391–402.

Brammer, L. (1988). *The helping relationship.* Englewood Cliffs, NJ: Prentice Hall.

Bricker, W. A., & Bricker, D. D. (1976). The infant, toddler, and preschool research and intervention project. In T. D. Tjossem (Ed.), *Intervention strategies for high risk infants and young children* (pp. 545–572). Baltimore: University Park Press.

Brightman, R. P., Baker, B. L., Clark, D. B., & Ambrose, S. A. (1982). Effectiveness of alternative parent training formats. *Journal of Behavior Therapy and Experimental Psychiatry, 13,* 113–117.

Bristol, M. M. (1984). The birth of a handicapped child—a wholistic model for grieving. *Family Relations, 33,* 25–32.

Bristol, M. M., & Gallagher, J. J. (1986). Research on fathers of young handicapped children: Evolution review, and some future directions. In J. Gallagher & P. Vietze (Eds.), *Families of handicapped persons* (pp. 81–100). Baltimore: Paul H. Brookes Publishing Co.

Bristol, M. M., & Schopler, E. (1983). Stress and coping in families with autistic adolescents. In E. Schopler & G. B. Mesibov (Eds.), *Autism in adolescents and adults* (pp. 251–278). New York: Plenum Press.

Brotherson, M. J. (1985). *Parents self report of future planning and its relationship to family functioning and family stress with sons and daughters who are disabled.* Unpublished doctoral dissertation, The University of Kansas.

Brotherson, M. J., Backus, L., Summers, J. A., & Turnbull, A. P. (1986). Transition to adulthood. In J. A. Summers (Ed.), *The right to grow up: Introduction to developmentally disabled adults* (pp. 17–44). Baltimore: Paul H. Brookes Publishing Co.

Brown, W. (1987). Review and evaluation: Rainbow connection instructional guide. *Techniques: A Journal for Remedial Education and Counseling, 3*(4), 257–259.

Browning, P., Thorin, E., & Rhoades, C. (1984). National profile of self-help/self-advocacy groups of people with mental retardation. *Mental Retardation, 22*(5), 226–230.

Bruch, C. B. (1984). Schooling for the gifted: Where do we go from here? *Gifted Child Quarterly, 28*(1), 12–16.

Budd, K. S., & Greenspan, S. (1984). Mentally retarded mothers. In E. A. Blechman (Ed.), *Behavior modification with women* (pp. 477–506). New York: The Guilford Press.

Budoff, M. (1979). Implementing due process safeguards: From the user's point of view. In Department of Health, Education, and Welfare, Office of Education, *Due process: Developing criteria for the evaluation of due process procedural safeguard provisions.* Philadelphia: Research for Better Schools, Inc.

Budoff, M., & Orenstein, A. (1982). *Due process in special education: On going to a hearing.* Cambridge, MA: The Ware Press.

Burton, K., & Rachlin, M. (1988). Priority: Integration in ESE. *A Separate Voice, 1*(1), 1–3.

Caplan, G. (1976). The family as a support system. In G. Caplan & M. Killilea (Eds.), *Support systems and mutual help: Multidisciplinary explorations* (pp. 19–36). New York: Grune & Stratton.

Carnes, P. (1981). *Family development I: Understanding us.* Minneapolis: Interpersonal Communications Programs, Inc.

Carter, E. A., & McGoldrick, M. (Eds.). (1980). *The family life cycle: A framework for family therapy.* New York: Gardner Press.

Carter, S., & Reynolds, K. (1984). *Parent to parent organizational handbook.* Athens: University of Georgia Affiliated Facility.

Chambers, D. (1972). Alternatives to civil commitment of the mentally ill: Practical guides and constitutional imperatives. *Michigan Law Review, 70,* 1108–1200.

Chapey, G. D., Trimarco, T. A., Crisci, P., & Capobianco, M. (1987). School–parent partnerships in gifted education: From paper to reality. *Educational Research Quarterly, 11*(3), 37–46.

Chase, S., Wright, J. H., & Ragade, R. (1981). Decision making in an interdisciplinary team. *Behavioral Science, 26,* 206–215.

Children's Defense Fund, Inc. (1974). *Children out of school in America: A report of the Children's Defense Fund, Washington Research Project, Inc.* Washington: Author.

Chilman, C. S. (1973). Programs for disadvantaged parents: Some major trends and related research. In H. H. Ricciuti & M. Caldwell (Eds.), *Review of child development research* (Vol. 3, pp. 403–465). Chicago: University of Chicago Press.

Clark, M. (1987). *A review of the literature regarding decelerative procedures.* Unpublished manuscript, University of Wisconsin, Madison.

Cleveland, D. W., & Miller, N. (1977). Attitudes and life commitments of older siblings of mentally retarded adults: An exploratory study. *Mental Retardation, 15*(3), 38–41.

Cobb, S. (1976). Social support as a mediator of life stress. *Psychosomatic Medicine, 38,* 300–314.

Code of Federal Regulations. (1984). Title 34, Part 300, Subparts A through G.

Cohen, S., & Warren, R. D. (1985). *Respite care: Principles, programs, and policies.* Austin, TX: Pro-Ed., Inc.

Coles, R. (1989). *The call of stories.* Boston: Houghton Mifflin Co.

Connolly, G., Morgan, S., Russell, F. F., & Richardson, B. (1980). Early intervention with Down syndrome children. *Physical Therapy, 60,* 1405–1408.

Cooley, S. A., McVey, D. L., & Barrett–Jones, K. (1987). *Evaluation of identification and preassessment procedures in Kansas.* Grant #G0085C3514. Kansas State Department of Education Research Report.

Cormier, W., & Cormier, L. (1979). *Interviewing strategies for helpers: A guide to assessment, treatment, and evaluation.* Monterey, CA: Brooks/Cole Publishing Co.

Corn, A. L. (1985). An independence matrix for visually handicapped learners. *Education of the Visually Handicapped, 17*(1), 3–10.

Council for Exceptional Children. (1983). Code of ethics and standards for professional practice. *Exceptional Children, 50*(3), 205–218.

Crary, D. (1980). Advocacy for children and families. *Educational Horizons, 59*(1), 47–53.

Crawford, D. (1978). Parent involvement in instructional planning. *Focus on Exceptional Children, 10*(7), 1–8.

Crump, I. M. (Ed.). (1987). *Nutrition and feeding of the handicapped child.* Boston: Little, Brown and Company.

Cummings, S. T. (1976). Impact of the child's deficiency on the father: A study of fathers of mentally retarded and chronically ill children. *American Journal of Orthopsychiatry, 46,* 246–255.

Cummings, S. T., Bayley, H. C., & Rie, H. E. (1966). Effects of the child's deficiency on the mother of mentally retarded, chronically ill, and neurotic children. *American Journal of Orthopsychiatry, 36,* 595–608.

Daniels, S. M. (1982). From parent advocacy to self advocacy: A problem of transition. *Exceptional Education Quarterly, 3*(2), 25–32.

Dardig, J. C., & Heward, W. L. (1981, Summer/Fall). A systematic procedure for prioritizing IEP goals. *The Directive Teacher, 5*82.

Daynard, C. (1980). *Due process: The appeals hearing under chapter 766.* Unpublished doctoral dissertation, Boston University.

DBS Corporation (1987, December). *1986 elementary and secondary school civil rights survey national summaries* (Contract Number 300-86-0062). Washington, DC: Office of Civil Rights, U.S. Department of Education.

Deford, F. (1983). *Alex: The life of a child.* East Rutherford, NJ: Viking Press.

Deiner, P. L. (1983). *Resources for teaching young children with special needs.* New York: Harcourt Brace Jovanovich.

DeLuca, K. D., & Solerno, S. C. (1984). *Helping professionals connect with families with handicapped children.* Springfield, IL: Thomas Press.

Dettman, D. F., & Colangelo, N. (1980). A functional model for counseling parents of gifted students. *Gifted Child Quarterly, 24*(4), 158–161.

DeWert, M., & Helsel, E. (1985). Update: The Helsel family today. In H. R. Turnbull & A. P. Turnbull (Eds.), *Parents speak out: Then and now* (pp. 101–106). Columbus, OH: Merrill Publishing Co.

Diamond, S. (1981). Growing up with parents of a handicapped child: A handicapped person's perspective. In J. L. Paul (Ed.), *Understanding and working with parents of children with special needs* (pp. 23–50). New York: Holt, Rinehart, & Winston.

Donnellan, A. M., & Mirenda, P. L. (1984). Issues related to professional involvement with families of individuals with autism and other severe handicaps. *Journal of the Association for Persons with Severe Handicaps, 9,* 16–24.

Donner, R. (1988). *Rest a bit: Respite care training manual for families of children with disabilities.* (Available from Families Together, Topeka, KS).

Dunlap, D. A., Ondelacy, J., & Sells, E. (1979). Videotape involves parents. *Journal of American Indian Education, 19*(1), 1–7.

Dunlap, W. R., & Hollingsworth, J. S. (1977). How does a handicapped child affect the family? Implications for practitioners. *The Family Coordinator, 26*(3), 286–293.

Dunst, C. J., Trivette, C., & Deal, A. (1988). *Enabling and empowering families: Principles and guidelines for practice.* Cambridge, MA: Brookline Books.

Dunst, C. J., Vance, S. D., & Cooper, C. S. (1986). A social systems perspective of adolescent pregnancy: Determinants of parent and parent-child behavior. *Infant Mental Health Journal, 7,* 34–48.

Duvall, E. (1957). *Family development.* Philadelphia: Lippincott. Education of the Handicapped Act, 20 U.S.C. Section 1401–1461 (P.L. 91–230), as amended by Education of All Handicapped Children Act (P.L. 94–142).

Eareckson-Tada, J. (1987). *Friendship unlimited: How you can help a disabled friend.* Wheaton, IL: Harold Shaw Publishers.

Edger, E. B., Reid, P. C., Pious, C. C. (1988). Special Sitters: Youth as respite care providers. *Mental Retardation, 26*(1), 33–37.

Edwards, M. (1986). Effects of training and self-evaluation upon special educators' communication and interaction skills when discussing emotion-laden information with parents of handicapped infants (Doctoral dissertation, University of Idaho). *Dissertation Abstracts International, 47,* 2996A.

Einstein, E., & Albert, L. (1986). *Strengthening stepfamilies.* Circle Pines, MN: American Guidance Service.

Embry, L. H. (1980). Family support for handicapped preschool children at risk for abuse. In J. J. Gallagher (Ed.), *New directions for exceptional children* (pp. 29–57). San Francisco: Jossey-Bass.

Engelhart, L. (1985). He changed. *Sibling Information Network Newsletter, 4*(3), 3.

Ensher, G., & Clark, D. (1986). *Newborns at risk: Medical care and psychoeducational intervention.* Rockville, MD: Aspen Publishers.

Epilepsy Foundation of America. (1988). Epilepsy month kit. Landover, MD: Author.

Epley, T. M. (1985). *Futuristics: A handbook for teachers of the gifted/talented.* Ventura, CA: Ventura County Superintendent of Schools Office.

Esquivel, G. (1985). Best practices in the assessment of limited English proficient and bilingual children. In A. Thomas & J. Grimes (Eds.), *Best Practies in school psychology* (pp. 113–124). Kent, OH: National Association of School Psychologists.

Essex, L. N. (1979). The development and evaluation of an inservice workshop training program in conflict management for school administrators. *Dissertation Abstracts International, 40,* 4822. (University Microfilms No. 8006605).

Evans, R. L., Smith, K. M., Werkhoven, W. S., Fox, H. R., & Pritzl, D. O. (1986). Cognitive telephone group therapy with physically disabled elderly persons. *The Gerontologist, 26*(1), 8–11.

Eversoll, D. (1979). A two generational view of fathering. *The Family Coordinator, 28,* 503–508.

Falicov, C. J. (1982). Mexican families. In M. McGoldrick, J. K. Pearce, & J. Giordano (Eds.), *Ethnicity in family therapy* (pp. 134–163). New York: The Guilford Press.

Farber, B. (1960). Family organization and crisis: Maintenance of integration in families with a severely retarded child. *Monographs of the Society for Research in Child Development, 25*(1).

Farber, B., Jenne, W., & Toigo, R. (1960). Family crisis and the decision to institutionalize the retarded child. *NEA Research Monograph Series.* Washington, DC: Council for Exceptional Children.

Farber, B., & Ryckman, D. B. (1965). Effects of severely mentally retarded children on family relationships. *Mental Retardation Abstracts, 2,* 1–17.

Featherstone, H. (1980). *A difference in the family: Living with a disabled child.* New York: Basic Books.

Federal Register. (1977, August). Washington, DC: U.S. Government Printing Office.

Federal Register. (1981, January, 19). Washington, DC: U.S. Government Printing Office.

Federation of Families for Children's Mental Health. (1989, March). *Mission statement.* Author.

Ferguson, D. L. (1984). Parent advocacy network. *The Exceptional Parent, 14,* 41–45.

Ferguson, J. T. (1978). *Starting a respite care co-op program.* Kalamazoo, MI: Family and Children's Services of the Kalamazoo Area.

Ferguson, P. M., Ferguson, D. L., & Jones, D. (1988). Generations of hope: Parental perspectives on the transitions of their children with severe retardation from school to adult life. *Journal of the Association for Persons with Severe Handicaps, 13*(3), 177–187.

Ferrell, K. A. (1984). *Parenting preschoolers: Suggestions for raising young blind and visually impaired children.* New York: American Foundation for the Blind.

Fielder, Craig, R. (1985). *Conflict prevention, containment, and resolution in special education due process disputes: Parents' and school personnel's perception of variables associated with the development and escalation of due process conflict.* Unpublished doctoral dissertation, The University of Kansas.

Fifield, V. J. (1978). *Parent and school staff attitudes toward meetings to develop individualized education programs which include/exclude the child.* Unpublished manuscript, Utah State University, Department of Special Education.

Figley, C. R., & McCubbin, H. I. (Eds.). (1983). *Stress and the family. Vol. I: Coping with normative transitions.* New York: Brunner/Mazel.

Fisher, R., & Ury, W. (1981). *Getting to Yes: Negotiating Agreement without giving in.* New York: Viking–Penguin, Inc.

Fithian, J. (Ed.). (1984). *Understanding the child with a chronic illness in the classroom.* Phoenix, AZ: Oryx Press.

Flake-Hobson, C., & Swick, K. J. (1984). Communication strategies for parents and teachers, or how to say what you mean. In M. L. Henniger & E. M. Nesselroad (Eds.), *Working with parents of handicapped children: A book of readings for school personnel* (pp. 141–149). Lanham, MD: University Press of America, Inc.

Flemming, E., & Flemming, D. (1987). Involvement of minors in special education decision-making. *Journal of Law and Education, 16*(4), 389–402.

Folberg, J., & Taylor, A. (1984). *Mediation: A comprehensive guide to resolving conflicts without litigation.* San Francisco: Jossey-Bass.

Forest, M. (1988). Full inclusion is possible. *Minnesota University Affiliated Program Impact, 1*(2), 3–4.

Fortier, L. M., & Wanlass, R. L. (1984). Family crisis following the diagnosis of a handicapped child. *Family Relations, 33,* 13–24.

Fotheringham, J. B., & Creal, D. (1974). Handicapped children and handicapped families. *International Review of Education, 20*(3), 353–371.

Fotheringham, J. B., Shelton, M., & Hoddinott, B. A. (1972). The effects on the family of the presence of a mentally retarded child. *Canadian Psychiatric Association Journal, 17,* 283–290.

Fowler, S. A., Chandler, L. K., Johnson, T. E., & Stella, M. E. (1988). Individualizing family involvement in school transitions: Gathering information and choosing the next program. *Journal of the Division of Early Childhood, 12*(3), 208–216.

Frankena, W. K. (1973). *Ethics* (2nd ed.). Englewood Cliffs, NJ: Prentice-Hall, Inc.

Freedman, S., Pierce, P., & Reiss, J. (1987, Fall). Model program reach: A family-centered community-based case management model for children with special health care needs. *Children's Health Care, 16*(2), 114–117.

Friedman, E. H. (1980). Systems and ceremonies: A family view of rites of passage. In E. A. Carter & M. McGoldrick (Eds.), *The family life cycle* (pp. 429–460). New York: Gardner Press.

Friedman, S. G., & Hofmeister, A. M. (1984). Matching technology to content and learners: A case study. *Exceptional Children, 51*(2), 130–134.

Friedrich, W. N. (1979). Predictors of coping behavior of mothers of handicapped children. *Journal of Consulting and Clinical Psychology, 47,* 1140–1141.

Frodi, A. M. (1981). Contribution of infant characteristics to child abuse. *American Journal on Mental Deficiency, 85,* 341–349.

Frost, J. L. (1986). Children in a changing society: Frontiers of challenge. *Childhood Education, 62*(4), 242–249.

Fuller, C., Vandiviere, P., & Kronberg, C. (1987). TALKLINE: An evaluation of a call-in telephone source for parents. *Journal of the Division for Early Childhood, 11*(3), 265–270.

Fulmer, R. H., Cohen, S., & Monaco, G. (1985). Using psychological assessment in structural family therapy. *Journal of Learning Disabilities, 18*(3), 145–150.

Gallagher, J., Beckman, P., & Cross, A. (1983). Families of handicapped children: Sources of stress and its amelioration. *Exceptional Children 50*(1), 10–19.

Gallagher, J. J., Cross, A., & Scharfman, W. (1981). The father's role. *Journal of the Division for Early Childhood, 3,* 3–14.

Gardner, N. E. S. (1980). *The self-advocacy workbook. The University of Kansas: Kansas Center for Mental Retardation and Human Development.*

Gardner, N. E. S. (1986). Sexuality. In J. A. Summers (Ed.), *The right to grow up: An introduction to adults with developmental disabilities* (pp. 45–66). Baltimore: Paul H. Brookes Publishing Co.

Gardner, R. A. (1971). The guilt reactions of parents of children with severe physical disease. In R. L. Noland (Ed.), *Counseling parents of the ill and the handicapped* (pp. 27–43). Springfield, IL: Charles C. Thomas.

Gath, A. (1974). Sibling reactions to mental handicaps: A comparison of the brothers and sisters of mongol children. *Journal of Child Psychology and Psychiatry and Allied Disciplines, 15*(3), 838–843.

Gath, A. (1977). The impact of an abnormal child upon the parents. *British Journal of Psychiatry, 130,* 405–410.

George, J. D. (1988). Therapeutic intervention for grandparents and extended family of children with developmental delays. *Mental Retardation, 26*(6), 369–375.

Gerber, P. J., Banbury, M. M., Miller, J. H., & Griffin, H. D. (1986). Special educators' perceptions of parental participation in the individual education plan process. *Psychology in the Schools, 23,* 158–163.

Germain, C. B., & Gitterman, A. (1980). *The life model of social work practice.* New York: Columbia University Press.

Gillespie, E., & Turnbull, A. P. (1983). Involving special education students in planning the IEP. *Teaching Exceptional Children, 16*(1), 27–29.

Gilliam, J. E., & Coleman, M. C. (1981). Who influences IEP committee decisions? *Exceptional Children, 47*(8), 642–644.

Glick, P. C. (1984). American household structure in transition. *Family planning perspectives, 16*(5), 205–211.

Gliedman, J., & Roth, W. (1980). *The unexpected minority: Handicapped children in America.* New York: Harcourt Brace Jovanovich.

Goddard, H. H. (1912). *The Kallikak family: A study in the heredity of feeblemindedness.* New York: Macmillan.

Goldenberg, I., & Goldenberg, H. (1980). *Family therapy: An overview.* Monterey, CA: Brooks/Cole Publishing Co.

Goldenson, L. H. (1965, March). *Remarks on the occasion of United Cerebral Palsy Associations' 15th anniversary.* Paper presented at the 15th annual meeting of the United Cerebral Palsy Associations, Los Angeles.

Goldfarb, L., Brotherson, M. J., Summers, J. A., & Turnbull, A. P. (1986). *Meeting the challenge of disability and chronic illness—A family guide.* Baltimore: Paul H. Brookes Publishing Co.

Goldstein, S., Strickland, B., Turnbull, A. P., & Curry, L. (1980). An observational analysis of the IEP conference. *Exceptional Children, 46*(4), 278–286.

Goldstein, S., & Turnbull, A. P. (1982). The use of two strategies to increase parent participation in IEP conferences. *Exceptional Children, 48*(4), 360–361.

Gordon, T. (1970). *Parent effectiveness training.* New York: Wyden.

Gottlieb, J. (1981). Mainstreaming: Fulfilling the promise? *American Journal of Mental Deficiency, 86,* 115–126.

Graden, J. L., Casey, A., & Bronstrom, O. (1985). Implementing a prereferral intervention system: Part II. The data. *Exceptional Children, 51,* 487–496.

Graden, J. L., Casey, A., & Christenson, S. L. (1985). Implementing a prereferral intervention system: Part I. The model. *Exceptional Children, 51,* 377–384.

Green, P. (1988). The national special education alliance: One year later. *Exceptional Parent, 18*(7), 48–51.

Grossman, F. K. (1972). *Brothers and sisters of retarded children: An exploratory study.* Syracuse, NY: Syracuse University Press.

Grotevant, H. D., & Carlson, C. I. (1989). *Family assessment: A guide to methods and measures.* New York: The Guilford Press.

Guess, P. D., Benson, H., & Siegel-Causey, E. (1985). Concepts and issues related to choice-making and autonomy among persons with severe handicaps. *Journal of the Association for Persons with Severe Handicaps, 10*(2), 79–86.

Guess, D., Bronicki, M. A., Firmender, K., Mann, J., Merrill, M., Olin-Zimmerman, S., Wanat, P., Zamarripa, E., & Turnbull, H. (1984). Legal and moral considerations in the education of a child with herpes. *Mental Retardation, 22*(5), 257–263.

Guess, D., & Siegel-Causey, E. (1985). Behavioral control and education of severely handicapped students: Who's doing what to whom? And why? In D. Bricker & J. Filler (Eds.), *Severe mental retardation: From theory to practice* (pp. 230–244). Reston, VA: The Council for Exceptional Children.

Gumz, E. J., & Gubrium, J. F. (1972). Comparative parental perceptions of a mentally retarded child. *American Journal of Mental Deficiency, 77,* 175–180.

Haavik, S. F., & Menninger, K. A. (1981). *Sexuality, law, and the developmentally disabled person.* Baltimore: Paul H. Brookes Publishing Co.

Hains, A. H., Fowler, S. A., & Chandler, L. K. (1988). Planning school transitions: Family and professional collaboration. *Journal of the Division for Early Childhood, 12*(2), 108–114.

Halperin, L. (1989). Encounters of the closest kind: A view from within. *NASP Communique, 17,* 6.

Halpern, R. (1982). Impact of P.L. 94–142 on the handicapped child and family: Institutional responses. *Exceptional Children, 49* 270–272.

Hamre-Nietupski, S., Krajewski, L., Nietupski, J., Ostercamp, D., Sensor, K., & Opheim, B. (1988). Parent/professional partnerships in advocacy: Developing integrated options within resistive systems. *Journal of the Association for Persons with Severe Handicaps, 13*(4), 251–259.

Hanline, M. F. (1988). Making the transition to preschool: Identification of parent needs. *Journal of the Division for Early Childhood, 12*(2), 98–107.

Hanline, M. F., & Knowlton, A. (1988). A collaborative model for providing support to parents during their child's transition from infant intervention to preschool special education public school programs. *Journal of the Division for Early Childhood, 12*(2), 116–125.

Hanson, M. J., & Harris, S. R. (1986). *Teaching the young child with motor delays: A guide for parents and professionals.* Austin, TX: Pro–Ed, Inc.

Hanson, S. M. H., & Sporakowski, M. J. (1986). Single parent families. *Family Relations, 35,* 3–8.

Hareven, T. K. (1982). American families in transition: Perspectives on change. In F. Walsh (Ed.), *Normal family processes* (pp. 446–466). New York: The Guilford Press.

Harrington, R. G., & Gibson, E. (1986). Preassessment procedures for learning disabled children: Are they effective? *Journal of Learning Disabilities, 19,* 538–541.

Harris, G. A. (1985). Fairy tales, beatlemania, and a handicapped child. In H. R. Turnbull & A. P. Turnbull (Eds.), *Parents speak out: Then and now* (pp. 261–270). Columbus, OH: Merrill Publishing Co.

Harrison, R., & Edwards, J. (1983). *Child abuse.* Portland, OR: Ednick Publications.

Hassell, C. M. (1982). A study of the consequences of excessive legal intervention on the local implementation of P.L. 94–142. *Dissertation Abstracts, 42,* 7.

Heifetz, L. J. (1977). Behavioral training for parents of retarded children: Alternative formats based on instructional manuals. *American Journal of Mental Deficiency, 82,* 194–203.

Helge, D. (1988). Serving at–risk populations in rural America. *Teaching Exceptional Children, 20*(4), 17–18.

Helsel Family. (1985). The Helsel's story of Robin. In H. R. Turnbull & A. P. Turnbull (Eds.), *Parents speak out: Then and now* (pp. 81–100). Columbus, OH: Merrill Publishing Co.

Hepner, P., & Silverstein, J. (1988a). Seeking an independent evaluation: Issues for parents to consider. *Exceptional Parent, 18*(2), 42–47.

Hepner, P., & Silverstein, J. (1988b). Seeking an independent evaluation: Part II: What will the assessment involve? *Exceptional Parent, 18*(2), 48–53.

Hepworth, D. H., & Larsen, J. A. (1982). *Direct social work practice: Theory and skills.* Homewood, IL: The Dorsey Press.

Heshusius, L. (1982). At the heart of the advocacy dilemma. *Exceptional Children, 49*(1), 6–13.

Heward, W. L., & Chapman, J. E. (1981). Improving parent-teacher communication through recorded telephone messages: Systematic replication in a special education classroom. *Journal of Special Education Technology, 4,* 11–19.

Heward, W. L., Dardig, J. C., & Rossett, A. (1979). *Working with parents of handicapped children.* Columbus, OH: Merrill Publishing Co.

Heward, W. L., & Orlansky, M. D. (1984). *Exceptional Children* (2nd ed.). Columbus, OH: Merrill Publishing Co.

Hill, R. (1949). *Families under stress.* New York: Harper and Row.

Hirsch, G. P. (1981). *Training developmental disability specialists in parent conference skills.* Unpublished doctoral dissertation, The University of Kansas.

Hirsch, G., & Altman, K. (1986). Training graduate students in parent conference skills. *Applied Research in Mental Retardation, 7*(3), 371–385.

Hochman, R. (1979). Communicating with parents about the classroom. *Exceptional Teacher, 1*(3), 6–7.

Hornby, G. (1988). *Fathers of handicapped children.* Unpublished manuscript, University of Hull, England.

Horner, C. M. (1987). Homework: A way to teach problem solving. *Academic Therapy, 22*(3), 239–244.

Horner, N. (1987). Parent involvement in special education (Doctoral dissertation, University of Oregon). *Dissertation Abstracts International, 47,* 3394A.

Houghton, J., Bronicki, G. J., & Guess, D. (1987). Opportunities to express preferences and make choices among students with severe disabilities in classroom settings. *JASH, 12*(1), 18–27.

Hoy, C. (1986). Preventing learned helplessness. *Academic Therapy, 22*(1), 11–18.

Hughes, J., & Beaty, N. (1986). *Rainbow connection: An instructional guide.* (Grant #G008530224, U.S. Department of Education, Office of SPED & Rehabilitation). Birmingham, AL: United Cerebral Palsy of Greater Birmingham.

Hunt, J. (Ed.). (1972). *Human intelligence.* New Brunswick: Transaction Books.

Huntington, F. (1984a). Home remedies. *inCider,* pp. 21–25.

Huntington, F. (1984b). Ten tips for choosing educational software. *inCider,* pp. 31–34.

Hyman, I., & Schreiber, K. (1975). Selected concepts and practices of child advocacy in school psychology. *Psychology in the Schools, 12*(7), 50–58.

Intagliata, S., & Doyle, N. (1984). Enhancing social support for parents of developmentally disabled children: Training in interpersonal problem solving skills. *Mental Retardation, 22,* 4–11.

Isbell, H. M. (1979). He looked the way a baby should look. In T. Dougan, L. Isbell, & P. Vyas (Eds.), *We have been there* (pp. 6–11). Nashville, TN: Abingdon Press.

Isbell, L. (1979a). Happy Valentine's Day. In T. Dougan, L. Isbell, & P. Vyas (Eds.), *We have been there: A guidebook for parents of people with mental retardation* (pp. 132–135). Salt Lake City: Dougan, Isbell, and Vyas Associates.

Isbell, L. (1979b). The conditional use permit. In T. Dougan, L. Isbell, & P. Vyas (Eds.), *We have been there* (pp. 237–240). Nashville, TN: Abingdon Press.

Isbell, L. (1979c). The meanest mommy on the block. In T. Dougan, L. Isbell, & P. Vyas (Eds.), *We have been there* (pp. 45–49). Nashville, TN: Abingdon Press.

Iverson, B. K., Brownlee, G. D., & Walberg, H. J. (1981). Parent-teacher contacts and student learning. *Journal of Educational Research, 74*, 394–396.

Ivey, A. P. (1986). *Developmental therapy: Theory into practice.* San Francisco: Jossey-Bass.

Jennings, J. (1987). Elderly parents as caregivers for their adult dependent children. *Social Work, 32*(5), 430–433.

Jesien, G. (1988). Rural families with special needs. *OSERS News in Print, 1*(4), 7.

Johnson, B., & Morse, H. A. (1968). Injured children and their parents. *Children, 15*, 147–152.

Johnson, B. H., McGonigel, M. J., & Kaufmann, R. K. (Eds.). (1989). *Guidelines and recommended practices for the individualized family service plan.* (Contract No. 300-87-0163). Washington, DC: U.S. Department of Education.

Johnson, D. W., & Johnson, R. T. (1986). Mainstreaming and cooperative learning strategies. *Exceptional Children, 52*(6), 553–561.

Joyce, K., Singer, M., & Isralowitz, R. (1983). Impact of respite care on parents' perceptions of quality of life. *Mental Retardation, 21*, 153–156.

Kabler, M. L. (1985). Best practices in procedural safeguards. In A. Thomas & J. Grimes (Eds.), *Best practices in school psychology* (pp. 237–250). Kent, OH: National Association of School Psychologists.

Kamerman, S. (1985). Young, poor, and a mother alone. In H. McAdoo & J. Parham (Eds.), *Services to young families* (pp. 1–38). Washington, DC: American Public Welfare Association.

Kammerlohr, B., Henderson, R. A., & Rock, S. (1983). Special education due process hearing in Illinois. *Exceptional Children, 49*(5), 417–422.

Kanner, L. (1949). Problems of nosology and psychodynamica of early infantile autism. *American Journal of Orthopsychiatry, 19*, 416–426.

Kantor, D., & Lehr, W. (1975). *Inside the family: Toward a theory of family process.* San Francisco: Jossey-Bass.

Karnes, F. A., & Karnes, M. R. (1982). Parents and schools: Educating gifted and talented children. *The Elementary School Journal, 82*(3), 236–248.

Karnes, M. B., & Teska, J. A. (1980). Toward successful parent involvement in programs for handicapped children. In J. J. Gallagher (Ed.), *New directions for exceptional children: Parents and families of handicapped children* (Vol. 4, pp. 85–109). San Francisco: Jossey-Bass.

Kaslow, S. W., & Cooper, B. (1978). Family therapy with learning disabled children and his or her family. *Marriage and Family Counseling, 4*(1), 41–49.

Katz, J. (1984). Why doctors don't disclose uncertainty. *The Hastings Center Report, 14*(1), 35–44.

Katzen, K. (1980). To the editor: An open letter to CEC. *Exceptional Children, 46*(8), 582.

Kauffman, J. M. (1984). Saving children in the age of big brother: The moral and ethical issue in the identification of deviance. *Behavioral Disorders, 10*(1), 60–70.

Kazak, A. E., & Marvin, R. S. (1984). Differences, difficulties and adaptation: Stress and social networks in families with a handicapped child. *Family Relations, 33*, 67–77.

Kermani, E. J. (1988). Handicapped children and the law: Children afflicted with AIDS. *American Academy of Child and Adolescent Psychiatry, 27*(2), 152–154.

Kibert, R. P. (1986). *A descriptive study of the perceptions of normal college siblings in families with a mentally retarded child.* Unpublished doctoral dissertation, University of Pittsburgh.

Kinloch, D. (1986). *An investigation of the impact of a preparation strategy on teachers' perceptions of parent participation in the IEP review conferences of learning disabled and educable mentally retarded students.* Unpublished doctoral dissertation, University of Missouri, Columbia.

Kirk, S. A. (1984). Introspection and prophecy. In B. Blatt & R. J. Morris (Eds.), *Perspectives in special education: Personal orientations* (pp. 25–55). Glenview, IL: Scott, Foresman, & Co.

Klein, B., Van Hasselt, V. B., Trefelner, M., Sandstrom, D. J., & Brandt–Snyder, P. (1988). The parent and toddler training project for visually impaired and blind multihandicapped children. *Journal of Visual Impairment and Blindness, 82*(2), 59–64.

Knapp, L. (1972). *Nonverbal communication in human interaction.* New York: Holt, Rinehart & Winston, Inc.

Knighton, C. E., & Knighton, W. (1985). The colors of the rainbow. In H. R. Turnbull & A. P. Turnbull (Eds.), *Parents speak out: Then and now* (pp. 271–280). Columbus, OH: Merrill Publishing Co.

Kolstoe, O. P. (1970). *Teaching educable mentally retarded children.* New York: Holt, Rinehart and Winston, Inc.

Kozol, J. (1988). *Rachel and her children: Homeless families in America.* New York: Fawcett Columbine.

Krents, E., Schulman, V., & Brenner, S. (1987). Child abuse and the disabled child: Perspectives for parents. *Volta Review 89*(5), 78–91.

Kronick, D. (1976). *Three families: The effect of family dynamics on social and conceptual learning.* San Rafael, CA: Academic Therapy Publications.

Kroth, R. L. (1975). *Communication with parents of exceptional children.* Denver: Love Publishing Co.

Kroth, R. L. (1985). *Communicating with parents of exceptional children: Improving parent-teacher relationships* (2nd ed.). Denver, CO: Love Publishing Co.

Kupfer, F. (1982). *Before and after Zachariah.* New York: Delacorte Press.

Kupfer, F. (1988, December). Not home for the holidays. *Family Circle,* p. 226.

Kushner, H. S. (1981). *When bad things happen to good people.* New York: Avon Books.

LaBarbera, J. D., & Lewis S. (1980). Fathers who undermine children's treatment: A challenge for the clinician. *Journal of Consulting and Clinical Psychology, 9,* 204–206.

Lane, G. (1989). AIDS and family grief. *Children with AIDS Newsletter, 1*(4), 6.

Latham, G. (1981). Serving the rural handicapped: Multiple methods. *Rural Educator, 2*(3), 25–30.

Lavine, J. (1986). De-mystifying professional evaluations. *Academic Therapy, 21*(5), 615–617.

Lay, C. A. (1977). Due process in special education. *Dissertation Abstracts International, 37,* 7687A.

Lechtenberg, R. (1984). *Epilepsy and the family.* Cambridge, MA: Harvard University Press.

Lee, G. R. (1982). *Family structure and interaction: A comparative analysis.* Minneapolis: University of Minnesota Press.

Lehr, S. (1989). Implications for parent training and information centers. *Coalition Quarterly, 6*(2&3). Boston: Technical Assistance for Parent Programs (TAPP).

Lennox, D., Miltenberger, R., Spengler, P., & Erfanian, N. (1988). Decelerative treatment practices with persons who have mental retardation: A review of five years of the literature. *American Journal on Mental Retardation, 92*(6), 492–501.

LePontois, J., Moel, D. I., & Cohn, R. A. (1987). Family adjustment to pediatric ambulatory dialysis. *American Journal of Orthopsychiatry, 57,* 78–83.

Leslie, G. R. (1979). The nature of the family. In G. R. Leslie (Ed.), *The family in social context* (4th ed., pp. 3–23). New York: Oxford University Press.

Levitt, M. (1988). Away from home for the first time. *The Exceptional Parent, 18*(5), 55.

Lewis, C. L., Busch, J. P., Proger, B. B., & Juska, P. J. (1981). Parents' perspectives concerning the IEP process. *Education Unlimited, 3*(3), 18–22.

Liebman, R. & Montalva, B. (Ed.). (1975). *Constructing a workable reality* [training videotape]. Philadelphia: Philadelphia Child Guidance Clinic.

Lipton, H. L., & Svarstad, B. (1977). Sources of variation in clinicians' communication to parents about mental retardation. *American Journal of Mental Deficiency, 82,* 155–161.

Lloyd, J. W., Crowley, E. P., Kohler, F. W., & Strain, P. S. (1988). Redefining the applied research agenda: Cooperative learning, prereferral, teacher consultation, and peer-mediated interventions. *Journal of Learning Disabilities, 21,* 43–52.

Lombana, J. H. (1983). *Home-school partnerships: Guidelines and strategies for educators.* New York: Grune & Stratton.

Lonsdale, G. (1978). Family life with a handicapped child: The parents speak. *Child: Care, Health and Development, 4,* 99–120.

Losen, S. M., & Diament, B. (1978). *Parent conference in the schools: Procedures for developing effective partnership.* Boston: Allyn and Bacon, Inc.

Lucito, L. J. (1963). Gifted children. In L. M. Dunn (Ed.), *Exceptional children in the schools* (pp. 179–238). New York: Holt, Rinehart & Winston, Inc.

Lusthaus, C. S., Lusthaus, E. W., & Gibbs, H. (1981). Parents' role in the decision process. *Exceptional Children, 48*(3), 256–257.

Luterman, D. (1979). *Counseling parents of hearing impaired children.* Boston: Little, Brown.

Lynch, E. W., & Bakley, S. (1989). Serving young children whose parents are mentally retarded. *Infants and Young Children, 1*(3), 26–38.

Lynch, E. W., & Stein, R. (1982). Perspectives on parent participation in special education. *Exceptional Education Quarterly, 3*(2), 56–63.

Lynch, E., & Stein, R. (1987). Parent participation by ethnicity: A comparison of Hispanic, Black, and Anglo families. *Exceptional Children, 54*(2), 105–111.

MacDonald, L., & Mare, D. L. (1988). Respite care—Who uses it? *Mental Retardation, 26*(2), 93–96.

MacMillan, D., Henrick, I., & Watkins, A. (1988). Impact of Diana, Larry P., & P.L. 94–142 on minority students. *Exceptional Children, 54*(5), 426–432.

MacMillan, D. L., & Turnbull, A. P. (1983). Parent involvement with special education: Respecting individual preferences. *Education and Training of the Mentally Retarded, 18*(1), 5–9.

MacMurphy, H. (1916). The relation of feeble mindedness to other social problems. *Journal of Psycho-Asthenics, 21,* 58–63.

Maddux, C. D., & Cummings, R. E. (1983). Parental home tutoring: Aids and cautions. *The Exceptional Parent, 13*(4), 30–33.

Malmberg, P. A. (1984). *Development of field tested special education placement committee parent education materials.* Unpublished doctoral dissertation, Virginia Polytechnic Institute at State University, Blacksburg.

Mangrum, C. T., & Strichart, S. S., (Eds.). (1988). *Peterson's Colleges with Programs for Learning Disabled Students* (2nd ed.). Princeton, NJ: Peterson's Guides.

Mann, J. A., & Kreyche, G. F. (1966). *Approaches to morality.* New York: Harcourt, Brace & World, Inc.

Marcus, L. M. (1977). Patterns of coping in families of psychotic children. *American Journal of Orthopsychiatry, 47*(3), 388–399.

Margalit, M. (1982). Learning disabled children and their families: Strategies of extension and adaption of family therapy. *Journal of Learning Disabilities, 15,* 594–595.

Margolis, H., & Brannigan, G. (1986). Building trust with parents. *Academic Therapy, 22*(1), 71–75.

Marion, R. (1979). Minority parent involvement in the IEP process: A systematic model approach. *Focus on Exceptional Children, 10*(8), 1–16.

Marion, R. (1981). *Educators, parents, and exceptional children.* Rockville, MD: Aspen Publishers.

Marriage and Divorce Today. (1987, July 13). *12* (#50).

Marshall, N. R., & Goldstein, S. G. (1969). Imparting diagnostic information to mothers: A comparison of methodologies. *Journal of Speech and Hearing Research, 12,* 65–72.

Mattson, B. D. (1977). Involving parents in special education: Did you really teach them? *Education and Training of the Mentally Retarded, 12*(4), 358–360.

May, J. (1988). Special needs children, special needs fathers. *Family Resource Coalition Report, 2,* 10.

McAndrew, I. (1976). Children with a handicap and their families. *Child: Care, Health and Development, 2,* 213–237.

McCarney, S. (1986). Preferred types of communication indicated by parents and teachers of emotionally disturbed students. *Behavioral Disorders, 11*(2), 118–123.

McConkey, R. (1988). Educating all parents: An approach based on video. In K. Marfo (Ed.), *Parent-child interaction and developmental disabilities: Theory, research, and intervention,* (pp. 253–272). New York: Praeger Publishers.

McCubbin, H. I., Joy, C. B., Cauble, A. E., Comeau, J. K., Patterson, J. M., & Needle, R. H. (1980). Family stress and coping: A decade review. *Journal of Marriage and the Family, 42,* 855–871.

McCullough, M. E. (1981). Parent and sibling definition of situation regarding transgenerational shift in care of a handicapped child. (Doctoral dissertation, University of Minnesota). *Dissertation Abstracts International, 42,* 161B.

McDonnell, A., & Hardman, M. (1988). A synthesis of best practice guidelines for early childhood services. *Journal of the Division for Early Childhood, 12*(4), 328–341.

McDonnell, J. (1987). Integration of students with severe handicaps into regular public schools: An analysis of parents' perceptions of potential outcomes. *Education and Training in Mental Retardation, 22*(2), 98–111.

McElroy, E. (1987). *Children and adolescents with mental illness: A parents guide.* Kensington, MD: Woodbine House.

McGill, D., & Pearce, J. K. (1982). British families. In M. Goldrick, J. K. Pearce, & J. Giordano (Eds.), *Ethnicity in family therapy* (pp. 457–482). New York: The Guilford Press.

McGinley, K. H. (1987). *Evaluating the effectiveness of mediation as an alternative to the sole use of the due process hearing in special education.* Unpublished doctoral dissertation, The University of Kansas.

McGoldrick, M. (1982). Ethnicity and family therapy: An overview. In M. McGoldrick, J. K. Pearce, & J. Giordano (Eds.), *Ethnicity in family therapy* (pp. 3–30). New York: The Guilford Press.

McGoldrick, M., & Gerson, R. (1985). *Genograms in family assessment.* New York: W. W. Norton & Company.

McGuire, J. M., & Shaw, S. F. (1987). A decision-making process for the college-bound student: Matching learner, institution and support program. *LD Quarterly, 10*(2), 106–111.

McHale, S. M., & Gamble, W. C. (1987). Sibling relationships and adjustment of children with disabled brothers and sisters. *Journal of Children in Contemporary Science, 19,* 131–138.

McLoughlin, J. A., Edge, D., Petrosko, J., & Strenecky, B. (1981). PL 94–142 and information dissemination: A step forward. *Journal of Special Education Technology, 4*(4), 50–56.

McNamara, B. (1986). Parents as partners in the IEP process. *Academic Therapy, 21*(3), 309–319.

Meier, J. H., & Sloan, M. P. (1984). The severely handicapped and child abuse. In J. Blacher (Ed.), *Severely handicapped young children and their families* (pp. 247–274). New York: Academic Press.

Mercer, J. R. (1973). *Labeling the mentally retarded child.* Berkeley, CA: University of California Press.

Mesibov, G. B., & LaGreca, A. M. (1981). Ethical issues in parent professional service interaction. In J. L. Paul (Ed.), *Understanding and working with parents of children with special needs* (pp. 154–179). New York: Holt, Rinehart and Winston.

Mest, G. M. (1988). With a little help from their friends: Use of social support systems by persons with retardation. *Journal of Social Issues, 44*(1), 117–125.

Meyer, D. J. (1986). Fathers of handicapped children. In R. R. Fewell and P. F. Vadasy (Eds.), *Families of handicapped children: Needs and supports across the life span* (pp. 35–73). Austin, TX: Pro-Ed, Inc.

Meyer, D. J., & Vadasy, P. F. (1986). *Grandparent workshops: How to organize workshops for grandparents of children with handicaps.* Seattle: University of Washington Press.

Meyer, D. J., Vadasy, P. F., & Fewell, R. R. (1985a). *Living with a brother or sister with special needs: A book for siblings.* Seattle: University of Washington Press.

Meyer, D. J., Vadasy, P. F., & Fewell, R. R. (1985b). *SIBSHOPS: A handbook for implementing workshops for siblings of children with special needs.* Seattle: University of Washington Press.

Meyer, D. J., Vadasy, P. F., Fewell, R. R., & Schell, G. C. (1985). *A handbook for the fathers program: How to organize a program for fathers and their handicapped children.* Seattle: University of Washington Press.

Michael, R. J. (1987). Evaluating the college of choice. *Academic Therapy, 22*(5), 485–488.

Michael, R. J. (1988). Library services for LD college students. *Academic Therapy, 23*(5), 529–532.

Michaelis, C. (1981). Mainstreaming: A mother's perspective. *Topics in Early Childhood Special Education, 1*(1), 11–16.

Miller, J. A., Bigner, J. J., Jacobson, R. B., & Turner, J. G. (1982). The value of children for farm families: A comparison of mothers and fathers. In N. Stinnett, J. DeFrain, K. King, H. Lingren, G. Rowe, S. VanZandt, & R. Williams (Eds.), *Family strengths 4: Positive support systems* (pp. 33–42). Lincoln: University of Nebraska Press.

Miller, M., & Diao, J. (1987). Family friends: New resources for psychosocial care of chronically ill children in families. *Children's Health Care, 15*(4), 259–264.

Miller, N. B., & Cantwell, D. P. (1976). Siblings as therapists: A behavioral approach. *American Journal of Psychiatry, 133*(4), 447–450.

Milofsky, C. (1974). Why special education isn't special. *Harvard Education Review, 44,* 437–458.

Minner, S., & Prater, G. (1987). Parental use of telephone answering equipment to assist handicapped children. *Techniques: A Journal for Remedial Education and Counseling, 3,* 51–56.

Minuchin, S. (1974). *Families and family therapy.* Cambridge, MA: Harvard University Press.

Mitchell, S. (1976). *Parental perceptions of their experiences with due process in special education: A preliminary report.* Cambridge, MA: Research Institute for Educational Problems. (ERIC Document Reproduction No. ED 130 482)

Moore, J. (1988). Online help from IBM. *Exceptional Parent, 18*(7), 56–60.

Morton, K. (1985). Identifying the enemey—A parent's complaint. In R. H. Turnbull & A. P. Turnbull (Eds.), *Parents speak out: Then and now* (pp. 143–148). Columbus, OH: Merrill Publishing Co.

Moses, K. I. (1983). The impact of initial diagnosis: Mobilizing family resources. In J. A. Mulick & S. M. Pueschel (Eds.), *Parent-professional partnerships in developmental disability services* (pp. 11–34). Cambridge, MA: The Ware Press.

Mullins, J. B. (1983). The uses of bibliotherapy in counseling families confronted with handicaps. In M. Seligman (Ed.), *The family with a handicapped child: Understanding and treatment* (pp. 235–251). New York: Grune and Stratton.

Murphy, A. T. (1982). The family with a handicapped child: A review of the literature. *Developmental and Behavioral Pediatrics, 3*(2), 73–82.

Nader, R., Petkas, P., & Blackwell, K. (Eds.). (1972). *Whistle-blowing.* New York: Grossman.

National Association of State Directors of Special Education (NASDSE). (1978). *The implementation of due process in Massachusetts.* Washington, DC: Author.

National Society for Autistic Children, Board of Directors and Professional Advisory Board. (1977). *A short definition of autism.* Albany, NY: Author.

Neal, B. (1988). Sharing the journey. *Let's Face It, 1*(2).

Nebraska Department of Education, Special Education Bureau. (1987). Adjusting our sails to the direction of the wind. *Sharing Connection. 3*(1), 1–6.

Nelson, P. T. (1986). Newsletters: An effective delivery mode for providing educational information and emotional support to single parent families? *Family Relations, 35,* 183–188.

Neubert, D. A., & Foster, J. (1988). LD students make the transition. *Teaching Exceptional Children, 20*(3), 42–44.

Neugarten, B. (1976). Adaptations and the life cycle. *The Counseling Psychologist, 6*(1), 16–20.

Neulicht, A. T. (1984). *Developing residential opportunities for persons with autism.* Overland Park, KS: Johnson County Mental Retardation Center.

Northern, H. (1982). *Clinical social work.* New York: Columbia University Press.

Norton, A. J., & Glick, P. C. (1986). One parent families: A social and economic profile. *Family Relations, 35*(1), 9–17.

Nye, J., Westling, K., & Laten, S. (1986). Communication skills for parents. *The Exceptional Parent, 16*(5), 30–36.

Office of Special Education, U.S. Department of Education. (1983). *Fifth Annual Report to Congress on the Implementation of P.L. 94–142.* Washington, DC: author.

Office of Special Education, U.S. Department of Education. (1984). *Sixth Annual Report to Congress on the Implementation of P.L. 94–142.* Washington, DC: author.

Office of Special Education, U.S. Department of Education. (1985). *Seventh Annual Report to Congress on the Implementation of P.L. 94–142.* Washington, DC: author.

Office of Special Education, U.S. Department of Education. (1986). *Eighth Annual Report to Congress on the Implementation of P.L. 94–142.* Washington, DC: author.

Office of Special Education, U.S. Department of Education. (1988). *Tenth Annual Report to Congress on the Implementation of P.L. 94–142.* Washington, DC: author.

O'Hara, D. M., & Levy, S. M. (1984). Family adaptation to learning disability: A framework for understanding and treatment. *Learning Disabilities, 3*(6), 63–77.

Olshansky, S. (1962). Chronic sorrow: A response to having a mentally defective child. *Social Casework, 43,* 191–194.

Olson, D. H., McCubbin, H. I., Barnes, H., Larsen, A., Muxen, M., & Wilson, M. (1983). *Families: What makes them work.* Beverly Hills, CA: Sage Publications.

Olson, D. H., Russell, C. S., & Sprenkle, D. H. (1980). Circumplex model of marital and family systems II: Empirical studies and clinical intervention. In J. P. Vincent (Ed.), *Advances in family intervention assessment and theory* (Vol. 1, pp. 129–179). Greenwich, CT: JAI Press.

Olson, D. H., Sprenkle, D. H., & Russell, C. S. (1979). Circumplex model of marital and family systems: I. Cohesion and adaptability dimensions, family types, and clinical applications. *Family Process, 18,* 3–28.

Osborne, D. (1988). Keeping a 'Grace'ful perspective. *Dialogue on Disabilities, 9*(4), 1–2.

Osterkamp, L., & Press, A. N. (1980). *Stress? Find your balance.* Lawrence, KS: Lynn Osterkamp and Allan N. Press, P.O. Box 763.

PACER Center, Inc. (1984). *Parents helping parents.* Evaluation report. Minneapolis, MN: Author.

PACER Center, Inc. (1987). Evaluation report: The parents helping parents and programs for students projects, 1986–1987, Minneapolis, MN: PACER Center, Inc.

Parent Involvement Center. (1985). Albuquerque Public Schools, Albuquerque, NM.

Parsons, T., & Bales, R. F. (1955). *Family, socialization and interaction process.* Glencoe, IL: Free Press.

Pasanella, A. L., & Volkmor, C. B. (Eds.). (1981). *Teaching handicapped students in the mainstream: Coming back or never leaving* (2nd ed.). Columbus, OH: Merrill Publishing Company.

Pask-McCartney, C., & Salomone, P. R. (1988). Difficult cases in career counseling: III—the multipotentialed client. *The Career Development Quarterly, 36,* 231–239.

Pearlin, L. I., & Schooler, C. (1978). The structure of coping. *Journal of Health and Social Behavior, 19*, 2–21.

Pepper, F. C. (1976). Teaching the American Indian child in mainstream settings. In R. L. Jones (Ed.), *Mainstreaming and the Minority Child* (pp. 108–122). New York: The Guilford Press.

Perino, S. C., & Perino, J. (1981). *Parenting the gifted: Developing the promise.* New York: R. R. Bowker Co.

Perls, F. S. (1969). *Gestalt therapy verbation.* Lafayette, CA: Real People Press.

Perske, R., Perske, M., Clifton, A., McLean, B., & Stein, J. (1986). *Mealtimes for persons with severe handicaps.* Baltimore: Paul H. Brookes Publishing Co.

Peterson, N. L. (1987). *Early Intervention for Handicapped at-risk Children.* Denver: Love Publishing Co.

Pfeiffer, S. I. (1980). The school-based interprofessional team: Recurring problems and some possible solutions. *Journal of School Psychology, 18*(4), 388–394.

Pfeiffer, S. I., & Tittler, B. I. (1983). Utilizing the multidisciplinary team to facilitate a school-family systems orientation. *School Psychology Review, 12*, 168–173.

Philage, M., & Kuna, D. (1985). The therapeutic contract and LD families. *Academic Therapy, 10*,(4), 407–411.

Pistono, W. J. (1977). The relationships between certain identified variables and parental participation during the educational planning and placement committee meeting for handicapped students in Michigan. *Dissertation Abstracts International, 38*(5A), 2705.

Powell, T. H., & Ogle, P. A. (1985). *Brothers and sisters—A special part of exceptional families.* Baltimore: Paul H. Brookes Publishing Co.

President's Committee on Mental Retardation. (1977). *Mental retardation: Past and present.* Washington, DC: U.S. Government Printing Office.

Price, J. A. (1976). North American Indian Families. In C. H. Mindel & R. W. Habestein (Eds.), *Ethnic families in America patterns and variations* (pp. 248–270). New York: Elsevier.

Price, M., & Goodman, L. (1980). Individualized education programs: A cost study. *Exceptional Children, 46*(6), 446–458.

Pruett, K. D. (1987). *The nurturing father.* New York: Pocket Books.

Pueschel, S. M. (1988). *Young person with Down syndrome: Transition from adolescence to adulthood.* Baltimore: Paul H. Brookes Publishing Co.

Pulver, R. (1988). You will grow because of this. *Exceptional Parent, 1*, 59–61.

Quine, L., & Paul, J. (1985). Examining the causes of stress in families with severely mentally handicapped children. *British Journal of Social Work, 15*, 501–517.

Ramirez, B. A. (1988). Culturally and linguistically diverse children. *Teaching Exceptional Children, 20*(4), 445–446.

Reed, E. W., & Reed, S. C. (1965). *Mental retardation: A family study.* Philadelphia: Saunders.

Reschly, D. J. (1988). Minority MMR overrepresentation and special education reform. *Exceptional Children, 54*, 316–323.

Reynolds, M. C. (1988). Past, present and future of school integration. *Minnesota University Affiliated Program Impact, 1*(2), 2.

Roberds-Baxter, S. (1984). The parent connection: Enhancing the affective component of parent conferences. *Teaching Exceptional Children, 17*(1), 55–58.

Rockowitz, R. J., & Davidson, P. W. (1979). Discussing diagnostic findings with parents. *Journal of Learning Disabilities, 12*(1), 11–16.

Rodriquez, F. (1987). *Equity education: An imperative for effective schools.* Dubuque, IA: Kendall-Hunt.

Rogers, C. (1951). *Client-centered therapy.* Boston: Houghton-Mifflin Co.

Rogers, C. (1965). *On becoming a person: A therapist's view of psychotherapy.* Boston: Houghton-Mifflin Co.

Roos, P. (1985). Parents of mentally retarded children—Misunderstood and mistreated. In H. R. Turnbull & A. P. Turnbull (Eds.), *Parents speak out: Then and now* (pp. 245–260). Columbus, OH: Merrill Publishing Co.

Rosenberg, H., Tesolowski, D., & Stein, R. (1983). Advocacy: Education responsibility to handicapped children. *Education and Training of the Mentally Retarded, 18*(4), 266–270.

Rosenberg, M. S., Reppucci, N. D., & Linney, J. A. (1983). Issues in the implementation of human service programs: Examples from a parent training project for high-risk families. *Analysis and Intervention in Developmental Disabilities, 3*, 215–225.

Rosenberg, S. A., & McTate, G. A. (1982). Intellectually handicapped mothers: Problems and prospects. *Children Today, 11*, 24–26.

Rotunno, M., & McGoldrick, M. (1982). Italian families. In M. McGoldrick, J. K. Pearce, & J. Giordano (Eds.), *Ethnicity in family therapy* (pp. 340–363). New York: The Guilford Press.

Rousso, H. (1982). Taking on the social scene. *The Exceptional Parent, 12*(1), 21–25.

Rousso, H. (1984). Fostering healthy self-esteem. *Exceptional Parent, 8*(14), 9–14.

Rubin, L. B. (1976). *Worlds of pain: Life in the working-class family.* New York: Basic Books.

Rutherford, R. G., & Edgar E. (1979). *Teachers and parents: A guide to interaction and cooperation.* Boston: Allyn & Bacon, Inc.

Safer, N. D., Morrissey, P. A., Kaufman, M. J., & Lewis, L. (1978). Implementation of IEPs: New teacher roles and requisite support systems. *Focus on Exceptional Children, 10*(1), 1–20.

Sager, C. J., Brown, H. S., Crohn, H., Engel, T., Rodstein, E., & Walker, L. (1983). *Treating the remarried family.* New York: Brunner/Mazel.

Salend, S. J., & Schliff, J. (1988). The many dimensions of homework. *Academic Therapy, 23*(4), 397–403.

Salisbury, C., & Evans, I. M. (1988). Comparison of parental involvement in regular and special education. *Journal of the Association for Persons with Severe Handicaps, 13*(4), 268–272.

Sarason, S. B., & Doris, J. (1979). *Educational handicap, public policy, and social history.* New York: The Free Press.

Sattler, J. M. (1988). *Assessment of children.* San Diego: Jerome M. Sattler.

Schalock, R. L. (1985). Comprehensive community services: A plea for interagency coordination. In R. H. Bruininks & K. C. Lakin (Eds.), *Living and learning in the least restrictive environment* (pp. 37–63). Baltimore: Paul H. Brookes Publishing Co.

Scheerenberger, R. C. (1983). *A history of mental retardation.* Baltimore: Paul H. Brookes Publishing Co.

Schilling, R. F., Kirkham, M. A., Snow, W. H., & Schinke, S. P. (1986). Single mothers with handicapped children: Different from their married counterparts? *Family Relations, 35*, 69–77.

Schradle, S. B., & Dougher, M. J. (1985). Social support as a mediator of stress: Theoretical and empirical issues. *Clinical Psychology Review, 5*, 641–661.

Schreibman, L., O'Neill, R. E., & Koegel, R. L. (1983). Behavioral training for siblings of autistic children. *Journal of Applied Behavior Analysis, 16*(2), 129–138.

Schulz, J. B. (1985a). Growing up together. In H. R. Turnbull & A. P. Turnbull (Eds.), *Parents Speak Out: Then and Now* (pp. 11–20). Columbus, OH: Merrill Publishing Co.

Schulz, J. B. (1985b). The parent-professional conflict. In H. R. Turnbull and A. P. Turnbull (Eds.), *Parents speak out: Then and now,* (pp. 3–11). Columbus, OH: Merrill Publishing Co.

Schulz, J. B., & Turnbull, A. P. (1984). *Mainstreaming handicapped students: A guide for the classroom teacher.* Newton, MA: Allyn & Bacon, Inc.

Select Committee on Children, Youth & Families. (December, 1988). *Children and Families: Key Trends in the 1980's.* Washington, D.C.: U.S. Government Printing Office.

Seligman, M. (1985). Handicapped children and their families. *Journal of Counseling and Development, 64*, 274–277.

Seligman, M., & Darling, R. B. (1989). *Ordinary families, special children: A systems approach to childhood disability.* New York: The Guilford Press.

Seligman, M., & Meyerson, R. (1982). Group approaches for parents of exceptional children. In M. Seligman (Ed.), *Group psychotherapy and counseling with special populations*, (pp. 99–116). Baltimore: University Park Press.

Shearer, D. E., & Loftin, C. R. (1984). The portage project: Teaching parents to teach their preschool children in the home. In R. F. Dangel & R. A. Polster (Eds.), *Parent training* (pp. 93–126). New York: The Guilford Press.

Shearer, M. S., & Shearer, D. E. (1977). Parent involvement. In J. B. Jordan, A. H. Hayden, M. B. Karnes, & M. M. Wood (Eds.), *Early childhood education for exceptional children* (pp. 208–235). Reston, VA: Council for Exceptional Children.

Shertzer, B. & Stone, S. C. (1981). *Fundamentals of Guidance* (4th ed.). Boston: Houghton-Mifflin Company.

Shevin, M., & Klein, N. K. (1984). The importance of choice-making skills for students with severe disabilities. *The Journal of the Association for Persons with Severe Handicaps, 9*(3), 159–166.

Shon, S. P., & Ja, D. Y. (1982). Asian families. In M. McGoldrick, J. K. Pearce, & J. Giordano (Eds.), *Ethnicity and family therapy* (pp. 208–228). New York: The Guilford Press.

Siegel, J. F., & Kantor, O. (1982). Self-advocacy: Change within the individual and the professional. *Social Work, 27*,(5), 451–453.

Silver, L. (1974). Emotional and social problems of a family with a child who has developmental disabilities. In R. E. Reber (Ed.), *Handbook on learning disabilities: A prognosis for the child, the adolescent, the adult.* Englewood Cliffs, NJ: Prentice Hall.

Simons, R. (1987). *After the tears: Parents talk about raising a child with a disability.* New York: Harcourt Brace Jovanovich.

Simpson, R. L. (1982). *Conferencing parents of exceptional children.* Rockville, MD: Aspen Publications.

Singer, J., Bossard, M., & Watkins, M. (1977). Effects of parental presence on attendance and input of interdisciplinary teams in an institutional setting. *Psychological Reports, 41*, 1031–1034.

Skarnulis, D. (1988). Realizing the vision for Michael. *Minnesota University Affiliated Impact, 1*(2), 4.

Skrtic, T. M., Summers, J. A., Brotherson, M. J., & Turnbull, A. P. (1984). Severely handicapped children and their brothers and sisters. In J. Blacher (Ed.), *Severely handicapped young children and their families* (pp. 215–246). New York: Academic Press.

Slater, M. A., Bates, M. A., Eicher, L., & Wikler, L. (1986). Survey: Statewide family support programs. *Applied Research in Mental Retardation, 7*, 241–257.

Somers, M. N. (1987). Parenting in the 1980s: Programming perspectives and issues. *Volta Review, 89*(5), 68–77.

Sonnenschein, P. (1984). Parents and professionals: An uneasy relationship. In M. L. Henniger & E. M. Nesselroad (Eds.), *Working with parents of handicapped children: A book of readings for school personnel* (pp. 129–139). Lanham, MD: University Press of America.

Sourkes, B. M. (1987). Siblings of the child with a life-threatening illness. *Journal of Children in Contemporary Science, 19*, 159–184.

Spradley, T. S., & Spradley, J. P. (1978). *Deaf like me.* New York: Random House.

Staff Report of the Select Committee on Children, Youth, and Families. (1987). *Abused children in America: Victims of Official Neglect.* Washington, DC: U.S. Government Printing Office.

Staples, R. (1988). The emerging majority: Resources for nonwhite families in the United States. *Family Relations, 37*, 348–354.

Stephens, T. M., & Wolf, J. S. (1980). *Effective skills in parent/teacher conferencing.* Columbus: Ohio State University, National Center for Educational Materials and Media for the Handicapped.

Stevens, S. H. (1984). *Classroom success for the learning disabled.* Winston-Salem, NC: John F. Blair, Publishing.

Stewart, C. J. (1986). *Counseling parents of exceptional children.* Columbus, OH: Merrill Publishing Co.

Strain, P. S. (1982). *Social development of exceptional children.* Rockville, MD: Aspen Publications.

Strickland, B. (1982). *Perceptions of parents and school representatives regarding their relationship before, during, and after the due process hearing.* Unpublished doctoral dissertation, The University of North Carolina.

Strickland, B. (1983). Legal issues that affect parents. In M. Seligman (Ed.), *The family with a handicapped child: Understanding and treatment* (pp. 27–39). New York: Grune & Stratton.

Strickland, B., & Turnbull, A. P. (1990). *Developing and Implementing Individualized Education Programs* (3rd ed.). Columbus, OH: Merrill.

Strukoff, P. M., McLaughlin, T. F., & Bialozor, R. C. (1987). The effects of a daily report card system in increasing homework completion and accuracy in a special education setting. *Techniques: A Journal for Remedial Education and Counseling, 3,* 19–26.

Suelzle, M., & Keenan, V. (1981). Changes in family support networks over the life cycle of mentally retarded persons. *American Journal of Mental Deficiency, 86,* 267–274.

Summers, J. A. (1987a). *Defining successful family life in families with and without disabilities: A qualitative study.* Unpublished doctoral dissertation, The University of Kansas.

Summers, J. A. (1987b). Family adjustment: Issues in research on families with developmentally disabled children. In V. B. Van Hasselt, P. S. Strain, & M. Hersen (Eds.), *Handbook of developmental disabilities* (pp. 79–90). New York: Pergamon Press.

Summers, J. A., Dell' Oliver, C., Turnbull, A. P., Benson, H. A., Santelli, E., Campbell M., & Siegel-Causey, E. (in press). Focusing in on the IFSP process: What are family and provider preferences? *Topics in Early Childhood Special Education.*

Swenson–Pierce, A., Kohl, F. L., & Egel, A. L. (1987). Siblings as home trainers: A strategy for teaching domestic skills to children. *Journal of the Association for Persons with Severe Handicaps, 12*(1), 53–60.

Switzer, L. S. (1985). Accepting the diagnosis: An educational intervention for parents of children with learning disabilities. *Journal of Learning Disabilities, 18*(3), 151–153.

Takacs, C. A. (1986). *Enjoy your gifted child.* Syracuse, NY: Syracuse University Press.

Tallman, I. (1965). Spousal role differentiation and the socialization of severely retarded children. *Journal of Marriage and the Family, 27,* 37–42.

Tawney, J. W., Aeschleman, S. R., Deaton, S. L., & Donaldson, R. M. (1979). Using telecommunications technology to instruct rural severely handicapped children. *Exceptional Children, 46,* 118–125.

Taylor, P. W. (1967). *Problems of moral philosophy: An introduction to ethics.* Belmont, CA: Dickenson Publishing Company, Inc.

Taylor, S. (1981). Caught in the continuum: A critical analysis of the principle of the least restrictive environment. *Journal of the Association for Persons with Severe Handicaps, 13*(1), 41–53.

Teglasi, H. (1985). Best practices in interpreting psychological assessment data to parents. In A. Thomas & J. Grimes (Eds.), *Best practices in school psychology* (pp. 415–430). Kent, OH: National Association of School Psychologists.

Terkelson, K. G. (1980). Toward a theory of family life cycle. In E. Carter & M. McGoldrick (Eds.), *The family life cycle: A framework of family therapy* (pp. 21–52). New York: Gardner Press.

Terman, L. (1916). *The measurement of intelligence.* Cambridge, MA: Riverside Press.

Tew, B. J., Payne, E. H., & Lawrence, K. M. (1974). Must a family with a handicapped child be a handicapped family? *Developmental Medicine and Child Neurology, 16,* Suppl. 32, 95–98.

Thompson, S. C. (1985). Finding positive meaning in a stressful event and coping. *Basic and Applied Social Psychology, 6*(4), 279–295.

Thompson, T. M. (1982). An investigation and comparison of public school personnel's perception and interpretation of P.L. 94–142. *Dissertation Abstracts International, 43,* 2840A.

Thurman, S. K., Whaley, A., & Weinraub, M. A. (1985). Studying families with handicapped parents: A rationale. In S. K. Thurman (Ed.), *Children of handicapped parents: research and clinical perspectives* (pp. 1–8). Orlando, FL: Academic Press.

Tomlan, P. (1985). Self–awareness, self–understanding, and self–concept. *Academic Therapy, 21*(2), 199–204.

Tomlinson, J. R., Acker, N., Canter, A., & Lindborg, S. (1977). Minority status, sex, and school psychological services. *Psychology in the Schools, 14*(4), 456–460.

Traux, C. B., & Mitchell, K. M. (1971). Research on certain therapist interpersonal skills in relation to process and outcome. In A. E. Bergin & S. L. Garfield (Eds.), *Handbook of psychotherapy and behavior change* (pp. 299–344). New York: Wiley.

Trevino, F. (1979). Siblings of handicapped children: Identifying those at risk. *Social Casework: The Journal of Contemporary Social Work, 60*, 488–492.

Trout, M. D. (1983). Birth of a sick or handicapped infant: Impact on the family. *Child Welfare, 62*, 337–348.

Trute, B., & Hauch, C. (1988). Building on family strength: A study of families with positive adjustment to the birth of a developmentally disabled child. *Journal of Marital and Family Therapy, 14*(2), 185–193.

Turnbull, A., & Bronicki, G. J. (1986). Changing second graders' attitudes toward people with mental retardation: Using kid power. *Mental Retardation, 24*(1), 44–45.

Turnbull, A., & Bronicki, G. J. (1987). Using kid power to teach kids about mental retardation: A long-term follow-up. *Journal of the Association for Persons with Severe Handicaps, 12*(3), 216–217.

Turnbull, A. P. (1983). Parental participation in the IEP process. In J. A. Mulick & S. M. Pueschel (Eds.), *Parent-professional participation in developmental disabilities services: Foundations and prospects* (pp. 107–123). Cambridge, MA: The Ware Press.

Turnbull, A. P. (1985a). The dual role of parent and professional. In H. R. Turnbbull & A. P. Turnbull (Eds.), *Parents speak out: Then and now* (pp. 137–142). Columbus, OH: Merrill Publishing Co.

Turnbull, A. P. (1985b). From professional to parent—A startling experience. In H. R. Turnbull & A. P. Turnbull (Eds.), *Parents speak out: Then and now* (pp. 127–135). Columbus, OH: Merrill Publishing Co.

Turnbull, A. P. (1988a). Accepting the challenge of providing comprehensive support to families. *Education and Training in Mental Retardation, 23*(4), 261–272.

Turnbull, A. P. (1988b). A life span perspective. *Family Resource Coalition Report, 7*(2), 13.

Turnbull, A. P., Brotherson, M. J., & Summers, J. A. (1985). The impact of deinstitutionalization on families: A family systems approach. In R. H. Bruininks (ed.), *Living and learning in the least restrictive environment* (pp. 115–152). Baltimore: Paul H. Brookes Publishing Co.

Turnbull, A. P., & Strickland, B. (1981). Parents and the educational system. In J. L. Paul (Ed.), *Understanding and working with parents of children with special needs* (pp. 231–263). New York: Holt, Rinehart, and Winston.

Turnbull, A. P., Strickland, B., & Brantley, J. C. (1982). *Developing and implementing individualized education programs.* Columbus, OH: Merrill Publishing Co.

Turnbull, A. P., & Summers, J. A. (1985, April). *From parent involvement to family support: Evolution to revolution.* Paper presented at the Down Syndrome State-of-the Art Conference, Boston.

Turnbull, A. P., & Summers, J. A. (1987). From parent involvement to family support: Evolution to revolution. In S. M. Pueschel, C. Tingey, J. W. Rynders, A. C. Crocher, & D. M. Crutcher (Eds.), *New perspectives on Down syndrome: Proceedings on the state-of-the-art conference* (pp. 289–306). Baltimore: Paul H. Brookes Publishing Co.

Turnbull, A. P., Summers, J. A., & Brotherson, M. J. (1984). *Working with families with disabled members: A family systems approach.* Lawrence: University of Kansas, Kansas University Affiliated Facility.

Turnbull, A. P., & Turnbull, H. R. (1982). Parent involvement in the education of handicapped children: A critique. *Mental Retardation, 20*(3), 115–122.

Turnbull, A. P., & Turnbull, H. R. (1984). Developing independence in adolescents with disabilities. *Journal of Adolescent Health Care. 6*(2), 108–124.

Turnbull, A. P., & Turnbull, H. R. (1985). Developing independence. *Journal of Adolescent Health Care, 6*(2), 108–119.

Turnbull, A. P., & Turnbull, H. R. (1985, October). *Stepping back from early intervention: An ethical perspective.* Paper presented at the DEC/CEC Early Childhood Conference, Denver.

Turnbull, A. P., & Turnbull, H. R. (1986). Stepping back from early intervention: An ethical perspective. *Journal of the Division for Early Childhood, 10,* 106–117.

Turnbull, A. P., & Turnbull, H. R. (1988). Toward great expectations for vocational opportunities: Family-professional partnerships. *Mental Retardation, 26*(6), 337–342.

Turnbull, A. P., & Winton, P. J. (1983). A comparison of specialized and mainstreamed preschools from the perspectives of parents of handicapped children. *Journal of Pediatric Psychology, 8*(1), 57–71.

Turnbull, A. P., & Winton, P. J. (1984). Parent involvement policy and practice: Current research and implications for families of young severely handicapped children. In J. Blacher (Ed.), *Severely handicapped children and their families: Research in review* (pp. 377–397). New York: Academic Press.

Turnbull, A. P., Winton, P. J., Blacher, J. B., & Salkind, N. (1983). Mainstreaming in the kindergarten classroom: Perspectives of parents of handicapped and nonhandicapped children. *Journal of the Division of Early Childhood, 6,* 14–20.

Turnbull, H. R. (Ed.). (1978). *The consent handbook.* Washington, DC: American Association on Mental Deficiency.

Turnbull, H. R. (Ed.). (1981). *The least restrictive alternative: Principles and practices.* Washington, DC: American Association on Mental Deficiency.

Turnbull, H. R. (1982). Youngberg v. Romeo: An essay. *The Journal of the Association for Persons with Severe Handicaps, 8,* 3–6.

Turnbull, H. R. (1985a). Jay's story. In H. R. Turnbull & A. P. Turnbull (Eds.), *Parents speak out: Then and now* (pp. 109–118). Columbus, OH: Merrill Publishing Co.

Turnbull, H. R. (1985b). Jay's story—The paradoxes. In H. R. Turnbull & A. P. Turnbull (Eds.), *Parents speak out: Then and now* (pp. 119–124). Columbus, OH: Merrill Publishing Co.

Turnbull, H. R. (1990). *Free appropriate public education: Law and interpretation.* Denver, CO: Love Publishing Co.

Turnbull, H. R., & Barber, P. (1984). Perspectives on public policy. In E. L. Meyen (Ed.), *Mental retardation: Topics of today—issues of tomorrow* (pp. 5–24). Reston, VA: Division on Mental Retardation of the Council for Exceptional Children.

Turnbull, H. R., et al. (1983). A policy analysis of the "least restrictive education" of handicapped children. *Rutgers Law Journal, 14*(3), 489–540.

Turnbull, H. R., Guess, D., with Backus, L., Barber, P., Fiedler, C., Helmstetter, E., & Summers, J. A. (1986). A model for analyzing the moral aspects of special education and behavioral interventions: The moral aspects of adversive therapy. In P. Dokecki & R. Zaner (Eds.), *Ethics of dealing with persons with severe handicaps: Toward a research agenda.* Baltimore: Paul H. Brookes Publishing Co.

Turnbull, H. R., Guess D., & Turnbull, A. P. (1988). Vox populi and Baby Doe. *Mental Retardation, 26*(3), 127–132.

Turnbull, H. R., & Turnbull, A. P. (1985). *Parents speak out: Then and now.* Columbus, OH: Merrill Publishing Co.

Turnbull, H. R., & Turnbull, A. P. (1987, May). *The Latin American family and public policy in the United States: Informal support and transition into adulthood.* Unpublished manuscript, The University of Kansas, Beach Center on Families and Disability.

Turnbull, H. R., Turnbull, A. P., Bronicki, G. J., Summers, J. A., & Roeder–Gordon, C. (1989). *Disability and the family: A guide to decisions for adulthood.* Baltimore: Paul H. Brookes Publishing Co.

Turnbull, H. R., Turnbull, A. P., & Strickland, B. (1979, Summer). Due process: The sword the untrained should not unsheath. *Boston University Journal of Education,* 40–59.

Turnbull, H. R., Turnbull, A. P., & Wheat, M. (1982). Assumptions about parental participation: A legislative history. *Exceptional Education Quarterly, 3*(2), 1–8.

Turnbull, H. R., & Wheat, M. (1983). Legal responses to classification of people as mentally retarded. In J. Mulick & J. Matson (Eds.), *A handbook of mental retardation* (pp. 157–170). New York: Pergamon Press.

Turnbull, K., & Bronicki, G. J. (1989). Children can teach other children. *Teaching Exceptional Children, 22*(1), 64–65.

Tymchuk, A. J. (1976). A perspective on ethics in mental retardation. *Mental Retardation, 14*(6), 44–45.

Ulrich, S. (1972). *Elizabeth*. Ann Arbor, MI: The University of Michigan Press.

University of New Mexico Institute for Parent Involvement. (1979). Albuquerque, NM.

Upshur, C. C. (1982). An evaluation of home-based respite care. *Mental Retardation, 20,* 58–63.

Urwin, C. A. (1988). AIDS in children: A family concern. *Family Relations, 37,* 154–159.

U.S. Department of Commerce. (1923). *Feeble-minded and epileptic in institutions*. Washington, DC: U.S. Government Printing Office.

U.S. Department of Commerce. (1934). *Mental defectives and epileptics in state institutions, 1929–1932*. Washington, DC: U.S. Government Printing Office.

Utley, C. A., & Marion, P. (1984, May). *Working with black families having mentally retarded members*. Paper presented at the annual meeting of the American Association on Mental Deficiency, Minneapolis.

Vacc, N. A., Vallecorsa, A. L., Parker, A., Bonner, S., Lester, C., Richardson, S., & Yates, C. (1985). Parents' and educators' participation in IEP conferences. *Education and Treatment of Children, 8*(2), 153–162.

Vadasy, P. F. (1986). Single mothers: A social phenomenon and population in need. in R. R. Fewell, & P. F. Vadasy (Eds.), *Families of handicapped children: Needs and supports across the life span* (pp. 221–249). Austin, TX: Pro-Ed, Inc.

Vadasy, P. F., & Fewell, R. R. (1986). Mothers of deaf-blind children. In R. R. Fewell & P. F. Vadasy (Eds.), *Families of handicapped children* (pp. 121–148). Austin, TX: Pro-Ed, Inc.

Vadasy, P. F., Fewell, R. R., Greenberg, M. T., Desmond, N. L., & Meyer, D. J. (1986). Follow up evaluation of the effects of involvement in the fathers program. *Topics in Early Childhood Education, 6,* 16–31.

Vadasy, P. F., Fewell, R. R., & Meyer, D. J. (1985). Supporting extended family members' roles: intergenerational supports provided by grandparents. *Journal of the Division for Early Childhood*.

Vadasy, P. F., Fewell, R. R., Meyer, D. J., & Greenberg, M. T. (1984). *Supporting fathers of handicapped young children: Preliminary findings of program effects*. Unpublished manuscript, University of Washington.

Vadasy, P. F., Fewell, R. R., Meyer, D. J., & Schell, G. (1984). Siblings of handicapped children: A developmental perspective on family interactions. *Family Relations, 33,* 155–167.

Vadasy, P. F., Fewell, R. R., Meyer, D. J., Schell, G., & Greenberg, M. T. (1984). Involved parents: Characteristics and resources of fathers and mothers of young handicapped children. *Journal of the Division for Early Childhood, 8,* 13–25.

Valero-Figueira, E. (1988). Hispanic children. In B. A. Ramirez (Ed.), Culturally and linguistically diverse children. *Teaching Exceptional Children, 20*(4), 47–48.

Vandercook, T., Fleetham, D., Sinclair, S., & Tetlie, R. R. (1988). Cath, Jess, Jules, and Ames . . . A story of friendship. *Minnesota University Affiliated Program Impact, 1*(2), 4.

Vandercook, T., York, J., & Forest, M. (1989). *MAPS: A strategy for building the vision*. University of Minnesota: Institute on Community Integration.

Van Reusen, A. K. (1984). *A study of the effects of training learning disabled adolescents in self-advocacy procedures for use in the IEP conference*. Unpublished doctoral dissertation, The University of Kansas.

Van Reusen, A. K., Bos, C. S., Schumaker, J. B., & Deshler, D. D. (1987). *The education planning strategy*. Lawrence, KS: Excell Enterprises, Inc.

Vaughn, S., Bos, C., Harrell, J., & Lasky, B. (1988). Parent participation in the initial placement/IEP conference ten years after mandated involvement. *Journal of Learning Disabilities, 21*(2), 82–89.

Ventura, J. N., & Boxx, P. G. (1983). The family coping inventory applied to parents with new babies. *Journal of Marriage and the Family, 45,* 867–875.

Vincent, L. J., Laten, S., Salisbury, C., Brown, P., & Baumgart, D. (1981). Family involvement in the educational processes of severely handicapped students: State of the art and directions for the future. In B. Wilcox & R. York (Eds.), *Quality educational services for the severely handicapped: The federal perspective* (pp. 164–179). Washington, DC: Division of Innovation and Development, Department of Education.

Visher, J. S., & Visher, E. B. (1982). Stepfamilies and stepparenting. In F. Walsh (Ed.), *Normal family processes* (pp. 331–353). New York: The Guilford Press.

Vyas, P. (1983a). Getting on with it. In T. Dougan, L. Isbell, & P. Vyas (Eds.), *We have been there* (pp. 17–19). Nashville, TN: Abingdon Press.

Vyas, P. (1983b). Just another little kid. In T. Dougan, L. Isbell, & P. Vyas (Eds.), *We have been there* (pp. 50–53). Nashville, TN: Abingdon, Press.

Wadsworth, H. G., & Wadsworth, J. B. (1971). A problem of involvement with parents of mildly retarded children. *The Family Coordinator, 28,* 141–147.

Walker, J. L. (1988). Young American Indian children. *Teaching Exceptional Children, 20*(4), 50–51.

Wallinga, C., Paquio, L., & Skeen, P. (1987). When a brother or sister is ill. *Psychology Today, 42,* 43.

Walsh, F. (1982). Conceptualizations of normal family functioning. In F. Walsh (Ed.), *Normal family processes* (pp. 3–42). New York: Guilford Press.

Walther-Thomas C., Hazel, J. S., Schumaker, J. B., Vernon, S., & Deshler, D. D. (in press). A program for families with children with learning disabilities. In M. J. Fine (Ed.), *Collaborative involvement with parents of exceptional children.*

Warren, F. (1985). A society that is going to kill your children. In H. R. Turnbull & A. P. Turnbull (Eds.), *Parents speak out: Then and now* (pp. 201–221). Columbus, OH: Merrill Publishing Co.

Warschaw, T. A. (1980). *Winning by negotiation.* New York: McGraw-Hill Book Co.

Wasserman, R. (1983). Identifying the counseling needs of the siblings of mentally retarded children. *The Personnel and Guidance Journal, 61*(10), 622–627.

Webster, E. J. (1977). *Counseling with parents of handicapped children: Guidelines for improving communication.* New York: Grune & Stratton, Inc.

Weicker, L. (1985). Sonny and public policy. In H. R. Turnbull & A. P. Turnbull (Eds.), *Parents speak out: Then and now* (pp. 281–287). Columbus, OH: Merrill Publishing Co.

Weinrott, M. R. (1974). A training program in behavior modification for siblings of the retarded. *American Journal of Orthopsychiatry, 44*(3), 362–375.

Weintraub, F. J., Abeson, A., Ballard, J., & Lavor, M. L. (1976). *Public policy and the education of exceptional children.* Reston, VA: Council for Exceptional Children.

Weintraub, F., & McCaffrey, M. (1976). Professional rights and responsibilities. In F. Weintraub, A. Abeson, J. Ballard, & M. La-Vor (Eds.), *Public policy and the education of exceptional children* (pp. 333–343). Reston, VA: Council for Exceptional Children.

Western Psychological Institute. (1980). *An intruder in the family: Families cope with cancer* [videotape]. Pittsburgh, PA: University of Pittsburgh.

Weyhing, M. C. (1983). Parental reactions to handicapped children and familial adjustments to routines of care. In J. A. Mulick & S. M. Pueschel (Eds.), *Parent-professional partnerships in developmental disabilities* (pp. 125–138). Cambridge, MA: The Ware Press.

White, R., Benedict, M. I., Wulff, L., & Kelley, M. (1987). Physical disabilities as risk factors for child maltreatment: A selected review. *American Journal of Orthopsychiatry 37,* 93–101.

Wiegel, R. R. (1982). Supporting today's farm family: An opportunity for family life educators. In N. Stinnet, J. DeFrain, K. King, H. Lingren, G. Rowe, S. VanZandt, & R. Williams (Eds.), *Family strengths 4: Positive support systems* (pp. 409–423). Lincoln: University of Nebraska Press.

Wikler, L., Wasow, M., & Hatfield, E. (1983, July–August). Seeking strengths in families of developmentally disabled children. *Social Work,* 313–315.

Willer, B., Intagliata, J., & Wicks, N. (1981). Return of retarded adults to natural families: Issues and results. In R. H. Bruininks, D. E. Meyers, B. B. Sigford, & K. C. Lakin (Eds.), *Deinstitutionalization and community adjustment of mentally retarded people* (pp. 207–216). Washington, DC: American Association on Mental Deficiency.

Williams, J. A., & Stockton, R. (1973). Black family structures and functions: An empirical examination of some suggestions made by Billingsley. *Journal of Marriage and the Family, 1,* 39–49.

Winer, M. E. (1982). Parental involvement in special education decision-making: Access and alienation. *Dissertation Abstracts International, 43,* 1116A. (University Microfilms No. DA8220975)

Winton, P. J., & Bailey, D. B. (1988). The family focused interview: A collaborative mechanism for family assessment and goal setting. *Journal of the Division for Early Childhood, 12*(3), 195–207.

Winton, P. J., & Turnbull, A. P. (1981). Parent involvement as viewed by parents of preschool handicapped children. *Topics in Early Childhood Special Education, 1*(3), 11–19.

Winton, P. J., Turnbull, A. P., & Blacher, J. B. (1984). *Selecting a preschool: A guide for parents of handicapped children.* Austin, TX: Pro-Ed, Inc.

Witt, J. C., Miller, C. D., McIntyre, R. M., & Smith, D. (1984). Effects of variables on parental perceptions of staffings. *Exceptional Children, 51*(1), 27–32.

Yaffa, C. (1987). A mother's thoughts. *Their World,* pp. 57–58.

Yee, L. Y. (1988). Special focus: Asian children. *Teaching Exceptional Children, 20*(4), 49–50.

Yehl, S. (n.d.) 20 dos and don'ts that will lessen the burden of grief for single-parent children. *Rainbows for All God's Children.* Schaumburg, IL: Rainbows for All God's Children, Inc.

Yockey, K. (1983). Facing the inquisition. In T. Dougan, L. Isbell, & P. Vyas (Eds.), *We have been there* (pp. 79–86). Nashville, TN: Abingdon Press.

York, J., Vandercook, T., Heise–Neff, C., & Caughey, E. (1988). Regular class integration at middle school: Feedback from classmates and teachers. *Minnesota University Affiliated Program Impact, 1*(2), 13–15.

Yoshida, R. K. (1979). *Developing assistance linkages for parents of handicapped children.* Washington, DC: Department of Health, Education and Welfare, Bureau of Education for the Handicapped.

Ysseldyke, J. E., Algozzine, B., & Mitchell, J. (1982). Special education team decision making: An analysis of current practice. *The Personnel and Guidance Journal, 60*(5), 308–313.

Ysseldyke, J. E., Thurlow, M., Graden, J., Wesson, C., Algozzine, B., & Deno, S. (1983). Generalizations from five years of research on assessment and decision making: The University of Minnesota Institute. *Exceptional Education Quarterly, 4,* 75–93.

Zigler, E., & Black, K. B. (1989). America's family support movement: Strengths and limitations. *American Journal of Orthopsychiatry, 59*(1), 6–19.

Zimmerman, W. (1982). A professional handles his child's diagnosis. *The Exceptional Parent, 12*(4), 27–29.

Zirpoli, T. J. (1986). Child abuse and children with handicaps. *Remedial and Special Education, 7*(2), 39–48.

Ziskin, L. (1985). Transition—From home to residential care. In H. R. Turnbull & A. P. Turnbull (Eds.), *Parents speak out: Then and now* (pp. 75–78). Columbus, OH: Merrill Publishing Co.

INDEX

ABOUT THE AUTHORS

Ann P. Turnbull is professor of special education, acting associate director of the Bureau of Child Research, and co-director of the Beach Center on Families and Disability at The University of Kansas at Lawrence. She received her Ed.D. from the University of Alabama, her M.Ed. from Auburn University, and her B.S.Ed. from the University of Georgia.

Dr. Turnbull is the author of numerous books and articles on disabilities, with a special focus on families, the integration of people with disabilities into the mainstream of school and community life, and the individualization of their education. In addition, she has co-edited *Parents Speak Out: Then and Now,* and has co-authored *Disability and the Family: A Guide to Decisions for Adulthood, Developing and Implementing Individualized Education Programs,* and *Mainstreaming Handicapped Students: A Guide for the Classroom Teacher.*

Dr. Turnbull serves on the Board of Directors of the National Center for Clinical Infant Programs and as Chair of the Family Committee of the International League of Societies for Persons with Mental Handicap. She is the former Vice President of the Education Division of the American Association on Mental Retardation. She has received awards for outstanding teaching from the North Carolina Association for Retarded Citizens and The University of Kansas; together with her husband, H. Rutherford Turnbull, III, she received the 1982 "Educator of the Year" award from the Association for Retarded Citizens—United States. During the 1988–1989 year, Dr. Turnbull was a Public Policy Fellow in Mental Retardation at the Joseph P. Kennedy, Jr., Foundation. In this role, she served as a Policy Fellow at the Select Committee on Children, Youth, and Families in the U.S. House of Representatives.

Dr. Turnbull has three children, one of whom, Jay, has mental retardation. He is a young adult who is currently working, living, and socializing in typical community settings.

H. Rutherford Turnbull, III, is professor of special education and law, senior research associate of the Bureau of Child Research, and co-director of the Beach Center on Families and Disability at The University of Kansas at Lawrence. He received his Ll.M. from Harvard University, his Ll.B. from the University of Maryland, and his B.A. from Johns Hopkins University.

Mr. Turnbull has published widely. He co-edited *Parents Speak Out: Then and Now,* is the author of *Free Appropriate Public Education: Law and Interpretation* and co-author of *Disability and the Family: A Guide to Decisions for Adulthood.* He has written books on consent, the doctrine of the least restrictive alternative, and disability-related issues of law, ethics, policy, and families. Mr. Turnbull has been legal counsel for the North Carolina legislature on disability matters and was the principal draftsman of that state's special education and limited guardianship laws. He has been an expert witness before committees of the U.S. House of Representatives and the U.S. Senate and served as special counsel on two disability cases in the United States Supreme Court.

Mr. Turnbull is Past-President, American Association on Mental Deficiency; former Secretary, Association for Retarded Citizens-United States; former Director, Foundation for Exceptional Children; and current member of the Board of Directors of the Association for Persons with Severe Handicaps.

Mr. Turnbull received the 1988 National Leadership Award from the National Association of Private Residential Resources, and was the co-recipient with, Ann P. Turnbull, in 1982 of the "Educator of the Year" award from the Association of Retarded Citizens—United States. In 1988, he worked as a special counsel at the U.S. Subcommittee on the Handicapped as a Kennedy Public Policy Fellow.

Mr. Turnbull has been an active parent advocate based on his experiences as the father of Jay Turnbull, who has mental retardation.

Drs. Jean Ann Summers (top), Mary Jane Brotherson (middle), and Holly Anne Benson (bottom) were collaborators in the first edition. At that time, they all were doctoral students in the Department of Special Education at The University of Kansas, emphasizing the study of policy and family. Currently, Dr. Summers is the Director of the Kansas University Affiliated Program at The University of Kansas, Dr. Brotherson is the Associate Director of the Interdisciplinary Human Development Institute at the University of Kentucky, and Dr. Benson is the Director of Training and Social Work at the Children's Rehabilitation Unit at The University of Kansas Medical Center.

The major contributors to the second edition of *Families, Professionals, and Exceptionality* are pictured below (in a celebration at the completion of the manuscript). From the front of the picture and moving counterclockwise are Chuck Rhodes, Betsy Santelli, Ann Turnbull, Chris Walther-Thomas, Karen Sorenson, Mary Beth Johnston, Lori Unruh, Laurie Ford, Julie Sergeant, and Marilyn Shank. Karen provided many of the photographs for the book and Mary Beth had major responsibility for the word processing. The others pictured, graduate students at The University of Kansas and some of them Research Associates of the Beach Center, all contributed to various chapters. Their particular contributions are noted in the preface. We regret that two of the contributors are not pictured—Gloria Grave, a graduate student who worked collaboratively on one of the chapters, and Opal Folks, who provided valuable assistance in word processing. A "family of contributors" meaningfully contributed to this family text.

WE VALUE YOUR OPINION—PLEASE SHARE IT WITH US

Merrill Publishing and our authors are most interested in your reactions to this textbook. Did it serve you well in the course? If it did, what aspects of the text were most helpful? If not, what didn't you like about it? Your comments will help us to write and develop better textbooks. We value your opinions and thank you for your help.

Text Title _____ Edition _____

Author(s) _____

Your Name (optional) _____

Address _____

City _____ State _____ Zip _____

School _____

Course Title _____

Instructor's Name _____

Your Major _____

Your Class Rank _____ Freshman _____ Sophomore _____ Junior _____ Senior

_____ Graduate Student

Were you required to take this course? _____ Required _____ Elective

Length of Course? _____ Quarter _____ Semester

1. Overall, how does this text compare to other texts you've used?

   _____ Superior _____ Better Than Most _____ Average _____ Poor

2. Please rate the text in the following areas:

	Superior	Better Than Most	Average	Poor
Author's Writing Style	_____	_____	_____	_____
Readability	_____	_____	_____	_____
Organization	_____	_____	_____	_____
Accuracy	_____	_____	_____	_____
Layout and Design	_____	_____	_____	_____
Illustrations/Photos/Tables	_____	_____	_____	_____
Examples	_____	_____	_____	_____
Problems/Exercises	_____	_____	_____	_____
Topic Selection	_____	_____	_____	_____
Currentness of Coverage	_____	_____	_____	_____
Explanation of Difficult Concepts	_____	_____	_____	_____
Match-up with Course Coverage	_____	_____	_____	_____
Applications to Real Life	_____	_____	_____	_____

3. Circle those chapters you especially liked:
   1   2   3   4   5   6   7   8   9   10   11   12   13   14   15   16   17   18   19   20
   What was your favorite chapter? _____
   Comments:

4. Circle those chapters you liked least:
   1   2   3   4   5   6   7   8   9   10   11   12   13   14   15   16   17   18   19   20
   What was your least favorite chapter? _____
   Comments:

5. List any chapters your instructor did not assign. _____

6. What topics did your instructor discuss that were not covered in the text?_____
   _____

7. Were you required to buy this book? _____ Yes _____ No

   Did you buy this book new or used? _____ New _____ Used

   If used, how much did you pay? _____

   Do you plan to keep or sell this book? _____ Keep _____ Sell

   If you plan to sell the book, how much do you expect to receive? _____

   Should the instructor continue to assign this book? _____ Yes _____ No

8. Please list any other learning materials you purchased to help you in this course (e.g., study guide, lab manual).
   _____

9. What did you like most about this text? _____
   _____

10. What did you like least about this text? _____
    _____

11. General comments:

    May we quote you in our advertising? _____ Yes _____ No

    Please mail to: Boyd Lane
                      College Division Research Department
                      P. O. Box 508
                      Columbus, Ohio 43216-0508

    Thank you!